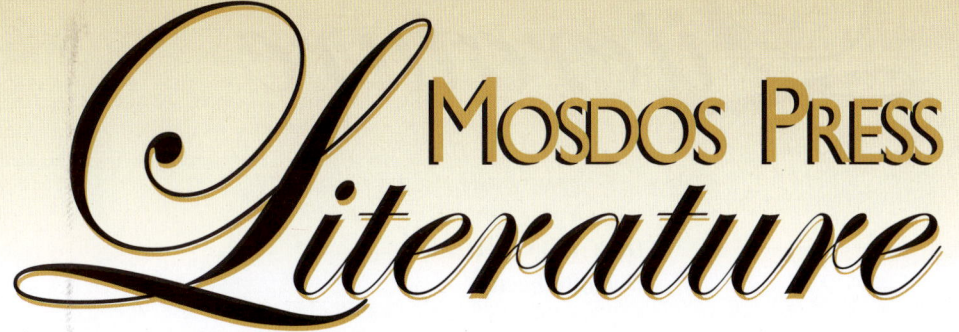

GOLD

EDITOR-IN-CHIEF
Judith Factor

EXECUTIVE EDITOR
Libby Spero

SENIOR EDITOR
Harold Males

ASSOCIATE EDITOR
Jill Brotman

COPY EDITOR
Laya Dewick

EDITORIAL STAFF
B. Resnicoff, S. Sperling, S. Zaidoff

INSTRUCTIONAL TEXT WRITERS
Rona Arato, Ruth C. Beach, Donna M. Caputo, Jill Cavano, E. Green,
E. L. Greenberger, Amy Greenspan, Monica M. Leigh, Susan Polster,
D. D. Segall, Jill E. Vining-Donovan

CREATIVE/ART DIRECTOR
Carla Martin

GRAPHICS
Eva Martin, S. Mendenhall, S. Merling, L. Neustadter, Olga Polner

TYPESETTING
Y. Dowek, F. Scheinbaum, K. Nisenbaum

TEXT AND CURRICULUM ADVISOR
Rabbi Ahron Dovid Goldberg

contents

Short Stories

Recognizing Plot

Arthur Gordon	**The Sea Devil**	16
Paul Annixter	**Accounts Settled**	30
O. Henry	**The Last Leaf**	42
MacKinlay Kantor	**A Man Who Had No Eyes**	52

Defining Character

Richard Y. Thurman	**The Countess and the Impossible**	60
Shirley Jackson	**Charles**	70
Kurt Vonnegut	**The No-Talent Kid**	78
Georges Carousso	**The Warden**	92
Bill Meissner	**In the Middle of a Pitch**	108

Exploring Setting

Jack London	**To Build a Fire**	118
Jesse Stuart	**This Farm for Sale**	136
Ray Bradbury	**The Drummer Boy of Shiloh**	148
John D. MacDonald	**Fire!**	156
Elsie Singmaster	**Mr. Brownlee's Roses**	164

Copyright © 2001 by Mosdos Press.

All rights reserved. Printed in Israel. 9th Printing.

No part of this publication may be reproduced or distributed in any form or by any means, or stored in a database or retrieval system, without prior permission in writing from Mosdos Press.

ISBN-10: 0-9671009-2-5
ISBN-13: 978-0-967-10092-0

contents

Point of View

George and Helen Papashvily	**The First Day**	176
Rumer Godden	**You Need to Go Upstairs**	186
Guy De Maupassant	**The Piece of String**	194
Lois Phillips Hudson	**Children of the Harvest**	204
Roald Dahl	**The Wish**	216

Understanding Theme

Paul Laurence Dunbar	**The Finish of Patsy Barnes**	225
Edward Everett Hale	**The Man Without a Country**	235
George P. McCallum	**The Song Caruso Sang**	256
D. H. Lawrence	**Adolf**	270
Ernest Hemingway	**Old Man at the Bridge**	280

Pulling It All Together

Robb White	**Fetch!**	285
Hugh Pentecost	**The Day the Children Vanished**	292

contents

Novella

Alexander Key   **The Forgotten Door** 316

Poetry

Poetic Diction

Don Marquis   **Takes Talent** 387
Edwin A. Hoey   **Foul Shot** 392

Poetic Images

Babette Deutsch   **Fireworks** 395
Elizabeth Bishop   **The Fish** 398
Deloras Lane   **Keepsakes** 403
Louis Untermeyer   **Dog at Night** 406
Joseph Bruchac   **Ellis Island** 409

Poetic Sound

John Masefield   **The West Wind** 413
Shel Silverstein   **The Garden** 417
Walt Whitman   **O Captain! My Captain!** 421
Deborah Austin   **Dandelions** 425

contents

Poetic Patterns

John Godfrey Saxe	The Blind Men and the Elephant	429
Walt Whitman	When I Heard the Learn'd Astronomer	433
Leroy V. Quintana	Legacy II	438

Poetic Form

Hal Summers	The Rescue	442
Lewis Carroll	The Walrus and the Carpenter	446

Lyric Poetry

Richard Garcia	The Clouds Pass	452
Richard Le Gallienne	I Meant to Do My Work Today	453

Poetic Theme

Elder Olson	Directions to the Armorer	458
Robert Frost	A Time to Talk	463
Naoshi Koriyama	Unfolding Bud	466

Pulling It All Together

Langston Hughes	As I Grew Older	470
Robert Frost	Stopping by Woods on a Snowy Evening	471

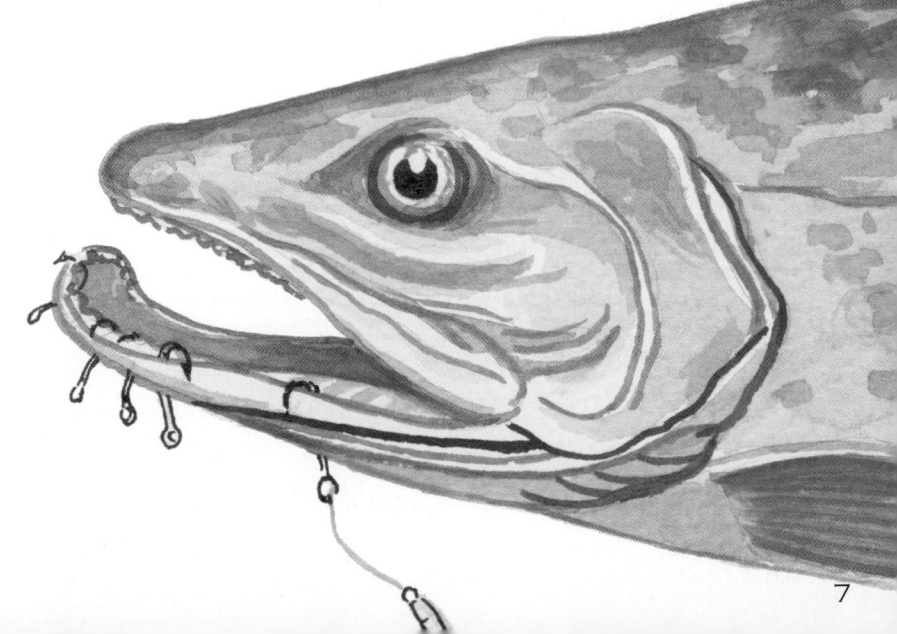

contents

Drama

Gordon Daviot **The Pen of My Aunt** 483

Nonfiction

Focus on the Persuasive Essay
Richard Lederer **The Case for Short Words** 502

Focus on Light Humor
Ralph Helfer **Fly Away** 510

Focus on the Autobiographical Anecdote
Roald Dahl **The Green Mamba** 518

Focus on the Memoir
Rita Dove **I Know What the Red Clay Looks Like** 530

contents

Focus on the Childhood Memoir

Bruce Brooks — **Animal Craftsmen** 540

Focus on Humor

James Herriot — **The Recital** 549

Focus on the Humorous Historical Recollection

James Thurber — **The Day the Dam Broke** 558

Focus on the Childhood Memoir

Santha Rama Rau — **By Any Other Name** 566

Focus on the Reminiscence

Ben Logan — **Drouth** 576

Novel

Jack Bennett — **The Voyage of the Lucky Dragon** 589

Glossary of Literary Terms 706
Glossary 722
Index of Authors and Titles 732

Mosdos Press

Educators transmitting appropriate values and academic excellence

Mosdos Press Literature Anthologies

Opal for 3rd Grade
Ruby for 4th Grade
Coral for 5th Grade
Pearl for 6th Grade
Jade for 7th Grade
Gold for 8th Grade

SHORT Stories

an amateur who didn't quit.

Blueprint for Reading

the *Author*

**Arthur Gordon
(1912-2002)**

Arthur Gordon was born in Savannah, Georgia. He graduated Yale University, later receiving a Rhodes Scholarship to Oxford University. He was managing editor of *Good Housekeeping* magazine as well as editor of *Cosmopolitan*. As a freelance writer, he turned out more than 200 stories and magazine articles, as well as a novel and several nonfiction books. His hobbies included fishing, hunting, and boating—all reflected in *The Sea Devil*.

Background Bytes

Which do *you* think is more important: work or play? In contemporary society, do we work so many hours, with such intensity, that we need to renew ourselves with mental and physical recreation? Do we also develop skills while playing that enable us to better focus when we are back at work?

We are no longer a society of farmers, hunters, and laborers. Appliances assist all of us with household tasks. Much of our professional work consists of thinking and sitting. To offset the absence of physical conditioning, many people go jogging each day. Others take yoga, go to exercise classes, or play sports regularly.

Are those folks who engage in strenuous and dangerous activities responding as well to the lack of physical challenge in modern society? Is the additional element of risk a big draw in mountain climbing and underwater exploration? The human neurological and physiological design may be exactly why some of us feel the call of the wild!

Into *The Sea Devil*

The Sea Devil is an action-adventure story about a person who ordinarily works with his head, not with his hands. His job requires clear thinking, but provides no physical challenge. Consequently, he seeks out a challenging hobby.

Night fishing is hard work and dangerous, with the additional satisfaction of yielding food for the practitioner's table. For the protagonist, night fishing allows him to experience his skill in activity fundamental to human survival, by himself. Here there is no boss nor the teamwork required at so many job sites.

However, this hunter who thinks he is safe is suddenly plummeted into the world of his prey and becomes one of the hunted. The pace of the narrative leaves the reader breathless. The action is described as it occurs chronologically, with the events in sequence. The theme of the story is revealed in the life-and-death struggle of the protagonist. A secondary theme is the enforced physical idleness and safety of contemporary culture. The protagonist is weary of this and seeks out a confrontation with natural forces. Another powerful thematic thread is the desire to return to an earlier, more primitive state that requires self-reliance and gives life deeper meaning.

The Sea Devil

Before you read the story:

Make two lists of at least five entries each. One list will have jobs requiring brains; the other list will have jobs requiring muscles. After making your lists, look them over. What are the advantages and disadvantages of each type of job? Then, write a brief statement telling what would be satisfying and unsatisfying about a job requiring only brains. Write the same kind of statement for a job requiring only muscles.

Focusing on the Plot

Every story has a **plot**. Simply put, this means every story has a beginning, a middle, and an end. More specifically, in literary terms, the beginning is the **exposition**, the part of the story that explains background, characters, and setting. The middle of the story includes the **rising action**, adding complications to the story's conflicts, the **climax**, or point of greatest suspense or interest, and the **falling action**, the logical result of the climax. The end of the story is the **resolution**, showing how the conflict is resolved.

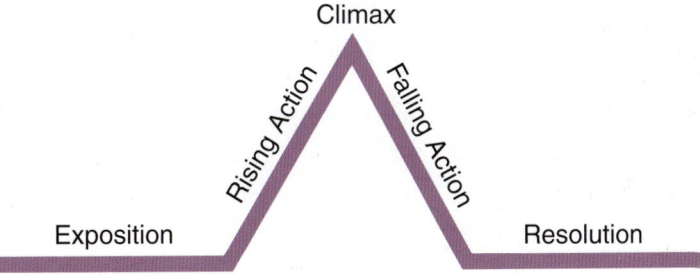

Word Bank

Lagoon is an odd word for the English language—with that funny "-oon" ending. What other words can you think of that end "-oon"? **Lagoon** has two sources: The Irish word *loch*, meaning "lake," as in the Loch Ness monster, and the Latin word *lacuna*, meaning "a pool, a pond" or "a gap"—as a gap in an old manuscript.

barnacle	imminent	placid	tenaciously
droning	impeding	preeminence	torrent
equilibrium	lagoon	respite	
furrow	mottled	simultaneously	
futile	perimeter	teeming	

The Sea Devil

Arthur Gordon

The man came out of the house and stood quite still, listening. Behind him, the lights glowed in the cheerful room, the books were neat and orderly in their cases, the radio talked importantly to itself. In front of him, the bay stretched dark and silent, one of the countless lagoons that border the coast where Florida thrusts its green thumb deep into the tropics.

It was late in September. The night was breathless; summer's dead hand still lay heavy on the land. The man moved forward six paces and stood on the sea wall. The tide was beginning to ebb.

Somewhere out in the blackness a mullet[1] jumped and fell back with a sullen splash. Heavy with roe,[2] they were jumping less often, now. They would not take a hook, but a practiced eye could see the swirls they made in the glassy water. In the dark of the moon, a skilled man with a cast net might take half a dozen in an hour's work. And a big mullet makes a meal for a family.

The man turned abruptly and went into the garage, where his cast net hung. He was in

---

1. A *mullet* (MUL it) is a spiny-finned fish that lives in shallow seas.
2. The term *roe* (RO) refers to fish eggs.

> **Word Bank**
> **lagoon** (luh GOON) *n*.: an area of shallow water open to the sea but separated from the ocean by low, sandy dunes

his late twenties, wide-shouldered and strong. He did not have to fish for a living, or even for food. He was a man who worked with his head, not with his hands. But he liked to go casting alone at night.

He liked the loneliness and the labor of it. He liked the clean taste of salt when he gripped the edge of the net with his teeth as a cast netter must. He liked the arching flight of sixteen pounds of lead and linen against the starlight, and the weltering crash[3] of the net into the unsuspecting water. He liked the harsh tug of the retrieving rope around his wrist, and the way the net came alive when the cast was true, and the thud of captured fish on the floorboards of the skiff.[4]

He liked all that because he found in it a reality that seemed to be missing from his twentieth-century job and from his daily life. He liked being the hunter, skilled and solitary and elemental.[5] There was no conscious cruelty in the way he felt. It was the way things had been in the beginning.

The man lifted the net down carefully and lowered it into a bucket. He put a paddle beside the bucket. Then he went into the house. When he came out, he was wearing swimming trunks and a pair of old tennis shoes.

The skiff, flat bottomed, was moored[6] off the sea wall. He would not go far, he told him-

---

3. A *weltering crash* is one that causes a lot of noise and movement in the water.
4. A *skiff* (SKIF) is a small, flat-bottomed boat suitable for one person.
5. Here, *elemental* (EL uh MEN til) means simple or basic.
6. When a boat is *moored* (MOORD), it is secured by an anchor or cable.

self. Just to the tumbledown dock half a mile away. Mullet had a way of feeding around old pilings after dark. If he moved quietly, he might pick up two or three in one cast close to the dock. And maybe a couple of others on the way down or back.

He shoved off and stood motionless for a moment, letting his eyes grow accustomed to the dark. Somewhere out in the channel a porpoise blew with a sound like steam escaping. The man smiled a little; porpoises were his friends. Once, fishing in the Gulf, he had seen the charter-boat captain reach overside and gaff[7] a baby porpoise through the sinewy[8] part of the tail. He had hoisted it aboard, had dropped it into the bait well, where it thrashed around, puzzled and unhappy. And the mother had swum alongside the boat and under the boat and around the boat, nudging the stout planking with her back, slapping it with her tail, until the man felt sorry for her and made the captain let the baby porpoise go.

He took the net from the bucket, slipped the noose in the retrieving rope over his wrist, pulled the slipknot tight. It was an old net, but still serviceable; he had rewoven the rents[9] made by underwater snags. He coiled the thirty-foot rope carefully, making sure there were no kinks. A tangled rope, he knew, would spoil any cast.

The basic design of the net had not changed in three thousand years. It was a mesh circle with a diameter of fourteen feet. It measured close to fifteen yards around the circumference and could, if thrown perfectly, blanket a hundred fifty square feet of sea water. In the center of this radial trap[10] was a small iron collar where the retrieving rope met the twenty-three separate drawstrings leading to the outer rim of the net. Along this rim, spaced an inch and a half apart, were the heavy lead sinkers.

The man raised the iron collar until it was a foot above his head. The net hung soft and pliant[11] and deadly. He shook it gently, making sure that the drawstrings were not tangled, that the sinkers were hanging true. Then he eased it down and picked up the paddle.

The night was black as a witch's cat; the stars looked fuzzy and dim. Down to the southward, the lights of a causeway made a yellow necklace across the sky. To the man's left were the tangled roots of a mangrove swamp;[12] to his right, the open waters of the bay. Most of it was fairly shallow, but there were channels eight feet deep. The man could not see the old dock, but he knew where it was. He pulled the paddle quietly through the water, and the phosphorescence[13] glowed and died.

For five minutes he paddled. Then, twenty feet ahead of the skiff, a mullet jumped. A big fish, close to three pounds. For a moment it hung in the still air, gleaming dully. Then it vanished. But

---

7. To *gaff* (GAF) a porpoise is to use a hook-like iron instrument to spear and capture it.
8. The *sinewy* (SIN yoo wee) part of the tail is the part that is tough and firm, without bone.
9. *Rents* (RENTS) are tears in the net.
10. *Radial trap* refers to the way the drawstrings of the net radiate from a small iron collar, like spokes from the center of a wheel.
11. Something that is *pliant* (PLY unt) is easily bent, or flexible.
12. A *mangrove swamp* is a grove of low trees with tangled roots growing on a tract of wet, spongy land.
13. *Phosphorescence* (FAHS fuh RESS intz) refers to the glowing or luminous appearance of some sea life at night.

the ripples marked the spot, and where there was one there were often others.

The man stood up quickly. He picked up the coiled rope, and with the same hand grasped the net at a point four feet below the iron collar. He raised the skirt to his mouth, gripped it strongly with his teeth. He slid his free hand as far as it would go down the circumference of the net, so that he had three points of contact with the mass of cordage[14] and metal. He made sure his feet were planted solidly. Then he waited, feeling the tension, the fierce exhilaration of the hunter at the moment of ambush, the atavistic desire[15] to capture and kill and ultimately consume.

A mullet swirled, ahead and to the left. The man swung the heavy net back, twisting his body and bending his knees so as to get more upward thrust. He shot it forward, letting go simultaneously with rope hand and with teeth, holding a fraction of a second longer with the other hand so as to give the net the necessary spin, impart the centrifugal force[16] that would make it flare into a circle. The skiff ducked sideways, but he kept his balance. The net fell with a splash.

The man waited for five seconds. Then he began to retrieve it, pulling in a series of sharp jerks so that the drawstrings would gather the net inward, like a giant fist closing on this segment of the teeming sea. He felt the net quiver, and he knew it was not empty. He swung it, dripping, over the gunwale,[17] saw the broad silver side of the mullet quivering, saw too the gleam of a smaller fish. He looked closely to make sure no stingray[18] was hidden in the mesh, then raised the iron collar and shook the net out. The mullet fell with a thud and flapped wildly. The other victim was an angelfish, beautifully marked, but too small to keep. The man picked it up gently and dropped it overboard. He coiled the rope, took up the paddle. He would cast no more until he came to the dock.

The skiff moved on. At last, ten feet apart, a pair of stakes rose up gauntly[19] out of the night. Barnacle-encrusted, they once had marked the approach from the main channel. The man guided the skiff between them, then put the paddle down softly. He stood up, reached for the net, tightened the noose around his wrist. From here he could drift down upon the dock. He could see it now, a ruined skeleton in the starshine. Beyond it a mullet jumped and fell back with a flat, liquid sound. The man raised the edge of the net, put it between his teeth. He would not cast at a single swirl, he decided; he would wait until he saw two or

---

14. *Cordage* (KOR dij) refers to the mass of cord or ropes making up the net.
15. An *atavistic desire* (AT uh VISS tik dih ZY ir) is a strong longing.
16. A *centrifugal force* (sen TRIF yoo gul FORSS) causes an object moving in a circle to move away from the center of the circle.
17. The *gunwale* (GUN il) is the upper edge of the side of a vessel.
18. A *stingray* (STING RAY) is a fish with a long, flexible tail, armed with a bony, poisonous spine.
19. Here *gauntly* (GAWNT lee) means desolately or grimly.

Word Bank

simultaneously (SY mul TAY nee iss lee) *adv.*: concurrently; occurring at the same time

teeming (TEEM ing) *adj.*: occurring or existing in great quantities or numbers; swarming

barnacle (BAR nih kul) *n.*: a sea-dwelling, hard-shelled creature that often attaches itself to ship bottoms and timber

three close together. The skiff was barely moving. He felt his muscles tense themselves, awaiting the signal from the brain.

Behind him in the channel he heard the porpoise blow again, nearer now. He frowned in the darkness. If the porpoise chose to fish this area, the mullet would scatter and vanish. There was no time to lose.

A school of sardines surfaced suddenly, skittering along like drops of mercury. Something, perhaps the shadow of the skiff, had frightened them. The old dock loomed very close. A mullet broke water just too far away; then another, nearer. The man marked[20] the spreading ripples and decided to wait no longer.

He swung back the net, heavier now that it was wet. He had to turn his head, but out of the corner of his eye he saw two swirls in the black water just off the starboard bow.[21] They were about eight feet apart, and they had the sluggish oily look that marks the presence of something big just below the surface. His conscious mind had no time to function, but instinct told him that the net was wide enough to cover both swirls if he could alter the direction of his cast. He could not halt the swing, but he shifted his feet slightly and made the cast off balance. He saw the net shoot forward, flare into an oval, and drop just where he wanted it.

Then the sea exploded in his face. In a frenzy of spray, a great horned thing shot like a huge bat out of the water. The man saw the mesh of his net etched against the mottled blackness of its body and he knew, in the split second in which thought was still possible, that those twin swirls had been made not by two mullet, but by the wing tips of the giant ray of the Gulf Coast, *Manta birostris,* also known as clam cracker, devil ray,

---

20. *Marked* (MARKT) means noticed or noted.
21. Facing the front of the boat, the *starboard bow* (STAR BORD BOU) is the right-hand side of the front of a vessel.

Word Bank

mottled (MAHT ild) *adj.*: marked with spots or blotches of different colors or shades

sea devil.

The man gave a hoarse cry. He tried to claw the slipknot off his wrist, but there was not time. The quarter-inch line snapped taut. He shot over the side of the skiff as if he had roped a runaway locomotive. He hit the water headfirst and seemed to bounce once. He plowed a blinding furrow for perhaps ten yards. Then the line went slack as the sea devil jumped again. It was not the full-grown manta of the deep Gulf, but it was close to nine feet from tip to tip and it weighed over a thousand pounds. Up into the air it went, pearl-colored underbelly gleaming as it twisted in a frantic effort to dislodge the clinging thing that had fallen upon it. Up into the starlight, a monstrous survival from the earliest of times.

The water was less than four feet deep. Sobbing and choking, the man struggled for a foothold on the slimy bottom. Sucking in great gulps of air, he fought to free himself from the rope. But the slipknot was jammed deep into his wrist; he might as well have tried to loosen a circle of steel.

The ray came down with a thunderous splash and drove forward again. The flexible net followed every movement, impeding it hardly at all. The man weighed a hundred seventy-five pounds, and he was braced for the shock, and he had the desperate strength that comes from looking into the blank eyes of death. It was useless. His arm straightened out with a jerk that seemed to dislocate his shoulder; his feet shot out from under him; his head went under again. Now at last he knew how the fish must feel when the line tightens and drags him toward the alien element that is his doom. Now he knew.

Desperately he dug the fingers of his free hand into the ooze, felt them dredge a futile channel through broken shells and the ribbon-like sea grasses. He tried to raise his head, but could not get it clear. Torrents of spray choked him as the ray plunged toward deep water.

His eyes were of no use to him in the foamstreaked blackness. He closed them tight, and at once an insane sequence of pictures flashed through his mind. He saw his wife sitting in their living room, reading, waiting calmly for his return. He saw the mullet he had just caught, gasping its life away on the floorboards of the skiff. He saw all these things and many others simultaneously in his mind as his body fought silently and tenaciously for its existence. His hand touched something hard and closed on it in a death grip, but it was only the sharp-edged helmet of a horseshoe crab, and after an instant he let go.

He had been underwater perhaps fifteen seconds now, and something in his brain told him quite calmly that he could last another forty or fifty and then the red flashes behind his eyes would merge into darkness, and the water would pour into his lungs in one sharp painful shock, and he would be finished.

This thought spurred him to a desperate

Word Bank

furrow (FUR oh) *n.*: a narrow groove-like or trench-like depression in any surface
impeding (im PEED ing) *v.*: causing delay, interruption, or difficulty
futile (FYOO till) *adj.*: incapable of producing any result; useless; not successful
torrent (TOR int) *n.*: a stream of water flowing with great rapidity and violence
tenaciously (tih NAY shiss lee) *adv.*: holding fast; characterized by keeping a firm hold

effort. He reached up and caught his pinioned[22] wrist with his free hand. He doubled up his knees to create more drag. He thrashed his body madly, like a fighting fish, from side to side. This did not disturb the ray, but now one of the great wings tore through the mesh, and the net slipped lower over the fins projecting like horns from below the nightmare head, and the sea devil jumped again.

And once more the man was able to get his feet on the bottom and his head above water, and he saw ahead of him the pair of ancient stakes that marked the approach to the channel. He knew that if he was dragged much beyond those stakes he would be in eight feet of water, and the ray would go down to hug the bottom as rays always do, and then no power on earth could save him. So in the moment of respite that was granted him, he flung himself toward them.

For a moment he thought his captor yielded a bit. Then the ray moved off again, but more slowly now, and for a few yards the man was able to keep his feet on the bottom. Twice he hurled himself back against the rope with all his strength, hoping that something would break. But nothing broke. The mesh of the net was ripped and torn, but the draw lines were strong, and the stout perimeter cord threaded through the sinkers was even stronger.

The man could feel nothing now in his trapped hand, it was numb; but the ray could feel the powerful lunges of the unknown thing that was trying to restrain it. It drove its great wings against the unyielding water and forged ahead, dragging the man and pushing a sullen wave in front of it.

The man had swung as far as he could toward the stakes. He plunged toward one and missed it by inches. His feet slipped and he went down on his knees. Then the ray swerved sharply and the second stake came right at him. He reached out with his free hand and caught it.

He caught it just above the surface, six or eight inches below high-water mark. He felt the razor-sharp barnacles bite into his hand, collapse under the pressure, drive their tiny slime-covered shell splinters deep into his flesh. He felt the pain, and he welcomed it, and he made his fingers into an iron claw that would hold until the tendons were severed or the skin was shredded from the bone. The ray felt the pressure increase with a jerk that stopped it dead in the water. For a moment all was still as the tremendous forces came into equilibrium.

Then the net slipped again, and the perimeter cord came down over the sea devil's eyes, blinding it momentarily. The great ray settled to the bottom and braced its wings against the mud and hurled itself forward and upward.

The stake was only a four-by-four of

---

22. His wrist was *pinioned* (PIN yund), or bound very tightly, to the net.

Word Bank

respite (RESS pit) *n.*: a delay or stopping for a time, especially of anything distressing or difficult; an interval of relief

perimeter (puh RIM ih ter) **cord** *n.*: a rope marking the boundary or outer limits of an area or object

equilibrium (E kwill LIB ree um) *n.*: a state of rest or balance

creosoted[23] pine, and it was old. Ten thousand tides had swirled around it. Worms had bored; parasites had clung. Under the crust of barnacles it still had some heart left, but not enough. The man's grip was five feet above the floor of the bay; the leverage was too great. The stake snapped off at its base.

The ray lunged upward, dragging the man and the useless timber. The man had his lungs full of air, but when the stake snapped he thought of expelling the air and inhaling the water so as to have it finished quickly. He thought of this, but he did not do it. And then, just at the channel's edge, the ray met the porpoise, coming in.

The porpoise had fed well this night and was in no hurry, but it was a methodical creature and it intended to make a sweep around the old dock before the tide dropped too low. It had no quarrel with any ray, but it feared no fish in the sea, and when the great black shadow came rushing blindly and unavoidably, it rolled fast and struck once with its massive horizontal tail.

The blow descended on the ray's flat body with a sound like a pistol shot. It would have broken a buffalo's back, and even the sea devil was half stunned. It veered wildly and turned back toward shallow water. It passed within ten feet of the man, face down in the water. It slowed and almost stopped, wing tips moving faintly, gathering strength for another rush.

The man had heard the tremendous slap of the great mammal's tail and the snorting gasp as it plunged away. He felt the line go slack again, and he raised his dripping face, and he reached for the bottom with his feet. He found it, but now the water was up to his neck. He plucked at the noose once more with his lacerated hand, but there was no strength in his fingers. He felt the tension come back into the line as the ray began to move again, and for half a second he was tempted to throw himself backward and fight as he had been doing, pitting his strength against the vastly superior strength of the brute.

But the acceptance of imminent death had done something to his brain. It had driven out the fear, and with the fear had gone the panic. He could think now, and he knew with absolute certainty that if he was to make any use of this last chance that had been given him, it would have to be based on the one faculty that had carried man to his preeminence above all beasts, the faculty of reason. Only by using his brain could he possibly survive, and he called on his brain for a solution, and his brain responded. It offered him one.

He did not know whether his body still had the strength to carry out the brain's commands, but he began to swim forward, toward the ray that was still moving hesitantly away from the channel. He swam forward, feeling the rope go slack as he gained on the creature.

Ahead of him he saw the one remaining stake, and he made himself swim faster until he was parallel with the ray and the rope trailed behind both of them

---

23. *Creosoted* (KREE uh SO tid) means treated with creosote, a strong-smelling, oily liquid used to preserve wood.

Word Bank

imminent (IM ih nint) *adj.*: likely to occur at any moment

preeminence (pree EM ih nintz) *n.*: superiority to all others

in a deep U. He swam with a surge of desperate energy that came from nowhere, so that he was slightly in the lead as they came to the stake. He passed on one side of it; the ray was on the other.

Then the man took one last deep breath, and he went down under the black water until he was sitting on the bottom of the bay. He put one foot over the line so that it passed under his bent knee. He drove both his heels into the mud, and he clutched the slimy grass with his bleeding hand, and he waited for the tension to come again.

The ray passed on the other side of the stake, moving faster now. The rope grew taut again, and it began to drag the man back toward the stake. He held his prisoned wrist close to the bottom, under his knee, and he prayed that the stake would not break. He felt the rope vibrate as the barnacles bit into it. He did not know whether the rope would crush the barnacles, or whether the barnacles would cut the rope. All he knew was that in five seconds or less he would be dragged into the stake and cut to ribbons if he tried to hold on, or drowned if he didn't.

He felt himself sliding slowly, and then faster, and suddenly the ray made a great leap forward, and the rope burned around the base of the stake, and the man's foot hit it hard. He kicked himself backward with his remaining strength, and the rope parted, and he was free.

He came slowly to the surface. Thirty feet away the sea devil made one tremendous leap and disappeared into the darkness. The man raised his wrist and looked at the frayed length of rope dangling from it. Twenty inches, perhaps. He lifted his other hand and felt the hot blood start instantly, but he didn't care. He put this hand on the stake above the barnacles and held on to the good, rough, honest wood. He heard a strange noise, and realized that it was himself, sobbing.

High above, there was a droning sound. Looking up, he saw the nightly plane from New Orleans inbound for Tampa. Calm and serene, it sailed, symbol of man's superiority. Its lights winked red and green for a moment; then it was gone.

Slowly, painfully, the man began to move through the placid water. He came to the skiff at last and climbed into it. The mullet, still alive, slapped convulsively with its tail. The man reached down with his torn hand, picked up the mullet, let it go.

He began to work on the slipknot doggedly with his teeth. His mind was almost a blank, but not quite. He knew one thing. He knew he would do no more casting alone at night. Not in the dark of the moon. No, not he.

Word Bank

droning (DRONE ing) *adj.*: continuous, low, monotonous

placid (PLASS id) *adj.*: pleasantly calm or peaceful

Studying the Selection

First Impressions

Which brief passage does most to bring the story to life for you? Which part do you find most amusing?

✔ Quick Review

1. What activity was the man engaged in? What method did he use?
2. What was the result of his first cast?
3. What was the result of his second cast?
4. What would happen if the man were pulled out past the old dock?

In-depth Thinking

5. Give three examples that show the man is skilled at cast-fishing.
6. Dragged by the ray, the man closes his eyes and imagines the scene at home. What is gained by contrasting the imagined scene with the present experience of the man?
7. Why are we told the man had saved a baby porpoise? How is it related to the story?
8. What does the author mean when he says the man feels "the tension … the fierce exhilaration of the hunter at the moment of ambush, the atavistic desire to capture and kill and ultimately consume"? Contrast this feeling with his usual way of obtaining food.

Drawing Conclusions

9. The author uses many contrasts in this story. The silence outdoors contrasts with the noise of the radio in the house. The wild struggle of the man and the stingray contrasts with the peaceful setting of the man's home. The man's job contrasts with his fishing experiences. Referring to these contrasts, explain how the author uses them to make a statement about the conflict between man and nature. What is the author's view of the conflict? Why do people challenge nature?
10. People who work in offices, at desks, looking at computer screens all day, often feel apart from the natural world. What kind of jobs put people in more direct contact with nature? Would these jobs be more satisfying than office jobs? Why or why not?

Focusing on the Plot

The **plot** of *The Sea Devil* is a series of events told in **chronological** order. There is a major **conflict**, encompassing minor conflicts as well. Complete the following activities to help you better understand plot.

1. Assign each part of the story to the proper plot element, explaining which action corresponds to which plot element: **exposition**, **rising action**, **climax**, **falling action**, and **resolution**.
2. Find the bits of **exposition** occurring in the middle of the action. Show how they reveal theme.
3. Another element of plot is foreshadowing. **Foreshadowing** is an early incident or comment hinting at or predicting a later action. Find an example of foreshadowing, and explain how it connects with a later event in the story.

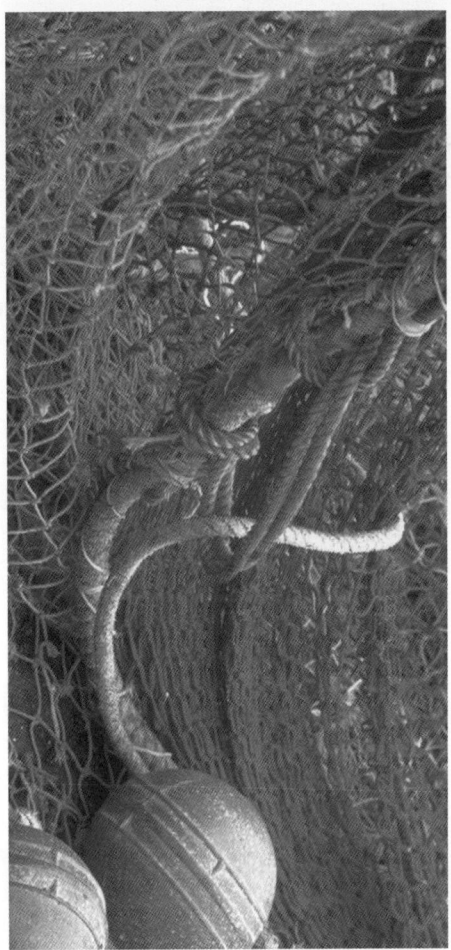

Creating and Writing

1. Discuss the character's irritation with everyday life and his desire for adventure. Does the author favor this quest for excitement, or does he disapprove? Is he neutral? Use specific references to the story to support your thesis.
2. Write a brief sketch in which a character's search for adventure takes a bad turn. Pay attention to setting, action, and the character's thoughts. Use vivid words.
3. Give an oral report on the differences between stingrays and porpoises. Explain why a porpoise is a good choice as the 'hero' of the story and the stingray is a good 'villain.'

Blueprint for Reading

the Author

**Paul Annixter
(1894-1985)**

Paul Annixter, whose real name was Howard Allison Sturtzel, was born in Minnesota. He lived much of his life in the back country and was fond of animals. For a year and a half, while still a young man, he worked alone on a timber section, cutting wood for money and hunting game for food. This experience is embedded in *Accounts Settled*. He and his wife Jane wrote more than 500 animal stories. They once said, "Our stories always deal with some phase of human and animal interrelation, which offers, to our mind, a different and deeper sort of heart interest."

Background Bytes

The traditional woodsman, or mountain man, is a colorful character in American history. These men, trappers for the fur trade, pushed the borders of colonial America and explored the great western and northern frontiers. The life of the mountain man was difficult, dangerous, and filled with adventure.

In the 20th century, fur farms furnish most pelts. Yet a few hardy souls continue to trap for fur. This life is still difficult, for the best pelts are gathered in winter when an animal's coat grows lush to protect against cold. Can you imagine spending days deep in the forest in bitter cold with only the barest of provisions? What might induce someone to live this kind of life?

Into *Accounts Settled*

Paul Annixter has created a story filled with tension and danger. The main character is sixteen-year-old Gordon Bent, forced to become "man of the house" when his father falls ill. Through his family situation, Gordon experiences loss, but also gain. This type of story, where childhood is left behind, is called a "coming of age" story. As you read, ask yourself what matters most to Gordon and why. In what way has he changed by the end of the story?

Accounts Settled

Focusing on Plot Development: Conflict

Tension is the glue that keeps the reader 'held' to the page. It keeps us reading to see what happens next. Tension is a result of **conflict** which, in *Accounts Settled*, is a matter of **man vs. nature**. Gordon, alone in the woods, senses that some unknown creature is stalking him. Annixter tells us of Gordon's fear from the outset. He builds upon this shadowy conflict, increasing the tension, until the source of Gordon's fear is suddenly revealed.

As in the story *The Sea Devil*, Paul Annixter has written *his* story using the basic principles of **plot development**: exposition, rising action, climax, falling action, and resolution. Plot without **conflict** weakens a story. Annixter understands the importance of conflict. We learn gradually about Gordon and his situation (*exposition*). As Gordon's fear and difficulties increase, the *action rises* to a suspenseful *climax*. The pace of the story quickens to match Gordon's situation. At the point where Gordon (and the reader!) can't take any more, events turn (*falling action*), eventually coming to a *resolution*. On your second reading of the story, note how the plot builds and moves. How do the author's descriptions hold your attention? How have the events in the story (basically, the plot) helped Gordon truly "come of age"?

Word Bank

Sinister: In ancient Rome, the left hand was called *sinistra*, or "unfavorable," and the right hand was called *dexta*, originally meaning "favorable," or "adroit, having skill." Certainly, for most people, the right hand has greater skill and strength. But left-handedness, in ancient times, apparently had ominous associations, as in a bad omen, and **sinister** acquired its current meaning of "threatening harm or evil."

attuned	inimical	petulance	undermining
cowardice	inordinately	semblance	vigilance
culminating	irate	sinister	waning
enigmatic	lithe	solitude	wolverine
ferocity	ludicrously	stripling	writhing
gnawing	lynx	subtler	
havoc	onslaught	tithe	

Accounts Settled

Paul Annixter

There it was again, that sinister feeling in the pine shadows and a sense of something watching, waiting among the dense trees up ahead. This spruce valley was a dark, forbidding place even in summer; now the winter silence under the blue-black trees was more than silence—it was like a spell. Queer, they had had to choose this place to lay their trapline, just a week before his father had come down with flu-pneumonia, leaving Gordon to cover the long line during the worst weeks of winter. He wouldn't have minded tending the old line along the lake shore, but this haunted place—

Gordon Bent was sixteen, turning seventeen, already six feet tall and scantling thin.[1] The first fuzz of beard showed like a faint gray lichen[2] along his lean cheek. Timber-bred, he knew the woods and creatures as well as his father, and never before had he feared any of them. But something about this valley had filled him with dread from the first.

It would have been all right but for the nights. The valley was a mile from home, and it took him two days to cover the trapline properly. So twice a week he had to make snow camp in the deep woods near the valley's head, sleeping out in the bark-covered, half-faced lean-to he and his father had set up for the storing of trapping gear.

Almost too much to bear, it had been at first—the deathly diamond stillness of the night, the tremendous onslaught of the cold, the emptiness and the loneliness. And then he began to see and feel all the things he had longed to know; the deep woods showing him their dark and secret face, their winter side, which few men ever had the need or hardihood to learn. Only because he had been raised to like the lonely places had he grown accustomed to it. Then, in the past week or so, had come this other thing—the growing sense that he was not alone, that inimical eyes were watching him from some unguessed vantage. The feeling was so strong that he would stop often to look behind him and sometimes go back over his trail, but he saw nothing; the silence of the winter woods remained enigmatic and complete.

Once he spoke to his father about it.

"Might be some young lynx, playin' hide an' seek with you," the elder Bent had smiled. "A lynx is a tomfool for followin' humans."

Gordon had let it go at that, but he knew by the occasional fuzz of nerves along his back that the secret shadowing still went on, and that it was more than an inquisitive surveillance.[3] There was threat and danger in it. He had thought at first it might be a wolverine, that bane[4] of all trappers, whose cunning is beyond belief; but a wolverine would have played hob with[5] his traps, and this prowler did not molest his line. His catch of fur continued to mount, and he was inordinately proud, for ill luck had long dogged the back-woods family, culminating in his father's illness coming just as the high tide of the trapping season began. Each outjourney now netted him from six to a dozen prime pelts.[6] His father, lying in his cord bunk, would carefully examine every pelt that spilled from Gordon's filled sack with expert appraisal,[7] while Gordon would stand by, the faint sweat of pride on his frost-darkened face. The elder Bent would hold up the skins, blowing expertly into the piled nap[8] where it was deepest, estimating their value, each one a rare mint[9] of the secret woods.

"How many now, Son?" he would ask, and Gordon, who kept careful record,

---

1. *Scantling thin* (SKANT ling thin) is a metaphor, telling us Gordon was very thin, as thin as a small piece of wood that is part of a much larger structure called a scantling.
2. The beginnings of his beard looked like *lichen* (LY kin), a fuzzy, leafless plant found clinging to tree bark, fences, and rocks.
3. An *inquisitive surveillance* (in KWIZ uh tiv sir VAY lintz) is simply an inspection out of curiosity.
4. The *bane* (BANE) of the trapper is anything that ruins or spoils his catch.
5. *Played hob with* (played HAHB with) means interfered or made mischief with.
6. A *pelt* (PELT) is the skin, including the fur, of a fur-bearing animal.
7. An *appraisal* (uh PRAY zil) is an act of judgment or evaluation.
8. The *piled nap* (PIE ild NAP) is the thickest part of the animal's fur. The thicker the fur, the more the skin was worth.
9. A *rare mint* (MINT) (a term taken from coin collecting) refers to a forest item of unusual value.

Word Bank

sinister (SIN iss ter) *adj.*: threatening or hinting at evil, harm, or trouble

onslaught (AHN slawt) *n.*: an onset or assault, especially a vigorous one

inimical (in IM ih kul) *adj.*: unfriendly; hostile

enigmatic (EN ig MAT ik) *adj.*: mysterious; perplexing

lynx (LINX) *n.*: a fierce wildcat with a short tail and tufted ears

wolverine (WOOL ver EEN) *n.*: a carnivore of the weasel family, native to Canada and the northern United States

inordinately (in OR dihn it lee) *adv.*: excessively; unrestrainedly

culminating (KUL min ate ing) *v.*: arriving at a final or climactic stage

would study his list. "Sixty-seven now, Pa. Thirty-five of them prime number ones, I figure."

"We're getting out of the woods for fair," his father would smile. "'Spite of my lying here hog-tied and halted. Old Hard Luck went and hunted him another range after layin' me low, I guess. Couldn't cope with you nohow."

"I aim to have more skins curing[10] here than a body'll know what to do with, come February," Gordon would say largely, holding hard against the tide of feeling roused by all this praise. He was bowed these days beneath the care of the line and all the chores about the place, trying to act like the man of the house, fighting against the undermining gnawing of exhaustion and the subtler gnawing of self-importance. At all times he was aware of his father's silent appraisal. Not for anything would he have shown by word or look the fear he felt in the lonely valley. For these were the crucial days that marked his initiation into the cult of finished woodsmen.

And the valley had kept giving up its daily tithe of treasure, the skins had kept coming in. Three great bundles of them now hung in the storehouse suspended from chains against the inroads of rodents, and the cabin walls were pegged with them from floor to rafter.[11] More than pelts, they were furry flags and banners of victory, proclaiming that the Bents were winning out at last in their long handicap fight against poverty, proclaiming, too, that Gordon was no longer a stripling, but a man.

Now it was late afternoon and Gordon was making another lonely round of the line. Tonight he was to sleep in the woods again. As the short winter day drew to a close, he felt the clutch of the empty solitude like a hand squeezing the valves of his heart. He came to his night camp in a dense stand of hemlocks. As usual, he stood for a time in silence, gazing down the blue-black aisles between the trees, listening to the ancient dirge[12] of the breeze in the treetops. Always he felt the deep woods here as nowhere else in the valley, and always that sense of surveillance was stronger here.

All around his camp the dark conifers[13] stood quiet, listening, as if they were tranced and hearing something too. They talked softly among themselves in winter tones. The tall firs with their heads together whispered and creaked; the hoary[14] matted hemlocks muttered low.

---

10. *Curing* (KYUR ing) is preparing (meat, fish, fur) for preservation by salting or smoking.
11. A *rafter* is a sloping roof beam.
12. A *dirge* (DIRJ) usually refers to a funeral march. In this case, it was a slow, mournful sound.
13. *Conifers* (KAHN ih furz) are evergreen trees, so-called because they bear pine cones.
14. When a thing is *hoary* (HOR ee), it is gray or white with age.

Word Bank

undermining (UN der MYN ing) *adj.*: impairing, weakening, or destroying (health, morale, etc.) in barely noticeable stages

gnawing (NAW ing) *n.*: biting on or chewing on persistently; troubling or tormenting by constant annoyance

subtler (SUT ler) *adj.*: finer or more delicate in meaning or intent; more difficult to perceive or understand

tithe (TYTH) *n.*: a tenth part or small part of something

stripling (STRIP ling) *n.*: a youth

solitude (SAHL ih tude) *n.*: a state of being or living alone

Sometimes they sighed.

Abruptly Gordon became aware of another sound, not of the trees. His nerves tautened, and automatically he loosed the safety catch of his rifle. Then high above him he saw the source of the sound. A porcupine had just emerged from a hole high up in the big hemlock. Gordon's rifle went up and he was about to shoot the animal in nervous reaction to the start it had given him, when he recalled something his father had told him. "Never kill a porcupine," the elder Bent had counseled him, and later Gordon had found that it was a sort of unwritten law among woodsmen to let the quill-pig go unmolested. The porcupine was an utterly harmless animal, abroad at all seasons, and many a time, according to record, hunters' lives had been saved in a pinch when they killed a porcupine for food.

Gordon let his rifle drop into the crook of his arm and watched the porky slowly descending the tree trunk, accompanied by the rasping of claws on bark and a total disregard for who or what might see him. Every now and then it emitted small grunts and chatterings of petulance or satisfaction. Once it turned its gray-black, gnomelike face to eye Gordon with an expression at once mild and ludicrously irate. Its quills rose and rattled and the whole animal seemed to pale with anger and irritation, as the gray-white underfur

Word Bank

petulance (PECH oo lintz) *n.*: sudden irritation
ludicrously (LOO dih kris lee) *adv.*: ridiculously
irate (i RATE) *adj.*: angry; enraged

came into view. Then it continued its downward progress, calm with a containment that few but the great achieve. About him, if one were sensitive enough to catch it, was the sense that he was as mystically attuned to nature as the silent, grand march of the forest trees.

Gordon passed on up the valley, for he had three more traps to cover before he turned in. Darkness had fallen when he returned, and it was then that he found out why the porky had been hanging around. His grub cache[15] had been robbed. He made a hurried checkup. Nearly all of his precious supply of bacon was gone. With infinite pains, Quills had gnawed a hole clear through the split-log cache with big yellow chisels, in search of food. In an uprush of anger, Gordon rated himself for a fool, for not having shot the porcupine. If he crossed the animal's trail again, he vowed, he would kill it on sight.

Because of the robbery, he rolled into his blankets with scarcely any supper. He did not sleep for a long time, but lay looking up through the hemlock branches to the cold sky pollened with stars. Finally he drowsed off. How long afterward it was that he awakened he never knew, nor what it was that seemed to cry a sharp warning through the mists of the unconscious. It must have been something akin to those guardian instincts that animals know, and without which all wild things would soon become extinct. The same thing that had warned him brought him back to full consciousness smoothly and subtly so that not the slightest jerk or start accompanied it. Almost before his eyelids parted, he was aware of the nature of the danger that threatened.

A segment of waning moon shone through the branches overhead and into the open-ended lean-to. In the faint light, Gordon half doubted the testimony of his eyes, though at the same time something within him did not. Something about the outline of the hemlock branch directly above him drew and fixed his attention. And all at once he knew that a great cougar was crouching up there; that it had been the grim fixity[16] of the beast's regard that had jerked him out of sleep.

The limb was nine feet above him, and Gordon knew in a flash how the cougar had reached it—by climbing a tree some hundreds of feet away and picking his way among the overlapping branches. The big cat was stretched out along the branch, its powerful foreclaws unsheathed and gripping the bark in tense but silent savagery. Its yellow-notch eyes glowed lambently[17] in the flat, down-thrust head. By the savage hunger of those eyes and by every contour of the crouching form, Gordon knew that had he made a single abrupt movement on awakening, the cat would have sprung.

Gordon knew the nature of the cougar to be about eighty percent ferocity, which is just another name for cowardice, and that

---

15. *Grub* (GRUB) is an informal term for food. A *cache* (KASH) is a hidden storage area.
16. The animal was staring with *grim fixity* (FIK sih tee), meaning the animal's eyes seemed permanently fixed on him in a frightening way.
17. Something that glows *lambently* (LAM bint lee) reflects soft, or dim light.

Word Bank

attuned (uh TOOND) *v.*: brought into harmony; was in tune with
waning (WAY ning) *adj.*: gradually decreasing in strength, intensity, or size
ferocity (fuh RAHS ih tee) *n.*: fierceness; wildness
cowardice (COW er diss) *n.*: lack of courage; lack of mental and emotional strength

under ordinary circumstances a man had nothing to fear from him. But there were certain times, under certain conditions, when there was no enemy in the wilderness more dangerous. Let age slow his speed and spoil his timing and hunger have its way with him, and the lion of America leans toward man-killing, just as the lion of Africa. In the eyes of this one, Gordon sensed fear and murder struggling for mastery. Here, he knew, was the unseen shadower that had been playing havoc with his nerves.

Instinct dictated his actions in the grim moments that followed. He kept his eyes almost closed, that the beast might not catch their gleam; and his whole body remained still, in a semblance of sleep. He knew that if he so much as stirred a hand the cat would spring. But if he remained utterly still there was a slim chance that the animal might go away.

Then began an ordeal which taxed every atom of Gordon's physical and mental control. His body was numb and full of aches from sleeping in one position. Already his muscles cried out to be eased and stretched. Yet he dared not move an inch.

Moments passed, horrible heart-thudding moments, during which neither man nor animal stirred. The cougar remained frozen in his attitude of vigilance, head sunk on paws, every muscle set except for the slow, unconscious twitching of his rounded tail tip. His eyes held the boy unwinkingly as he waited in the fiendish way of cats for the moment when the man must stir, or make an attempt to escape, the moment when his ingrained fear of man would be swallowed up by the rising tide of his blood-lust.

Gordon began to feel that he was going mad. Sweat stood out on his body now, prickling sensations ran along his cramped limbs, and he could hear the pumping of blood in his temples like the beating of a great drum. He knew he could not hold out much longer, that soon his tormented nerves and muscles must assert an involuntary rebellion of their own, even though his will stood out against it.

He had located the exact position of his rifle, propped against the side of the lean-to, but he knew that a single move to reach it would precipitate[18] a lightning spring. An almost overwhelming impulse to risk all on a desperate grab for the gun obsessed him; but his cooler faculties told him he would never live to fire a shot. The cougar would be on him in a flash, his great claws like steel hooks, ripping, tearing. Yet the torture was too great for calm judgment now. He must move, in another minute, another second—

And then, even as he was on the verge of desperate action, came interruption.

A sound smote upon his overstretched nerves—slight, yet magnified a hundred times in the breathless stillness of the forest night. It was exactly timed to upset the dramatic situation at the moment of crisis, for it electrified the cougar on his high perch.

---

18. To *precipitate* (pree SIP ih tayt) is to bring about suddenly. He was afraid that any movement on his part would cause the animal to pounce on him.

Word Bank

havoc (HAV ok) *n.*: great destruction or devastation
semblance (SEM blintz) *n.*: an appearance or outward aspect; slightest appearance or trace
vigilance (VIJ uh lintz) *n.*: the state or quality of being on guard; watchfulness; alertness

Gordon saw a tremor pass over the lithe form of the killer. For a taut instant he held his breath. The slightest thing now, he knew, might draw a swift attack. Then he gasped in silent relief, for he had located the sound. So had the cougar. The flat head lifted in attention; then the eyes glared downward on the other side of the branch.

Quills, the porcupine, had recalled his stolen meal of bacon in Gordon's cache, and was returning in search of more. He had approached from behind the lean-to and was investigating the hole he had gnawed, giving vent to short grunts and faint rodent-like chatterings of anticipation. Fearless and one-pointed in his quest, he was oblivious to both man and cougar.

Above him, Gordon saw the cougar quiver slightly, its tail lashing softly. For a moment or two, he knew, the cat would not leap; for its shallow brain could focus upon but one thing at a time, and

---

Word Bank

lithe (LYTH) *adj.*: bending readily; supple; flexible

the porcupine now held the stage.

Stealthily[19] Gordon lifted the blankets and reached for his rifle, his eyes never leaving the crouched form above. His hand closed on the weapon and with a single follow-through movement he dropped to his back again and fired.

Almost in the same instant the cougar launched himself frenziedly downward. Gordon fired again from his prone position, and in mid-air the lithe outstretched body buckled and crumpled, the leap falling just short of the boy, who had flung himself aside. Again the rifle blazed death at the writhing body in the snow, and that shot took vengeance for the ordeal Gordon had undergone, and the weeks of fear that had gone before.

As the breathless silence of the night and the forest fell once more over the camp, Gordon found himself trembling all over with a cold that had nothing to do with the frost. A sort of whimper escaped him, the first sound he had made, and two hot tears sprang from his eyes and bounced off his cheeks. They were the final tears of boyhood, and he was glad he was alone with them. Never would he cry again, and never again, he felt, would he be afraid of any beast that prowled.

His eye was drawn now to the squat form of the porcupine, every quill erect and faintly limned[20] in the patch of milky moonlight. At the report of the rifle, Quills had quickly doubled up in self-defense, thrusting his nose between his forefeet. As Gordon watched, the panoply[21] of spines began slowly to lower and the little meddler took a crafty look around. The unseemly ruckus that had startled him was apparently over. Disregarding the watching boy, he returned to his rummaging, and Gordon, grinning, made no move to stop him.

Sleep was gone for him for the night. Dawn was not far off. He built a fire near the opening of the lean-to and got out his skinning knife. Only then did he sense how very near the end he had been. In the light of the flames, he saw the yellowed and broken fangs in the cougar's open jaws, the ragged, moulting[22] look of the fur and other signs of age. It had been a long time since the killer had been able to bring down his usual prey among the deer herds. Months of desperate hunger had led up to the big cat's act of daring madness.

Gordon thought with a shiver of the inevitable outcome had he shot the porcupine that afternoon as he had been tempted to do. The porcupine had repaid his little act of tolerance a hundredfold.

What a tale he'd have to tell when people gathered round hearth or campfire. No longer would he be a stripling, sitting back in the shadows, listening to the sights and feats of other hunters. He'd have a marvel to relate that matched the oldest of them now, and a pelt to prove it, as a trophy.

---

19. Here, *stealthily* (STEL thuh lee) means his actions are quiet and secretive.
20. When an object is *limned* (LIMD), it is outlined by light shining from behind. Here, the porcupine's quills were faintly outlined by the moonlight shining from behind them.
21. A *panoply* (PAN uh plee) is a magnificent covering or array. Here, the term *panoply* refers to the porcupine's needle-like covering.
22. *Moulting* (MOLT ing) is the shedding of an animal's fur. The animal's fur may be missing in spots because of old age and ill health.

Word Bank

writhing (RYTH ing) *adj.*: twisting about, as in pain or effort

Studying the Selection

First Impressions

You have read about Gordon Bent's character and his family situation. Can we separate these two parts of the equation? What might he be had his father not become ill? How have his responsibilities affected his personality?

✔ Quick Review

1. Why does Gordon know "the woods and the creatures as well as his father"?
2. What does his father think might be following Gordon?
3. Why doesn't Gordon shoot the porcupine when he first encounters it?
4. What led up to the cougar's "act of daring madness"?

In-depth Thinking

5. After first telling his father of his feeling that he was being followed in the forest, why doesn't Gordon speak of his fear again?
6. Gordon's father praises him. Touched by this pride, Gordon fights "hard against the tide of feeling roused by all this praise." Why?
7. When Gordon discovers the cougar above him, what keeps him from moving, even when the urge to do so is overwhelming?
8. Think about the title of the story and what it means to have "accounts settled." In what way have accounts been settled by the end of the story?

Drawing Conclusions

9. What might have made Mr. Bent stay a trapper, despite the hardship of earning a living from the woods and despite his family's poverty? Do you suppose Gordon will continue trapping for a living? Why or why not?
10. Have you ever experienced Gordon's need to be viewed as an equal by others in a particular group? Drawing on your own experience, why do you think being considered a "finished woodsm[a]n" is so important to Gordon? Give evidence that he has met this goal and comes of age by the end of the story.

Focusing on Plot Development: Conflict

As we have seen, conflict underlies a good story—it keeps it interesting. Other types of conflict are man vs. man, man vs. machine, and man vs. himself. Undoubtedly, you've seen examples of these conflicts before, without perhaps noticing the formula. In each instance, the protagonist, or main character and first half of the "vs." equation, is confronted by and must overcome the antagonist, or second half of the equation. The following activities will help you understand these literary terms.

1. Think of conflicts experienced by you or someone else. Perhaps an argument with a friend didn't get resolved (man vs. man); maybe you walked home from school during a sudden snowstorm (man vs. nature); or perhaps you've struggled to write a paper on a temperamental computer (man vs. machine). Finally, you might have been in a situation where you acted badly, yet pride kept you from admitting your error (man vs. himself). Choose a conflict-filled, personal situation, or one from a friend, or an imagined situation. Use the plot development pyramid in the **Blueprint for Reading** section of *The Sea Devil* as your model. Jot down the material you would put in each category to build a story around your conflict.

2. As we have seen, and perhaps you've experienced, coming of age involves conflict. Interview an adult close to you, a parent, teacher, grandparent, aunt or uncle, or perhaps a neighbor, to record a story of their coming of age. Listen carefully while they talk to you. Ask questions to draw out details of the times and places they discuss. What brought about this change to adulthood? Who were the important people in their lives? When and where did this event take place? Did they feel good about the change or were they filled with regret? Perhaps both? If so, why? Write an essay about this person's life-changing experience. In the essay, include what you learned from the story.

3. Many of the greatest stories revolve around conflict and the resulting coming of age. Think about one of your favorite stories. What makes the story interesting? Can you outline the story using the plot pyramid?

Creating and Writing

1. The porcupine in *Accounts Settled* plays a major role in the story. How does its presence affect the mood of the story? What lessons does Gordon learn from his encounters with the animal? In what way is Gordon changed because of their encounters? Write a short essay concerning these questions.

2. Write a story, using your pyramid notes from activity one or activity three in **Focusing on Conflict**. Think of the vivid details Annixter uses in *Accounts Settled* to help his readers *see* what is happening. Use similar details in your piece to make the conflict real to your readers.

3. We have learned something of forest life through *Accounts Settled*. Our country was built by risk-takers, people who sought adventure, and survived hardship. Farmers, woodsmen, mountain men, and pioneers, among others—all shaped our country. Research one of these "risk takers" to find out what these workers faced, where they came from, what skills ensured success, and what motivated them to continue. Create a collage or poster presentation highlighting the answers to these questions.

Blueprint for Reading

the Author

**O. Henry
(1862-1910)**

"O. Henry" is the pen name of William Sydney Porter, who was a gifted writer of short stories. Porter grew up in Greensboro, North Carolina. He left school at an early age, and moved to Austin, Texas, where he was employed as a bank teller. He was convicted of embezzling money and sent to prison. It was there that he began writing. His first short story was published while he was serving his sentence. At the time of his release, he was a well-known writer.

O. Henry's stories reveal the inherent goodness of man. The "common man" is depicted with tenderness, realism, and humor. His short stories are prized for their "twist" endings, which hold a surprise that is much like a wonderful dessert at the end of a good meal. One of the most prestigious literary honors, the O. Henry Award, is given each year for outstanding short fiction.

Background Bytes

As in *Accounts Settled*, pneumonia underlies the plot of *The Last Leaf*. The disease is a result of a viral or bacterial upper-respiratory infection. Pneumonia is still common today, particularly in winter. However, the threat of death from this illness receded with the arrival of antibiotics in the 1940s. In the early 20th century, when *The Last Leaf* was written, pneumonia was the most common cause of death in adults.

Into *The Last Leaf*

Two major themes dominate *The Last Leaf*. The first theme has long intrigued scientists, physicians, and psychologists: the way emotional health affects physical health. A recent magazine article discussed one aspect of this theme, the 'placebo effect.' The placebo effect occurs when physicians provide sugar pills or similar neutral medicines to patients. Just the hope of treatment can sometimes improve a patient's outlook and promote healing. The article mentions an experiment with young asthma patients. The children were given medicine with vanilla scent added. Eventually the patients "started responding to the vanilla scent alone." As the article states, "Clearly the mind can heal the body when bolstered by hope and expectation."

The other theme in the story relates to friendship of the truest kind. You have met people who care deeply for one another, who work endlessly to help a sick friend. In reading *The Last Leaf*, ask yourself what might have been Johnsy's fate without friends to stand by her. What happens to improve her outlook and change her chance of recovery? This story is a beautiful example of the positive impact of friendship, if we allow our deepest concerns to guide us.

The Last Leaf

Focusing on the Twist Ending

O. Henry is renowned for his **twist endings**. In fact, this type of ending is now called an O. Henry ending. To get the most out of his wonderful tales of the struggling poor, with their displays of quiet heroism, you should read them twice. First read *The Last Leaf* for pure enjoyment, to experience the impact of the surprise ending. A second reading offers an opportunity to play detective. Search the story for clues to the ending, clues you missed on the first reading.

Unlike *The Sea Devil* and *Accounts Settled*, where the conflict concerns man vs. nature, *The Last Leaf* deals with **inner conflict**, or **man vs. himself**. Johnsy is her own worst enemy, having lost all will to live. O. Henry slowly and gently builds the change in Johnsy, reflecting her weakness and inner turmoil. Then he skillfully uses setting and season to enhance the conflict. To lighten the dark plot, O. Henry provides humor, especially with the eccentric Mr. Behrman. His rough German accent contrasts with the rest of the prose. His playful teasing of Sue also helps lift the mood. Ask yourself how the deep friendship of the two roommates alters the bleak tone as well.

As you view the three 'actors,' pay attention to the seemingly passive Johnsy. Consider a simple magnifying lens. We use it to examine otherwise overlooked features and patterns, but we are interested in the item, not the lens. How closely could we observe Sue and Mr. Behrman if Johnsy did not serve as our 'lens'?

Word Bank

Traverse: Many English words use the Latin root *uertere*, "to turn," with a Latin prefix, such as *a-* (meaning "away"), *ad-* ("to, towards"), *con-* ("thoroughly"), *di-* ("aside"), *extro-* (outside), *trans-* ("beyond, across"). The Latin *uertere* became *vert-*. Do you know what it means to *avert* your eyes? What is an *extrovert*? Have you ever had *vertigo*? **Traverse** literally means "to turn across." Now it means "to extend or move over, across, or through."

chivalric	eaves	morbid	smiting
congenial	gnarled	ravager	solicitously
dissolution	mite	serrated	traversing

The Last Leaf

O. Henry

In a little district west of Washington Square[1] the streets have run crazy and broken themselves into small strips called "places." These "places" make strange angles and curves. One street crosses itself a time or two. An artist once discovered a valuable possibility in this street. Suppose a collector with a bill for paints, paper, and canvas should in traversing this route suddenly meet himself coming back, without a cent having been paid on account!

So, to quaint[2] old Greenwich Village[3] the art people soon came prowling, hunting for north windows and eighteenth-century gables and Dutch attics[4] and low rents. Then they imported some pewter mugs and a chafing dish[5] or two from Sixth Avenue, and became a "colony."

At the top of a squatty, three-story brick Sue and Johnsy had their studio. "Johnsy"

---

1. *Washington Square* is a famous park in the Greenwich Village section of New York City.
2. Here, the term *quaint* (KWAINT) refers to Greenwich Village's unusual, old-fashioned look.
3. *Greenwich Village* (GREN ich VILL ij) is a section of New York City, in lower Manhattan, frequented by artists and students.
4. The artists were looking for inexpensive accommodations that let in light. A *gable* (GAY bul) is a decorative, peaked structure that reaches from the roof down to its lower edge. A *Dutch attic* (DUTCH ATT ik) is an attic shaped like a barn roof, usually with a large window to let in the light.
5. A *chafing dish* (CHAY fing DISH) contains a candle, and is used to keep food warm at the table.

Word Bank

traversing (truh VERS ing) *v*.: passing or moving over, along, or through; crossing

was familiar for Joanna. One was from Maine; the other from California. They had met at the table d'hôte[6] of an Eighth Street "Delmonico's,"[7] and found their tastes in art, chicory salad, and bishop sleeves[8] so congenial that the joint studio resulted.

That was in May. In November a cold, unseen stranger, whom the doctors called Pneumonia, stalked about the colony, touching one here and there with his icy fingers. Over on the east side this ravager strode boldly, smiting his victims by scores, but his feet trod slowly through the maze of the narrow and moss-grown "places."

Mr. Pneumonia was not what you would call a chivalric old gentleman. A mite of a little woman with blood thinned by California zephyrs[9] was hardly fair game for the red-fisted, short-breathed old duffer.[10] But Johnsy he smote; and she lay, scarcely moving, on her painted iron bedstead looking through the small Dutch windowpanes at the blank side of the next brick house.

One morning the busy doctor invited Sue into the hallway with a shaggy, gray eyebrow.

"She has one chance in—let us say, ten," he said, as he shook down the mercury in his clinical thermometer. "And that chance is for her to want to live. This way people have of lining-up on the side of the undertaker makes the entire pharmacopoeia[11] look silly. Your little lady has made up her mind that she's not going to get well. Has she anything on her mind?"

"She—wanted to paint the Bay of Naples someday," said Sue.

"Paint?—bosh! Has she anything on her mind worth thinking about twice?"

"No, doctor, there is nothing."

"Well, it is the weakness, then," said the doctor. "I will do all that science, so far as it may filter through my efforts, can accomplish. But whenever my patient begins to count the carriages in her funeral procession I subtract 50 percent from the curative power of medicines. If you will get her to ask one question about the new winter styles in cloak sleeves I will promise you a one-in-five chance for her, instead of one-in-ten."

After the doctor had gone Sue went into the workroom and cried a Japanese paper

---

6. *Table d'hote* (TAHB leh DOTE) (table of the host) refers to the common table where everyone eats together.
7. *Delmonico's* (dell MAHN ih KOZE) is a fancy restaurant that is *not* located on Eighth Street. The artists met at a poor man's version of *Delmonico's*.
8. *Chicory* (CHIK ur ee) *salad* is a green, leafy salad. *Bishop sleeves* is a loose style of clothing worn like a robe.
9. *California zephyrs* (ZEF irz) are gentle mild breezes.
10. Here, the pneumonia is described as an old *duffer* (DUFF er): an incompetent, clumsy old man.
11. The doctor explains that without the will to live, the entire *pharmacopoeia* (FAR muh kooh PEE uh), or array of drugs, is useless.

Word Bank

congenial (kun JEEN yil) *adj.*: suited in tastes, temperament; compatible
ravager (RAV ij er) *n.*: someone or something that damages or destroys
smiting (SMYT ing) *v.*: afflicting or attacking with deadly or disastrous effect
chivalric (shiv AL rik) *adj.*: considerate and courteous; knightly in behavior
mite (MYT) *n.*: a very small creature, person, or thing

napkin to a pulp. Then she swaggered into Johnsy's room with her drawing board, whistling ragtime.[12]

Johnsy lay, scarcely making a ripple under the bedclothes, with her face towards the window. Sue stopped whistling, thinking she was asleep.

She arranged her board and began a pen-and-ink drawing to illustrate a magazine story. Young artists must pave their way to Art by drawing pictures for magazine stories that young authors write to pave their way to Literature.

As Sue was sketching a pair of elegant horseshow riding trousers and a monocle[13] on the figure of the hero, an Idaho cowboy, she heard a low sound, several times repeated. She went quickly to the bedside.

Johnsy's eyes were open wide. She was looking out the window and counting—counting backward.

"Twelve," she said, and a little later "eleven"; and then "ten," and "nine"; and then "eight" and "seven," almost together.

Sue looked solicitously out of the window. What was there to count? There was only a bare, dreary yard to be seen, and the blank side of the brick house twenty feet away. An old, old ivy vine, gnarled and decayed at the roots, climbed half way up the brick wall. The cold breath of autumn had stricken its leaves from the vine until its skeleton branches clung, almost bare, to the crumbling bricks.

"What is it, dear?" asked Sue.

"Six," said Johnsy, in almost a whisper.

"They're falling faster now. Three days ago there were almost a hundred. It made my head ache to count them. But now it's easy. There goes another one. There are only five left now."

"Five what, dear? Tell your friend, Sudie."

"Leaves. On the ivy vine. When the last one falls I must go, too. I've known that for three days. Didn't the doctor tell you?"

"Oh, I never heard such nonsense," complained Sue, with magnificent scorn. "What have old ivy leaves to do with your getting well? And you used to love that vine, so, you naughty girl. Don't be a goosey. Why, the doctor told me this morning that your chances for getting well real soon were—let's see exactly what he said—he said the chances were ten to one! Why, that's almost as good a chance as we have in New York when we ride on the streetcars or walk past a new building. Try to take some broth now, and let Sudie go back to her drawing, so she can sell the editor man with it, and buy some port wine for her sick child, and lamb chops for her greedy self."

"You needn't get any more wine," said Johnsy, keeping her eyes fixed out the window. "There goes another. No, I don't want any broth. That leaves just four. I

---

12. *Ragtime* (RAG TIME) was a type of music popular in the early part of the 20th century.
13. *A monocle* (MAHN uh kul) was an eyeglass for one eye. It was used much as we would use a magnifying glass.

Word Bank

solicitously (suh LISS ih tuss lee) *adv.*: anxiously or concernedly; in a kindly way

gnarled (NAR uld) *adj.*: full of or covered with knot-like shapes; bent; twisted

want to see the last one fall before it gets dark. Then I'll go, too."

"Johnsy, dear," said Sue, bending over her, "will you promise me to keep your eyes closed, and not look out the window until I am done working? I must hand those drawings in by tomorrow. I need the light, or I would draw the shade down."

"Couldn't you draw in the other room?" asked Johnsy, coldly.

"I'd rather be here by you," said Sue. "Besides, I don't want you to keep looking at those silly ivy leaves."

"Tell me as soon as you have finished," said Johnsy, closing her eyes, and lying white and still as a fallen statue, "because I want to see the last one fall. I'm tired of waiting. I'm tired of thinking, I want to turn loose my hold on everything, and go sailing down, down, just like one of those poor, tired leaves."

"Try to sleep," said Sue. "I must call Behrman up to be a model for the old hermit miner. I'll not be gone a minute. Don't try to move 'til I come back."

Old Behrman was a painter who lived on the ground floor beneath them. He was past sixty. Behrman was a failure in art. Forty years he had wielded the brush without recognition or success. He had been always about to paint a masterpiece, but had never yet begun it. For several years he had painted nothing except now and then a daub[14] in the line of commerce or advertising. He earned a little by serving as a model to those young artists in the colony who could not pay the price of a professional. He still talked of his coming masterpiece. For the rest he was a fierce little old man, who scoffed terribly at softness in anyone, and who regarded himself as especial mastiff[15]-in-waiting to protect the two young artists in the studio above.

Sue found Behrman in his dimly lighted

---

14. A *daub* (DAHB) is a painting that is not very good or well-developed.
15. A *mastiff* (MAST if) is a large, powerful dog. The old man considered himself their protector.

den below. In one corner was a blank canvas on an easel that had been waiting there for twenty-five years to receive the first line of the masterpiece. She told him of Johnsy's fancy, and how she feared she would, indeed, light and fragile as a leaf herself, float away, when her slight hold upon the world grew weaker.

Old Behrman, with his red eyes plainly streaming, shouted his contempt and derision[16] for such idiotic imaginings.

"Vaas!" he cried. "Is dere people in de world mit der foolishness to die because leafs dey drop off from a confounded vine? I haf not heard of such a thing. No, I will not bose as a model for your fool hermit-dunderhead. Vy do you allow dot silly pusiness to come in der brain of her? Ach, dot poor leetle Miss Yohnsy."

"She is very ill and weak," said Sue, "and the fever has left her mind morbid and full of strange fancies. Very well, Mr. Behrman, if you do not care to pose for me, you needn't. But I think you are a horrid old—old flibbertigibbet."

"You are just like a woman!" yelled Behrman. "Who said I will not bose? Go on, I come mit you. For half an hour I haf peen trying to say dot I am ready to bose. Dis is not any blace in which one so goot as Miss Yohnsy shall lie sick. Someday I will paint a masterpiece, and ve shall all go away. Yes."

Johnsy was sleeping when they went upstairs. Sue pulled the shade down to the window-sill, and motioned Behrman into the other room. In there they peered out the window fearfully at the ivy vine. Then they looked at each other for a moment without speaking. A persistent, cold rain was falling, mingled with snow. Behrman, in his old blue shirt, took his seat as the hermit miner on an upturned kettle for a rock.

When Sue awoke from an hour's sleep the next morning she found Johnsy with dull, wide-open eyes staring at the drawn green shade.

"Put it up; I want to see," she ordered, in a whisper.

Wearily Sue obeyed.

But, lo! after the beating rain and fierce gusts of wind that had endured through the livelong night, there yet stood out against the brick wall one ivy leaf. It was the last on the vine. Still dark green near its stem, but with its serrated edges tinted with the yellow of dissolution and decay, it hung bravely from a branch some twenty feet above the ground.

"It is the last one," said Johnsy. "I thought it would surely fall during the night. I heard the wind. It will fall today, and I shall die at the same time."

"Dear, dear!" said Sue, leaning her worn face down to the pillow, "think of me, if you won't think of yourself. What would I do?"

But Johnsy did not answer. The lonesomest thing in all the world is a soul

---

16. *Derision* (duh RIZH in) means scorn.

Word Bank

morbid (MOR bid) *adj.*: suggesting an unhealthy mental attitude; unwholesomely gloomy

serrated (SIR ayt id) *adj.*: notched on the edge like a saw

dissolution (DISS uh LOO shun) *n.*: separation into parts or elements; disintegration

when it is making ready to go on its mysterious, far journey. The fancy seemed to possess her more strongly as one by one the ties that bound her to friendship and to earth were loosed.

The day wore away, and even through the twilight they could see the lone ivy leaf clinging to its stem against the wall. And then, with the coming of the night the north wind was again loosed, while the rain still beat against the windows and pattered down from the low Dutch eaves.

When it was light enough Johnsy, the merciless, commanded that the shade be raised.

The ivy leaf was still there.

Johnsy lay for a long time looking at it. And then she called to Sue, who was stirring her chicken broth over the gas stove.

"I've been a bad girl, Sudie," said Johnsy. "Something has made that last leaf stay there to show me how wicked I was. It is a sin to want to die. You may bring me a little broth now, and some milk with a little port in it, and—no; bring me a hand-mirror first, and then pack some pillows about me, and I will sit up and watch you cook."

An hour later she said:

"Sudie, someday I hope to paint the Bay of Naples."

The doctor came in the afternoon, and Sue had an excuse to go into the hallway as he left.

"Even chances," said the doctor, looking kindly at Sue. "With good nursing you'll win. And now I must see another case I have downstairs. Behrman, his name is—some kind of artist, I believe. Pneumonia, too. He is an old, weak man, and the attack is acute. There is no hope for him; but he goes to the hospital today to be made more comfortable."

The next day the doctor said to Sue: "She's out of danger. You've won. Nutrition and care now—that's all."

And that afternoon Sue came to the bed where Johnsy lay, contentedly knitting a very blue and very useless woolen shoulder scarf, and put one arm around her, pillows and all.

"I have something to tell you, white mouse," she said. "Mr. Behrman died of pneumonia today in the hospital. He was ill only two days. The janitor found him on the morning of the first day in his room downstairs helpless with pain. His shoes and clothing were wet through and icy cold. They couldn't imagine where he had been on such a dreadful night. And then they found a lantern, still lighted, and a ladder that had been dragged from its place, and some scattered brushes, and a palette with green and yellow colors mixed on it, and—look out the window, dear, at the last ivy leaf on the wall. Didn't you wonder why it never fluttered or moved when the wind blew? Ah, darling, it's Behrman's masterpiece—he painted it there the night that the leaf fell."

Word Bank

eaves (EEVZ) *n.*: the overhanging lower edge of a roof

Studying the Selection

First Impressions

Sue and Johnsy are close friends. Do both interact with Mr. Behrman? At what point, if any, did you spot the plot twist? Did the ending surprise you?

✔ Quick Review

1. In which part of New York City do the artists live? Why did so many artists choose to live there?
2. What does the doctor say is hampering Johnsy's chances of recovering? What is causing her state of mind?
3. Johnsy has one obsession while she lies ill. What is it?
4. What role does Old Behrman assign himself in regard to the two young artists living above him?

In-depth Thinking

5. O. Henry uses personification to describe pneumonia, calling it "an unseen stranger" who "stalked about the colony, touching one here and there with his icy fingers." What effect does this description have on the reader?
6. Why is Sue's statement that Johnsy wants to "…paint the Bay of Naples someday" significant?
7. After the doctor leaves, Sue goes into the workroom and "cried a Japanese paper napkin to a pulp." Next she "swaggers" (or struts) into Johnsy's room "whistling ragtime." What does this description say about Sue's feelings for Johnsy?
8. What accounts for Mr. Behrman's outbursts and contradictions when Sue describes Johnsy's illness and obsession?

📁 Drawing Conclusions

9. Do you think Sue was as surprised as Johnsy at the staying power of the last leaf? Are there any clues in the story to indicate that Sue knew the leaf was painted, *before* she tells Johnsy the facts surrounding Mr. Behrman's death?
10. When this story was written, more men than women made a living as artists. What might be the significance of the main characters being women?

Focusing on the Twist Ending

The surprise—or **twist**—ending is most effective when supported by carefully placed events in the story. **Surprise endings** miss the mark if writers use them only for shock value, without justification. Consider how a skillful author uses details, tone, characterization, dialogue, and description to 'weave' a plot leading to a satisfying end.

1. With your teacher's help, find an O. Henry anthology, and read three stories. Jot down your initial reaction to each story, noting if the ending was satisfying or not. Choose a story to study more closely, preferably the one that most affected you, noting the effective ending. A list of clues leading to the 'twist' might help. Finally, write a review, pretending that O. Henry is an unknown author and has submitted the story to your magazine. Note the most effective elements in the story, and tell him why you are accepting the story.

2. Working with a partner, come up with a different ending for *The Last Leaf*. What events will you need to alter to fit your new ending? What changes would the characters undergo because of this ending? In what way will the tone be affected? What new title, if any, would you need to give the story? Share your revised version of the story with the class.

3. Think about the inner conflicts people undergo in their daily lives and write a list of your ideas. On a poster board, draw a line dividing the space in half. On one half, create a collage to illustrate various inner conflicts. On the other side, create a collage that shows how each conflict might be resolved. Use pens, markers, and materials from old magazines or newspapers supplied by your teacher. Other objects can also be glued to your poster board.

Creating and Writing

1. In *The Last Leaf*, the care and love of Johnsy's friends are key to her recovery. She probably would not have survived without Sue and Mr. Behrman. Think about a person who is your "life saver," someone you can't imagine being without, whose presence truly makes a difference. Write an essay about that person describing the quality you admire. Present that person with a copy of your essay.

2. Many interesting studies have been done about the influence of mind on one's health. Some studies deal with the elderly and their will to live, some with infants denied physical contact, others with the effects of stress. Locate information on this aspect of health. You might interview a doctor with first-hand experience. Often a phone interview is most convenient. Remember, doctors are busy, and you will need to make an appointment for the interview. Write a brief essay about your findings.

3. You can gain experience in helping others through volunteer work. Visit the children's ward of a local hospital or a nursing home. You may have an ailing relative who would benefit from your company. Consider visiting on a regular basis. After several visits, see if you notice a change in attitude. Has the person warmed up to you and now looks forward to your visits? Have the visits changed you in any way? Report your experience to your class. Please continue the visits!

Blueprint for Reading

the Author

**MacKinlay Kantor
(1904-1977)**

MacKinlay Kantor was born in Webster City, Iowa. When he was seventeen, his articles appeared in the *Webster City Daily News*, the newspaper his father edited. Kantor's first novel, *Diversey*, was published when he was 24, but it wasn't until 1934 that he had his first bestseller, *Long Remember*. Kantor was a war correspondent in World War II and covered the air battles of Europe. He later won a Pulitzer Prize for his Civil War novel *Andersonville*. Kantor also wrote essays, articles, poems, and short stories.

Background Bytes

As the title states, a main character in this story is blind. He wasn't born that way. Rather, he became blind as an adult, in an accident. Yet most blindness does not result from accidents. Half of all blind people are over 65, and lose their sight to cataracts, glaucoma, or macular degeneration. A small percentage of infants lose their sight to illness or malnutrition. Indeed health problems are responsible for most loss of sight. Two people in a thousand face the reality of blindness; many live full lives.

Formal education for the blind did not begin until the late 1700s, and progress was slow. During the 20th century, many rehabilitation programs were developed, opening new fields to the blind. Employers are sometimes reluctant to hire blind workers. But opportunities are limited as well by a lack of self-confidence. As often with challenging circumstances, our personalities and drive may determine how well we fare.

Into *A Man Who Had No Eyes*

In MacKinlay Kantor's story, we meet two very different characters. One man peddles cigarette lighters for a living; the author calls him a beggar. The other man has a respected job in an insurance office. As the story unfolds, we learn something surprising about the characters; the surprise holds the theme of the story.

It has been said: "Poor eyes limit your sight. Poor vision limits your deeds." How does the title of the story relate to this statement? Is the beggar truly without eyes, or does he lack *internal eyes*—vision? Why are the two characters so different—how has each handled adversity?

A Man Who Had No Eyes

Focusing on Dialogue and the Ironic Ending

As with *The Last Leaf*, *A Man Who Had No Eyes* ends unpredictably. Kantor's story differs from O. Henry's in that the conclusion not only surprises, but also contains an **ironic** "twist." **Irony** is defined as inconsistency between the actual result of a sequence of events and the expected result. Irony comes from the Greek word *eiron*. An *eiron* was a person who deliberately pretended to be less intelligent than he was. He triumphed over the *alazon*—the self-deceiving and stupid braggart. This "dissembling" or "hiding what is actually the case" remains a feature of irony.

Through the twist ending, we learn a great deal about the characters. We find our early impression misleading. As with *The Last Leaf*, you should reread this story to see how Kantor builds to his ending. What clues let us appreciate the twist at the end? Was the end satisfying? If so, why? Authors must find the right balance between revealing too much and giving enough information to make the end logical, even inevitable. Well-chosen clues along the way make a surprise ending believable. When you finish reading *A Man Who Had No Eyes*, ask yourself what details Kantor included to make the story believable, and what information he excluded to keep the ending a surprise.

The other important literary component to consider is **dialogue**. In this story much of our knowledge of character and plot development comes to us through conversation, dialogue. Do the *voices* of the characters differ? What information regarding their situation and their central conflict is revealed by the dialogue? Note how Kantor intersperses description with dialogue to help the reader *see* the events. What effect does this style of writing have on the reader?

Word Bank

Guv'nor: A frequently used term is *guv'nor*, a form of *governor*. The beggar calls Mr. Parsons *guv'nor* not because he is one, but in deference to his supposedly higher social standing. The beggar assumes Mr. Parsons will be more generous if called *guv'nor*. Notice how the beggar has adjusted to his world by becoming sensitive to the personality of his target. He is not unintelligent.

fiendishly   reminiscence   unamiably   wheedled

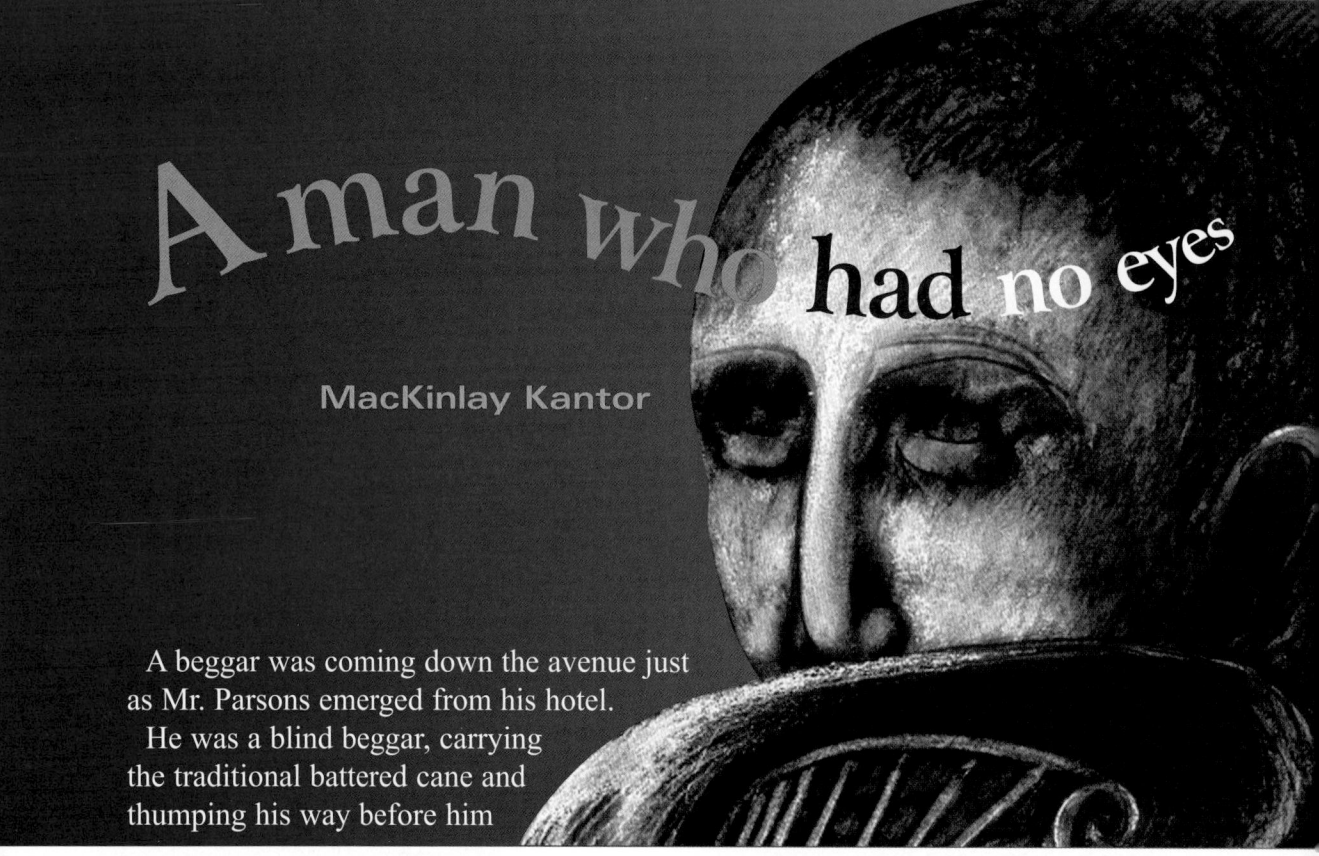

A man who had no eyes

MacKinlay Kantor

A beggar was coming down the avenue just as Mr. Parsons emerged from his hotel.

He was a blind beggar, carrying the traditional battered cane and thumping his way before him with the cautious, half-furtive[1] effort of the sightless. He was a shaggy, thick-necked fellow; his coat was greasy about the lapels and pockets, and his hand splayed[2] over the cane's crook with a futile sort of clinging. He wore a black pouch slung over his shoulder. Apparently he had something to sell.

The air was rich with spring; sun was warm and yellowed on the asphalt. Mr. Parsons, standing there in front of his hotel and noting the clack-clack approach of the sightless man, felt a sudden and foolish sort of pity for all blind creatures.

And, thought Mr. Parsons, he was very glad to be alive. A few years ago he had been little more than a skilled laborer; now he was successful, respected, admired….Insurance…And he had done it alone, unaided, struggling beneath handicaps….And he was still young. The blue air of spring, fresh from its memories of windy pools and lush shrubbery, could thrill him with eagerness.

He took a step forward just as the tap-tapping blind man passed him by. Quickly the shabby fellow turned.

"Listen, guv'nor.[3] Just a minute

---

1. The blind man moved *half-furtively* (HAF FUR tiv lee), as if trying to hide his movements.
2. The blind man *splayed* (SPLAYD) his fingers over the top of his cane; that is, he spread his fingers over the top of his cane in order to get a better grip.
3. The term *guv'nor* (GUV ner) is short for *Governor*, a term of respect used to address a man of superior rank or status.

of your time."

Mr. Parsons said, "It's late. I have an appointment. Do you want me to give you something?"

"I ain't no beggar, guv'nor. You bet I ain't. I got a handy little article here"—he fumbled until he could press a small object into Mr. Parsons' hand—"that I sell. One buck. Best cigarette lighter made."

Mr. Parsons stood there, somewhat annoyed and embarrassed. He was a handsome figure, with his immaculate gray suit and gray hat and a malacca stick.[4] Of course the man with the cigarette lighters could not see him.... "But I don't smoke," he said.

"Listen. I bet you know plenty people who smoke. Nice little present," wheedled the man. "And, mister, you wouldn't mind helping a poor guy out?" He clung to Mr. Parsons' sleeve.

Mr. Parsons sighed and felt in his vest pocket. He brought out two half dollars and pressed them into the man's hand. "Certainly. I'll help you out. As you say, I can give it to someone. Maybe the elevator boy would—" He hesitated, not wishing to be boorish[5] and inquisitive, even with a blind peddler. "Have you lost your sight entirely?"

The shabby man pocketed the two half dollars. "Fourteen years, guv'nor." Then he added with an insane sort of pride: "Westbury, sir. I was one of 'em."

"Westbury," repeated Mr. Parsons. "Ah, yes. The chemical explosion.... The papers haven't mentioned it for years. But at the time it was supposed to be one of the greatest disasters in—"

"They've all forgot about it." The fellow shifted his feet wearily. "I tell you, guv'nor, a man who was in it don't forget about it. Last thing I ever saw was C shop going up in one grand smudge, and that awful gas pouring in at all the busted windows."

Mr. Parsons coughed. But the blind peddler was caught up

---

4. A *malacca stick* (muh LAHK uh STIK) is a cane made from the stem of a palm tree found in Malaysia. In those times an important person often carried a polished stick as part of his attire.
5. A *boorish* (BORE ish) person shows a lack of manners or sensitivity.

Word Bank

wheedled (WEED ihld) *v.*: tried to influence by, using flattering words or acts

with the train of his one dramatic reminiscence. And, also, he was thinking that there might be more half dollars in Mr. Parsons' pocket.

"Just think about it, guv'nor. There was a hundred and eight people killed, about two hundred injured, and over fifty of them lost their eyes. Blind as bats—" He groped forward until his dirty hand rested against Mr. Parsons' coat. "I tell you, sir, there wasn't nothing worse than that in the war. If I had lost my eyes in the war, okay. I would have been well took care of. But I was just a workman, working for what was in it. And I got it. You're so right I got it, while the capitalists[6] were making their dough! They was insured, don't worry about that. They—"

"Insured," repeated his listener. "Yes. That's what I sell—"

"You want to know how I lost my eyes?" cried the man. "Well,

---

6. As used here, the term *capitalist* (KAP ih tul ist) is used negatively, it refers to a wealthy businessman who takes advantage of his workers.

Word Bank

reminiscence (REM ih NISS intz) *n.*: a recalling of the past; a personal remembrance from the past

here it is!" His words fell with the bitter and studied drama of a story often told, and told for money. "I was there in C shop, last of all the folks rushing out. Out in the air there was a chance, even with buildings exploding right and left. A lot of guys made it safe out the door and got away. And just when I was about there, crawling along between those big vats, a guy behind me grabs my leg. He says, 'Let me past, you——!' Maybe he was nuts. I dunno. I try to forgive him in my heart, guv'nor. But he was bigger than me. He hauls me back and climbs right over me! Tramples me into the dirt. And he gets out, and I lie there with all that poison gas pouring down on all sides of me, and flames and stuff...." He swallowed—a studied sob—and stood dumbly expectant. He could imagine the next words: Tough luck, my man. Awfully tough. Now, I want to— "That's the story, guv'nor."

The spring wind shrilled past them, damp and quivering.

"Not quite," said Mr. Parsons.

The blind peddler shivered crazily. "Not quite? What you mean, you—?"

"The story is true," Mr. Parsons said, "except that it was the other way around."

"Other way around?" He croaked unamiably. "Say, guv'nor—"

"I was in C shop," said Mr. Parsons. "It was the other way around. You were the fellow who hauled back on me and climbed over me. You were bigger than I was, Markwardt."

The blind man stood for a long time, swallowing hoarsely. He gulped: "Parsons. By heaven! By heaven! I thought you—" And then he screamed fiendishly: "Yes. Maybe so. Maybe so. But I'm blind! I'm blind, and you've been standing here letting me spout to you, and laughing at me every minute! I'm blind!"

People in the street turned to stare at him.

"You got away, but I'm blind! Do you hear? I'm—"

"Well," said Parsons, "don't make such a row[7] about it, Markwardt....So am I."

---

7. A *row* (ROU) is a noisy quarrel.

Word Bank

unamiably (un A mee uh blee) *adv.*: unpleasantly; in an unfriendly way
fiendishly (FEEN dish lee) *adv.*: in an outrageously cruel way; wickedly

Studying the Selection

First Impressions *Did you predict the ending of this story, or were you surprised? Did your impression of the characters change at the conclusion? How effective would this story be with a different ending? In this story the twist ending makes us stop and reconsider the previously read material. Yet we can't say that this story, except for the type of ending, resembles The Last Leaf. Can you see any major difference?*

✔ Quick Review

1. What does Mr. Parsons feel upon "noting the clack-clack approach of the sightless man"?
2. Although the author begins the story "A beggar was coming down the avenue…," the character denies he is a beggar. What reason does he give to support his denial?
3. How did the beggar become blind?
4. When Mr. Parsons recognizes the beggar, why does he say the actual event "was the other way around"?

In-depth Thinking

5. We are told that Mr. Parsons "was very glad to be alive." What does the rest of the paragraph with that phrase tell the reader about Mr. Parsons?
6. Why might the beggar have spoken of Westbury and the accident "with an insane sort of pride"?
7. Mr. Parsons coughs when the beggar mentions Westbury. What does this simple action reveal about Mr. Parsons? What do the next two sentences in the paragraph reveal about the beggar?
8. Early in the story the day is described as "rich with spring." We're told the "blue air of spring, fresh from its memories of windy pools and lush shrubbery, could thrill [Mr. Parsons] with eagerness." After the beggar relates his story to Mr. Parsons, the author switches and says the "spring wind shrilled past them, damp and quivering." What accounts for the difference in tone, and what purpose might this description play in the story?

Drawing Conclusions

9. Compare the physical descriptions of the beggar and Mr. Parsons. The beggar "was a shaggy, thick-necked fellow; his coat was greasy about the lapels and pockets, and his hand splayed over the cane's crook with a futile sort of clinging." Mr. Parsons, on the other hand, "was a handsome figure, with his immaculate gray suit and gray hat and malacca stick." How does this visual distinction support the ending of the story?
10. Both men are salesmen. What is ironic about the goods they sell?

Focusing on Dialogue and the Ironic Ending

Each of these activities deals with a literary device used for emotional effect. Complete the following activities, using the story as your model.

1. Plays rely heavily on the use of dialogue to build plot. Ask your teacher or librarian to recommend a short play to read. Notice how stage directions act in a manner similar to Kantor's selective description. Note how character is revealed through dialogue. Now write a two-part essay about Kantor's short story. In the first part, use the "I" voice (first-person narrative) of one character to describe the other. Then reverse the situation, writing about the second character. Your descriptions should reflect the characters' feelings about each other and hint at the central conflict of the story.

2. It is said that life is stranger than fiction, in large part because of the ironies of daily life. Interview friends, family, and teachers to find real-life ironic situations. Provide the person you are interviewing with a definition and examples of irony if they are unsure how to respond. Choose the most unusual situation, and recount it in an essay. The ironic situation will often have a twist ending. Use enough description to allow your readers to experience fully the ironic twist.

3. Try your hand at writing a short story depending on dialogue between the two main characters. Build the story around a central conflict. Plan the story, knowing the ending in advance. Decide what can be revealed by dialogue and what can be shown through description. Share your story with the class.

Creating and Writing

1. People often change their past to excuse present behavior. Mr. Markwardt did so, but to what advantage? In an essay, discuss how his view of the past affected his life. Compare the result of his living a lie with Mr. Parsons' way of dealing with the truth.

2. Helen Keller became deaf and blind at 19 months, from a high fever. With the aid of her teacher, Anne Sullivan, she learned to read and write. Helen Keller inspired many by writing and speaking about her experiences as a deaf-blind person. Find out more about this famous woman by reading any of her writings. Report your findings to the class.

3. Find out what social service programs are available for the blind in your community. Call an agency for the blind to see what volunteer opportunities exist; then make an effort to help. You will learn much about the blind through your active involvement.

Blueprint for Reading

Background Bytes

Countess is a title for a woman of noble birth. In the story, we do not know whether the woman *is* a Countess, nor do we know anything about her history. Apparently, she does not mix easily with the people in the town. Her style of living and her precise language suggests she feels superior to others—or perhaps this is simply the way she has been raised to be.

When the Countess meets the boy who narrates the story, we have a clash of cultures. He behaves casually—he's young and American and she finds him cutting through her hedge. She is a foreigner, a lady with standards, and she stops him. It is clear that she has come to a land where the natives are in need of a strong hand. She accepts her responsibility: She asks the boy a series of questions and when he leaves he has committed himself to the job of cutting her lawn. She *will* impose civilization on a backward land. The boy—as an American and a young person—will benefit from the lessons learned. This is *not* an article about lawn care.

Into *The Countess and the Impossible*

The narrator of this story has grown as a result of meeting the Countess. She has assigned a goal, a seemingly impossible goal, and he has performed beyond his own expectations. Now, as an adult, he looks back, and appreciates her demanding personality. The "young man"—we never learn his name—has been shaped by her, and for the better. Her lesson remains with him.

We see this simple—yet powerful—narrative unfolding before us, and we watch the young man rise to the challenge. Only at the end is the theme stated directly, as the young man realizes he has been asked to "…grow an inch or a foot, or a mile…" in order that he might "…come to a fuller life."

The Countess has set the narrative in motion, but the theme becomes real through the internal struggles of a young boy discovering this truth for himself. What is he worth? How can he grow? How can he achieve the impossible?

Have you asked these same questions? How might you find your answers?

The Countess and the IMPOSSIBLE

Focusing on the Protagonist and Antagonist

Throughout his narrative, the **protagonist** (or main character), gives us a first-person viewpoint. He describes the Countess vividly as the focus of his small world. But the role of the storyteller changes, as he steps back into the past, becoming a boy of thirteen again, the main character in his remembered drama.

The Countess is the **antagonist**, the person opposing the main character. In reality, her standards are the psychological and physical barriers that become the **internal conflict** for the main character. When the boy first begins the job, he is motivated by money. As he is paid each week, the Countess assesses his efforts, often in a seemingly patronizing manner. Yet her remarks prove to be the very stimulus he needs for success.

The clear writing pictures a young boy coming of age, giving us a sense of a small Utah town in a vanished America. The story line allows the reader a glimpse into an encounter that forever changes a young boy's life.

Word Bank

Expiring: Expire is another example from Latin, with a root word (*spirare*, to breath) and a prefix (*ex-*, out), that has dozens of sister words in English. To name only a few, there's *spirit, aspirate, aspire, conspiracy, inspire, perspire,* and *respirator*. Can you think of any others? If we learn the meanings of the prefixes, our vocabularies are increased immeasurably. When a person expires, he or she breathes out.

chastise	expiring	inaccessible	symmetrical
clod			

The Countess and the IMPOSSIBLE

Richard Y. Thurman

No one in our Utah town knew where the Countess had come from; her carefully precise English indicated that she was not a native American. From the size of her house and staff, we knew that she must be wealthy, but she never entertained, and she made it clear that when she was at home she was completely inaccessible. Only when she stepped outdoors did she become at all a public figure—and then chiefly to the small fry[1] of the town, who lived in awe of her.

The Countess always carried a cane, not only for support but as a means of chastising any youngster she thought needed disciplining. And at one time or another most of the kids in our neighborhood seemed to display that need. By running fast and staying alert I had managed to keep out of her reach. But one day when I was thirteen, as I was short-cutting through her hedge, she got close enough to rap my head with her stick. "Ouch!" I yelled, jumping a couple of feet.

"Young man, I want to talk to you," she said. I was expecting a lecture on the evils of trespassing, but as she looked at me, half-smiling, she seemed to change her mind. "Don't you live in that green house with the willow trees, in the next block?"

"Yes, ma'am."

"Do you take care of your lawn? Water it? clip it? mow it?"

---

1. *Small fry* (*fry* are young fish) is an endearing way to refer to young children.

Word Bank

inaccessible (IN ak SESS uh bul) *adj.*: impossible to approach; unreachable

chastise (chass TYZ) *v.*: discipline, especially using physical punishment; criticize severely

THE COUNTESS AND THE IMPOSSIBLE / 61

"Yes, ma'am."

"Good. I've lost my gardener. Be at my house Thursday morning at seven, and don't tell me you have something else to do. I've seen you slouching around on Thursdays."

When the Countess gave an order, it was carried out. I didn't dare not come on that next Thursday. I went over the whole lawn three times with a mower before she was satisfied, and then she had me down on all fours looking for weeds until my knees were as green as the grass. She finally called me up to the porch.

"Well, young man, how much do you want for your day's work?"

"I don't know. Fifty cents maybe."

"Is that what you figure you're worth?"

"Yes'm. About that."

"Very well. Here's the fifty cents you say you're worth, and here's the dollar and a half more that I've earned for you by pushing you. Now I'm going to tell you something about how you and I are going to work together. There are as many ways of mowing a lawn as there are people, and they may be worth anywhere from a penny to five dollars. Let's say that a three-dollar job would be just what you've done today, except that you would do it all by yourself. A four-dollar job would be so perfect that you'd have to be something of a fool to spend that much time on a lawn. A five-dollar lawn is—well, it's impossible, so we'll forget about that. Now then, each week I'm going to pay you according to your own evaluation of your work."

I left with my two dollars, richer than I remembered being in my whole life and determined that I would get four dollars out of her the next week. But I failed to reach even the three-dollar mark. My will began faltering the second time around her yard.

"Two dollars again, eh? That kind of job puts you right in the edge of being dismissed, young man."

"Yes'm. But I'll do better next week."

And somehow I did. The last time around the lawn I was exhausted, but I found I could spur myself on.[2] In the exhilaration[3] of that new feeling, I had no hesitation in asking the Countess for three dollars.

Each Thursday for the next four or five weeks, I varied between a three- and a three-and-a-half-dollar job. The more I became acquainted with her lawn, places where the ground was a little high or a little low, places where it needed to be clipped short or left long on the edges to make a more satisfying curve along the garden, the more aware I became of just what a four-dollar lawn would consist of. And each week I would resolve to do just that kind of job. But by the time I had made my three- or three-and-a-half-dollar mark, I was too tired to remember ever having had the ambition to go beyond

---

2. To *spur myself on* means to push myself, as a rider spurs a horse forward.
3. *Exhilaration* (eg ZIL uh RAY shun) refers to the excitement felt by the young worker.

that point.

"You look like a good, consistent three-fifty man," she would say as she handed me the money.

"I guess so," I would say, too happy at the sight of the money to remember that I had shot for something higher.

"Well, don't feel too bad," she would comfort me. "After all, there are only a handful of people in the world who could do a four-dollar job."

And her words *were* a comfort at first. But then, without my noticing what was happening, her comfort became an irritant that made me resolve to do that four-dollar job, even if it killed me. In the fever of my resolve, I could see myself expiring on her lawn, with the Countess leaning over me, handing me the four dollars with a tear in her eye, and begging my forgiveness for having thought I couldn't do it.

It was in the middle of such a fever, one Thursday night when I was trying to forget that day's defeat and get some sleep, that the truth hit me so hard I sat upright, half-choking in my excitement. It was the *five-dollar* job I had to do, not the four-dollar one! I had to do the job that no one could do because it was impossible.

I was well acquainted with the difficulties ahead. I had the problem, for example, of doing something about the worm mounds in the lawn. The Countess might not even have noticed them yet, they were so small; but in my bare feet, I knew about them and I had to do something about them. And I *could* go on trimming the garden edges with shears, but I knew that a five-dollar lawn demanded that I line up each edge exactly with a yardstick and then trim it precisely with the edger. And there were other problems that only I and my bare feet knew about.

I started the next Thursday by ironing out the worm mounds with a heavy roller. After two hours of that, I was ready to give up for the day. Nine o'clock in the morning and my will was already gone! It was only by accident that I discovered how to regain it. Sitting under a walnut tree for a few minutes after finishing the rolling, I fell asleep. When I woke up minutes later, the lawn looked so good through my fresh eyes and felt so good under my feet that I was anxious to get on with the job.

I followed this secret for the rest of the day, dozing a few minutes every

Word Bank **expiring** (ek SPY ir ing) *v.*: breathing the last breath; dying

hour to regain my perspective and replenish my strength. Between naps I mowed four times, two times lengthwise, two times across, until the lawn looked like a green velvet checkerboard. Then I dug around every tree, crumbling the big clods and smoothing the soil with my hand, then finished with the edger, meticulously lining up each stroke so the effect would be perfectly symmetrical. And I carefully trimmed the grass between the flagstones[4] of the front walk. The shears wore my fingers raw, but the walk never looked better.

Finally about eight o'clock that evening, after I had run home at five for a bite of supper, it was all completed. I was so proud I didn't even feel tired when I went up to her door.

"Well, what is it today?" she asked.

"Five dollars," I said, trying for a little calm and sophistication.

---

4. *Flagstones* (FLAG STONEZ) are stones used, without cement, to pave the front path leading to the house.

Word Bank

clod (CLAHD) *n.*: a lump or mass of earth or clay

symmetrical (sih MET rih kul) *adj.*: well-balanced; having harmonious proportions in shape, size; having corresponding parts, so that the right and left sides are mirror images

"Five dollars? You mean four dollars, don't you? I told you that a five-dollar lawn isn't possible."

"Yes it is. I just did it."

"Well, young man, the first five-dollar lawn in history certainly deserves some looking around."

We walked about the lawn together in the last light of evening, and even I was quite overcome by the impossibility of what I had done.

"Young man," she said, putting her hand on my shoulder, "what on earth made you do such a crazy, wonderful thing?"

I didn't know why, but even if I had, I couldn't have explained it in the excitement of hearing that I *had* done it.

"I think I know," she continued, "how you felt when this idea came to you of mowing a lawn that I had told you was impossible. It made you very happy when it first came, then a little frightened. Am I right?"

She could see she was right by the startled look on my face.

"I know how you felt because the same thing happens to almost everybody. They feel this sudden burst in them of wanting to do some great thing. They feel a wonderful happiness. But then it passes because they have said, 'No, I can't do that. It's impossible.' Whenever something in you says 'It's impossible,' remember to take a careful look. See if it isn't really G-d asking you to grow an inch, or a foot, or a mile, that you may come to a fuller life."

She folded my hand around the money. "You've been a great man today. It's not often a man gets paid for a thing like greatness. You're getting paid because you're lucky and I like you. Now run along."

Since that time, some twenty-five years ago, when I have felt myself at an end with nothing before me, suddenly with the appearance of that word "impossible" I have experienced again the unexpected lift, the leap inside me, and known that the only possible way lay through the very middle of the impossible.

Studying the Selection

First Impressions

The Countess was effective in encouraging the boy. Would you recommend her method as a general technique? How would you react to such a challenge?

✔ Quick Review

1. Describe the Countess. Why is she so unusual in this town?
2. What does the Countess tell the boy to do? How is she going to pay him?
3. What accidentally learned trick helps the boy regain his will to work?
4. When did the boy actually complete the five-dollar job?

In-depth Thinking

5. Compare the boy's initial motivation for working for the Countess to his later motivation.
6. Analyze how the Countess inspired the boy to do a five-dollar job.
7. Why do you think that the four-dollar job wasn't enough?
8. What lessons did the boy learn from his experiences?

Drawing Conclusions

9. Have you ever known a person with a disposition similar to that of the Countess? How did he or she get that way? Use your knowledge to create a past for the Countess. Write a short character sketch, building on the information given by the narrator.
10. Can you apply the theme of this story to your own life? Write a brief essay about a challenge you are facing.

Focusing on the Protagonist and Antagonist

Earlier we learned two literary terms relating to character: **protagonist** and **antagonist**. Once again, the **protagonist** *is* the main character. The **antagonist** is the character in conflict with the main character in a story.

1. Your teacher will suggest sources for this assignment. Cut out five or more newspaper articles dealing with conflict. See if you can identify and highlight the antagonist and protagonist in each case.

2. Choose a theme revolving around a goal you would like to achieve. Write two sample conversations centering on your theme.

    a. First, imagine an antagonist speaking against your goal. How would the antagonist stop you from achieving your goal? Is the obstacle another person, a lack of finances, your own fears, or some other element of the situation?

    b. Now write the conversation again. Neutralize the attacks of the antagonist and show how your dream can become a reality.

3. List five characters who play the part of the protagonist or antagonist in any of your favorite stories.

Creating and Writing

1. Write a plan showing how you would convince your best friend to keep trying to achieve a goal, even in an impossible situation.
2. Make an entry in a diary, as if you are an adult looking back on a real event that is currently happening.
3. Aim for the impossible. Create a "Class Guinness Book of World Records" or "Fun Olympics." Assemble a group of friends and do the following activities. Feel free to come up with a few of your own challenges (with permission from your teacher).
    - See who can sing a note the longest without stopping to take a breath.
    - See who can stare the longest without blinking.
    - See who can jump the highest.
    - See who can hold his or her breath the longest.
    - See who can stand on one foot for the longest time.

    After the contest, talk about what it felt like to win or lose these different contests. Was there anything in particular that motivated you? How does this simple exercise relate to the story?

Blueprint for Reading

the Author

Shirley Jackson (1919-1965)

Born in San Francisco, California, Shirley Jackson went to school in New York, attending the University of Rochester and Syracuse University. She wrote novels, short stories, and media scripts. She was noted for her haunting works of fiction and horror. She often inserted unexpected disturbances into her humorous stories about suburban life.

Background Bytes

This story, like *The Last Leaf* and *A Man Who Had No Eyes*, ends with a surprise. Like many kindergarten children, Laurie tells stories, but his stories are always about a child named Charles. From the start, Charles, a fellow student, challenges all rules. Laurie's parents become more and more involved in the "Charles saga," even giving Charles a role in the family humor, never questioning their son's tales. Told from the viewpoint of Laurie's mother, *Charles* offers us a humorous peek into Laurie's world.

Into *Charles*

Why do people act as they do? Literature tackles this fascinating question again and again. In *Charles* we have a child leaving home to attend kindergarten. His classmate Charles, clever and strong-willed, handles the demands of school in an interesting way—at least as described by Laurie (the **main character** or **protagonist**). Why does Charles act that way? Why do Laurie's parents accept his account of classroom events? For that matter, why do they accept Laurie's behavior at home?

Before you read the story, think about people you have met. Write a short description of someone who often challenges authority or acts disobediently. Why do you suppose the person behaves that way?

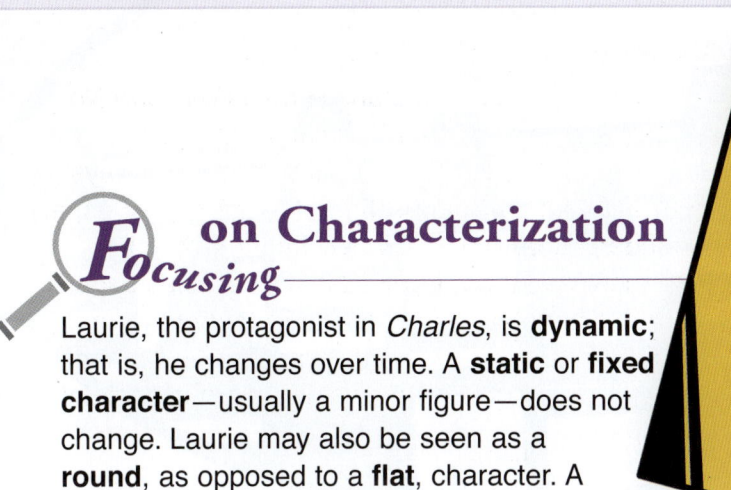

Focusing on Characterization

Laurie, the protagonist in *Charles*, is **dynamic**; that is, he changes over time. A **static** or **fixed character**—usually a minor figure—does not change. Laurie may also be seen as a **round**, as opposed to a **flat**, character. A **round** character has various personality traits and characteristics. A **flat** character has one unchanging trait. Laurie's personality suggests depth and complexity.

Jackson uses both **direct** and **indirect characterization** to portray her main character. We learn about him through Jackson's **direct** descriptions. **Indirectly** we learn about him by taking in his comments and behavior, and through his descriptions of Charles. We think we know him. Then Jackson, with a surprise ending, makes us reconsider Laurie.

Word Bank

Maneuver: The Latin word for "hand" is *manus*. The word for "work," is *opus*, or *operare*. Therefore, the Latin *manuopera* meant "to work by hand." In French, the 'p' was changed to a 'v,' for *manoeuvre*, manual labor. The meaning changed over time. The word **maneuver** came into English and today means "to move skillfully, avoiding obstacles."

insolently   maneuvered   primly   solemnly

Charles

By Shirley Jackson

The day my son Laurie started kindergarten he renounced[1] corduroy overalls with bibs and began wearing blue jeans with a belt: I watched him go off the first morning with the older girl next door, seeing clearly that an era of my life was ended, my sweet-voiced, nursery-school tot replaced by a long-trousered, swaggering[2] character who forgot to stop at the corner and wave goodbye to me.

He came home the same way, the front door slamming open, his cap on the floor, and the voice suddenly became raucous[3] shouting, "Isn't anybody *here*?"

At lunch he spoke insolently to his father, spilled his baby sister's milk, and remarked that his teacher said we were not to take the name of the L-rd in vain.

"How *was* school today?" I asked, elaborately casual.

"All right," he said.

"Did you learn anything?" his father asked.

Laurie regarded his father coldly. "I didn't learn nothing," he said.

---

1. To *renounce* (re NOWNS) is to give up or put aside.
2. One who is *swaggering* (SWAG ger ing) walks in a very proud, aggressive way.
3. *Raucous* (RAW cuss) means rough-sounding.

"Anything," I said. "Didn't learn anything."

"The teacher spanked a boy, though," Laurie said, addressing his bread and butter. "For being fresh," he added, with his mouth full.

"What did he do?" I asked. "Who was it?"

Laurie thought. "It was Charles," he said. "He was fresh. The teacher spanked him and made him stand in a corner. He was awfully fresh."

"What did he do?" I asked again, but Laurie slid off his chair, took a cookie, and left, while his father was still saying, "See here, young man."

The next day Laurie remarked at lunch, as soon as he sat down, "Well, Charles was bad again today." He grinned enormously and said, "Today Charles hit the teacher."

"Good heavens," I said, mindful of the L-rd's name, "I suppose he got spanked again?"

"He sure did," Laurie said.

"Why did Charles hit the teacher?" I asked quickly.

"Because she tried to make him color with red crayons," Laurie said. "Charles wanted to color with green crayons so he hit the teacher and she spanked him and said nobody play with Charles but everybody did."

The third day—it was Wednesday of the first week—Charles bounced a seesaw onto the head of a little girl and made her bleed, and the teacher made him stay inside all during recess. Thursday Charles had to stand in a corner during storytime because he kept pounding his feet on the floor. Friday Charles was deprived of blackboard privileges because he threw chalk.

On Saturday I remarked to my husband, "Do you think kindergarten is too unsettling for Laurie? All this toughness, and bad grammar, and this Charles boy sounds like such a bad influence."

"It'll be all right," my husband said reassuringly. "Bound to be people like Charles in the world. Might as well meet them now as later."

On Monday Laurie came home late, full of news, "Charles," he shouted as he came up the hill; I was waiting anxiously on the front steps. "Charles," Laurie yelled all the way up the hill, "Charles was bad again."

"Come right in," I said, as soon as he came close enough. "Lunch is waiting."

"You know what Charles did?" he demanded, following me through the door. "Charles yelled so in school they sent a boy in from first grade to tell the teacher she had to make Charles keep quiet, and so Charles had to stay after school. And so all the children stayed to watch him."

"What did he do?" I asked.

"He just sat there," Laurie said, climbing into his chair at the table. "Hi, Pop."

"Charles had to stay after school today," I told my husband. "Everyone stayed with him."

"What does this Charles look like?" my husband asked Laurie. "What's his other name?"

"He's bigger than me," Laurie said. "And he doesn't have any rubbers and he doesn't ever wear a jacket."

Monday night was the first Parent-

Word Bank

insolently (IN suh lint lee) *adv.*: disrespectfully; in a boldly rude way

Teachers meeting, and only the fact that the baby had a cold kept me from going; I wanted passionately to meet Charles's mother. On Tuesday Laurie remarked suddenly, "Our teacher had a friend come to see her in school today."

"Charles's mother?" my husband and I asked simultaneously.

"Naaah," Laurie said scornfully. "It was a man who came and made us do exercises, we had to touch our toes. Look." He climbed down from his chair and squatted down and touched his toes. "Like this," he said. He got solemnly back into his chair and said, picking up his fork, "Charles didn't even *do* exercises."

"That's fine," I said heartily. "Didn't Charles want to do exercises?"

"Naaah," Laurie said. "Charles was so fresh to the teacher's friend he wasn't *let* do exercises."

"Fresh again?" I said.

"He kicked the teacher's friend," Laurie said. "The teacher's friend told Charles to touch his toes like I just did and Charles kicked him."

"What are they going to do about Charles, do you suppose?" Laurie's father asked him.

Laurie shrugged elaborately. "Throw him out of school, I guess," he said.

Wednesday and Thursday were routine; Charles yelled during story hour and hit a boy in the stomach and made him cry. On Friday Charles stayed after school again and so did all the other children.

With the third week of kindergarten Charles was an institution in our family; the baby was being a Charles when she cried all afternoon; Laurie did a Charles when he filled his wagon full of mud and pulled it through the kitchen; even my husband, when he caught his elbow in the telephone cord and pulled telephone, ashtray, and a bowl of flowers off the table, said, after the first minute, "Looks like Charles."

During the third and fourth weeks it looked like a reformation[4] in Charles; Laurie reported grimly at lunch on Thursday of the third week, "Charles was so good today the teacher gave him an apple."

"What?" I said, and my husband added warily,[5] "You mean Charles?"

"Charles," Laurie said. "He gave the crayons around and he picked up the books afterward and the teacher said he was her helper."

"What happened?" I asked incredulously.[6]

"He was her helper, that's all," Laurie said, and shrugged.

"Can this be true, about Charles?" I asked my husband that night. "Can something like this happen?"

"Wait and see," my husband said cynically.[7] "When you've got a Charles to deal with, this may mean he's only plotting."

He seemed to be wrong. For over a week Charles was the teacher's helper; each day he handed things out and he picked things

---

4. *Reformation* (REF or MAY shun) refers to a complete turnaround or improvement in Charles's behavior.
5. To respond *warily* (WAIR ih lee) is to respond guardedly. Laurie's father was not sure whether to be happy or not.
6. Laurie's mother responded *incredulously* (in KREJ yuh liss lee); that is, she did not or could not believe that Charles had really improved.
7. Laurie's father spoke *cynically* (SIN ih klee), in a way that showed he did not fully trust Charles.

Word Bank

solemnly (SAHL em lee) *adv.*: seriously; earnestly

up; no one had to stay after school.

"The P.T.A. meeting's next week again," I told my husband one evening. "I'm going to find Charles's mother there."

"Ask her what happened to Charles," my husband said. "I'd like to know."

"I'd like to know myself," I said.

On Friday of that week things were back to normal. "You know what Charles did today?" Laurie demanded at the lunch table, in a voice slightly awed. "He told a little girl to say a word and she said it and the teacher washed her mouth out with soap and Charles laughed."

"What word?" his father asked unwisely, and Laurie said, "I'll have to whisper it to you, it's so bad." He got down off his chair and went around to his father. His father bent his head down and Laurie whispered joyfully. His father's eyes widened.

"Did Charles tell the little girl to say *that*?" he asked respectfully.

"She said it *twice*," Laurie said. "Charles told her to say it *twice*."

"What happened to Charles?" my husband asked.

"Nothing," Laurie said. "He was passing out the crayons."

Monday morning Charles abandoned the little girl and said the evil word himself three or four times, getting his mouth washed out with soap each time. He also threw chalk.

My husband came to the door with me that evening as I set out for the P.T.A. meeting. "Invite her over for a cup of tea after the meeting," he said. "I want to get a look at her."

"If only she's there," I said prayerfully.

"She'll be there," my husband said. "I don't see how they could hold a P.T.A. meeting without Charles's mother."

At the meeting I sat restlessly, scanning each comfortable matronly face, trying to determine which one hid the secret of Charles. None of them looked to me haggard[8] enough. No one stood up in the meeting and apologized for the way her son had been acting. No one mentioned Charles.

After the meeting I identified and sought out Laurie's kindergarten teacher. She had a plate with a cup of tea and a piece of chocolate cake; I had a plate with a cup of tea and a piece of marshmallow cake. We maneuvered up to one another cautiously, and smiled.

"I've been so anxious to meet you," I said. "I'm Laurie's mother."

"We're all so interested in Laurie," she said.

"Well, he certainly likes kindergarten," I said. "He talks about it all the time."

"We had a little trouble adjusting, the first week or so," she said primly, "but now he's a fine little helper. With occasional lapses,[9] of course."

"Laurie usually adjusts very quickly," I said. "I suppose this time it's Charles's influence."

"Charles?"

"Yes," I said laughing, "you must have had your hands full in that kindergarten, with Charles."

"Charles?" she said. "We don't have any Charles in the kindergarten."

---

8. To appear *haggard* (HAG urd) is to look exhausted and worn out from pain or suffering.
9. *With occasional lapses* (LAP siz) means reverting to old ways, as in misbehavior.

Word Bank

maneuvered (muh NOO verd) *v.*: moved skillfully to avoid obstacles

primly (PRIM lee) *adv.*: properly; in a formally precise way

Studying the Selection

First Impressions

First write a few paragraphs about Laurie, focusing on why you think he behaves as he does, and why he tells his parents such fantastic stories about Charles.

Now consider Laurie's parents. Why might they be so tolerant of his sudden change in behavior? Why haven't they told the school of their concerns and why did they wait until PTA night to ask about Charles? Now return to your essay. Are your impressions still the same regarding Laurie's behavior?

✔ Quick Review

1. What two details in the first paragraph of the story signal to the narrator that her son is growing up?
2. List four of the behaviors that get Charles in trouble at school.
3. Why doesn't Laurie's mother attend the first Parent-Teachers meeting?
4. How does Charles reform during the third and fourth weeks of school?

In-depth Thinking

5. Why do you think Laurie feels the need to report on Charles's behavior?
6. Why might Laurie's parents be slow to learn Charles's true identity?
7. Why doesn't the kindergarten teacher contact Laurie's parents about his misbehavior?
8. Why does Charles's behavior change for the better?

Drawing Conclusions

9. Speculate on the parents' reaction after learning Charles does not exist.
10. Based upon your knowledge of real life, is Laurie's behavior typical?

Focusing on Characterization

1. Laurie's personality unfolds via both **direct** and **indirect characterization**. Identify at least three details that directly characterize him (Laurie's own actions or language). Then identify three details that indirectly characterize him (what others say about him or what he says about Charles).
2. As a **dynamic character**, Laurie changes over time. What evidence do we have of this change?
3. It can be instructive to 'look in the mirror,' to view oneself as others do. Write a description of yourself as if you were writing about someone else. (Be gentle!)

Creating and Writing

1. Assume the voice of Laurie's kindergarten teacher and write a letter about his behavior for placement in his permanent file. Speculate on the motivations for his actions and how you see him developing. Include a note about meeting Laurie's mother.
2. Write a memoir of your first month of school. How did you respond to the new surroundings, your teacher, the other children? Were you frightened or excited by the independence gained at school? Did your parents or siblings help you adjust? Include details that bring your five-year-old self to life.
3. In groups of two or three, act out a scene in which a person must deal with one of life's milestones (going off to camp for the first time, transferring from one school to another, moving up a grade). Dramatize the struggles faced in passing these milestones.

Blueprint for Reading

the Author

Kurt Vonnegut Jr. (1922-2007)

Kurt Vonnegut was born in Indianapolis, Indiana. He attended Cornell University, the Carnegie Institute of Technology, and the University of Chicago. While serving in World War II he was captured and imprisoned in Dresden, the setting of his novel *Slaughterhouse-Five* (1969). After the war, he worked as a reporter and then for General Electric. He taught at various schools before settling in New York City, where he wrote nonfiction pieces, novels, short stories, and plays.

Background Bytes

The No-Talent Kid differs greatly from Kurt Vonnegut's usual fantasy or science fiction stories. Here we have a realistic but revealing tale about a music teacher and a member of a high school band. Within a recognizable and—at first glance—ordinary world, Vonnegut presents a fascinating character and an important message about individual strengths and weaknesses. Vonnegut's trademark writing style, with its tongue-in-cheek sense of humor, works well here.

Into *The No-Talent Kid*

Each of us is born with special gifts and talents. This is the major theme of the apparently misnamed *The No-Talent Kid*. We have different talents, and it takes some work, for many of us, to identify them. Our title character is, as you may have guessed, highly talented. Before reading the story, list *your* talents. Do your friends agree with your judgment? Might they see other talents in you?

THE *No-Talent Kid*

*F*ocusing on Dialogue as a Key to Character

Vonnegut, a gifted craftsman, defines personality through **dialogue**. As Mr. Helmholtz and Walter Plummer, the two main characters, engage in verbal ping-pong, they do more than advance the plot: They reveal their motivations, their strengths and weaknesses. It may help to read the dialogue aloud with a friend. Vonnegut is particularly skilled at the **direct characterization** of characters through their own words. Also note the interior monologue Vonnegut provides, giving us access to the private thoughts of Mr. Helmholtz. Without the interior monologue, we wouldn't have the same story. The additional reflections, seen from his point of view, let us appreciate his feelings.

> **Word Bank**
>
> **Gait:** When you see a short, one-syllable word, it often comes from Old English, the Germanic, or Scandinavian languages. Such words don't provide the clues that the Latin roots give us. **Gait**, which has the alternative spelling, *gate*, is related to its English homonym, *gate*. **Gait**, which means "a manner of walking," comes from Old Norse *gata*, a lane, and probably was brought to England by the Goths.
>
> | | | | |
> |---|---|---|---|
> | appraisingly | inaudible | persevered | virtuosity |
> | arbitrarily | judiciously | rebuked | |
> | gait | ovation | sullenly | |

The No-Talent Kid

— Kurt Vonnegut Jr.

It was autumn, and the leaves outside Lincoln High School were turning the same rusty color as the bare brick walls in the band-rehearsal room. George M. Helmholtz, head of the music department and director of the band, was ringed by folding chairs and instrument cases; and on each chair sat a very young man, nervously prepared to blow through something, or, in the case of the percussion section, to hit something, the instant Mr. Helmholtz lowered his white baton.

Mr. Helmholtz, a man of forty, who believed that his great belly was a sign of health, strength and dignity, smiled angelically, as though he were about to release the most exquisite sounds ever heard by men. Down came his baton.

"Blooooomp!" went the big sousaphones.

"Blat! Blat!" echoed the French horns, and the plodding, shrieking, querulous[1] waltz was begun.

Mr. Helmholtz's expression did not change as the brasses lost their places, as the

---

1. A *querulous* (KWER ih liss) waltz is music that sounds like a complaint. In other words, it did not sound very good.

woodwinds' nerve failed and they became inaudible rather than have their mistakes heard, as the percussion section shifted into a rhythm pattern belonging to a march they knew and liked better.

"A-a-a-a-ta-ta, a-a-a-a-a-a, ta-ta-ta-ta!" sang Mr. Helmholtz in a loud tenor, singing the first cornet part when the first cornetist, florid[2] and perspiring, gave up and slouched in his chair, his instrument in his lap.

"Saxophones, let me hear you," called Mr. Helmholtz. "Good!"

This was the C Band, and, for the C Band, the performance was good; it couldn't have been more polished for the fifth session of the school year. Most of the youngsters were just starting out as bandsmen, and in the years ahead of them they would acquire artistry enough to move into the B Band, which met in the next hour. And finally the best of them would gain positions in the pride of the city, the Lincoln High School Ten Square Band.

The football team lost half its games and the basketball team lost two thirds of its, but the band, in the ten years Mr. Helmholtz had been running it, had been second to none until last June. It had been first in the state to use flag twirlers, the first to use choral as well as instrumental numbers, the first to use triple-tonguing[3] extensively, the first to march in breathtaking double time, the first to put a light in its bass drum. Lincoln High School awarded letter sweaters to the members of the A Band, and the sweaters were deeply respected—and properly so. The band had won every statewide high school band competition in the last ten years—every one save the one in June.

As the members of the C Band dropped out of the waltz, one by one, as though mustard gas[4] were coming out of the ventilators, Mr. Helmholtz continued to smile and wave his baton for the survivors, and to brood inwardly over the defeat his band had sustained in June, when Johnstown High School had won with a secret weapon, a bass drum seven feet in diameter. The judges, who were not musicians but politicians, had had eyes and ears for nothing but this eighth wonder of the world, and since then Mr. Helmholtz had thought of little else. But the school budget was already lopsided with band expenses. When the school board had given him the last special appropriation[5] he'd begged so desperately—money to wire the plumes of the bandsmen's hats with flashlight bulbs and batteries for night games—the board had made him promise that this was the last time.

Only two members of the C Band were playing now, a clarinetist and a snare drummer, both playing loudly, proudly, confidently, and all wrong. Mr. Helmholtz, coming out of his wistful dream of a bass drum bigger than the one

---

2. Someone who is *florid* (FLOR id) is red-faced with exertion.
3. *Triple-tonguing* (TRIP il TUNG ing) is a way to play rapid notes on a brass wind instrument.
4. *Mustard gas* (MUSS terd GASS) is poisonous. The students stopped playing, as if overcome by poison gas.
5. Here, *appropriation* (uh PRO pree AY shun) refers to money the school board authorized to be paid to the high school for band expenses.

Word Bank

inaudible (in AW dih bul) *adj.*: too quiet or distant to be heard

that had beaten him, administered the *coup de grâce*[6] to the waltz by clattering his stick against his music stand. "All righty, all righty," he said cheerily, and he nodded his congratulations to the two who had persevered to the bitter end.

Walter Plummer, the clarinetist, nodded back soberly, like a concert soloist receiving an ovation led by the director of a symphony orchestra. He was small, but with a thick chest developed in summers spent at the bottom of swimming pools, and he could hold a note longer than anyone in the A Band, much longer, but that was all he could do. He drew back his tired, reddened lips, showing the two large front teeth that gave him the look of a squirrel, adjusted his reed,[7] limbered his fingers, and awaited the next challenge to his virtuosity.

This would be Plummer's third year in the C Band, Mr. Helmholtz thought, with a mixture of pity and fear. Nothing, apparently, could shake Plummer's determination to earn the right to wear one of the sacred letters of the A Band, so far, terribly far away.

Mr. Helmholtz had tried to tell Plummer how misplaced his ambitions were, to recommend other fields for his great lungs and enthusiasm, where pitch[8] would be unimportant. But Plummer was blindly in love, not with music, but with the letter sweaters, and, being as tone-deaf as boiled cabbage, he could detect nothing in his own playing to be discouraged about.

"Remember, now," said Mr. Helmholtz to the C Band, "Friday is challenge day, so be on your toes. The chairs you have now were assigned arbitrarily. On challenge day it'll be up to you to prove which chair you deserve." He avoided the narrowed, confident eyes of Plummer, who had taken the first clarinetist's chair without consulting the seating plan posted on the bulletin board. Challenge day occurred every two weeks, and on that day any bandsman could challenge anyone ahead of him to a contest for his position, with Mr. Helmholtz as utterly dispassionate[9] judge.

Plummer's hand was raised, its fingers snapping urgently.

"Yes, Plummer?" said Mr. Helmholtz, smiling bleakly. He had come to dread challenge days because of Plummer, and had come to think of it as Plummer's day. Plummer never challenged anybody in the C Band or even in the B Band, but stormed the organization at the very top, challenging, as was unfortunately the privilege of all, only members of the A Band. The waste of the A Band's time

---

6. A *coup de grace* (KOO DAY GRAH) is a blow to end suffering. Here it means the last stroke of the band. The suffering players were permitted to stop playing.
7. A *reed* is a small, flexible piece of wood set into the mouthpiece of a wind instrument.
8. Here, *pitch* (PICH) refers to the musician's ability to create the correct tone with his instrument.
9. To be *dispassionate* (dis PASH ih nit) is to be without personal feeling or bias: to be impartial.

Word Bank

persevered (PUR suh VEERD) *v.*: persisted in pursuing a goal in spite of obstacles or opposition

ovation (oh VAY shun) *n.*: an enthusiastic, public show of approval, marked especially by loud, prolonged applause

virtuosity (VUR choo AH sih tee) *n.*: excellence in a skill or performance

arbitrarily (AR bih TRAIR ih lee) *adv.*: unreasonably; done according to one individual's will; on a whim

was troubling enough, but infinitely more painful for Mr. Helmholtz were Plummer's looks of stunned disbelief when he heard Mr. Helmholtz's decision that he hadn't outplayed the men he'd challenged. And Mr. Helmholtz was thus **rebuked** not just on challenge days, but every day, just before supper, when Plummer delivered the evening paper. "Something about challenge day, Plummer?" said Mr. Helmholtz uneasily.

"Mr. Helmholtz," said Plummer coolly, "I'd like to come to A Band session that day."

"All right—if you feel up to it." Plummer always felt up to it, and it would have been more of a surprise if Plummer had announced that he wouldn't be at the A Band session.

"I'd like to challenge Flammer."

Word Bank

rebuked (ree BYOOKT) *v*.: sternly disapproved of; reprimanded

THE NO-TALENT KID / 81

The rustling of sheet music and clicking of instrument-case latches stopped. Flammer was the first clarinetist in the A Band, a genius that not even members of the A Band would have the gall[10] to challenge.

Mr. Helmholtz cleared his throat. "I admire your spirit, Plummer, but isn't that rather ambitious for the first of the year? Perhaps you should start out with, say, challenging Ed Delaney." Delaney held down the last chair in the B Band.

"You don't understand," said Plummer patiently. "You haven't noticed I have a new clarinet."

"H'm'm? Oh—well, so you do."

Plummer stroked the satin-black barrel of the instrument as though it were like King Arthur's sword, giving magical powers to whoever possessed it. "It's as good as Flammer's," said Plummer. "Better, even."

There was a warning in his voice, telling Mr. Helmholtz that the days of discrimination were over, that nobody in his right mind would dare to hold back a man with an instrument like this.

"Um," said Mr. Helmholtz. "Well, we'll see, we'll see."

After practice, he was forced into close quarters with Plummer again in the crowded hallway. Plummer was talking darkly to a wide-eyed freshman bandsman.

"Know why the band lost to Johnstown High last June?" asked Plummer, seemingly ignorant of the fact that he was back to back with Mr. Helmholtz. "Because," said Plummer triumphantly, "they stopped running the band on the merit system. Keep your eyes open on Friday."

Mr. George Helmholtz lived in a world of music, and even the throbbing of his headaches came to him musically, if painfully, as the deep-throated boom of a cart-borne bass drum seven feet in diameter. It was late afternoon on the first challenge day of the new school year. He was sitting in his living room, his eyes covered, awaiting another sort of thump—the impact of the evening paper, hurled against the clapboard of the front of the house by Walter Plummer.

As Mr. Helmholtz was telling himself that he would rather not have his newspaper on challenge day, since Plummer came with it, the paper was delivered with a crash that would have done credit to a siege gun.

"Plummer!" he cried furiously, shaken.

"Yes, sir?" said Plummer solicitously[11] from the sidewalk.

Mr. Helmholtz shuffled to the door in his carpet slippers. "Please, my boy," he said plaintively,[12] "can't we be friends?"

"Sure—why not?" said Plummer, shrugging. "Let bygones be bygones, is what I say." He gave a bitter imitation of an amiable chuckle.[13] "Water over the dam. It's been two hours now since the knife was stuck in me and twisted."

Mr. Helmholtz sighed. "Have you got a moment? It's time we had a talk, my boy."

Plummer kicked down the standard on his bicycle, hid his papers under shrubbery,

---

10. To have *gall* (GAWL) is to have great impudence, boldness, or daring.
11. Plummer spoke *solicitously* (suh LISS ih tiss lee), anxiously; eagerly with deep concern to his teacher.
12. His teacher spoke to him *plaintively* (PLAIN tiv lee), sorrowfully, regretting earlier events.
13. An *amiable chuckle* is a friendly, short laugh.

and walked in sullenly. Mr. Helmholtz gestured at the most comfortable chair in the room, the one in which he'd been sitting, but Plummer chose instead to sit on the edge of a hard one with a straight back.

Mr. Helmholtz, forming careful sentences in his mind before speaking, opened his newspaper, and laid it open on the coffee table.

"My boy," he said at last, "G-d made all kinds of people: some who can run fast, some who can write wonderful stories, some who can paint pictures, some who can sell anything, some who can make beautiful music. But He didn't make anybody who could do everything well. Part of the growing-up process is finding out what we can do well and what we can't do well." He patted Plummer's shoulder gently. "The last part, finding out what we can't do, is what hurts most about growing up. But everybody has to face it, and then go in search of his true self."

Plummer's head was sinking lower and lower on his chest and Mr. Helmholtz hastily pointed out a silver lining. "For instance, Flammer could never run a business like a paper route, keeping records, getting new customers. He hasn't that kind of a mind, and couldn't do that sort of thing if his life depended on it."

"You've got a point," said Plummer, looking up suddenly with unexpected brightness. "A guy's got to be awful one-sided to be as good at one thing as Flammer is. I think it's more worthwhile to try to be better-rounded. No, Flammer beat me fair and square today, and I don't want you to think I'm a bad sport about that. It isn't that that gets to me."

"That's very mature of you," said Mr. Helmholtz. "But what I was trying to point out to you was that we've all got weak points, and—"

Plummer charitably waved him to silence. "You don't have to explain to me, Mr. Helmholtz. With a job as big as you've got, it'd be a miracle if you did the whole thing right."

"Now, hold on, Plummer!" said Mr. Helmholtz.

"All I'm asking is that you look at it from my point of view," said Plummer. "No sooner'd I come back from challenging A Band material, no sooner'd I come back from playing my heart out, than you turned those C Band kids loose on me. You and I know we were just giving 'em the feel of challenge days, and that I was all played out. But did you tell them that? No, you didn't, Mr. Helmholtz, and those kids all think they can play better than me. That's all I'm sore about, Mr. Helmholtz. They think it means something, me in the last chair of the C Band."

"Plummer," said Mr. Helmholtz evenly, "I have been trying to tell you something as kindly as possible, but apparently the only way to get it across to you is to tell it to you straight."

"Go ahead and quash[14] criticism," said Plummer, standing.

"Quash?"

"Quash," said Plummer with finality. He headed for the door. "I'm probably ruining my chances for getting into the A Band by speaking out like this, Mr.

---

14. To *quash* (KWAHSH) is to put down or put a stop to.

Word Bank

sullenly (SUL in lee) *adv.*: gloomily and irritably

Helmholtz, but frankly, it's incidents like what happened to me today that lost you the band competition last June."

"It was a seven-foot bass drum!"

"Well, get one for Lincoln High and see how you make out then."

"I'd give my right arm for one!" said Mr. Helmholtz, forgetting the point at issue and remembering his all-consuming dream.

Plummer paused on the threshold. "One like the Knights of Kandahar use in their parades?"

"That's the ticket!" Mr. Helmholtz imagined the Knights of Kandahar's huge drum, the showpiece of every local parade. He tried to think of it with the Lincoln High School black panther painted on it. "Yes, sir!" When he returned to earth, Plummer was on his bicycle.

Mr. Helmholtz started to shout after Plummer, to bring him back and tell him bluntly that he didn't have the remotest chance of getting out of C Band ever; that he would never be able to understand that the mission of a band wasn't simply to make noises, but to make special kinds of noises. But Plummer was off and away.

Temporarily relieved until next challenge day, Mr. Helmholtz sat down to enjoy his paper, to read that the treasurer of the Knights of Kandahar, a respected citizen, had disappeared with the organization's funds, leaving behind and unpaid the Knights' bills for the past year and a half. "We'll pay a hundred cents on the dollar, if we have to sell everything but the special Mace," the Sublime Chamberlain of the Inner Circle was on record as saying.

Mr. Helmholtz didn't know any of the people involved, and he yawned and turned to the funnies. He gasped suddenly, turned to the front page again, looked up a number in the phone book, and dialed feverishly.

"Zum-zum-zum-zum," went the busy signal in his ear. He dropped the telephone clattering into its cradle. Hundreds of people, he thought, must be trying to get in touch with the Sublime Chamberlain of the Inner Circle of the Knights of Kandahar at this moment. He looked up at his flaking ceiling in deep thought. But none of them were after a bargain in a cart-borne bass drum.

He dialed again and again, always getting the busy signal, and walked out on his porch to relieve some of the tension building up in him. He would be the only one bidding on the drum, he told himself, and he could name his own price. If he offered fifty dollars for it, he could probably have it! He'd put up his own money, and get the school to pay him back in three years, when the plumes with the electric lights in them were paid for in full.

He laughed at this magnificent stroke of fortune. As he exhaled happily, his gaze dropped to his lawn, and he saw Plummer's undelivered newspapers lying beneath the shrubbery.

He went inside and called the Sublime Chamberlain again, with the same results. To make the time go, and to do a good turn, he called Plummer's home to let him know where the papers were mislaid. But the Plummers' line was busy too.

He dialed alternately the Plummers' number and the Sublime Chamberlain's number for fifteen minutes before getting a ringing signal.

"Yes?" said Mrs. Plummer.

"This is Mr. Helmholtz, Mrs. Plummer.

Is Walter there?"

"He was here a minute ago, telephoning, but he just went out of here like a shot."

"Looking for his papers? He left them under my spiraea."[15]

"He did? Oh my, I have no idea where he was going. He didn't say anything about his papers, but I thought I overheard something about selling his clarinet." She sighed and then laughed nervously. "Having money of their own makes them awfully independent. He never tells me anything."

"Well, you tell him I think maybe it's for the best, his selling his clarinet. And tell him where his papers are."

It was unexpected good news that Plummer had at last seen the light about his musical career, and Mr. Helmholtz now called the Sublime Chamberlain's home again for more good news. He got through this time, but was momentarily disappointed to learn that the man had just left on some sort of lodge business. For years Mr. Helmholtz had managed to smile and keep his wits about him in C Band practice sessions. But on the day after his fruitless efforts to find out anything about the Knights of Kandahar's bass drum, his defenses were down, and the poisonous music penetrated to the roots of his soul.

"No, no, no!" he cried in pain, and he threw his white baton against the brick wall. The springy stick bounded off the bricks and fell into an empty folding chair at the rear of the clarinet section—Plummer's empty chair.

As Mr. Helmholtz, red-faced and apologetic, retrieved the baton, he found himself unexpectedly moved by the symbol of the empty chair. No one else, he realized, no matter how untalented, could ever fill the last chair in the organization as well as Plummer had. He looked up to find many of the bandsmen contemplating the chair with him, as though they, too, sensed that something great, in a fantastic way, had disappeared, and that life would be a good bit duller on account of it.

During the ten minutes between the C Band and B Band sessions, Mr. Helmholtz hurried to his office and again tried to get in touch with the Sublime Chamberlain of the Knights of Kandahar, and was again told what he'd been told substantially several times during the night before and again in the morning.

"L—rd knows where he's off to now. He was in for just a second, but went right out again. I gave him your name, so I expect he'll call you when he gets a minute. You're the drum gentleman, aren't you?"

"That's right—the drum gentleman."

The buzzers in the hall were sounding, marking the beginning of another class period. Mr. Helmholtz wanted to stay by the phone until he'd caught the Sublime

---

15. A *spiraea* (spy REE uh) is a roselike shrub that has clusters of small white or pink flowers.

Chamberlain and closed the deal, but the B Band was waiting—and after that it would be the A Band.

An inspiration came to him. He called Western Union, and sent a telegram to the man, offering fifty dollars for the drum, and requesting a reply collect.

But no reply came during B Band practice. Nor had one come by the halfway point of the A Band session. The bandsmen, a sensitive, high-strung lot, knew immediately that their director was on edge about something, and the rehearsal went badly. Mr. Helmholtz was growing so nervous about the drum that he stopped a march in the middle because of a small noise coming from the large double doors at one end of the room, where someone out-of-doors was apparently working on the lock.

"All right, all right, let's wait until the racket dies down so we can hear ourselves," he said.

At that moment, a student messenger handed him a telegram. Mr. Helmholtz beamed, tore open the envelope, and read:

DRUM SOLD STOP COULD YOU USE A STUFFED CAMEL ON WHEELS STOP.

The wooden doors opened with a shriek of rusty hinges, and a snappy autumn gust showered the band with leaves. Plummer stood in the great opening, winded and perspiring, harnessed to a drum on wheels that could have contained a dozen youngsters his size.

"I know this isn't challenge day," said Plummer, "but I thought you might make an exception in my case."

He walked in with splendid dignity, the huge apparatus grumbling along behind him.

Mr. Helmholtz rushed to meet him, and crushed Plummer's right hand between both of his. "Plummer, boy! You got it for us! Good boy! I'll pay you whatever you paid for it," he cried, and in his joy he added rashly, "and a nice little profit besides. Good boy!"

Plummer laughed modestly. "Sell it?" he said. "I'll give it to you when I graduate," he said grandly. "All I want to do is play it in the A Band while I'm here."

"But, Plummer," said Mr. Helmholtz uneasily, "you don't know anything about drums."

"I'll practice hard," said Plummer reassuringly. He started to back his instrument into an aisle between the tubas and the trombones—like a man backing a trailer truck into a narrow alley—backing it toward the percussion section, where the amazed musicians were hastily making room.

"Now, just a minute," said Mr. Helmholtz, chuckling as though Plummer were joking, and knowing full well he wasn't. "There's more to drum playing than just lambasting[16] the thing whenever you take a notion to, you know. It takes years to be a drummer."

"Well," said Plummer cheerfully, "the quicker I get at it, the quicker I'll get good."

"What I meant was that I'm afraid you won't be quite ready for the A Band for a little while."

Plummer stopped his backing. "How long?" he asked suspiciously.

---

16. *Lambasting* (lam BAYS ting) refers to the way an amateur will beat a drum, very hard without regard for tune or rhythm.

"Oh, sometime in your senior year, perhaps. Meanwhile, you could let the band have your drum to use until you're ready."

Mr. Helmholtz's skin began to itch all over as Plummer stared at him coldly, appraisingly. "Until it snows in August?" Plummer said at last.

Mr. Helmholtz sighed resignedly. "I'm afraid that's about right." He shook his head sadly. "It's what I tried to tell you yesterday afternoon: nobody can do everything well, and we've all got to face up to our limitations. You're a fine boy, Plummer, but you'll never be a musician—not in a million years. The only thing to do is what we all have to do now and then: smile, shrug, and say, 'Well, that's just one of those things that's not for me.' "

Tears formed on the rims of Plummer's eyes, but went no farther. He walked slowly toward the doorway, with the drum tagging after him. He paused on the doorsill for one more wistful look at the A Band that would never have a chair for him. He smiled feebly and shrugged. "Some people have eight-foot drums," he said kindly, "and others don't, and that's just the way life is. You're a fine man, Mr. Helmholtz, but you'll never get this drum in a million years, because I'm going to give it to my mother for a coffee table."

"Plummer!" cried Mr. Helmholtz. His plaintive voice was drowned out by the rumble and rattle of the big drum as it followed its small master down the school's concrete driveway.

Mr. Helmholtz ran after him with a floundering, foot-slapping gait. Plummer and his drum had stopped at an intersection to wait for a light to change, and Mr. Helmholtz caught him there, and seized his arm. "We've got to have that drum," he panted. "How much do you want?"

"Smile," said Plummer. "Shrug! That's what I did." Plummer did it again. "See? So I can't get into the A Band, so you can't have the drum. Who cares? All part of the growing-up process."

"The situations aren't the same!" said Mr. Helmholtz furiously. "Not at all the same!"

The light changed, and Plummer left Mr. Helmholtz on the corner, stunned.

Mr. Helmholtz had to run after him again. "Plummer," he said sweetly, "you'll never be able to play it well."

"Rub it in," said Plummer, bitterly.

"But you're doing a beautiful job of pulling it, and if we got it, I don't think we'd ever be able to find anybody who could do it as well."

Plummer stopped, backed and turned the instrument on the narrow sidewalk with speed and hair-breadth precision, and headed back for Lincoln High School, skipping once to get in step with Mr. Helmholtz.

As they approached the school they both loved, they met and passed a group of youngsters from the C Band, who carried unscarred instrument cases and spoke self-consciously of music.

"Got a good bunch of kids coming up this year," said Plummer judiciously. "All they need's a little seasoning."

Word Bank

appraisingly (uh PRAY zing lee) *adv.*: with an eye towards estimating the nature, quality, or importance of

gait (GAYT) *n.*: the manner of walking, stepping, or running

judiciously (joo DISH iss lee) *adv.*: having or characterized by good judgment

Studying the Selection

First Impressions

List Walter Plummer's most obvious talents. Which actions show these talents? Think ahead twenty years. Do you think you might read about Walter Plummer some day? What might his future hold?

✔ Quick Review

1. Name three Lincoln High School bands. Describe the skill level in each.
2. Why does Mr. Helmholtz think Lincoln lost to Johnstown in the last band competition?
3. Describe Walter Plummer's skills as a musician.
4. How did Mr. Helmholtz and Walter finally get what they wanted?

In-depth Thinking

5. Why does Walter insist on challenging members of the A Band, despite his past failures?
6. When Walter misses a day of C Band practice, his absence is noticed. What does Walter bring to this organization?
7. Analyze Mr. Helmholtz's skills as a band teacher. Do you feel he treats Walter fairly? Why or why not?
8. Look at Plummer's final speech. How has he become Mr. Helmholtz's equal?

Drawing Conclusions

9. How might Walter use his special talents later in life?
10. How does this story provide a model for reconciliation (settling a disagreement) between antagonists?

Focusing on Dialogue as a Key to Character

Character is revealed by speech, by action, and by the comments of others. In the following questions, focus on the role of **speech** in revealing character.

1. "Language most shows a man: speak that I may see thee" (Ben Jonson, *Timber*). If language "shows a man," what do we learn about Walter Plummer from his language and tone? Use specific examples.
2. Write a short dialogue between two characters to reveal unmistakable personality traits. Read your dialogue to two friends and see if each can identify the traits you had in mind. Do they agree? If not, why?
3. Imagine a story in which only one character speaks. What would such a story lack? Why is it so difficult to write good dialogue? Choose your favorite ten to fifteen lines of dialogue from this story and analyze their effectiveness.

Creating and Writing

1. "Talent is insignificant. I know a lot of talented ruins. Beyond talent lie all the usual words: discipline, love, luck, but, most of all, endurance" (James Baldwin). In a short essay, respond to Baldwin's statement. Do you agree with him? How might this quotation apply to Walter Plummer?
2. Write a poem (15-20 lines) entitled "Talent is…" Include the name of a tree, the name of a color, and the name of an emotion. Now copy a dictionary definition of *talent*. Which do you prefer?
3. Report to your class on a historical figure who was thought to lack talent but ended up achieving greatness.

Blueprint for Reading

Background Bytes

Judging others is easy—or so we may think, since it happens so often and so effortlessly. We simply look outward and pronounce sentence. Yet what happens when we look within? Do we judge ourselves by the same standards that we apply to others? Can we even see ourselves as we see others? When we do look within, are we happy with our findings? Or humbled?

The discovery of self is a frequent theme in literature—often crucial in stories that use harsh landscapes to test character. *The Warden* uses a wilderness setting, but not just to show man in conflict with nature. The larger drama here is Harlan Bellamy's internal conflict: the conflict he has within himself.

Bellamy, the protagonist, has grown up in this wilderness setting. He identifies himself with wilderness skills. But he has grown away from the special demands of the region, because of the tasks that occupy him as game warden. Game wardens may be responsible for large tracts of state lands, but their jobs involve monitoring hunters, supervising road and trail repairs, overseeing maintenance, and processing administrative paperwork. They are desk-bound.

Although Bellamy is not entirely isolated from the Big Panther range of the story, he is no longer at home in the woods. Does he know this? Can he bear to know that he "has lost his edge"?

Into *The Warden*

As we grow up and develop an identity, we face the expectations of others. We may feel trapped in a **persona** or role. We may feel we are not perceived accurately by others. Or we may feel that we need to keep up a façade, in order to be liked or respected by others. Sometimes, we may feel that we ourselves, the persons we feel ourselves to be inside, do not count; only our accomplishments matter. What then happens when we fail at something? Write in your journal about a time when the expectations of others felt more important than anything else.

The Warden

Focusing on Character: Self-Awareness

Most major characters face both **internal** and **external conflicts**. **Internal conflicts** occur within—self-doubt, guilt, ambivalent feelings. **External conflicts** occur outside—quarreling with a neighbor, driving on a slick road, breaking a leg. Carousso, like many authors, uses his major character's external conflict (getting lost in the Big Panther range) to uncover an internal conflict (his unwillingness to face his own weaknesses). As you read, notice how Harlan Bellamy avoids confronting his own vulnerabilities. Why does he do this?

When characters come to self-knowledge, we say they have an epiphany (eh PIH fah nee), a deeper understanding of self, of others, or society. The warden comes close to such a moment, but ultimately avoids true understanding. Note how Carousso italicizes the messages Bellamy should be accepting from his subconscious.

Word Bank

Grotesque: When we see a word ending *–que*, it often comes to us from French. The French word usually has come from Latin. The Italian *grottos*, or underground vaults, were decorated in a way that was fashionable in ancient Rome. But tastes change, and such ornamentation came to be seen as ridiculous. The French **grotesque**, and its English counterpart, came to mean "absurdly incongruous, departing markedly from the natural, the expected, or the typical, bizarre."

converge	integral	traipsing
grotesquely	rend	wraith

The Warden

Georges Carousso

The searching party was gathered on the open hotel porch, smoking silently, casting uneasy glances up at the shrouded[1] mountains. It was snowing hard up there. It would be a nasty search. Harlan Bellamy, the game warden, walked heavily up and down the porch, chewing viciously on the stem of his pipe. There was a man lost somewhere on the Big Panther range. Some fool tenderfoot[2] deer hunter with not enough sense to carry a compass, or know how to use it if he did.

Having a man lost in your district meant trouble. It meant you had to make out reports to the Department; you had to gather up state troopers and the fire ranger and what guides did not happen to be working and as many natives as you could get; you had to go out and find the dumb tenderfoot, and then you had to start making reports all over again. And all that while, every violator who had a piece of illegal doe meat could sneak right out of the country without a man to check him. If Game Warden Bellamy had his way, lost hunters could stay lost.

A little apart from the natives, the lost man's hunting companions formed a small, restless group. They were city slickers. They talked too much. They argued too much, in nervous little sentences that blamed Bill, the lost man, and the weather, and Joe, who should have stuck by Bill, and the country in general, and Big Panther Mountain in particular. The natives sat passively by. They listened and said nothing.

"What are we waiting around here

---

1. Something *shrouded* (SHROU did) is covered or hidden from view. The mountains were *shrouded* by the falling snow.
2. A *tenderfoot* (TEN der FOOT) is a raw, inexperienced person: a novice.

for?" a big man asked. He seemed to be the leader of the hunting party.

Bellamy looked the man over coolly. "We're waiting for Bert Ellis," he said, trying to keep the anger out of his voice. "Best guide up Big Panther country. Knows it better than any of us."

Then suddenly, because he was scared, anger came into his voice. "We don't go off half-cocked,"[3] he said irritably. "And if you folks didn't go off half-cocked, there wouldn't be men getting lost around here!" He knew he was scared. Big Panther country was plenty big. And Bear Trap Swamp, in back of it, was bigger still. The chances of finding the lost hunter were small. Bellamy faced the hunters, hemming them in with his bulk and anger.

"Just because there's a hard-surface road through here, you city folks think that this is tame country. It ain't! It's seventy-five miles of mountains and swamps and lakes straight west to the next road. You fellers think you can hunt this country without guides or compasses, or without even studying a topographical map.[4] Every year some of you get lost. And when you get lost, you panic. And the panic kills you, if the cold don't."

The hunters did not answer but they looked up at the snow clouds on the mountains. A battered jitney[5] pulled up and Bert Ellis, a small, wiry middle-aged man with a week's growth of beard, got out. He passed a critical eye over the men on the porch.

"This is all the men you got?" he asked.

The warden nodded. "That's all, Bert."

The little man shrugged. "That Panther country's mighty big," he said thoughtfully. He got back in his car. Bellamy got in beside him. The rest of the men walked to their cars and started piling in.

"How're you goin' to run this search?" the warden asked.

"Dunno," said Ellis. "Most lost men sort of swing around the shoulder of the mountain and get theirselves tangled up in Bear Trap Swamp. Need a thousand men to spook 'em out of there."

"This feller's pals claim he ain't lost," the warden said. "Claim he must be hurt because they didn't hear no signal shots."

"Most likely throwed his gun away minute he found he was lost. Most of 'em do. They get excited."

They drove the cars to the foot of Panther Mountain and pulled them in along the old tote road[6] that cut off the main highway. They went single file along the tote road, Ellis leading, then the natives, then the city hunters. Bellamy brought up the rear.

Ellis walked with his shoulders hunched against the snow, his hands in his pockets, and the gun hanging loosely from the crook of his arm. Most of the natives walked that way, loose-hipped, slouched, their guns an

---

3. To go off *half-cocked* (HAF KAHKT) is to go into the wilderness unprepared, without the supplies necessary for survival.
4. A *topographical map* (TAHP uh GRAF ih kul MAP) shows mountains, hills, and valleys, as well as roads and towns.
5. A *jitney* (JIT nee) is a small passenger bus or taxi that follows a regular route.
6. Here, an *old tote* (TOTE) *road* refers to an old road used to transport people or supplies to the forest.

integral part of them. They walked fast—faster now that they had a bunch of city slickers[7] with them, showing off a bit with a subconscious mixture of pride and malice.

The hunters were walking stiffly, their bodies tensed against the dangers of the unfamiliar footing. The guns they carried were alien to them, and they shifted them from one hand to the other, from one shoulder to the other, unable to make them part of the balance of their motions. The gap between them was widening. One of them kept at the heels of the close-packed group of natives for a while, then he too dropped back.

Ellis sure is setting a pace, Bellamy thought. *He sure is giving them the works.*

Bellamy himself was puffing. Well, he was not as young as he had been, and he had put on a bit of weight, too. There had been a time, ten–fifteen years ago, when he could have walked the whole bunch of them off their feet—Ellis included. In those days he could shoulder a pack basket full of traps and grub, head out over the range and drop down to Little Wolf Pond without even stopping to roll a smoke or get a breather. Fifteen—? It must have been a good twenty years ago. He had been in the Service that long. In the Service there wasn't much call for a warden to go traipsing around the woods. A warden had to cover a lot of territory, but he covered most of it in a car. Now a wiry little squirt like Bert Ellis could walk the legs off him.

Ellis stopped up ahead, and the thin single line of men blunted around him. He had rolled and smoked half a cigarette before the last of the hunters and Bellamy reached the group. Yes, sir, he had certainly set a pace! You could see the steam coming off the hunters. It must be cold to see steam like that, but Bellamy didn't feel cold. Sweat drenched his backbone. He took out a red bandanna and blew his nose, fumbling with it before his face so they

---

7. Rural people use *city slicker* (SIT ee SLIK er) to refer to a sophisticated, usually well-dressed, city dweller.

Word Bank

integral (in TUH gril) *adj.*: essential to the whole; necessary to completeness

traipsing (TRAYP sing) *v.*: walking or going aimlessly or idly, without finding or reaching a goal

would not notice his gasping breaths.

"I guess we'd better start droppin' off men from here," Ellis said. "You take this here end of the line, Warden. I'll take the rest up yonder along the tote road, and drop them off say every couple or three hundred yard. I'll drop one of you folks next, then somebody who knows the woods. We're gonna keep hollering, 'Hey, Jack!'—or whatever the feller's name is."

"Bill," one of the hunters volunteered.

"Okay, then, 'Hey, Bill!' And keep listenin' for the man on your right and left. I ain't aimin' to get any more of you lost. I got chores aplenty to do." He dropped his cigarette in the snow and stepped on it from force of habit. "And no shootin' unless we find this feller Bill. Shoot two quick ones if you find him. We'll answer with one. Shoot a couple every fifteen minutes to guide us to you."

He turned to Bellamy. "We'll spread out and work up the range, far as the rock cliffs. If he's hurt down here somewhere, we might find him. I dunno what else to say."

The warden nodded. He wanted to offer some suggestions, but breath was still choking in his throat. Ellis's plan was good enough.

"How about the swamp?" one of the hunters asked.

"A man ain't got no call to go into that swamp. It'd take the Army, with some Marines to boot, to find a man in there unless he signals. Your friend don't seem to be the signaling kind." He turned away and led the searching party on.

There was a half-rotted log at the side of the trail, and the warden sat down. He could breathe more evenly now but his knees trembled from the exertion.

I guess I'm not as young as I was, he thought. *Ellis sure set a pace.* Dry pellets of snow almost as heavy as hail hissed through the evergreens. Bellamy shivered. The cold was already working inside of him, spreading along his spine. After a while he got up and started beating his arms together, and twice he looked at his watch to see how long it was since Ellis had left him.

He began to think maybe the starting signal had gone down the line and he had not heard it in the hissing of the wind and snow. When he strained his ears, he could hear "Hey, Bill! Hey, Bill!" far away, blending into the sounds of the wind, and he was ready to shout himself when he heard other voices calling, and far away the strains of ghostly music, and the bugle tones of a hound baying, and the voice of his wife saying, "The wood…the wood…the wood…."

When the real voices came, they were unmistakable, and the ghost sounds of the woods disappeared instantly. He heard a faint voice shouting "Hey, Bill!" Then another voice, nearer, repeating the cry, and then the man directly to his left, so near that it startled him. He started to shout and his voice croaked in his tight throat and he swallowed a couple of times and cleared it and then shouted.

I could always hear things in the sound of running water, he thought. *When I was a kid, I used to sit by the brook and hear whole conversations.*

He cut at right angles from the trail and headed into the thicket of young beech seedlings[8] not much higher than his head, but so thick that he had to shoulder his way through them. The beech seedlings kept tangling him up and whipping across his face. To his left, the man shouted, "Hey, Bill!" and he stopped and shouted back.

The ground sloped upward, and he came out of the belt of young beeches to a small clearing where the trees had been cut down. The logs had been dragged out but the tops lay in a tangled heap. He was breathing hard again when he came out into the hardwood timber. He wanted to rest, but the cry of the man on his left sounded, fainter this time and farther up the slope, and he kept on going.

"City slicker," he murmured. "Race horse." Showing off up there somewhere, going fast just because the going under *his* feet was good and solid. No thought that somebody else might have it tough. Well, it would take more than a burst of speed by a city hunter to leave him behind, even if he wasn't as young as he used to be.

The snow stopped for a few moments, and he could see the mist-shrouded hulk of the mountain through the bare tree branches. It looked immense in the dim light. A tough mountain, uncompromising and sinister, and for a moment Bellamy felt sympathy for the man who was lost somewhere in its grasp.

Poor feller, he thought. *What chance has he got?* And then the resentment welled up in him again. *Well, they got no business tanglin' with mountains like this one. They ain't got no right to be so sassy.*

It began to snow again, big soft flakes. The giant mountain drew back into the haze and disappeared. He could no longer see the crest of the ridges in front of him. Once he had scrambled to their tops, he could not see the bottoms of the ravines he had left. *It's like walking inside of a cocoon*, he thought. He stopped and called the lost man's name, feeling the futility of it for the first time. If the man had slipped and fallen and knocked himself out, his body would long ago have been covered by the snow.

It occurred to him that he had not heard the man on his left for some time. He cupped his hands and called out. He shouted again and again, trying to pierce the muffling snow, but it was like shouting with his face buried in a pillow. He needed a rest and the comfort of tobacco, but here was another guy straying off his post. He took off his mittens and tried whistling through his fingers. Only a couple of off-key sounds came out. He walked on for a few hundred yards, calling all the while, then suddenly stopped.

There was something wrong. He was supposed to be skirting the base of the mountain. The swamp had been to his right, and now it should be in back of him. The man to his left should be uphill from him. Yet, in spite of the rise and fall of the ground, he was definitely going downhill. He tried to peer through the thick curtain of snow. He took a few steps in one direction, stopped and looked around him again.

---

8. A thicket of *beech seedlings* (BEECH SEED lingz) is a grove of small, young beech trees.

Then he trotted back to where the snow was churned up by his turning feet. He looked all around. But there was nothing to see, and he felt fear growing inside him.

It was ridiculous. The swamp had been to his right. The other man had been to his left and farther up the slope. But the ground was dipping away from him. He cupped his hands to his mouth and shouted. In the mute fluttering of the snow, he heard an answer to his cry. He stood still and held his breath. He heard the cry again. It was from the direction he had expected and he thought with relief, *I was right all the time.*

Then he heard the cry again and it came from in back of him, and then it came from his right and from his left, until it was all around him, until it became a part of the soft music he had not noticed before and the sound of his wife's voice saying, "The wood…the wood…."

I can back track, he thought. *I can follow my own tracks until I get to a spot I recognize, then set myself right again.* He looked around him, picked up his dim track in the snow, and started to follow it. But after a few steps, the track curved back, and came to the churned place in the snow where he had been standing. The tight fist of fear in his chest grew bigger.

"That's the track I made looking around trying to get located," he muttered. "Sure! The other one must head off that way."

He started to circle, looking for the track, and he almost stepped over it before he saw the dim rounded outline in the snow. The snow was filling the track fast; he followed it, bent almost double. Once he thought he had lost it but he was able to pick it up again where his boot had brushed the snow off a stump. He began to trot, racing against time, racing against the endless curtain of snow, against the inevitability of defeat softly stamped in each dimming print.

The prints disappeared. He stopped. His eyes darted in all directions. There was no avenue of escape, no opening in the white cocoon of snow.

"I'm lost," he said. The mute voices of the woods echoed his words and flung them back at him, the voices blending with the music and his wife's words. Lost—

He began to run, as if running would rend the invisible veil that hemmed him in, and still the mute voices. He scrambled up the side of the ravine that he did not remember crossing, his mouth gaping, his breath coming in wheezing gasps. He almost reached its crest when the choking feathers in his chest filled it completely. Hot wires of pain tightened across his chest. They crossed and recrossed in a spot over his heart. They touched and exploded in a blinding shower of pain-filled sparks. He clutched at his chest, staggered a few steps, and sank against the base of a tree.

Take it easy, he thought. *Got to take it easy*.

He was not conscious of the pain diminishing, but he began to hear the sharp rasping of his breath and feel the rapid thumping of his heart. He sat where he had fallen, his cheek pressed against the rough bark of the tree, and stared at his mittened hand lying palm upward in the snow, and watched the snowflakes settling softly on it. The pain over his heart gradually diminished.

Word Bank   **rend** (REND) *v.*: separate into parts with force or violence; tear apart

I'm lost, he thought. *Lost!*

The desire to run swept over him in uncontrollable waves. He would have started running if he had been standing up instead of lying in the snow. He would have started running again, blindly, unthinkingly. But in the time and effort of raising his body, of clawing his way upward along the tree trunk, he stifled the impulse. He stood up with his arms still clutched around the tree trunk, holding himself from running.

You're acting like a tenderfoot, he thought. *You're acting like a city slicker. You've got to stop and think.*

He dug out his pipe and tobacco, and took off his mittens. But his hands were trembling so that the tobacco spilled. He dropped the pipe and, in an unreasoning fit of anger, threw the tobacco pouch down. He forgot them immediately and started to put on his mittens. He got the right one on but when the left one fell in the snow at his feet, he forgot that, too, in the welter of thoughts[9] racing through his mind.

He was lost. A mile from the trail. Maybe more. Maybe a lot more. The snow was a heavy, muffling curtain that closed in all around him. The trail was somewhere to the south of him. Only there was no way of telling which way was south. The wind usually blew in from the north and the snow was usually stuck on the north sides of the trees. But it did not work out that way all the time. Some of the worst storms came in from the south. The mountains made their own wind currents. You couldn't tell, except with a compass, and he never carried one. No native ever carried one.

"Shucks, I wouldn't give pocket room to one of them things. All's I got to do is follow my nose back to one of Ma's pies." All natives said that to city slickers. Or else they said, "Comes a time I get turned around, I just set my gun down on its feet and follow it plumb into camp."

There was a bunch of men in the woods. There might be one of them just beyond the curtain of snow, for all he knew, and if there was he could set himself right; he wouldn't have to admit that he was lost. He cupped his hands around his mouth and shouted, "Hey, Bill!" He was not thinking of the lost man; he shouted that name because he'd shouted it before. He walked and he shouted, lifting his face to the falling snow, but there was no answer.

He thought of the pistol then—the .45 strapped around his waist. They would hear that. They were bound to, in spite of the muffling snow. He opened the holster, rested his hand on the butt. But he didn't draw the gun out. "No shooting unless we find the lost man," Ellis had said. He hadn't found the lost man. If he shot, they would answer him, and they would converge on him, the

---

9. A *welter of thoughts* is a confused mixture of thoughts.

Word Bank   **converge** (kun VURJ) *v.*: move toward one point; come together by gradual approach

THE WARDEN / 99

natives and the city hunters. He couldn't tell them that he had shot because *he* was lost. He couldn't stand before them and say, "I'm the warden, but I got lost. I got lost and panicky, and I got a pain across my heart, and I needed help." He couldn't say that to the city slickers. Not even to the natives. He couldn't be the warden and say that.

He kept on walking, shuffling with heavy feet through the snow. He was lost and he must get out of there, and walking was the only way that he could get out. He must not run. If he started to run, he must wind his arms around a tree and hold on until the impulse to run left him. *I'm lost*, he thought. *Lost—lost—lost*—The words became the rhythm of his motions, the total of his reasoning. When the pain returned to his chest, now dull and heavy and constant, he did not think of it as pain containing a meaning and a warning of its own but only as part of being lost.

He walked with head lolling on his neck and downcast eyes that seldom raised above the obstacles before his feet. The wind had begun to blow again. The snowflakes were heavy and hard-driven. It was getting much colder, but he did not notice that. He stumbled blindly forward, sometimes falling. Once he twisted his wrist in a fall, but the pain of it mingled with the rhythm throbbing in his head.

Time became a blank infinity that held no meaning for him. Once he ran headlong into a tree, and the shock startled him. He touched his skinned forehead with his hand and looked vaguely at the blood on his fingers. A deer bounded out of its bed beside a small fir; he watched it dully as it disappeared into the haze with noiseless leaps. He came to a spruce thicket and crashed through the dead, interlocked branches with the full weight of his body.

It was much lighter now. But he failed to notice he was out of the big timber, walking in tall, matted beaver-meadow grass. His feet broke through the surface of small ice-crusted puddles. He did not notice them until he stepped into one deeper than the others, and the water welled over his boot tops.

He was in a swamp clustered with thickets of alder.[10] On the drier ground, here and there, were even thicker clusters of spruce and cedar. He climbed over rotted tree trunks, half hidden in the tall grass. He skirted many ice-covered pools and once, very carefully, crossed a large one along the branch network of an old beaver dam. He felt proud of having crossed the beaver dam; floundering forward, he thought about it, but there was no meaning to his thoughts.

He was shouldering his way through a thicket of low snow-covered spruce when suddenly he stopped. It was the first time he had stopped voluntarily. He raised his head and looked dully around him. He became aware of the pelting of the wind-driven snow, of the heavy pain in his chest, and the dull pain of his forehead, and the sharper pain of his wrist. He became conscious of the icy water inside his boots and

---

10. An *alder* (AWL der) is a type of tree or shrub that grows in moist land. It is related to the birch tree.

the throbbing of his leg muscles.

I'm lost, he thought in surprise. The thought held a meaning once more.

He looked around carefully. He was standing on a low, flat ridge that rose out of the swamp like a whale's back out of a heaving sea. He was somewhere out on a swamp. On Bear Trap Swamp—the terror of the whole district! Yet, somehow, the thought did not startle him. The *thing* that had stopped him suddenly still lingered in his subconscious, driving out panic. He turned slowly, looked all around him. His senses were alert. Suddenly, he knew, he had smelled wood smoke!

He sniffed the air hungrily. There it was! Unmistakable! It had been there all along—a thin link between the wilderness that surrounded him and civilization. His eyes spied a twisting, transparent wraith, thicker than the haze of snow. A cry escaped his lips. He started to run. But he stopped suddenly and his eyes narrowed. It must be the lost hunter. He had forgotten completely about him. There would be no one else out here in this dismal swamp but that fool hunter hunching over a little fire. It would never do to go up to him, panting and gasping like a worn-out old engine.

He moved cautiously through the screen of spruce until he saw the

---

Word Bank **wraith** (RAITH) *n.*: a vision or apparition cone of rising smoke, and then the small fire and the figure of the man hunched down beside it. Bellamy crouched down out of sight and breathed carefully until the fierce panting of his chest subsided. Then he stood up and walked toward the man.

He said evenly, "Hi, Bill. Kind of cold out, ain't it?"

The man by the fire leaped up with a strangled cry. He gazed with wide, terrified eyes for a moment; then the cry came from his open lips again, and he stumbled toward the warden, hopping on one leg and dragging the other one grotesquely behind him. He threw his arms around the warden and sagged against him, and buried his face against his coat, and sobbed.

"Easy, feller," the warden said. "Take it easy. You're all right now." The sobbing slowed and stopped. The man rubbed his face back and forth against the warden's coat, then straightened himself up slowly. "You'll be all right," the warden said. "Here, lean on me, and let's get over to that fire."

"I'm all right now," the man said.

He leaned on the warden's shoulder and hobbled back to the fire.

"Pulled my ankle sometime yesterday. Guess it was yesterday——"

"It was," said the warden. "Here—you lie down here and let me pile up some wood on this fire. I guess I'd better signal. There's a reg'lar army out lookin' for you."

He took out his pistol and fired two quick shots. There was no answer for a moment, and fear inside him began to mount again. Then he heard an answer dimly from somewhere in back of him. He turned and faced that way, and the gust of wind in his face brought the sound of other shots more clearly.

"Have a gang here in less than an hour," he said cheerily.

The hunter smiled up at him.

"Here, let me take a look at that foot," Bellamy said.

"It's all right," the hunter said.

Bellamy found a dead spruce nearby, and broke off an armful of branches and piled them on the fire. "That's what I call a fire," he said. "Only city folks believe that bunk about Indians building little fires. Any man wants to keep from freezing builds a heaping big fire."

Suddenly he remembered something. He dug into his pocket and brought out a small vacuum of coffee and poured out a steaming cup. The hunter reached out for it. His eyes opened in sudden amazement.

"Say, I've got a sandwich in my pocket!" he said. "I thought a while ago that I was going to starve to death out here—and I never remembered that sandwich in my pocket."

"Lost men do mighty queer things," the warden said. "Why didn't you shoot when you found out you was lost?"

The man sipped the hot coffee thoughtfully as if trying to remember.

Word Bank   **grotesquely** (gro TESK lee) *adv.*: in an odd or unnatural way

"I couldn't," he said at last. "I slipped and fell and banged my head. Knocked myself cold. When I came to, it was just getting dark and my ankle was on fire. I started to look for the gun, but I couldn't find it. Then I started out for home. I—I guess I got lost then—I found myself out here when it got light."

"You mean you traveled all night?"

"Yes, I think I did."

"You ought to be glad you didn't drown yourself in one of them ponds down there. The ice would never hold you up. Of all the stupid——"

"I know," the man said.

The warden got up and fired two quick shots with his pistol. The answers were much more distinct.

"I'm sorry," the man said. "I guess I led you through some tough going. That's a nasty cut on your forehead."

Bellamy reached up his unmittened hand and touched the spot tenderly. "Ducked one branch and ran smack into another I hadn't seen."

His hat was gone, too. He didn't remember losing it. He remembered going through a real tough thicket once. That must have been the place he lost it. It would be just like Ellis to find it in that thicket and start asking questions. Ellis had a nose for such things. The two men sat by the fire, staring into the leaping flames and thinking their own thoughts. The hunter finally said:

"Warden, when I first saw you—I mean—I guess I acted sort of like a fool."

"Shucks," the warden said. "Rest easy. There's some things one man never tells about another."

"Thanks," the man said.

And later, when a new armful of branches blazed high against the darkening sky, the hunter looked up once more.

"I've been wondering how you found me," he said.

Warden Bellamy thought for a long time before answering. "Years ago, when we used to run deer with dogs," he said slowly, "every deer we started on a certain mountain would go pretty near along the same ridges, and through the same notches, and finally cross the brooks at certain places. A wounded deer will pretty near always travel over a certain way. Maybe the going is easier that way—maybe, for generations, they've gone that way, to some thicket or swamp, to die. I guess maybe all lost men travel in the same paths without even knowin' it——"

The hunter thought that over, nodding slowly. "You ever been lost, Warden?"

This time there was no need to stop and think.

"Shucks, no! Been turned around for two–three days, a couple of times. But lost——"

He chuckled at the idea, and his arm came up and he rubbed his sleeve absently over his badge, the way he always chuckled, the way he always rubbed his badge when he was telling it to a tenderfoot, to a fool city slicker. The hunter believed him. They all did. Sometime, he might even grow to believe it himself again. He had to. He was a native. He belonged to these mountains. He was the warden.

Studying the Selection

First Impressions Make two columns. Label one column The Warden and the other Harlan Bellamy. In the first list those personality traits and characteristics that the general public would expect a game warden to have. In the second, list Harlan Bellamy's actual traits and characteristics. Then, as a class, compare the two lists.

✔ Quick Review

1. Describe the search plan as outlined by Bert Ellis.
2. What initial clues suggest that Harlan Bellamy is out of shape?
3. At what point does Bellamy realize he is lost? How does he react?
4. Where and how does Bellamy discover the lost hunter?

In-depth Thinking

5. Compare and contrast the "city slickers" and the "natives."
6. Why does Harlan Bellamy begin to hear music and his wife's voice?
7. Discuss the role of the following items in Bellamy's plight: no compass, chest pains, failure to observe the landscape, his unwillingness to fire his pistol.
8. Why doesn't Bellamy tell the hunter that he, too, was lost?

Drawing Conclusions

9. Psychologists say we are offended by traits in others that we dislike in ourselves. How does Harlan Bellamy behave toward the city slickers?
10. Speculate on what effects, if any, this experience will have on Bellamy.

Focusing on Character: Self-Awareness

It often requires an **external conflict** to bring about an encounter with self. Occasionally, these encounters lead to moments of **self-awareness**. Answer the following questions in writing, using specific examples to support your views.

1. Identify three moments in the story when an external conflict triggered an internal conflict.
2. The American philosopher Eric Hoffer said, "We lie loudest when we lie to ourselves." Discuss how this quotation applies to Harlan Bellamy.
3. Choose three high-profile professions—such as doctor, teacher, president—and list the characteristics that we, as a society, expect these individuals to possess. What happens when an individual does not meet our expectations?

Creating and Writing

1. Trapped by the **persona** of game warden, Bellamy nearly dies in the Big Panther range. But his encounter with the lost hunter suggests that the codes defining his behavior, were also felt by the other man. Discuss how our society sets up rules of behavior for individuals. Do these rules help or hurt?
2. Write a short play (3-4 pages) in which your major character faces both external and internal conflicts and experiences a moment of self-awareness. Then, with the help of classmates, perform your play for the class.
3. Identify an external and an internal conflict you (or someone close) may be currently experiencing. Write an action plan for solving both conflicts; then work to carry out your plan.

Blueprint for Reading

the Author

**Bill Meissner
(1948-)**

Bill Meissner grew up in Iowa and Wisconsin, with baseball a major part of his life. He has compared baseball with life: "I know the meaning of the home run. It's the slow circling of the bases, and then the return. I know it well. My father was a traveling salesman with the highway wrapped around his wrist like a gray sweatband." Meissner has won many awards for fiction. He lives with his wife and son in St. Cloud, Minnesota. He is Director of Writing at St. Cloud State University.

Background Bytes

Some of us know people who were hurt playing team sports. Surely, they did not accept being suddenly taken out of the game with equanimity (composure, evenness of temper). Were they able to watch calmly as the team played without them? The story of the 'fallen athlete' is a favorite of authors. Although we are all at risk of accident, and individuals are injured in various circumstances, the plight of the injured athlete may be particularly affecting. Why is this so? Perhaps the young and gifted athlete seems a superhero, beyond the reach of misfortune. *In the Middle of a Pitch* reminds us that a single incident can alter the course of a life. Perhaps this is why life is so unpredictable, but also—paradoxically—why it is so precious.

Into *In the Middle of a Pitch*

As long as human beings competed at sports, there have been tales of athletes achieving fame only to suffer an injury that ended a career. Imagine building a life around a physical talent—a talent that must fade over time.

Before you read the story, discuss this problem with your classmates. See if you can come up with a list of athletes or well-known personalities who have suffered career-ending injuries. How did these individuals pick up the pieces of their lives?

In the Middle of a Pitch

Focusing on Introspection and Maturation

It has been said that, "The unexamined life is not worth living." This age-old truth is reminding us to think about our lives and how we are living them. We meet the main character of this story during just such a period of **introspection**. Defined as self-observation and examination, **introspection** is necessary for emotional and spiritual growth.

Each of us mature differently as we experience our own individual problems. This is an important theme in literature. Notice how the aging Sikarsky finally gives in to reflection and introspection.

Word Bank

Ledgers: When is it correct to use a noun as a verb? The word, **ledgers**, is currently only correct as a noun meaning "an account book, in which business transactions are recorded." However, you may hear people using it as a verb sometimes, if they say that they *ledgered* something. A more popular change, considered incorrect until very recently, is the use of the word *impact* as a verb meaning "to have an impact on or to affect." The powers that be have decided that it is all right (two words, two ll's) to say, for example, "The dog's behavior *impacted* the entire family, when she rescued Charlie, the cat."

adept	curt	hefts	potential
aromatic	elaborate	hulls	subtle
citations	façade	ledgers	warped
corroded	gaudily	mirage	

In the Middle of a Pitch

Bill Meissner

He wakes before his alarm to the faraway song of an umpire calling a third strike. Standing in front of the bathroom mirror, he leans forward, narrowing his eyes at himself as if he were peering at the catcher for his sign. Then he stretches, his hands high, almost touches the plaster ceiling where the spiderweb cracks seem to lengthen a little each week. When he brings his right arm down in an imaginary pitch, a strike, he feels the old aching. Staring at the arm in the mirror, he wonders how the flesh got so flabby. *It didn't look that way yesterday, did it?* he thinks. Yesterday the tendons were taut[1] and ready like some finely tuned musical instrument; yesterday he was sure he could hear every muscle humming.

Everything happens so fast, he thinks, *everything happens in a day.* One day he's Dusty Sikarsky, starting pitcher for a major league team. The next day he's Dusty Sikarsky, used car salesman, tossing curves at the off-balance customers. As he dresses for work, his mind spans twenty years to the baseball days. He thinks about how you work your way up through the leagues: First it's town ball, where he pitched his team into the tournaments with his fastball. The photographer for the local paper could hardly catch that pitch with his flashbulb. Next the minor league scouts stood waiting for him after a game, their smiles like piano keys, and everything speeded up, as if someone had tilted the whole world and it started sliding toward him. A minor league coach watched him, chin on his hand, for three months in Class A, then, at midseason, the coach nodded at him once. The next day Dusty was moved up to Triple A, the bleachers bigger and more freshly painted, the fans louder. He kept moving up, faster and quicker. His life seemed to be rushing toward him and flying away from him at the same moment. His arm felt great, and the more he threw, the better it felt. The leather ball loved his fingertips. "The kid's so good he could pitch blindfolded and still strike out the side," a coach once remarked. On the mound, Dusty went through his motion: kicking, reaching way back in the still air with his right arm. Then he whirled down hard, and the ball was

---

1. The expression *tendons were taut* refers to his muscles being in good shape. The tendon is the cord connecting the end of a muscle to the bone.

nestled in the catcher's mitt long before Dusty's cap, jolted from his head, had a chance to fall to the grass in front of the mound. The ball was like music that passed so fast you never really heard it.

He remembers the rush as he was called to the bigs:[2] the flutter of a paper contract, the tingling static electricity as he slid a major league uniform over his head for the first time in the locker room, the click and spark of spikes on concrete as he jogged down the ramp to the dugout.

The next thing he knew, the game was starting, and the first batter stepped to the plate. Then, the funniest thing happened—everything slowed down. It took half an hour to reach up to adjust the bill of his cap. His windup[3] felt like an elaborate dance performed underwater. When he threw that first pitch, the ball seemed to take a year to reach home plate, like some kind of satellite aimed for the moon, just rotating over and over slowly in the soft, endless vacuum of space.

Somehow, he made it through the first game and he did all right. He pitched six innings, gave up a couple of hits, but no runs. Not bad for a first outing. The guys patted him on the back after the game. The catcher congratulated him and told him later how his eyes always widened each time he delivered the ball. He had a great year, and the papers called him the Rookie Sensation. The sportswriters always used the word *potential* when they wrote about him; they predicted he'd be the best in the game.

The seasons passed. One, two, three of them. He chalked up fifty wins. Then, one night in Chicago, too cool for June, when the bases were loaded in the late innings, he reached as far back as he could to fire a fastball and felt something snap in his arm. Not *snap*, exactly—it was more of a ping, like the off-key sound of a thin wire or guitar string being plucked. It didn't hurt at first, though he remembers shaking his arm a few times as if it had ants on it.

When he threw his next pitch, and the next, he knew something was wrong. The ball didn't quite go where it was aimed. Just an inch or two off target, but that's all it takes. He lost that game on a double. After that, the batters began hitting his curve, his slider. His fastball lost its jump, no longer appeared to be rising as it reached the batter, but instead drew a straight line to the sweet spot of their bats.

That's when the music slowed down, his career like a record clicked off in the middle of its playing, the needle dragging across the vinyl. The team put him

---

2. *Bigs* (BIGZ) is slang for the highest level of competition. He was good enough to play in the major leagues.
3. A pitcher's *windup* (WYND UP) is the beginning movements before the ball is thrown.

Word Bank

elaborate (ee LAB rit) *adj.*: worked out in great detail; painstaking
potential (po TEN shill) *n.*: possibility; latent ability that may not be developed

on the disabled list and he sat it out for a couple of weeks. He worked with the trainer in the clubhouse, rotating the arm, wrapping it with heat, kneading the muscle as if it were bread dough about to rise. After he gave up six or seven runs in each of his next three starts, the manager shook his head and said the owners wanted him sent down to the minors.

"How long?" Dusty remembers asking the manager. He felt suddenly short of breath, unable to exhale a full sentence.

The manager stood chewing a toothpick, staring only at Dusty's arm. "Just a while. That's all. A month, maybe. You'll be back, kid."

"Yeah," he responded. "A month."

A month became the rest of the season. He struggled in the minors, too—even the rookies were hitting his best pitches, taking them to the gaudily painted wooden fences advertising CHEER and BRYL CREEM—A LITTLE DAB'LL, and COLGATE WITH GARDOL.

The next February, he got a letter from the club. He remembers staring at the outside of the long beige envelope that morning, not certain if he should open it or not. He set it down on the desk. After lunch, he picked the letter up again. As he tore it open, the ripping paper made the sound of crackling ice. The letter told him, in a few curt sentences, that his contract wouldn't be renewed. The last sentences read: *Thank you for your contribution to the club. Best wishes in the future.*

He remembers crumpling the letter in his fist, tossing it into the wastebasket, and jogging out to the nearby sandlot field. Though it was cold outside and patches of ice still plastered themselves to the field, Dusty threw fastball after fastball toward the warped black and white plate, none of them strikes. The pain in his arm seemed to make a noise that grew louder and louder, like a scream caught beneath the skin.

The shrill sound of his alarm clock brings him back to his apartment. He jogs into the bedroom, clicks off the ringing alarm. All that was years ago, he thinks as he brushes his teeth, combs his graying slicked-back hair, slides on his snappy brown striped tie and brown suit jacket, then slips out the front door for work. He's got a new career, and he's a different man now—he's Dusty Sikarsky, best car salesman in El Dorado, Kansas. He's got his sales pitch[4] down perfect, and he's got plaques on

---

4. Here, a *pitch* (PICH) is a high-pressure sales talk.

Word Bank

gaudily (GAW dil lee) *adv.*: showily and tastelessly; flashily
curt (KERT) *adj.*: rudely brief, abrupt in manner
warped (WORPT) *adj.*: bent or twisted, especially from a straight or flat shape

the wall of his office at Edge Motors and citations from the El Dorado Businessmen's Club to prove it. He's got a quick, bright smile on his face and the music in his voice; his boss once said he could sell any car on the lot blindfolded.

Dusty tastes the first warmth of April air as he walks through the town. It's a taste he's almost forgotten, a taste aromatic and rich that seems to come from deep inside himself at the same moment. By the time he reaches the low, tin-sided building at the car lot, he's puffing. He grins at his co-workers as he lopes toward his dark paneled office. Inside, as he waits for the first customer, he pours a mug of coffee, and, cupping a powdered sugar donut in his palm, stares beyond the hulls of the cars to the shimmering water mirage beginning to form at the far end of the asphalt lot.

The whole town seems to know about his days in the majors. As he walks down Main in front of the crumbling two-story brick façades, a little heavier and a little grayer, the kids open their eyes wide as they pass and then whisper behind him: "You know who *that* is? That's Dusty Sikarsky. He pitched in the majors." Some of the older guys at work smile and say, "Hey Dusty, what was it like, pitching in the big leagues?" Dusty usually just shakes his head. He wants to reply, *What's there to say? You just throw a ball at a glove.* But he doesn't want to sound flip so he just says something pat like "Good. It was real good."

He never talks much about the big leagues, never mentions the injury. For years now, he's managed to avoid talking about it, has become adept at a subtle curve of conversation, a change of subject. He never goes to the town league baseball games on the weekends, though his buddies sometimes ask him to take in a game. Once in a while, as a gag, he'll ball up an old invoice, go into his windup, pitch it hard through the bright light of the

---

Word Bank

citations (sy TAY shunz) *n.*: awards for outstanding achievement

aromatic (OW ROH MAT ik) *adj.*: having a pleasant smell; fragrant or sweet-scented

hulls (HULZ) *n.*: outer coverings of seeds, fruits, or other objects

mirage (mih RAHZH) *n.*: something illusory; an optical effect created by the reflection of light over hot sand or pavement

façade (fuh SAHD) *n.*: the front of a building, especially an imposing or decorative one

adept (uh DEPT) *adj.*: very skilled; proficient; expert

subtle (SUT il) *adj.*: so slight as to be difficult to detect; not obvious

open doorway, and the guys nod at him and know he remembers.

"You should pick up a baseball sometime, Dusty," the boss told him once.

"Ever think of coaching or something?" Dusty just took a slurp of coffee, pretending not to hear. "With no wife, no kids," the boss added, "you got all the time in the world."

His arm doesn't hurt like it used to the first couple years after he was cut from the team. It only aches a little once in a while as he lifts a pile of ledgers or when he leans his weight the wrong way on the waxed fender of a Chevy while making a pitch about what a workhorse the V6 engine is, how fast this machine would be on the highway even though it's got a few miles on the ol' speedometer.

This April day passes with its usual blur of stats and sales, printouts and receipts. Another day passes beneath his fingertips and it feels dry to the touch. In the late afternoon, an ad appears in the *El Dorado Weekly* proclaiming SHINY CLEAN USED CARS FOR SPRING. In the picture, Dusty, pudgy and not quite smiling, poses stiffly beside a Dodge, like he doesn't know what to do with his hands.

After work, on his way home, Dusty takes a detour to the town ball field. Shouldering through the creaking fence gate, he pulls off his wide striped tie, unbuttons the top button of his white

> **Word Bank**
>
> **ledgers** (LEJ urz) *n.*: account books for keeping records

shirt. He sits down on the front row of the bleachers, slips off his brown suit jacket, tosses it over a corroded railing. He can hear the whistle of the wind through the high backstop, a rusty music. He sits there a while, gazing at the empty sunlit field from behind the barrier of wires. Rolling up his sleeves, he massages the muscle of his right arm. Then he notices, directly behind the plate, widened gaps in the backstop wires. *A wild pitch could get caught in there easy*, Dusty thinks. *It could get caught for years between the bent wires.*

Turning his head, Dusty notices two boys biking across the grass. He thinks at first that they're cutting across the field on their way to the games at the arcade, but they stop in the middle of the infield. One skinny kid who looks about seven keeps trying to pitch from the gravelly mound sixty feet away, but can't quite get his throws to home plate. He hefts the ball like a shotput,[5] and the ball skitters in the dirt a few feet from the plate where another boy, short and chunky, stands with a catcher's mitt that's too big for his hand. The boy who's pitching moves a few steps closer. An idea crosses Dusty's mind that he should go out there and give the kid a few tips. The kid brings his arm down pretty well, but he's bending all wrong at the elbow. *Naw*, he thinks. *Let the kids have their game.* The boy tosses another one, a rounded throw that skips in front of the catcher's mitt, rolls all the way to the backstop. The skinny kid runs from the mound to retrieve it. By the time the boy reaches the backstop, Dusty is stretching his arm through the bent wires to pick up the baseball, snagging the sleeve of his white shirt on a sharp, loose wire.

"You stuck, mister?" the kid asks.

Dusty smiles up at the boy from his knees.

"Nope," Dusty blurts. "Yeah. I mean, I don't know."

A little embarrassed, Dusty manages a chuckle. Still clutching the baseball, he hears something in the sleeve tear as he pulls his arm back. *It's okay*, he thinks, *you can replace a shirt. You can put a Band-Aid on a scratched arm.*

He stands with the ball, faces the boy through the wires, and grins. The boy cups his hands as if expecting Dusty to toss the ball over, as if expecting a brief spring shower. But Dusty doesn't toss the ball. Instead, he finds himself stepping through a gate in the fence, hears his voice ask, "Wanna learn some pitches?" Instead, Dusty finds himself slipping off his polished shoes and brown dress socks, then climbing the small mountain of the pitcher's mound, all that gravel suddenly tender and welcoming beneath his bare feet.

---

5. Here, the ball is compared to a *shotput*; a field event in which a heavy ball or shot is thrown or put for distance.

Word Bank

corroded (kuh RODE id) *adj.*: rusted; eaten or worn away gradually

hefts (HEFTS) *v.*: lifts; heaves

Studying the Selection

First Impressions

Imagine you are Dusty Sikarsky and have received the letter canceling your major league contract. Write a journal entry detailing your thoughts and feelings.

✔ Quick Review

1. What happened to end Dusty Sikarsky's career in the major leagues?
2. What does he do for a living now?
3. At work, how does Sikarsky sometimes show he recalls his former career?
4. What incident brings Sikarsky back to baseball?

In-depth Thinking

5. How does the author suggest Sikarsky's dissatisfaction with his current life?
6. Discuss the ironic nature of Sikarsky's career-ending injury.
7. Analyze Sikarsky's response to the little boy's question, "You stuck, mister?"
8. Why does Sikarsky decide to help the boys, and how is this moment important for him?

Drawing Conclusions

9. State—as simply as possible—the theme of this story.
10. Why is it appropriate for Sikarsky's turnaround to take place in this 'reduced' baseball situation?

Focusing on Introspection and Maturation

As we grow up, we must also try to gain wisdom. We need to develop the habit of introspection, examining our motives and actions. Challenges and setbacks often serve to promote growth. Complete the following activities, using suitable examples to support your judgments.

1. A life free of trials would offer fewer opportunities for growth. Fortunately (or so we say, at a later date) such a life is not possible. What wisdom might have been denied Dusty Sikarsky had he not left baseball prematurely?
2. Write of a challenge you faced that allowed for introspection and growth. Would you have learned these lessons any other way?
3. Will you know when you are fully mature? Does the maturing process ever end? Is it possible to be an old, immature person?

Creating and Writing

1. Read A. E. Housman's "To An Athlete Dying Young." Compare the theme of the Housman poem to the theme of *In the Middle of a Pitch*.
2. Write a character sketch of a fictional person who is stuck in the past. Perhaps this person can't stop reliving a senior year in high school, or wishes to be a child with no responsibilities. Be sure to suggest the dangers of this lifestyle.
3. Interview three people your grandparents' age about their experience of getting older. What lessons have they learned as they age? What things do they now appreciate or miss? Discuss your findings with your class in a round-table format.

Blueprint for Reading

the Author

**Jack London
(1876-1916)**

Born in San Francisco, California, London had almost no formal schooling, but he was an avid reader. He loved the waterfront and worked many odd jobs there. Given to wandering, London spent a year on a ship hunting seals from the Arctic to Japan. He wandered the U.S. and Canada, with no permanent residence, working odd jobs. He returned to California briefly, enrolled at the University of California, and tried to sell some early writings. Then he took to wandering again. He worked as a gold miner in the Klondike, Yukon Territory from 1897-1898, then returned again to California where he finally started to sell his fiction. Some of his earlier pieces, based on his experiences in the wild North, were *Call of the Wild* (1903), *The Sea Wolf* (1904), and *White Fang* (1906).

Background Bytes

The setting is the Klondike Gold Rush of 1898. Forty-nine years earlier, during the Gold Rush of 1849, Americans rushed to California to stake claims and mine gold, often bringing their families with them. The work was hard, and many families struggled to adapt, but at least the climate was warm. During the Klondike Gold Rush, however, miners found themselves battling treacherous weather conditions and an unforgiving environment. The terrain was rugged, and isolation in the wilderness often threatened their mental stability. Many lives were lost to the cold and geography of Alaska during the Gold Rush of 1898.

In this story a lone traveler struggles to survive the double blows of weather and isolation. London, who experienced firsthand the conditions he writes about, is able to capture the man's grim situation with strikingly realistic detail. The narrative's matter-of-fact tone reflects the harsh and forbidding landscape.

Into *To Build a Fire*

Few of us experience life-threatening hardships on a regular basis. In fact, most of us may never have had such an experience. Consider the situations that firefighters or inner-city police officers encounter on a daily basis. These people put their lives in danger as a matter of course, all in the line of duty. However, they are carefully trained to handle emergencies: they are rigorously drilled, they work with experienced mentors, they use special tools, and they wear protective equipment and clothing. The work is dangerous, but because of these safeguards, fatalities are not common.

The man in the story wasn't prepared for his experience. This is the basic difference between these individuals and the main character in *To Build a Fire*. Before you read the story, think how you might increase your chances of survival in a barren Alaskan landscape, alone, at 75° below zero. Make a list of provisions and equipment you think might be useful.

To Build a Fire

Focusing on Setting

Setting is central to this story. It is so vividly described that it takes on a personality and nearly becomes another character. At times, it almost has a will of its own.

Setting means when and where a story takes place. This story begins and ends during the early 1900s in northwestern Canada, where temperatures are bitterly cold and the terrain is mountainous. The forces of nature are cold and without mercy. Its laws are hard and unbending, and at times deadly for human beings.

You have just studied **characterization** (how a character is described and given life in a story). Now notice how nature is **personified** or brought to life in *To Build a Fire*. Here, the landscape seems to have a will of its own, a desire to crush foolish man in the sub-zero weather. Contrast the vivid description of setting with the shallow characterization of the man. In the contrast, he appears non-human: His absence of emotion robs him of his humanity.

Word Bank

Apathetically: Do you know what it means to be *apathetic*? *Apathy*, which means not having concern for, or interest in, things that others find moving or exciting, can be an uncomfortable feeling—especially if it comes from being "blue," or, to use another idiom, "down in the dumps." Does *apathetic* sound like any other words you know? Most English words that have *–path* as a root word are related to *feelings.* Which other related words can you think of, besides *sympathy*? The Greek word *pathos* means 'suffering.'

apathetically	apprehension	gait	imperceptible
appeasingly	capsized	imperative	intangible

To Build a Fire

Jack London

Day had broken cold and gray, exceedingly cold and gray, when the man turned aside from the main Yukon trail[1] and climbed the high earth bank, where a dim and little-traveled trail led eastward through the fat spruce timberland. It was a steep bank, and he paused for breath at the top, excusing the act to himself by looking at his watch. It was nine o'clock. There was no sun or hint of sun, though there was not a cloud in the sky. It was a clear day, and yet there seemed an intangible pall[2] over the face of things, a subtle gloom that made the day dark and that was due to the absence of sun. This fact did not worry the man. He was used to the lack of sun. It had been days since he had seen the sun, and he knew that a few more days must pass before that cheerful orb,[3] due south, would just peep above the skyline and dip immediately from view.

The man flung a look back along the way he had come. The Yukon lay a mile wide and hidden under three feet of ice. On top of this ice were as many feet of snow. It was all pure white, rolling in gentle undulations[4] where the ice jams of the freeze-up had formed. North and south, as far as his eye could see, it was unbroken white, save for a dark hairline that curved and twisted from around the spruce-covered island to the south and that curved and twisted away into the north, where it disappeared behind another spruce-covered island. This dark hairline was the trail—the main trail—that led south five hundred miles to the Chilcoot Pass,[5] Dyea,[6] and salt water, and

---

1. The *Yukon trail* (U kahn TRAY il) goes through the Yukon, a territory in northwestern Canada.
2. A *pall* (PAWL) is something that covers, especially with darkness or gloom.
3. The *orb* (ORB) is a reference to the rounded shape of the sun.
4. The term *undulations* (UN dyuh LAY shunz) refers to the way the thick snow seemed wavy in the distance.
5. The *Chilcoot Pass* (CHILL koot PASS) is on the boundary between southeast Alaska and British Columbia, Canada.
6. At the time of the story, *Dyea* (DY uh) was a town south of the Chilcoot Pass in western British Columbia.

Word Bank

intangible (in TAN jih bul) *adj*.: not definite or clear to the mind; vague; elusive

that led north seventy miles to Dawson,[7] and still on to the north a thousand miles to Nulato,[7] and finally to St. Michael on the Bering Sea,[8] a thousand miles and half a thousand more.

But all this—the mysterious, far reaching hairline trail, the absence of sun from the sky, the tremendous cold, and the strangeness and weirdness of it all—made no impression on the man. It was not because he was long used to it. He was a newcomer in the land, a *chechaquo*,[9] and this was his first winter. The trouble with him was that he was without imagination. He was quick and alert in the things of life, but only in the things, not in the significances. Fifty degrees below zero meant eighty-odd degrees of frost. Such a fact impressed him as being cold and uncomfortable, and that was all. It did not lead him to meditate upon his frailty as a creature of temperature, and upon man's frailty in general, able only to live within certain narrow limits of heat and cold. Fifty degrees below zero stood for a bite of frost that hurt and that must be guarded against by the use of mittens, ear flaps, warm moccasins, and thick socks. Fifty degrees below zero was to him just precisely fifty degrees below zero. That there should be anything more to it than that was a thought that never entered his head.

As he turned to go on, he spat speculatively.[10] There was a sharp, explosive crackle that startled him. He spat again. And again, in the air, before it could fall to the snow, the spittle crackled. He knew that at fifty below spittle cracked on the snow, but this spittle[11] had crackled in the air. Undoubtedly it was colder than fifty below—how much colder he did not know. But the temperature did not matter. He was bound for the old claim on the left fork of Henderson Creek where the boys were already. They had come over across the divide from the Indian Creek country, while he had come the roundabout way to take a look at the possibilities of getting out logs in the spring from the islands in the Yukon. He would be in to camp by six o'clock; a bit after dark, it was true, but the boys would be there, a fire would be going, and a hot supper would be ready. As for lunch, he pressed his hand against the protruding[12] bundle under his jacket. It was also under his shirt, wrapped up in a handkerchief and lying against his skin. It was the only way to keep the biscuits from freezing. He smiled agreeably to himself as he thought of those biscuits, each cut open and sopped in grease, and each enclosing a generous slice of fried meat.

He plunged in among the big spruce trees. The trail was faint. A foot of snow had fallen since the last sled had passed over, and he was glad he was without a sled, traveling light. In fact, he carried nothing but the lunch wrapped in the handkerchief. He was surprised, however, at the cold. It certainly was cold, he concluded, as he rubbed his numb nose and cheekbones with his mittened hand. He was a warm-whiskered man, but the hair

---

7. *Dawson* (DAW sin) is a city in western Yukon Territory, Canada, on the eastern bank of the Yukon River. *Nulato* (new LA toe) is a city in western Alaska.
8. *St. Michael on the Bering Sea* (SAINT MY kil on the BEAR ing SEE) is a port city on the western coast of Alaska.
9. The term *chechaquo* (chee CHAH ko) is local language for tenderfoot, or newcomer.
10. To act *speculatively* (SPEK yoo LAY tiv lee) is to do something to test a theory. He thought perhaps it was colder than minus fifty. He spat to test his theory.
11. *Spittle* (SPIT il) is saliva, or spit.
12. Something that is *protruding* (pro TROOD ing), bulges or pushes forward or outward.

on his face did not protect the high cheekbones and the eager nose that thrust itself into the frosty air.

At the man's heels trotted a dog, a big native husky, the proper wolf dog, gray-coated and without any visible or temperamental difference from its brother, the wild wolf. The animal was depressed by the tremendous cold. It knew that it was no time for traveling. Its instinct told it a truer tale than was told to the man by the man's judgment. In reality, it was not merely colder than fifty below zero; it was colder than sixty below, than seventy below. It was seventy-five below zero. Since the freezing point is thirty-two above zero, it meant that one hundred and seven degrees of frost was achieved. The dog did not know anything about thermometers. Possibly in its brain there was no sharp consciousness of a condition of very cold such as was in the man's brain. But the brute had its instinct. It experienced a vague but menacing apprehension that subdued it and made it slink along at the man's heels, and that made it question eagerly every unwonted movement of the man as if expecting him to go into camp or to seek shelter somewhere and build a fire. The dog had learned fire, and it wanted fire, or else to burrow under the snow and cuddle its warmth away from the air.

The frozen moisture of its breathing had settled on its fur in a fine powder of frost, and especially were its jowls,[13] muzzle, and eyelashes whitened by its crystaled breath. The man's red beard and mustache were likewise frosted, but more solidly, the deposit taking the form of ice and increasing with every warm, moist breath he exhaled. Also, the man was chewing tobacco, and the muzzle of ice held his lips so rigidly that he was unable to clear his chin when he expelled the juice. The result was that a crystal beard of the color and solidity of amber was increasing its length on his chin. If he fell down it would shatter itself, like glass, into brittle fragments. But he did not mind the appendage.[14] It was the penalty all tobacco chewers paid in that country, and he had been out before in two cold snaps. They had not been so cold as this, he knew, but by the spirit thermometer at Sixty Mile[15] he knew they had been registered at fifty below and at fifty-five.

He held on through the level stretch of woods for several miles, and dropped down a bank to the frozen bed of a small stream. This was Henderson Creek, and he knew he was ten miles from the forks. He looked at his watch. It was ten o'clock. He was making four miles an hour, and he calculated that he would arrive at the forks at half-past twelve. He decided to celebrate that event by eating his lunch there.

The dog dropped in again at his heels, with a tail drooping discouragement, as the man swung along the creek bed. The furrow[16] of the old sled trail was plainly visible, but a dozen inches of snow covered

---

13. The dog's *jowls* (JOW ilz) are the fleshy part of its jaws.
14. An *appendage* (uh PEN dij) is an attached part of a larger thing. Ice and tobacco juice became a 'beard,' an appendage.
15. *Sixty Mile* (SIX tee MILE) is a village in western Yukon Territory, near the Alaskan border.
16. *Furrow* (FUR oh) refers to the long groove-like area in the snow, marking an old sled trail.

Word Bank

apprehension (AP ree HEN shun) *n.*: suspicion or fear of future trouble

the marks of the last runners. In a month no man had come up or down that silent creek. The man held steadily on. He was not much given to thinking, and just then, particularly, he had nothing to think about save that he would eat lunch at the forks and that at six o'clock he would be in camp with the boys. There was nobody to talk to, and, had there been, speech would have been impossible because of the ice muzzle on his mouth. So he continued monotonously to chew tobacco and to increase the length of his amber beard.

Once in a while the thought reiterated[17] itself that it was very cold and that he had never experienced such cold. As he walked along he rubbed his cheekbones and nose with the back of his mittened hand. He did this automatically, now and again changing hands. But, rub as he would, the instant he stopped his cheekbones went numb and the following instant the end of his nose went numb.

He was sure to get frostbite; he knew that, and experienced a pang of regret that he had not devised a nose strap of the sort Bud wore in cold snaps. Such a strap passed across the cheeks as well and saved them. But it didn't matter much, after all. What were frosted cheeks? A bit painful, that was all; they were never serious.

Empty as the man's mind was of thoughts, he was keenly observant, and he noticed the changes in the creek, the curves and bends and timber jams, and always he sharply noted where he placed his feet. Once, coming around a bend, he shied abruptly, like a startled horse, curved away from the place where he had been walking, and retreated several paces back along the trail. The creek he knew was frozen clear to the bottom—no creek

---

17. *Reiterated* (ree IT er RAY tid) means repeated.

could contain water in that arctic winter—but he knew also that there were springs that bubbled out from the hillsides and ran along under the snow and on top of the ice of the creek. He knew that the coldest snaps never froze these springs, and he knew likewise their danger. They were traps. They hid pools of water under the snow that might be three inches deep, or three feet. Sometimes a skin of ice half an inch thick covered them, and in turn was covered by the snow. Sometimes there were alternate layers of water and ice skin, so that when one broke through, he kept on breaking through for a while, sometimes wetting himself to the waist.

   That was why he had shied in such panic. He had felt the give under his feet and heard the crackle of a snow-hidden ice skin. And to get his feet wet in such a temperature meant trouble and danger. At the very least it meant delay, for he would be forced to stop and build a fire, and, under its protection, to bare his feet while he dried his socks and moccasins. He stood and studied the creek bed and its banks and decided that the flow of water came from the right. He reflected awhile, rubbing his nose and cheeks, then skirted to the left, stepping gingerly and testing the footing for each step. Once clear of the danger, he took a fresh chew of tobacco and swung along at his four-mile gait.

   In the course of the next two hours he came upon several similar traps. Usually the snow above the hidden pools had a sunken, candied appearance that advertised the danger. Once again, however, he had a close call, and once, suspecting danger, he compelled the dog to go on in front. The dog did not want to go. It hung back until the man shoved it forward, and then it went quickly across the white, unbroken surface. Suddenly it broke through, floundered to one side, and got away to firmer footing. It had wet its forefeet and legs, and almost immediately the water that clung to it turned to ice. It made quick efforts to lick the ice off its legs, then dropped down in the snow and began to bite out the ice that had formed between the toes. To permit the ice to remain would mean sore feet. It did not know this. This was a matter of instinct. But the man knew, having achieved a judgment on the subject, and he removed the mitten from his right hand and helped tear out the ice particles. He did not expose his fingers more than a minute, and was astonished at the swift numbness that smote them. It certainly was cold. He pulled on the mitten hastily, and beat the hand savagely across his chest.

   At twelve o'clock the day was at its brightest. Yet the sun was too far south on its winter journey to clear the horizon. The bulge of the earth intervened between it and Henderson Creek, where the man walked under a clear sky at noon and cast no shadow. At half-past twelve, to the minute, he arrived at the forks of the creek. He was pleased at the speed he had made. If he kept it up, he would certainly be with the boys by six. He unbuttoned his jacket and shirt and drew forth his lunch. The action consumed no more than a quarter of a minute, yet in that brief moment the numbness laid hold of the

---

Word Bank

gait (GAYT) *n*.: a manner of walking, stepping, or running exposed fingers. He did not put the mitten on, but, instead, struck the fingers a dozen sharp smashes against his leg. Then he sat down on a snow-covered log to eat. The sting that followed upon the striking of his fingers against his leg ceased so quickly that he was startled. He had no chance to take a bite of biscuit. He struck the fingers repeatedly and returned them to the mitten, baring the other hand for the purpose of eating. He tried to take a mouthful but the ice muzzle prevented. He had forgotten to build a fire and thaw out. He chuckled at his foolishness, and as he chuckled he noted the numbness creeping into the exposed fingers. Also, he noted that the stinging which had first come to his toes when he sat down was already passing away. He wondered whether the toes were warm or numb. He moved them inside the moccasins and decided that they were numb.

He pulled the mitten on hurriedly and stood up. He was a bit frightened. He stamped up and down until the stinging returned into the feet. It certainly *was* cold, was his thought. That man from Sulphur Creek had spoken the truth when telling how cold it sometimes got in the country. And he had laughed at him at the time! That showed one must not be too sure of things. There was no mistake about it, it was cold. He strode up and down, stamping his feet and threshing his arms, until reassured by the returning warmth. Then he got out matches and proceeded to make a fire. From the undergrowth, where high water of the previous spring had lodged a supply of seasoned twigs, he got his firewood. Working carefully from a small beginning, he soon had a roaring fire, over which he thawed the ice from his face and in the protection of which he ate his biscuits. For the moment the cold of space was outwitted. The dog took satisfaction in the fire, stretching out close enough for warmth and far enough away to escape being singed.[18]

When the man had finished, he filled his pipe and took his comfortable time over a smoke. Then he pulled on his mittens, settled the ear flaps of his cap firmly about his ears, and took the creek trail up the left fork. The dog was disappointed and yearned back toward the fire. This man did not know cold. Possibly all the generations of his ancestry had been ignorant of cold, of real cold, of cold one hundred and seven degrees below freezing point. But the dog knew; all its ancestry knew, and it had inherited the knowledge. And it knew that it was not good to walk abroad in such fearful cold. It was the time to lie snug in a hole in the snow and wait for a curtain of cloud to be drawn across the face of outer space whence this cold came. On the other hand, there was no keen closeness between the dog and the man. The one was the toil slave of the other, and the only caresses it had ever received were the caresses of the whip lash and of harsh and menacing throat sounds that threatened the whip lash. So the dog made no effort to communicate its apprehension to the man. It was not concerned in the welfare of the man; it was for its own sake that it yearned back toward the fire. But the man whistled and spoke to it with the sound of whip lashes, and the dog swung in at the man's heels and followed after.

The man took a chew of tobacco and proceeded to start a new amber beard. Also, his moist breath quickly powdered with white his mustache, eyebrows, and lashes. There did not seem to be so many

---

18. *Singed* (SINJD) means to be burnt superficially or slightly.

springs on the left fork of the Henderson, and for half an hour the man saw no signs of any. And then it happened. At a place where there were no signs, where the soft, unbroken snow seemed to advertise solidity beneath, the man broke through. It was not deep. He wet himself halfway to the knees before he floundered out to the firm crust.

He was angry. He had hoped to get into camp with the boys at six o'clock, and this would delay him an hour, for he would have to build a fire and dry out his footgear. This was imperative at that low temperature—he knew that much; and he turned aside to the bank which he climbed. On top, tangled in the underbrush about the trunks of several small spruce trees, was a high-water deposit of dry firewood—sticks and twigs, principally, but also larger portions of seasoned branches and fine, dry, last year's grasses. He threw down several large pieces on top of the snow. This served for a foundation and prevented the young flame from drowning itself in the snow it otherwise would melt. The flame he got by touching a match to a small shred of birch bark that he took from his pocket. This burned even more readily than paper. Placing it on the foundation, he fed the young flame with wisps of dry grass and with the tiniest dry twigs.

He worked slowly and carefully, keenly aware of his danger. Gradually, as the flame grew stronger, he increased the size

Word Bank   **imperative** (im PAIR uh tiv) *adj.*: absolutely necessary or required

of the twigs with which he fed it. He squatted in the snow, pulling the twigs out from their entanglement in the brush and feeding directly to the flame. He knew there must be no failure. When it is seventy-five below zero, a man must not fail in his first attempt to build a fire— that is, if his feet are wet. If his feet are dry, and he fails, he can run along the trail for half a mile and restore his circulation. But the circulation of wet and freezing feet cannot be restored by running when it is seventy-five below. No matter how fast he runs, the wet feet will freeze the harder.

All this the man knew. The old-timer on Sulphur Creek had told him about it the previous fall, and now he was appreciating the advice. Already all sensation had gone out of his feet. To build a fire he had been forced to remove his mittens, and the fingers had quickly gone numb. His pace of four miles an hour had kept his heart pumping blood to the surface of his body and to all the extremities. But the instant he stopped, the action of the pump eased down. The cold of space smote the unprotected tip of the planet, and he, being of that unprotected tip, received the full force of the blow. The blood of his body recoiled[19] before it. The blood was alive, like the dog, and like the dog it wanted to hide away and cover itself up from the fearful cold. So long as he walked four miles an hour, he pumped that blood, willy-nilly, to the surface, but now it ebbed away and sank down into the recesses of his body. The extremities were the first to feel its absence. His wet feet froze the faster, and his exposed fingers numbed the faster, though they had not yet begun to freeze. Nose and cheeks were already freezing, while the skin of all his body chilled as it lost its blood.

But he was safe. Toes and nose and cheeks would be only touched by the frost, for the fire was beginning to burn with strength. He was feeding it with twigs the size of his finger. In another minute he would be able to feed it with branches the size of his wrist, and then he could remove his wet footgear, and, while it dried, he could keep his naked feet warm by the fire, rubbing them at first, of course, with snow. The fire was a success. He was safe. He remembered the advice of the old-timer on Sulphur Creek and smiled. The old-timer had been very serious in laying down the law that no man must travel alone in the Klondike[20] after fifty below. Well, here he was; he had had the accident; he was alone; and he had saved himself. Those old-timers were worriers, some of them, he thought. All a man had to do was to keep his head, and he was all right. Any man who was a man could travel alone. But it was surprising, the rapidity with which his cheeks and nose were freezing. And he had not thought his fingers could go lifeless in so short a time. Lifeless they were, for he could scarcely make them move together to grip a twig, and they seemed remote from his body and from him. When he touched a twig, he had to look and see whether or not he had hold of it. The wires were pretty well down between him and his finger ends.

All of which counted for little. There was the fire, snapping and crackling and promising life with every dancing flame. He started to untie his moccasins. They were coated with ice; the thick German

---

19. *Recoiled* (REE KOYLD) means go back, in alarm, horror, or disgust. His blood moved back deeper into his body to protect itself from the cold.
20. The *Klondike* (KLAHN dyk) is a region in the western part of the Yukon Territory.

socks were like sheaths[21] of iron halfway to the knees; and the moccasin strings were like rods of steel all twisted and knotted as by some conflagration.[22] For a moment he tugged with his numb fingers; then, realizing the folly of it, he drew his sheath knife.

But before he could cut the strings, it happened. It was his own fault or, rather, his mistake. He should not have built the fire under the spruce tree. He should not have built it in the open. But it had been easier to pull the twigs from the brush and drop them directly on the fire. Now the tree under which he had done this carried a weight of snow on its boughs. No wind had blown for weeks, and each bough was fully freighted. Each time he had pulled a twig he had communicated a slight agitation to the tree—an imperceptible agitation, so far as he was concerned, but an agitation sufficient to bring about the disaster. High up in the tree one bough capsized its load of snow. This fell on the boughs beneath, capsizing them. This process continued, spreading out and involving the whole tree. It grew like an avalanche, and it descended without warning upon the man and the fire, and the fire was blotted out! Where it had burned was a mantle of fresh and disordered snow.

The man was shocked. It was as though he had just heard his own sentence of death. For a moment he sat and stared at the spot where the fire had been. Then he grew very calm. Perhaps the old-timer on Sulphur Creek was right. If he had only had a trail mate he would have been in no danger now. The trail mate could have built the fire. Well, it was up to him to build the fire over again, and this second time there must be no failure. Even if he succeeded, he would most likely lose some toes. His feet must be badly frozen by now, and there would be some time before the second fire was ready.

Such were his thoughts, but he did not sit and think them. He was busy all the time they were passing through his mind. He made a new foundation for a fire, this time in the open, where no treacherous tree could blot it out. Next he gathered dry grasses and tiny twigs from the high-water flotsam.[23] He could not bring his fingers together to pull them out, but he was able to gather them by the handful. In this way he got many rotten twigs and bits of green moss that were undesirable, but it was the best he could do. He worked methodically, even collecting an armful of the larger branches to be used later when the fire gathered strength. And all the while the dog sat and watched him, a certain yearning wistfulness[24] in its eyes, for it looked upon him as the fire provider, and the fire was slow in coming.

When all was ready, the man reached in his pocket for a second piece of birch bark. He knew the bark was there, and, though he could not feel it with his fingers, he could hear its crisp rustling as he

---

21. The ice on his socks is compared to a *sheath* (SHEETH), a close-fitting covering for a sword or other sharp weapon.
22. A *conflagration* (KAHN fluh GRAY shun) is a destructive fire.
23. *Flotsam* (FLOHT sum) is refuse floating on water.
24. To be filled with *wistfulness* (WIST full niss) is to yearn sadly. The dog longed for the warmth of a fire.

Word Bank

imperceptible (IM pur SEPT ih bul) *adj.*: very slight, gradual, or subtle

capsized (KAP syzd) *v.*: turned bottom up; overturned

fumbled for it. Try as he would, he could not clutch hold of it. And all the time, in his consciousness, was the knowledge that each instant his feet were freezing. This thought tended to put him in a panic, but he fought against it and kept calm. He pulled on his mittens with his teeth, and threshed his arms back and forth, beating his hands with all his might against his sides. He did this sitting down, and he stood up to do it; and all the while the dog sat in the snow, its wolf brush of a tail curled around warmly over its forefeet, its sharp wolf ears pricked forward intently as it watched the man. And the man, as he beat and threshed with his arms and hands, felt a great surge of envy as he regarded the creature that was warm and secure in its natural covering.

After a time he was aware of the first faraway signals of sensation in his beaten fingers. The faint tingling grew stronger till it evolved into a stinging ache that was excruciating but which the man hailed with satisfaction. He stripped the mitten from his right hand and fetched forth the birch bark. The exposed fingers were quickly going numb again. Next he brought out his bunch of sulphur matches. But the tremendous cold had already driven the life out of his fingers. In his effort to separate one match from the others, the whole bunch fell in the snow. He tried to pick it out of the snow, but failed. The dead fingers could neither touch nor clutch. He was very careful. He drove the thought of his freezing feet, and nose, and cheeks, out of his mind, devoting his whole being to the matches. He watched, using the sense of vision in place of that of touch, and when he saw his fingers on each side of the bunch, he closed them—that is, he willed to close them, for the wires were down, and the fingers did not obey. He pulled the mitten on the right hand, and beat it fiercely against his knee. Then, with both mittened hands, he scooped the bunch of matches, along with much snow, into his lap. Yet he was no better off.

After some manipulation he managed to get the bunch between the heels of his mittened hands. In this fashion he carried it to his mouth. The ice crackled and snapped when, by a violent effort, he opened his mouth. He drew the lower jaw in, curled the upper lip out of the way, and scraped the bunch with his upper teeth in order to separate a match. He succeeded in getting one, which he dropped on his lap. He was no better off. He could not pick it up. Then he devised a way. He picked it up in his teeth and scratched it on his leg. Twenty times he scratched before he succeeded in lighting it. As it flamed he held it with his teeth to the birch bark. But the burning brimstone[25] went up his nostrils and into his lungs, causing him to cough spasmodically.[26] The match fell into the snow and went out.

The old-timer on Sulphur Creek was right, he thought in the moment of controlled despair that ensued: after fifty below, a man should travel with a partner. He beat his hands but failed in exciting any sensation. Suddenly he bared both hands, removing the mittens with his teeth. He caught the whole bunch between the heels of his hands. His arm muscles not being frozen enabled him to press the hand heels tightly against the matches. Then he scratched the bunch

---

25. *Brimstone* (BRIM STONE) is another word for sulphur, an ingredient used in making matches.
26. To cough *spasmodically* (spaz MAHD ik lee) means to cough with sudden, quick coughs.

along his leg. It flared into flame, seventy sulphur matches at once! There was no wind to blow them out. He kept his head to one side to escape the strangling fumes, and held the blazing bunch to the birch bark. As he so held it, he became aware of sensation in his hand. His flesh was burning. Deep down below the surface he could feel it. The sensation developed into pain that grew acute. And still he endured it, holding the flame of the matches clumsily to the bark that would not light readily because his own burning hands were in the way.

At last, when he could endure no more, he jerked his hands apart. The blazing matches fell sizzling into the snow, but the birch bark was alight. He began laying dry grasses and the tiniest twigs on the flame. He could not pick and choose, for he had to lift the fuel between the heels of his hands. Small pieces of rotten wood and green moss clung to the twigs, and he bit them off as well as he could with his teeth. He cherished the flame carefully and awkwardly. It meant life, and it must not perish. The withdrawal of blood from the surface of his body now made him begin to shiver, and he grew more awkward. A large piece of green moss fell squarely on the little fire. He tried to poke it out with his fingers, but his shivering frame made him poke too far, and he disrupted the nucleus of the little fire, the burning grasses and tiny twigs separating and scattering. He tried to poke them together again, but in spite of the tenseness of the effort, his shivering got away with him, and the twigs were hopelessly scattered. Each twig gushed a puff of smoke and went out.

The fire provider had failed. As he looked apathetically about him, his eyes chanced on the dog, sitting across the ruins of the fire from him, in the snow, making restless, hunching movements, slightly lifting one forefoot and then the other, shifting its weight back and forth on them with wistful eagerness.

The sight of the dog put a wild idea into his head. He remembered the tale of the man, caught in a blizzard, who killed a steer and crawled inside the carcass and so was saved. He would kill the dog and bury his hands in the warm body until the numbness went out of them. Then he could build another fire. He spoke to the dog, calling it to him, but in his voice was a strange note of fear that frightened the animal, who had never known the man to speak in such a way before. Something was the matter, and its suspicious nature sensed danger—it knew not what danger, but somewhere, somehow, in its brain arose an apprehension of the man. It flattened its ears down at the sound of the man's voice, and its restless, hunching movements and the liftings and shiftings of its forefeet became more pronounced; but it would not come to the man. He got on his hands and knees and crawled toward the dog. This unusual posture again excited suspicion, and the animal sidled mincingly[27] away.

The man sat up in the snow for a moment and struggled for calmness. Then he pulled on his mittens, by means of his teeth, and got up on his feet. He glanced down at first in order to assure himself

---

27. *Sidled mincingly* (SY dild MIN sing lee) means to edge away from something with short steps. The dog is backing away from the man.

Word Bank

apathetically (AP uh THET ik lee) *adv.*: having or showing little or no emotion

that he was really standing up, for the absence of sensation in his feet left him unrelated to the earth. His erect position in itself started to drive the webs of suspicion from the dog's mind, and when he spoke peremptorily,[28] with the sound of whip lashes in his voice, the dog rendered its customary allegiance and came to him. As it came within reaching distance, the man lost his control. His arms flashed out to the dog, and he experienced genuine surprise when he discovered that his hands could not clutch, that there was neither bend nor feeling in the fingers. He had forgotten for the moment that they were frozen and that they were freezing more and more. All this happened quickly, and before the animal could get away, he encircled its body with his arms. He sat down in the snow and in this fashion held the dog, while it snarled and whined and struggled.

But it was all he could do, hold its body encircled in his arms and sit there. He realized that he could not kill the dog. There was no way to do it. With his helpless hands he could neither draw nor hold his sheath knife nor throttle the animal. He released it, and it plunged wildly away, with tail between its legs and still snarling. It halted forty feet away and surveyed him curiously, with ears sharply pricked forward.

The man looked down at his hands in order to locate them, and found them hanging on the ends of his arms. It struck him as curious that one should have to use his eyes in order to find out where his hands were. He began threshing his arms back and forth, beating the mittened hands against his sides. He did this for five minutes, violently, and his heart

---

28. The man spoke *peremptorily* (pur EMPT er ih lee), meaning he gave the dog no opportunity for refusal.

pumped enough blood up to the surface to put a stop to his shivering. But no sensation was aroused in the hands. He had an impression that they hung like weights on the ends of his arms, but when he tried to run the impression down, he could not find it.

A certain fear of death, dull and oppressive, came to him. This fear quickly became poignant[29] as he realized that it was no longer a mere matter of freezing his fingers and toes, or of losing his hands and feet, but that it was a matter of life and death with the chances against him. This threw him into a panic, and he turned and ran up the creek bed along the old, dim trail. The dog joined in behind and kept up with him. He ran blindly, without intention, in fear such as he had never known in his life. Slowly, as he plowed and floundered through the snow, he began to see things again—the banks of the creek, the old timber jams, the leafless aspens, and the sky. The running made him feel better. He did not shiver. Maybe, if he ran on, his feet would thaw out, and, anyway, if he ran far enough, he would reach camp and the boys. Without doubt he would lose some fingers and toes and some of his face, but the boys would take care of him, and save the rest of him when he got there. And at the same time there was another thought in his mind that said he would never get to the camp and the boys, that it was too many miles away, that the freezing had too great a start on him, and that he would soon be stiff and dead. This thought he kept in the background and refused to consider. Sometimes it pushed itself forward and demanded to be heard, but he thrust it back and strove to think of other things.

It struck him as curious that he could run at all on feet so frozen that he could not feel them when they struck the earth and took the weight of his body. He seemed to himself to skim along above the surface and to have no connection with the earth.

His theory of running until he reached camp and the boys had one flaw in it: he lacked the endurance. Several times he stumbled, and finally he tottered, crumpled up, and fell. When he tried to rise, he failed. He must sit and rest, he decided, and next time he would merely walk and keep on going. As he sat and regained his breath, he noted that he was feeling quite warm and comfortable. He was not shivering, and it even seemed that a warm glow had come to his chest and trunk. And yet, when he touched his nose and cheeks, there was no sensation. Running would not thaw them out. Nor would it thaw out his hands and feet. Then the thought came to him that the frozen portions of his body must be extending. He tried to keep this thought down, to forget it, to think of something else; he was aware of the panicky feeling that it caused, and he was afraid of the panic. But the thought asserted itself and persisted, until it produced a vision of his body totally frozen. This was too much, and he made another wild run along the trail. Once he slowed down to a walk, but the thought of the freezing extending itself made him run again.

And all the time the dog ran with him, at his heels. When he fell down a second time, it curled its tail over its forefeet and sat in front of him, facing him, curiously eager and intent. The warmth and security of the animal angered him, and he lashed out at it till it flattened down its

---

29. *Poignant* (POYN yint) means deeply emotional.

ears appeasingly. This time the shivering came more quickly upon the man. He was losing in his battle with the frost. It was creeping into his body from all sides. The thought of it drove him on, but he ran no more than a hundred feet when he staggered and pitched headlong. It was his last panic. When he had recovered his breath and control, he sat up and entertained in his mind the conception of meeting death with dignity. However, the conception did not come to him in such terms. His idea of it was that he had been making a fool of himself, running around like a chicken with its head cut off—such was the simile that occurred to him. Well, he was bound to freeze anyway, and he might as well take it decently. With this new-found peace of mind came the first glimmerings of drowsiness. A good idea, he thought, to sleep off to death. It was like taking an anesthetic. Freezing was not so bad as people thought. There were lots worse ways to die.

He pictured the boys finding his body next day. Suddenly he found himself with them, coming along the trail and looking for himself. And, still with them, he came around a turn in the trail and found himself lying in the snow. He did not belong with himself any more, for even then he was out of himself, standing with the boys and looking at himself in the snow. It certainly was cold, was his thought. When he got back to the States he could tell the folks what real cold was. He drifted on from this to a vision of the old-timer on Sulphur Creek. He could see him quite clearly, warm and comfortable, and smoking a pipe.

"You were right, old hoss; you were right," the man mumbled to the old-timer of Sulphur Creek.

Then the man drowsed off into what seemed to him the most comfortable and satisfying sleep he had ever known. The dog sat facing him and waiting. The brief day drew to a close in a long, slow twilight. There were no signs of a fire to be made, and, besides, never in the dog's experience had it known a man to sit like that in the snow and make no fire. As the twilight drew on, its eager yearning for the fire mastered it, and with a great lifting and shifting of forefeet, it whined softly, then flattened its ears down in anticipation of being chidden[30] by the man. But the man remained silent. Later the dog whined loudly. And still later it crept close to the man and caught the scent of death. This made the animal bristle and back away. A little longer it delayed, howling under the stars that leaped and danced and shone brightly in the cold sky. Then it turned and trotted up the trail in the direction of the camp it knew, where were the other food providers and fire providers.

---

30. To be *chidden* (CHID in) (from "to chide") means to be scolded or reproached.

Word Bank

appeasingly (uh PEEZ ing lee) *adv.*: in a pacifying way; in such a way as to please

Studying the Selection

First Impressions

Now that you have finished the story, answer the following questions in a well-written paragraph or two: What mistakes did the man make that led to his death, and how might he have been better prepared for this situation?

✔ Quick Review

1. What is a *chechaquo*?
2. What destination was the man trying to reach?
3. What was in the bundle under the man's shirt? Why did he carry it there?
4. What is an "amber beard"?

In-depth Thinking

5. How did the man first know the temperature was colder than fifty below zero?
6. Describe the dog in the story. How does the dog's knowledge of the landscape, and preparation for the conditions he encounters, compare to the man's awareness?
7. Discuss the stages involved in freezing to death. Were you surprised by the man's calm demeanor at the very end of his life?
8. Summarize the old-timer's advice. How do the man's feelings about this advice change as the story progresses?

Drawing Conclusions

9. Did the man in the story learn a lesson before he died? If so, what did he learn?
10. Imagine that the dog reached the camp and convinced the boys to return with him to find the man. Is this a good possibility?

Focusing on Setting

Complete these activities keeping in mind that **setting** is where and when a story takes place.

1. Write a paragraph describing a setting that can be life-threatening to its inhabitants; for example, a seaport hit by a hurricane or a rural town threatened by a forest fire.
2. Write about two places that evoke opposite moods; for instance, the beach on a sunny afternoon and a deserted street during a thunderstorm. Experiment with descriptive language, creating images that bring specific moods to life.
3. Go back to the story and copy 15-20 phrases that suggest the cold, menacing, and/or isolating nature of the setting. Include paragraph and page numbers for reference.

Creating and Writing

1. In what specific ways did the dog's instincts serve him better than the man's knowledge and experience? For support, include quotes from the story.
2. Write a story about a loyal friendship between an adult and a dog, or a child and a dog. Include an incident in which the dog has the opportunity to save its owner's life. At the end of your story, write a separate paragraph contrasting this relationship with the one shown in the story. Analyze the differences.
3. **Wax Hands:** Your teacher will distribute a list of instructions for this "hands-on" project. It is designed to help you experience the numbing sensation felt by the man in the story as his extremities began to freeze. You will see how difficult it is to sense heat once your hands are numb. When you are done, you will also have a wax mold of your hand.

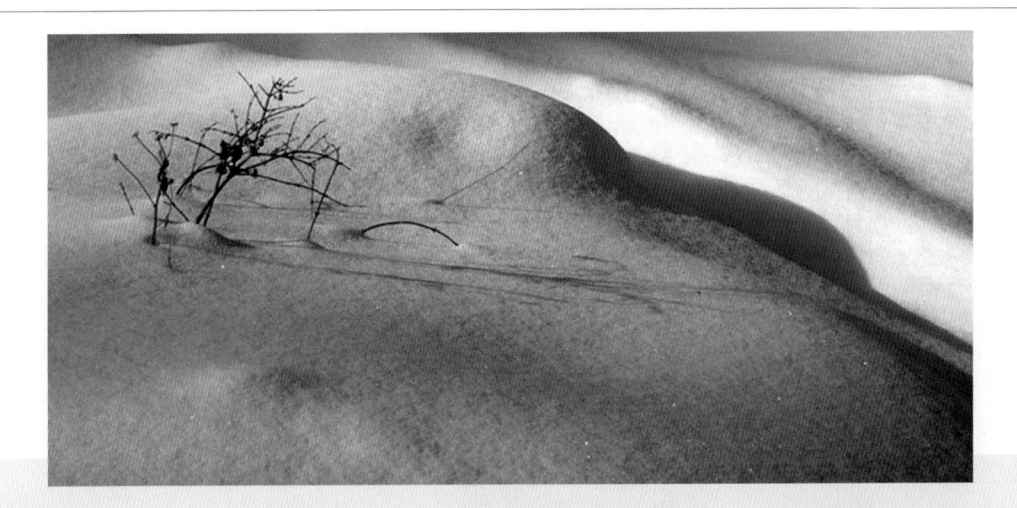

Blueprint for Reading

the Author

**Jesse Stuart
(1906-1984)**

Jesse Stuart was born in Kentucky, the second of seven children. In high school, an English teacher encouraged him to write. Later he was accepted at Lincoln Memorial University in Harrogate, Tennessee. From 1931-1932, Stuart attended graduate school at Vanderbilt University. Throughout much of his life, he did farm chores, helping to raise the family crops. His work is widely praised for its treatment of Appalachian experiences.

Background Bytes

Have you ever gone to a flea market? If so, you've seen people crowding around stalls, picking through goods. You may have heard a shriek of delight as a shopper found the exact item he or she wanted. Flea markets survive because everyone loves a bargain; and because one person's trash is another person's treasure. For one person to find the *most* charming hat, an antique, or an old book at *such* a price means that someone else is willing to sell it. The exchange works and flea markets thrive. Sometimes, a customer's enthusiasm gives the seller a new perspective on the item being sold!

Into *This Farm for Sale*

As you read *This Farm for Sale*, consider the saying, "The grass is always greener on the other side." The story takes place in the country. The protagonists don't know the worth of their farm, until they see it through the eyes of an outsider. Since the land has passed from one generation to the next, it is too "close to home" for the family to value it fully. They are selling the farm and moving to the city, where they will have modern appliances and less mud.

The family also feels isolated on their land which can only be reached by horseback. The isolation has kept the homestead primitive. The farm is surrounded by natural boundaries, with no easy link to civilization. Yet this very seclusion charms the realtor who comes to appraise the property.

Before you read, write a paragraph about a time when you thought "the grass [was] greener on the other side." Try to state why it might be hard to appreciate a situation with which you have become too familiar.

This Farm for Sale

Focusing on Setting and Perspective

The author uses **setting** in a unique way. Usually, the setting of a story tells us where the story takes place. For example, a story may take place, like this one, in the country, or it may take place in a city. Indeed, the whole story may take place in a room, if the characters never leave the room. This is also true if the narrator's perspective never leaves the room to 'show' the reader the world beyond. **Perspective** is how something is seen. Think of a toddler's perspective; a child will see things a bit differently, since he or she is closer to the ground. Imagine your perspective, if you were always craning your neck to look up at the 'giants.'

In *This Farm for Sale*, the author uses setting as a device to gain perspective. Notice how the family describes the farm, and how the wording changes in the advertisement. Only when the salesman 'sets the stage' for a possible buyer in his newspaper ad does the family 'see' the farm differently.

As you approach the story, consider the narrator's identity. Why might his perspective differ somewhat from that of the family?

Word Bank

Galoshes: *Galoshes* is a funny-sounding word that was formerly used much more than it is today. Perhaps this is because clothing fashions and shoe styles have changed. Perhaps, as our society grows more affluent (that is, rich), many people can afford to own both shoes *and* boots. Do you know anyone who uses the word? Do you know what *galoshes* look like? The singular of the word is *galosh* or *galoshe*, but people rarely talk about one galoshe! Galoshe comes from the words Romans used for the shoes worn by the people of Gaul (France): *solea gallica*, or Gaulish sandal.

cane	drove	galoshes	sorghum
deed	exploited	persimmon	

This Farm for Sale

Jesse Stuart

"This time we're goin' to sell this farm," Uncle Dick said to Aunt Emma. "I've just learned how to sell a farm. Funny, I never thought of it myself."

My cousins—Olive, Helen, Oliver, and Little Dick—all stopped eating and looked at one another and then looked at Uncle Dick and Aunt Emma. When Aunt Emma smiled, they smiled, too. Everybody seemed happy because Uncle Dick, who had just come from Blakesburg, had found a way to sell the farm. Everybody was happy but me. I was sorry Uncle Dick was going to sell the farm.

"This farm is just as good as sold!" Uncle Dick talked on. "I've got a real estate man, my old friend Melvin Spencer, coming here tomorrow to look the place over. He's goin' to sell it for me."

"I'd like to get enough for it to make a big payment on a fine house in Blakesburg," Aunt Emma said. "I've got the one picked out that I want. It's the beautiful Coswell house. I understand it's up for sale now and no one's livin' in it!"

"Gee, that will be wonderful," Cousin Olive said. "Right on the street and not any mud. We wouldn't have to wear galoshes all winter if we lived there!"

"I'll say it will be wonderful," Helen said, with a smile. "Daddy, I hope Mr. Spencer can sell this place."

I wanted to tell Aunt Emma the reason why no one was living in the Coswell house. Every time Big River rose to flood stage, the water got on the first floor in the house; and this was the reason why the Coswells had built a house on higher ground outside Blakesburg and had moved to it. And this was the reason why they couldn't keep a renter any longer than it took Big River to rise to flood stage. But this wasn't my business, so I didn't say anything.

"Mel Spencer will come here to look this farm over," Uncle Dick said, puffing on his cigar until he'd almost filled

---

Word Bank

galoshes (guh LAHSH iz) *n.*: waterproof boots or overshoes, usually high ones

the dining room with smoke. "Then he'll put an ad in the Blakesburg Gazette."

"What will we do about the cows, horses, hogs, honeybees, hay in the barn lofts and in the stacks, and corn in the bins?" Cousin Oliver asked.

"Sell them, too," Uncle Dick said. "When we sell, let's sell everything we have but our house plunder."[1]

It was ten o'clock the next day before Melvin Spencer came. Since he couldn't drive his car all the way to Uncle Dick's farm, he rode the mail truck to Red Hot. Red Hot is a store and post office on the Tiber River. And at Red Hot, Uncle Dick met him with an extra horse and empty saddle. So Melvin Spencer came riding up with Uncle Dick. And I'll never forget the first words he said when he climbed down from the saddle.

"Richard, it's a great experience to be in the saddle again," he said, breathing deeply of the fresh air. "All this reminds me of another day and time."

Oliver, Little Dick, and I followed Melvin Spencer and Uncle Dick as they started walking toward the Tiber bottoms.[2]

"How many acres in this farm, Richard?" Melvin Spencer asked.

"The deed calls for three hundred, more or less," Uncle Dick said.

"How many acres of bottom land?" he asked Uncle Dick.

"I'd say about sixty-five," Uncle Dick replied.

We walked down the jolt-wagon road, where my cousins and I had often ridden Nell and Jerry to and from the field.

"What kind of land is this?" Melvin Spencer asked. He had to look up to see the bright heads of cane.

"It's limestone land," Uncle Dick bragged. "Never had to use fertilizer. My people have farmed these bottoms over a hundred years."

Then Uncle Dick showed Melvin Spencer the corn we had laid by. It was August, and our growing corn was maturing. Melvin Spencer looked at the big cornfield. He was very silent. We walked on to the five acres of tobacco, where the broad leaves crossed the balks[3] and a man couldn't walk through. Then we went down to the river.

"My farm comes to this river," Uncle Dick said. "I've often thought what a difference it would be if we had a bridge across this river. Then I could reach the Tiber road and go east to Blakesburg and west to Darter

---

1. *House plunder* refers to movable personal belongings, such as furniture, clothing, or jewelry.
2. *Tiber bottoms* (TY ber BAHT umz) are low-lying fields near the river. They are very fertile, containing soil and nutrients deposited during flood season.
3. The *balks* (BAWLX) is a reference to the strips of land left unplowed.

Word Bank

deed *n.*: an official document, delivered to finalize an acquisition, especially of real estate

cane *n.*: sugarcane

City. But we don't have a bridge; and until we go down the river seven miles to Red Hot where we can cross to the Tiber road, we'll always be in the mud. I've heard all my life that the county would build a bridge. My father heard it, too, in his lifetime."

"You *are* shut in here," Melvin Spencer agreed, as he looked beyond the Tiber River at the road.

"Now, we'll go to the house and get some dinner," Uncle Dick said. "Then I'll take you up on the hill this afternoon and show you my timber and the rest of the farm."

When we reached the big house, Melvin Spencer stopped for a minute and looked at the house and yard.

"You know, when I sell a piece of property, I want to look it over," he told Uncle Dick. "I want to know all about it. How old is this house?"

"The date was cut on the chimney," Uncle Dick said.

Melvin Spencer looked over the big squat log house with the plank door, big stone steps, small windows, the moss-covered roof. Then we went inside, and he started looking again. That is, he did until Uncle Dick introduced him to Aunt Emma and Aunt Emma introduced him to a table that made him stand and look some more.

"I've never seen anything like this since I was a boy," Melvin Spencer said, showing more interest in the loaded table than he had in the farm.

"All of this came from our farm here," Uncle Dick said.

I never saw a man eat like Melvin Spencer. He ate like I did when I first came to Uncle Dick's and Aunt Emma's each spring when school was over. He tried to eat something of everything on the table, but he couldn't get around to it all.

"If I could sell this farm like you can prepare a meal, I'd get a whopping big price for it," he said with a chuckle as he looked at Aunt Emma.

"I hope you can," Aunt Emma said. "We're too far back here. Our children have to wade the winter mud to get to school. And we don't have electricity. We don't have the things that city people have. And I think every country woman wants them."

Melvin Spencer didn't listen to all that Aunt Emma said. He was much too busy eating. And long before he had finished, Uncle Dick pulled a cigar from his inside coat pocket, struck a match under the table, lit it, and blew a big cloud of smoke toward the ceiling in evident enjoyment.

He looked at Aunt Emma and smiled.

"The old place is as good as sold, Mother," Uncle Dick said with a wink. "You're a-goin' to be out of the mud. We'll let some other woman slave around here and wear galoshes all winter. We'll be on the bright, clean streets wearin' well-shined shoes—every one of us. We'll have an electric washer, a radio where we won't have to have the batteries charged, a bathroom, and an electric stove. No more of this stove-wood choppin' for the boys and me."

When Uncle Dick said this, Olive and Helen looked at Aunt Emma and smiled. I looked at Oliver and Little

Dick, and they were grinning. But Melvin Spencer never looked up from his plate.

When we got up from the table, Melvin Spencer thanked Aunt Emma, Cousin Olive, and Helen for the "best dinner" he'd had since he was a young man. Then he asked Aunt Emma for a picture of the house.

Aunt Emma sent Helen to get it. "If you can, just sell this place for us," Aunt Emma said to Melvin Spencer.

"I'll do my best," he promised her. "But as you ought to know, it will be a hard place to sell, located way back here and without a road."

"Are you a-goin' to put a picture of this old house in the paper?" Uncle Dick asked, as Helen came running with the picture.

"I might," Melvin Spencer said. "I never say much in an ad, since I have to make my words count. A picture means a sale sometimes. Of course, this expense will come from the sale of the property."

He said good-by to Aunt Emma, Olive, and Helen. Little Dick, Oliver, and I followed him and Uncle Dick out of the house and up the hill where the yellow poplars and the pines grow.

"Why hasn't this timber been cut long ago?" Melvin Spencer asked, looking up at the trees.

"Not any way to haul it out," Uncle Dick told him.

"That's right," Melvin Spencer said.

"I'd forgot about the road. If a body doesn't have a road to his farm, Richard, he's not got much of a place."

"These old trees get hollow and blow down in storms," Uncle Dick said. "They should have been cut down a long time ago."

"Yes, they should have," Melvin Spencer agreed, as he put his hand on the bark of a yellow poplar. "We used to have trees like this in Pike County. But not any more."

While we walked under the beech grove,[4] we came upon a drove of slender hogs eating beechnuts.

"Old Skinny bacon hogs," Uncle Dick said, as they scurried past us. "They feed on the mast[5] of the beeches and oaks, on saw-briar, greenbriar, and pine-tree roots, and on mulberries, persimmons, and pawpaws."[6]

When we climbed to the top of a hill, the land slanted in all directions.

"Show me from here what you own," Melvin Spencer said.

"It's very easy, Mel," Uncle Dick said. "The stream on the right and the one on the left are the left and right forks of Wolfe Creek. They are boundary lines. I own all the land

---

4. A *beech grove* is a small group of beech trees growing close together.
5. The term *mast* refers to the nuts of forest trees, such as oak and beech, when used as food for hogs.
6. A *pawpaw* (PAW PAW) is the fleshy fruit of the pawpaw tree.

Word Bank

drove (DROVE) *n.*: a number of oxen, sheep or swine driven in a group; herd; flock

persimmon (per SIM in) *n.*: a large orange fruit that is edible and sweet when very ripe and soft

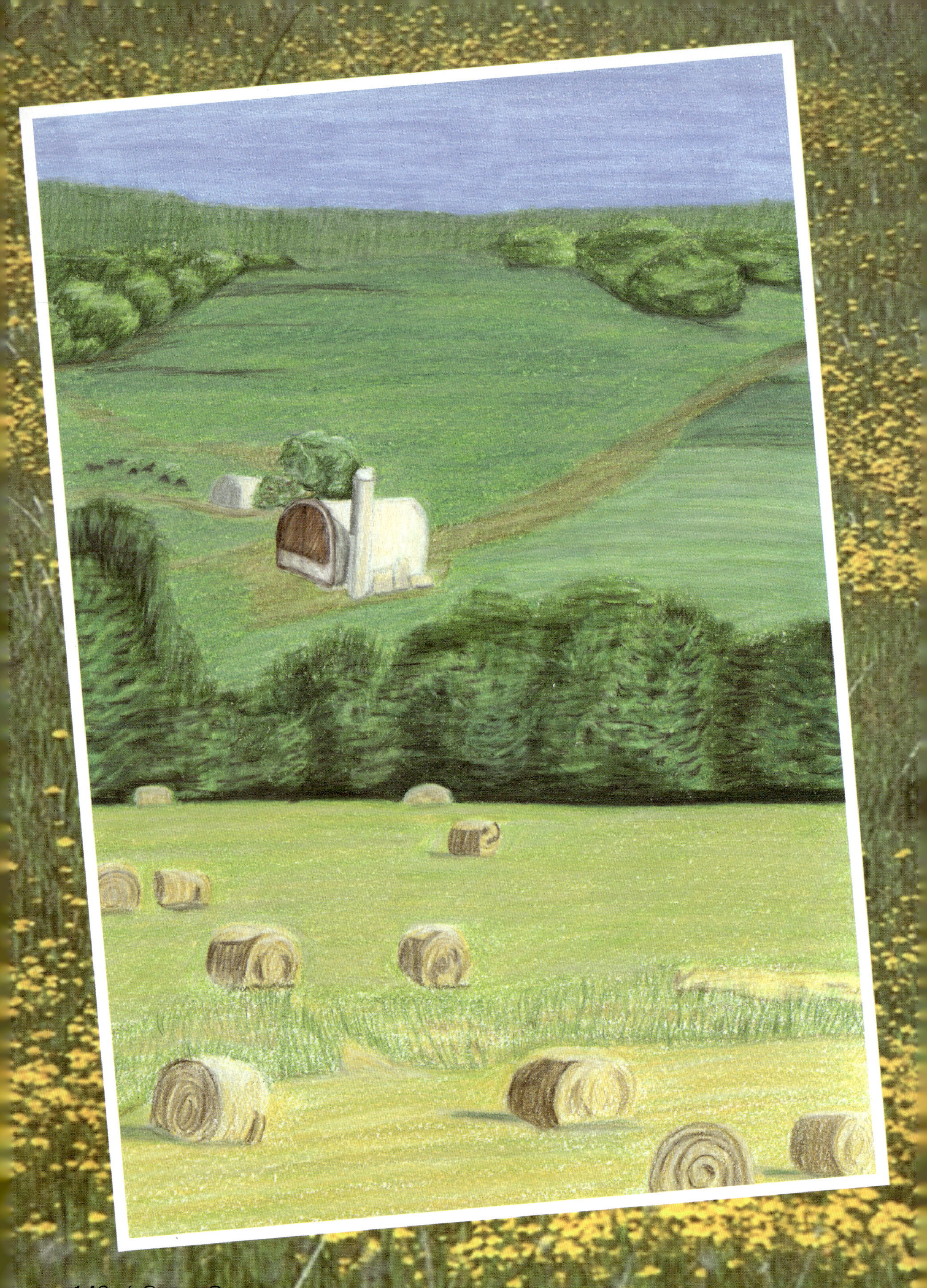

between them. I own all the bottom land from where the forks join, down to that big bend in the Tiber. And I own down where the Tiber flows against those white limestone cliffs."

"You are fenced in by natural boundaries," Melvin Spencer said. "They're almost impossible to cross. This place will be hard to sell, Richard."

Then we went back down the hill, and Melvin and Uncle Dick climbed into the saddles and were off down the little narrow road toward Red Hot. Their horses went away at a gallop, because Melvin Spencer had to catch the mail truck, and he was already behind schedule.

On Saturday, Uncle Dick rode to Red Hot to get the paper. Since he didn't read very well, he asked me to read what Melvin Spencer had said about his house. When I opened the paper and turned to the picture of the house, everybody gathered around.

"Think of a picture of this old house in the paper," Aunt Emma said.

"But there are pictures of other houses for sale in the paper," Uncle Dick told her. "That's not anything to crow[7] about."

"But it's the best-looking of the four," Cousin Olive said.

"It does look better than I thought it would," Aunt Emma sighed.

"Look, here's two columns all the way down the page," I said. "The other four places advertised here have only a paragraph about them."

"Read it," Uncle Dick said. "I'd like to know what Mel said about this place. Something good, I hope."

So I read this aloud:

Yesterday, I had a unique experience when I visited the farm of Mr. and Mrs. Richard Stone, which they have asked me to sell. I cannot write an ad about this farm. I must tell you about it.

I went up a winding road on horseback. Hazelnut bushes, with clusters of green hazelnuts bending their slender stems, swished across my face. Pawpaws, heavy with green clusters of fruit, grew along this road. Persimmons with bending boughs covered one slope below the road. Here are wild fruits and nuts of Nature's cultivation for the one who possesses land like this. Not any work but just to go out and gather the fruit. How many of you city dwellers would love this?

"What about him a-mentionin' the persimmons, pawpaws, and hazelnuts!" Uncle Dick broke in. "I'd never have thought of them. They're common things!"

When we put the horses in the big barn, Mr. Stone, his two sons, his nephew, and I walked down into his Tiber-bottom farm land. And, like the soil along the Nile River, this overflowed land, rich with limestone, never has to be fertilized. I saw cane as high as a giraffe, and as dark green as the waves of the Atlantic. It grew in long, straight rows with brown clusters of seed that looked to be up against the blue of the sky. I have never seen such dark clouds of

---

7. To *crow* (KROE) about something is to boast or brag about it.

This Farm for Sale / 141

corn grow out of the earth. Five acres of tobacco, with leaves as broad as a mountaineer's shoulders. Pleasant meadows with giant haystacks here and there. It is a land rich with fertility and abundant with crops.

"That sounds wonderful," Aunt Emma said, smiling.

This peaceful Tiber River, flowing dreamily down the valley, is a boundary to his farm. Here one can see to the bottoms of the deep holes, the water is so clear and blue. One can catch fish from the river for his next meal. Elder bushes,[8] where they gather the berries to make the finest jelly in the world, grow along this riverbank as thick as ragweeds. The Stones have farmed this land for four generations, have lived in the same house, have gathered elderberries for their jelly along the Tiber riverbanks, and fished in its sky-blue waters that long—and yet they will sell this land.

"Just a minute, Shan," Uncle Dick said as he got up from his chair. "Stop just a minute."

Uncle Dick pulled a handkerchief from his pocket and wiped the sweat from his forehead. His face seemed a bit flushed. He walked a little circle around the living room and then sat back down in his chair. But the sweat broke out on his face again when I started reading.

The proof of what a farm produces is at the farm table. I wish that whoever reads what I have written here could have seen the table prepared by Mrs. Stone and her two daughters. Hot fluffy biscuits with light-brown tops, brown-crusted corn-bread, buttermilk, sweet milk (cooled in a freestone well), wild-grape jelly, wild-crabapple jelly, mast-fed lean bacon that melted in my mouth, fresh apple pie, wild-blackberry cobbler, honey-colored sorghum from the limestone bottoms of the Tiber, and wild honey from the beehives.

"Oh, no one ever said that about a meal I cooked before," Aunt Emma broke in.

"Just a minute, Shan," Uncle Dick said, as he got up from his chair and with his handkerchief in his hand again.

This time Uncle Dick went a bit faster as he circled the living room. He wiped sweat from his face as he walked. He had a worried look on his face. I read on:

The house, eight rooms and two halls, would be a show place if close to some of our modern cities. The house itself would be worth the price I will later quote you on this farm. Giant yellow poplar logs with twenty- to thirty-inch facings, hewed smooth with broadaxes by the mighty hands of Stone pioneers, make the sturdy walls in this termite-proof house. Two planks make the broad doors in this

---

8. An *elder bush* (ELL der BUSH) is a type of honeysuckle bush, with clusters of small red, black, or yellow berries.

Word Bank

sorghum (SORE gum) *n.*: a sweet syrup made from the sorgo plant

house that is one-hundred-and-six years old. This beautiful home of pioneer architecture is without modern conveniences, but since a power line will be constructed up the Tiber River early next spring, a few modern conveniences will be possible.

"I didn't know that!" Aunt Emma was excited. "I guess it's just talk, like about the bridge across the Tiber."

After lunch I climbed a high hill to look at the rest of this farm. I walked through a valley of virgin trees, where there were yellow poplars and pine sixty feet to the first limb. Beech trees with tops big enough to shade twenty-five head of cattle. Beechnuts streaming down like golden coins, to be gathered by the hogs running wild. A farm with wild game and fowl, and a river bountiful with fish! And yet, this farm is for sale!

Uncle Dick walked over beside his chair. He looked as if he were going to fall over.

Go see for yourself roads not exploited by the county or state, where the horse's shoe makes music on the clay, where apple orchards with fruit are bending down, and barns and bins are full. Go see a way of life, a richness and fulfillment that make America great, that put solid foundation stones under America! This beautiful farm, fifty head of livestock, honeybees, crops old and new, and a home for only $22,000!

"Oh!" Aunt Emma screamed. I thought she was going to faint. "Oh, he's killed it with that price. It's unheard of, Richard! You couldn't get $6,000 for it."

Uncle Dick still paced the floor.

"What's the matter, Pa?" Oliver finally asked.

"I didn't know I had so much," Uncle Dick said. "I'm a rich man and didn't know it. I'm not selling this farm!"

"Don't worry, Richard," Aunt Emma said. "You won't sell it at that price!"

I never saw such disappointed looks as there were on my cousins' faces.

"But what will you do with Mr. Spencer?" Aunt Emma asked. "You've put the farm in his hands to sell."

"Pay him for his day and what he put in the paper," Uncle Dick told her. "I know we're not goin' to sell now, for it takes two to sign the deed. I'll be willing to pay Mel Spencer a little extra because he showed me what we have."

Then I laid the paper down and walked quietly from the room. Evening was coming on. I walked toward the meadows. I wanted to share the beauty of this farm with Melvin Spencer. I was never so happy.

Word Bank **exploited** (eks PLOY tid) *v*.: taken advantage of; used or abused

Studying the Selection

First Impressions

Now that you have read the story, have you identified the narrator? Why wasn't he as excited as his cousins when Uncle Dick decided to sell the farm? What key factor lets him see things a little bit differently?

✓ Quick Review

1. Why does Aunt Emma want to move to Blakesburg?
2. What crops do the Stones grow on the farm?
3. What kinds of fruits grow naturally on the land?
4. Why doesn't the family need to use fertilizer on the land?

In-depth Thinking

5. Compare and contrast the cousins' facial expressions at the beginning and end of the story as the sale of the farm is discussed. Explain the reasons for the difference.
6. Compare and contrast the narrator's feelings at the beginning and end of the story.
7. Throughout the story, the family says the country has one thing the city doesn't have. What is it and why is this the main reason they want to live "right on the street"?
8. Find the two parts in the story where the pigs are described, first by Uncle Dick and then by Mr. Spencer. Explain why this is a good example of how the family and the salesman see the farm differently.

Drawing Conclusions

9. In this story, the salesman seems to feel **nostalgia** when he visits the farm. Nostalgia is the sentimental feeling you have when remembering a past experience, like recalling a special moment from your childhood. There is one critical moment in the story when the salesman 'steps into' this way of thinking. He has stepped out of the city setting and into the country setting with the family. Can you find this moment in the story?
10. During the events of the story, the narrator says little. In fact, the only time he actually speaks to the others is when he reads the newspaper ad aloud to the family. Notice, however, he is not speaking his own words. Rather he is reading the words of the salesman. How are these two characters, the narrator and the salesman, similar? A parallel seems to be drawn between them. Explain why you think the author chose to have the narrator read the ad and not another family member.

Focusing on Setting and Perspective

Remember—**setting** is where a story takes place and **perspective** is how something is seen.

1. Describe the setting of your classroom.
2. Describe the setting of your neighborhood.
3. Describe the things you would see at eye-level if you were a toddler.

Creating and Writing

1. Mr. Spencer's ad said, "This beautiful home of pioneer architecture is without modern conveniences, but since a power line will be constructed up the Tiber River early next spring, a few modern conveniences will be possible," to which Aunt Emma replied, "I didn't know that! I guess it's just talk, like about the bridge across the Tiber." How might things change on the farm if it gets the "modern conveniences" of electricity and a bridge "to the other side" and is no longer so isolated?
2. Do you have a friend who spends a lot of time with you, either at home or where you spend your summers? Write a real estate ad for one of these places. Be realistic in your descriptions. Now ask your friend to write the same ad. Are they similar? Write a short essay dealing with the differences in the ads.
3. Imagine the perspective of a fish in a bowl of water, sitting on a table in the corner of a room. Write a paragraph describing how the room looks to you. Think how things might look if you saw them through water. Give details of the things in this room. Tell us how noises sound if heard through the water. Also, consider telling us how the water smells, tastes, and feels in your bowl. Who feeds you, and what is this experience like?

Blueprint for Reading

the Author

**Ray Bradbury
(1920-2012)**

Ray Bradbury was born in Waukegan, Illinois. After high school, he lived in Los Angeles where he joined a theater group. In 1941, he began publishing stories. Although best known for science fiction, he also has written other types of fiction, dramas, essays, and poetry. Bradbury has long been concerned with the freedom to think; he said, "You don't have to burn books to destroy a culture, just get people to stop reading them." This is a startling statement by the author of *Fahrenheit 451*, a story of government-sponsored book burning.

Background Bytes

The Civil War battle of Shiloh was fought in a town called Shiloh, in southwestern Tennessee, on April 6-7, 1862. There, 25,000 men died in one of the most horrifying battles of the war. During the Civil War over 600,000 men died in action or from infection, and more than one million were wounded. Improved heavy artillery, "better" rifles, and outdated battlefield tactics created havoc; limited medical knowledge, terrible battlefield hospitals, and lack of antibiotics made even minor wounds deadly.

Into *The Drummer Boy of Shiloh*

The story opens as soldiers prepare to fight and die. With dreams of storybook battles filling their heads, these "man-boys" have only a dim awareness of the harsh realities awaiting them. Many are innocents who are not even ready to shave, let alone stand up to the horrors of war.

The story begins and ends before a single bullet is fired, before the sun even rises, but the sense of impending doom builds against a serene backdrop of innocent youth and delicate nature. The theme is of "ripeness" and budding forth—the promise of youth.

Before you read, use the sensory skills you sharpened while studying *To Build a Fire.* Look closely at a peach. Examine it and observe its color and shape. Hold the peach and feel its weight, its fuzzy texture, and its ripeness (determined by gentle squeezing). Now smell it. Peaches have a very distinct, sweet smell, especially if ripe. Open the fruit and compare its fuzzy outside to its wet, soft inside. Take a bite. Did juice run down your chin? Did the fuzz tickle your lips? When you are done, drop the pit onto your desk. Think about the noise it makes. Was it loud or faint? A *thud* or a *tap*? Discuss these observations with your classmates. Remember the observations as you read.

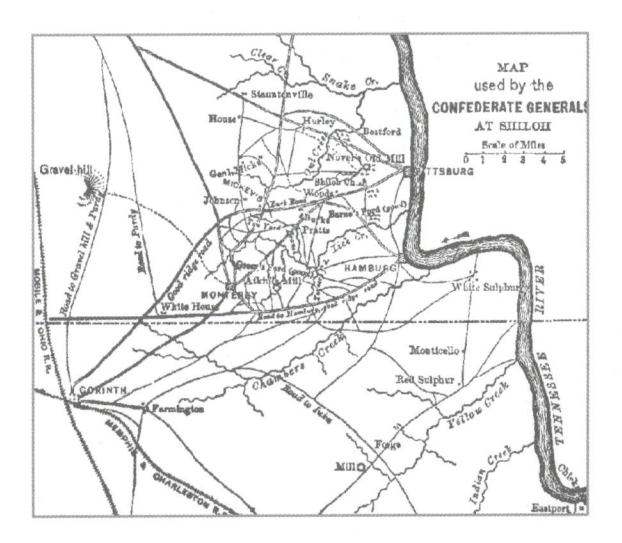

The Drummer Boy of Shiloh

Focusing on Creating Mood Through Setting

The setting of the story is a military camp; the mood is subdued, taut, and ominous. But the story conveys images of beauty and delicacy: This is youth that will never grow old.

Although thousands of young men will meet their deaths, Bradbury describes a peach orchard, the hush of whispering men, the touch of a moth. The mood is almost serene, peaceful, even dreamlike.

Consider how the setting—the land and the peach orchard—will change at daybreak. As gentle as it is now, a haven, as the sun rises it will become a bloody battleground, the air rent by screams. Consider how the contrast heightens the tragedy and the drama not yet unfolded.

Word Bank

Helter-skelter: An interesting rhyming word is found in footnote 1. What does *helter-skelter* mean? If you say that your little brother is *running helter-skelter* all over the house, you mean he is running "in confused haste." If you say that you left your clothes *scattered helter-skelter* about the floor, you mean that you left your clothes "without any regard for order"—which is closer to the meaning of the word in the story. Words such as *helter-skelter* and *willy-nilly* are said by linguists to be formed from the process of **echoic** (like an echo) **reduplication** (the making of doubles or copies).

askew   lunar   resolute

The Drummer Boy of Shiloh

Ray Bradbury

In the April night, more than once, blossoms fell from the orchard trees and lighted with rustling taps on the drumhead. At midnight a peach stone left miraculously on a branch through winter, flicked by a bird, fell swift and unseen; it struck once, like panic, and jerked the boy upright. In silence he listened to his own heart ruffle away, away—at last gone from his ears and back in his chest again.

After that he turned the drum on its side, where its great lunar face peered at him whenever he opened his eyes.

His face, alert or at rest, was solemn. It was a solemn time and a solemn night for a boy just turned fourteen in the peach orchard near Owl Creek not far from Shiloh.

"...thirty-one...thirty-two...thirty-three." Unable to see, he stopped counting.

Beyond the thirty-three familiar shadows forty thousand men, exhausted by nervous expectation and unable to sleep for romantic dreams of battles yet unfought, lay crazily askew in their uniforms. A mile farther on, another army was strewn helter-skelter,[1] turning slowly, basting themselves[2] with the thought of what they would do when the time came—a leap, a yell, a blind plunge their strategy, raw youth their protection and benediction.[3]

Now and again the boy heard a vast wind come up that gently stirred the air. But he knew what it was—the army here, the army there, whispering to itself in the dark. Some men talking to others, others murmuring to themselves, and all so quiet it was like a natural element arisen from South or North with the motion of the earth toward dawn.

What the men whispered the boy could only guess and he guessed that it was "Me, I'm the one, I'm the one of all the rest who won't die. I'll live through it. I'll go home. The band will play. And I'll be there to hear it."

Yes, thought the boy, *that's all very well for them, they can give as good as they get!*

For with the careless bones of the young

---

1. The other army also lay *helter-skelter* (HELT er SKELT er): haphazardly, without regard for order.
2. Here, *basting themselves* refers to holding their emotions together to ward off the fear of the unknown.
3. Here, *benediction* (BEN uh DIK shun) means the positive benefit of the strength of youth.

Word Bank

lunar (LOON er) *adj.*: resembling the moon; round or crescent-shaped

askew (uh SKYOO) *adj.*: to one side; crooked

men, harvested by night and bindled[4] around campfires, were the similarly strewn steel bones of their rifles with bayonets fixed like eternal lightning lost in the orchard grass.

Me, thought the boy, *I got only a drum, two sticks to beat it, and no shield.*

There wasn't a man-boy on this ground tonight who did not have a shield he cast, riveted,[5] or carved himself on his way to his first attack, compounded of remote but nonetheless firm and fiery family devotion, flag-blown patriotism, and self-sure immortality strengthened by the very real gunpowder, ramrod,[6] Minié ball,[7] and flint.[8] But without these last, the boy felt his family move yet farther off in the dark, as if one of those great prairie-burning trains had chanted them away, never to return—leaving him with this drum which was worse than a toy in the game to be played tomorrow or someday much too soon.

The boy turned on his side. A moth brushed his face, but it was peach blossom. A peach blossom flicked him, but it was a moth. Nothing stayed put. Nothing had a name. Nothing was as it once was.

If he stayed very still, when the dawn came up and the soldiers put on their bravery with their caps, perhaps they might go away, the war with them, and not notice him living small here, no more than a toy himself.

"Well, by thunder now," said a voice. The boy shut his eyes to hide himself, but it was too late. Someone, walking by in the night, stood over him. "Well," said the voice quietly, "here's a soldier crying *before* the fight. Good. Get it over. Won't be time once it all starts."

And the voice was about to move on when the boy, startled, touched the drum at his elbow. The man above, hearing this, stopped. The boy could feel his eyes, sense him slowly bending near. A hand must have come down out of the night, for there was a little *rat-tat* as the fingernails brushed and the man's breath fanned the boy's face.

"Why, it's the drummer boy, isn't it?"

The boy nodded, not knowing if his nod was seen. "Sir, is that you?" he said.

"I assume it is." The man's knees cracked as he bent still closer. He smelled as all fathers should smell, of salt-sweat, tobacco, horse and boot leather, and the earth he walked upon. He had many eyes. No, not eyes, brass buttons that watched the boy.

He could only be, and was, the general.

"What's your name, boy?" he asked.

"Joby, sir," whispered the boy, starting to sit up.

"All right, Joby, don't stir." A hand pressed his chest gently, and the boy relaxed. "How long you been with us, Joby?"

"Three weeks, sir."

"Run off from home or join legitimate, boy?"

Silence.

"Fool question," said the general. "Do you shave yet, boy? Even more of a fool. There's your cheek, fell right off the tree overhead. And the others here, not much older. Raw,

---

4. *Bindled* (BIN dild) means gathered.
5. *Riveted* (RIV it id) means to fasten or fix firmly.
6. A *ramrod* is a metal rod used to push down the ammunition on top of the powder.
7. A *Minié ball* (MIN ee BAWL) was a cone-shaped bullet with a hollow base that expanded when fired. It was named for Claude Etienne Minié, the French Army officer who designed it.
8. The *flint* is struck to create a spark that sets off the powder.

raw, the lot of you. You ready for tomorrow or the next day, Joby?"

"I think so, sir."

"You want to cry some more, go on ahead. I did the same last night."

"You, sir?"

"It's the truth. Thinking of everything ahead. Both sides figuring the other side will just give up, and soon, and the war done in weeks and us all home. Well, that's not how it's going to be. And maybe that's why I cried."

"Yes, sir," said Joby.

The general must have taken out a cigar now, for the dark was suddenly filled with the Indian smell of tobacco unlighted yet, but chewed as the man thought what next to say.

"It's going to be a crazy time," said the general. "Counting both sides, there's a hundred thousand men—give or take a few thousand—out there tonight, not one as can spit a sparrow off a tree, or knows a horse clod from a Minié ball. Stand up, ask to be a target, thank them and sit down, that's us, that's them. We should turn tail and train four months, they should do the same. But here we are, taken with spring fever and thinking it blood lust, taking our sulphur[9] with cannons instead of with molasses, as it should be—going to be a hero, going to live forever. And I can see all them over there nodding agreement, save the other way around. It's wrong, boy, it's wrong as a head put on hindside front and a man marching backward through life. Sometime this week more innocents will get shot out of pure Cherokee enthusiasm than ever got shot before. Owl Creek was full of boys splashing around in the noonday sun just a few hours ago. I fear it will be full of boys again, just floating, at sundown tomorrow, not caring where the current takes them."

The general stopped and made a little pile of winter leaves and twigs in the dark as if he might at any moment strike fire to them to see his way through the coming days when the sun might not show its face because of what was happening here and just beyond.

The boy watched the hand stirring the leaves and opened his lips to say something, but did not say it. The general heard the boy's breath and spoke himself.

"Why am I telling you this? That's what you wanted to ask, eh? Well, when you got a bunch of wild horses on a loose rein somewhere, somehow you got to bring order, rein them in. These lads, fresh out of the milkshed, don't know what I know; and I can't tell them—men actually die in war. So each is his own army. I got to make one army of them. And for that, boy, I need you."

"Me!" The boy's lips barely twitched.

"You, boy," said the general quietly. "You are the heart of the army. Think about that. You are the heart of the army. Listen to

---

9. *Sulphur* (SUL fir) is a nonmetallic element used in making gunpowder. It is also used as an ingredient in homemade medicine—sulphur and blackstrap molasses. These young men are not getting sulphur as part of a childhood tonic, as they should be, but rather as deadly gunfire.

me, now."

And lying there, Joby listened. And the general spoke. If he, Joby, beat slow tomorrow, the heart would beat slow in the men. They would lag by the wayside. They would drowse in the fields on their muskets. They would sleep forever after that—in those same fields, their hearts slowed by a drummer boy and stopped by enemy lead.

But if he beat a sure, steady, ever faster rhythm, then, then, their knees would come up in a long line down over that hill, one knee after the other, like a wave on the ocean shore. Had he seen the ocean ever? Seen the waves rolling in like a well-ordered cavalry charge? Well, that was it, that's what he wanted, that's what was needed. Joby was his right hand and his left. He gave the orders, but Joby set the pace.

So bring the right knee up and the right foot out and the left knee up and the left foot out, one following the other in good time, in brisk time. Move the blood up the body and make the head proud and the spine stiff and the jaw resolute. Focus the eye and set the teeth, flare the nostril and tighten the hands, put steel armor all over the men, for blood moving fast in them does indeed make men feel as if they'd put on steel. He must keep at it, at it! Long and steady, steady and long! Then, even though shot or torn, those wounds got in hot blood—in blood he'd helped stir—would feel less pain. If their blood was cold, it would be more than slaughter, it would be murderous nightmare and pain best not told and no one to guess.

The general spoke and stopped, letting his breath slack off. Then, after a moment, he said, "So there you are, that's it. Will you do that, boy? Do you know now you're general of the army when the general's left behind?"

The boy nodded mutely.

"You'll run them through for me then, boy?"

"Yes, sir."

"Good. And, maybe, many nights from tonight, many years from now, when you're as old or far much older than me, when they ask you what you did in this awful time, you will tell them—one part humble and one part proud—I was the drummer boy at the battle of Owl Creek or the Tennessee River. I was the drummer boy at Shiloh. Good grief, that has a beat and sound to it fitting for Mr. Longfellow.[10] 'I was the drummer boy at Shiloh.' Who will ever hear those words and not know you, boy, or what you thought this night, or what you'll think tomorrow or the next day when we must get up on our legs and move."

The general stood up. "Well, then. G-d bless you, boy. Good night."

"Good night, sir." And tobacco, brass, boot polish, salt-sweat, and leather, the man moved away through the grass.

Joby lay for a moment staring, but unable to see where the man had gone. He swallowed. He wiped his eyes. He cleared his throat. He settled himself. Then, at last, very slowly and firmly he turned the drum so it faced up toward the sky.

He lay next to it, his arm around it, feeling the tremor, the touch, the muted thunder as all the rest of the April night in the year 1862, near the Tennessee River, not far from the Owl Creek, very close to Shiloh, the peach blossoms fell on the drum.

---

10. Henry Wadsworth *Longfellow* (LONG fell oh) was a famous U.S. poet who lived during the 19th century.

Word Bank   **resolute** (REZ uh loot) *adj.*: firmly set in purpose or opinion; determined

Studying the Selection

First Impressions

Imagine yourself in the story, lying in the field. Assume the voice of a restless, young soldier. Write about what you see, hear, and smell as the long night unfolds. Include your feelings about where you are and what might happen once day breaks.

✔ Quick Review

1. How many men were lying in the field that night?
2. How did the general smell?
3. What is a Minié ball?
4. What was the boy's name?

In-depth Thinking

5. Why did the general first notice the boy?
6. According to the general, what effect would slow drumming have on the soldiers?
7. What effect would steady and sure drumming have?
8. Why would the boy want to be remembered as "the drummer boy of Shiloh"?

Drawing Conclusions

9. Speculate on the scene that will unfold the next morning. Will the young drummer's romantic dreams of battle be fulfilled? What kinds of scenes are likely to play out?
10. An epitaph is a message carved on a tombstone. Examples are "Loving Mother" or "Kindly Remembered." Look at the last sentence of the story and reword it as the boy's epitaph. How might this epitaph strike someone coming across his grave in the future?

Focusing on Creating Mood Through Setting

Mood is the feeling created by an author through the use of vivid words in description and dialogue. **Setting** is also important in creating mood. The author's world is a simplified one. By deciding which elements to place in this simpler world, the author can exclude items that don't contribute to the mood.

1. Describe a setting that makes you feel happy.
2. Describe a setting that makes you feel sad.
3. Write a suspenseful introductory paragraph, one describing a scary setting (for example, a paragraph introducing a detective or mystery novel).

Creating and Writing

1. A **symbol** is an event, an object, or a character in a story that represents an important but intangible idea. (Intangible means something you cannot touch, like "honor.") The "peach fuzz" on the fruit in the orchard represents the soft hair on the faces of the boys who have yet to shave. For some people, shaving is considered a rite of passage, an indication that a boy is maturing.

   Likewise, the buds on the trees mark places where fruit will grow and become ripe with the warmth of the sun. These buds also represent the young boys who have not matured.

   Look through the story and find other symbols of freshness or "unripeness." List them in the order in which they appear, and include page numbers.

2. For this writing assignment, you will need to pick an object and an idea it might represent. For example, you might write about an old piece of furniture and how it reminds you of your grandfather; or a playground and how it makes you think of your childhood. Try to focus on a specific memory and object. For example, if you are writing about the playground, think of one particular event—how you were finally tall enough to reach the monkey bars. Then connect this event with growing up.

3. It used to be more common for children the age of this drummer boy or younger to enter the workforce. Your teacher may take you on a class field trip to an old age home. Interview the residents about their earliest work experiences. The following are some questions you can ask: How old were they when they first entered the workforce? Did they work only with other young people? Did anyone make any special allowance for the age of the young workers? Did anyone try to keep them in school? How old were their employers or supervisors? Did these retired people think there was anything unusual about their early work experiences? How do they regard young workers today?

Blueprint for Reading

the Author

John D. MacDonald (1916-1986)

John MacDonald was born in Sharon, Pennsylvania, graduated from Syracuse University, and then earned his MBA from Harvard. He did not consider himself a writer for quite some time, since he felt writers were born with special talents he did not possess. He wrote more than 500 short stories and saw his first novel published in 1950. He received many awards and was respected by his fellow authors.

Background Bytes

Fire! is set in the western United States, on a small family farm surrounded by woodlands. It takes place during a hot, dry autumn marked by drought and frequent forest fires. MacDonald does not date the story exactly, but there are clues that link the story's events to the early decades of the 20th century.

The narrator tells the story as a flashback, a childhood memory. It is October, but he is not always in school. As one of seven children raised by his mother and grandfather, he is a valued worker on the family farm. In reality, the narrator's experience was not unusual in rural areas. School vacations revolved around farm needs, coinciding with planting and harvesting. Schooling was important, but survival took precedence. Even if non-farm children attended the same school, lessons stopped during spring and fall. Only when the vast majority of children lived in town communities did the school calendar change, and even then some children would miss school, if their help was needed on the farm.

Into *Fire!*

The narrator, well aware of the fragility of his surroundings, has been careless—causing significant damage. Now he must come to terms with his putting his physical environment and his family's well-being in jeopardy.

The theme of this story is about taking responsibility for one's actions. Before you read, think about a time when you failed to take full responsibility for something you did. What was the outcome? Why is it so important to admit our errors?

Fire!

Focusing on the Sensory Details of Setting

As you read, notice how carefully MacDonald fills in his landscape. Look for the **sensory details** that bring the sights and smells to life. Are there descriptive passages you find particularly interesting? Now compare *this* farm setting to the one in *This Farm for Sale*, noting any specific similarities or differences. Be prepared to discuss them in class.

Word Bank

Sullen: Have you ever felt sullen? It is not a pleasant feeling. For those who have to deal with a sullen person it is also difficult, but it is *surely* no fun for the person who is feeling sullen. However, the word sullen is often used negatively, or as if it were deliberate bad behavior *especially* from a child, as when someone says, "Don't be so sullen!" Actually, the word has a very respectable history. Etymologists say that it comes from either of two roots: the word *solemn*, meaning "serious, sedate, grave, profound"; or the word *solitude*, "the state of being alone or lonely." So, if you see someone who is sullen, don't get mad—reach out and help that person!

anguish   ember   sullen

Fire!

John D. MacDonald

Not long ago, coming back home on a night flight, I saw the sullen ember of a distant forest fire in the hills and felt a small twist of anguish. I knew it was the memory of the injustice of my grandfather toward my big brother Paul in a long-ago October.

There were seven of us children in all. Now, when we all get together with wives and husbands and children, we end up telling Grandfather stories, marveling at that strange old man who raised us, with our mother acting more as referee than parent. Sometimes we judge him quite mad. At other times we think he was full of wisdom. Perhaps it was both. He never explained. Paul and I can laugh about the fire now.

It was a strange October that year. Hot and still and dry, day after day, the sun rising and setting in a weird mist. The creek ran nearly dry. We all lugged water to the growing things and worried about the well. I remember that the three littlest ones, Tom, Nan, and Bunny volunteered to give up washing—as an effort to save water. It was denied. The woodlands which began a half dozen miles north of the farm had dozens of fires. When the winds were right, you could smell the stink of burning forest, a strange dirty stench,[1] somehow frightening.

Paul was fifteen that year, and I was twelve. I did the thoughtless, stupid thing on the way back from the creek. I'd gone down there with Paul on a hot Sunday afternoon to see if any fish were trapped in the pools. We were walking back. I had some kitchen matches in my pocket. When out in the wide world I liked to carry one in the corner of my mouth. I felt it gave me a certain carefree air.

---

1. A *stench* (STENCH) is an offensive smell or odor.

In those years all small boys knew that if you hold a match in a certain way and throw it downward at a stone or a sidewalk, it will pop and burn. I was not skilled, but I had tried so many times it required no thought. As we passed a gray rock half buried in the dry weeds along the fence line, I hurled my match at it. It struck properly for once. The head popped and bounced into the weeds, and in an instant the sun-paled flames were high and spreading. For once Paul did not take time out to tell me how stupid I was. He yanked his shirt off and began stomping and flailing,[2] and yelled at me to run for help and water.

I was a hundred yards from the dooryard, and I think I made as good time and as much noise as a fire engine. In a very short and confusing time, all seven kids and my mother and my grandfather were out there with wet sacks and blankets. It was a very near thing. I think that if there had been eight of us instead of nine, it might have gotten away. As it was, it burned off a very large area.

Tom was nine, and as responsible as any of us, and Grandfather left him out there with a bucket of water and orders to patrol the edges, looking for any spark which could have survived the battle.

---

2. *Flailing* (FLAY ling) refers to the way Paul beat at the flames—hard, again and again, in order to smother them.

Word Bank

sullen (SUL in) *adj.*: gloomy or cheerless

ember (EM ber) *n.*: a small burning piece of coal or wood, as in a dying fire

anguish (AYN gwish) *n.*: acute suffering or pain

When we got back to the porch, Grandfather sat down to catch his wind. He had been wonderful out in the pasture, like a great windmill hammering at the flames, yelling at them as he beat them out.

"Who was there?" he demanded.

That was one area where he had always been predictable. When any punishable offense occurred, Grandfather solved the problem of blame by walloping[3] everyone who had been in the immediate area. Thus we were forever united, policing each other, with no tattletales.

Paul and I admitted our presence at the scene, knowing that we would sit down very carefully for the next day or so. The other kids drifted away, and we were left there facing the old man. I remember the black streaks of burned grasses on his big hands.

"All right," he said. "Which one of you did it?"

The simple question surprised us. Without warning he had changed the rules. Paul straightened himself slightly and said, "I did it!" He was fifteen. He used a tone of voice we younger ones did not dare to use. Grandfather sighed and he looked at me, blue eyes under those angry white brows. I believe I tried to speak. But the thing I had done was so shamefully stupid, I wasted too much time trying to think of a way to confess which would make it believable.

Before I could find the beginning words, Grandfather got up and went into the house, Mother trotting along behind him, asking nervous questions.

I tried to explain myself to Paul, but he turned away. There was a great silence that night at the supper table. I was an outcast. I wanted the normal punishment. The change of ground rules made me feel lost and sick.

Grandfather got up from the table and looked at Paul and said, "I made some arrangements. You are excused from school. You'll get a better look at a fire, boy."

Early Monday morning one of the county trucks stopped and picked up Grandfather and Paul. There was a crew of rough, weary[4] men aboard the truck and a crude bunch of tools in a steel drum—axes, shovels, mattocks.[5] I remember Mother pleading with Grandfather, saying, "But he's just a boy!"

I did not hear his answer. I know now they needed every strong pair of arms they could round up. It was a fearful time in the powder-dry forests.

I went off to school with the others. I did not hear much that day in school. I had the horrible vision of Paul encircled by a roar of flames, running and screaming. It was a horrible injustice. It was all my fault. I plotted to sneak off that night and join them in the hills. Somehow I would rescue Paul, and everyone would forgive me.

When the five of us got home from school, we learned that the well had gone dry. And that too seemed to be my fault. We had used a lot of water fighting that stupid grass fire. Mother got me aside and said, "What do you think we should do?"

---

3. *Walloping* (WAHL ih ping) means whipping or beating, as in punishment.
4. One who is *weary* (WEER ee) is physically or mentally exhausted.
5. A *mattock* (MAT ik) is a digging tool shaped like a pickax, but with one end wide instead of pointed.

The question astonished me. It made me realize that with Grandfather and Paul gone, I was the eldest male on the farm. I forgot the feeling of being an outcast. The creek water was sweet. The creek was nearly three hundred yards from the well. Mother had turned off the pump when it had sucked dry.

I organized the four eldest of us, Christine, Sheila, Tom, and me, into a water brigade.[6] We scoured[7] out big containers and loaded them on the pickup, and I drove it as close to the creek as I could get it. Then we filled them, bucket by bucket, drove back, and dumped the water into the well. It was very hard work. After several loads, I primed[8] the old pump and started it again. After Tom and Sheila were too exhausted to continue, Christine and I managed two more trips by ourselves.

As I lay in my bed that moonlight night, a smell of burning forest came in the window. I was in a soft bed, while Paul and Grandfather were in the hills. There was more penance[9] to do. I could not manage the truck system by myself, but I could carry water. I dressed and went quietly out into the night. I could not guess how many trips I made that night. Toward the end I could not manage full buckets.

I remember sitting on the edge of the well, the dawn rose-gray at the horizon line, opening and closing my aching hands, summoning up the will to make yet another trip to the creek. I remember seeing my mother come across the side yard in her robe. She led me back to the house. I can remember fighting tears, and losing just as we reached the steps.

The heavy rains began at dawn on Thursday, and before we left for school, Paul and our grandfather were home, dirty, exhausted, walking in a strange dazed, dragging way, as though they were walking up hill. When we came home from school, they were still sleeping. Grandfather got up for supper, but Paul did not, and Mother had me take him up hot soup and milk and apple pie. He told me of digging endless trenches,[10] chopping through thousands of tough forest roots. He showed me his hands. We were friends again, somehow, but in a different way.

When I went back downstairs to my place at the table, I found Mother telling Grandfather how well I had managed the water problem. When there was a pause I blurted, "I set that fire Sunday."

"Don't interrupt your mother," he said.

I sat with my head bowed. I could not eat. When she had finished, Grandfather said, "Mary, if I didn't think the boy could manage, I wouldn't have taken Paul with me."

He gave me a rough pat on the shoulder as he left the table. I wore it like medals. And suddenly I was hungry. Grandfather never explained, and we never knew what he would do next. He was as wild and random as the winds that blew.

---

6. *Brigade* (brih GADE) refers to a group organized to do a job. Paul and his family formed a brigade to bring water from the creek to the well.
7. He *scoured* (SKOW erd) the big containers, or cleaned them.
8. He poured water down the metal well lining to *prime* (PRYM) (to make ready) the pump, allowing the pump to 'pull' against water instead of air.
9. *Penance* (PEN intz) means voluntary self-punishment.
10. *Trenches* (TREN chiz) are the long furrows dug by firefighters beyond a forest fire to stop it from reaching new fuel.

Studying the Selection

First Impressions

Consider the grandfather's reaction to the fire started by the narrator. Do you think the grandfather knows who did it? If so, why does he punish Paul? Is it really a punishment? How does the grandfather's decision affect the narrator?

✔ Quick Review

1. How did the narrator start the fire that almost destroyed his family's farm?
2. What disciplinary step did the grandfather take?
3. How old were Paul and the narrator?
4. What did the narrator do while Paul and his grandfather were off fighting fires?

In-depth Thinking

5. Why do you think the grandfather "changed the rules" of his disciplinary routine?
6. Why do you think Paul took the blame for his younger brother?
7. Why didn't the narrator admit he started the fire?
8. At the end of the story, the narrator says of his older brother, "We were friends again, somehow, but in a different way." What does he mean?

Drawing Conclusions

9. When the narrator finally confesses he started the fire, his grandfather's only answer is, "Don't interrupt your mother." Later he gives the narrator a rough pat on the shoulder. Explain the significance of these reactions.
10. How was the narrator affected by his experience in organizing the water brigade?

Focusing on the Sensory Details of Setting

As you can see from examining the stories in this section and others, **setting** plays a significant role in shaping the mood, the dramatic impact, and the theme of a piece.

1. Write about the overall importance of setting in one of the stories you have already read. Consider how setting impacts character, mood, and theme.
2. Look at the next story in your book. After reading only the first three or four paragraphs, describe the setting. How might this setting affect the characters?
3. Compare and contrast the settings in any two stories in this book. Note ways in which the similarities and differences are appropriate to each story's theme.

Creating and Writing

1. Why do you think the author chose to tell this story as a flashback? What does the framework of a flashback add to the story or the author's perspective? (Recall your perspective activity from *This Farm for Sale*.)
2. Consider how you might use the five senses—sight, sound, touch, smell, and taste—to write about fire. How many of these senses can you write about in a poem? You can write about the beneficial uses of fire as well as the harmful effects.
3. Interview an adult about a youthful episode gone bad. What was learned from the mistake, and was this understanding achieved immediately or much later?

Blueprint for Reading

the Author

Elsie Singmaster (1879-1958)

Elsie Singmaster was born in Pennsylvania and lived much of her life in Gettysburg, eventually writing about Civil War events there. She is known for her stories of local miners and the Pennsylvania Dutch. Her first story appeared in a teacher's journal when she was eleven. When asked about the story, she said, "The plot was not wholly original; when the story was printed, my conscience began to trouble me and has ever since."

Background Bytes

This story is set in eastern Pennsylvania, in a bleak coal-mining town that had grown as coal replaced wood as the major industrial fuel. That happened in the 1840s when there was an influx of immigrants to the United States who constituted a large, willing labor force. These newcomers to America, eager to succeed in a new country, often had to work under desperately unsafe conditions. The accident that killed the protagonist's father is one of many such disasters that plagued the coal-mining industry until federal legislation in the 1930s encouraged mine safety. As you read, notice Jennie's drive to become a productive, hard-working American, despite the many obstacles in her path.

Mr. Brownlee's Roses

Into *Mr. Brownlee's Roses*

The town described in the story is grim. Cold and impoverished, covered by black soot, it is at the mercy of the needs of the coal industry. Only Mr. Brownlee's greenhouse, filled with the pink and yellow blooms of his roses, provides color and life. The delicacy and hope represented by these wondrous plants, especially in the face of the surrounding bleak conditions, will become a key symbol in the story.

Before you read, write a brief description of a desolate place you have visited. What makes it so bleak? Does anything brighten the harsh landscape?

Focusing on External and Internal Settings

The focus in this story is on the contrasts between **external** and **internal settings**. The town itself is dirty and cold, whipped by fierce winds and whirling snow. But the Yonsons' home, however small and sparsely furnished, is a warm and loving place, filled with laughter and sweet treats. Likewise, the greenhouse, even with its fires burning low, is a paradise of color and warmth.

Word Bank

Refuse, when it is a noun, is pronounced REF yoos. Since the verb *refuse*, with which most of us are more familiar, is pronounced re FYOOZ, this is an example of a word whose context we have to look at carefully, to see both what it means and how we should say it. The noun **refuse** (REF yoos) means "trash, rubbish, or garbage"—clearly something that isn't wanted. The verb *refuse* (re FYOOZ) means "to decline to accept (something offered)" or "to decline to give; deny a request." The noun form of the verb *refuse* (re FYOOZ) is *refusal*, which also has the accent on the second syllable.

blight	incomprehensible	refuse
delusion	insoluble	

Mr. Brownlee's Roses

As Jennie Swenson closed the outer door of her mother's kitchen, pulling with all her strength against the wind, she heard far up the street a man's loud singing.

I went to a ball one night,
　　It was a fancy hop;
I danced until the lights went out,
　　And the music it did stop.

Stanislaus Sobieski, usually called Stan Sobski, night fireman at Mr. Brownlee's greenhouse, was going to his work. His song was old; new songs, he said, did not fit his voice. He was apparently not disturbed by the fact that work began at six o'clock and it was now seven.

To Jennie, Mr. Brownlee's greenhouse was paradise; she did not understand how anyone could be late for work there. All else in the mining town was black and grim; there was no money for paint, and there was no time for cultivating gardens. At each end of Main Street towered a frame structure called a breaker, to whose lofty summit ran cars filled with coal. Beside each breaker grows a mountain of black refuse, separated from the coal as it descended in long chutes.

There had been a third mine along the hillside, and its owner, Mr. Brownlee's father, had built a small greenhouse for his own pleasure. As the mine grew lean, he began to sell flowers. Presently he was shipping a thousand American Beauties each night to New York. The present Mr. Brownlee was shipping three thousand before he went to war. Now he and his sister were once more sending roses, five thousand in a night—not American Beauties, but newer and more fashionable varieties: Premier and

Word Bank	**refuse** (REF yoos) *n.*: something that is discarded as worthless or useless

Columbia and Radiance, in various shades of rose and pink; Talisman, a blending of pink and apricot and gold; double white Killarneys and long yellow buds of Souvenir de Claudius Pernet.[1]

Jennie did not know their names or even their distinct and lovely odors; she knew only their colors, seen when she walked slowly by, looking eagerly for panes of glass on which the white paint was worn away. She often watched Mr. Brownlee and his sister. He was tall and a little lame, and his hair was slightly gray; Miss Brownlee was short and broad, but not stout. She had clear blue eyes, wavy hair, and a broad white forehead. Her brother could do no strenuous work; but she worked from morning till night, directing the laborers, inspecting rows of plants, and superintending the packing of roses.

At the same instant that Jennie heard Stan singing, she wound her scarf more tightly around her neck, locked the door, and hung the key behind a shutter. For hours a light snow had been falling, and now an east wind was beginning to blow. Stan had now reached the middle of his song.

    And this is what I ate:
    A dozen raw, a plate of slaw,
    A chicken and a roast,
    Some oyster stew and ice cream too,
    And several quail on toast.

In the moment while she waited for Stan to pass, Jennie was tempted to turn back to the kitchen and study. There was a good light and perfect quiet—for Mrs. Swenson, a nurse, was on a case, and Jennie's sisters, Anna and Gertrude, lived in Wilkes-Barre.[2]

But what Jennie required for study was not quiet—it was company. There were incomprehensible passages in her Latin lesson; insoluble problems in her alg-

---

1. *Souvenir de Claudis Pernet* (soov NEER DEE KLAW dee iss peer NAY) is a type of rose.
2. *Wilkes-Barre* (WILKS BARE ee) was the largest city in the Wyoming Valley in northeastern Pennsylvania.

Word Bank

incomprehensible (IN kahm pree HEN sih bul) *adj.*: impossible to understand
insoluble (in SAHL yuh bul) *adj.*: incapable of being solved

ebra. If she did not graduate in June, she could not get a position. Better the storm and the long walk to Hilda Yonson's kitchen, where there were no less than eight younger children, than peace and quiet and blankness of mind.

Gertrude and Anna were astonished at her dullness. She could not be a stenographer[3] because she was too slow; she could not teach because she was too dull; she could not be a nurse because she was too timid. The teachers gave aptitude tests, but she showed no aptitude for anything. When she was excited or embarrassed her Swedish tongue refused to say "j"; it refused now.

"I *must* get a yob!" wailed Jennie aloud to the storm.

She stepped from the boardwalk, already swept bare, into a drift up to her knees. Instantly she laughed and shook the tears out of her eyes. She was a true Swede, tall and broad and strong. She started briskly down the street. The lights in the neighbors' houses were dimmed by whirling snow, but far above them hung a light at the top of the breaker.

She heard a shrill bell which heralded[4] the rising of the elevator from the mine. In a moment a line of tired men would pass the corner. Five years ago there had been an evening when the loud whistle blew and everyone went running and crying to the pit head. Mrs. Swenson had been the first to get there and first to know that she was widowed.

At the third corner Jennie halted. There were two ways to the Yonson house: one down Main Street; the other through side streets, past Mr. Brownlee's greenhouse. Jennie took a step in that direction; then, laughing at herself, ran on down Main Street, then up a sharp hill.

From the Yonsons' porch the whole of the Wyoming Valley was visible in daylight—cities and towns and roads, schools and factories; and in every town and village a towering breaker. A part of the valley had a strange and solemn name, "The Shades of Death," a memorial of Colonial war and massacre.

Tim Yonson sat before the stove, in a coal-blackened rocker reserved for his use. His face and hands were clean, but they were not white. He smoked a long pipe and talked to Mrs. Yonson, who was washing dishes. There was a child on each side of the table, each pair of eyes on a book.

"Good efening,[5] Yennie," said Tim.

"Good efening," said Mrs. Yonson.

Hilda looked up. "Hello! Thought you weren't coming."

As Jennie unwound her scarf, Mrs. Yonson set a large plate of Swedish cookies on the table to lighten the evening's labors, and it was not until half past nine that Jennie rose to leave. Mr. Yonson had gone to bed and so had five or six children.

"I certainly am grateful," sighed Jennie.

Mrs. Yonson had difficulty with many English letters. "Come efery night till you are old, and Hilda will not yet pay what your moder done for us."

Jennie had expected to have the wind in her face, but it blew from every direction in turn. Regardless of the stinging snow, she turned down the dark street

---

3. A *stenographer* (stuh NAHG rih fur) is a person who specializes in taking dictation in shorthand; either on a special machine or by hand.
4. *Heralded* (HAIR ul did) means announced.
5. *Efening* is 'evening' with a Swedish accent.

which led to Mr. Brownlee's greenhouse. A new section had been added, and the low, dimly lighted buildings occupied a solid block.

She walked slowly past. There they were, the pinks, the yellows, the shades of rose! She stood still, though the wind seemed to blow through her. The snow hissed against the glass. How could this thin protection keep the roses safe?

The office was furnished with two broad desks, a half-dozen chairs, a bookcase, and many files. Neither of the Brownlees was in sight; but Mr. Brownlee's gray overcoat hung on a hook, his soft gray hat above it, and a crumpled newspaper lay on the floor beside his chair. At the back of the room a door opened on a stairway leading to the boiler room. The door was ajar; perhaps he was down there with Stan. Probably he would stay in the greenhouse all night. She would, in his place!

In ten minutes she was at home. The house rocked a little in the wind. She shook down the fire, put on fresh coal, and, while it caught, sat near the stove.

Though she was warm in bed, she could not sleep. She shut her eyes, determined not to open them again; then, startled by a sound, she sat up. "Mother?" she called.

There was no answer. The sound came from outside and grew each moment louder.

"I took my friend to a ball one night!" shouted Stan Sobieski at the gate. "To a ball! Fifty cents!"

Jennie was terrified. But Stan was an honest fellow—he would not break into a house! That is, when he was sober! She sprang out of bed and went to the window. She could not see him, but she could hear him. "I took my friend to a social hop!"

He was not going toward the greenhouse; he was going in the opposite direction!

"And this is what I ate! And this is what I ate—" he yelled, from far away. "I ate—".

It was not until Jennie had one knee on her bed and was about to creep back that she was really awake. It was a bitter night, and Mr. Brownlee's roses were in the midst of their most profitable bloom. Suppose the fires should go out? But Mr. Brownlee was there! But suppose Mr. Brownlee had gone home?

Foolish though it seemed, she put on her slippers and went downstairs. In the pale glow from the fire she could see her clothes spread on the chair; they seemed to say, "Put us on! Put us on!"

"How silly!" said Jennie. "I'm going back to bed."

Instantly she had another delusion; she saw thousands of roses standing with drooping heads. No, as plants froze they got stiffer and stiffer and held their heads straight. It was only after the sun came out that they got limp and black.

"I don't care if I am crazy," she said, and began to dress.

As she opened the door, the wind seemed to drag her out, rather than drive her back. It blew with a roaring sound, far above her head. She heard a loud

---

Word Bank   **delusion** (dih LOO zhin) *n.*: a type of mental turmoil; a false belief

crash, as though the roof of a house had been blown off. She could see the breaker light when the clouds of snow blew away, but no other.

She laughed hysterically and ran. Stan had another old song—"I don't know where I'm going, but I'm on my way."

"That's me!" said Jennie.

The great area of dim light was as it had been. She slowed her step; there were the roses, beautiful and unchanged. The office was brightly lighted and still empty of human beings; but Mr. Brownlee's coat hung on its hook, and the door to the boiler room was open.

"It's all right!" thought Jennie.

Above Mr. Brownlee's desk hung a clock with a large face. "Look at me, Jennie!" it seemed to say. It was half-past one! At the same instant she saw that Mr. Brownlee's crumpled newspaper lay exactly where it had been at half-past nine.

Jennie went up the step and opened the door. How warm it was, how sweet, how like paradise!

"Mr. Brownlee!" she called faintly.

There was no answer.

"Mr. Brownlee!" Alarm sharpened her voice.

"Who is there?" Undoubtedly it was Mr. Brownlee, speaking from the boiler room.

"Jennie Swenson." She could not help giggling. What did "Jennie Swenson" mean to Mr. Brownlee?

"In the name of mercy, Jennie Swenson, come down here!"

The words were pitiful, yet there was an undertone of amusement. Trembling, Jennie went down the steps. The room was low and paved with brick. At one end was a huge boiler; along one side were coalbins and piles of wood, and along the other shelves filled with cans and bottles of insecticides and sprays. Before the boiler stood an old couch, and on it lay Mr. Brownlee.

"Open that firebox door quick, will you, and pile in wood."

Jennie picked up a chunk as she dashed to the furnace.

"Finer pieces, plenty of them! Pretty low, isn't it?"

"Not so very bad," said Jennie.

"What are you crying for?"

"Will they die?"

"Humph!" said Mr. Brownlee. "Go to my desk and take the flashlight you'll find there; then go to the farthest corner of every greenhouse and read the thermometers. And you might pray as you go!"

"Did Stan tie you?"[6] asked Jennie, running up the stairs swiftly.

"Lumbago[7] tied me."

Jennie came running back. The wood in the firebox was burning briskly. Mr. Brownlee's eyes shone like points of fire.

"Forty-eight degrees is the lowest."

Mr. Brownlee threw up his arm. It covered his eyes and mouth. "What did you say your name is?"

"Jennie Swenson."

"Where do you come from?"

"Up the street."

"You come from heaven!" Mr. Brownlee still kept his eyes covered. "Can you put coal on the fire?"

"Sure!"

"Have you no father who may be out looking for you? No mother who is anxious? Are you real?"

"My father was killed in Shaft Eighteen. I guess you remember that time."

"Remember!" exclaimed Mr. Brownlee.

"My mother's a nurse, Mrs. Swenson. She has a case all night. I heard Stan Sobieski going home and I thought of the flowers. He was singing loud."

"Close that lower door," ordered Mr. Brownlee. "Then make the rounds with your flashlight. When you come back, bring yourself a chair."

"The lowest is now above forty-eight," reported Jennie a few minutes later.

"Sit down, Jennie," said Mr. Brownlee. "Now tell me again how you happen to be here."

"I vas"—excited and embarrassed, Jennie spoke rapidly—"I vas studying mine lesson by Hilda Yonson, and I vas coming past so I could see the flowers." Then she recovered her English. "There was no one in the office, but a newspaper was lying all mussed on the floor. When I was in bed, I heard Stan going home."

"He wasn't here," said Brownlee. "He

---

6. The expression *"Did Stan tie you?"* means 'did Stan cause this?'
7. *Lumbago* (lum BAY go) is a chronic or recurring pain in the lower back region.

never came. I was shoveling coal when this attack of lumbago caught me. It's happened before. All I could do was lie down on Stan's couch. It'll take a stretcher to get me home. My sister is in New York; otherwise she would have been here long ago. Now go on. So you heard Stan going home?"

"Then I came," said Jennie.

"Then you came," repeated Mr. Brownlee. "You got up in the middle of the night in a blizzard and you came."

"I saw the newspaper in the same place," she explained, "and I felt something was wrong."

Again Mr. Brownlee covered his eyes. "Better make another round, Jennie, and you might fetch my overcoat along."

"It's now fifty at the lowest," she reported on her return. "I'll cover you up. I can hear water bubbling in the pipe. I could take a few of those bottles, fill them with hot water, and put them behind you."

"Why, so you could! Open that spigot and you can fill them. Do you go to school?"

"Yes." Jennie sat down in her chair. "But I'm not good at Latin and algebra and geometry. I don't know if I can graduate in June. And I don't know if I can find a"—this time Jennie knew that she had made a slip—"a yob. I'm strong, but I'm not bright."

"No?" said Mr. Brownlee. "Will you kindly take another look at the thermometers?"

"Fifty-two everywhere," she told him jubilantly. "It's three o'clock now, not long till daylight."

"At five-forty my sister's train is due. She'll see the light in the office as they come into the station. Whatever has been our pain and anxiety, Jennie, we shall have the fun of seeing her come down those stairs. While I was at war, you know, the government shut down on luxuries. We couldn't use our own coal to run our own greenhouse, and we lost sixteen thousand plants in one night."

"I have heard of that," Jennie wept.

"You've got to keep the houses fifty-seven at night and fifty-five by day. Below forty-eight is blight and mildew. Will you please put more coal on, and make another round?"

"Sure!"

At six o'clock that morning the outer door opened, and there was a brisk tap of feet on the linoleum.

"Dick!" called a frightened voice. "Where are you?"

Already Miss Brownlee was on the steps. At the bottom she stood looking from her brother to his guest. Jennie rose, the flashlight in her hand.

"You might take that flash, Alice, and read the thermometers," said Mr. Brownlee in a tired voice.

Like an old woman, Miss Brownlee crept up the steps. Then she ran.

"It's fifty-seven everywhere," she cried, returning. "Have you lumbago? You've been shoveling coal! Where's Stan? What's the matter?"

"Alice, this is Jennie Swenson, Harriet

Word Bank **blight** (BLYT) *n.*: a disease in plants that causes them to stop growing and wither

Swenson's daughter," said Mr. Brownlee. "Last night at one o'clock, lying in her bed, she heard Stan going home, singing as he went. Now Jennie is something of a prowler herself. She comes here—has been coming for a good many years—to peer in at our windows. She looks at the roses; she doesn't handle them, she doesn't even smell them. She has never been in the greenhouse. But, hearing Stan yelling, she dressed and came down, just to look in and see that everything was all right. She says that she's dull, but she observed that my newspaper was lying exactly where she had seen it at nine-thirty."

"I'll put on a little more coal," offered Jennie.

Miss Brownlee looked hard at her. "You certainly have common sense, and you're certainly strong, and you certainly love flowers," she said at last. "Would you come here and work as an assistant? I would teach you all I know."

"When school closes, you mean," put in Mr. Brownlee. "In the meantime we'll help her with her Latin, her Greek, her Hebrew, her calculus, and her what not."

If he thought Jennie would laugh, he was mistaken. She lifted her hand to cover her trembling lips.

"Sure I'd come!" said she.

At half-past six Jennie went up the street. The snow was whirling through the air. Traveling was uncertain because you stepped now on bare, slippery flagstones, now into deep drifts. Jennie had a box on her arm; she carried it as though it were a baby.

Jennie opened the kitchen door of her home. The light was burning and her mother sat before the fire, taking off her shoes. She turned with a start. She had pleasant, tired eyes and a braid of thick light hair.

"Why, Yennie!" she exclaimed. "Where were you out in the night? What have you?"

Jennie sat down, the box in her arms.

"I've got roses in this box," she said. "Red and pink and white and yellow. They have long, long stems. And— moder—oh, moder! I've got a yob!"

Studying the Selection

First Impressions

Jennie is single-mindedly focused on success, yet she appreciates the warmth and friendship of the Yonson home. She is equally drawn to the greenhouse. In a few paragraphs explain why the greenhouse is so appealing to Jennie. How is she similar to Mr. Brownlee's roses?

✓ Quick Review

1. What are American Beauties?
2. Summarize Stan Sobieski's role in the story.
3. Describe Mr. Brownlee and his sister.
4. What happened to Jennie's father?

In-depth Thinking

5. Why is Jennie so worried about her studies? What evidence do we have that she is *not* a "dull girl"?
6. What do we learn about the Yonson family from Jennie's visit there?
7. Describe the conditions necessary for the roses' survival. How is their delicacy symbolic?
8. How might you state the theme of this story?

Drawing Conclusions

9. Jenny laughs at herself three different times in this story. Describe each occurrence. What do these incidents say about her character?
10. Write about a time in your own life when an interest or hobby led to a personal opportunity.

Focusing on External and Internal Settings

Setting helps create mood. When a place is described as dark and cold, we react negatively towards it. Conversely, a warm and well-lit setting attracts us. Use descriptive and precise language in the following assignments.

1. Write a paragraph about an outdoor setting that produces a negative mood.
2. Write a paragraph about an indoor setting that produces a positive mood.
3. Write in detail about a place that *instantly* cheered or depressed you.

Creating and Writing

1. Write a short essay about the effect of Mr. Brownlee's greenhouse. Consider not only its impact on Jennie but on the town as a whole. In general, what do roses symbolize? Specifically, what might Mr. Brownlee's roses symbolize?
2. A **synonym** is a word with the same or approximate meaning as another word. An **antonym** is a word with the opposite meaning. A synonym for *happy* is *glad*; an antonym for *happy* is *sad*.

    Think of one word to describe Mr. Brownlee's greenhouse. Then list five synonyms and five antonyms for that word. Define each word. Most likely you will find that some of the antonyms will describe the town. Using these descriptive antonyms, write a paragraph describing the bleak mining town in the story.
3. Using charcoal pastels, sketch a town scene on a piece of paper. Use only black to sketch the entire scene—the sidewalks, streets, buildings, and people. Now use color to draw a single object, such as a flower or tree. Place it at or near the center of your picture. Notice how the one bit of color brightens the whole page. Think how Mr. Brownlee's greenhouse does this for the people of the mining town.

    Now, notice the black dust on your skin, on your fingers, and imagine this dust as being always there. If you were a coal miner, or if you lived in a mining town, this dust would be all around you. When you wash your hands, notice if any of the black dust sticks to your skin or stays under your fingernails. Now, recall how Jennie described Tim Yonson's hands, clean but not white.

Blueprint for Reading

the Author

**George and Helen Papashvily
(1898-1978) (1906-1996)**

George Papashvily was born on a farm in Russia and apprenticed to a harnessmaker at the age of nine. Later he was hired by a swordmaker. When he was fourteen, he joined the Czar's army and served in World War I. After emigrating to the United States, he worked as a miner and factory worker until he could devote himself to sculpting and storytelling. He never took classes or lessons but still became an accomplished sculptor. Not fluent in English, he told stories to his wife Helen, who wrote them down. Together they wrote *Anything Can Happen*, *Thanks to Noah*, *Dogs and People*, and *Yes and No Stories*.

Background Bytes

The speaker of this story is Georgian; that is, he is from Georgia, a republic on the border of Russia. He is a recent immigrant to the United States, having landed at an unnamed island, which we can assume is the real Ellis Island.

Today Ellis Island is a memorial with a museum. But in the late 1800s and early 1900s it was the point of entry to the United States for millions of immigrants. This was a time when a relatively empty America needed willing workers and farmers to help a booming economy. Immigrants needed only to be healthy—mentally and physically—and show they would not become a public burden.

Ellis Island was the answer. Doctors employed by the United States Public Health Service examined the new arrivals as they came off the boat. After weeding out people with mental problems (actually few in number), they moved on to more serious concerns. Those immigrants who still exhibited eye diseases or lung problems, after a specific period of isolation, were sorted out and sent back to the countries they came from. Often families were broken up. Only those who passed the examinations could enter the land of opportunity.

Into *The First Day*

In part, this is a story of language, and it is told by the main character speaking in the first-person, using the pronoun "I." As you read, listen to the voice of this narrator. Does he use recognizable English? Are there times when he is truly hampered by a lack of English language skills?

As the story develops, notice how the narrator's language skills affect his dealings with others. Note places in the story where the narration or quotations do not use proper English. Is this a flaw, or is it an effective technique?

The First Day
George and Helen Papashvily

Focusing on First-Person Narration

The narrator of *The First Day* is a Georgian immigrant telling us of his first day in the United States. The **first-person narrative** lets the reader see events as the narrator sees them. This **point of view** keeps the narrator's lack of ease with both the language and the customs of his new country vivid.

Your teachers may tell you to **show, don't tell** in your own writing. The authors of *The First Day* don't tell us the narrator is uncomfortable in America; they show us. They use the first-person viewpoint to show us what is going on in the main character's head. The narrator's unfamiliarity with English leads him to create a sort of dialect. He puts Georgian words into English sentences, speaking a language that is definitely not Georgian, but is not English either.

Word Bank

Greenhorn has a variety of meanings. Usually it refers to an untrained or inexperienced person. It can also mean someone who is naïve or gullible. **Greenhorn** is the sort of word that might make a person stop and wonder, Where did that come from? Why should a *green*horn be a newly arrived immigrant? Why should someone who is a newcomer be described as a *horn*, in any case? When we say someone is *green*, it makes sense that *green = new*, because when trees bud and plants push up from the soil in spring, the buds are green. In fact, **greenhorn** entered English in the 1400s and was originally a term for young cattle, whose new horns were described as green.

steerage   visor

The First Day

George and Helen Papashvily

At five in the morning the engines stopped, and after thirty-seven days the boat was quiet.

We were in America.

I got up and stepped over the other men and looked out the porthole. Water and fog. We were anchoring off an island. I dressed and went on deck.

Now began my troubles. What to do? This was a Greek boat and I was steerage, so of course by the time we were halfway out I had spent all my landing money for extra food.

Hassan, the Turk, one of the six who slept in the cabin with me, came up the ladder.

"I told you so," he said as soon as he saw me. "Now we are in America and you have no money to land. They send you home. No money, no going ashore. What a disgrace. In your position, frankly, I would kill myself."

Hassan had been satisfied to starve on black olives and salt cheese all the way from Gibraltar, and he begrudged every skewer[1] of lamb I bribed away from the first-cabin steward.

We went down the gangplank into the big room. Passengers with pictures in their hands were rushing around to match them to a relative. Before their tables the inspectors were busy with long lines of people.

The visitors' door opened and a fellow with a big pile of caps, striped blue-and-white cotton caps with visors and a top button, came in. He went first to an old man with a karakul[2] hat near the window, then to a Cossack[3] in the line. At last he came to me.

"Look," he said in Russian, "look at your hat. You want to be a greenhorn[4] all your life? A karakul hat! Do you expect to see anybody in the U.S.A. still with a fur hat? The customs inspector, the doctor, the captain—are they wearing fur hats? Certainly not."

I didn't say anything.

"Look," he said. "I'm sorry for you. I was a greenhorn once myself. I wouldn't

---

1. A *skewer* (SKYOO er) of lamb refers to chunks of lamb meat cooked on a stick, as in shish kebab.
2. A *karakul* (car AH kool) hat is a black or silver lambskin hat worn by Eastern Europeans.
3. A *Cossack* (kuh ZAHK) is a Russian cavalryman.
4. The term *greenhorn* (GREEN HORN) refers to a new immigrant.

Word Bank

steerage (STEER ij) *n.*: the cheapest accommodations for travelers, usually providing minimal comfort and convenience

visor (VY zer) *n.*: the projecting front brim of a cap

want to see anybody make my mistakes. Look, I have caps. See, from such rich striped material. Like wears railroad engineers, and house painters, and coal miners." He spun one around on his finger. "Don't be afraid. It's a cap in real American style. With this cap on your head, they couldn't tell you from a citizen. I'm positively guaranteeing. And I'm trading you this cap even for your old karakul hat. Trading even. You don't have to give me one penny."

Now it is true I bought my karakul *coudie*[5] new for the trip. It was fine skin, a silver lamb, and in Georgia[6] it would have lasted me a lifetime. Still——

"I'll tell you," the cap man said. "So you can remember all your life you made money the first hour you were in America, I give you a cap and a dollar besides. Done?"

I took off my *coudie* and put on his cap. It was small and sat well up on my head, but then in America one dresses like an American and it is a satisfaction always to be in the best style. So I got my first dollar.

Ysaacs, a Syrian, sat on the bench and smoked brown paper cigarettes and watched all through the bargain. He was from our cabin, too, and he knew I was worried about the money to show the examiners. But now, as soon as the cap man went on to the next customer, Ysaacs explained a way to get me by the examiners—a good way.

Such a very good way, in fact, that when the Inspector looked over my passport and entry permit I was ready.

"Do you have friends meeting you?" he asked me. "Do you have money to support yourself?"

I pulled out a round fat roll of green American money—tens, twenties—a nice thick pile with a rubber band around.

"O.K." he said. "Go ahead." He stamped my papers.

I got my baggage and took the money roll back again to Ysaac's friend, Arapoulaopolus, the money lender, so he could rent it over again to another man. One dollar was all he charged to use it for each landing. Really a bargain.

On the outer platform I met Zurabeg, an Ossetian,[7] who had been down in steerage, too. But Zurabeg was no greenhorn coming for the first time. Zurabeg was an American citizen with papers to prove it, and a friend of Gospadin[8] Buffalo Bill besides. This Zurabeg came first to America twenty years before as a trick show rider, and later he was boss cook on the road with the Gospadin Buffalo Bill. Every few years, Zurabeg, whenever he saved enough money, went home to find a

---

5. *Coudie* is the Russian word for 'hat.'
6. *Georgia* (JOR juh) is a republic in the southeast part of the former Soviet Union, between the Black and Caspian Seas.
7. An *Ossetian* (AH set EEN) is one from a region of Russia between the Black and the Caspian Seas.
8. *Gospadin* (gahss puh DEEN) is the Russian word for 'Mister.'

wife—but so far with no luck.

"Can't land?" he asked me.

"No, I can land," I said, "but I have no money to pay the little boat to carry me to shore." A small boat went chuffing back and forth taking off the discharged passengers. "I try to make up my mind to swim, but if I swim how will I carry my baggage? It would need two trips at least."

"Listen, donkey-head," Zurabeg said, "this is America. The carrying boat is free. It belongs to my government. They take us for nothing. Come on."

So we got to the shore.

And there—the streets, the people, the noise! The faces flashing by—and by again. The screams and chatter and cries. But most of all the motion, back and forth, back and forth, pressing deeper and deeper on my eyeballs.

We walked a few blocks through this before I remembered my landing cards and passport and visas. I took them out and tore them into little pieces and threw them all in an ash can. "They can't prove I'm not citizen, now," I said. "What we do next?"

"We get jobs," Zurabeg told me. "I show you."

We went to an employment agency. Conveniently, the man spoke Russian. He gave Zurabeg a ticket right away to start in Russian restaurant as first cook.

"Now, your friend? What can you do?" he asked me.

"I," I said, "am a worker in decorative leathers particularly specializing in the ornamenting of crop handles according to the traditional designs."

"Good night!" the man said. "This is the U.S.A. No horses. Automobiles. What else can you do?"

Fortunately my father was a man of great foresight and I have two trades. His idea was that in the days when a man starves with one, by the other he may eat.

"I am also," I said, "a sword-maker. Short blades or long; daggers[9] with or without chasing;[10] hunting knives, plain or ornamented; tempering, fitting, pointing——" I took my certificate of successful completion of apprenticeship out of my *chemidon*.[11]

"What next? A crop maker—a sword pointer. You better take him along for a dishwasher," he said to Zurabeg. "They can always use another dishwasher."

We went down into the earth and flew through tunnels in a train. It was like

---

9. A *dagger* (DAG ur) is a short, sword-like weapon with a pointed blade and handle.
10. *Chasing* (CHAY sing) refers to decorative engraving; *tempering* strengthens the metal by heating and cooling; *fitting* means attaching the knife handle; and *pointing* means to shape or sharpen the point of the knife.
11. A *chemidon* (chim uh DAHN) refers to a type of wallet or holder for official papers.

the caves under the Kazbeck[12] where the giant bats sleep, and it smelled even worse.

The restaurant was on a side street and the lady owner, the *hasaika*,[13] spoke kindly. "I remember you from the tearoom," she said to Zurabeg. "I congratulate myself on getting you. You are excellent on the *piroshkis*,[14] isn't it?"

"On everything, madame," Zurabeg said grandly. "On everything. Buffalo Bill, an old friend of mine, has eaten thirty of my *piroshkis* at a meal. My friend—" he waved toward me "—will be a dishwasher."

I made a bow.

The kitchen was small and hot and fat—like inside of a pig's stomach. Zurabeg unpacked his knives, put on his cap, and, at home at once, started to dice celery.

"You can wash these," the *hasaika* said to me. "At four we have party."

It was a trayful of glasses. And such glasses—thin bubbles that would hardly hold a sip—set on stems. The first one snapped in my hand, the second dissolved, the third to tenth I got washed, the eleventh was already cracked, the twelfth rang once on the pan edge and was silent.

Perhaps I might be there yet, but just as I carried the first trayful to the service slot, the restaurant cat ran between my feet.

When I got all the glass swept up, I told Zurabeg, "Now, we have to eat. It's noon. I watch the customers eat. It makes me hungry. Prepare a *shashlik*[15] and some cucumbers, and we enjoy our first meal for good luck in the New World."

"This is a restaurant," Zurabeg said, "not a *duquani*[16] on the side of the Georgian road where the proprietor and the house eat with the guests together at one table. This is a restaurant with very strict organization. We get to eat when the customers go, and you get what the customers leave. Try again with the glasses and remember my reputation. Please."

I found a quart of sour cream and went into the back alley and ate that and some bread and a jar of caviar which was very salty—packed for export, no doubt.

The *hasaika* found me. I stood up. "Please," she said, "please go on. Eat sour cream. But after, could you go away? Far away? With no hard feelings. The glasses—the caviar—it's expensive for me—and at the same time I don't want to make your friend mad. I need a good cook. If you could just go away? Quietly? Just disappear, so to speak? I give you five dollars."

"I didn't do anything," I said, "so you don't have to pay me. All in all, a restaurant probably isn't my fate. You can tell Zurabeg afterward."

She brought my cap and a paper bag. I went down through the alley and into the street. I walked. I walked until my feet took fire in my shoes and my neck

---

12. The *Kazbeck* (kahz BEK) is a mountain that rises over 16,000 feet in the Caucasus Mountains in Russia.
13. The *hasaika* (huh ZY kuh) is the female owner of a restaurant.
14. *Piroshkis* (peer RUSH keez) are small turnovers with a filling, such as meat or vegetables.
15. *Shashlik* is shish kebab.
16. A *duquani* (doo KWAN nee) is a small inn, where the guests eat at the owner's table.

ached from looking. I walked for hours. I couldn't even be sure it was the same day. I tried some English on a few men that passed. "What watch?" I said. But they pushed by me so I knew I had it wrong. I tried another man. "How many clock?" he showed me on his wrist. Four-thirty.

A wonderful place. Rapidly, if one applies oneself, one speaks the English.

I came to a park and went in and found a place under a tree and took off my shoes and lay down. I looked in the bag the *hasaika* gave me. A sandwich from bologna and a nickel—to begin in America with.

What to do? While I decided, I slept.

A policeman was waking me up. He spoke. I shook my head I can't understand. Then with hands, with legs, rolling his eyes, turning his head, with motions, with gestures (really he was as good as marionettes[17] I saw once in Tiflis[18]), he showed me to lie on the grass is forbidden. But one is welcome to the seats instead. All free seats in this park. No charge for anybody. What a country.

But I was puzzled. There were iron arm rests every two feet along the benches. How could I distribute myself under them? I tried one leg. Then the other. But when I was under, how could I turn around? Then, whatever way I got in, my chin was always caught by the hoop. While I thought this over, I walked and bought peanuts for my nickel and fed the squirrels.

Lights began to come on in the towers around the park. It was almost dark. I found a sandy patch under a rock on little bluff above the drive. I cut a *shashlik* stick and built a fire of twigs and broiled my bologna over it and ate the bread. It lasted very short. Then I rolled up my coat for a pillow like the days during the war and went to sleep.

I was tired from America and I slept some hours. It must have been almost midnight when the light flashed in my face. I sat up. It was from the head lamp of a touring car choking along on the road below me. While I watched, the engine coughed and died. A man got out. For more than an hour he knocked with tools and opened the hood and closed it again.

Then I slid down the bank. In the war there were airplanes, and of course cars are much the same except, naturally, for the wings. I showed him with my hands and feet and head, like the policeman: "Give me the tools and let me try." He handed them over and sat down on the bench.

---

17. A *marionette* (MAIR ee uh NET) is a puppet manipulated by strings attached to its jointed limbs.
18. *Tiflis* (tif LEESE) is the capital city of Russian Georgia.

I checked the spark plugs and the distributor, the timer and the coils. I looked at the feed line, at the ignition, at the gas. In between, I cranked.[19] I cranked until I cranked my heart out onto the ground. Still the car wouldn't move.

I got mad. I cursed it. When I finished all I knew in Georgian I said it again in Russian to pick up the loose ends. Then I kicked the radiator as hard as I could. The car was an old Model T, and it started with a snort that shook the chassis[20] like an aspen.

The man came running up. He was laughing and he shook my hands and talked at me and asked questions. But the policeman's method didn't work. Signs weren't enough. I remembered my dictionary—English-Russian, Russian-English—it went both ways. I took it from my blouse pocket and showed the man. Holding it under the headlights, he thumbed through.

"Work?" he found in English.

I looked at the Russian word beside it and shook my head.

"Home?" he turned to that.

"No," again.

I took the dictionary. "Boat. Today."

"Come home—" he showed me the words—"with me—" he pointed to himself. "Eat. Sleep. Job." It took him quite a time between words. "Job. Tomorrow."

"Automobiles?" I said. We have the same word in Georgian.

"Automobiles!" He was pleased we found one word together.

We got in his car, and he took me through miles and miles of streets with houses on both sides of every one of them until we came to his own. We went in and we ate and we drank and ate and drank again. For that, fortunately, you need no words.

Then his wife showed me a room and I went to bed. As I fell asleep, I thought to myself: Well, now, I have lived one whole day in America and—just like they say—America is a country where anything, anything at all can happen.

And in twenty years—about this—I never changed my mind.

---

19. When he *cranked* (KRAINKT) the engine, he was attempting to start the car manually.
20. The *chassis* (CHASS ee) is the frame to which the wheels, engine, and body are attached. Since an *aspen* (AS pin) is a type of tree with oval-shaped leaves that tremble in the slightest breeze, we see that the car shook like a leaf.

Studying the Selection

First Impressions

a) How did the first-person viewpoint give us information about the narrator that a third-person viewpoint could not?

b) How would an author-omniscient narrative—where we know what every character is thinking—change the focus of the story?

✓ Quick Review

1. How does the narrator travel to America?
2. How does the narrator get his first dollar?
3. Why is the narrator fired from his first job of washing dishes?
4. Where does the narrator spend his first full night in America?

In-depth Thinking

5. Describe two early scenes that indicate the narrator's vulnerability.
6. Reread the paragraphs in which the narrator describes his skills to the employment agent. Do the sentences seem suitable for a new immigrant? Why might they be written this way? Why do you think these quotes are so much more complex than the others in the story?
7. Do you think Zurabeg really knows Buffalo Bill as well as he claims? Why might he lie or exaggerate about knowing Buffalo Bill?
8. Why does the narrator mention sword-making and leather-working as his skills, but not auto repair?

Drawing Conclusions

9. Was the narrator dishonest in eating the restaurant's food?
10. Do you think the narrator was successful in the years following his first day? Does the narrator have skills that will help him get ahead in life?

Focusing on First-Person Narration

A first-person narrative focuses the story on one person, the narrator. The narrator's thoughts, feelings, and reasons for actions are the only ones we can know. If the viewpoint were author-omniscient, we might learn more about the others, but we would lose something. We would only observe, look on; we would not be involved. A first-person narrator with a particular way of speaking (in this case, a man struggling with the English language) brings us into his world.

1. Rewrite or discuss the scene with the cap buyer in the first-person, from the cap buyer's point of view. How does the scene differ?
2. Rewrite or discuss the scene with the policeman in the park, this time from the policeman's point of view. How does the scene differ?
3. Rewrite the first scene of the story (stopping before the cap buyer enters) in the third person. Use "he," not "I." Since you will not be an author-omniscient, you can not know what any character is thinking. Notice how the scene changes if the reader doesn't know the narrator's thoughts.

Creating and Writing

1. Look at the Georgian words used by the narrator. If you disregard the footnotes, can you still define these words? Does it matter if you cannot define them exactly? Why do you think the authors included such words?
2. Write a first-person account of your own first day somewhere—a new school, summer camp. Show us—don't tell us—your feelings.
3. Interview a person who came to the United States as an adult. What is most memorable about that first day in the United States?

Blueprint for Reading

the Author

**Rumer Godden
(1907–1997)**

Margaret Rumer Godden was born in Eastbourne, England. When she was 6 months old, her family took her to India, where her father managed a steamship company. She started writing poetry when she was five. Godden was sent to school in England with her sister but returned to India in 1925. Her first novel was published in 1935. She would get up at 4 A.M. to write and return to her desk at 11 P.M. when her children had gone to bed. She wrote several books in the 1950s and 1960s—poetry, translations, a biography of Hans Christian Andersen, books for her children, and two volumes of autobiography. She said of her writing, "Nobody took notice of me, which was very healthy. To be ignored is the best thing for a writer."

Background Bytes

Learning to rely on oneself is not merely an important part of growing up—it *is* growing up. Of necessity, people assert their independence at different times, and in different ways.

This is the story of Ally, a young girl determined to go from her yard up to her bathroom, without any help. An ordinary task for an ordinary person—but Ally is blind. Ally's desire to go upstairs on her own shows us just how ready Ally is to declare her independence—and how brave she is! We also see that even the brave need help, even if that help sometimes consists of knowing when to stand aside.

Into *You Need to Go Upstairs*

An infant sees the world from only one point of view—his own. As he grows, he becomes aware of other people and of their needs and wants. The more mature a person is, the more he grasps and feels how *others* feel. Yet, no matter how understanding of others we become, we never lose our own individual point of view.

You Need to Go Upstairs is a story told by a blind girl about an experience she had. For most of us, the brief experience would not be a story—we would not even give it a second thought! But for a young girl who is blind, finding her way upstairs from the garden all by herself is a milestone in her life. As the girl tells the story, she brings us into her world, almost asking us to walk in her shoes for a while. We see her thin and knobbly legs through *her* eyes, we hear the visitor talking to us through *her* ears, and we smell the cinders through *her* nose. We recall things Mother has told her through *her* memory, and we hear Mother's warnings through *her* imagination. When she finally reaches the "loo," we feel as though *her* victory is ours.

YOU NEED TO GO Upstairs

*F*ocusing on Point of View

How does the author help us to temporarily experience life from Ally's point of view? She does this by describing how Ally, who cannot see, finds her way upstairs with the help of her other senses. Things that, to us, would be just sounds, sights, or smells become, for a blind girl, helpful markers and guides. Can you spot places where the sense of touch is very important to Ally? Does she use her sense of smell to guide her? Is her hearing more sensitive and acute than that of a sighted person? What about her sixth sense—that is to say, her intuition? Can you find some places where she reads the minds of those around her in a way that is beyond what most girls of her age could do? By describing things the way a blind person thinks about them, the author creates a story with a unique and memorable point of view.

Word Bank

In this story, Ally keeps from falling, when the smell of **ashes** reminds her of the little brick edge hidden in the grass by the path. She had fallen over it once before. This sounds like the opposite of what occurs in the nursery rhyme, Ring O' Roses. As children hold hands and walk in a circle, they recite, "Ring around the roses, A pocket full of posies, Ashes! Ashes! We all fall down." Actually, the words of the rhyme are *not* ashes, but "A-tishoo! A-tishoo!" mimicking the sound of sneezing. Some scholars believe that the circle rhyme dates from the days of the Black Plague: They say that a rosy rash was a symptom of the plague, posies of herbs were carried as protection, and those who fell ill had fits of sneezing. "All fall down" was what happened in the end.

YOU NEED TO GO Upstairs

RUMER GODDEN

And just when everything is comfortably settled you need to go upstairs.

You are sitting in the garden for the first time this year, sitting on a cushion on the grass by Mother. The feel of the grass is good; when you press it down and lift your hand the blades spring up again at once as strong as ever; they will not be kept lying down.

You sit with your legs straight in front of you; they have come out from their winter stockings and are very thin and knobbly, but the sun is beginning to warm them gently as if it were glad to see them again.

Your back is against Mother's chair and occasionally she puts her finger between your collar and your skin, to feel if you are warm; you are warm and you pick up your knitting because you can knit; with your finger you follow the wool along the big wooden pins and you say, "Knit one—knit another"; with the slow puffs of wind. The wind brings the garden scents and the sounds to you; sounds of birds and neighbors and the street.

"I like it, Mother."

"So do I."

Then Doreen, who comes in the afternoons to help, brings out a visitor; voices and footsteps; Mother has to get up but you hang your head and go on knitting. Voices creaking and rustling and a sigh. The visitor has sat down. Presently she whispers to Mother, "What is her name?"

"Her name is Alice," says Mother loudly and clearly to blot out the whisper. "We call her Ally. Ally, stand up and say how do you do."

"Ah, don't!" says the visitor and you do not stand up; you press the grass down flat with your hand. It is then that you know you need to go upstairs. The cloakroom[1] is out of order; you have to go upstairs.

The visitor's voice falls from high up, almost into your lap, cutting off the wind and the birds, cutting off Mother, so that you have to stand up.

"Yes, Ally?"

"Mother, I need to go upstairs," and you hurry to say, "I can go by myself, Mother."

---

1. A *cloakroom* is actually a closet for coats; here, another term for bathroom.

Mother is looking at your face—you cannot look yourself, yet you can always feel Mother's look; now she is doubtful, but she is proud, and after a moment she says, "Very well, dear." You understand what she does not say, *"Be careful! Be careful!"*

"Alone?" breathes the visitor, and prickles seem to rise up all over you. You have said you will do it alone, and you will. You turn your back on the visitor.

From the chairs to the poplars is easy; you can hear them straining and moving their branches just enough to tell you where they are. There are two, and when you are up to them, you separate your hands the distance apart you think they will be and you do not hit them, you find them; their trunks are under your hands and you stay to feel those trunks; they are rough and smooth together; they are like people, they are alive.

On the other side of the trees is a smell of cinders where, last winter, ashes were thrown down on the snow. The smell warns you. Move your feet along the grass, don't lift them, because the path is there and it has a little brick-edge hidden in the grass. You fell over it last summer; suddenly you were down on the grass and you have a fright about falling. You won't fall, the cinder smell has warned you. You find the path. Lift your feet—one—two. The cinders are crunching, now you can go along the path to where the flowers are.

"It's wonderful," says the visitor and her voice sounds like tears. "Her…little blue…jacket."

"It's a nice jacket, isn't it?" says

Mother. "We got it at Pollard's bargain counter. Ally feels it's warm and gay."

The visitor there would be surprised if you picked the flowers, one by one, and took them to her and told her what they were. "I see no reason why you should not know your flowers," Mother has often told you. "Flowers have shapes and smells as well as colors." This is the hyacinth[2] bed; hyacinths are easy, strong in scent and shaped like little pagodas[3]—"Remember, I told you about pagodas"—and these are crocuses[4] and these are aconites[5]—but Mother is not close and you remember that Schiff may be out on the path.

Schiff! You stop. Schiff is so small that you might easily step on him, but Schiff is large enough for you to fall over. Mother…but you must not call, you must go on. You think of falling, you can't help thinking of falling—down—into nothing until you get hit. Mother! Schiff! Mother! But you have not called and Mother is saying in what seems an ordinary voice to the visitor, but is her special loud voice for you. "How strange! With all this sun, our tortoise has not come out on the path today."

At the end of the path are two orange bushes with bitter-smelling leaves; they are bad little bushes, with twigs that catch on your coat; you don't like them and you think you will hurry past. There are two bushes in two tubs, and there are four steps; you can remember that, twice two are four. One—two—three—four, and your foot is on the last step, but you catch at the air, catch at the door with a sharp pain ringing in your shin, catch your breath and catch the door and save yourself.

Someone, somebody, has left the scraper[6] on the step. It has been pulled right out. You stand there shaking, boiling with anger, the pain hurting in your leg, but there is no sound from the garden; the visitor has not seen.

Now you are in the house. At first it is always curiously still; and then always out of the stillness you find it. This is the hall and in it are the smells and sounds of all the rooms: furniture cream and hot pipes, carpet and dried roses from the drawing-room, tobacco and a little of pickles from the dining-room, mint and hot cake from the kitchen, and down the stairs comes soap from the bathroom. The loo[7] is up, next door to the bathroom—it has a piece of pine-smelling brick in a wire holder on the wall.

With the smells come the house sounds, all so familiar: Doreen's footsteps in the kitchen; a whirring like

---

2. *Hyacinth* (HY yuh SINTH) is a flower of the lily family with a cylindrical cluster that is fragrant and colorful.
3. A *pagoda* (puh GO duh) is a building found in the Far East; it has a series of roofs, with the topmost coming to a point.
4. *Crocuses* (KRO kuss siz) are small flowers of the iris family that bloom in early Spring and are grown for their showy colors.
5. *Aconites* (AK eh NYTS) are plants of the buttercup family with loose flowers in clusters; some have medicinal use.
6. A *scraper* (SKRAY per) is a tool used for scraping dried paint off surfaces; also a decorative figure with a blade used to scrape mud from boots.
7. The *loo* (LOO) comes from a mispronunciation of *l'eau* (LOH), the French word for 'water,' and is a room with a toilet.

insects from the refrigerator and the clocks; a curtain flapping in the wind and a tapping, a tiny rustle from the canary. You know all these things better than anyone else.

Now you let go of the door—like this—and you go across the hall. Of course you could have gone round by the wall to the stairs, feeling around the hat rack and the chest, but you would not do that any more than you would go up the stairs on your hands and knees. No, you go across—like this—like this—and the big round knob at the bottom of the stairs is in your hands. Dear knob. You put your cheek against the wood; it is smooth and firm. Now you can go upstairs.

You are not at all afraid of the stairs. Why? Because Mother has put signals there for you, under the rail where no one can find them, and they guide you all the way up; now your legs go up the stairs as quickly as notes up a piano—almost. At the top is a small wooden heart for you to feel with your fingers; when you reach it, it is like a message and your own heart gets steady. It was not quite steady up the stairs.

"Ally, always, always be careful of the landing." Mother has said that so many times. The landing feels the same to you as the hall but it isn't. Once you dropped a ball over, and the sound came from far away down; if you tripped on the landing you might drop like the ball.

Now? Or not now? Are you facing the right way? That is an old fright. Did you turn round without noticing? You feel the stairs behind you with your foot and they are still there but now you are afraid to let go in case you can't step away. It is steep —steep behind you. Suppose you don't move away? Suppose you hit something—like the chair —and pitch down backwards? Little stickers come out along your back and neck; the back of your neck is cold, your fingers are sticky too, holding the heart signal. Suddenly you can't move away from the stairs. Mother. Mother, but you bite your lips. You must not call out.

Through the window you hear voices—voices from the path.

Drops of water burst out on your neck and under your hair, and you leave the rail and step out on to the carpet and walk very boldly towards the verbena[8] and warm towelling and the hot-metal-from-the-bath-taps smell.

"Is she all right? Is she?"

"Ally, are you managing?" calls Mother.

"Perfectly," you answer, and you shut the loo door.

---

8. *Verbena* (ver BEE nuh) is a type of flowering plant.

Studying the Selection

First Impressions

a) What made Ally, who had never gone upstairs on her own, decide to try to do it now? b) The narrator calls Ally "you." How does this help the reader come closer to seeing the world from Ally's point of view?

✓ Quick Review

1. Why does Ally need to go upstairs?
2. Why is it a major accomplishment for Ally to go upstairs alone?
3. What happens to Ally as she reaches the top step on her way into the house?
4. How does Ally climb the stairs to the bathroom so quickly, and how does she know she is at the top?

In-depth Thinking

5. Reread these sentences: "'Ah, don't!' says the visitor and you do not stand up; you press the grass down flat with your hand. It is then that you know you need to go upstairs." This is the second time Ally presses down the grass. How does this repetition of the action tell us why Ally now chooses to go upstairs?
6. What are the early clues the author supplies to let us know Ally is blind?
7. Look at the scene where the mother responds to the visitor's mention of Ally's jacket. What does the visitor mean by her comments? Does she really think Ally's jacket is wonderful? Compare the mother's response with her earlier reaction to the whispered question about Ally's name. What is Ally's mother trying to do?
8. Examine the following sentences: "Of course you could have gone round by the wall to the stairs, feeling around the hat rack and the chest, but you would not do that any more than you would go up the stairs on your hands and knees. No, you go across…" Why would Ally not go up the stairs on her hands and knees? What do these sentences tell us about Ally's sense of self?

Drawing Conclusions

9. Reread the scene where Ally becomes angry because someone has left the scraper on the step. What are the housekeeping responsibilities of sighted people if they share space with the blind?
10. At the end of the story, why does Mother ask Ally if she is "managing" rather than ask if she needs any help? Do you think Mother knows what Ally's answer will be? Why or why not?

Focusing on Point of View

Any story can be rewritten from another **point of view**. With the change in point of view, there is a change in our understanding of a character's actions. In *The First Day*, the only character whose intentions we know is the narrator. As you read any story, think about the point of view the author has chosen and how that choice affects the reader's knowledge of what is going on.

1. Rewrite, in the **first-person**, the scene with the visitor, using the visitor's **point of view**. Begin with the visitor sitting down, and end with Ally getting up and moving between the poplar trees. Look for the author's clues to the visitor's feelings as she becomes aware of Ally's blindness.
2. Write, in the **first-person** from Mother's **point of view**, about her decision to hide signals under the stair-rail for Ally. Be sure to consider her decision to hide them rather then place them, for example, along the top of the railing.
3. Using **omniscient narration**, rewrite any paragraph from *You Need to Go Upstairs*. Pay special attention to what Ally is thinking.

Creating and Writing

1. If the story were written in the **third person** (with the reader not knowing the thoughts of any character unless they are stated) would Ally's relationship with her mother be as clear? Why or why not?

2. Notice how much Ally knows about her house. She can identify every room by smell, sound, and touch. Describe your own house, telling how a blind person might move from the front door to either your bedroom or the kitchen using smell, sound, and touch.

3. Spend an afternoon volunteering at a center for the blind, perhaps reading aloud to a blind person or helping someone to answer mail. Notice how some blind people have compensated for their disability by refining their senses of hearing, smell, touch, and taste.

Blueprint for Reading

the Author

Guy de Maupassant (1850-1893)

A French-born writer, Guy de Maupassant spent his life in Normandy, France. He was a soldier and a clerk for the government, who was encouraged to write by his countryman, the renowned novelist, Gustave Flaubert. Flaubert was a close friend of the de Maupassant family. De Maupassant was extremely prolific and wrote more than three hundred short stories. His other works include several novels.

Background Bytes

The Piece of String takes place in the 19th century, thirty years after the French Revolution. The revolutionary slogan *"Liberty, Equality, Fraternity"* has long faded into historic lore and life for the majority of France's peasants is oppressively hard. The people are isolated and worn down by their poverty and the spirit of brotherhood is only a slogan. There is very little relief from the monotony of hard physical labor and material deprivation. Therefore, when Maître Malandain (MET tr mahl len DEN) pokes fun at Maître Hauchecome (MET tr howsh COMB), the townspeople are eager to join in the torture. It offers them a diversion from the tediousness of daily life.

Into *The Piece of String*

The main character of *The Piece of String* is Maître Hauchecome, a peasant whose life is torn apart when he picks up a piece of string. He is no different from his fellow men, except that he is the victim of a bad conscience and a vicious neighbor. In fact, given the opportunity Maître Hauchecome might even have done what he was accused of. The reader learns this both by entering into his thoughts, and from the stated opinions of the author.

The Piece of String

Focusing on the Omniscient Narrator's Comments

The **author-omniscient narrative** of *The Piece of String* offers two paths into the story. First we have the thoughts and actions of Maître Hauchecome (the main character) as well as others. We also have the narrator's stated opinions, filled with well-chosen adjectives and nouns. Our attitudes are shaped as much by the author's pronouncements as the events of the story.

As you read:

1. Note the narrator's editorial comments, as he describes his subjects. Is there a common denominator? What is his attitude toward these people?
2. Note the scenes—some quite lengthy—where the narrator moves inside Maître Hauchecome's head. How does this material differ from the external description of the village?
3. Note where the narrator tells the thoughts or intentions of other characters. Is there any change of tone?

Word Bank

Burgh: Have you ever thought about where names of places come from? Names of places that end in *–ton*, such as Hampton, Middleton, Newton, are actually ending with the word *town.* Many place names incorporate the directions North, East, South, and West, sometimes in an abbreviated fashion. For example, Norton is short for *North Town*; Eaton, for *East Town*; Suffolk, for *South Folk.* Various forms of the word **burgh**, which means town, figure in place names: Middle**boro**, Pitts**burgh**, New**bury**port, and Attle**borough**. **Burgh** is related to the words *hamburger, bury, burrow, burglar, harbor,* and *bourgeois.*

affirmation	impassive	mutton	scanty
aristocracy	incredulous	nag	shaft
burgh	indignation	perceived	spare
credence	interminable	protruded	spits
haunches	jeers	robust	vender

The Piece of String

Guy de Maupassant

Along all the roads around Goderville[1] the peasants and their wives were coming toward the burgh because it was market day. The men were proceeding with slow steps, the whole body bent forward at each movement of their long twisted legs; deformed by their hard work, by the weight on the plow which, at the same time, raised the left shoulder and swerved the figure; by the reaping of the wheat which made the knees spread to make a firm "purchase,"[2] by all the slow and painful labors of the country. Their blouses, blue, "stiff-starched," shining as if varnished, ornamented with a little design in white at the neck and wrists, puffed about their bony bodies, seemed like balloons ready to carry them off. From each of them a head, two arms and two feet protruded.

Some led a cow or a calf by a cord, and their wives, walking behind the animal, whipped its haunches with a leafy branch to hasten its progress. They carried large baskets on their arms from which, in some cases, chickens and, in others, ducks thrust out their heads. And they walked with a quicker, livelier step than their husbands. Their spare straight figures were wrapped in a scanty little pinned shawl, and their heads were enveloped in a white cloth glued to the hair and surmounted by a cap.

Then a wagon passed at the jerky trot of a nag, shaking strangely, two men seated side by side and a woman in the bottom of the vehicle, the latter holding onto the sides to lessen the hard jolts.

In the public square of Goderville there was a crowd, a throng of human beings and animals mixed together. The horns of the cattle, the tall hats, with long nap,[3] of the rich peasant and the headgear of the peasant women rose above the surface of the assembly.

And the clamorous,[4] shrill, screaming voices made a continuous and savage din which sometimes was dominated by the

---

1. *Goderville* (goh dare VEE)
2. *Purchase* means to get leverage on or to get an effective hold on. If one has *firm purchase*, one can grasp something securely.
3. The tall hats, with long *nap*, refers to the *nap* in clothing: the short, fuzzy ends of fiber on the surface of cloth.
4. *Clamorous* (KLAM or us) voices are full of demands or complaints.

Word Bank

burgh (BERG) *n.*: a town; an incorporated town
protruded (pro TROOD id) *v.*: projected; jutted out
haunches (HAWN chez) *n.*: the hips or fleshy part of the body about the hips; the hindquarters of an animal
spare (SPAIR) *adj.*: lean or thin
scanty (SKAN tee) *adj.*: insufficient; very brief
nag (NAG) *n.*: an old horse

robust lungs of some countryman's laugh or the long lowing[5] of a cow tied to the wall of a house.

All that smacked of the stable,[6] the dairy and the dirt heap, hay and sweat, giving forth that unpleasant odor, human and animal, peculiar to the people of the field.

Maître[7] Hauchecome of Breaute[8] had just arrived at Goderville, and he was directing his steps toward the public square when he perceived upon the ground a little piece of string. Maître Hauchecome, economical like a true Norman,[9] thought that everything useful ought to be picked up, and he bent painfully, for he suffered from rheumatism. He took the bit of thin cord from the ground and began to roll it carefully when he noticed Maître Malandain,[10] the harness maker, on the threshold of his door, looking at him. They had heretofore had business together on the subject of a halter, and they were on bad terms, both being good haters. Maître Hauchecome was seized with a sort of shame to be seen thus by his enemy, picking a bit of string out of the dirt. He concealed his "find" quickly under his blouse, then in his trousers' pocket; then he pretended to be still looking on the ground for something which he did not find, and he went toward the market, his head forward, bent double by his pains.

He was soon lost in the noisy and slowly moving crowd which was busy with interminable bargainings. The peasants milled, went and came, perplexed, always in fear of being cheated, not daring to decide, watching the vender's eye, ever trying to find the trick in the man and the flaw in the beast.

The women, having placed their great baskets at their feet, had taken out the poultry which lay upon the ground, tied together by the feet, with terrified eyes and scarlet crests.

They heard offers, stated their prices with a dry air and impassive face, or perhaps, suddenly deciding on some proposed reduction, shouted to the customer who was slowly going away: "All right, Maître Authirne,[11] I'll give it to you for that."

Then little by little the square was deserted, and the ringing at noon, those who had stayed too long scattered to their shops.

At Jourdain's[12] the great room was full of people eating, as the big court[13] was

---

5. *To low* is to utter the deep sound characteristic of cattle: to moo.
6. In *smacked* of the stable, *smacked* means to have the taste, flavor, trace, or suggestion of: here it suggests the smell of the stable.
7. This term, *Maître* (MET tr), is used when addressing men, and is the equivalent of the English 'Mister.'
8. *Hauchecome* (howsh COMB) of *Breaute* (BROHT)
9. At the time of this story, a *Norman* (the word comes from *Northman*) was a French person from a region in northwest France called Normandy.
10. *Maître Malandain* (MET tr mahl len DEN)
11. *Maître Authirne* (MET tr ooh TEERN)
12. *Jourdain's* (zhoor DEHNHZ)
13. As used here, a *court* (KORT) is an area open to the sky that is mostly or entirely surrounded by walls and buildings.

Word Bank

robust (roh BUST) *adj.*: strong, healthy, hearty
perceived (per SEEVD) *v.*: became aware of, identified by means of the senses; recognized
interminable (in TUR min uh bul) *adj.*: having no apparent limit or end
vender (VEN dur) *n.*: (also spelled vendor) a seller
impassive (ihm PASS iv) *adj.*: showing or feeling no emotion

full of vehicles of all kinds, carts, gigs,[14] wagons, dumpcarts, yellow with dirt, mended and patched, raising their shafts to the sky like two arms or perhaps with their shafts in the ground and their backs in the air.

Just opposite the diners seated at the table the immense fireplace, filled with bright flames, cast a lively heat on the backs of the row on the right. Three spits were turning on which were chickens, pigeons and legs of mutton, and an appetizing odor of roast beef and gravy dripping over the nicely browned skin rose from the hearth, increased the jovialness[15] and made everybody's mouth water.

All the aristocracy of the plow ate there at Maître Jourdain's, tavern keeper and horse dealer, a rascal who had money.

The dishes were passed and emptied, as were the jugs of yellow cider.

Everyone told his affairs, his purchases and sales. They discussed the crops. The weather was favorable for the green things but not for the wheat.

Suddenly the drum beat in the court before the house. Everybody rose, except a few indifferent persons, and ran to the door or to the windows, their mouths still full and napkins in their hands.

After the public crier had ceased his drumbeating he called out in a jerky voice, speaking his phrases irregularly: "It is hereby made known to the inhabitants of Goderville, and in general to all persons present at the market, that there was lost this morning on the road to Benzeville,[16] between nine and ten o'clock, a black leather pocket-book containing five hundred francs and some business papers. The finder is requested to return same with all haste to the mayor's office or to Maître Fortune Houlbreque[17] of Manneville;[18] there will be twenty francs reward."

Then the man went away. The heavy roll of the drum and the crier's voice were again heard at a distance.

Then they began to talk of this event, discussing the chances that Maître Houlbreque had of finding or not finding his pocketbook.

And the meal concluded. They were finishing their coffee when a chief of the

---

14. A *gig* is a light, two-wheeled, one-horse carriage.
15. The smell of the good food cooking on the spit added to the *jovialness* (JO vee il niss), or happy mood, of the people there.
16. *Benzeville* (bohn zh VEE)
17. *Maître Fortune Houlbreque* (MET tr for TYEENH oohl BREH)
18. *Manneville* (mahn nuh VEE)

Word Bank

shaft (SHAFT) *n.*: a long pole or handle serving to balance a weapon or tool
spits *n.*: pointed rods for skewering and holding meat over a fire for cooking
mutton (MUTT un) *n.*: the flesh of a mature sheep, used as food
aristocracy (AIR iss TAHK rih see) *n.*: a class of persons holding high rank and privileges, especially the nobility

gendarmes[19] appeared upon the threshold.

He inquired:

"Is Maître Hauchecome of Breaute here?"

Maître Hauchecome, seated at the other end of the table, replied:

"Here I am."

And the officer resumed:

"Maître Hauchecome, will you have the goodness to accompany me to the mayor's office? The mayor would like to talk to you."

The peasant, surprised and disturbed, swallowed at a draught[20] his tiny glass of brandy, rose and, even more bent than in the morning, for the first steps after each rest were specially difficult, set out, repeating: "Here I am, here I am."

The mayor was awaiting him, seated on an armchair. He was the notary[21] of the vicinity, a stout, serious man with pompous phrases.[22]

"Maître Hauchecome," said he, "you were seen this morning to pick up, on the road to Benzeville, the pocketbook lost by Maître Houlbreque of Manneville."

The countryman, astounded, looked at the mayor, already terrified by this suspicion resting on him without his knowing why.

"Me? Me? Me pick up the pocketbook?"

"Yes, you yourself."

"Word of honor, I never heard of it."

"But you were seen."

"I was seen, me? Who says he saw me?"

"Monsieur[23] Malandain, the harness maker."

The old man remembered, understood and flushed with anger.

"Ah, he saw me, the clodhopper, he saw me pick up this string here, M'sieu[24] the Mayor." And rummaging in his pocket, he drew out the little piece of string.

But the mayor, incredulous, shook his head.

"You will not make me believe, Maître Hauchecome, that Monsieur Malandain, who is a man worthy of credence, mistook this cord for a pocketbook."

The peasant, furious, lifted his hand, spat at one side to attest his honor, repeating:

"It is nevertheless the truth of the good G-d, the sacred truth, M'sieu the Mayor."

The mayor resumed:

"After picking up the object you stood like a stilt, looking a long while in the mud to see if any piece of money had fallen out." The good old man choked with indignation and fear.

"How anyone can tell—how anyone can tell—such lies to take away an honest

---

19. *Gendarmes* (zhan DARMZ) are police officers, literally "gentleman of arms."
20. The expression *at a draught* (DRAFT) means in a single gulp, as if it were inhaled.
21. A *notary* (NOH turr ee) is an official clerk or secretary, performing such functions as witnessing the signing of documents.
22. *With pompous phrases* refers to the mayor's habit of talking in a manner that showed him to be very important and dignified.
23. *Monsieur* (mih SYOUR) means mister.
24. *M'sieu* (mihs YH) is a colloquialism meaning *Monsieur*.

Word Bank

incredulous (in KRED you lus) *adj.*: disbelieving

credence (KREED intz) *n.*: belief in the truth of something

indignation (in dig NAY shun) *n.*: strong displeasure at something considered unjust or insulting; righteous anger

man's reputation! How can anyone——"

There was no use in his protesting; nobody believed him. He was confronted with Monsieur Malandain, who repeated and maintained his affirmation. They abused each other for an hour. At his own request Maître Hauchecome was searched; nothing was found on him.

Finally the mayor, very much perplexed, discharged him with the warning that he would consult the public prosecutor and ask for further orders.

The news had spread. As he left the mayor's office the old man was surrounded and questioned with a serious or bantering[25] curiosity in which there was no indignation. He began to tell the story of the string. No one believed him. They laughed at him.

He went along, stopping his friends, beginning endlessly his statement and his protestations, showing his pockets turned inside out to prove that he had nothing.

They said:

"Old rascal, get out!"

And he grew angry, becoming exasperated, hot and distressed at not being believed, not knowing what to do and always repeating himself.

Night came. He must depart. He started on his way with three neighbors to whom he pointed out the place where he had picked up the bit of string, and all along the road he spoke of his adventure.

In the evening he took a turn in the village of Breaute in order to tell it to everybody. He only met with incredulity.

It made him ill at night.

The next day about one o'clock in the afternoon Marius Paumelle,[26] a hired man in the employ of Maître Breton,[27] husbandman[28] at Ymanville,[29] returned the pocketbook and its contents to Maître Houlbreque of Manneville.

This man claimed to have found the object in the road, but not knowing how to read, he had carried it to the house and given it to his employer.

The news spread through the neighborhood. Maître Hauchecome was informed of it. He immediately went the circuit and began to recount his story completed by the happy climax. He was in triumph.

"What grieved me so much was not the thing itself as the lying. There is nothing so shameful as to be placed under a cloud on account of a lie."

He talked of his adventure all day long; he told it on the highway to people who were passing by, and in the wineshop to people who were drinking there. He stopped strangers to tell them about it. He was calm now, and yet something disturbed him without his knowing exactly what it was. People had the air of joking while they listened. They did not seem convinced. He seemed to feel that remarks were being made behind his back.

On Tuesday of the next week he went to the market at Goderville, urged solely by

---

25. *Bantering* means good-natured.
26. *Marius Paumelle* (mahr ree OOO poh MELL)
27. *Maître Breton* (MET tr bray TAHNH)
28. A *husbandman* (HUZ bind man) is a farmer.
29. *Ymanville* (ee mahnh VEE)

Word Bank **affirmation** (AF er MAY shun) *n.*: the assertion that something exists or is true

the necessity he felt of discussing the case.

Malandain, standing at his door, began to laugh on seeing him pass. Why?

He approached a farmer from Crequetot[30] who did not let him finish and, giving him a thump in the stomach, said to his face:

"You big rascal."

Then he turned his back on him.

Maître Hauchecome was confused; why was he called a big rascal?

When he was seated at the table in Jourdain's tavern he commenced to explain "the affair."

A horse dealer from Montvilliers[31] called to him:

"Come, come, old sharper, that's an old trick; I know all about your piece of string!"

Hauchecome stammered:

"But since the pocketbook was found."

But the other man replied:

"Quiet, papa, there is one that finds and there is one that reports. At any rate you are mixed with it."

The peasant stood choking. He understood. They accused him of having had the pocketbook returned by a confederate,[32] by an accomplice.

He tried to protest. All the table began to laugh.

He could not finish his dinner and went away in the midst of jeers.

He went home ashamed and indignant, choking with anger and confusion. He was dejected by the thought that they considered him capable, with his Norman cunning, of doing what they had accused him of and even boasting about it. His innocence to him, in a confused way, was impossible to prove, as his sharpness was known. And he was stricken to the heart by the injustice of the suspicion.

Then he began to recount the adventures again, prolonging his history every day, adding each time new reasons, more energetic protestations, which he imagined and prepared in his hours of solitude, his whole mind given up to the story of the string. He was believed so much the less as his defense was more complicated and his arguing more subtle.[33]

"Those are lying excuses," they said behind his back.

He felt it, consumed his heart over it and wore himself out with useless efforts. He wasted away before their very eyes.

The wags now made him tell about the string to amuse them, as they make a soldier who has been on a campaign tell about his battles. His mind, touched to the depth, began to weaken.

Toward the end of December he took to his bed.

He died in the first days of January, and in the delirium of his death struggles he kept claiming his innocence, reiterating:

"A piece of string, a piece of string—look—here it is, M'sieu the Mayor."

---

30. *Crequetot* (krek TOH)
31. *Montvilliers* (mohn vee lee AY)
32. A *confederate* (kun FED er it) is a person, group, or nation united with others; an ally. Here, the word is used to mean a partner-in-crime.
33. As his arguments grew more *subtile* (SUT il) (an old spelling of subtle), or skillful and clever, he was believed less and less.

Word Bank

jeers (JEERZ) *n.*: rude and mocking shouts or taunts

Studying the Selection

First Impressions

a) Write a few paragraphs, giving your overall impression of the peasants, based on the narrator's treatment of them, both at the square and as they listen to Maître Hauchecome's tale.

b) What crucial piece of information would we know if the story were told from the first-person point of view of Maître Malandain?

✓ Quick Review

1. Is the market scene calm and orderly? Note specific descriptive passages.
2. Why, according to the narrator, does Maître Hauchecome pretend to look around for something he has lost?
3. Is Maître Hauchecome effective in protesting his innocence to the mayor? What are some of the phrases used?
4. What finally "consumes [Maître Hauchecome's] heart" and causes him to waste away and die?

In-depth Thinking

5. Why is Maître Hauchecome "seized with a sort of shame" when he realizes Maître Malandain has seen him picking up a piece of string?
6. Notice where the narrator describes the peasants as being similar, having little individualism. List these instances. Why do these details become important?
7. The narrator speaks of people questioning Maître Hauchecome outside the mayor's office "...with a serious or bantering curiosity *in which there was no indignation.*" What is meant by this phrase? Why is it a significant observation?
8. Why does the matter of the string finally lead to Maître Hauchecome's death?

Drawing Conclusions

9. Does Maître Malandain truly believe Maître Hauchecome stole the pocketbook, or is he lying to the mayor? What clues does the narrator give to help answer this question?
10. Look again at this passage:

    [Maître Hauchecome] went home ashamed and indignant, choking with anger and confusion. He was dejected by the thought that they considered him capable, with his Norman cunning, of doing what they had accused him of and ever boasting about it. His innocence to him, in a confused way, was impossible to prove, as his sharpness was known.

    What does this statement mean? How does it tell us why Maître Hauchecome continues protesting his innocence, even as he realizes he is being ridiculed? Who is Maître Hauchecome really trying to convince?

Focusing on the Omniscient Narrator's Comments

1. How do the narrator's inserted comments influence us as we examine Maître Hauchecome's situation?
2. Discuss one of the scenes in which Maître Hauchecome protests his innocence, this time using the **first-person point of view** of one of the peasants being addressed. What important piece of knowledge about the peasant do we now have that wasn't available in de Maupassant's story?
3. Discuss the death of Maître Hauchecome. If **third-person narration** were used, so that the character's thoughts would remain unknown, what couldn't we learn about Maître Hauchecome's motives for telling his story again and again?

Creating and Writing

1. Rewrite the scene of Maître Hauchecome picking up the string while being observed. Use **first-person narration** (the "I" voice) so that only the thoughts of Maître Malandain are known. How does the scene differ?
2. Write your own account of an event when you were innocent of an accusation made against you. For example, perhaps a sibling broke something, and your parent mistakenly thought you had done it. How did you feel? How did you react?
3. Draw a scene at the market. How will the narrator's descriptions help you in choosing details to include in your picture?

Blueprint for Reading

the Author

Lois Phillips Hudson (1927-2010)

Lois Phillips Hudson was born in 1927 and raised in the western United States. Her family was poor and lived on the prairie. Her experiences are part of *Children of the Harvest*. About this story, she wrote: "…not one school in a hundred makes any real effort to educate the children of laborers. [Readers] might find it hard to understand that migrant children are not welcome in ANY school! My own family tramped the fruit only one season, and most of that time, as I said in the story, we were not in school…I sometimes wonder if even one of the many children I knew in the migrant camps even got out of high school…I wrote this story because it was a story that had to be told. It is based on things that happened, but it has many fictional elements. Barbara, the owner's daughter, was real, but the dirty Okie boy who sat in front of me is not. Thus the story is, like almost all fiction, a…combination of real and imagined details and incidents."

Background Bytes

Putting food on the table, for most of us, means a trip to the store. Today most food is grown by relatively few farmers. Science and technology have lightened the work involved in farming and reduced the negative effects of the elements and insects. Still, some crops must be picked by hand, and the labor is exhausting. While migrant workers may be better paid than they once were, their earnings are still insufficient for them to move out of poverty. Many people (some from other countries) still follow the harvest, picking our crops as they mature, and then moving on.

Children of the Harvest, set in 1937, tells of these people. The narrator and her family are migrant workers. Forced to abandon their own roots, they travel from place to place, hiring themselves out to pick the ripening crops owned by others. With the harvest complete, they move on, for there is no more work. The narrator and her family move from a berry patch, to a hops yard, to an apple orchard. They are always on the move traveling to the next crop that is ready for picking. The crops change; the work remains the same. In the midst of this endless drudgery, family is more important than ever.

Into *Children of the Harvest*

The word **memoir** comes from *memoire*, French for *memory*. A **memoir** is an account of the author's own memories. It is usually, but not always, written using a **first-person point of view**. Sometimes an author will write in the **third-person** ("he" or "she," as opposed to "I"), to emphasize the emotional distance gained with time, or to show that the author feels very different now. *Children of the Harvest* is a fictional **first-person memoir**. The main character is never named in the story. But Lois Phillips Hudson wrote this short story as an adult, perhaps to examine her childhood experiences and show (not tell) others how migrant children lived.

Children of the Harvest

Focusing on the Memoir as Fiction

A **memoir** is the author's personal story. The reader's awareness of any character is limited by the author's perception. In this story, the author's youth and inexperience limits how she judged other characters at the time the story took place. This limited judgment is what she presents to the reader.

Even years later, when the author reflects on her life, she still has no sure way of knowing the thoughts or feelings of the others in her drama. She remembers only their actions—and judges them accordingly.

"The workers come...stripping a field, moving to the next, filling their boxes or crates or sacks..."

Word Bank

Mélange, Prestige: **Mélange** (may LAHNZH) and **prestige** (press TEEZH) are two French words that appear in this story. Although they have become part of the English language, they entered later than words we talk about as having roots in French, and their spellings and pronunciation are close to the French. In fact, it may be surprising to learn just how many English words are really French. Some with which you may be familiar are *ballet*, *façade*, *grotesque*, *bureau*, *chic*, *charade*, *blonde*, *naïve*, and *promenade*. Do you know how to pronounce these words? Do you know any others? Notice that in French, the accent is typically on the final syllable.

access	dissociate	incorrigible	phenomena
acute	dubious	inscrutable	prestige
assurance	elicited	insinuated	scoured
augmented	entice	intercepted	transient
disconcerting	habitation	minute	

Children of the Harvest

Lois Phillips Hudson

On a suffocating summer day in 1937, the thirteenth year of the drought[1] and the seventh year of depression,[2] with our mouths, nostrils, and eyes full of the dust blowing from our bare fields, my family sold to our neighbors at auction most of the accouterments[3] of our existence. Then we loaded what was left into a trailer my father had made and drove West to find water and survival on the Washington coast.

During the auction the two classmates with whom I had just finished the fourth grade hung about the desultory[4] bidders giving me looks of respect and undisguised envy. They envied me not so much for the things they could imagine as for the things they couldn't—the unimaginable distance I was going and the unimaginable things along it and at the end of it.

And though we all could have imagined most of Montana well enough, how could any of us have imagined an end to the prairie's limitless sky and the giddy encroachments[5] rising higher and higher against that sky that were the Rocky Mountains? How could we have imagined how, in burning summer, the forested profiles of the Cascades[7] could echo everywhere the shouts of white falls above us and green rivers below? Who could have imagined, once confronted with their gray expanse, that the waters of Puget Sound were not actually the Pacific, but only a minute stray squiggle of it? Who, finally, could have imagined that there were so many people in the world or that the world could offer them so hospitable a habitation?

---

1. A *drought* (DROWT) is a long period of dry weather that destroys crops.
2. Here, *depression* (dee PRESH in) refers to the Great Depression in the United States which began with the stock-market crash of 1929, and left millions of people financially ruined.
3. The family sold most of their *accouterments* (uh KOO ter mintz), or personal clothing, accessories, and equipment.
4. Here, *desultory* (DESS ul TOR ee) means simply random, disconnected, or aloof. The bidders were not personally connected to the items which they were bidding on.
5. The *giddy encroachments* (in KROACH mintz) refer to the beginnings of the dizzyingly high Rocky Mountains jutting up from the flat prairie.
6. The *Cascades* (kas KAIDZ) are a mountain range in the Northwestern United States. Its highest peak is Mount Rainier.

Word Bank

minute (my NOOT) *adj*.: extremely small, as in size, amount, extent, or degree
habitation (HAB ih TAY shun) *n*.: a place of residence; dwelling; community

There were so many things I could scarcely believe even when I was doing them or looking at them or eating them. We lived in a cabin on an island for a few weeks after we arrived, and it always seemed impossible to me that we could be surrounded by so much water. I spent every moment of the hour-long ferry trip from the mainland hanging over the rail gazing down at the exhilarating wake of my first boat ride. The island was exactly what any island should be—lavish green acres covered with woods and orchards and fields of berries, ringed by glistening sandy beaches richly stocked with driftwood. Once in North Dakota my aunt had brought a very small basket of black cherries to my grandfather's house, and I had made the four or five that were my share last all afternoon. I would take tiny bites of each cherry, then suck the pit and roll it around with my tongue to get the faint remaining taste, till it came out as clean and smooth as a brook-bottom pebble. But on the island I would climb into the trees with my five-year-old sister and have contests with her, seeing which of us could get the most cherries in our mouths at once. Then we would shoot the wet pits, no longer hungrily scoured of their slipperiness, at each other and at the robins who perched above us. Sometimes I would go into the fields with my mother and father and spend an hour helping pick raspberries or blackberries or loganberries or any of the other things they worked in, but there were really only two important things to do—play on the beaches and eat fruit.

It didn't occur to me that things would ever be different again, but one day early in August the last berry was picked and we took the ferry into Seattle, where we bought a big brown tent and a camp stove. We added them to our trailer load and drove back over the green-and-white Cascades, beneath the glacial sunrise face of Mount Rainier, and down into the sweaty outdoor factory that is the Yakima Valley. There the Yakima River is bled for transfusions to the millions of rows of roots, its depleted currents finally dragging themselves muddily to their relieved merger with the undiminishable[7] Columbia. One can follow the Yakima for miles and miles and see nothing but irrigated fields and orchards—and the gaunt[8] camps of transient laborers.

The workers come like a horde of salvaging locusts, stripping a field, moving to the next, filling their boxes or crates or sacks, weighing in, collecting the bonuses offered to entice them to stay till the end of the season, and disappearing again. They spend their repetitive days in rows of things to be picked and their sweltering nights in rows of tents and trailers. We pitched our tent beside the others, far from our pleasant island where the owners of the fields were neighbors who invited my sister and me among their cherry trees. Here the sauntering[9] owners and their bristling foremen never smiled at those children who ran through the fields playing games, and only occasionally at those who worked beside their parents.

In North Dakota I had worked on our farm—tramping hay, driving a team of horses,

---

7. *Undiminishable* (UN dih MIN ish a bull) means it would be impossible to make the Columbia smaller.
8. Something *gaunt* (GAWNT) is bleak, desolate, or grim. (A *gaunt* person, however, is thin, malnourished.)
9. *Sauntering* (SAWN ter ing) means to walk in a confident, leisurely way.

Word Bank

scoured (SKOW erd) *v.*: removed by hard rubbing
transient (TRAN shint) *adj.*: not lasting or enduring, temporary
entice (en TYC) *v.*: lead on by exciting hope or desire; tempt

fetching cows, feeding calves and chickens—but of course that had all been only my duty as a member of the family, not a way to earn money. Now I was surrounded by grownups who wanted to pay me for working, and by children my own age who were stepping up to the pay window every night with weighing tags[10] in their hands and collecting money. I saw that the time had come for me to assume a place of adult independence in the world.

I made up my mind I was going to earn a dollar all in one day. We were picking hops[11] then, and of all the rows I have toiled my way up and down, I remember hop rows the most vividly. Trained up on their wires fifteen feet overhead, the giant vines resemble monster grape arbors hung with bunches of weird unripe fruit. A man who does not pick things for a living comes and cuts them down with a knife tied to a ten-foot pole so the people below can strip them off into sacks. Hops don't really look like any other growing thing but instead like something artificially constructed—pine cones, perhaps, with segments cleverly cut from the soft, limp, clinging leaves that lie next to the kernels of an ear of corn. A hop in your hand is like a feather, and it will almost float on a puff of air. Hops are good only for making beer, so you can't even get healthily sick of them by eating them all day long, the way you can berries or peas.

Pickers are paid by the pound, and picking is a messy business. Sometimes you run into a whole cluster that is gummy with the honeydew of hop aphids,[12] and gray and musty with the mildew growing on the sticky stuff. Tiny red spiders rush from the green petals and flow up your arms, like more of the spots the heat makes you see.

The professionals could earn up to six dollars a day. One toothless grandmother discouraged us all by making as much as anybody in the row and at the same time never getting out of her rocking chair except to drag it behind her from vine to vine. My father and mother each made over three dollars a day, but though I tried to work almost as long hours as they did, my pay at the end of the day would usually be somewhere between eighty and ninety cents.

Then one day in the second week of picking, when the hops were good and I stayed grimly sweating over my long gray sack hung on a child-sized frame, I knew that this was going to be the day. As the afternoon waned[13] and I added the figures on my weight tags over and over again in my head, I could feel the excitement begin to make spasms in my stomach. That night the man at the pay window handed me a silver dollar and three pennies. He must have seen that this was a day not for paper, but for silver. The big coin, so neatly and brightly stamped, was coolly distant from the blurred mélange[14] of piled vines and melting heat that had put it into my hand. Only its solid heaviness connected it in a businesslike way with the work it represented. For the first time in my life I truly comprehended the relationship between toil and media of exchange, and I saw how exacting and yet how satisfying were the terms of the world. Perhaps because of this insight, I did not want the significance of my dollar dimmed by the common touch of copper pettiness. I gave the vulgar pennies to my little sister, who was amazed but grateful. Then I felt even more grown-up than before, because not everybody my age was in a position to give pennies to kids.

That night I hardly slept, lying uncovered beside my sister on our mattress on the

---

10. Each *weighing tag* (WAY ing TAG) represented the amount picked. Each tag was worth a certain amount of money.
11. *Hops* (HAHPS) is the fruit of the hop plant, used for brewing beer.
12. An *aphid* (A fid) is a soft-bodied insect that sucks sap from the leaves and stem of various plants.
13. As the afternoon *waned* (WAIND), means the afternoon drew to a close.
14. The French word *mélange* (may LAHNZH) means simply a mixture.

ground, sticking my hand out under the bottom of the tent to lay it on the cooling earth between the clumps of dry grass. Tired as I was, I had written post cards to three people in North Dakota before going to bed. I had told my grandmother, my aunt, and my friend Doris that I had earned a dollar in one day. Then, because I did not want to sound impolitely proud of myself, and to fill up the card, I added on each one, "I'm fine and I plan to pick again tomorrow. How are you?"

I couldn't wait to get to the field the next day and earn another dollar. Back home none of my friends would have dreamed of being able to earn so much in one day. The only thing to do back there for money was to trap gophers[15] for the bounty; and even the big kids, who ran a fairly long trap line and had the nerve to cut the longest tails in half, couldn't make more than twenty cents on a good day, with tails at two cents apiece. I earned a dollar and forty cents the next day and the day after that, and at least a dollar every day for another week, until we moved to another place of picking—a pear orchard.

By that time it was September, and most of us children from the rows of tents stood out at the gateway of the camp and waited each day for the long yellow school bus. I had never seen a school bus before, and my sister and I were shy about how to act in such a grand vehicle. We sat together, holding our lunch buckets on our knees, looking out at the trees beside the roads, trying to catch a glimpse of our mother and father on the ladders.

The school had about three times as many pupils in it as there were people in the town back in North Dakota where we used to go to buy coal and groceries. The pupils who were planning to attend this school all year were separated from those who, like me, did not know how many days or weeks we would be in that one spot. In our special classes we did a great deal of drawing and saw a number of movies. School was so luxurious in comparison with the hard work I had done in North Dakota the previous year that I wrote another post card to Doris, telling her that we never had to do fractions and that we got colored construction paper to play with almost every day. I copied a picture of a donkey with such accuracy that my teacher thought I had traced it until she held the two to the window and saw that the lines were indisputably[16] my own. After that I got extra drawing periods and became very good at copying, which always elicited more praise than my few original compositions.

I was understandably sad when we left that school after two weeks and went to Wenatchee. For the first time, we were not in a regular camp. The previous year my father, recognizing that the crops had not brought in enough to get us through the winter, had taken the train to Wenatchee after the sparse harvest was in and picked apples for a man named Jim Baumann. Baumann wanted him back, so he let us pitch our tent on his land not far from his house. We made camp, and after supper Baumann came down to talk about the next day's arrangements. The school was not so large as the other one, and there was no school bus for us because we were only a half mile away from it. Baumann was shorthanded in the packing shed and needed my mother early in the morning. Besides, there was no reason why she should

---

15. A *gopher* (GO fur) is a small, burrowing, rat-like creature with a stout body and short tail.
16. The drawing was *indisputably* (IN diss PYOOT uh blee), or undeniably, her own.

Word Bank

elicited (ee LISS ih tid) *v.*: drew out or brought forth

have to take us to school, because he had a daughter in my grade who could walk with us and take us to our respective rooms.

"Why, isn't that lovely!" my mother exclaimed with unwonted[17] enthusiasm. "Now you'll have a nice little girl to play with right here and to be your friend at school."

Her excitement was rather remarkable, considering the dubious reaction she had had to everybody else I had played with since we started camping. It hadn't seemed to me that she had liked even the child who made me a pair of stilts and taught me to walk on them. Now here she was favorably predisposed[18] toward somebody I didn't even know. I agreed that it would be nice to have a nice little girl to play with.

The next morning my sister and I sat on the steps of the Baumanns' front porch, where Barbara's mother had told us to make ourselves at home, waiting for her to finish her breakfast. We had already been up so long that it seemed to me we must surely be late for school; I began picturing the humiliating tardy entrance into a roomful of strange faces.

Two of Barbara's friends came down the driveway to wait for her. They both wore the kind of plaid skirts I had been wondering if I could ask my mother about buying —after all, she *had* said all my dresses were too short this fall because of all the inches I'd grown in the summer. The two girls looked at us for a moment, then uncoiled shiny-handled jump ropes and commenced loudly shouting two different rhymes to accompany their jumping.

Barbara came out on the porch, greeted her friends with a disconcerting assurance, jumped down the steps past us, insinuated herself between them and clasped their hands. "I have to show these kids where the school is," she told them. Turning her head slightly she called, "Well, come if you're coming. We're going to be late." Swinging their arms together, they began to skip down the driveway.

A couple of times on the way to school they stopped and waited until we got near them; I yanked irritably on my little sis-

---
17. *Unwonted* (un WONE tid) *enthusiasm* is not the usual enthusiasm.
18. To be favorably *predisposed* (PREE diss POZED) toward somebody is to be favorably inclined or biased toward that person.

Word Bank

dubious (DOO bee iss) *adj.*: marked by doubt; questionable; inclined to doubt
disconcerting (DISS kun SURT ing) *adj.*: disturbing; unsettling; throw into confusion
assurance (uh SHUR intz) *n.*: a positive declaration intended to give confidence; freedom from doubt; self-confidence
insinuated (in SIN yoo ate id) *v.*: suggested or hinted; placed (herself) into a position between

ter's arm and thought about how her shorter legs had been holding me back ever since she was born. I always seemed to be the one who had to drag a little kid along.

The teacher kept me standing at her desk while she called the roll and started the class on a reading assignment. When she looked up at me, I got the irrational impression that I had already managed to do something wrong. She asked where I had come from and I said "North Dakota," thinking it would be simpler than trying to tell all the places I had been in the last three months. She gave me the last seat in a row behind a boy in dirty clothes. As she passed by him she made the faintest sound of exhalation,[19] as though she was ridding her nostrils of a disagreeable smell.

At recess a boy in a bright shirt and new cream-colored corduroy pants yelled "North Dakota, North Dakota" in a funny way as he ran past me to the ball field. The boy who sat ahead of me came up and said confidentially, "We been out all around here for two years. We come from Oklahoma. We're Okies.[20] That's what you are too, even if you didn't come from Oklahoma." I knew I could never be anything that sounded so crummy as "Okie," and I said so. "Oh, yeah!" he rejoined stiffly. I walked away before he could argue any more and went to find my sister, but the primary grades had recess at a different time, so I went and stood by the door until the period was over. That afternoon I stayed in my seat reading a history book, but the teacher, who seemed to want to go outdoors herself, said, "It's better for the room if everybody goes outside for recess." So I went out and stood around the fringes of two or three games and wondered what was funny about North Dakota. Somehow I had the feeling that it would hurt my mother if I asked her.

The last part of the day was given to a discussion period, when each of us who wanted to was given a chance to tell about an important day in his life. The important days of my classmates, all about having a part in a play or learning to ride a bike, seemed so pathetically juvenile that I was impelled[21] to speak. I stood at my seat and told about how before we had gone to the pear orchard, which was before we had come here, I had earned a dollar all in one day in the hop fields.

From two sides of the room Barbara's friends turned to send her looks which I intercepted but found inscrutable. I had been looking at her too, watching for her reaction. A boy near me poked another and whispered in mocking awe, "A whole dollar!"

The boy ahead of me jumped suddenly to his feet, banging his leg against the desk so hard that the entire row shook. "So what," he cried, "we just come from there, too, and I made more'n a buck and a half *every* day." He gave me a triumphant smile and sat down. Then I knew I hated that boy. That night I told my mother about how there was a mean boy just like those other mean boys at the camps and how the teacher *would* have to put me right behind him. "Well," she sighed, "just try not to pay any attention to him."

By the time I had found my sister after school, Barbara and her friends had gone. The next morning when we went to the big house she was gone, too.

---

19. Here, *exhalation* (EX huh LAY shun) is the act of breathing out after holding one's breath.
20. *Okies* (O keez) are farm workers who travel from farm to farm. The term originally referred only to workers from Oklahoma, but became a negative term for all migrant workers.
21. To be *impelled* (im PELD) is to be driven or forced to do something.

Word Bank

intercepted (IN ter SEPT id) *v.*: secretly listened to or recorded; took, seized, or halted
inscrutable (in SKROOT uh bul) *adj.*: mysterious; impossible to understand

After that, my sister and I walked together. Sometimes we would be close enough to hear Barbara's friends, who were always with her, laugh and call her "Bobby." I had never known any Barbaras before, and the name seemed full of unapproachable prestige and sophistication; it was the kind of name that could belong only to a girl who had as many dresses as Barbara Baumann had. At school, if I recited in class, she acted queerly self-conscious, as though she were responsible for me—the way I often felt around my sister when she said something silly to kids my age.

For various reasons I had that same embarrassed feeling of an enforced distasteful relationship with the boy who sat ahead of me. Once in a while somebody in the class would tease me about him or would say something about "the hop pickers." I was bitterly determined to dissociate myself from the boy, and whenever he turned around to talk to me I would pretend he was trying to copy my paper. I would put my hand over it while I kept my eyes glued to the desk and felt my face grow hot.

There were some things about the school I liked very much. We were allowed to use the library a great deal; and for the first time in my life I had access to numbers of books I hadn't already read. By reading at noon and recess I could finish a book at school every two days. I would also have a book at home that I would read in a couple of nights. One of the nice things about living in a tent was that there were hardly any household chores to do and I could read as much as I wanted.

Frosty mornings came with October, and my sister and I would try to dress under the quilts before we got up to eat our oatmeal. Leaves began to blow across the road, apples grew redder with each cold night, pickers hurried from tree to tree, filling the orchards with the soft thunder of hard round fruit rolling out of picking sacks into boxes, and packers worked faster and faster, trying to get the apples twisted up in fancy tissue and into boxes before they jammed up too thickly on the perpetually moving belts. After school my sister and I would go to the box shed behind the big house where Harry, Barbara's big brother, would be nailing boxes together for a nickel apiece. He was always glad to have company, and would let us stand at a respectful distance and watch him pound in nail after nail with two strokes—a tap to set it, then a mighty clout to send it in—three to an end, six to a side.

One afternoon, with the chill blue sky brilliant behind the orange and black cutouts on the windows, I was sitting at my desk dreamily drawing when the teacher called my name. She told me that she wanted me to take all my books out of my desk and take them to the front of the room. Then she told everybody in my row to pack up his books and move one seat back. My heart banged alarmingly up in my throat and I nearly gagged from the sudden acute sensations in my viscera.[22] In North Dakota such drastic action was taken only when an offender, after repeated warnings, had proved too incorrigible to sit anywhere except right in front of the teacher's desk. The fact that I had no idea of why I was now classified as such an incor-

---

22. The *viscera* (VISS ur uh) are a person's intestines.

> **Word Bank**
>
> **prestige** (press TEEZH) *n.*: reputation or influence arising from success
> **dissociate** (dih SO shee ate) *v.*: to draw apart from; disconnect; separate
> **access** (AK sess) *n.*: the ability or right to enter or use
> **acute** (uh KYOOT) *adj.*: sharp or severe in effect; intense
> **incorrigible** (in KOR ih juh bul) *adj.*: unruly; uncontrollable; bad beyond reform

rigible only augmented my anguish. While books, papers, and pencils fell to the floor and boys jostled each other in the aisle, I managed to sidle[23] numbly up to the front. I sat down in my new seat, trying not to notice how shamefully close it was to the big desk facing it, and I was careful not to raise my eyes higher than the vase of zinnias standing on the corner nearest me.

When school was out I hurried to find my sister and get out of the schoolyard before seeing anybody in my class. But Barbara and her friends had beaten us to the playground entrance and they seemed to be waiting for us. Barbara said, "So now you're in the A class." She sounded impressed.

"What's the A class?" I asked.

Everybody made superior yet faintly envious giggling sounds. "Well, why did you think the teacher moved you to the front of the room, dopey? Didn't you know you were in the C class before, way in the back of the room?"

Of course I hadn't known. The Wenatchee fifth grade was bigger than my whole school had been in North Dakota, and the idea of subdivisions within a grade had never occurred to me. The subdividing for the first marking period had been done before I came to the school, and I had never, in the six weeks I'd been there, talked to anyone long enough to find out about the A, B, and C classes.

I still could not understand why that had made such a difference to Barbara and her friends. I didn't yet know that it was disgraceful and dirty to be a transient laborer and ridiculous to be from North Dakota. I thought living in a tent was more fun than living in a house. I didn't know that we were gypsies, really (how that thought would have thrilled me then!), and that we were regarded with the suspicion felt by those who plant toward those who do not plant. It didn't occur to me that we were all looked upon as one more of the untrustworthy natural phenomena, drifting here and there like mists or winds, that farmers of certain crops are resentfully forced to rely on. I didn't know that I was the only child who had camped on the Baumanns' land ever to get out of the C class. I did not know that school administrators and civic leaders held conferences to talk about the problem of transient laborers.

I only knew that for two happy days I walked to school with Barbara and her friends, played hopscotch and jump rope with them at recess, and was even invited into the house for some ginger ale—an exotic drink I had never tasted before.

Then we took down our tent and packed it in the trailer with our mattresses and stove and drove on, because the last apples were picked and sorted and boxed and shipped to the people all over the world, whoever they were, who could afford to buy them in 1937. My teacher wrote a letter for me to take to my next school. In it, she told me, she had informed my next teacher that I should be put into the A class immediately. But there wasn't any A class in my room, the new teacher explained.

By then I was traveled enough to realize that it was another special class for transients. The teacher showed us movies almost every day.

---

23. To *sidle* (SYD il) is to walk with a sideways movement.

Word Bank

augmented (awg MEN tid) *v.*: enlarged in size, number, strength, or extent; increased

phenomena (feh NAHM ih nuh) *n.*: facts, occurrences, or circumstances that are observable; things that are remarkable or extraordinary

Studying the Selection

First Impressions

As a child, how did the narrator react to her treatment by the local residents?

How does the adult narrator now feel about attitudes toward migrant workers during the Depression?

✔ Quick Review

1. Why does the family sell their farm and move west?
2. Why does the family leave the island they move to?
3. What difference does the narrator note in regard to working on the family farm in North Dakota and working in Yakima Valley?
4. How does the narrator's relationship with Barbara Baumann change when the narrator is put in the A class?

In-depth Thinking

5. Reread the third paragraph of the story. ("And though we all could have imagined most of Montana well enough, how could any of us have imagined an end to the prairie's limitless sky and the giddy encroachments rising higher and higher against the sky that were the Rocky Mountains?") How does the narrator know this information? Is she speaking in her voice of 1937, or is she speaking from a different perspective?
6. Why was the narrator's mother so happy the narrator had a chance to walk to school with Barbara?
7. Why were the picker children called "Okies" if they were not from Oklahoma?
8. Why was the narrator uncomfortable around the transient picker boy seated in front of her? Who does she resemble when she is so embarrassed by him?

Drawing Conclusions

9. Why are the transient children put into classes separate from local children? How do the classes differ?
10. In *You Need to Go Upstairs*, Ally achieves independence when she goes upstairs alone. How is independence achieved in *Children of the Harvest*?

Focusing on the Memoir as Fiction

1. Discuss or rewrite the scene in which the teacher walks by the boy in the narrator's class, acting as if she has smelled something unpleasant. Use a **first-person viewpoint**, seen through the boy's eyes. How does the passage change?
2. Rewrite or discuss the scene in which the narrator tells her classmates about earning a dollar a day. Use the **author-omniscient viewpoint**. Focus on Barbara and her friends. What details can you provide that the narrator was unaware of?
3. Rewrite the passage where the narrator goes to the pay window on the day she first earns a dollar. Use an **author-omniscient** approach, allowing the reader to learn the thoughts of both the man at the window and the main character.

Creating and Writing

1. In order to avoid talking with the boy sitting in front of her, the narrator pretended he was trying to copy her work. What does her adult response to this situation tell us about the healing that comes with time?
2. Talk to someone at a bank—perhaps making an appointment first—about an FDIC Insured savings account. What is it? How did it come about? You should be able to get a pamphlet on the subject. Share your information with the class.
3. Interview relatives or acquaintances who lived through the Great Depression. What do they remember about those difficult economic times?

Blueprint for Reading

the Author

**Roald Dahl
(1916-1990)**

Roald Dahl's parents were Norwegian immigrants who settled in South Wales, where Dahl spent his childhood. As a boy, he derived enormous pleasure from listening to his grandmother's fascinating tales of giants, witches, and magic. His father died when Dahl was very young, and his mother subsequently struggled to provide for the family. He attended a series of boarding schools, where he experienced the cruelty of other children and the neglect of teachers and staff.

Following his graduation from high school, he took a job in Africa so that he could see the world. Both the short story, *The Wish*, and the nonfiction piece, *The Green Mamba*, come out of his sojourn there. Regarding his work for children, he is best known for the book, *Charlie and the Chocolate Factory*. Many of his stories have a quality of strangeness, and touch on human feelings and fears.

Background Bytes

It has been said that play is the work of children—and it is very important work, indeed. As part of this play, fantasy allows the child to relate to the surrounding world—a way of taking complicated and seemingly random facts and making some sort of patterned sense of them. Because play is key to the child's world, it is also the key used by others in understanding the child's fears and anxieties.

Play therapy is an important tool for psychologists working with children. When there are concerns about a child's inner world, one step is to observe the child at play. Which toys are selected? How are the toys used? How do the child's "characters" interact? Healthy play includes a wide range of behaviors, so we must be careful not to over-analyze!

Into *The Wish*

The Wish is a story of a boy who invents a challenge to determine whether he will get his desired birthday gift. As you read, ask yourself whether the story is about his wish, his personal test, or additional issues not stated clearly. Have you ever become involved in this sort of "challenge" (for example, walking on the pavement without stepping on the cracks)? Why does the boy continue the game, when he becomes terrified? What is real and what is unreal here? Is Dahl's protagonist too absorbed by the demons he imagines, or do we all have such powerful fantasies from time to time?

The Wish

Focusing on Third-Person Point of View

We have considered various perspectives in this section on point of view. *The Wish* is written in the **third-person**, using an omniscient (all-knowing) narrator. This narrator, however, *limits* himself to the boy's perspective. We meet only the boy in the story. It is as if he exists in a world without adults. In the final sentence, the boy's mother is mentioned, almost as an afterthought. She is remote, outside the boy's nightmare, looking for him in the wrong place.

Because we see the events through the boy's eyes, his perspective is absolutely reliable: He is the creator of this perilous world. Has he confused the real and unreal? Does he survive in the end? What can the reader know? Does it matter what is "real," if it is real to the boy? Dahl uses the boy's eyes, and the carpet of snakes comes alive.

Point of view is a powerful tool—it cannot be separated from the author's purpose. As you read, ask why Dahl didn't just write this in the first-person, since the story emerges from the boy's perspective. What does **third-person narration** add to the story? Keep in mind that this story borders on fantasy. The job of the fantasy writer is to make the unreal believable.

Word Bank

Gingerly: Have you ever tasted the spice, *ginger*? It is used to make gingersnaps—cookies flavored with ginger—gingerbread, ginger ale, ginger beer, as well as a variety of Asian dishes. Some of you may be familiar with the nursery story of the gingerbread man, who "runs as fast as he can." If you were to taste ginger, you might be sure it was the source of gingerly, because of its tingly taste. To do something gingerly, is to do it with great care or caution. One samples *ginger*, gingerly. But the two words have different roots. *Ginger* comes from *Zingiber*, a reedlike plant in Southeast Asia, where it is used for cooking and medicinal purposes. **Gingerly** comes from a Latin word meaning "gentle, gracious, or well-born."

banister	gingerly	intent	uncoiling
channel	gravely	tapestry	widish
compelled	instinctively	triumphantly	

The Wish

Roald Dahl

Under the palm of one hand the child became aware of the scab of an old cut on his kneecap. He bent forward to examine it closely. A scab was always a fascinating thing; it presented a special challenge he was never able to resist.

Yes, he thought, I will pick it off, even if it isn't ready, even if the middle of it sticks, even if it hurts like anything.

With a fingernail he began to explore cautiously around the edges of the scab. He got the nail underneath, and when he raised it, but ever so slightly, it suddenly came off, the whole hard brown scab came off beautifully, leaving an interesting little circle of smooth red skin.

Nice. Very nice indeed. He rubbed the circle and it didn't hurt. He picked up the scab, put it on his thigh, and flipped it with a finger so that it flew away and landed on the edge of the carpet, the enormous red and black and yellow carpet that stretched the whole length of the hall from the stairs on which he sat to the front door in the distance. A tremendous carpet. Bigger than the tennis lawn. Much bigger than that. He regarded it gravely, setting his eyes upon it with mild pleasure. He had never really noticed it before, but now, all of a sudden, the colors seemed to brighten mysteriously and spring out at him in a most dazzling way.

You see, he told himself, I know how it is. The red parts of the carpet are red-hot lumps of coal. What I must do is this: I must walk all the way along it to the front door without touching them. If I touch the red I will be burnt. As a matter of fact, I will be burnt up completely. And the black parts of the carpet...yes, the black parts are snakes, poisonous snakes, adders[1] mostly, and cobras,[2] thick like tree trunks round the middle, and if I touch one of *them*, I'll be bitten and I'll die before tea time.[3] And if I get across safely, without being burnt and without being bitten I will be given a puppy for my birthday tomorrow.

He got to his feet and climbed higher up the stairs to obtain a better view of this vast tapestry of color and death. Was it possible? Was there enough yellow? Yellow was the only color he was allowed to walk on. Could it be done? This was not a journey to be undertaken lightly: the risks were too great for that. The child's face—a fringe of white-gold hair, two large blue eyes, a small pointed chin—peered anxiously over the banisters. The yellow was a bit thin in places and there were one or two widish gaps, but it did seem to go all the way along to the other end. For someone who had only yesterday triumphantly traveled the whole length of the brick path from the stables to the summerhouse without touching the cracks, this carpet thing should not be too difficult. Except for the snakes. The mere thought of snakes sent a fine electricity of fear running like pins down the backs of his legs and under the soles of his feet.

He came slowly down the stairs and advanced to the edge of the carpet. He extended one small sandaled foot and placed it cautiously upon a patch of yellow. Then he brought the other foot up, and there was just enough room for him to stand with the two feet together. There! He had started! His bright oval face was curiously intent, a shade whiter perhaps than before, and he was holding his arms out sideways to assist his balance.

---

1. *Adders* (ADD ers) are common European vipers. A *viper* is a poisonous snake with a pair of hollow fangs.
2. *Cobras* (KOH bruhs) are poisonous snakes, found especially in India and Africa, that have the ability to flatten their necks into a hood.
3. *Tea time* is the late-afternoon time at which tea and assorted cakes are served in Britain and in countries that were part of the British Commonwealth of Nations.

Word Bank

gravely (GRAYV lee) *adv.*: seriously or solemnly

tapestry (TAP iss tree) *n.*: a woven, ornamental fabric

banister (BAN iss tur) *n.*: a handrail and its supporting posts, especially on a staircase

widish (WYD ish) *adj.*: rather wide; tending to be wide

triumphantly (try UMF ant lee) *adv.*: successfully; victoriously

intent (in TENT) *adj.*: firmly or steadfastly fixed or directed; having the attention sharply focused on something

He took another step, lifting his foot high over a patch of black, aiming carefully with his toe for a narrow channel of yellow on the other side. When he had completed the second step he paused to rest, standing very stiff and still. The narrow channel of yellow ran forward unbroken for at least five yards and he advanced gingerly along it, bit by bit, as though walking a tightrope. Where it finally curled[4] off sideways, he had to take another long stride, this time over a vicious looking mixture of black and red. Halfway across he began to wobble. He waved his arms around wildly, windmill fashion,[5] to keep his balance, and he got across safely and rested again on the other side. He was quite breathless now, and so tense he stood high on his toes all the time, arms out sideways, fists clenched. He was on a big safe island of yellow. There was lots of room on it—he couldn't possibly fall off—and he stood there resting, hesitating, wishing he could stay forever on this big safe yellow island. But the fear of not getting the puppy compelled him to go on.

Step by step, he edged further ahead, and between each one he paused to decide exactly where next he should put his foot. Once, he had a choice of ways, either to left or right, and he chose the left because although it seemed the more difficult, there was not so much black in that direction. The black was what made him nervous. He glanced quickly over his shoulder to see how far he had come. Nearly halfway. There could be no turning back now. He was in the middle and he couldn't turn back and he couldn't jump off sideways either because it was too far, and when he looked at all the red and all the black that lay ahead of him, he felt that old sudden sickening surge of panic in his chest—like last holiday time, that afternoon when he got lost all alone in the darkest part of Piper's Wood.

He took another step, placing his foot carefully upon the only little piece of yel-

---

4. *Curled* (KURLD) means it moved and progressed in a curving direction or path.
5. He waved his arms *windmill fashion* means that he stuck his arms straight out to the side and rotated them like propeller blades in the air, to keep his balance.

Word Bank

channel (CHAN nul) *n.*: a navigable route between two bodies of water; a waterway; a route along which anything passes
gingerly (JINJ er lee) *adv.*: with great care or caution; warily
compelled (kom PELD) *v.*: forced or driven to a course of action

low within reach, and this time the point of the foot came within a centimeter[6] of some black. It wasn't touching the black, he could see it wasn't touching, he could see the small line of yellow separating the toe of his sandal from the black; but the snake stirred as though sensing the nearness, and raised its head and gazed at the foot with bright beady eyes, watching to see if it was going to touch.

"I'm not touching you! You mustn't bite me! You know I'm not touching you!"

Another snake slid up noiselessly beside the first, raised its head, two heads now, two pairs of eyes staring at the foot, gazing at a little place just below the sandal strap where the skin showed through. The child went high up on his toes and stayed there, frozen stiff with terror. It was minutes before he dared to move again.

The next step would have to be a really long one. There was this deep curling river of black that ran clear across the width of the carpet, and he was forced by his position to cross it at its widest part. He thought first of trying to jump it, but decided he couldn't be sure of landing accurately on the narrow band of yellow on the other side. He took a deep breath, lifted one foot, and inch by inch he pushed it out in front of him, far far out, then down and down until at last the tip of his sandal was across and resting safely on the edge of the yellow. He leaned forward, transferring his weight to this front foot. Then he tried to bring the back foot up as well. He strained and pulled and jerked his body, but the legs were too wide apart and he couldn't make it. He tried to get back again. He couldn't do that either. He was doing the splits[7] and he was properly stuck. He glanced down and saw this deep curling river of black underneath him. Parts of it were stirring now, and uncoiling and sliding and beginning to shine with a dreadful oily glister.[8] He wobbled, waved his arms frantically to keep his balance, but that seemed to make it worse. He was starting to go over. He was going over to the right, quite slowly he was going over, then faster and faster, and at the last moment, instinctively he put out a hand to break the fall and the next thing he saw was this bare hand of his going right into the middle of a great glistening mass of black and he gave one piercing cry of terror as it touched.

Outside in the sunshine, far away behind the house, the mother was looking for her son.

---

6. In the metric system, a *centimeter* (SENT ih MEE ter) is a unit of measurement equal to one-hundredth of a meter. About 2.5 centimeters equal an inch.
7. Doing the *splits* refers to the physical feat of separating the legs and keeping them straight while sinking to the floor, until they extend at right angles to the body.
8. *Glister* (GLISS ter) refers to the shine of a snake's skin exposed to the light.

Word Bank

uncoiling (un KOY ling) *v.*: unwinding from a spiral
instinctively (in STINKT iv lee) *adv.*: arising from a natural or inborn impulse, inclination, or tendency

Studying the Selection

First Impressions

What do you think really happens at the end of the story? Why is his mother mentioned in the last line?

✔ Quick Review

1. What is the first challenge the little boy encounters?
2. What does the boy say will happen if he gets across the carpet without touching the red and black parts?
3. At one point the boy has "a choice of ways" along the carpet. Why does he choose the more difficult way?
4. When had the boy felt "that old sudden sickening surge of panic" before?

In-depth Thinking

5. At the beginning of the story Dahl describes, in lengthy detail, the boy's scab. Why does he spend so much time on this seemingly insignificant detail?
6. Think about the contrast between these two phrases: "if I touch one of *them*, I'll be bitten and I'll die before tea time" and "If I get across safely…I will be given a puppy for my birthday tomorrow." What does this reveal about the little boy? How does it lay the groundwork for the plot?
7. The boy compares this panic to the time he was lost "…all alone in the darkest part of Piper's Wood." How might his past affect his present actions?
8. We are never told the boy's age in this story. How old do you think he is? Supply details from the story to support your answer.

Drawing Conclusions

9. At what point in the story does the game become fantastic? How do we know it's not, after all, real?
10. Dahl describes the journey across the carpet in detail. His 'realism' creates tension in the story. What is gained by using the boy's perspective?

Focusing on Third-Person Point of View

1. Change the point of view in *The Wish* to see how the switch affects a story. Either tell the story in the first-person (the "I" voice) from the boy's perspective, or use an *objective* third-person voice, describing actions without the character's thoughts. Dialogue becomes more important with the objective, third-person voice. Think about

other characters who might be part of the boy's life. We know he has a mother, but he might also have a father, siblings, grandparents, or a nanny close to him. Relate this incident through one of their perspectives, using either first- or third-person narration. What does the new version bring to the story? How does it detract from it?

2. Review three other stories you have read. In each, identify the point of view. For example: One story might use a first-person viewpoint showing us the main character's perspective. One might use an omniscient third-person viewpoint to relate the thoughts and feelings of many characters. In another an objective third-person viewpoint relates only action and dialogue. Now take one of your three stories and change the point of view. Discuss how the tone and meaning of the story change with this other perspective.

3. Ask your teacher or librarian to recommend a good, short fantasy. After reading the story, write about it. Did you feel involved in the action? Why? Even if the events were not realistic, were they believable—did they make sense in terms of the plot and characters? If so, what made them believable? What was your favorite part of the story? Discuss why you particularly liked this part.

Creating and Writing

1. The boy in *The Wish* has an extremely active imagination. Think back to your own childhood. Did you ever have an "imagination game" that came to seem real? Did you play this game alone or with others? What was exciting about this game? In a brief essay, describe it. If you don't remember such a game, try to invent one.

2. Sometimes a traumatic incident can result in unreasonable fears. In *The Wish*, the little boy was once lost in the woods, perhaps increasing his fear of snakes or influencing his imaginative play. In a poem or story, create a persona or character that has survived a traumatic experience. Put this person in a situation reflecting a reaction to the past experience. Use Dahl's technique of only briefly mentioning the past, just hinting at its influence on the present. Let the character's actions *show* the influence.

3. Look for an opportunity to be around small children. Perhaps you have younger brothers or sisters, young neighbors, or you can baby-sit. If not, arrange to visit an after-school program or a day-care facility. Sit quietly, and observe the children at play. What games do they play, and how involved are they? What can you discover about children by observing the roles they play and how absorbed they are? After you've observed long enough to report your findings to your class, spend some active time with the children. Thank them for your visit by reading them a story or playing a game with them.

Using your research, present an oral report comparing the activities of *these* children and the activity of the little boy in *The Wish*.

Blueprint for Reading

Background Bytes

Often we think a story is just that—a story. But when the author deals with beliefs and values, we are permitted to wonder how much is personal history. Keep this in mind as you read *The Finish of Patsy Barnes*.

Paul Laurence Dunbar was born in 1872 to Matilda and Joshua Dunbar, both former slaves. Matilda took in washing to keep food on the table. Paul and his two half-brothers did odd jobs to supplement the family income. Although they were poor, Matilda instilled in her sons a love of songs, poetry, and storytelling as well as the desire to achieve.

Dunbar was, indeed, an achiever, the only black student at Dayton's Central High School. Yet, because of discrimination, he had to work as an elevator boy after graduation. Still he added to his wages by writing for various national newspapers and magazines.

Eventually Dunbar became a renowned poet and author, writing about his fellow black Americans. Some works were written in Southern dialect, reflecting his mother's storytelling influence. Others were written in standard English.

By the time of his death in 1906, Dunbar was well-recognized by critics and writers. He was a major influence on the Harlem Renaissance, the high point of black writing and culture in New York City during the 1920s and 1930s. Dunbar's life, in aiming for equality and respect, is symbolic of the struggle for racial equality in the United States in the 20th century.

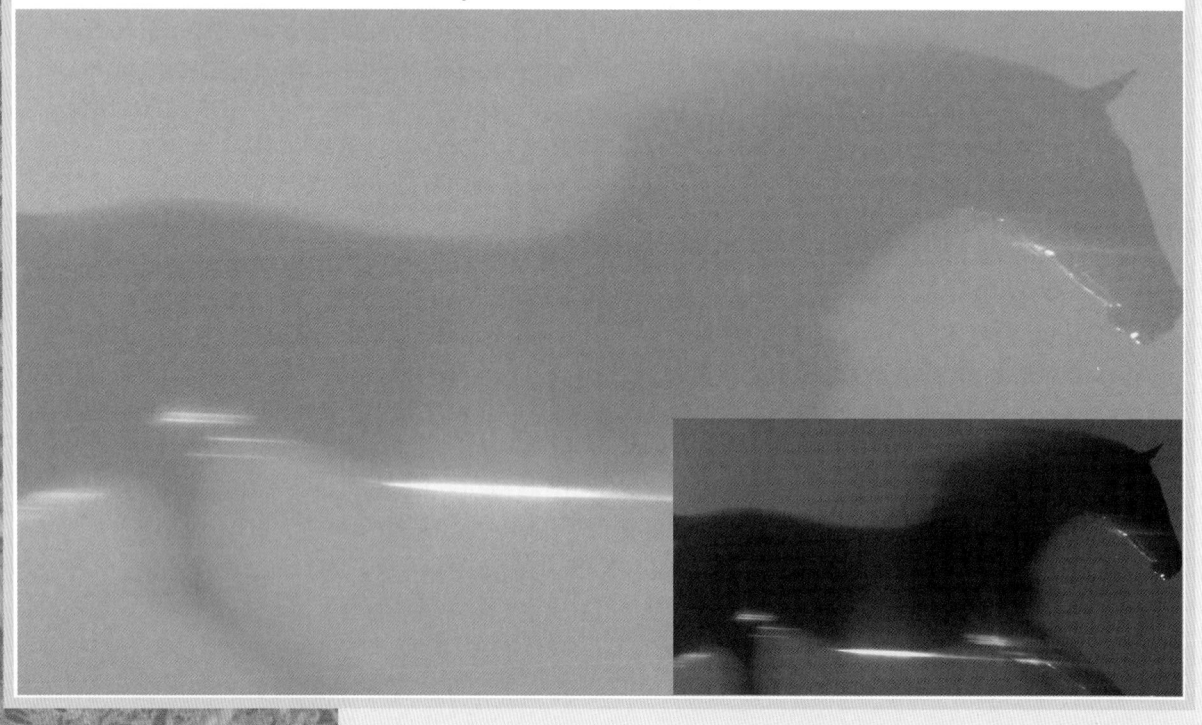

The Finish of Patsy Barnes

Into *The Finish of Patsy Barnes*

Life is often difficult. But Patsy Barnes seems to have more troubles than most. Perhaps an adult could deal with these problems, but Patsy is only fourteen years old. How does he view life? Is he an optimist or pessimist? What motivates him to overcome obstacles?

In looking for the **theme** of a story, think about why it was written. It may have had an intriguing plot, great characters, a conflict, climax, and resolution, but its meaning is derived from its theme. The theme of a story is what settles deeply into the reader.

A theme is seldom stated as such, rather, it remains to be uncovered. If you don't grasp the idea of theme, consider the fable, *The Tortoise and the Hare*. The slow Tortoise wins the race, because he is persistent. The Hare loses, because he is too confident. The subject of the fable is a race. The moral, or theme, which in this case is actually given at the end, is "slow and steady wins the race." In modern fiction, a theme is not so obvious and is not often stated at the end. Still, a careful reader should be able to uncover a story's theme by just letting the story settle within and just thinking about one's own reaction to it.

With this in mind, what is the theme of *The Finish of Patsy Barnes*? How did you figure it out? List the phrases or sentences supporting your opinion.

Focusing on the Aspects of Theme

The theme of the story is reinforced by other literary devices. One such device is **motif**, the careful placement of supporting ideas. Here are some of those ideas:

- ◇ "A man goes where he is appreciated."
- ◇ "For a single moment Patsy thinks of the sick woman at home…."
- ◇ "When Patsy told his story, it was Eliza's pride that started her on the road to recovery…."

What ideas are presented here? Do they support the theme of the story?

In the section on **Point of View** we discussed the various voices a writer can use. Here again we look at **viewpoint**—as it relates to theme. **Viewpoint** is where the author stands, in relation to the characters, as they act out the story for the reader. Generally, two points of view are options: the **first-person** and the **third-person**. The first-person point of view lets the reader see, hear, and know what the *narra-*

tor sees, hears, and knows. This kind of narration provides a sense of closeness. The reader experiences the drama as it happens to one of the participants.

In the third-person narrative, the all-knowing author stands outside the story, knowing all that has happened, is happening, and will happen. The advantage of using this approach is its unlimited scope; the disadvantage is the extra distance from the reader. Don't confuse the voice of the all-knowing narrator with an individual viewpoint of a character. In other words, the statements below are not observed facts but are judgments on events seen from a character's point of view.

> "It was with a king's pride that Patsy marched home with his first considerable earnings. Eliza was inordinately proud, and it was this pride that gave her strength…."

> "When Patsy told his story, it was Eliza's pride that started her on the road to recovery."

From whose point of view are these statements made? Why do you think this is done?

The literary component of **characterization** plays a basic role in this story. Patsy is incorrigible, cheerful, adventurous, stubborn, honest, and forthright. He shows these traits in taking a "heroic resolution to make the best of what he had" in order to care for his mother. Again, characterization shows us the triumph over adversity. Had Patsy been less positive, less confident in his abilities, we would have a different story—and theme.

Finally, *The Finish of Patsy Barnes* is written in a rather old-fashioned style. Note such lines as "but she [Eliza] never murmured, for she loved the boy with a deep affection" and "her complainings were loud in the land." This style adds to the *mood* of the story, one given to exaggerated emotions, one likely to arouse pity in the reader. This intense prose adds an additional emotional level, making the resolution of *The Finish of Patsy Barnes* that much more dramatic.

Word Bank

What is the difference between a *citizen* and a **denizen**? A **denizen** typically means "a resident or inhabitant," and comes from a Latin word that means *within*. Denizens can also be animals—mammals, reptiles, and fish, for example. Have you ever heard the expression, *denizens of the deep*? It is used to describe the creatures of the ocean. A *citizen* is a member of a state or nation; a citizen has obligations and privileges. *Citizen* comes from the word *city*.

The Finish of Patsy Barnes

Paul Laurence Dunbar

His name was Patsy Barnes, and he was a denizen[1] of Little Africa. In fact, he lived on Douglass Street. By all the laws governing the relations between people and their names, he should have been Irish—but he was not. He was black, and very much so. That was the reason he lived on Douglass Street. The Negro has very strong within him the instinct of colonization, and it was in accordance with this that Patsy's mother had found her way to Little Africa when she had come North from Kentucky.

Patsy was incorrigible.[2] Even into the confines of Little Africa had penetrated the truant officer and the terrible penalty of the compulsory education law. Time and time again had poor Eliza Barnes been brought up on account of the shortcomings of that son of hers. She was a hard-working, honest woman, and day by day bent over her tub, scrubbing away to keep Patsy in shoes and jackets that would wear out so much faster than they could be bought. But she never murmured, for she loved the boy with a deep affection, though his misdeeds were a sore thorn in her side.

She wanted him to go to school. She wanted him to learn. She had the notion that he might become something better, something higher than she had been. But for him school had no charms; his school was the cool stalls in the big livery stable[3] near at hand; the arena of his pursuits, its sawdust floor; the height of his ambition, to be a horseman. Either here or in the racing

---

1. A *denizen* (DEN ih zin) is an inhabitant or resident of an area.
2. Here *incorrigible* (en KOR ih jih bul) means unruly and uncontrollable.
3. A *livery stable* (LIV er ee STAY bul) is a place where horses and vehicles are cared for or rented out.

stables at the fair grounds he spent his truant hours. It was a school that taught much, and Patsy was as apt a pupil as he was a constant attendant. He learned strange things about horses, and fine, sonorous[4] oaths that sounded eerie on his young lips, for he had only turned into his fourteenth year.

A man goes where he is appreciated; then could this slim black boy be blamed for doing the same thing? He was a great favorite with the horsemen, and picked up many a dime or nickel for dancing or singing, or even a quarter for warming up a horse for its owner. He was not to be blamed for this, for, first of all, he was born in Kentucky, and had spent the very days of his infancy about the paddocks[5] near Lexington, where his father had sacrificed his life on account of his love for horses. The little fellow had shed silent tears when he looked at his father's bleeding body, bruised and broken by the fiery young two-year-old he was trying to subdue. Patsy did not sob aloud or whimper, though his heart ached, for over all the feeling of his grief was a mad, burning desire to ride that horse.

His tears were shed anew, when, actuated[6] by the idea that times would be easier up North, they moved to Dalesford. Then, when he learned that he must leave his old friends, the horses and their masters, whom he had known, he wept. The comparatively meager appointments of the fair grounds at Dalesford proved a poor compensation for all these. For the first few weeks Patsy had dreams of running away—back to Kentucky and horses and stables. Then after a while he settled himself with heroic resolution to make the best of what he had, and with a mighty effort took up the burden of life away from his beloved home.

Eliza Barnes, older and more experienced though she was, took up her burden with a less cheerful philosophy than her son. She worked hard, and made a scanty livelihood, it is true, but she did not make the best of what she had. Her complainings were loud in the land, and her wailings for her old home smote the ears of any who would listen to her.

They had been living in Dalesford for a year nearly, when hard work and exposure brought the woman down to bed with pneumonia. They were very poor—too poor even to call in a doctor, so there was nothing to do but to call in the city physician. Now this medical man had too frequent calls into Little Africa, and he did not like to go there. So he was very gruff when any of its denizens called him, and it was even said that he was careless of his patients.

Patsy's heart bled as he heard the doctor talking to his mother:

"Now, there can't be any foolishness about this," he said. "You've got to stay in bed and not get yourself damp."

"How long you think I got to lay hyeah, doctah?" she asked.

"I'm a doctor, not a fortuneteller," was the reply. "You'll lie there as long as the disease holds you."

"But I can't lay hyeah long, doctah, case I ain't got nuffin' to go on."

"Well, take your choice: the bed or the boneyard."

Eliza began to cry.

"You needn't sniffle," said the doctor; "I don't see what you people want to come up here for anyhow. Why don't you stay down South where you belong? You come up here and you're just a burden and a trouble to the city. The South deals with all of you better, both in poverty and crime." He knew that

---

4. *Sonorous* (SAHN ur iss) oaths are loud and full in sound.
5. *Paddocks* (PAD iks) are the enclosures where horses are saddled and mounted before a race.
6. *Actuated* (AK choo AYT id) means started.

these people did not understand him, but he wanted an outlet for the heat within him.

There was another angry being in the room, and that was Patsy. His eyes were full of tears that scorched him and would not fall. Oh! to have a stone—to be across the street from that man!

When the physician walked out, Patsy went to the bed, took his mother's hand, and bent over shamefacedly to kiss her. He did not know that with that act he blotted out many a curious flaw of his.

The little mark of affection comforted Eliza unspeakably. The mother-feeling overwhelmed her in one burst of tears. Then she dried her eyes and smiled at him.

"Honey," she said; "mammy ain' gwine lay hyeah long. She be all right putty soon."

"Nevah you min'," said Patsy with a choke in his voice. "I can do somep'n', an' we'll have anothah doctah."

"La, listen at de chile; what kin you do?"

"I'm goin' down to McCarthy's stable and see if I kin git some horses to exercise."

A sad look came into Eliza's eyes as she said: "You'd bettah not go, Patsy; dem hosses'll kill you yit, des lak dey did yo' pappy."

But the boy, used to doing pretty much as he pleased, was obdurate,[7] and even while she was talking, put on his ragged jacket and left the room.

Patsy was not wise enough to be diplomatic. He went right to the point with McCarthy, the liveryman.[8]

The big red-faced fellow slapped him until he spun round and round. Then he said, "Ye little devil, ye, I've a mind to knock the whole head off o' ye. Ye want harses to exercise, do ye? Well git on that 'un, an' see what ye kin do with him."

The boy's honest desire to be helpful had tickled the big, generous Irishman's peculiar sense of humor, and from now on, instead of giving Patsy a horse to ride now and then as he had formerly done, he put into his charge all the animals that needed exercise.

It was with a king's pride that Patsy marched home with his first considerable earnings.

They were small yet, and would go for food rather than a doctor, but Eliza was inordinately[9] proud, and it was this pride that gave her strength and the desire of life to carry her through the days approaching the crisis of her disease.

As Patsy saw his mother growing worse, saw her gasping for breath, heard the rattling as she drew in the little air that kept going through her clogged lungs, felt the heat of her burning hands, and saw the pitiful appeal in her poor eyes, he became convinced that the city doctor was not helping her. She must have another. But the money? That afternoon, after his work with McCarthy, found him at the fair grounds. The spring races were on, and he thought he might get a job warming up the horse of some independent jockey. He hung around the stables, listening to the talk of men he knew and some he had never seen before. Among the latter was a tall, lanky man, holding forth to a group of men.

"No, suh," he was saying to them generally, "I'm goin' to withdraw my hoss, because thaih ain't nobody to ride him as he ought to be rode. I haven't brought a jockey along with me, so I've got to depend on pickups. Now, the talent's set against my hoss, Black Boy, because he's been losin' regular, but that hoss has lost for the want of ridin',

---

7. To be *obdurate* (AHB doo rit) is to be stubborn or unyielding.
8. The *liveryman* (LIV er ee MAN) is the owner or employee of a livery stable.
9. When one is *inordinately* (in OR din it lee) proud one is expressing uncontrolled feelings and emotions.

that's all."

The crowd looked in at the slim-legged, raw-boned horse, and walked away laughing.

"The fools!" muttered the stranger. "If I could ride myself I'd show 'em!"

Patsy was gazing into the stall at the horse.

"What are you doing thaih?" called the owner to him.

"Look hyeah, mistah," said Patsy, "ain't that a bluegrass hoss?"

"Of co'se it is, an' one o' the fastest that evah grazed."

"I'll ride that hoss, mistah."

"What do you know 'bout ridin'?"

"I used to gin'ally be' roun' Mistah Boone's paddock in Lexington, an'—"

"Aroun' Boone's paddock—what! Look here, little boy, if you can ride that hoss to a winnin' I'll give you more money than you ever seen before."

"I'll ride him."

Patsy's heart was beating very wildly beneath his jacket. That horse. He knew that glossy coat. He knew that raw-boned frame and those flashing nostrils. That black horse owed something to the orphan he had made.

The horse was to run in the race before the last. Somehow out of odds and ends, his owner scraped together a suit and colors for Patsy. The colors were maroon and green, a curious combination. But then it was a curious horse, a curious rider, and a more curious combination that brought the two together.

Long before the time for the race Patsy went into the stall to become better acquainted with his horse. The animal turned its wild eyes upon him and neighed. He patted the long, slender head, and grinned as the horse stepped aside as gently as a lady.

"He sholy is full o' ginger," he said to the owner, whose name he had found to be Brackett.

"He'll show 'em a thing or two," laughed Brackett.

"His mother was a fast one," said Patsy, unconsciously.

Brackett whirled on him in a flash. "What do you know about his mother?" he asked.

The boy would have retracted,[10] but it was too late. Stammeringly he told the story of his father's death and the horse's connection therewith.

"Well," said Brackett, "if you don't turn out a nothin', you're a winner, sure. But I'll be—if this don't sound like a story! But I've heard that story before. The man I got Black Boy from, no matter how I got him, told it to me."

When the bell sounded and Patsy went out to warm up, he felt as if he were riding on air. Some of the jockeys laughed at his getup, but there was something in him—or under him, maybe—that made him scorn their derision.[11] He saw a sea of faces about him, then saw no more. Only a shining white track loomed ahead of him, and a restless steed was cantering[12] with him around the curve. Then the bell called him back to the stand.

They did not get away at first, and back they trooped. A second trial was a failure. But at the third they were off in a line as straight as a chalk mark. There were Essex and Firefly, Queen Bess and Mosquito, galloping away side by side, and Black Boy a neck ahead. Patsy knew the family reputation of his horse for endurance as well as fire, and began riding the race from the first.

---

10. To have *retracted* (ree TRAKT id) a statement means to take it back as if it were not said in the first place.
11. *Derision* (dih RIZH in) means mocking or ridicule; to laugh at someone or something.
12. *Cantering* (KAN ter ing) means riding at an easy gallop.

Black Boy came of blood that would not be passed, and to this his rider trusted. At the eighth the line was hardly broken, but as the quarter was reached Black Boy had forged a length ahead, and Mosquito was at his flank. Then, like a flash, Essex shot out ahead under whip and spur, his jockey standing straight in the stirrups.

The crowd in the stand screamed; but Patsy smiled as he lay low over his horse's neck. He saw that Essex had made his best spurt. His only fear was for Mosquito, who hugged and hugged his flank. They were nearing the three-quarter post, and he was tightening his grip on the black. Essex fell back; his spurt was over. The whip fell unheeded on his sides. The spurs dug him in vain.

Black Boy's breath touches the leader's ear. They are neck and neck—nose to nose. The black stallion passes him.

Another cheer from the stand, and again Patsy smiles as they turn into the stretch. Mosquito has gained a head. The black boy flashes one glance at the horse and rider who are so surely gaining upon him, and his lips close in a grim line. They are half-way down the stretch, and Mosquito's head is at the stallion's neck.

For a single moment Patsy thinks of the sick woman at home and what that race will mean to her, and then his knees close against the horse's sides with a firmer dig. The spurs shoot deeper into the steaming flanks. Black Boy shall win; he must win. The horse that has taken away his father shall give him back his mother. The stallion leaps away like a flash, and goes under the wire—a length ahead.

Then the band thundered, and Patsy was off his horse, very warm and very happy, following his mount to the stable. There, a little later, Brackett found him. He rushed to him, and flung his arms around him.

"You little imp," he cried, "you rode like you were kin to that hoss! We've won! We've won!" And he began sticking banknotes at the boy. At first Patsy's eyes bulged, and then he seized the money and got into his clothes.

"Goin' out to spend it?" asked Brackett.

"I'm goin' for a doctah fu' my mother," said Patsy, "she's sick."

"Don't let me lose sight of you."

"Oh, I'll see you again. So long," said the boy.

An hour later he walked into his mother's room with a very big doctor, the greatest the druggist could direct him to. The doctor left his medicines and his orders, but, when Patsy told his story, it was Eliza's pride that started her on the road to recovery. Patsy did not tell his horse's name.

Studying the Selection

First Impressions

What is the theme of *The Finish of Patsy Barnes*? Share your opinion with the class. Find passages in the story to support your conclusions.

✔ Quick Review

1. Name (a) Patsy's mother; (b) the horse that Patsy rides; (c) the horse's owner.
2. Why did Patsy and Eliza move from Kentucky to Dalesford?
3. What is Eliza's illness called?
4. How is Patsy able to provide a good doctor for Eliza?

In-depth Thinking

5. Compare the attitudes of Patsy and Eliza as they settled in Dalesford. How do they differ in their philosophy and outlook on life?
6. We are told the city physician did not like to go to Little Africa. Why? Is he prejudiced?
7. Does the name of the horse—"Black Boy"—have any significance?
8. What is meant when Brackett says to Patsy, " 'You rode like you were kin to that hoss!' "?

Drawing Conclusions

9. Why do you feel the story ends with the sentence "Patsy did not tell his horse's name"?
10. Is there more than one meaning to *The Finish of Patsy Barnes*? In other words, does the title mean more than a first-place finish with Black Boy? List various possibilities.

Focusing on the Aspects of Theme

Life can be rich and rewarding when an individual strives to live a life of strength and joy. Patsy Barnes was triumphant in his horse race, able to afford the best medical care he could find for his mother. The following three exercises focus on the theme of triumph over adversity, on the theme of "finishing the race."

1. Look in magazines and other publications provided by your teacher to find stories about ordinary people triumphing over adversity. Consider such topics as the triumph over poverty, disability, or discrimination. Then make a class presentation, telling why these people are so inspiring. Present your material in the form of an oral short story.
2. Read about Paul Laurence Dunbar or another member of a minority group who succeeded. Write a report about this person's struggles to achieve in an America that so often discriminated against members of minority groups.
3. Read about early job opportunities in America. Why did so many young children go to work instead of school? Did government authorities try to keep children in school? Make a class presentation describing a day in the life of one of these young workers.

Creating and Writing

1. The United States has often been called 'a melting pot'—a kettle accepting many nationalities, boiling away their unique cultures and customs, to combine them into a single form—Americans. Now some scholars want the United States to call itself a tapestry—a weaving together of different colors and textures. These will remain distinct, forming a work of art from the different languages, traditions, and religions. Which term appeals to you as a description of Americans? Write an essay explaining your views. In addition, you might include a drawing that illustrates the point you are making.
2. Write about an obstacle you have overcome, or are overcoming—or ask a family member to be the subject of your essay. Consider reading it to the class.
3. Volunteer at a local community service center, by yourself or with your class. Write a report about your experiences with the people being served.

Blueprint for Reading

the Author

Edward Everett Hale (1822-1901)

Edward Everett Hale wrote *The Man Without a Country* in 1863. Already known as a writer and clergyman before the Civil War, he vigorously opposed slavery. Hale is thought to have written the story of Philip Nolan to encourage Unionists. He later served as chaplain of the U.S. Senate (1903-1909). Hale died in 1909, having witnessed his beloved country grow from twenty to forty-eight states.

Background Bytes

In *The Man Without a Country*, the fictional character Philip Nolan receives his sentence in 1807. For the rest of his life, he will never hear the name "the United States" or set foot on her shores. By the time he dies in 1863, he has missed fifty-six years of American growth and prosperity, not to mention friends and family.

In 1807, the United States was less than thirty years old and had twenty states. By 1863, when Nolan died, there were thirty-four states, with twenty-three million people. Two wars had been fought—The War of 1812 and the Mexican-American War—and the country was locked in a fierce struggle between Union and Confederate forces. (Although the South had seceded from the Union by that time, President Lincoln refused to remove any stars from the flag.) The farmlands of the South and the Midwest were producing huge crops, and the Middle Atlantic and New England states were centers of manufacturing, trade, and finance. Principal products of the Eastern Seaboard were woolen goods, leather, clothing, textiles, lumber, and machinery.

To distribute these goods throughout the world, shipping vessels crossed the seas, proudly displaying the Stars and Stripes. During these exciting days of commerce and adventure, Philip Nolan sat alone in his quarters, exiled from the United States and unaware of her tremendous growth.

The Man Without a Country

Into *The Man Without a Country*

Have you heard the expression "write about what you know"? In the case of Edward Everett Hale, that adage should read "write about what you *love*." Hale obviously loved the United States, and his story imagines the tragic life of a man who would be forced to forsake his homeland. It is a salute to patriotism.

The name of the protagonist and the title of the story further the theme. Why? Look closely at the name "Nolan." Why is that name relevant to the story? Why would Nolan be "*the* man without a country" as opposed to "*a* man without a country"?

Sometimes the theme of a story is **implicit**, meaning that the theme is not readily apparent. Such themes can be detected only after thoughtful reading. However, the theme is quite obvious in *The Man Without a Country*. What is that theme? How did the story make you feel? How would you feel if you had no homeland to call your own?

The Man Without a Country is certainly a patriotic tale, but today it also seems to ask, "What *is* patriotism?" In a time when flag burning is considered freedom of expression, is *The Man Without a Country* too old-fashioned? Can an American disagree with a government policy or policies and *still* be considered patriotic?

Focusing on Theme: A Frame Story

The Man Without a Country consists of a series of supposedly factual episodes. The narrator states he spent only a short period of time in Nolan's company. He provides 'authenticity' by consulting documents, letters, and acquaintances of Nolan to complete the tale. This makes *The Man Without a Country* a **frame story**—a story fleshed out by the conversations and letters within. Even the narrator, from whose viewpoint the story is told, is not named until he receives a letter from a fellow officer late in the story.

In writing this piece, Hale used a **limited omniscient viewpoint**, focusing on the thoughts, feelings, and actions of one character alone—Philip Nolan. However, he also reveals his own attitude toward that main character. He is sympathetic, which contributes greatly to the tragic mood of the story. Count how many times in the first four paragraphs the narrator uses the adjective *poor* to describe the main character. Note adjectives and phrases throughout the story that make you feel sorry for Nolan. List the many ways he is shown to be a kind, wise man. Finally, identify significant events in the story that illustrate how great was the treasure Nolan lost—his own country!

Word Bank

Courts-martial: Footnote 6 highlights the appropriate way to make many compound, hyphenated words plural. Although it may sound strange to our ears, in the word **courts-martial**, *courts* is the noun that needs to be plural; *martial* is just the verb. For the most part, in such compound expressions, it is the noun that takes the **s**. The chief law officer of the United States is the *attorney general*. If there were more than one, the correct form would be *attorneys general*. Here, *attorney* is the noun and *general* is just an adjective. Two more examples are *teaspoonsful* and *mothers-in-law*. Can you think of any others?

allusion	expedition	hold	schooner
availed	fervent	infernal	sovereignty
chivalry	frigate	insignia	spontaneous
crimson	garrison	liberality	treason
dispatches	grandeur	overhauled	wretched
etiquette	hogshead	pardoned	

The Man Without a Country

Edward Everett Hale

Part One

I suppose that very few readers of the New York *Herald* of August 13, 1863, observed in an obscure corner, among the "Deaths" the announcement:

> NOLAN. Died on board U.S. Corvette *Levant*,[1] Lat. 2° 11′ S., Long. 131° W., on the 11th of May, PHILIP NOLAN.

Hundreds of readers would have paused at that announcement, if it had read thus: "Died, May 11, THE MAN WITHOUT A COUNTRY." For it was as *The Man Without a Country* that poor Philip Nolan had generally been known by the officers who had him in charge during some fifty years, as, indeed, by all the men who sailed under them.

There can now be no possible harm in telling this poor creature's story. Reason enough there has been till now for very strict secrecy, the secrecy of honor itself, among the gentlemen of the Navy who have had Nolan in charge. And certainly it speaks well for the profession, and the personal honor of its members, that to the press this man's story has been wholly unknown—and I think, to the country at large also. This I do know, that no naval officer has mentioned Nolan in his report of a cruise.

But, there is no need for secrecy any longer. Now the poor creature is dead, it seems to me worthwhile to tell a little of his story, by way of showing young Americans of today what it is to be *A Man Without a Country*.

NOLAN'S FATAL WISH

Philip Nolan was as fine a young officer as there was in the "Legion of the West," as the Western division of our army was then called. When Aaron Burr[2] made his first dashing expedition

---

1. The *Corvette Levant* (kor VET luh VANT) was a small fighting ship in the Navy. It was similar to the modern destroyer.
2. *Aaron Burr* (AIR in BUR) (1756-1836), a former vice president of the United States, was later suspected of plotting to set up an empire in the Southwest. He was tried for treason, but was found innocent.

Word Bank

expedition (EK spuh DISH un) *n.*: a journey or voyage made for a specific purpose

down to New Orleans in 1805, he met this carefree, bright young fellow. Burr marked him, talked to him, walked with him, took him a day or two's voyage in his flatboat, and, in short, fascinated him. For the next year, barrack life was very tame to poor Nolan. He occasionally availed himself of the permission the great man had given him to write to him. Long, stilted letters the poor boy wrote and rewrote and copied. But never a line did he have in reply. The other boys in the garrison sneered at him, because he lost the fun which they found in shooting or rowing while he was working away on these grand letters to his grand friend. But before long the young fellow had his revenge. For this time His Excellency, Honorable Aaron Burr, appeared again under a very different aspect. There were rumors that he had an army behind him and an empire before him. At that time the youngsters all envied him. Burr had not been talking twenty minutes with the commander before he asked him to send for Lieutenant Nolan. Then after a little talk he asked Nolan if he could show him something of the great river and the plans for the new post. He asked Nolan to take him out in his skiff[3] to show him a canebrake[4] or a cottonwood tree, as he said—really to win him over; and by the time the sail was over, Nolan was enlisted body and soul. From that time, though he did not yet know it, he lived as a man without a country.

What Burr meant to do I know no more than you. It is none of our business just now. Only, when the grand catastrophe came, the great treason trial at Richmond,[5] Fort Adams got up a string of courts-martial[6] on the officers there. One and another of the colonels and majors were tried, and, to fill out the list, little Nolan, against whom there was evidence enough—that he was sick of the service, had been willing to be false to it, and would have obeyed any order to march anywhere had the order been signed, "By command of His Exc. A. Burr." The courts dragged on. The big flies[7] escaped—rightly for all I know. Nolan was proved guilty enough, yet you and I would never have heard of him but that, when the president of the court asked him at the close whether he wished to say anything to show that he had always been faithful to the United States, he cried out, in a fit of frenzy:

"I hate the United States! I wish I may never hear of the United States again!"

---

3. A *skiff* (SKIF) is a vessel small enough for sailing or rowing by one person.
4. A *canebrake* (KANE BRAKE) is a dense growth of tall reeds, frequently found in wet creek bottoms in Louisiana.
5. *Richmond* (RICH mund), Virginia was the place where Aaron Burr was tried.
6. *Courts-martial* (KORTZ MAR shil) means military courts, where military men are tried for service-related offenses.
7. *Big flies* means the important people who might have plotted with Burr.

Word Bank

availed (uh VAY ild) *v.*: used to his advantage, made use of
garrison (GAIR ih sun) *n.*: a body of troops stationed in a fortified place
treason (TREE zohn) *n.*: violation of allegiance to one's state; the betrayal of a trust or confidence; treachery

NOLAN'S PUNISHMENT

I suppose he did not know how the words shocked old Colonel Morgan, who was holding the court. Half the officers who sat in it had served through the Revolution, and their lives, not to say their necks, had been risked for the very idea which he cursed in his madness. He, on his part, had grown up in the West of those days. He had been educated on a plantation where the finest company was a Spanish officer or a French merchant from Orleans. His education had been perfected in commercial expeditions to Veracruz,[8] and I think he told me his father once hired an Englishman to be a private tutor for a winter on the plantation. He had spent half his youth with an older brother, hunting horses in Texas; and to him *United States* was scarcely a reality. I do not excuse Nolan; I only explain to the reader why he cursed his country, and wished he might never hear her name again.

From that moment, September 23, 1807, till the day he died, May 11, 1863, he never heard her name again. For that half-century and more he was a man without a country.

Old Morgan, as I said, was terribly shocked. If Nolan had compared George Washington to Benedict Arnold,[9] or had cried, "G-d save King George,"[10] Morgan would not have felt worse. He called the court into his private room, and returned in fifteen minutes with a face like a sheet, to say:

"Prisoner, hear the sentence of the Court! The Court decides, subject to the approval of the President, that you never hear the name of the United States again."

Nolan laughed. But nobody else laughed. Old Morgan was too solemn, and the whole room was hushed dead as night for a minute. Even Nolan lost his swagger in a moment. Then Morgan added:

"Mr. Marshal, take the prisoner to Orleans, in an armed boat, and deliver him to the naval commander there."

The marshal gave his orders and the prisoner was taken out of court.

"Mr. Marshal," continued old Morgan, "see that no one mentions the United States to the prisoner. Mr. Marshal, make my respects to Lieutenant Mitchell at Orleans, and request him to order that no one shall mention the United States to the prisoner while he is on board ship. You will receive your written orders from the officer on duty here this evening. The court is adjourned."

Before the *Nautilus*[11] got round from New Orleans to the northern Atlantic coast with the prisoner on board, the sentence had been approved by the President, and he was a man without a country.

The plan then adopted was substantially the same which was necessarily followed ever after. The Secretary of the Navy was requested to put Nolan on board a government vessel bound on a long cruise, and to direct that he should be only so far confined there as

---

8. *Veracruz* (VAIR uh KROOZ) is the chief port of Mexico.
9. During the American Revolution, *Benedict Arnold* (BEN uh dikt AR nild) was a traitor to the American cause.
10. *King George* ruled England at the time.
11. *Nautilus* (NAW till iss) was the naval ship to which Nolan was delivered.

to make it certain that he never saw or heard of the country. We had few long cruises then, and I do not know certainly what his first cruise was. But the commander to whom he was entrusted regulated the etiquette and the precautions of the affair, and according to his scheme they were carried out till Nolan died.

When I was second officer of the *Intrepid*, some thirty years after, I saw the original paper of instruction. I have been sorry ever since that I did not copy the whole of it. It ran, however, much in this way:

WASHINGTON (with a date, which must have been late in 1807)

Sir,—You will receive from Lieutenant Neale the person of Philip Nolan, late a lieutenant in the United States Army.

This person on trial by court-martial expressed, with an oath, the wish that he might "never hear of the United States again."

The court sentenced him to have his wish fulfilled.

For the present, the execution of the order is entrusted by the President to this Department.

You will take the prisoner on board your ship, and keep him there with such precautions as shall prevent his escape.

You will provide him with such quarters, rations,[12] and clothing as would be proper for an officer of his late rank, if he were a passenger on your vessel on the business of his Government.

The gentlemen on board will make any arrangements agreeable to themselves regarding his society.[13] He is to be exposed to no indignity of any kind, nor is he ever unnecessarily to be reminded that he is a prisoner.

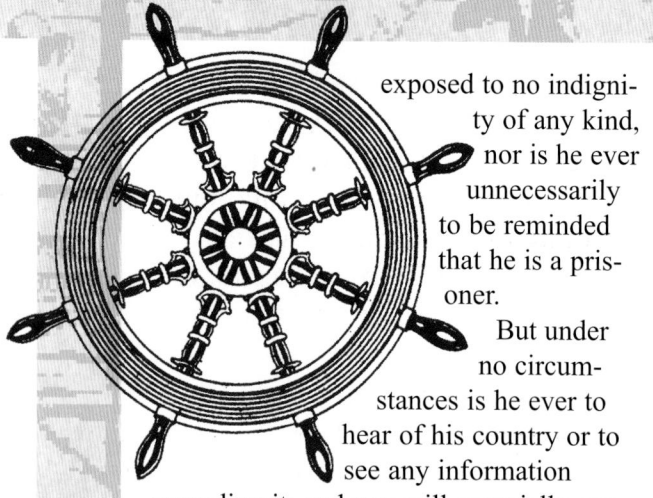

But under no circumstances is he ever to hear of his country or to see any information regarding it; and you will especially caution all the officers under your command to take care that this rule, in which his punishment is involved, shall not be broken.

It is the intention of the Government that he shall never again see the country which he has disowned. Before the end of your cruise you will receive orders which will give effect to this intention.[14]

Respectfully yours,
W. SOUTHARD,
for the Secretary of the Navy.

The rule adopted on board the ships on which I have met The Man Without a Country was, I think, transmitted from the beginning. No mess[15] liked to have him permanently, because his presence cut off all talk of home or of the prospect of return, of politics or

---

12. *Quarters* (KWOR turz) refers to living quarters, or rooms; *rations* (RASH inz) refers to food.
13. *Regarding his society* refers to the people he was permitted to socialize with.
14. The phrase *give effect to these intentions* means official orders stating the punishment.
15. Here, *mess* is an area where a group of officers eat their meals together.

Word Bank

etiquette (ET ih kit) *n.*: formally approved requirements for proper behavior in a given situation

letters, of peace or of war—cut off more than half the talk men liked to have at sea. But it was always thought too hard that he should never meet the rest of us, except to touch hats, in a sort of half-salute, and we finally sank into one system. He was not permitted to talk with the men, unless an officer was by. With officers he had unrestrained conversations, as far as they and he chose. But he grew shy, though he had favorites: I was one. Then the captain always asked him to dinner on Monday. Every mess in succession took up the invitation in its turn. According to the size of the ship, you had him at your mess more or less often at dinner. His breakfast he ate in his own stateroom. Whatever else he ate or drank, he ate or drank alone. Sometimes, when the marines or sailors had any special jollification,[16] they were permitted to invite "Plain-Buttons," as they called him. Then Nolan was sent with some officer, and the men were forbidden to speak of home while he was there. I believe the theory was that the sight of his punishment did them good. They called him "Plain-Buttons," because, while he always chose to wear a regulation army uniform, he was not permitted to wear the army button, for the reason that it bore either the initials or the insignia of the country he had disowned.

THE READING

I remember, soon after I joined the Navy, I was on shore with some of the older officers from our ship, and some of the gentlemen fell to talking about Nolan, and someone told the system which was adopted from the first about his books and other reading. As he was almost never permitted to go on shore, even though the vessel lay in port for months, his time at the best hung heavy. Everybody was permitted to lend him books, if they were not published in America and made no allusion to it. These were common enough in the old days. He had almost all the foreign papers that came into the ship, sooner or later; only somebody must go over them first, and cut out any advertisement or stray paragraph that referred to America. This was a little cruel sometimes, when the back of what was cut out might be innocent. Right in the midst of one of Napoleon's battles, poor Nolan would find a great hole, because on the back of the page of that paper there had been an advertisement of a packet[17] for New York, or a scrap from the President's message. This was the first time I ever heard of this plan. I remember it, because poor Phillips, who was of the party, told a story of

---

16. A *jollification* (JAHL if fuh KAY shun) is anything that brings extra joy or happiness, such as a special event in the sailors' lives.
17. A *packet* (PAK it) is a ship carrying mail and goods as well as passengers.

Word Bank

allusion (uh LOO zhin) *n.*: a passing or casual reference to something, either directly or implied

insignia (inn SIG nih yuh) *n.*: a badge or distinguishing mark of office or honor

something which happened at the Cape of Good Hope on Nolan's first voyage. They had touched at the Cape, paid their respects to the English admiral and the fleet, and then Phillips had borrowed a lot of English books from an officer. Among them was *The Last Minstrel*,[18] which they had all of them heard of, but which most of them had never seen. I think it could not have been published long. Well, nobody thought there could be any risk of anything national in that. So Nolan was permitted to join the circle one afternoon when a lot of them sat on deck smoking and reading aloud. In his turn Nolan took the book and read to the others; and he read very well, as I know. Nobody in the circle knew a line of the poem, only it was all magic and Border[19] chivalry, and was thousands of years ago. Poor Nolan read steadily through the fifth canto,[20] stopped a minute and drank something, and then began, without a thought of what was coming:

Breathes there a man with soul so dead,
Who never to himself hath said—

It seems impossible to us that anybody ever heard this for the first time; but all these fellows did then, and poor Nolan himself went on, still unconsciously or mechanically:

This is my own, my native land!

Then they all saw that something was to pay;[21] but he expected to get through, I suppose, turned a little pale, but plunged on:

Whose heart hath ne'er within him burned,
As home his footsteps he hath turned
From wandering on a foreign strand?
If such there breathe, go mark him well—

By this time the men were all beside themselves, wishing there was any way to make him turn over two pages; but he had not quite presence of mind for that; he gagged a little, colored crimson, and staggered on:

For him no minstrel raptures swell;[22]
High though his titles, proud his name,
Boundless his wealth as wish can claim,
Despite these titles, power and pelf,[23]
The wretch, concentered all in self[24]—

---

18. *The Last Minstrel* is a famous poem by Sir Walter Scott.
19. The *Border* (BORD er) is between Scotland and England, the scene of many conflicts before the countries were united.
20. A *canto* (KAN toe) is one of the main or larger divisions of a long poem.
21. *Something was to pay* means 'trouble was coming.'
22. *No minstrel raptures swell* means no music plays.
23. *Pelf* is money.
24. *Concentered all in self* means concentrated on himself.

Word Bank

chivalry (SHIV il ree) *n.*: a combination of qualities that include courage, generosity, and courtesy

crimson (KRIM zen) *n.*: deep purplish red

and here the poor fellow choked, could not go on, but started up, swung the book into the sea, vanished into his stateroom, "And by Jove," said Phillips, "we did not see him for two months again. And I had to make up some story to that English surgeon why I did not return his Walter Scott to him."

That story shows about the time when Nolan's braggadocio[25] must have broken down. At first, they said, he took a very high tone, considered his imprisonment a mere farce, affected[26] to enjoy the voyage, and all that; but Phillips said that after he came out of his stateroom he never was the same man again. He never read aloud again, unless it was the Bible or Shakespeare, or something else he was sure of. But it was not that merely. He never entered in with the other young men exactly as a companion again. He was always shy afterward, when I knew him—very seldom spoke unless he was spoken to, except to a very few friends. He lighted up occasionally, but generally he had the nervous, tired look of a heart-wounded man.

When Captain Shaw was coming home, rather to the surprise of everybody they made one of the Windward Islands,[27] and lay off and on for nearly a week. The boys said the officers were sick of salt-junk,[28] and meant to have turtle-soup before they came home. But after several days the *Warren* came to the same rendezvous;[29] they exchanged signals; she told them she was outward-bound, perhaps to the Mediterranean, and took poor Nolan on the boat back to try his second cruise. He looked very blank when he was told to get ready to join her. He had known enough of the signs of the sky to know that till that moment he was going "home." But this was a distinct evidence of something he had not thought of, perhaps—that there was no going home for him, even to a prison. And this was the first of some twenty such transfers, which brought him sooner or later into half our best vessels, but which kept him all his life at least some hundred miles from the country he had hoped he might never hear of again.

---

25. *Braggadocio* (BRAG uh DOE shee oh) means acting boastfully. Here, it refers to his pretense that he did not mind his punishment.
26. *Affected* (uh FEK tid) means pretended.
27. The *Windward Islands* (WIND werd I lindz) is a group of islands in the West Indies.
28. They were tired of eating *salt-junk*, the kind of salted meat that would not spoil on board ship.
29. A *rendezvous* (RAHN day voo) is a previously agreed place for a meeting.

Studying the Selection

✓ Quick Review

1. Name (a) the person who conducted Nolan's court-martial and handed down the sentence; (b) the nickname the sailors gave Nolan; (c) the name of the poem Nolan read aloud.
2. What was the Western division of the Army called when Philip Nolan served there?
3. What were the rumors about Aaron Burr?
4. The naval officers were permitted to lend books to Nolan on two conditions. What were they?

📑 In-depth Thinking

5. How does the protagonist's last name advance the theme of the story?
6. Nolan has quarters, food, and clothing—he has a home aboard any naval vessel that carries him. Why is he so unhappy?
7. Why did Nolan lose his braggadocio after reading the poem?
8. Did the other naval officers feel sorry for Nolan? Why or why not? Support your answer with passages from the story.

📁 Drawing Conclusions

9. Did Nolan's punishment fit the crime? In other words, did he deserve such a life-changing sentence?
10. What does patriotism mean to you?

Creating and Writing

1. Could a punishment such as Nolan's happen today? Write an essay explaining your views.
2. Which thirty-four states comprised the United States in 1863, the year Nolan died? (Remember, some southern states did secede, but President Lincoln did not remove any stars from the flag. Include all thirty-four states.)
3. With a group, create a timeline of important events in American history that occurred between 1807-1863. Your teacher will assign the general subject for your group's timeline.

Part Two

NOLAN'S COURAGE

A happier story than the other I have told is of the war.[30] That came along soon after. I have heard this affair told in three or four ways—and, indeed, it may have happened more than once. In one of the great frigate duels with the English, in which the Navy was really sunk, it happened that a round-shot[31] from the enemy entered one of our ports[32] square, and took right down the officer of the gun himself, and almost every man of the gun's crew. Now you may say what you choose about courage, but that is not a nice thing to see. But, as the men who were not killed picked themselves up, and as they and the surgeon's people were carrying off the bodies, there appeared Nolan, in his shirt-sleeves, with the rammer[33] in his hand, and, just as if he had been the officer, told them off with authority—who should go to the cockpit with the wounded men, who should stay with him, perfectly cheery, and with that way which makes men feel sure all is right and is going to be right. And he finished loading the gun with his own hands, aimed it, and bade the men fire. And there he stayed, captain of that gun, keeping those fellows in spirits, till the enemy struck[34]—sitting on the carriage while the gun was cooling, though he was exposed all the time—showing them easier ways to handle heavy shot—making the raw deck hands laugh at their own blunders—and when the gun cooled again, getting it loaded and fired twice as often as any other gun on the ship. The captain walked forward by way of encouraging the men, and Nolan touched his hat and said:

"I am showing them how we do this in the artillery, sir."

And this is the part of the story where all the legends agree; the commodore said:

"I see you are, and I thank you, sir; and I shall never forget this day, sir, and you never shall, sir."

After the whole thing was over, and

---

30. *The war* refers to the war of 1812, between the United States and England.
31. A *round-shot* is a cannon ball.
32. *Ports* are the cannon openings in the side of the ship.
33. A *rammer* (RAM mer) is a stick used to push the cannonball against the gunpowder.
34. Here *struck* means hauled down their flag to admit defeat.

Word Bank

frigate (FRIG it) *n.*: a fast naval vessel of the late 18th and early 19th centuries

he had the Englishman's sword,³⁵ in the midst of the state and ceremony of the quarter-deck,³⁶ he said:

"Where is Mr. Nolan? Ask Mr. Nolan to come here."

And when Nolan came, he said:

"Mr. Nolan, we are all very grateful to you today; you are one of us today; you will be named in the dispatches."

And then the old man took off his own sword of ceremony, and gave it to Nolan and made him put it on. The man who told me this saw it. Nolan cried like a baby, and well he might. He had not worn a sword since that infernal day at Fort Adams. But always afterwards on occasions of ceremony, he wore that quaint old French sword.

The captain did mention him in the dispatches. It was always said he asked that he might be pardoned. He wrote a special letter to the Secretary of War. But nothing ever came of it.

All that was near fifty years ago. If Nolan was thirty then, he must have been near eighty when he died. He looked sixty when he was forty. But he never seemed to me to change a hair afterward. As I imagine his life, from what I have seen and heard of it, he must have been in every sea, and yet almost never on land. Till he grew very old, he went aloft³⁷ a great deal. He always kept up his exercise; and I never heard that he was ill. If any other man was ill, he was the kindest nurse in the world; and he knew more than half the surgeons do. Then if anybody was sick or died, or if the captain wanted him to, on any other occasion, he was always ready to read prayers. I have said that he read beautifully.

THE SLAVES

My own acquaintance with Philip Nolan began six or eight years after the English war,³⁸ on my first voyage after I was appointed a midshipman.³⁹ From the time I joined, I believe I thought Nolan was a sort of lay chaplain⁴⁰—a chaplain with a blue coat. I never asked about him. Everything in the ship was strange to me. I knew it was green to ask questions, and I suppose I thought there was a "Plain-Buttons" on every ship. We had him to dine in our mess once a week, and the caution was given that on that day nothing was to be said about home. But if they had told us not to say anything about the planet Mars or the book of Deuteronomy, I should not have asked why; there were a great

---

35. He had the *Englishman's sword*, since a defeated commander gave up his sword to the victor.
36. The *quarter-deck* is the part of the upper deck where all important ceremonies are held.
37. To go *aloft* (uh LAWFT) means to climb on the masts high up in the rigging and upper rigging.
38. The *English war* was the War of 1812.
39. A *midshipman* (MID SHIP men) is someone training to be an officer in the U.S. Navy.
40. A *lay chaplain* (LAY CHAP lin) is someone who performs the services of a clergyman without being officially installed.

Word Bank

dispatches (diss PATCH iz) *n.*: messages or official communications sent with speed
infernal (in FUR nil) *adj.*: extremely troublesome, annoying; outrageous
pardoned (PAHR dund) *v.*: forgave, especially an offender

many things which seemed to me to have as little reason. I first came to understand anything about The Man Without a Country one day when we overhauled a dirty little schooner which had slaves on board. An officer named Vaughan was sent to take charge of her, and, after a few minutes, he sent back his boat to ask that someone might be sent who could speak Portuguese. None of the officers did; and just as the captain was sending forward to ask if any of the people could, Nolan stepped out and said he should be glad to interpret, if the captain wished, as he understood the language. The captain thanked him, fitted out another boat with him, and in this boat it was my luck to go.

When we got there, it was such a scene as you seldom see, and never want to. Nastiness beyond account, and chaos run loose in the midst of the nastiness. There were not a great many of the Negroes; but by way of making what there were understand that they were free, Vaughan had had their handcuffs and ankle cuffs knocked off. The Negroes were, most of them, out of the hold, and swarming all around the dirty deck, with a central throng surrounding Vaughan and addressing him in every dialect.

As we came on deck, Vaughan looked down from a hogshead, on which he had mounted in desperation, and said:

"Is there anybody who can make these wretches understand something?"

Nolan said he could speak Portuguese, and one or two fine-looking Krumen[41] were dragged out, who had worked for the Portuguese on the coast.

"Tell them they are free," said Vaughan.

Nolan explained it in such Portuguese as the Krumen could understand, and they in turn to such of the Negroes as could understand them. Then there was such a yell of delight, clinching of fists, leaping and dancing, kissing of Nolan's feet, and a general rush made to the hogshead by way of spontaneous celebration of the occasion.

"Tell them," said Vaughan, well pleased, "that I will take them all to Cape Palmas."

This did not answer so well. Cape Palmas was practically as far from the homes of most of them as New Orleans or Rio do Janeiro was; that is, they would be eternally separated from home there. And their inter-

---

41. *Krumen* (KROO men) are members of an African tribe.

Word Bank

overhauled (O ver HAWLD) *v.*: gained upon, caught up with; overtook
schooner (SKOON er) *n.*: any sailing vessel with both a foremast and a mainmast
hold (HOLD) *n.*: the cargo space in the hull of a vessel, especially between the lowermost deck and the bottom
hogshead (HAWGZ HED) *n.*: a large wooden barrel
spontaneous (spahn TAY nee iss) *adj.*: coming from a natural feeling without effort; unplanned

preters as we could understand, instantly said, *"Ah, no Palmas!"* and began to protest loudly. Vaughan was rather disappointed at this result of his liberality, and asked Nolan eagerly what they said. The drops stood on poor Nolan's white forehead, as he hushed the men down, and said:

"He says, 'Not Palmas.' He says, 'Take us home, take us to our own country, take us to our own house, take us to our own children and our own families.' He says he has an old father and mother who will die if they do not see him. And this one says he left his people all sick, and paddled down to Fernando to beg the white doctor to come and help them, and that these devils[42] caught him in the bay just in sight of home, and that he has never seen anybody from home since then. And this one says," choked out Nolan, "that he has not heard a word from his home in six months."

Vaughan always said Nolan grew gray himself while he struggled through this interpretation. I, who did not understand anything of the passion involved in it, saw that the very elements were melting with fervent heat, and that something was to pay somewhere. Even the Negroes themselves stopped howling, as they saw Nolan's agony, and Vaughan's almost equal agony of sympathy. As quick as he could get words, he said:

"Tell them yes, yes, yes; tell them they shall go to the Mountains of the Moon, if they will. If I sail the schooner through the Great White Desert, they shall go home!"

And after some fashion Nolan said so. And then they all fell to kissing him again, and wanted to rub his nose[43] with theirs. But he could not stand it long; and getting Vaughan to say he might go back, he beckoned me down into our boat. As we started back he said to me: "Youngster, let that show you what it is to be without a family, without a home, and without a country. If you are ever tempted to say a word or to do a thing that shall put a bar between you and your family, your home, and your country, pray G-d in His mercy to take you that instant home to His own heaven. Think of your home, boy; write and send, and talk about it. Let it be nearer and nearer to your thought, the farther you have to travel from it; and rush back to it when you are free, as that poor slave is doing now. And for your

---

42. *These devils* is a reference to the slave traders.
43. To *rub his nose* is a way of showing affection, among some people.

Word Bank

liberality (LIB er AL ih tee) *n*.: generosity and open-mindedness
fervent (FUR vint) *adj*.: very warm or intense

THE MAN WITHOUT A COUNTRY / 247

country, boy," and the words rattled in his throat, "and for that flag," and he pointed to the ship, "never dream a dream but of serving her as she bids you, though the service carry you through a thousand battles. No matter what happens to you, no matter who flatters you or who abuses you, never look at another flag, never let a night pass but you pray G-d to bless the flag. Remember, boy, that behind all these men you have to do with, behind officers, and government, and people even, there is the Country herself, your Country, and that you belong to her as you belong to your own mother. Stand by her, boy, as you would stand by your mother!"

I was frightened to death by his calm, hard passion; but I blundered out that I would, by all that was holy, and that I had never thought of doing anything else. He hardly seemed to hear me; but he did, almost in a whisper, say, "Oh, if anybody had said so to me when I was of your age!"

I think it was this half-confidence of his, which I never abused, which afterward made us great friends. He was very kind to me. Often he sat up, or even got up, at night, to walk the deck with me, when it was my watch.[44] He explained to me a great deal of my mathematics and I owe him my taste for mathematics. He lent me books, and helped me about my reading. He never referred so directly to his story again; but from one and another officer I have learned, in thirty years, what I am telling.

Nolan's Repentance

After that cruise I never saw Nolan again. The other men tell me that in those fifteen years he aged very fast, but that he was still the same gentle, uncomplaining, silent sufferer that he ever was, bearing as best he could his self-appointed punishment. And now it seems the dear old fellow is dead. He has found a home at last, and a country.

Since writing this, and while considering whether or not I would print it, as a warning to the young Nolans of today of what it is to throw away a country, I have received from Danforth, who is on board the *Levant*, a letter which gives an account of Nolan's last hours. It removes all my doubts about telling this story.

Here is the letter:

Dear Fred:—

I try to find heart and life to tell you that it is all over with dear old Nolan. I have been with him on this voyage more than I ever was, and I can understand wholly now the way in which you used to speak of the dear old fellow. I could see that he was not strong, but I had no idea the end was so near. The doctor has been watching him very carefully, and yesterday morning came to me and told me that Nolan was not so well, and had not left his stateroom—a thing I never remember before. He had let the doctor come and

---

44. His *watch* is his turn to stay on duty on deck.

see him as he lay there—the first time the doctor had been in the stateroom—and he said he should like to see me. Do you remember the mysteries we boys used to invent about his room in the old *Intrepid* days?[45] Well, I went in, and there, to be sure, the poor fellow lay in his berth, smiling pleasantly as he gave me his hand, but looking very frail. I could not help a glance round. The stars and stripes were draped up above and around a picture of Washington, and he had painted a majestic eagle, with lightnings blazing from his beak and his foot just clasping the whole globe, which his wings overshadowed. The dear old boy saw my glance, and said, with a sad smile, "Here, you see, I have a country!" Then he pointed to the foot of his bed, where I had not seen before a great map of the United States, as he had drawn it from memory, and which he had there to look upon as he lay. Quaint, queer old names were on it, in large letters: "Indiana Territory,"[46] "Mississippi Territory," and "Louisiana Territory," as I suppose our fathers learned such things: but the old fellow had patched in Texas, too; he had carried his western boundary all the way to the Pacific, but on that shore he had defined nothing.

"Oh Captain," he said, "I know I am dying. I cannot get home. Surely you will tell me something now?—Stop! stop! Do not speak till I say what I am sure you know, that there is not in this ship, that there is not in America—G-d bless her!—a more loyal man than I. There cannot be a man who loves the old flag as I do, or prays for it as I do, or hopes for it as I do. There are thirty-four stars in it now, Danforth. I thank G-d for that, though I do not know what their names are. There has never been one taken away: I thank G-d for that. I know by that that there has never been any successful Burr. Oh Danforth, Danforth," he sighed out, "how like a wretched night's dream a boy's idea of personal fame or of separate sovereignty seems, when one looks back on it after such a life as mine! But tell me—tell me something—tell me everything, Danforth, before I die!"

I swear to you that I felt like a monster, that I had not told him everything before. "Mr. Nolan," said I, "I will tell you everything you ask about. Only, where shall I begin?"

Oh, the blessed smile that crept over his white face! And he pressed my hand and said, "G-d bless you! Tell me their names," he said, and he pointed to the stars on the flag. "The last I know is Ohio. My father lived in Kentucky. But I have guessed Michigan, and Indiana, and Mississippi—that was where Fort Adams is—they make twenty. But where are your other fourteen? You have not cut up any of the old ones, I hope?"

Well, that was not a bad text, and I told him the names in as good order as I could, and he bade me take down his beautiful map and draw them in as I best could with my pencil. He was wild with delight about Texas, told me how his cousin died there; he had placed a gold mark near where he supposed his grave was; and he had guessed

---

45. *Intrepid days* (in TREP id DAYZ) refer to the time when they were all aboard the ship *Intrepid*.
46. *Indiana Territory* refers to the U.S. area west of the Appalachian Mountains, which had not been settled enough to become states at the time Nolan was sentenced.

Word Bank

wretched (RECH id) *adj*.: characterized by misery and sorrow; miserable
sovereignty (SAHV rin tee) *n*.: supreme and independent power or authority

at Texas. Then he was delighted as he saw California and Oregon—that, he said, he had suspected partly, because he had never been permitted to land on that shore, though the ships were there so much. Then he asked about the old war—told me the story of his serving the gun the day we took the *Java.* Then he settled down more quietly, and very happily, to hear me tell in an hour the history of fifty years.

How I wish it had been somebody who knew something! But I did as well as I could. I told him of the English war. I told him of Fulton and the steamboat beginning. I told him about old Scott,[47] and Jackson,[48] told him all I could think of about the Mississippi, and New Orleans, and Texas, and his own old Kentucky.

I tell you, it was a hard thing to condense the history of half a century into that talk with a sick man. And I do not now know what I told him—of emigration[49] and the means of it—of steamboats, and railroads, and telegraphs—of inventions, and books, and literature—of the colleges, and West Point, and the Naval School, but with the queerest interruptions that ever you heard. You see it was Robinson Crusoe asking all the accumulated questions of fifty-six years!

I remember he asked, all of a sudden, who was President now; and when I told him, he asked if Old Abe was General Benjamin Lincoln's son. He said he met old General Lincoln, when he was quite a boy himself, at some Indian Treaty. I said no, that Old Abe was a Kentuckian like himself, but I could not tell him of what family; he had worked up from the ranks. "Good for him!" cried Nolan; "I am glad of that." Then I got talking about my visit to Washington. I told him everything I could think of that would show the grandeur of his country and its prosperity.

And he drank it in and enjoyed it as I cannot tell you. He grew more and more silent, yet I never thought he was tired or faint. I gave him a glass of water, but he just wet his lips, and told me not to go away. The he asked me to bring him his book of prayers which lay there and said, with a smile, that it would open at the right place—and so it did. There was his double red mark down the page; and I read and he repeated with me, *For ourselves and our country, we are thankful that, notwithstanding our manifold transgressions*[50] *we have continued to receive marvelous kindness*—And so to the end of that thanksgiving. Then he turned to the end of the same book, and I read the words more familiar to me: *Most heartily we ask that the President of the United States, and all others in authority be granted favor.* "Danforth," he said, "I

---

47. General Winfield *Scott* was the commander during the War of 1812 and the Mexican War.
48. Andrew *Jackson* won the battle of New Orleans and was later president of the United States.
49. *Emigration* (EM ih GRAY shun) refers to the steady stream of settlers moving westward and filling up the new land.
50. *Transgressions* (tranz GRESH inz) are violations of laws or moral rules; sins.

Word Bank

grandeur (GRAN jer) *n.*: impressiveness, importance, distinction

have repeated those prayers night and morning, it is now fifty-five years." And then he said he would go to sleep. He bent me down over him and kissed me: and he said, "Look in my prayers, Captain, when I am gone." And I went away.

But I had no thought it was the end. I thought he was tired and would sleep. I knew he was happy, and I wanted him to be alone.

But in an hour, when the doctor went in gently, he found Nolan had breathed his life away with a smile.

We looked in his prayers and there was a slip of paper at the place where he had marked the text. On this slip of paper he had written: "Bury me in the sea; it has been my home, and I love it. But will not someone set up a stone for my memory, that my disgrace may not be more than I ought to bear? Say on it:

In Memory of
PHILIP NOLAN,
*Lieutenant in the Army
of the United States*

"He loved his country
as no other man has loved her;
but no man deserved less
at her hands."

Studying the Selection

First Impressions *How do you feel after reading this story? How do you feel about your country? How does your country connect to your world, beyond school? Is this connection a work in progress, or is it merely there? What happens to patriotism if the need for it is no longer obvious?*

✔ Quick Review

1. Name (a) the officer sent to take charge of the schooner which held the slaves; (b) the slaves who could speak Portuguese; (c) the name of the letter writer who gave an account of Nolan's last hours; (d) Nolan's home state.
2. What was the last state Nolan had been aware of?
3. What three territories had Nolan named in large letters on his map?
4. We are told Nolan was delighted that three states in particular had joined the United States. Name them.

In-depth Thinking

5. Why did Nolan feel the need to wear "that quaint old French sword" at ceremonial occasions?
6. Why did the narrator suppose there was a "Plain-Buttons" on every ship?
7. Why would Nolan have looked sixty when he was forty?
8. We are told "The Negroes stopped howling as they saw Nolan's agony" aboard the slave ship. Why?

Drawing Conclusions

9. The words Nolan wanted engraved on his gravestone were: "He loved his country as no other man loved her; but no man deserved less at her hands." Is Nolan being too hard on himself?
10. Which of the major events in the story do you think was the most difficult for Nolan? Support your answer with statements from the story.

Focusing on Theme: A Frame Story

Viewpoint, characterization, and the development of events to create a **frame story**, enhance the most important component of *The Man Without a Country*—its theme.

1. Write a letter from Nolan to the narrator. Use as your subject matter an event from the story—such as the reading of the poem or the encounter with the slave ship. When your work is done, you will have created a frame story of your own, from the viewpoint of the story's protagonist, not as an observer.
2. Compare the encounter with the slave ship to Nolan's life aboard ship. How do these become parallel themes? Alone or with a partner, list the similar and dissimilar aspects of the slave experience and Nolan's exile.
3. Nolan is quite a sympathetic character. Develop a list of his characteristics; then on another list, write the opposite of those traits. For example, one list will state that Nolan is kind; the other will state he is cruel. Consider how the story would be altered had Nolan been less virtuous. Now rewrite a part of the story using these negative characteristics. Share your story with the class.

Creating and Writing

1. It has been said *The Man Without a Country* was written to inspire Union soldiers during the Civil War. What passages in the story could be a special message to these soldiers? Cite the passages and explain why they seem to relate to the Union cause.
2. Interview a family member or a friend who has served in the U.S. military during wartime. Ask in what war that person served, in which branch of the armed forces—Army, Navy, Marines, Air Force—and how they felt about their country then and now. (If you don't know of anyone who served in the military, look for newspaper or magazine articles about famous veterans, such as political figures.) Make a short presentation to the class.
3. With your group, perform a skit of any of the events that occurred in *The Man Without a Country*. In addition to the main events of the story (the poem, the encounter with the slave ship), this could include other aspects of Nolan's life, such as his early days in the military or his court-martial.

Blueprint for Reading

Background Bytes

Enrico Caruso, the great Italian tenor, was born in Naples, Italy in 1873. He made his operatic debut there in 1894, but achieved his first great success in Milan in 1898. Engagements soon followed in Rome, Lisbon, Monte Carlo, London, and St. Petersburg.

From his first appearance, Caruso, with his powerful voice, became the chief attraction of the Metropolitan Opera House. However, Caruso became universally famous through phonograph recordings in the early 1900s. Several of his recordings have been reissued in new formats and are still available. His position as the greatest dramatic tenor was unchallenged to the end of his life.

Caruso's last appearance was at the Metropolitan Opera House on December 24, 1920. He died in 1921. In 1987, the National Academy of Recording Arts & Sciences recognized Caruso by awarding a posthumous Grammy Lifetime Achievement Award.

Into *The Song Caruso Sang*

Comedy sometimes obscures profound truths behind lighthearted laughter. *The Song Caruso Sang* is a delightful, heartwarming story with important themes: Family unity and togetherness are more important than material wealth; some things are too valuable to sell no matter how much money one may be offered.

Through characterization, the use of symbols, and humor, the narrator—George Washington Esposito—brings these themes to life. The reader is invited into the Esposito home, as if a member of the family, with its warmth and intimacy. At the beginning of the memoir, George assures the reader that "it's all over now and everything is okay again." He wraps up the tale by suggesting that the reader come by and join them sometime. The intimacy of the writing style is expressive of the story itself, as much like home as "the smell of garlic in the kitchen."

As you read *The Song Caruso Sang*, pay attention to the informal colloquial language.

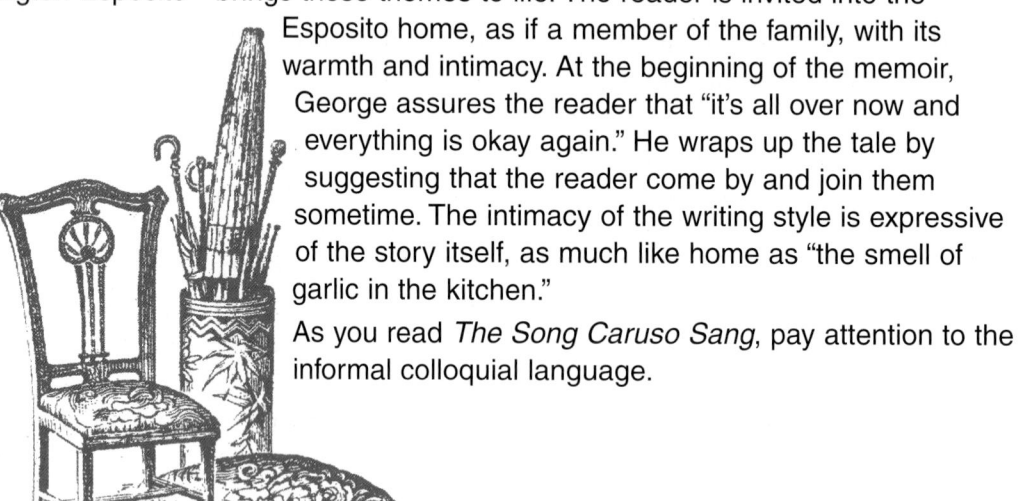

The Song Caruso Sang

Focusing on Symbolism in Theme

Have you ever read a story that you found too sweet? Had *The Song Caruso Sang* been written in a more serious style, it could have been overly sweet and melodramatic. The first-person, humorous voice of the narrator delivers an important theme in a lighthearted 'package.' Comedy lightens the mood, but not the message.

Literary comedy is a written work dealing with familiar situations that involve ordinary people using everyday language, while making us smile along the way. In contrast we have **tragedy**, which usually begins in happy circumstances and ends in disaster. Comedy often begins with its characters in difficult but amusing situations that are happily resolved in the end. Tragic characters tend to be idealized, noble, or of mythic stature; comic characters are usually average human beings.

Characterization plays a major role in *The Song Caruso Sang*. The people in the story exemplify the theme: the joy of family life. As comic characters, the Espositos are certainly "average human beings." They have real jobs, attend school, and enjoy the simple things in life, such as music and good food. These characters are authentic as they act and interact, especially with the "outsiders" Dick Mantini and Mr. Kamp. These interactions create the conflict of the story—should the record, the symbol of family togetherness, be sold to strangers?

The literary component of **symbolism** is central to *The Song Caruso Sang*, even to the title. Papa's prized Caruso recording symbolizes all that is good in the Esposito family, all that connects them to one another. Their Sunday evening ritual had begun with Papa bringing records home from Sheeler's music store; it soon revolved around Papa's own Caruso record. George even states that the record "was just part of our lives; we never knew any different." It is a symbol of all things Italian and everything dear to the family—love, togetherness, simplicity, and happiness.

Note the ellipses used throughout, the dots (…) that pepper the tale. When ellipses are used, the omitted words are as important as those expressed. 'Read between the lines,' noting what has been said leading up to the ellipses, and you should understand what the narrator is trying to say. Sometimes what is unsaid speaks volumes.

The Song Caruso Sang

Patrick McCallum

Well, it's all over now and everything is okay again, although not very long ago it looked like the whole Esposito family was going to bust right up. That would have been pretty bad, because we're a big family—Mamma and Papa and six kids, counting Beppe,[1] who is married now and last year made me an uncle.

My name is George Washington Esposito[2] because I was born the day Papa became an American citizen. He was so proud that he named me after our first President. I sort of think he hoped some day I might be a President, too. But that was fourteen years ago, and so far there's been no sign of me heading in that direction.

What I want to tell you about is the record, and what happened to it and to the Espositos because of it. I know it sounds crazy when I tell you all the things that a recording of "*Celeste Aïda*"[3] by Enrico Caruso did to us, but it's the truth, all of it.

As long as I can remember anything at all, I remember the Sunday evenings in our parlor, even when I was little and we lived on the East Side of Manhattan. It's gone on the same right here in Brooklyn, too.

The whole family was always together then—Papa and Mamma, of course, and Angelina, Beppe (now with Rosa and little Peppino[4]), Enrico, Giovanni,[5] Mary Alice, and me, George Washington. We last two are the only Espositos who have real American names, though Mamma calls us "Maria" and "Giorgio."[6]

Let me tell you it was a roomful, especially when the Pezzullos from next door came over. You can imagine how we squeezed together on the horsehair sofa and filled all the chairs, the straight-backed ones with the round knobs that pressed against our spines when we sat up straight like we ought to in them, as well as the ones from the kitchen; and still some of us had to sit on the floor. But we didn't mind. What did it matter where you sat when you were listening

---

1. *Beppe* (BEH pea)
2. *Esposito* (ESS poh ZEE toe)
3. The song "*Celeste Aida*," (suh LEST i EE duh) from the opera "Aida," became even more famous when sung by Enrico Caruso (en REE koh kah RUH soe).
4. *Peppino* (peh PEA no)
5. *Giovanni* (gee oh VAHN ee)
6. *Giorgio* (GEORGE ee oh)

to beautiful music? That's something to be enjoyed anywhere.

You see, Papa had this job at Sheeler's, the big music store just off Times Square. It wasn't much of a job in those days, but even if he was only a janitor, it paid enough for him to take care of his family, and he could be near music. Before he came to America, Papa played the violincello in the string quartet at the Ristorante Ricco,[7] one of the best places to eat in Naples in case you ever go there. But after the first big war, when times got bad, Papa wrote to Uncle Guido[8] in America, and Uncle Guido said to come over, so he and Mamma and Beppe came to New York. That was clear back in 1920.

I was telling you about Papa's job. Like I said, he didn't mind being a janitor, because it meant he was where he could hear music all day. Mr. Sheeler took a liking to Papa and let him bring records home over the weekend, so we could all hear the wonderful music that Papa listened to every day at the store as he swept and mopped the floors.

So that's the way the Sunday evenings began. We had a phonograph, a second-hand one that Papa got at the store real cheap; not the latest model, of course, but it had a clear tone, and that's what counts. It was my job to wind it up[9] between records, but that's as much as Papa would let any of us do; he always changed the records himself. In all the years he brought records home only one was broken and two scratched. That's pretty good, I'd say.

We all love music. From the very beginning, even back in Italy before my oldest brother, Beppe, was born, the Esposito house had music in it. And after Mamma and Papa got to America and could afford it, there was a piano, and Angelina and Beppe took lessons. Later there was a violin for Giovanni; and Mamma, who had done some singing herself before she got married, taught Enrico to sing, because he had the best voice, and maybe just a little because his name was Enrico. As for me, I'm learning to play the piccolo[10] in the school band.

There was more than music to our Sundays in the parlor. There was the being together, and for me that was best of all. During the week we were all running in and out of the house to and from school and work; only at supper could we be together, and then only for a little while, because Angelina had her night classes at business college, and Beppe and Giovanni were turning out for basketball at the YMCA, and Enrico practiced his singing in the bedroom with the door closed, and Mary Alice and I had our homework. So it was really only Sunday in the evening that we could gather in the parlor with the lights dim and listen while Papa played the operas of Verdi and the symphonies of Beethoven.

For over an hour we would listen. Then Papa would say, "That's all tonight," and start to close down the top of the phonograph.

---

7. *Ristorante Ricco* (rist toh run TAY REE koh)
8. *Guido* (GWEE doe)
9. *To wind up* a phonograph means to physically wind up a crank to make the turntable go round so the record could play.
10. A *piccolo* (PIH keh loe) is a small high-pitched flute.

"But the record, Papa!" Everyone in the room chimed in. "We want to hear the record!"

Papa would look mystified, as though he didn't know what we were talking about. "The record? What record?"

"The Caruso record, Papa!" we would come back at him, everyone grinning. "You know which one we mean!"

"Ah!" he would nod as though just barely remembering. "The Caruso record." He would smile then. "Well, *bambini*,[11] if you insist." He would shake his head. "But I do not understand why you want every time this same record."

Papa knew his part in the game. He would pick up the record, the one I mentioned before, *"Celeste Aïda,"* from the table, where he had placed it, knowing that we would demand to hear it.

To me, it is the best recording Caruso ever made of that lovely aria[12] of Verdi's. Maybe it's because I've heard it almost every Sunday since I can remember; maybe it's because this is the only one of its kind, since no other copies were made, and it is ours.

Well, here is how it came to be: You see, long ago Papa had known Caruso in Naples, because sometimes the great tenor would come to Ricco's for a late supper when he was singing at the San Carlo. He even sang with the quartet when he felt like it—just got up in the middle of supper and sang. It was really something to hear, Papa says.

Papa had written Caruso that he and Mamma and Beppe would soon be in New York. The great man had made him promise to write if ever the Espositos came to America. He was not one to forget his old friends. If he had been, there wouldn't have been the record nor the thing that happened to us because of it.

I've heard so many times the story of Papa's meeting in New York with the man my brother Enrico was named after that now I almost feel I was there, myself, that day when Papa, following Caruso's instructions, went to the recording studio where the famous tenor was making an album of opera selections.

It was while he was singing into the

---

11. *Bambini* (bahm BEE nee) is a phrase of endearment, like dear children.
12. An *aria* (AR ee uh) is a solo performance, with instrumental accompaniment, of a melody or tune.

big, flower-shaped horn of the recording machine that Papa entered the studio, having been permitted with the card that Caruso had sent him.

The aria was nearly over, the high, clear notes of that difficult solo going onto the soft wax disc so easily. *Ay! Mamma mia!* There was a voice straight out of heaven!

He turned away from the horn as he let go of the last note, and it was then he saw Papa through the glass and waved and smiled, crying out, *"Eh, Pasqualino, cumme stai?"*[13] and even before Papa could answer that he was fine, Caruso came rushing out of the studio and embraced him joyfully. "Come!" he said in Italian—this was before Papa knew any English. "We shall hear the record and then have some lunch. A feast it shall be! A feast to welcome my old friend to his new home!" Then he laughed and embraced Papa again.

They sat down to listen to the record.

The last note of *"Celeste Aïda"* faded away. There was a pause, then *"Eh, Pasqualino, cumme stai?"* came out of the loud-speaker as clearly as the aria just finished.

Papa said Caruso turned speechlessly and pointed his finger at Papa and then at himself in astonishment.

The engineers in the recording room had funny looks on their faces as they hurried out. "I'm afraid you'll have to do it over, Mr. Caruso," one of them said. "It'd be pretty hard to cut out that last part without ruining the music; there isn't enough of a pause between the last note of the singing and the words you spoke afterward."

Caruso shrugged his shoulders. "Okay," he said, and grinned. "Then we do it over." He got up and started into the studio again. "I will not be long, Pasqualino," he promised. "Then we go eat."

Papa says his heart seemed to quiver and his voice would hardly come as he stopped the singer. "Enrico," he said, "what is to become of the one you just made?"

Caruso went through the motions of breaking an invisible record over his knee, grinning as he did so.

Papa nodded gravely, his voice trembling as he continued. "Enrico, may I have it?" he asked, almost in a whisper.

The tenor did not seem to understand. "You want that record, Pasqualino?" he asked. "But why? It is no good. I can make you a better one right now."

"No, no, my friend!" Papa begged. "Please, I want only that one, the one where you speak to me and call my name."

Caruso laughed and slapped Papa on the back. "Ah, now I see!" he said. "Of course you may have it! One *'Celeste Aïda'* just for you!" And he added, "With my special autograph!"

So, nearly every Sunday since, we have heard the golden voice of Enrico Caruso singing *"Celeste Aïda,"* then felt proud and happy as we heard this greatest tenor of all time call out joyfully to our own father, *"Eh, Pasqualino, cumme stai?"* as if he were right in our parlor with us.

You can understand now why we all thought so much of the record. It was

---

13. *Pasqualino,* (pahs kwa LEEN oh) *Cumme stai* (KOME uh STAH) is Italian for "How are you?"

more than just a recording of *"Celeste Aïda"* by Enrico Caruso. Yet, I don't think I could tell you all the things it was to us. Like red wine on the table, the smell of garlic in the kitchen, and the sound of Neapolitan Italian being spoken, it was just part of our lives; we never knew any different. It isn't easy to explain things like that….

Well, the years passed and we all grew older. Beppe got married, and Angelina got a secretarial position, a good one with an import-export firm because she knew both English and Italian and was a good secretary besides.

The Sunday evenings continued through all these changes in our lives. By now Papa had a better job at Sheeler's and no longer had to sweep and mop the floors; he didn't have to borrow records, either. We saved our money through the years and bought our own. One year we all put together, my brothers and sisters and I, and bought Papa and Mamma a new radio-phonograph, the best there is; they were so surprised and happy that they both cried when they saw it.

Papa's record by Caruso, though, was still the prize possession of the Espositos, and it never seemed to get scratched or worn. Of course, no one touched it but Papa, and he was very careful, playing it only once a week, and always with a new needle.

It was after that first Sunday when Dick Mantini, Angelina's boss, came to supper and our concert afterward, that things began to change. Dick's just a young guy, but he's got a swell position in this export outfit. He sure got a funny look on his face when we began our act of "The record, Papa! Let us hear the record!" Then Angelina explained what it was all about, and Dick smiled politely as Papa carefully lowered the needle onto the whirling disc.

I never saw anyone spring to life as quickly as Dick when he realized that *"Eh, Pasqualino, cumme stai?"* was on the record.

"Hey, that's terrific!" Dick exclaimed. "There's a real collector's item, I'd say. Ought to be worth a lot of money." The parlor got real quiet when he asked Papa, "Have you ever tried to sell it?"

Papa didn't seem to understand. "Sell? What you mean, sell?"

"Why, there are people would pay you a lot of money for that record, Mr. Esposito; I couldn't say how much, but plenty, I'll bet. The singing alone, this being the only copy, would be worth a lot." He shook his head in amazement. "And with that business at the end, you could make a small fortune on it."

The room became awfully quiet, a different quiet than when we were listening to the music.

"Well," Papa sighed, "it's not for sale. It is mine, given by my friend Enrico Caruso. I will sell first my right arm."

Beppe, on the horsehair sofa with Rosa and Peppino, started to speak. "But, Papa," he began—only, when Papa looked in his direction he didn't finish what he started to say.

There was an atmosphere of uneasiness in the parlor that night and I had a feeling that Dick's idea would not just fade away by itself….

The following Sunday, Beppe got up after we had heard the record and made a little speech. "Papa," he began, and everyone in the parlor knew what he was going to say.

"This week I have been thinking, and I have talked with Dick and with Enrico and Giovanni."

Papa sat up stiff but didn't say anything. Mamma looked like she'd rather be out in the kitchen making *lasagne.*

"Papa," Beppe went on, "for a long time now you've dreamed of owning a little piece of land out in Jersey, where you could have a garden and grow some grapes and fruit trees. You and Mamma have worked hard, and now it is time you took life easy. You owe it to yourselves."

Papa still did not speak. Beppe looked around him like maybe he wished Enrico or Giovanni was doing the talking.

"Well, Papa," he continued, after a pause that was nearly a sigh, "we think you ought to sell the record. Dick says he knows a man who is interested in such things and probably would give you plenty of money for it. Maybe a thousand dollars, even."

We all blinked our eyes at Beppe's words. A thousand dollars! For a record? Even if it is by Caruso? Not possible! Yet I'd never seen Beppe with a more serious expression on his face. Believe me, he wasn't kidding.

Papa spoke at last. "My record is not for sale," he said quietly but firmly. "I said before, I say again, not for a thousand or five thousand. We talk about it no more." He got up and left the parlor.

Beppe and Rosa and the baby went home, and the rest of us went to bed. I thought the talk of the record was finished, and, without knowing why, I was kind of relieved. Still, letting myself dream for a minute, it would be nice to have a little farm in New Jersey. We often talked about it and dreamed of our own grapes and a few apple and cherry trees. But to sell the record? Somehow, even the little farm we wanted so much didn't seem worth that sacrifice.

It was the next day, just as I was sure the matter was closed, that Beppe came to the house all excited; while we were eating supper it was.

Beppe's eyes were bright as he told Papa about the new idea. "You wouldn't even have to sell the record, Papa!" he said breathlessly. "I talked to Dick about it again today. He says he thinks you could just sell the rights to it; you'd only have to let one of the big companies borrow the record and make a copy of it. You might get even more money than from a private collector. Think of it, Papa!" He leaned clear across the table and looked into Papa's face, waiting for him to say something.

Papa kept right on eating his supper. Then he took a sip of Chianti[14] from the glass beside his plate, and after what seemed a long, long time, said, "I will think." But there was not even a trace of a smile on his face when he said it. "Can I find out how to get in touch with the right party at the recording company, just in case?" Beppe asked, still leaning across the table.

Papa took another sip of wine, then nodded slowly. I could tell he wanted to forget the whole business.

---

14. *Chianti* (kee AHN tee) is a dry, red, Italian table wine. It is named for the region in Italy, Chianti, where it is produced.

Speaking of forgetting, I'd be just as glad to forget that next couple of weeks after Papa said okay to Beppe. For the first time in my memory we didn't even have the music in the parlor. You see, except for Papa and Mamma, nobody was speaking to anybody.

After Papa had agreed to Beppe's suggestion, my oldest brother contacted someone who was interested in the record and wanted to hear it. "The way they talk," Beppe explained, "I think they might give even more than a thousand for the record."

Papa finally agreed that the people from the recording company could hear the Caruso record, but they'd have to come to our house to do so; he wouldn't let the record out of the house.

It was then the unhappiness began. All my brothers and sisters, and with shame I must include myself, began thinking of the different ways we could spend the money, even before we had any idea how much it would be. Only Papa and Mamma said nothing. They were like two lost children who didn't know which way to turn; they would sit and listen to Angelina and Enrico and Giovanni and Mary Alice and me, and Beppe when he came from his house, quarreling about the money.

Giovanni wanted us to have a car, a big, new one. We'd never had a car, but he could think of all the reasons why we really needed one.

Angelina said that it would be nice to have a home out on Long Island and commute to work on the train.

Enrico thought we should all take a trip back to Italy, and he could study voice there.

Beppe and Rosa still held out for the farm in New Jersey, as it would be a good place to bring the baby on sunny weekends.

I don't think Mary Alice and I knew what we wanted, because we changed our minds every day. All of us were guilty of stretching the amount we thought we'd get for the record to cover whatever it was we wanted….

The man from the recording company was coming on Sunday evening to listen to the record and decide whether or not it was what his company wanted. By that Sunday our house was not a place to be in if you were in a good mood and wanted to stay that way. Once, when I looked into Mamma's face I could tell she'd been crying, and Papa, who was always cheerful, never smiled anymore.

Mamma had insisted that everybody come to dinner that Sunday, just like always, even if we were all mad at each other.

"Such faces," Papa said with a sigh as we all sat down at the table. "Only Peppino looks happy."

The little boy laughed when he heard his name. The rest of us looked down at our plates, just as we had when we were little and Papa scolded us for fighting.

"It is over two weeks now," Papa went on, "that Dick Mantini tells us maybe we can get much money for our record. I feel this is not good, but as to give only the use of the record does not really seem bad I say nothing."

Papa sighed and shook his head sadly. "But, *si*, it is bad, very bad. I know this now. Ever since we think to sell I watch this family, and I see it is no more a family. Before, it is happy, and this house is filled with love and much laughing. Now there is only angry faces and fighting. Always before this time I hurry home from my work at night; now I stay away."

I could hear Mamma beginning to sniffle at the other end of the table.

"Why is this?" Papa continued. "It is because of a record, a record by my dear friend Enrico Caruso which for many years brings much joy to the Espositos." His voice sounded strange, not Papa's voice at all. "Now the thing that for many years is happiness for Pasqualino Esposito is unhappiness. I ask myself can I buy with money this happiness once again, and I find the only answer is *No*."

You could almost hear the silence in the room. Finally Giovanni spoke. "But, Papa," he reminded, "you'd still have your record and the little farm in Jersey with the apples and grapes…"

"Apples and grapes I can buy at the fruit stand of Pezzullo," Papa interrupted. "A family I cannot buy in any place." He left the room.

Mamma got up, too, and looked at us as though to say something, but then she turned without saying it and followed Papa into the parlor and closed the door.

Beppe was the first to speak after they had gone. "Papa's right," he said. "It's all my fault."

"Your fault?" Giovanni asked.

Beppe nodded. "I insisted that Papa consider selling after he'd said he didn't want to. If only I'd—"

"Don't say that, Beppe!" Giovanni interrupted. "You were right to insist. You were just thinking of the good of the family. Once this is all over and the record is sold, Papa will see it is right. Like you said just now, he'll have his record and the money, too."

"But the family?" Beppe asked. "Didn't you hear Papa and see his face just now? And Mamma, too? That's what made me realize it. We stand a chance of losing more than we could ever gain in dollars."

They argued on, everybody pitching in, until finally Beppe banged his fist on the table and said, "We're not going to sell the record, so what's the use of arguing?"

The others stopped talking, although Giovanni did remind Beppe that in any case it was too late to call up Mr. Kamp, the man from the recording company, and tell him not to bother to come.

I found myself awfully glad about what Beppe had said. I knew now that the last thing I wanted was for us to sell the Caruso record. If it went out of our house, then something awfully important would be gone out of our family, perhaps forever….

The recording-company representative, Mr. Kamp, a bald-headed little man, came on the dot of seven-thirty, just as he was supposed to. We all went into the parlor and sat down. Mr. Kamp sat alone on the horsehair sofa. The room was deadly quiet, like just before a thunderstorm.

Papa picked up the record from its place among the others on the table and put it on the turntable. It began to turn, and he lowered the needle carefully into the outside groove. His hand was shaking noticeably.

We all looked at each other in surprise. It wasn't *"Celeste Aïda"* at all! In confusion, Papa had put on *"Vesti la giubba,"*[15] instead. Both records, the big, thick kind they used to make before I was born, looked exactly alike.

Papa asked Mr. Kamp's pardon for the mistake and took *"Celeste Aïda"* from the table and put it on the machine.

The little man from the recording company leaned forward and stared at the floor as he listened to the record. When it was finished he merely nodded and asked to hear it again.

Papa sat by the phonograph looking intently at each of us as Caruso sang. Following Papa's gaze, I saw Angelina and Beppe and Enrico and Giovanni and Mary Alice all with the same worried expression, one just like the next. They were not like my brothers and sisters at all, nor was this the happy time of those other Sundays.

"Best *'Celeste Aïda'* ever recorded by Caruso, I'm convinced," Mr. Kamp said in a businesslike tone after hearing it the second time. He was the authority on Caruso for his company, he told us, and had heard all the great tenor's records, "but none quite like this." He was smiling for the first time. "That little personal touch at the end would make it a record seller, too," he told us, and laughed as though he thought he'd said something funny.

He got up off the sofa and, jamming his hands down into his pockets, paced across the parlor twice, his bald head almost glowing. He seemed very excited. "Mr. Esposito," he said in an even more businesslike tone than before, "my company will pay you five thousand dollars for all rights to the use of this recording if it's what we want, and I do not hesitate to assure you that it is." He began to explain the details.

There were little gasps all over the room. Five thousand dollars! We had never really dreamed of so much!

Papa nodded, but looked as though he weren't even listening to Mr. Kamp.

It was then that Beppe stood up and told Mr. Kamp the record was not for sale.

"Sorry you had to come out to Brooklyn for nothing," Beppe apologized. "We just this afternoon decided not to sell the record or the rights to it."

Both Papa and Mamma just sat looking at Beppe as though they couldn't believe what they were hearing.

Enrico and Giovanni didn't just sit there, though. They both began talking at once, each having forgotten that it would be better for the whole family, as they'd agreed, if we didn't sell our record. The offer of five thousand dollars had been too much for them. I began to tremble, and wanted to speak but couldn't.

Mr. Kamp stood up, too, as Beppe, his arms folded across his chest, stood facing Enrico and Giovanni defiantly, shaking his head. "If I might get a word in here," the record-company representa-

---

15. *Vesti la guibba* (VES tee lah GWEE bah)

tive said, "I would like to tell you I have been authorized to go as high as six thousand if necessary."

"Six thousand!" Enrico and Giovanni shouted together. Angelina and Mary Alice looked as though they might weaken, but Beppe stood his ground.

I still could not speak, and there were tears in my eyes which almost blinded me. I turned my head away so no one could see that I was crying. Through a blur I could see the record on the table.

I'll never be able to explain, not even to myself, just how it happened, but, with a sob of "No! No!" I grabbed the record from off the table and slammed it onto the floor, breaking it into a thousand pieces.

Everything in the room stopped dead-still where it was. Giovanni's hands hovered above Beppe's shoulders, where they were about to grab and shake him good. Papa's face had an expression of sorrow and joy and relief all at once as he took my hand. Mamma broke the silence sobbing and saying over and over in Italian, "Good son!" The others just stood staring at me in disbelief.

Mr. Kamp finally grabbed his hat and left, muttering to himself, "Crazy as loons, all of them!"

I ran into the kitchen, no longer able to control my sobs. The others followed, all except Beppe, and they were crying and hugging me and saying I had done the right thing, that it was the only way to bring them to their senses. Papa, his arm around my shoulder, assured me, "This is a family again, and nothing else matters."

Mamma began pouring wine and passing it around, stopping only to brush away a tear from time to time; she was smiling for the first time in two weeks.

We became conscious of the sound of music drifting in from the parlor. A few seconds later Beppe appeared at the kitchen door. "Listen," he said.

We could hardly believe our ears. It was *"Celeste Aïda!"*

Beppe grinned at me. "I guess we'll have to get a new *'Vesti la giubba,'*" he said. "It seems like our old one got broken somehow."

In my rush I had grabbed the wrong record from off the table!

"Celeste Aïda" never sounded so beautiful as it did then. We listened as though for the first time. When it was over and Caruso called out, *"Eh, Pasqualino, cumme stai?"* Papa answered, "Happy again, my friend, very happy." He spoke for all of us….

Well, that's all there is. We're a family again and still have the record. Maybe someday we'll save enough money to move to that farm in Jersey. Right now it's just something nice to dream about.

The Sunday evenings are once again as before, except that Angelina has now married, and now the couple join with us every Sunday. Maybe sometime you would like to come hear the record with us, too. Caruso never sang *"Celeste Aïda"* better, and we all still get a big kick out of *"Eh, Pasqualino, cumme stai?"* at the very end.

Studying the Selection

First Impressions

Look over the story, and note the touches that indicate it is written in an intimate, friendly style. Jot these down. Be prepared to discuss how the author gets close to us.

✔ Quick Review

1. Who are the only Espositos with American names?
2. What musical instrument had Papa played when he lived in Naples, Italy?
3. How had Papa come to know Caruso?
4. What was the name of the recording company representative?

In-depth Thinking

5. The Caruso record is just that—a record. Selling it could have made life much easier for Papa and Mamma. Why did they resist doing so?
6. Why was Mamma always crying?
7. Why was the Caruso recording worth at least a thousand dollars?
8. Why did Papa look intently at each of his children as Caruso sang *Celeste Aïda*?

Drawing Conclusions

9. Throughout *The Song Caruso Sang*, each Esposito child has a selfish plan for spending the money from the sale of the record. The thought of gaining a thousand dollars, then five thousand, then six thousand, greatly excites them. Why didn't George's siblings react angrily after he broke the record? Why did they say it "was the only way to bring them to their senses"? Does this sudden change in attitude ring true to you? Why or why not? Support your answer with passages from the story.
10. From the evidence in the story, do you think the family will ever have "enough money to move to that farm in Jersey"? Why or why not? Again, refer to the story to support your answer.

Focusing on Symbolism in Theme

Whether written as a comedy or a tragedy, a short story must have a theme or it will mean nothing to the reader. The theme of a story is usually something universal, a truth or attitude that makes the reader *think* or *feel* about the human condition. Comedy entertains us as we learn to understand that truth or attitude. This is the case with *The Song Caruso Sang*.

1. By yourself, or with a partner, list instances of George telling the story in a friendly, intimate manner. Write a shorter version of the story using a more formal style.
2. Write a character study of Papa as if he were the *only* family member who wanted to sell the record.
3. Reread the information on **tragedy** provided in the **Focusing** section. As part of a small group, rewrite the story as a tragedy. You might put it on as a play for the class.

Creating and Writing

1. The *"Celeste Aïda"* record is a symbol in the story. In a one-page essay, explain what it symbolizes.
2. Write a short article about a family tradition that is special to you. Consider holidays, religious activities, or even ordinary weekly events.
3. Research what life was like in America for new immigrants. If your relatives came to the United States in the previous century, you have a great source of information for this exercise. Otherwise, you may want to focus on a certain ethnic group in a particular time period—the Irish, Spanish, or Italians, in the late 1800s—or even interview someone who is a relatively new arrival, such as the Vietnamese. In your research, find out the difficulties and challenges posed by living in a new land far from one's homeland. Present your findings to the class.

Blueprint for Reading

the Author

D. H. Lawrence (1885-1930)

David Herbert Richard Lawrence was born in Eastwood in Nottinghamshire, England. After studying at University College, Nottingham, he became a teacher, but left to write, having achieved a mild success with his first novel, *The White Peacock* (1911). He married Frieda Weekley in 1914 and lived in Italy, Australia, and Mexico before returning to England. Besides short stories and novels, Lawrence wrote poetry and essays, all quite different from the usual polite English offerings. Referring to his writing, Lawrence said, "Whoever reads me will be in the thick of the scrimmage, and if he doesn't like it—if he wants a safe seat in the audience—let him read someone else." He died of tuberculosis at the age of forty-five.

Background Bytes

To some extent, writing is always autobiographical. The author's background, experience, education, beliefs, and gender leave traces. If the author wants to use personal raw material, the reader will not have to look far.

D. H. Lawrence wrote about what he knew and felt and left that imprint throughout his work. He grew up in the coal-mining town of Eastwood in Nottinghamshire, England, the fourth child of an illiterate miner and an educated mother. At the turn of the century, Lawrence's father and the other workers could walk through beautiful fields to gritty jobs in the mines. Many of Lawrence's works, including *Adolf*, explore the contrast between the mining town and the unspoiled countryside, between the spoiled rich and the noble poor, and examined the life and culture of the coal miners.

D. H. Lawrence was fascinated by the gap between the green world of the region and the grime of the mines, the weary routine of labor set against the freedom of wild creatures. The result is seen in *Adolf*, as Lawrence explores the difference between man and nature. The conflict is obvious as the very domestic mother tries to control wildness: the rabbit, disorder at home, children. A powerful short story is created. It remains with the reader long after it is put down.

Into *Adolf*

Have you ever written about a holiday, a school event, or a childhood episode? The result was probably a **vignette** (pronounced *vin-yet*), a sharply focused piece of nonfiction prose. Had you changed the names, altered events for greater impact, and included the literary components of theme and conflict, you would have had a short story.

Adolf is, likely, a vignette from Lawrence's childhood. How does he end the story? Note the narrator's reaction in the last paragraph. Is this a summing up of the theme? For whom does Lawrence have greater respect—man or beast?

Adolf

Focusing on Conflict as Theme

Normally, conflict serves to bring out theme. In *Adolf,* the conflicts *are* the theme. The story is, essentially a study of conflict. All three conflicts in literature are present in *Adolf*—**man vs. nature**, **man vs. man**, and **man vs. self**.

- Man vs. nature: a family tries to tame a wild animal that won't be tamed.
- Man vs. man: Mother argues with her family about keeping the creature.
- Man vs. self: the narrator must work to control emotions that can't be returned by "the wild and loveless" rabbit.

The sharp contrasts between **man and nature** cause the conflicts. Nature is pure and free; Father is dirty from the mine and tired. He feels compassion for Adolf and hopes he can survive indoors; Mother doesn't want the wild creature in her house. The narrator is drawn to Adolf but fights not to love him.

The conflicts are rooted in character. Sensible Mother lives by convention; animals may not eat at the table! Father, as unpredictable as Adolf, returns home soiled and weary at dawn, sips tea from a saucer like a cat, uses his forearm as a napkin, and grunts his comments.

The theme is a serious one, but Lawrence keeps a light tone. The rabbit is amusing, causing disorder yet fleeing the uproar. At first indifferent to the family, he becomes a nuisance, kicking and scratching the children. At story's end, conflict is usually resolved. Does that happen here? What lingers?

Word Bank

Enigmatically: What does it mean, to speak **enigmatically**? Do you know what an *enigma* is? An *enigma* is a puzzle or a riddle, and has come to mean a puzzling or contradictory situation or person. In both ancient Greece and Rome, the word meant *to speak darkly* or *in riddles*. Another word in the story, **obscure**, "not clear or plain, vague, indistinct," is also related to the absence of light. The Latin *obscurus* meant 'dark.' The word **oblivious**, "unmindful or unaware; without remembrance of memory," describes a state of mind in which there is a spiritual or psychological loss of light.

affronted	deluged	insolent	pensively
cajoling	elongation	oblivious	rend
circumvent	enigmatically	obscure	
clamor	extricated	palpitated	

Adolf

D. H. Lawrence

When we were children our father often worked on the night-shift. Once it was spring-time, and he used to arrive home, black and tired, just as we were downstairs in our nightdresses. Then night met morning face to face, and the contact was not always happy. Perhaps it was painful to my father to see us gaily entering upon the day into which he dragged himself soiled and weary. He didn't like going to bed in the spring morning sunshine.

But sometimes he was happy, because of his long walk through the dewy fields in the first daybreak. He loved the open morning, the crystal and the space, after a night down pit.[1] He watched every bird, every stir in the trembling grass, answered the whinnying of the peewits[2] and tweeted to the wrens. If he could, he also would have whinnied and tweeted and whistled in a native language that was not human. He liked non-human things best.

One sunny morning we were all sitting at table when we heard his heavy slurring walk up the entry. We became uneasy. His presence was always trammelling.[3] He passed the window darkly, and we heard him go into the scullery[4] and put down his tin bottle. But directly he came into the kitchen. We felt at once that he had something to communicate. No one spoke. We watched his black face for a second.

"Give me a drink," he said.

My mother hastily poured out his tea.

---

1. A night *down pit* is a night spent working in the coal mines.
2. A *peewit* (PEE wit) is any of various birds with a high, shrill cry, such as the lapwing.
3. *Trammelling* (TRAM uh ling) refers to the father's presence restraining the children from doing as they pleased.
4. A *scullery* (SKULL er ee) is a small room off a kitchen where food is prepared and utensils are cleaned and stored.

He went to pour it out into his saucer. But instead of drinking he suddenly put something on the table among the teacups. A tiny brown rabbit! A small rabbit, a mere morsel, sitting against the bread as still as if it were a made thing.

"A rabbit! A young one! Who gave it to you, Father?"

But he laughed enigmatically, with a sliding motion of his yellow-grey eyes, and went to take off his coat. We pounced on the rabbit.

"Is it alive? Can you feel its heart beat?"

My father came back and sat down heavily in his armchair. He dragged his saucer to him, and blew his tea, pushing out his red lips under his black moustache.

"Where did you get it, Father?"

"I picked it up," he said, wiping his forearm over his mouth and beard.

"Where?"

"It is a wild one!" came my mother's quick voice.

"Yes it is."

"Then why did you bring it?" cried my mother.

"Oh, we wanted it," came our cry.

"Yes, I've no doubt you did—" retorted my mother. But she was drowned in our clamor of questions.

On the field path my father had found a dead mother rabbit and three dead little ones—this one alive, but unmoving.

"But what had killed them, Daddy?"

"I couldn't say, my child. I s'd think she'd aten something."[5]

"Why did you bring it!" again my mother's voice of condemnation. "You know what it will be."

My father made no answer, but we were loud in protest.

"He must bring it. It's not big enough to live by itself. It would die," we shouted.

"Yes, and it will die now. And then there'll be *another* outcry."

My mother set her face against the tragedy of dead pets. Our hearts sank.

"It won't die, Father, will it? Why will it? It won't."

"I s'd think not," said my father.

"You know well enough it will. Haven't we had it all before!" said my mother.

"They dunna always pine,"[6] replied my father testily.

But my mother reminded him of other little wild animals he had brought, which had sulked and refused to live, and brought storms of tears and trouble in our house of lunatics.[7]

Trouble fell on us. The little rabbit sat on our lap, unmoving, its eye wide and dark. We brought it milk, warm milk, and held it to its nose. It sat still as if it was far away, retreated down some deep burrow, hidden, oblivious. We wetted its mouth and whiskers with drops of milk. It gave no sign, did not even shake off the wet white drops. Somebody began to shed a few secret tears.

"What did I say?" cried my mother. "Take it and put it down in the field."

Her command was in vain. We were driven to get dressed for school. There sat

---

5. "*I s'd think she'd aten something*": I should think she would have eaten something.
6. "*They dunna always pine*": They don't always waste away with hunger, grief, and homesickness.
7. A *lunatic* (LOON uh tik) is a person acting crazy-like.

Word Bank

enigmatically (EN ig MAT ih klee) *adv.*: perplexingly; mysteriously
clamor (KLAM er) *n.*: a loud uproar, as from a crowd of people
oblivious (uh BLIV ee us) *adj.*: unmindful or unaware

the rabbit. It was like a tiny obscure cloud. Watching it, our emotions died. Useless to love it, to yearn over it. A little wild thing, it became more mute and still, when we approached with love. We must not love it. We must circumvent it, for its own existence.

So I passed the order to my sister and my mother. The rabbit was not to be spoken to, nor even looked at. Wrapping it in a piece of flannel I put it in an obscure corner of the cold parlor, and put a saucer of milk before its nose. My mother was forbidden to enter the parlor while we were at school.

"As if I should take any notice of your nonsense," she cried affronted. Yet I doubt if she ventured into the parlor.

At midday, after school, creeping into the front room, there we saw the rabbit still and unmoving in the piece of flannel. Strange grey-brown neutralization of life, still living! It was a sore problem to us.

"Why won't it drink its milk, Mother?" we whispered. Our father was asleep.

"It prefers to sulk its life away, silly little thing." A profound problem. Prefers to sulk its life away! We put young dandelion leaves to its nose. The sphinx[8] was not more oblivious. Yet its eye was bright.

At tea-time, however, it had hopped a few inches, out of its flannel, and there it sat again, uncovered, a little solid cloud of muteness, brown, with unmoving whiskers. Only its side palpitated slightly with life.

Darkness came; my father set off to work. The rabbit was still unmoving. Dumb despair was coming over the sisters, a threat of tears came before bed-time. Clouds of my mother's anger gathered as she muttered against my father's wantonness.[9]

Once more the rabbit was wrapped in the old pit-singlet.[10] But now it was carried into the scullery and put under the copper fire-place, that it might imagine itself inside a burrow. The saucers were placed about, four or five, here and there on the floor, so that if the little creature *should* chance to hop abroad, it could not fail to come upon some food. After this my mother was allowed to take from the scullery what she wanted and then she was forbidden to open the door.

When morning came and it was light, I went downstairs. Opening the scullery door, I heard a slight scuffle. Then I saw dabbles of milk all over the floor and tiny rabbit droppings in the saucers. And there the miscreant,[11] the tips of his ears showing behind a pair of boots. I peeped at him. He sat bright-eyed and askance,[12] twitching his nose and looking at me while not looking at me.

He was alive—very much alive. But still we were afraid to trespass much on his confidence.

"Father!" My father was arrested[13] at the

---

8. The term *sphinx* (SFINX) refers to a still and mysterious thing.
9. In this context, *wantonness* (WAN tih niss) means playfulness.
10. *Pit-singlet* (PIT SING lit) is a woolen or flannel undershirt worn by coal miners.
11. A *miscreant* (MISS kree unt) is an evildoer without a conscience.
12. To sit *askance* (uh SKANTZ) means to sit, glancing sideways with a hint of disapproval.
13. Here, *arrested* means forcibly stopped.

Word Bank

obscure (ub SKYOOR) *adj.*: not readily seen, heard, noticed, or understood
circumvent (SIR kum VENT) *v.*: go around or bypass
affronted (uh FRUNT id) *adj.*: offended by an open display of disrespect; insulted
palpitated (PAL pih tayt id) *v.*: quivered; trembled; pulsated

door. "Father, the rabbit's alive."

"Sure on you it is," said my father. "Mind how you go in."

By evening, however, the little creature was tame, quite tame. He was named Adolf. We were enchanted by him. We couldn't really love him, because he was wild and loveless to the end. But he was an unmixed delight.

We decided he was too small to live in a hutch—he must live at large in the house. My mother protested, but in vain. He was so tiny. So we had him upstairs, and he dropped his tiny pills on the bed and we were enchanted.

Adolf made himself instantly at home. He had the run of the house, and was perfectly happy, with his tunnels and his holes behind the furniture.

We loved him to take meals with us. He would sit on the table humping his back, sipping his milk, shaking his whiskers and his tender ears, hopping off and hobbling back to his saucer, with an air of supreme unconcern. Suddenly he was alert. He hobbled a few tiny paces, and reared himself up inquisitively at the sugar basin.[14] He fluttered his tiny fore-paws and then reached and laid them on the edge of the basin, while he craned his thin neck and peeped in. He trembled his whiskers at the sugar, then he did the best to lift down a lump.

"*Do* you think I will have it! Animals in the sugar pot!" cried my mother, with a rap of her hand on the table.

Which so delighted the electric Adolf that he flung his hind-quarters and knocked over a cup.

He continued to take tea with us. He rather liked warm tea. And he loved sugar. Having nibbled a lump, he would turn to the butter. There he was shooed off by our parent. He soon learned to treat her shooing with indifference. Still, she hated him to put his nose in the food. And he loved to do it. And one day between them they overturned the cream-jug. Adolf deluged his little chest, bounced back in terror, was seized by his little ears by my mother and bounced down on the hearth rug. There he shivered in momentary discomfort, and suddenly set off in a wild flight to the parlor.

This was his happy hunting ground. He had cultivated the bad habit of pensively nibbling certain bits of cloth in the hearthrug. When chased from this pasture he would retreat under the sofa. There he would twinkle in meditation until suddenly, no one knew why, he would go off like an alarm clock. With a sudden bumping scuffle he would whirl out of the room,

---

14. The *sugar basin* is the sugar bowl.

Word Bank

deluged (DEL yoojd) *v*.: covered with liquid; flooded

pensively (PEN siv lee) *adv*.: in a dreamily or wistfully thoughtful way

going through the doorway with his little ears flying. Then we would hear his thunderbolt hurtling in the parlor, but before we could follow, the wild streak of Adolf would flash past us, on an electric wind that swept him round the scullery and carried him back, a little mad thing, flying possessed like a ball round the parlor. After which ebullition[15] he would sit in a corner composed and distant, twitching his whiskers in abstract meditation. And it was in vain we questioned him about his outburst. He just went off like a gun, and was as calm after it as a gun that smokes placidly.

Alas, he grew up rapidly. It was almost impossible to keep him from the outer door.

One day, as we were playing by the stile,[16] I saw his brown shadow loiter across the road and pass into the field that faced the houses. Instantly a cry of "Adolf!"—a cry he knew full well. And instantly a wind swept him away down the sloping meadow, his tail twinkling and zigzagging through the grass. After him we pelted. It was a strange sight to see him, ears back, his little loins so powerful, flinging the world behind him. We ran ourselves out of breath, but could not catch him. Then somebody headed him off, and he sat with sudden unconcern, twitching his nose under a bunch of nettles.[17]

His wanderings cost him a shock. One Sunday morning my father had just been quarrelling with a pedlar, and we were hearing the aftermath indoors, when there came a sudden unearthly scream from the yard. We flew out. There sat Adolf cowering under a bench, while a great black and white cat glowered intently at him, a few yards away. Sight not to be forgotten. Adolf rolling back his eyes and parting his strange muzzle in another scream, the cat stretching forward in a slow elongation.

Ha, how we hated that cat! How we pur-

---

15. Here, *ebullition* (EB uh LISH in) means an outburst of spontaneous, wild energy.
16. A *stile* (STY il) refers to a set of steps leading over a fence or wall.
17. *Nettles* (NET ilz) are shrubs with coarse, stinging hairs.

Word Bank   **elongation** (EE long GAY shun) *n.*: a lengthening or extending

sued him over the wall and across the neighbors' gardens.

Adolf was still only half grown.

"Cats!" said my mother. "Hideous detestable animals, why do people harbor them?"

But Adolf was becoming too much for her. He dropped too many pills. And suddenly to hear him clumping downstairs when she was alone in the house was startling. And to keep him from the door was impossible. Cats prowled outside. It was worse than having a child to look after.

Yet we would not have him shut up. He became more lusty, more callous[18] than ever. He was a strong kicker, and many a scratch on face and arms did we owe to him. But he brought his own doom on himself. The lace curtains in the parlor—my mother was rather proud of them—fell on the floor very full. One of Adolf's joys was to scuffle wildly through them as though through some foamy undergrowth. He had already torn rents in them.

One day he entangled himself altogether. He kicked, he whirled round in a mad nebulous[19] inferno. He screamed—and brought down the curtain-rod with a smash, right on the best beloved pelargonium,[20] just as my mother rushed in. She extricated him, but she never forgave him. And he never forgave either. A heartless wildness had come over him.

Even we understood that he must go. It was decided, after a long deliberation, that my father should carry him back to the wild-woods. Once again he was stowed into the great pocket of the pit-jacket.

"Best pop him i' th' pot," said my father, who enjoyed raising the wind of indignation.

And so, next day, our father said that Adolf, set down on the edge of the coppice,[21] had hopped away with utmost indifference, neither elated nor moved. We heard it and believed. But many, many were the heartsearchings. How would the other rabbits receive him? Would they smell his tameness, his humanized degradation,[22] and rend him? My mother pooh-poohed the extravagant idea.

However, he was gone, and we were rather relieved. My father kept an eye open for him. He declared that several times passing the coppice in the early morning, he had seen Adolf peeping through the nettle stalks. He had called him, in an odd-voiced, cajoling fashion. But Adolf had not responded. Wildness gains so soon upon its creatures. And they become so contemptuous then of our tame presence. So it seemed to me. I myself would go to the edge of the coppice and call softly. I myself would imagine bright eyes between the nettle-stalks, flash of a white, scornful tail past the bracken.[23] That insolent white tail, as Adolf turned his flank on us!

---

18. *Callous* (KAL iss) means hardened.
19. A *nebulous* (NEB yuh liss) inferno is a cloudy or cloudlike area of intense heat.
20. The term *pelargonium* (PEL ahr GO nee um) is the Latin term for geranium, a woody flowering plant.
21. A *coppice* (KAHP iss) is a thicket of small trees or bushes.
22. *Degradation* (DEG rih DAY shun) refers to Adolf's supposed loss of dignity by his associating with humans.
23. *Bracken* (BRAK in) refers to clusters of large ferns.

Word Bank

extricated (EX trih kayt id) *v.*: freed or released from entanglement; disengaged
rend *v.*: separate into parts with force or violence; tear apart
cajoling (kuh JOE ling) *adj.*: persuading by flattery or promises; wheedling; coaxing
insolent (IN suh lint) *adj.*: haughtily contemptuous, extremely disrespectful

Studying the Selection

First Impressions

Father rescues Adolf. Can a rabbit acknowledge such a gesture? Even imagining a final snub, the narrator tries to live with Adolf but cannot. At story's end, has the narrator accepted that some 'wildness' cannot be tamed?

✔ Quick Review

1. What made Father happy after a long night's work?
2. Where had Father found the rabbit?
3. Where was Adolf moved after spending the first night in the parlor?
4. What other animal did Adolf encounter in the yard one day?

In-depth Thinking

5. Why does Father think the dead mother rabbit has eaten something that killed her and her little ones?
6. How is Father's behavior similar to that of the rabbit?
7. Explain the phrase "Strange grey-brown neutralization of life, still living."
8. If Adolf enchants the family, why does the narrator feel he should not love the animal?

Drawing Conclusions

9. How does Mother differ from the rest of the family?
10. Why does Father seem so uncomfortable in his own home?

Focusing on Conflict as Theme

1. Adolf is brought home after the mother rabbit dies. Without Father's help, Adolf could not survive. Has Father 'solved' the conflict between man and nature? Write a few paragraphs about Father's dealings with the rabbit.
2. Have you been part of a **man vs. nature** conflict? Write about it, changing details as you turn *your* childhood vignette into a short story.
3. A formal debate usually consists of an opening statement—either for or against a position—followed by supporting material. Then you present material that exposes the weakness of your opponent's position. In closing, you sum up, stating your position even more strongly. Each part needn't take more than two minutes.

   Choose a classmate for a partner, and prepare to debate another team.

   Use one of these topics:
   - Most of us prefer safe *wildness* (zoos or theme parks) over real wilderness.
   - Animals should be left in their natural habitats.
   - Endangered animals should be safeguarded in 'recreated' habitats.

Creating and Writing

1. Write about a beloved pet. Was the pet allowed to run free in the home, or were boundaries established? Were all boundaries physical?
2. Take a nature hike, and look for signs of animal life. Use all your senses (sight, sound, touch, smell, taste—well, maybe not taste!). Nature is ready to teach if we pay attention. Prepare a short speech for the class, entitled "What Nature Can Teach Us."
3. Ask your teacher to suggest further readings on this theme.

Blueprint for Reading

the Author

Ernest Hemingway (1899-1961)

Ernest Hemingway was the second son of a physician. He grew up in a suburb of Chicago, Illinois. He began writing in high school, and worked briefly as a reporter for the *Kansas City Times* following his graduation.

In World War I, Hemingway worked for the Red Cross as a volunteer ambulance driver. He was wounded in Italy, and received a medal for bravery in the field. During World War II, he worked overseas as a reporter.

Hemingway once said, "My aim is to put down on paper what I see and what I feel in the best and simplest way." He was a fine writer and did exactly as he said. His language is plain, his writing not overly complex, and his personal philosophy simple. He is known for not wasting words.

Hemingway is recognized as one of the most important writers of 20th century literature. He was awarded both the Pulitzer Prize for Fiction and the Nobel Prize in Literature.

Background Bytes

If in reading *Old Man at the Bridge*, you feel the author was literally at this battle in Spain, your impression is correct. Ernest Hemingway first wrote *Old Man at the Bridge* as a news dispatch during the Spanish Civil War (1936–1939). This was one of a series of stories featuring the substitute-self *Edwin Henry*, acting as the voice of Hemingway.

The bare writing style seems to be a typical, no-nonsense newspaper report. Yet it is more—because it is less! You are looking at the invention of a style, an economical prose that tells us more than the words say. The story must be read for deeper meaning, as if it *were* a poem. Today critics often refer to a story as being Hemingway-esque, even if it is written by someone else.

Into *Old Man at the Bridge*

In most war stories, the horror is off-stage, hidden from an audience expecting entertainment and excitement, but shunning the accompanying blood or terror. Certainly, the horror of war is not usually found in a soft-spoken, weary old man, yet Hemingway takes this path in *Old Man at the Bridge*. Here is an old man, barely aware of the surrounding disorder, worrying about animals left behind when he was forced to leave home. In only two pages, Hemingway captures the subject and with it, the theme of hopelessness.

Keep in mind—that the literary component of theme makes us *think* about the human condition. With Hemingway's themes we have to think yet again, as they don't reveal themselves with a single reading. He has mastered understatement, reporting what he sees, but forcing us to read 'between the lines.' He doesn't use an emotional writing style, yet the story will jolt you.

Old Man at the Bridge

Finally, pay close attention to the way Hemingway structures the story. Hemingway does not open with emotional remarks. His character, Edwin Henry, reveals little feeling until the closing line of this tale. Had Henry's final statements been placed at the beginning of *Old Man at the Bridge*, they would not have been powerful. Hemingway gives Henry's sentiments even greater impact by relating his thoughts flatly and casually.

Focusing on the Understated Theme

Given his journalistic background, Hemingway seemingly gives us what he sees, as a photographer would take a picture. He uses simple nouns and verbs to capture scenes, giving the reader the *who*, *what*, *where*, *when*, and *why* of the experience, as seen by a reporter. The reader knows "just the facts," but finds meaning in the material left unsaid.

Hemingway's *economical writing style* is used for complex purposes. Through simple dialogue that advances the story and the intervening narrative passages, Hemingway makes a statement about the horrors of war, as the old man shows he is losing his hold on reality.

Irony means *incongruous*, the difference between what we expect and what we get. Irony plays a key role in Hemingway's writing. In *Old Man at the Bridge* the old man sits passively as refugees flee to safety. Facing an approaching enemy, he is concerned with his animals. Without politics, he is swept up in a political conflict. Irony underlies *Old Man at the Bridge*, making a powerful, yet implied, statement that war is not concerned with its victims.

Old Man at the Bridge

Ernest Hemingway

An old man with steel-rimmed spectacles and very dusty clothes sat by the side of the road. There was a pontoon bridge[1] across the river and carts, trucks, and men, women, and children were crossing it. The mule-drawn carts staggered up the steep bank from the bridge with soldiers helping push against the spokes of the wheels. The trucks ground up and away heading out of it all and the peasants plodded along in the ankle deep dust. But the old man sat there without moving. He was too tired to go any farther.

It was my business to cross the bridge, explore the bridgehead beyond, and find out to what point the enemy had advanced. I did this and returned over the bridge. There were not so many carts now and very few people on foot, but the old man was still there.

"Where do you come from?" I asked him.

"From San Carlos," he said, and smiled.

That was his native town and so it gave him pleasure to mention it and he smiled.

"I was taking care of animals," he explained.

"Oh," I said, not quite understanding.

"Yes," he said, "I stayed, you see, taking care of animals. I was the last one to leave the town of San Carlos."

He did not look like a shepherd nor a herdsman and I looked at his black dusty clothes and his gray dusty face and his steel-rimmed spectacles and said, "What animals were they?"

"Various animals," he said, and shook his head. "I had to leave them."

I was watching the bridge and the African-looking country of the Ebro Delta[2] and wondering how long now it would be before we would see the enemy, and listening all the while for the first noises that would signal that ever-mysterious event called contact, and the old man still sat there.

"What animals were they?" I asked.

"There were three animals altogether," he explained. "There were two goats and a cat and then there were four pairs of pigeons."

"And you had to leave them?" I asked.

"Yes. Because of the artillery.[3] The captain told me to go because of the artillery."

"And you have no family?" I asked, watching the far end of the bridge where a few last carts were hurrying down the slope of the bank.

"No," he said, "only the animals I

---

1. A *pontoon* (pahn TOON) *bridge* is a temporary bridge supported by boats or other floating structures.
2. The *Ebro Delta* is the fan-shaped outpouring of silt at the mouth of the Ebro River in Spain.
3. *Artillery* (ar TILL uh ree) refers to the mounted guns and missile launchers.

stated. The cat, of course, will be all right. A cat can look out for itself, but I cannot think what will become of the others."

"What politics have you?" I asked.

"I am without politics," he said. "I am seventy-six years old. I have come twelve kilometers[4] now and I think now I can go no further."

"This is not a good place to stop," I said. "If you can make it, there are trucks up the road where it forks for Tortosa."

"I will wait a while," he said, "and then I will go. Where do the trucks go?"

"Towards Barcelona," I told him.

"I know no one in that direction," he said, "but thank you very much. Thank you again very much."

He looked at me very blankly and tiredly, then said, having to share his worry with someone, "The cat will be all right, I am sure. There is no need to be unquiet[5] about the cat. But the others. Now what do you think about the others?"

"Why, they'll probably come through it all right."

"You think so?"

"Why not?" I said, watching the far bank where now there were no carts.

"But what will they do under the artillery when I was told to leave because of the artillery?"

"Did you leave the dove cage unlocked?" I asked.

"Yes."

"Then they'll fly."

"Yes, certainly they'll fly. But the others. It's better not to think about the others," he said.

"If you are rested I would go," I urged. "Get up and try to walk now."

"Thank you," he said and got to his feet, swayed from side to side and then sat down backwards in the dust.

"I was taking care of animals," he said dully, but no longer to me. "I was only taking care of animals."

There was nothing to do about him. It was Sunday and the Fascists[6] were advancing toward the Ebro. It was a gray overcast day with a low ceiling so their planes were not up. That and the fact that cats know how to look after themselves was all the good luck that old man would ever have.

---

4. A *kilometer* (kih LAHM ih ter), or 1000 meters, is equivalent to 0.62 miles.
5. Here *unquiet* means uneasy.
6. The *Fascists* (FASH ists) were the army forces supported by Germany during the Spanish Civil War (1936-1939).

Studying the Selection

First Impressions When did you realize this is a story rather than a nonfiction news report? Is the flat, unemotional language appropriate to a war story? What is your initial emotional reaction to the story? Write a few paragraphs about Hemingway's focus on the old man rather than on the approaching battle.

✓ Quick Review

1. What is the narrator's job?
2. Where had the old man lived?
3. What animals did he leave behind in that town?
4. Where are the trucks headed?

In-depth Thinking

5. Does the narrator lack compassion?
6. Is the narrator concerned about the animals the old man left behind?
7. Can we assume the old man has lost touch with reality? List passages that support your answer.
8. Compare the old man's worries about his animals to the narrator's concern for the old man. How do their concerns differ?

Drawing Conclusions

9. Knowing that the Spanish Civil War was about extremist politics, why is it important to know that the old man is "without politics"?
10. Hemingway was obviously a talented reporter. What skills do you think are needed to become a journalist?

Focusing on the Understated Theme

Old Man at the Bridge is a haunting story, gaining strength from its understated presentation. In the hands of another writer, it might have been emotionally overdone. The following exercises will help you examine the seemingly simple writing of Ernest Hemingway.

1. Rewrite the story as an article that might have appeared in a newspaper in the 1930s. Remember *who*, *what*, *where*, *when*, and *why*, the 'Five W's' of journalism; report "just the facts." Objectivity matters—you should not insert your personal feelings about the old man in your article.
2. List instances of Hemingway using irony as a literary device.
3. Look at the ending of the story. Imagine it is now one day later. Rewrite the ending to reflect this new information. In what way is this new ending at odds with Hemingway's use of ironic understatement?

Creating and Writing

1. Write an essay about the insanity of war and how the old man reacts to that insanity.
2. Look at the writing style of other authors in this unit—Dunbar, Hale, McCallum, and Lawrence. Rewrite a part of *Old Man at the Bridge* using the style of one of these writers. The theme of the rewritten story should be more readily apparent than Hemingway's.
3. Visit veterans at a local veterans' hospital or interview a war veteran in your family or neighborhood. Ask how being involved in a war has changed his or her life, and then let the veteran talk. What is the focus of these recollections?

Blueprint for Reading

the Author

**Robb White
(1909-1990)**

Robb White was born in the Caribbean and spent much of his childhood on tropical islands. Many of his stories are about these experiences. White went to high school in Virginia and attended the Naval Academy in Annapolis, Maryland. He later married and moved to the British Virgin Islands where he wrote a story about life there called *Our Virgin Island*.

Background Bytes

This story, set in the present, is not trying to express a theme or teach a lesson, unless it's the lesson that reading is fun.

We are introduced to a character and a situation. Then we're taken on a wild ride to a surprising conclusion. Look for the various literary techniques the author uses to maintain the suspense, delay the outcome, and overcome normal reader disbelief.

Into *Fetch!*

The author's purpose in *Fetch!* is to entertain, using two *colliding* (rather than *interacting*) characters and a plot device that drives the story forward. We meet a student and a professor, acting as job seeker and potential employer. The author doesn't bother much with characterization; the situation drives the story forward. Think—how would you test a friend's loyalty or resourcefulness?

Focusing on a Just for Fun Read

As you read, keep in mind the author's purpose—entertainment. Then notice how characters, setting, plot, and point of view interact to divert the reader's attention and create a short but satisfying read.

Word Bank

Artifacts: These days, the word **artifact** is mostly used to describe handmade objects dug up at archaeological sites, such as tools, or the remains of handmade objects, such as shards of pottery. Although **artifact** simply means something made by human beings for *use*, its *connotative meaning* is an object that comes from an earlier culture—something left over or representative. The Latin word *facere*, 'to make,' is the source of literally dozens of English words. In order to show past tense, the form of the Latin verb changes and includes such spellings as *fec-*, *fic-*, and *fact-*. Examples include *counterfeit, beneficent, factory, manufacture, faculty, perfect, sufficient.* How many English words can you find with this root? Do you know what their prefixes and suffixes mean?

artifacts   inestimable

FETCH!

Robb White

The last thing George Dixon expected, or wanted, to meet in an apartment on the seventeenth floor was this enormous Great Dane with an old tennis ball in his mouth. When Professor Werner called, "Come on in," and George opened the door, the only thing that greeted him was that dog, who knocked him back against the wall.

"Play with the dog, Dixon. I'll be out in a minute," the professor said from somewhere back in the apartment.

With that dog you did what that dog wanted you to do: Throw the ball so he could go galloping around and bring it back to you.

George had a lot more on his mind than playing with a dog. Six of his friends in Werner's archaeology[1] class already had been interviewed for the job and been turned down. Now it was his turn and he wanted to rehearse his speech, but this dog was jumping all over him and the furniture, dropping the drool-soaked ball on his best pants.

Then the idea came and George took the slimy ball and held it up. "OK, Fido, you're so smart, go get this one."

Instead of throwing the ball, George rolled it gently across the floor and, with great satisfaction, watched it roll under a low Oriental chest placed beneath an open window.

The Great Dane bounded across the room, his tail knocking a vase of flowers off a table.

The dog did not stop, nor even slow down.

With sudden horror George watched him leap from the floor. He cleared the top of the chest and went on, stretched out, flying. Outside a gentle rain was lit by the streetlights far below. The enormous dog sailed out into the rainy darkness. For what seemed a century to George the body of the dog seemed to float in the air. Then it slowly sank out of sight, falling down through the rain.

The Great Dane did not make a sound as he fell toward the pavement seventeen stories down.

For a moment George just sat there, paralyzed with agony for the dog.

Then he was on his feet running, looking only at the open, dark, and empty window.

Something grabbed his arm, stopping him in mid-stride and spinning him around.

---

1. *Archaeology* (AR kee AHL uh jee) is the scientific study of ancient peoples and their cultures.

"Come on!" Professor Werner said. "I'm late for an appointment so we'll talk in the elevator."

"Wait!" George begged, trying to pull his arm free.

"Come *on!*" the professor ordered, yanking him to the door.

"No! Wait!" George said, but the professor pulled him out of the room and locked the door.

Without a word Werner dragged George to the elevator, shoved him into it, and pushed the button for the lobby.

It was only after the elevator began to sink that George really understood the enormity of the thing. In his mind's eye he could still see that beautiful dog sailing out into the darkness and, in his body, almost feel the long, dreadful fall. Some of the windows the dog would fall past would have lights in them; some would be dark. The pavement would be wet with rain.

Gradually George realized that the professor had been talking to him all the time. They were going to dig in a remote cave in Kurdistan.[2] They might find gold artifacts of inestimable value. There might be clues to the missing chapters in the history of the human race.

George couldn't listen to him, couldn't pay attention.

That great dog, with the ball in his mouth, leaping so happily around that room. Those huge, soft eyes asking him to throw the ball again. The dirty trick he had pulled on him.

The professor kept talking and talking. It would be rugged in Kurdistan, and dangerous. They would explore a cave with a deep hole in the floor, perhaps a thousand feet deep. A hole down which some ancient man may have fallen thousands of years ago.

The dog had fallen *now*, tonight.

Slowly, as the elevator dial went past ten and nine and eight, George tried to erase the picture of that dog and to think about himself: this job he wanted so badly, this interview on which everything depended.

Had it been his fault? A dog had made a mistake and leaped out an open window. Had that been his fault? Was he to blame for that? Did he have to admit it?

Should he lose this job because of a dog?

George realized slowly that the professor had been asking him a direct question.

The elevator dial read three.

"Dixon," the professor asked again, "what's your definition of courage?" It took all his mental strength to force his mind to pay attention.

"Courage, sir? Er. Courage? I guess it's doing the right thing when you don't have to. Even though no one is watching. Nobody saw anything."

---

2. *Kurdistan* (KUR dih STAN) is a land of mountains and plateaus in southeast Turkey, northwestern Iran, and northern Iraq. Although the Kurds are geographically dispersed, they are united by a common language.

Word Bank

artifacts (AR tih FAKTZ) *n.*: handmade objects, or their remains from an earlier time, found at an archaeological excavation

inestimable (in ESS tih muh bul) *adj.*: too precious to be estimated or appreciated; invaluable

Werner laughed. "That's a definition I'd never thought of. But it's not bad. Anyway, this expedition you and I are going on is going to take a lot of it."

You and I. That's what he'd said. *You and I.*

People would be standing in the rain now, looking down at that beautiful dog lying crushed on the wet pavement.

The elevator stopped and the doors slid silently open.

As Werner started out, George pushed the CLOSE DOORS button and then turned and put both hands on Werner's shoulders, pushing him back against the wall.

"I killed your dog," George said.

Werner stared at him.

"I was playing with him. Throwing the ball. He went out the window. Just out. Into the rain."

Werner said nothing as he pushed George's hands aside and then walked to the front of the elevator and pushed the seventeen button.

The elevator going up made no sound at all and Werner stood in silence with his back to George.

"He was a beautiful dog," George said. "I'm sorry."

Werner said nothing as the doors opened and he stepped out. Without looking at George or waiting for him, he walked down the silent corridor, unlocked the door, reached in and turned on the lights and then, at last, turned and waited for George.

Feeling sick, and seeing again that dark, open window, George walked slowly into the room.

A great, moving weight struck him from behind, knocking him down flat on his face.

For a moment he just wanted to lie there, his face down on the carpet, his body waiting for more of the attack he knew he deserved.

Then something gently nudged him and he turned his head.

There was the Great Dane with that soggy tennis ball in his mouth, his tail flailing away, knocking things off a table.

"It was a mean thing to do to you, Dixon," Werner said. "But I need to know what sort of man I'm taking on this dangerous expedition."

George put his arms around the dog's neck and then got to his feet.

"There's a balcony outside that window," Werner said, smiling. "And this mutt loves to show off."

Studying the Selection

First Impressions

A rainy night, an open window, a playful dog, a nervous job seeker—these are the elements of the author's extended joke. Is it clever or silly—satisfying or contrived?

✔ Quick Review

1. Why is George in the professor's apartment? What is George's state of mind when he first arrives?
2. What is George told to do while the professor gets ready?
3. Why does George roll the ball under the chest?
4. Where is the professor's apartment located?

In-depth Thinking

5. Why doesn't George immediately tell the professor what happened to the dog?
6. Why doesn't George hear what the professor says in the elevator?
7. Why does George close the elevator doors to tell the professor about the dog?

Drawing Conclusions

8. What is ironic about George's definition of the word *courage*?
9. How do you know the professor was always aware of George's inner torment?

Focusing on a Just for Fun Read

In *Fetch!*, underlying plot weaknesses are well-hidden, as the author concentrates on providing a satisfying reading experience. George is put in a trying situation, and we do more than watch his reaction. The omniscient narrator has put us into George's mind as he works through his internal conflict. In effect, the narrow viewpoint keeps us from paying too much attention to any narrative flaws. For instance, why was a window left open on a rainy night? (Answer: The author needs to have the dog jump through it.) However, if George can ignore it, we might as well do so.

1. Can you find any other plot weaknesses?
2. How does the narrator draw out the suspense?
3. How does the conflict change as the story continues?
4. Look up the definitions of **round** and **flat characters** in the **Index of Literary Terms** in the back of your textbook. Are the characters of George and the professor round or flat? Why?

Creating and Writing

1. Explain how the point of view contributes to the suspense of the story. How does the narrator manipulate the reader's perception of time, to deepen emotional involvement in the story? Examine where the author arouses feelings of sympathy or empathy for George, and explain how he does it.
2. Imagine you are George and have undergone this experience. Write a letter thanking the professor for the interview. Mention the incident with the dog, and the lesson learned, being as polite as possible. Or, you can thank the professor for the interview, but decline the job, using polite but firm language to explain yourself.
3. Create a skit with three characters in which one character is being put through a test. Two characters are aware of the situation; the test-taker doesn't know what is happening.

Blueprint for Reading

the Author

Hugh Pentecost (1903-1989)

Hugh Pentecost's real name was Judson Phillips. As a mystery writer using a pen-name, he was a bit mysterious himself. He was best known for his mystery novels and wrote more than thirty. In 1939, he won the Dodd Mead Red Badge Mystery Story Award.

Background Bytes

Pat Mahoney, a main character in this story, is a retired stage entertainer. His background in vaudeville has shaped him. He dresses, acts, and speaks with a theatrical flair. Every conversation is a chance to perform, as his voice drops, leaving the listener hanging, wanting more.

His kind of theater, the vaudeville stage, is long gone, but until the 1950s it hosted more entertainers than any other branch of live theater. Basically, vaudeville was a variety show, a series of acts featuring singers, dancers, comedians, magicians, even animal trainers with their comic dogs and monkeys. They traveled the country, appearing for a week or two in each city. Then entertainment fashions changed; the country grew up, and vaudeville was only a memory—except to Pat Mahoney, for whom it is still very much alive!

Into *The Day the Children Vanished*

Although the story takes place in a small American town, the actions and reactions of the various characters are universal. The story has a mysterious plot, and is written in a style that creates and prolongs suspense. The major characters are interesting: concerned parents, a baffled young lady, a clever investigator, and a seemingly bewildered old vaudevillian. Their interaction moves the story along, even as the suspense builds. The theme of the story is a common one—the difference between appearance and reality.

When faced with the seemingly unexplainable, how does the creative problem solver proceed? Where in the story might you question what seems to be real?

The Day the Children Vanished

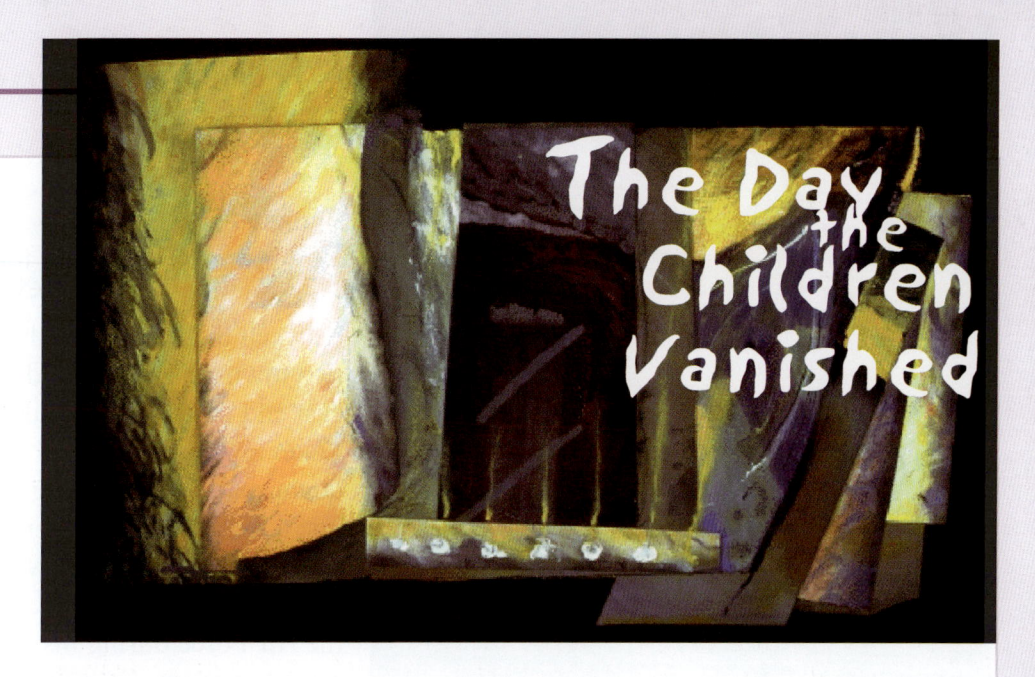

Focusing on Pulling It All Together

The **theme** of the story—the difficulty of establishing reality—underlies the main **plot** of the story but is seen in smaller details as well. One **character** may appear to be out of touch with reality, while another seems levelheaded. Which is which? The situation is played out in a **setting** that looks obvious, but appearances may be deceiving.

Why is the difference between appearance and reality such a common literary theme? Is this concern part of our own lives? Think of some real-life examples when a person has to separate appearance from reality.

Word Bank

Mesmerized: The word, **mesmerized**, is an example of an eponym—a word derived from a person's name. The Austrian physician, Franz (or Friedrich) Anton Mesmer, who lived from 1733 to 1815, worked with hypnosis, and apparently mesmerized his patients!

adequately	charade	incompetence	novel	routine
annals	expedient	inexplicable	objective	stance
bereaved	gaudy	mesmerized	quarry	writhing
callous	impenetrable			

The Day the Children Vanished

Hugh Pentecost

On a bright, clear winter's afternoon the nine children in the town of Clayton who traveled each day to the Regional School in Lakeview disappeared from the face of the earth, along with the bus in which they traveled and its driver, as completely as if they had been sucked up into outer space by some monstrous interplanetary[1] vacuum cleaner.

There was, of course, nothing interplanetary or supernatural[2] about the disappearance of nine children, one adult, and a special-bodied station wagon which was used as a school bus. It was the result of callous human villainy.[3] But, because there was no possible explanation for it, it assumed all the aspects of black magic in the minds of tortured parents and a bewildered citizenry.

Lakeview, considerably larger and with a long history of planning for growth, recently built a new school. It was agreed between the boards of education of the two towns that nine children living at the east end of Clayton should be sent to the Lakeview School where there was adequate space and teaching staff. It was to be just a temporary expedient.

Jerry Mahoney, the driver, was well liked and respected. He had been a mechanic in the Air Force during his tour of duty in the armed services. He was a wizard with engines. He was engaged to be married to Elizabeth Deering, who worked in the Clayton Bank. They were both nice people, responsible people.

The disappearance of the station wagon, the nine children and Jerry Mahoney took place on a two-mile stretch of road where disappearance was impossible. It was called the "dugway," and it wound along the side of the lake. Heavy wire guard rails protected the road from the lake for the full two miles. There was not a gap in it anywhere.

The ground on the other side of the road rose abruptly upward into thousands of acres of mountain woodlands, so thickly grown that not even a tractor could have

---

1. *Interplanetary* (IN ter PLAN uh TAIR ee) refers to something occurring between planets.
2. A *supernatural* occurrence is an occurrence that is above nature or unexplainable by natural law.
3. The term *villainy* (VILL uh nee) means outrageous wickedness.

Word Bank

callous (KAL iss) *adj.*: insensitive; indifferent; unsympathetic
expedient (eks PEED ee int) *n.*: a handy means to an end

made its way up any part of it except for a few yards of deserted road that led to an abandoned quarry. Even over this old road nothing could have passed without leaving a trail of torn brush and broken saplings.

At the Lakeview end of the dugway was a filling station owned by old Jake Nugent. On the afternoon of the disappearance the bus, with Jerry Mahoney at the wheel and his carload of kids laughing and shouting at each other, stopped at old man Nugent's. Jerry Mahoney had brought the old man a special delivery letter from the post office, thus saving the RFD[4] driver from making a special trip. Jerry and old Jake exchanged greetings, the old man signed the receipt for his letter, and Jerry drove off into the dugway with his cargo of kids.

At the Clayton end of the dugway was Joe Gorman's diner, and one of the children in Jerry's bus was Peter Gorman, Joe's son. The Diner was Jerry's first stop coming out of the dugway with his cargo of kids.

It was four-thirty in the afternoon when Joe Gorman realized that the bus was nearly three-quarters of an hour late. Worried, he called the school in Lakeview and was told by Miss Bromfield, the principal, that the bus had left on schedule.

This was one of seven calls Miss Bromfield was to get in the next half hour, all inquiring about the bus. Nine children; seven families.

Joe Gorman was the first to do anything about it seriously. He called Jake Nugent's filling station to ask about the bus, and old Jake told him it had gone through from his place on schedule. So something had happened to Jerry and his busload of kids in the dugway. Joe got out his jeep and headed through the dugway toward Lakeview. He got all the way to Jake Nugent's without seeing the bus or passing anyone coming the other way.

He used Jake's phone to call the Dicklers in Clayton. The Dicklers' two children, Dorothy and Donald, were part of Jerry's load and they were the next stop after Joe's Diner. The Dicklers were already alarmed because the children hadn't appeared.

Joe didn't offer any theories. He was scared, though. He called the trooper barracks in Lakeview and told them about the missing bus. They didn't take it too seriously, but they said they'd send a man out.

Joe headed back for Clayton. This time his heart was a lump in his throat. He drove slowly, staring at every inch of the wire guard rails. There was not a break anywhere, not a broken or bent post. The bus simply couldn't have skidded over the embankment into the lake without smashing through the wire guard rail.

Five minutes after Joe came out at his diner, Trooper Teliski came whizzing through from Lakeview and stopped his car.

"What's the gag?" he asked Joe.

Joe tried to light a cigarette and his hands were shaking so badly he couldn't make it. "Look," he said. "The bus started through the dugway at the regular time." He told about Jerry's stop at Nugent's. "It never came out this end."

A nerve twitched in Teliski's cheek. "The Lake," he said.

Joe shook his head. "I—I thought of that, right off. I just came through ahead of you—

---

4. *RFD* is an abbreviation for Rural Free Delivery which indicates the outlying areas of major cities where mail is still delivered to the homes.

Word Bank quarry (KWOR ee) *n.*: an excavation or pit from which building stone and slate are obtained by cutting or blasting

looking. Not a break in the guard rail anywhere. Not a scratch. Not a bent post. The bus didn't go into the lake. I'll stake my life on that."

"Then what else?" Teliski asked. "It couldn't go up the mountain."

"I know," Joe said, and the two men stared at each other.

"It's some kind of joke," Teliski said.

"It's no joke to me."

"Maybe they had permission to go to a special movie," Teliski said.

"Without notifying the parents? I talked to Miss Bromfield. She would have told me. Listen, Teliski. The bus went into the dugway and it didn't come out. It's not in the dugway now and it didn't go into the lake."

Teliski was silent for a moment; then he spoke with a solid attempt at common sense. "It didn't come out this end," he said. "We'll check back on that guard rail, but let's say you're right. It didn't skid into the lake. It couldn't go up the mountain. So where does that leave us?"

"Going nuts!" Joe said.

"It leaves us with one answer. The station wagon never went into the dugway."

Joe Gorman nodded. "That's logic," he said. "But Jake Nugent wouldn't lie. Jerry's bus is an hour and three-quarters late now. If he didn't go into the dugway, where is he? Where *could* he go? Why hasn't he telephoned if everything is okay?"

A car drove up and stopped. A man got out and came running toward them. It was Karl Dickler, whose two children were on the missing bus. He wanted to know what had happened.

"We can't figure it out," Teliski said. "The bus never came through the dugway."

"But it did!" Karl Dickler said.

"It never came out this end," Joe Gorman said. "I was watching for Pete."

"But it did come through!" Dickler said. "I passed them myself on the way to Lakeview. They were about half a mile this way from Jake Nugent's. I saw them! I waved at my own kids!"

The three men stared at each other.

"It never came out this end," Joe Gorman said, in a choked voice.

Dickler swayed and reached out to the trooper to steady himself. "The Lake!" he whispered.

But they were not in the lake. Joe Gorman's survey proved accurate; no broken wire, no bent post, not even a scratch…

It was nearly dark when the real search began. Troopers, the families of the children, the selectmen,[5] the sheriff and twenty-five or thirty volunteer deputies, a hundred or more school friends of the missing children.

The lake was definitely out. Not only was the guard rail intact, but the lake was frozen over with about an inch of ice. There wasn't a break in the smooth surface of the ice anywhere along the two miles of shore bordering the dugway.

Men and women and children swarmed through the woods on the other side of the road, knowing all the time it was useless. The road was called the "dugway" because it had been dug out of the side of the mountain. There was a gravel bank about seven feet high running almost unbrokenly along that side of the road. There was the one old abandoned trail leading to the quarry. It was clear, after walking the first ten yards of it, that no car had come that way. It couldn't.

A hundred phone calls were made to surrounding towns and villages. No one had seen the station wagon, the children or Jerry Mahoney. The impossible had to be faced.

The bus had gone into the dugway and it hadn't come out. It hadn't skidded into the lake and it hadn't climbed the impenetrable brush of the mountain. It was just gone! Vanished into thin air!

Everyone was deeply concerned for and sympathetic with the Dicklers, and Joe Gorman, and the Williams, the Trents, the Ishams, the Nortons, and the Jennings, parents of the missing children. Nobody thought much about Jerry Mahoney's family, or his fiancée.

It wasn't reasonable, but as the evening wore on and not one speck of evidence was found or one reasonable theory advanced, people began to talk about Jerry Mahoney. He was the driver. The bus had to have been driven somewhere. It couldn't navigate without Jerry Mahoney at the wheel. Jerry was the only adult involved. However it had been worked—this disappearance—Jerry must have had a hand in it.

It didn't matter that, until an hour ago, Jerry had been respected, trusted, liked. Their children were gone and Jerry had taken them somewhere. Why? Ransom. They would all get ransom letters in the morning, they said. A mass kidnapping. Jerry had the kids somewhere. There weren't any rich kids in Clayton so he was going to demand ransom from all seven families.

At nine-thirty Sergeant Mason and Trooper Teliski of the State Police, George Peabody, the sheriff, and a dozen others of the community including Joe Gorman and Karl Dickler stormed into the living room of Jerry Mahoney's house where an old man with silvery white hair sat in an overstuffed armchair with Elizabeth Deering, Jerry's fiancée, huddled on the floor beside him. She was crying.

The old man wore a rather sharply cut gray flannel suit, a bright scarlet vest with brass buttons and a green necktie that must have been designed for a special parade. As he stroked his hair, the light from the lamp reflected glittering shafts from a square-cut

---

5. *Selectmen* are members of a board of town officers, chosen to manage certain public affairs.

Word Bank

impenetrable (im PEN ih truh bul) *adj.*: incapable of being penetrated, pierced, or entered

diamond in a heavy gold setting which he wore on his little finger.

"All right, Pat," Sergeant Mason said. "What's Jerry done with those kids?" Pat Mahoney's pale blue eyes met the Sergeant's stare steadily.

There are those who are old enough to remember the days when Mahoney and Faye were listed about fourth on a bill of eight star acts all around the Keith-Orpheum vaudeville circuit.[6] Pat Mahoney was an Irish comic with dancing feet, and Nora Faye—Mrs. Mahoney to you—could match him at dancing and had the soprano voice of an angel.

If you were alone with Pat for more than five minutes, he went back to the old days.

Mahoney and Faye had never played the Palace, the Broadway goal of all vaudevillians. Pat had worked on a dozen acts that would crack the ice and finally he'd made it.

"We'd come out in cowboy suits, all covered with jewels, and jeweled guns, and jeweled boots, and we'd do a little soft shoe routine, and then suddenly all the lights would go out and only the jewels would show—they were made special for that—and we'd go into a fast routine, pulling the guns, and twirling and juggling them, and the roof would fall in! Oh, we tried it out of town, and our agent finally got us the booking at the Palace we'd always dreamed of."

There'd be long silence then, and Pat would take a gaudy handkerchief from his hip pocket and blow his nose with a kind of angry violence. "I can show you the costumes still. They're packed away in a trunk in the attic. Just the way we wore them—me and Nora—the last time we ever played. Atlantic City it was. And she came off after the act with the cheers still ringing in our ears, and down she went on the floor of the dressing room, writhing in pain.

"Then she told me. It had been getting worse for months. She didn't want me to know. The doctor had told her straight out. She'd only a few months she could count on. She'd never said a word to me—working toward the Palace—knowing I'd dreamed of it. And only three weeks after that—she left us. Me and Jerry—she left us. We were standing by her bed when she left—and the last words she spoke were to Jerry. 'Take care of Pat,' she says to him. 'He'll be helpless without someone to take care of him.' And then she smiled at me, and all the years were in that smile."

And then, wherever he happened to be when he told the story, Pat Mahoney would wipe the back of his hand across his eyes and say: "If you'll excuse me, I think I'll be going home...."

Now Pat said, "You asked me what Nora's boy has done with those kids. There's no answer to that question. Do I hear you saying, 'I know what you must be feeling, Pat Mahoney, and you, Elizabeth Deering? And is there anything we can do for you in this hour of your terrible anxiety?' I don't hear you saying that, Sergeant."

"I'm sorry, Pat," Mason said. "Those kids are missing. Jerry had to take them somewhere."

"No!" Liz Deering cried. "You all know Jerry better than that!"

---

6. The term *vaudeville circuit* (VAWD vill SIR kit) refers to a form of popular entertainment in the U.S., from the late 1800s to the early 1900s.

Word Bank

routine (roo TEEN) *n.*: a rehearsed act, performance, or part of a performance
gaudy (GAW dee) *adj.*: showy in a tasteless way; flashy
writhing (WRY thing) *v.*: twisting the body about, as in pain or effort

They didn't, it seemed, but they could be forgiven. You can't confront people with the inexplicable without frightening them and throwing them off balance. You can't endanger their children and expect a sane reaction. They muttered angrily, and old Pat saw the tortured faces of Joe Gorman and Karl Dickler and the swollen red eyes of Mrs. Jennings.

"Has he talked in any way queerly to you, Pat?" Mason asked. "Has he acted normal of late?"

"Nora's boy is the most normal boy you ever met," Pat Mahoney said. "You know that, Sergeant. Why, you've known him since he was a child."

Mrs. Jennings screamed out: "He'd protect his son. Naturally he'd protect his son. But he's stolen our children!"

"The Pied Piper rides again," Pat Mahoney said.

"Make him talk!" Mrs. Jennings cried, and the crowd around her muttered louder.

"When did you last see Jerry, Pat?"

"Breakfast," Pat said. "He has his lunch at Joe Gorman's Diner." The corner of his mouth twitched. "He should have been home for dinner long ago."

"Did he have a need for money?" Mason asked.

"Money? He was a man respected—until now—wasn't he? What need would he have for money?"

"Make him answer sensibly!" Mrs. Jennings pleaded in a despairing voice.

Joe Gorman stepped forward. "Pat, maybe Jerry got sick all of a sudden. It's happened to men who saw action overseas. Maybe you saw signs of something and wouldn't want to tell of it. But my Pete was on that bus, and Karl's two and Mrs. Jennings' two. We're nowhere, Pat—so if you can tell us anything! Our kids were on that bus!"

Pat Mahoney's eyes, as he listened to Joe Gorman, filled with pain. "My kid is on that bus, too, Joe," he said.

They all stared at him, some with hatred. And then, in the distance, they heard the wail of a siren. The troopers' car was coming from Lakeview!

"Maybe it's news!" someone shouted. "News!"

And they all went stumbling out of the house to meet the approaching car—all but Elizabeth Deering and the old man.

"I don't understand it," she said, her voice shaken, "They think he's harmed their children, Pat! Why? Why would they think he'd do such a thing? Why?"

Old Pat's eyes had a faraway look in them. "Did I ever tell you about The Great Thurston?" he asked. "Greatest magic act I ever saw."

"Pat!" Elizabeth said, her eyes widening in horror.

"First time I ever caught his act was in Sioux City," Pat said. "He came out in a flowing cape, and a silk hat, and he…"

Dear G-d, he's losing his reason, Elizabeth Deering told herself. Let the news be good! Let them be found safe!

Outside the siren drew close.

The police car with its wailing siren carried news, but it was not the sort the people of Clayton were hoping to hear.

It was reassuring to know that within a few hours of the tragedy the entire area was alerted, that the moment daylight came a fleet of

---

Word Bank   **inexplicable** (IN ex PLIK uh bul) *n.*: the unexplainable

THE DAY THE CHILDREN VANISHED / 297

army helicopters would cover the area for hundreds of miles around, that a five-state alarm was out for the missing station wagon and its passengers, and the Attorney General had sent the best man on his staff to direct and coordinate the search.

Top officials had a theory. Of course there had to be a rational explanation of the disappearance of the bus, and Clyde Haviland, tall, stoop-shouldered, scholarly looking investigator from the Attorney General's office, was ordered to produce that explanation as soon as possible upon his arrival in Clayton. But beyond that, officials had no doubt as to the reason for the disappearance: this was a mass kidnapping; something novel in the annals of crime.

Since none of the families involved had means, Haviland and his superiors were convinced the next move in this strange charade would be a demand on the whole community to pay ransom for the children. The FBI was alerted to be ready to act the moment there was any indication of involvement across state lines.

The Air Force turned over its complete data on Technical Sergeant Jerry Mahoney to the FBI. Men who had known Jerry in the service were waked from their sleep or pulled out of restaurants or theatres to be questioned. Had he ever said anything that would indicate he might move into a world of violence? Did his medical history contain any record of mental illness?

Sitting at a desk in the town hall, Clyde Haviland reported on some of this to George Peabody, the sheriff, the town's three selectmen, Sergeant Mason and a couple of other troopers. Haviland, carefully polishing his shell-rimmed glasses, was a quiet, reassuring sort of man. He had a fine reputation in the state. He was not an unfamiliar figure to people in Clayton because he had solved a particularly brutal murder in the neighboring town of Johnsville, and his investigation had brought him in and out of Clayton for several weeks.

"So far," he said, with a faint smile, "the report on Jerry Mahoney is quite extraordinary."

"In what way?" Sergeant Mason asked, eager for the scent of blood.

"Model Citizen," Haviland said. "No one has a bad word for him. No bad temper. Never held grudges. Never chiseled.[7] Saves his money. His savings account in the Clayton bank would surprise some of you. On the face of it, this is the last person in the world to suspect."

"There has to be a first time for everything," Karl Dickler said. He was a selectman as well as one of the bereaved parents.

---

7. Someone who has been *chiseled* (CHIZ ild) has been tricked or cheated.

Word Bank

novel (NAHV il) *adj.*: of a new kind; different from anything seen or known before
annals (AN ilz) *n.*: historical records; chronicles
charade (shuh RAYD) *n.*: an obvious fake or deception; a mockery
bereaved (bih REEVD) *adj.*: greatly saddened by the loss of a loved one

"It's going down toward zero tonight," George Peabody, the sheriff, said, glumly. "If those kids are out anywhere——"

"They're a long way from here by now, if you ask me," Sergeant Mason said.

Haviland looked at him, his eyes unblinking behind the lenses of his glasses. "Except that they never came out of the dugway."

"Nobody saw them," Mason said. "But they're not there so they did come out."

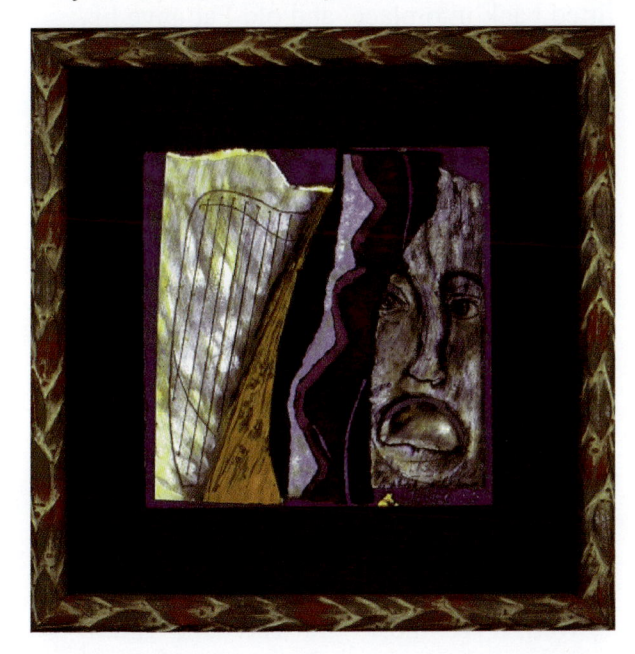

"They didn't come out," Joe Gorman said. "I was watching for them from the window of my diner at this end."

"That was the three seconds you were getting something out of the icebox in your pantry," Mason said.

"And I suppose everyone else along Main Street had his head in a closet at just that time!" Joe Gorman said.

"Or someone reached down out of the heavens and snatched that station wagon up into space," Haviland said. He was looking at Peabody's pudgy face as he spoke, and something he saw there made him add quickly: "I'm kidding, of course."

Peabody laughed nervously. "It's the only good explanation we've had so far."

Karl Dickler put his hand up to his cheek. There was a nerve there that had started to twitch, regularly as the tick of a clock. "I like Jerry. I'd give the same kind of report on him you've been getting, Mr. Haviland. But you can't pass up the facts. I'd have said he'd defend those kids with his life. But did he? And the old man—his father. He won't answer questions directly. There's something queer about him. Listen, Mr. Haviland, my kids are—out there, somewhere!" He waved toward the frost-coated window panes.

"Every highway within two hundred miles of here is being patrolled, Mr. Dickler," Haviland said. "If you'd ever investigated a crime, you'd know we usually are swamped with calls from people who think they've seen the wanted man. A bus—a busload of kids. Somebody *had* to see it! But there isn't even a crackpot report."

Dickler pinched savagely at his twitching cheek. "What are you going to *do*, Haviland?"

"Unless we're wrong," Haviland said, "we're going to hear from the kidnappers soon. Tonight—or maybe in the morning—by mail, or phone or in some unexpected way. But we'll hear. They'll demand money. What other purpose can there be?"

"Meanwhile you just sit here and wait!" Dickler said, a kind of despair rising in his voice.

"I think all the parents of the children should go home. You may be the one the kidnappers contact. It may be your child they put on the phone to convince you the kids are safe," Haviland said.

Elizabeth was sick with anxiety. Jerry was foremost in her mind; Jerry, missing with the children; Jerry, worse than that, suspected by his friends. But on top of that

THE DAY THE CHILDREN VANISHED / 299

was old Pat Mahoney.

He hadn't made the slightest sense since the angry crowd had left his house. He had talked on endlessly about the old days in vaudeville. He seemed obsessed with the memory of the first time he had seen the Great Thurston in Sioux City. He seemed to remember everything he had seen the great man do.

Elizabeth tried, but she could not bring Pat back to the present. The tragedy seemed to have tipped him right out of the world of reason. She was relieved when she heard firm steps on the front porch and saw Sergeant Mason and the tall stranger.

She took them into the living room where old Pat still sat in the overstuffed armchair.

Mason introduced Haviland. "Mr. Haviland is a special investigator from the Attorney General's office, Pat."

Pat's eyes brightened. "Say, you're the fellow that solved that murder over in Johnsville, aren't you?" he said. "Smart piece of work."

"Thanks," Haviland said. He looked at Pat, astonished at his gaudy vest and tie and the glittering diamond on his finger. He had been prepared for Pat, but not adequately.

"Sit down," Pat said. "Maybe Liz would make us some coffee if we asked her nicely."

Mason nodded to Liz, who went out into the kitchen. He followed her to tell her there was no news. Haviland sat down on the couch next to Pat.

"You go to vaudeville in the old days, Mr. Haviland?"

"When I was a kid," Haviland said. "I never had the pleasure of seeing you though, Mr. Mahoney."

"I was nothing, Mr. Haviland. Just a third-rate song-and-dance man. But Nora—well, if you ever saw my Nora——"

Haviland waited for him to go on, but Pat seemed lost in his precious memories.

"You must be worried about your son, Pat," Haviland said.

For a fractional moment the mask of pleasant incompetence seemed to be stripped from Pat's face. "Wouldn't you be?" he asked harshly. Then, almost instantly, the mask was fitted back into place, and old Pat gave his cackling laugh. "You got theories, Mr. Haviland? How're you going to handle this case?"

"I think," Haviland said, conversationally, "the children and your son have been kidnapped. I think we'll hear from the kidnappers soon. I think, in all probability, the whole town will be asked to get up a large ransom."

Pat turned his bright eyes directly on Haviland. "You figured out how the bus disappeared?"

"No," Haviland said.

"Of course it doesn't really matter, does it?" Pat said.

"Well, if we knew——" Haviland said.

"It wouldn't really matter," Pat said. "It's what's going to happen now that matters."

"You mean the demand for money?"

"If that's what's going to happen," Pat said. The cackling laugh suddenly grated on Haviland's nerves. The old joker did know something!

"You have a different theory, Pat?" Haviland asked, keeping his exasperation out of his voice.

"You ever see The Great Thurston on the Keith-Orpheum circuit?" Pat asked.

Word Bank

adequately (AD ih kwit lee) *adv.*: sufficiently

incompetence (in KAHM pih tintz) *n.*: lack of ability or fitness; mental deficiency

"I'm afraid not," Haviland said.

"Greatest magic act I ever saw," Pat said. "Better than Houdini. Better than anyone. I first saw him in Sioux City——"

"About the case here, Pat," Haviland interrupted. "You have a theory?"

"I got no theory," Pat said. "But I know what's going to happen."

Haviland leaned forward. "What's going to happen?"

"One of two things," Pat said. "Everybody in this town is going to be looking for that station wagon in the lake, where they know it isn't, and they're going to be looking for it in the woods, where they know it isn't. That's one thing that may happen. The other thing is, they buy this theory of yours, Mr. Haviland—and it's a good theory, mind you —and they all stay home and wait to hear something. There's one same result from both things, isn't there?"

"Same result?"

"Sure. Nobody in Clayton goes to work. The quarries don't operate. The small businesses will shut down. People will be looking and people will be waiting…"

"So?"

"So what good will that do anyone?" Pat asked.

"It won't do anyone any good. The quarry owners will lose some money. The small businesses will lose some money."

"Not much point in it, is there?" Pat said, grinning.

Haviland rose. He'd had about enough. Mason and Elizabeth were coming back from the kitchen with coffee. "There isn't much point to anything you're saying, Mr. Mahoney."

Pat's eyes twinkled. "Ah, coffee! Smells real good. Pull up a chair, Sergeant. By the way, Mr. Haviland, I'll make you a bet," Pat said.

"I'm not a betting man," Haviland said.

"I'll make you a bet that tomorrow morning they'll be out searching. I'll make you a bet that even if you order them to stay home and wait, they'll be out searching."

"Look here, Pat, if you know something—"

A dreamy look came into Pat's eyes. "Nora was so taken with The Great Thurston that time in Sioux City I went around to see him afterwards. I thought he'd show me how to do a few simple tricks. He wouldn't tell me anything—that is, not about any of his tricks. But he told me the whole principle of his business.

"The principle is," Pat said, "to make your audience think only what you want them to think, and see only what you want them to see." His eyes brightened. "Which reminds me, there's something I'd like to have you see, Mr. Haviland."

Haviland gulped his coffee. Somehow he felt mesmerized by the old man. Pat was at the foot of the stairs, beckoning.[8] Haviland followed.

Elizabeth looked at Mason and there were tears in her eyes. "It's thrown him completely off base," she said. "You know what he's going to show Mr. Haviland?" Sergeant Mason shook his head.

"A cowboy suit!" Elizabeth said, and dropped down on the couch, crying softly. "He's going to show him a cowboy suit."

---

8. *Beckoning* (BEK in ing) is to summons by a nod or gesture.

Word Bank

mesmerized (MEZ mer ized) *adj.*: hypnotized; spellbound; fascinated

And she was right. Haviland found himself in the attic, his head bowed to keep from bumping into the sloping beams. Old Pat had opened a wardrobe trunk and, with the gesture of a waiter taking the silver lid off a tomato surprise, revealed two cowboy suits, one hanging neatly on each side of the trunk—Nora's and his. Chaps,[9] shirt, vest, boots, Stetsons,[9] and gun belts—all studded with stage jewelry.

"… and when the lights went out," Pat was saying, "all you could see was these gewgaws, sparkling. And we'd take out the guns…" and suddenly Pat had the two jeweled six-shooters in his hands, twirling and spinning them. "In the old days I could draw these guns and twirl 'em into position faster than Jesse James!"

The spell was broken for Haviland. The old guy was cuckoo. "I enjoyed seeing them, Mr. Mahoney," he said. "But now, I'm afraid I've got to get back——"

As soon as dawn broke, Haviland had Sergeant Mason and Sheriff George Peabody out at the scene of the disappearance. Everyone else was at home, waiting to hear from the kidnappers. It had been a terrible night for the whole town, a night filled with forebodings[10] and dark imaginings. Haviland covered every inch of the two-mile stretch of the dugway. You couldn't get away from the facts. There was no way for it to have happened—but it had happened.

About eight-thirty he was back in Clayton in Joe's Diner, stamping his feet to warm them and waiting eagerly for eggs and toast to go with his steaming cup of black coffee. All the parents had been checked. There'd been no phone calls, no notes slipped under doors, nothing in the early-morning mail.

Haviland never got his breakfast. Trooper Teliski came charging into the diner just as Joe Gorman was taking the eggs off the grill. Teliski was white as parchment.[11] "We've found 'em," he said. "Or at least we know where they are. Helicopters spotted 'em. I just finished passing the word in town."

Joe Gorman dropped the plate of eggs on the floor behind the counter. Haviland spun around on his counter stool. Just looking at Teliski made the hair rise on the back of his neck.

"The old quarry off the dugway," Teliski said, and gulped for air. "No sign of the bus. It didn't drive up there. But the kids." Teliski steadied himself on the counter. "Schoolbooks," he said. "A couple of coats—lying at the edge of the quarry. And in the quarry—more of the same. A red beret belonging to one of the kids—"

"Peter!" Joe Gorman cried out.

Haviland headed for the door. The main street of Clayton was frightening to see. People ran out of houses, screaming at each

---

9. *Chaps* (CHAPS) are sturdy, trouser-like, leather leggings worn by cowboys. Although the *Stetson* (STET sin) was actually made by The Stetson Company, the term now refers to a type of felt hat with a broad brim and a high crown.

10. A *foreboding* (for BO ding) refers to a strong feeling that something bad is going to happen.

11. *Parchment* (PARCH mint) is a thick writing material made from the skins of sheep, goats, and other animals.

other, heading crazily toward the dugway. There was no order—only blind panic.

Haviland stood on the curb outside the diner, ice in his veins. He looked down the street just in time to see a wildly weeping woman pick up a stone and throw it through the front window of Pat's house.

"Come on—what's the matter with you?" Teliski shouted from behind the wheel of the State Police car.

Haviland stood where he was, frozen, staring at the broken window of Pat Mahoney's house. The abandoned quarry, he knew, was sixty feet deep, full to within six feet of the top with icy water fed in by constantly bubbling springs.

A fire engine roared past. They were going to try to pump out the quarry. It would be like bailing out the Atlantic Ocean with a tea cup.

"Haviland!" Teliski called desperately.

Haviland still stared at Pat Mahoney's house. A cackling old voice rang in his ears. "I'll make you a bet, Mr. Haviland. I'll make you a bet that even if you order them to stay home and wait, they'll be out searching."

Rage such as he had never known flooded the ice out of Haviland's veins. So Pat had known! The old codger[12] had known *last night*!

Haviland had never witnessed anything like the scene at the quarry.

The old road, long since overgrown, which ran about 200 yards in from the dugway to the quarry, had been trampled down as if by a herd of buffalo.

Within three-quarters of an hour of the news reaching town, it seemed as if everyone from Clayton and half the population of Lakeview had arrived at the quarry's edge.

One of the very first army helicopters which had taken to the air at dawn had spotted the clothes and books at the edge of the abandoned stone pit.

The pilot had dropped down close enough to identify the strange objects and radioed immediately to State Police. The stampede had followed.

---

12. The expression *old codger* (KAHJ er) refers to an odd or strange old man.

Haviland was trained to be objective in the face of tragedy, but he found himself torn to pieces by what he saw. Women crowded forward, screaming, trying to examine the articles of clothing and the books. Maybe not all the children were in this icy grave. It was only the hope of desperation. No one really believed it. It seemed, as Trooper Teliski had said, to be the work of a maniac.

Haviland collected as many facts about the quarry as he could from a shaken Sheriff Peabody.

"Marble's always been Clayton's business," Peabody said. "Half the big buildings in New York have got their marble out of Clayton quarries. This was one of the first quarries opened up by the Clayton Marble Company nearly sixty years ago. When they started up new ones, this one was abandoned."

In spite of the cold, Peabody was sweating. He wiped the sleeve of his plaid hunting shirt across his face. "Sixty feet down, and sheer walls," he said. "They took the blocks out at ten-foot levels, so there is a little ledge about every ten feet going down. A kid couldn't climb out of it if it was empty."

Haviland glanced over at the fire engine which had started to pump water from the quarry. "Not much use in that," he said.

"The springs are feeding it faster than they can pump it out," Peabody said. "There's no use telling them. They got to feel they're doing something." The fat sheriff's mouth set in a grim slit. "Why would Jerry Mahoney do a thing like this? *Why?* I guess you can only say the old man is a little crazy, and the son has gone off his rocker too."

"There are some things that don't fit," Haviland said. The hysterical shrieking of one of the women near the edge of the quarry grated on his nerves. "Where is the station wagon?"

"He must have driven up here and—and done what he did to the kids," Peabody said. "Then waited till after dark to make a getaway."

"But you searched this part of the woods before dark last night," Haviland said.

"We missed it somehow, that's all," Peabody said, stubbornly.

"A nine-passenger station wagon is pretty hard to miss," Haviland said.

"So we missed it," Peabody said. "I don't know how, but we missed it." He shook his head. "I suppose the only thing that'll work here is grappling hooks.[13] They're sending a crane[13] over from one of the active quarries. Take an hour or more to get it here. Nobody'll leave here till the hooks have scraped the bottom of that place and they've brought up the kids."

Unless, Haviland thought to himself, the lynching spirit[14] gets into them. He was thinking of an old man in a red vest and a green necktie and a diamond twinkling on his little finger. He was thinking of a broken window pane—and of the way he'd seen mobs act before in his time.

Someone gripped the sleeve of Haviland's coat and he looked down into the horror-struck face of Elizabeth Deering, Jerry Mahoney's fiancée.

---

13. *Grappling hooks* (GRAP ling HOOKS) are used when dragging for something under water. A *crane* (KRAYN) is a device that lifts and moves heavy objects.
14. A *lynching spirit* (LINCH ing SPEER it) occurs when a mob works itself into a frenzy, or wild state, as a prelude to killing or hanging someone.

Word Bank   **objective** (ub JEK tiv) *adj.*: not influenced by personal feelings or prejudice; unbiased

"It's true then," she whispered. She swayed on her feet.

"It's true they found some things belonging to the kids," he said. "That's all that's true at the moment, Miss Deering." He was a little astonished by his own words. He realized that, instinctively, he was not believing everything that he saw in front of him. "This whole area was searched last night before dark," he said. "No one found any schoolbooks or coats or berets then. No one saw the station wagon."

"What's the use of talking that way?" Peabody said. His eyes were narrowed, staring at Liz Deering. "I don't want to believe what I see either, Mr. Haviland. But I got to."

Liz Deering looked at Haviland, sobbing. The tall man stared over her head at the hundreds of people grouped around the quarry's edge. He was reminded of a mine disaster he had seen once in Pennsylvania: a whole town waiting at the head of the mine shaft for the dead to be brought to the surface.

"Let's get out of here," he said to Liz Deering, with sudden energy…

Clayton was a dead town. Stores were closed. Joe's Diner was closed. The railroad station agent was on the job, handling dozens of telegrams that were coming in from friends and relatives of the parents of the missing children. The two girls in the telephone office, across the street from the bank, were at their posts.

Old Mr. Granger, a teller in the bank, and one of the stenographers were all of the bank staff that had stayed on the job. Old Mr. Granger was preparing the payroll for the Clayton Marble Company. He didn't know whether the truck from the company's offices with the two guards would show up for the money or not.

Nothing else was working on schedule today. The hotel down the street had shut up shop. One or two salesmen had driven into town, heard the news, and gone off down the dugway toward the scene of the tragedy. A few very old people tottered in and out the front doors of houses, looking anxiously down Main Street toward the dugway. Even the clinic was closed. The town's doctors and nurses had all gone to the scene of the disaster.

Down the street a piece of newspaper had been taped over the hole in Pat Mahoney's front window. Pat Mahoney sat in the big overstuffed armchair in his living room. He rocked slowly back and forth, staring at an open scrapbook spread across his knees. A big black headline from a show-business paper was pasted across the top.

MAHONEY AND FAYE
BOFFO[15] BUFFALO

Under it were pictures of Pat and Nora in their jeweled cowboy suits, their six-shooters drawn, pointing straight at the camera. There was a description of the act, the dance in the dark with only the jewels showing and the six-shooters spouting flame. "Most original number of its kind seen in years," a Buffalo critic had written.

Pat closed the scrapbook and put it down on the floor beside him. He got up from his chair and moved toward the stairway. People who knew him would have been surprised. No one had ever seen Pat when his movements weren't brisk and youthful. He could still go into a tap routine at the drop of a hat, and he always gave the impression that he was on the verge of doing so. Now he moved slowly, almost painfully—a tired old man, with no need to hide it from anyone. There was no one to hide it from; Jerry was missing, Liz

---

15. A *boffo* (BAHF fo) is a hugely successful vaudeville act.

was gone.

He climbed to the attic. There he opened the wardrobe trunk he'd shown Haviland and took out the cowboy outfit—the chaps, the boots, the vest and shirt and Stetson hat, and the gun belt with the two jeweled six-shooters. Slowly he carried them down to his bedroom on the second floor. There Pat Mahoney proceeded to get into costume.

Then, slowly, he turned away to a silver picture frame on his bureau. Nora, as a very young girl, looked out at him with her gentle smile.

"It'll be all right, honey," Pat said. "You'll see. It'll be another boffo, honey. Don't you worry about your boy. Don't you ever worry about him while I'm around. You'll see."

It was a terrible day for Clayton, but Gertrude Naylor, the chief operator in the telephone office, said afterward that perhaps the worst moment for her was when she spotted old Pat Mahoney walking down the main street—right in the middle of the street—dressed in that crazy cowboy outfit. He walked slowly, looking from right to left, staying right on the white line that divided the street.

"I'd seen it a hundred times before in the movies," Gertrude Naylor said, afterward. "A cowboy, walking down the street of a deserted town, waiting for his enemy to appear—waiting for the moment to draw his guns. Old Pat's hands floated just above those crazy guns in his holster, and he kept rubbing the tips of his fingers against his thumb. I showed him to Millie, and we started to laugh, and then, somehow, it seemed about the most awful thing of all. Jerry Mahoney had murdered those kids and here was his old man, gone nutty as a fruitcake."

Old Mr. Granger, in the bank, had much the same reaction when the aged, bejeweled gun toter walked up to the teller's window.

"Good morning, Mr. Granger," Pat said, cheerfully.

Mr. Granger moistened his pale lips. "Good morning, Pat."

"You're not too busy this morning, I see," Pat said.

"N-no," Mr. Granger said. The killer's father—dressed up like a kid for the circus. He's ready for a padded cell, Mr. Granger thought.

"Since you're not so busy," Pat said, "I'd like to have a look at the detailed statement of my account for the last three months." As he spoke, he turned and leaned against the counter, staring out through the plate-glass bank window at the street. His hands stayed near the guns, and he kept rubbing his fingertips against the ball of his thumb.

"You get a statement each month, Pat," Mr. Granger said.

"Just the same, I'd like to see the detailed statement for the last three months," Pat said.

"I had to humor him, I thought," Mr. Granger said later. "So I went back in the vault to get his records out of the files. Well, I was just inside the vault door when he spoke again, in the most natural way. 'If I were you, Mr. Granger,' he said, 'I'd close that vault door, and I'd stay inside, and I'd set off all the alarms I could lay my hands on. You're about to be stuck up, Mr. Granger.'

"Well, I thought it was part of his craziness," Mr. Granger said, later. "I thought he meant *he* was going to stick up the bank. I thought that was why he'd got all dressed up in that cowboy outfit. Gone back to his childhood, I thought. I was scared, because I figured he was crazy. So I *did* close the vault door. And I *did* set off the alarm, only it didn't work. I didn't know then all the electric wires into the bank had been cut."

Gertrude and Millie, the telephone operators, had a box seat for the rest of it. They saw the black sedan draw up in front of the bank and they saw the four men in dark suits and hats get out of it and start up the steps of the bank. Two of them were carrying small suitcases and two of them were carrying guns.

Then suddenly the bank doors burst open and an ancient cowboy appeared, hands poised over his guns. He did a curious little jig step that brought him out in a solid square stance. The four men were so astonished at the sight of him they seemed to freeze.

"Stick 'em up, you lily-livered rats!" old Pat shouted. The guns were out of the holsters, twirling. Suddenly they belched flame, straight at the bandits.

The four men dived for safety, like men plunging off the deck of a sinking ship. One of them made the corner of the bank building. Two of them got to the safe side of the car. The fourth, trying to scramble back into the car, was caught in the line of fire.

"I shot over your heads that first time!" Pat shouted. "Move another inch and I'll blow you all to pieces!" The guns twirled again and then suddenly aimed steadily at the exposed bandit. "All right, come forward and throw your guns down," Pat ordered.

The man in the direct line of fire obeyed at once. His gun bounced on the pavement a few feet from Pat and he raised his arms slowly. Pat inched his way toward the discarded gun.

The other men didn't move. And then Gertrude and Millie saw the one who had gotten around the corner of the bank slowly raise his gun and take deliberate aim at Pat. She and Millie both screamed, and it made old Pat jerk his head around. In that instant there was a roar of gunfire.

Old Pat went down, clutching at his shoulder. But so did the bandit who'd shot him and so did one of the men behind the car. Then Mr. Haviland came around the corner of the hotel next door, a smoking gun in his hand. He must have spoken very quietly because Gertrude and Millie couldn't hear him, but whatever he said made the other bandits give up. Then they saw Liz Deering running across the street to where old Pat lay, blood dripping through the fingers that clutched at his shoulder.

Twenty minutes later Clayton was a madhouse. People running, people driving, people hanging onto the running boards of cars and clinging to bumpers. And in the middle of the town, right opposite the bank, was a station wagon with a yellow school bus sign on its roof, and children were spilling out of it, waving and shouting at their parents, who laughed and wept. And a young Irishman with bright blue eyes was standing with his fiancée, Elizabeth Deering…

"You can't see him yet," Haviland said to Jerry Mahoney. "The doctor's with him. In a few minutes."

"I still don't get it," Jerry said. "People thought *I* had harmed those kids?"

Word Bank stance (STANTZ) *n.*: position or posture of the body while standing

"You don't know what it's been like here," Liz Deering said.

Jerry Mahoney turned and saw the newspaper taped over the broken front window, and his face hardened. "Try and tell me, plain and simple, about Pop," he said.

Haviland shook his head, smiling like a man still dazed. "Your Pop is an amazing man, Mr. Mahoney," he said. "His mind works in its own peculiar ways. The disappearance of the bus affected him differently from some others. He saw it as a magic trick, and he thought of it as a magic trick—or rather, as *part* of a magic trick. He said it to me and I wouldn't listen. He said it is a magician's job to get you to think what he wants you to think and see what he wants you to see. The disappearance of the children, the ghastly faking of their death in the quarry—it meant one thing to your Pop, Mr. Mahoney. Someone wanted all the people in Clayton to be out of town. Why?

"There was only one good reason that remarkable Pop of yours could think of. The quarry payroll. Nearly a hundred thousand dollars in cash, and not a soul in town to protect it. Everyone would be looking for the children, and all the bandits had to do was walk into the bank and take the money. No cops, no nothing to interfere with them."

"But why didn't Pop tell you his idea?" Jerry asked.

"You still don't know what it was like here, Mr. Mahoney," Haviland said. "People thought you had done something to those kids; they imagined your Pop knew something about it. If he'd told his story, even to me, I think I'd have thought he was either touched in the head or covering up. So he kept still— although he did throw me a couple of hints. And suddenly, he was, to all intents and purposes, alone in the town. So he went upstairs, got dressed in those cowboy clothes and went, calm as you please, to the bank to meet the bandits he knew must be coming. And they came."

"But why the cowboy suit?" Liz Deering asked.

"A strange and wonderful mind," Haviland said. "He thought the sight of him would be screwy enough to throw the bandits a little off balance. He thought if he started blasting away with his guns they might panic. They almost did."

"What I don't understand," Liz said, "is how, when he fired straight at them, he never hit anybody!"

"Those were stage guns—prop guns,"[16] Jerry said. "They only fire blanks."

Haviland nodded. "He thought he could get them to drop their own guns and then he'd have a real weapon and have the drop on them. It almost worked. But the one man who'd ducked around the corner of the building got in a clean shot at him. Fortunately, I arrived at exactly the same minute, and I had them all from behind."

"But how did you happen to turn up?" Jerry asked.

"I couldn't get your father out of my mind," Haviland said. "He seemed to know what was going to happen. He said they'd be searching for the kids, whether I told them to wait at home or not. Suddenly I had to know why he'd said that."

"Thank G-d," Jerry said. "I gather you got them to tell you where we were?"

Haviland nodded. "I'm still not dead clear how it worked, Jerry."

"It was simple as pie à la mode,"[17] Jerry said. "I was about a half mile into the dugway

---

16. *Prop guns* (PRAHP GUNZ) are fake guns used on stage, to shoot fire, but no bullets.
17. It was as simple as *pie á la mode* (PIE AH LAH MODE) or pie with ice cream, is an expression similar to 'easy as pie'; in other words, it was very simple.

on the home trip with the kids. We'd just passed Karl Dickler headed the other way when a big trailer truck loomed up ahead of me on the road. It was stopped, and a couple of guys were standing around the tail end of it.

"Broken down, I thought. I pulled up. All of a sudden guns were pointed at me and the kids. They didn't talk much. They just said to do as I was told. They opened the back of the big truck and rolled out a ramp. Then I was ordered to drive the station wagon right up into the body of the truck. I might have tried to make a break for it except for the kids. I drove up into the truck, they closed up the rear end, and that was that. They drove off with us—right through the main street of town here!"

Haviland shook his head. "An old trick used hundreds of times back in bootleg[18] days. And I never thought of it!"

"Not ten minutes later," Jerry went on, "they pulled into that big deserted barn on the Haskell place. We've been shut up there ever since. They were real decent to the kids—hot dogs, ice cream cones, soda.

"So we just waited there, not knowing why, but nobody hurt, and the kids not as scared as you might think," Jerry laughed. "Oh, we came out of the dugway all right—and right by everybody in town. But nobody saw us."

The doctor appeared in the doorway. "You can see him for a minute now, Jerry," he said. "I had to give him a pretty strong sedative. Dug the bullet out of his shoulder and it hurt a bit. He's pretty sleepy—but he'll do better if he sees you, I think. Don't stay too long, though."

Jerry bounded up the stairs and into the bedroom where Pat Mahoney lay, his face very pale, his eyes half closed.

"Pop," he whispered. "You wonderful old galoot!"[19]

Pat opened his eyes. "You okay, Jerry?"

"Okay, Pop."

"And the kids?"

"Fine. Not a hair of their heads touched."

Jerry reached out and covered Pat's hand with his. "Now look here, Two-Gun Mahoney——"

Pat grinned at him. "It was a boffo, Jerry. A real boffo."

"It sure was," Jerry said. He started to speak, but he saw that Pat was looking past him at the silver picture frame on the dresser.

Then he grinned at Jerry, and his eyes closed and he was asleep.

---

18. The old *bootleg* (BOOT LEG) days refer to the years between 1919 and 1933, known as the Prohibition era, when liquor and other alcoholic beverages were manufactured and sold illegally.
20. A *galoot* (guh LOOT) is slang for a strange or odd person.

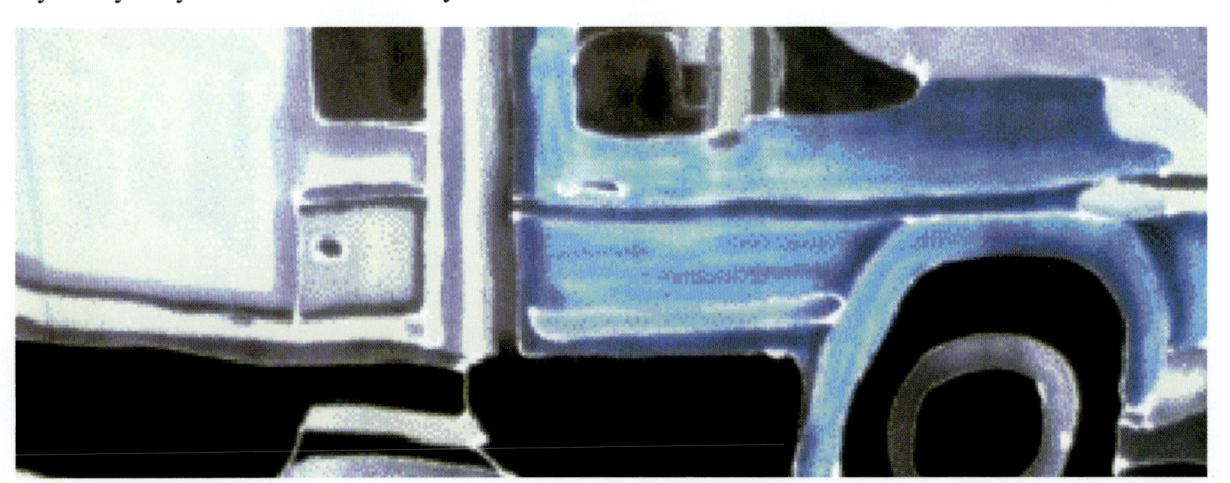

Studying the Selection

First Impressions As logical creatures, we are troubled by the seemingly impossible. We are even more disturbed if we are led astray by false clues. Did the ending surprise you, or had you solved the riddle of the children's disappearance? Where did you look for clues? Were you misdirected? Why is the solution obvious only to Pat Mahoney?

✓ Quick Review

1. Describe the dugway.
2. Name the two witnesses who saw the bus enter the dugway.
3. Why do the concerned parents begin to suspect Jerry Mahoney of wrongdoing?
4. Describe Pat Mahoney.

In-depth Thinking

5. The bus's disappearance is a paradox, a seemingly impossible event. What theories are put forward as possible explanations?
6. How do Pat Mahoney's memories about The Great Thurston shed light on this case?
7. Why is Haviland skeptical when the kids' personal items show up in the quarry?
8. Compare Pat Mahoney's efforts to save the day to those of the classic Western hero.

Drawing Conclusions

9. Fear and panic often breed irrationality and violence. What might have happened in Clayton if the mystery had not been solved?
10. What can we learn about problem solving by examining Pat Mahoney's approach?

Focusing on Pulling It All Together

In a well-crafted story, all the literary components work to support the theme. Answer the following questions, using specific examples from the story as support.

1. The basic aim of mystery writers is suspense. The basic way to create suspense is to make the reader or audience wait. How does Pentecost build suspense into his plotting and characterization?
2. How does the setting of this story enhance the theme? Supply three examples.
3. What would happen if this story were told from the perspective of Joe Gorman or Elizabeth Deering? Would the new story be as suspenseful?

Creating and Writing

1. Police work, laboratory studies, legal investigations—all rely on logic and reserving judgment. Why is it so dangerous to rush to conclusions in these (and other) kinds of situations? In what ways does this story remind and warn us of this danger?
2. Write about a time in your own life when the seemingly impossible occurred. How did you respond? How was the situation resolved?
3. Research and report to your classmates on a famous unsolved mystery. What were the circumstances? What theories have been put forward as explanation? What are your own theories regarding this mystery?

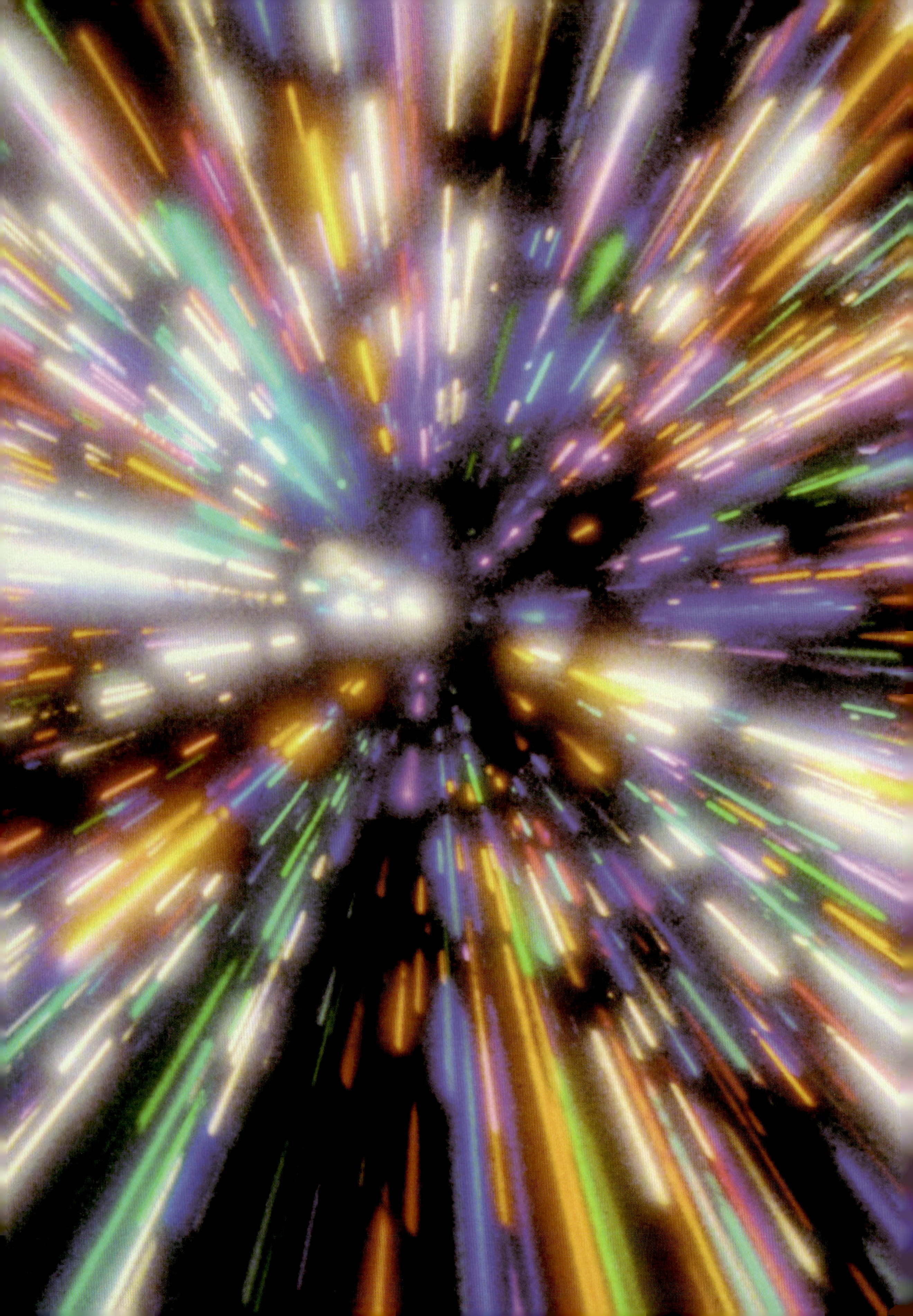

novella

"I have always wanted to write in such a way that will make people think, 'Why, I've always thought that but never found the words for it.'"

Blueprint for Reading

Background Bytes

The human brain stores, analyzes, processes, and communicates information. Sometimes, through injury, illness, or shock, an individual will experience the loss of a large block of interrelated memories. If the brain, itself, has not been physically damaged, these memories may still be present in the brain. But the individual has lost—and must relearn—the ability to access them. This is called having *amnesia*, from a Greek word meaning *oblivion*—"the state of being completely forgotten."

What is remembered and what is lost, when one has amnesia? How much of what we know of amnesia has been learned from scientific observation, and how much comes from rumor and popular stories? Could a person forget his or her name, but keep a deeply ingrained sense of right and wrong? Would skills and talents be retained, but long-time friends go unrecognized? Discuss this with your teacher and class. Then see what you can find out in a good reference text.

Into *The Forgotten Door*—Part One

The Forgotten Door is **science-fiction** adventure, because the plot is based on events that realistically are not possible. Nonetheless, the story is believable, engaging, and suspenseful, convincing in its realism. The title is drawn from the door that the protagonists assume is the portal between two worlds—two very different societies that exist, unaware, side by side. Although this is science fiction, the door may also be a symbol of the gate between opposite kinds of behavior: the alien and the familiar, the good and the evil, the innocent and the spoiled or corrupt. Watch how Alexander Key uses the device of parallel worlds to set up both the scheme and the theme of contrasting values.

Before You Read the Story

All societies are regulated by spoken and unspoken rules. In the United States, for example, our laws, the Constitution and the Bill of Rights, and most public policies are examples of "spoken" or written rules. Unspoken social rules include customs, traditions, rites of passage, and mores (MOHR rays) (moral views). The unspoken rules are generally accepted without question and include the basic moral attitudes of a group.

Individuals are usually brought up by their parents and communities to have some moral sense: principles, values, and ethics that are the basis for a sense of right conduct, a sense of honor, and a sense of shame. Much of what we learn about ourselves and others and about "correct" social behavior, we learn through the eyes of our parents, who teach us how to *see*. We begin to learn before we can even speak.

In *The Forgotten Door*, Little Jon is amnesiac and has come from a parallel world that he cannot recall. Nonetheless, he seems to have retained his values—he is shocked by behaviors he observes in his new setting. Thus, Little Jon is the author's primary vehicle for making a statement about values.

THE Forgotten Door
Part I

Before you read the selection, think about your own values and traditions. How do the people you know celebrate the birth of a new baby? What customs are observed when someone in the community dies? What rules are supposed to guide your behavior towards other people? What have you been taught about making accusations against someone, with or without having full information? Is it ever okay to lie? When is it appropriate to conceal your true feelings? Have you ever gone hunting? Can you think earnestly about why other people might think hunting is wrong (or right)? Have you ever spoken negatively about someone new to your group or about someone who is different from you and lives in a different social group?

Make brief, but honest, notes in response to each of these questions. Does your own behavior always meet the standards and the code of ethics you have been taught? When you finish reading the selection, think about how your values match, or would be at odds with, the social mores of Little Jon's world.

Focusing on the Novella: Characterization

In the short story selections, we discussed **round** and **flat** characters. **Flat** characters have simple personalities and do not grow in the story. Often, a flat character is just a symbol or a foil that makes the round characters come alive. **Round** characters are more complex and more fully engage the reader—they have conflicts and they struggle like the rest of us. The richness and depth of round characters drive the plot. Round characters, like people, change and evolve.

Since the author writes the story, all of the characters serve the same master. Out of their interaction comes the author's viewpoint, the plot, and the theme. Are all of the characters in *The Forgotten Door* believable? In life, is anyone all good or all bad? Are we ever really in a position to make that judgment about another person?

Word Bank

Footnote 1 in *The Forgotten Door* defines the word *cleft*, as "a split or crevice." In fact, *cleft* is one of a class of English words that mean both itself and its opposite. For example, a *cleft* is both the split and the indentation formed by such a split. It refers to both what *was* and what *is*. *Cleft* comes from the word *cleave*, which means "to split or divide." It also means "to cling to or adhere to closely." Another such word is *sanction*, which also has two contrary meanings: "to authorize or approve" and "to impose a penalty."

concussion	geology	prey	ravine
cowered	mercenary	primitive	surveyed
edible	misgivings	quench	vicious
enthralled	plaintively	ravenously	warily

THE Forgotten Door
Alexander Key

Chapter 1

HE IS LOST AND FOUND

It happened so quickly, so unexpectedly, that Little Jon's cry was almost instantly cut short as the blackness closed over him. No one knew the hole was there. It hadn't been there the day before, and in the twilight no one had noticed it.

At the moment it happened, the first shooting stars were crossing the sky—they were beginning to stream across like strings of jewels flung from another planet—and everyone was watching them. The smaller children were exclaiming in delight, while the older ones stood silent and enthralled. Here on the hill, where the valley people often came to watch the glittering night unfold, you could see the whole magic sweep around you, and you felt close to everything in the heavens. Other people, you knew, were standing on other hills on other worlds, watching even as you watched.

Word Bank

enthralled (en THRAHLD) *adj.*: captivated or charmed; spellbound

PART ONE

Little Jon, whose eyes were quicker than most, should have seen the hole, but all his attention was on the stars. Small for his age, he had moved away from the rest for a better view, and as he stepped backward, there was suddenly nothing under his feet.

It was astonishing at that moment to find himself falling swiftly into the hill at a spot where he had walked safely all his life. But in the brief seconds before the blackness swallowed him, he realized what must have happened: there had been a cave-in over the old Door—the Door that led to another place, the one that had been closed so long.

He cried out and tried to break his fall in the way he had been taught, but the effort came an instant too late. His head struck something, and darkness swirled over him.

Long later, when Little Jon was able to sit up, he had no idea where he was or what had happened. Memory had fled, and he ached all over. He would have been shivering with cold, but his thick jacket and trousers and heavy, woven boots kept him warm.

He seemed to be in a narrow cleft[1] of broken rock. There were mossy stones around him, and just ahead he could make out a bed of ferns where water trickled from a spring. He was still too dazed to be frightened, but now he realized he was thirsty, terribly so. He crawled painfully for-

---

1. A *cleft* (KLEFT) is a split or crevice.

ward and lay with his face in the water while he drank.

The coldness of the water startled him at first, but it was wonderfully sweet and satisfying. He bathed his face and hands in it, then sat up at last and looked around again.

Where was he? How did he get here? He pondered these questions, but no answers came. He felt as if he had fallen. Only—where could he have fallen *from?* The rocky walls met overhead, sloping outward into a tangle of leafy branches.

There was another question his mind carefully tiptoed around, because it was more upsetting than the others. Whenever he approached it, it caused a dull aching in his forehead. Finally, however, he gave his head a small shake and faced it squarely.

Who am I?

He didn't know. He simply didn't know, and it made everything terribly wrong.

All at once, trembling, he got to his feet and fled limping toward a shaft of sunlight ahead. Thick shrubs barred his way. He fought blindly through them, tripped, and fell sprawling. Fortunately he missed the boulders on either side, and landed in a soft bed of old leaves under a tree. He scrambled up in panic, started to run again, then stopped himself just in time.

This wasn't the sort of country where you could run. There were steep ledges here, and below them the ground sloped sharply downward for a great distance. All of it was covered with a wild tangle of forest. Little Jon rubbed his eyes and looked around him with growing wonder and fright.

Nothing here was familiar. He was *sure* of that. He had never seen trees quite like the ones around him. Many of the smaller trees were in bloom, covered with showers of white blossoms—these were *almost* familiar, as were the ferns and lichens[2] on the rocks. But there was a difference. But what the difference was, he was unable to tell.

Carefully he worked down to an open area below the ledge, and stood listening. The *sounds* were familiar, and hearing them made him feel a bit better. Birdsong, the gurgling of hidden springs, the faint clatter and fuss of a rushing stream somewhere. And there were the hesitant steps of wild creatures that came pleasantly to his sharp ears. Without quite realizing his ability, which was as natural as breathing, his mind reached toward them and found nothing strange in them—except that they were afraid. Afraid of him!

"Don't be afraid," he told them, so softly that his lips barely moved. "I'd *never* hurt you."

After a minute, two of the creatures—they were a doe and her fawn—moved hesitantly down the slope and stood looking at him curiously. Little Jon held out his hands, and presently the doe came close and nuzzled his cheek with her cold nose.

"Where am I?" he asked her plaintively. "Can you tell me?"

The doe couldn't answer, and all he could gather was that she was hungry, and that food could be found in the valley below.

"Lead the way," he told her. "I'll follow."

The doe and the fawn started down through the tangle. Little Jon went scrambling and limping behind them. Walking was difficult,

---

2. *Lichens* (LY kinz) are flowerless, leafless plants that grow on tree bark, fences, and rocks.

Word Bank

plaintively (PLAIN tiv lee) *adv.*: sadly; with sorrow or melancholy; mournfully

for both his knees were badly bruised and one ankle pained with every step. Soon, however, they reached a winding game trail and the going was much easier. Even so, it was hard to keep up with the doe, and several times in the next hour he had to beg her to stop and wait for him.

It did not seem at all strange to be following her. Her presence was very comforting and kept the unanswered questions from troubling him.

As they wound down near the bottom of the slope, the trees thinned and they passed through an open gate. Ahead he could see bright sunlight on a small greening field. Around a corner of the field ran a clattering stream—a stream different from the one he had heard earlier.

At the sight of the field Little Jon caught his breath. Fields and cultivated things were familiar. There would be people near. Soon he would meet them and find out about himself.

The doe paused at the edge of the field, sniffing the air currents. Little Jon could feel her uneasiness, though he could not understand it. He sniffed too, but all he could smell were the pleasant scents of fresh earth and blossoms, and the richness of the forest behind them. He was disappointed that he couldn't make out the scent of humans near, but maybe this was because the air was flowing down from the mountain, away from him.

As the doe stepped daintily into the field and began to nibble the young plants, Little Jon unconsciously did what he should have done earlier. His mind reached out, searching hopefully. He had no thought of danger. The sudden discovery that there *was* danger was so shocking that he could only spring forward with a strangled cry as he tried to tell the doe to run.

The doe whirled instantly and leaped, just as the sharp report of a rifle shattered the peace of the morning.

Little Jon had never heard a rifle shot before, but he was aware of the hot slash of pain across the doe's flank, and he could see the weapon in the hands of the man who rose from his hiding place at the edge of the stream. He was a lean man in overalls, with one shoulder higher than the other. The harsh features under the cap showed surprise and disbelief as he stared at Little Jon. Then the thin mouth twisted in fury.

"What you doin' in my field?" the man roared, striding forward. "You ruint my aim!"

Little Jon could make nothing of the words. The language was strange, but the hate-driven thoughts behind it were clear enough. For a moment he stood incredulous,[3] his mind trying to fight through the shock of what had happened. Surely the man approaching was a being like himself. But why the intent to kill another creature? Why the sudden hate? How could anyone ever, ever….

The anger that rose in him was a new thing. It was something he had never experienced before, at least in this measure. His small hands balled into fists and he trembled. But just as quickly, he realized that he couldn't quench hate with hate, and that now there was danger to himself. He turned abruptly and fled.

"Stop!" the man bellowed, close behind him. "I know you—you're one o' them

---

3. He was *incredulous* (IN kreh DYOO lis) means he was unable to believe what was happening.

Word Bank

quench (KWENCH) *v.*: satisfy, extinguish

Cherokees from over the ridge! I'll teach you to come meddlin' on my land!"

Little Jon tried to lighten his feet and put distance between himself and his pursuer. Ordinarily he might have managed it in spite of his pains, but he knew nothing of barbed-wire fences. The rusty wires were hidden by the shrubbery until he was almost on them. When he attempted to slide through them, the barbs caught his jacket. The tough material refused to tear. In another second he was squirming in the man's firm grasp.

The man dragged him roughly back to the field, then turned at the sound of an approaching motor. Presently a small farm truck whirled around the bend of the creek and stopped close by. A large woman, wearing faded overalls, got out and waddled over to them. She had a fleshy face, with small, shrewd eyes as hard and round as creek pebbles.

Little Jon had never seen a woman like her. Though he was repelled by her, she drew his attention far more than the truck, which was equally strange.

"I declare!" she muttered, staring. "What you got there, Gilby?"

"Not what I was aimin' at," the man growled. "The thievin' varmint[4] spoiled my shot."

"Just as well, I reckon, or he'd tell. Whose kid is he?"

"Dunno, Emma. Figured 'im for a Cherokee, but—"

"Pshaw, *he* ain't no Indian," she interrupted, peering closer.

"Got black hair like one, near long as a girl's. Could be half an' half."

"H'mp! Look at them *clothes*! Seems more foreignlike. Gypsy, maybe. Where you from, boy?"

Little Jon clenched his teeth and looked stonily back at her. Though her speech was strange, the rising questions and ugly thoughts in her mind were easily understood. She was a person to be avoided, and he wouldn't have answered her even if he had known how.

"Cat got your tongue?" she snapped. "Well, I reckon I can loosen it." Abruptly she slapped him, hard.

He knew the slap was coming, and he managed in time to go limp and roll his head. As he did so, the man unclenched his hand to get a better grip on him. Immediately Little Jon twisted free and ran.

This time he was able to lighten his feet, and went over the fence in a bound. He heard gasps of astonishment behind him, then shouts, and the man's pursuing footsteps. Presently these sounds faded, and the forest was quiet.

Little Jon ran on until he was nearly exhausted. He would have followed the doe and the fawn, but they had gone over a ridge where the way was too steep for his throbbing ankle.

Finally he huddled by a fallen log, removed one boot, and rubbed his swollen ankle while he gained his breath. Tears rolled down his cheeks. He missed the doe terribly. She was his only friend in all this strangeness.

Suddenly he dug his knuckles into his eyes, drew on his boot, and struggled to his feet. He couldn't stay here all day. It solved nothing. He had to keep moving, searching….

Resolutely[5] he began limping around the curve of the slope, taking the easiest course. Somewhere there must be other people—people unlike those behind him. But when he found them he would have to be careful. Very

---

4. In this context, a *varmint* (VAR mint) refers to an annoying person.
5. *Resolutely* (rez uh LOOT lee) means he went on with determination.

careful.

He heard the soft slither of the snake ahead before he saw it, even before it rattled its deadly warning. Its sudden rattle astonished him. He stared at it with more curiosity than fear. What a strange creature, legless and covered with scales, and with a rattle on the end of its tail! It seemed he had heard of such things, vaguely, just as he had heard of the odd kind of vehicle the woman had driven. But where?

Troubled, he limped carefully around the snake. With the thought that there might be other dangers here, dangers he knew nothing about, he drew a small knife from his belt and cut a staff from the shrubbery. The knife felt so much a part of him that he hardly questioned it till he had finished using it. It was only a tool—it seemed that someone had given it to him long ago —but he couldn't remember any more about it.

The staff made walking easier for a while, and he trudged painfully on, stopping at times to rest or to drink from one of the many springs. The sun, which he could glimpse only at intervals through the trees, began to sink behind him. He was very hungry, and his eyes searched continually for food. There ought to be berries. He had noticed some earlier, growing near the barbed-wire fence where the man had caught him.

Edible things, he decided finally, must grow in the open places, lower down.

Warily, slowly, he began to angle toward the valley. He reached the bottom of the slope much sooner than he had expected, only to discover that the valley had vanished. Another slope rose immediately ahead. In sudden alarm he realized he could no longer see the sun. With every step the gloom was deepening. The forest had chilled, and for the first time he saw the gray mist creeping down from above.

The gloom, the chill, and the creeping mist in this strange and bewildering land, together with his growing hunger and lameness, were almost too much. A sob broke from his lips, and he began to tremble with a black dread. He couldn't go much farther. What would he do when darkness came?

Then, like a glow of warmth in the chill, he felt the comforting knowledge of wild creatures near. They were friendly, but timid. He was on the point of calling to them when he heard the distant sound of a motor.

He stiffened, his hands clenched tightly on his staff. Memory of the angry man and the ugly woman rose like a warning. He shook off the thought of them. He *had* to go on. It was the only way....

Abruptly he began plunging toward the sound, following the narrow gully that curved away on his right.

A half hour later he broke through a tangle of evergreens and stared in amazement at the scene ahead.

He was on the edge of a steep bank that dropped down to a winding gravel road. Beyond the road a broad valley opened. The valley was ringed by wave on wave of blue

> This time he was able to lighten his feet, and went over the fence in a bound.

Word Bank

edible (ED ih bul) *adj.*: fit to be eaten as food; eatable

warily (WEAR ih lee) *adv.*: watchfully; watching against danger

and purple mountains that rose to the clouds. The valley was in shadow, but he could make out the farms with their little white houses, and see animals grazing in the pastures.

The motor he had heard earlier had passed, but a second one was approaching. Instantly his mind went out to it, exploring. There were several people in the vehicle, and they were very different from the ones he had met—but not different in a way that mattered. As the machine swung into sight, he allowed himself only a curious glimpse of its bright newness, before he cowered back into the tangle.

The shadows deepened in the valley, and began to creep over the distant mountains. Three more vehicles passed, and once a man on a horse went by. The horse sensed his presence and whinnied. Little Jon liked the horse, but he fought down the urge to call to it, for the man filled him with uneasiness.

It was nearly dark when he heard the final motor. This time, aware of the friendliness of its occupants—and something beyond friendliness—he did not hesitate. It was a small truck, and as it swung around the bend in the road, he slid quickly down the bank to meet it.

Chapter 2

HE GAINS A HOME

As his boots struck the edge of the road, his bad ankle gave way under him, and Little Jon fell in a heap. For a moment he was afraid the truck would go past without anyone noticing him. Its headlights were on, but the beams were sweeping beyond him around the curve.

He managed to struggle upright for a moment, then sank weakly to his knees. He had dropped his staff, and found that he could hardly stand without it.

The truck braked suddenly, and stopped. A man leaned out and said in quick concern, "Hey there, young fellow! What seems to be wrong?"

Little Jon opened his mouth soundlessly, and raised one hand. He heard a woman's

> There's something very strange about him. It isn't just his long hair. His features are so—so sensitive.

voice say, "For heaven's sake, children, let me out—I think the boy's hurt!"

Both doors of the truck flew open. The man stepped from the driver's side, and a boy and a girl tumbled from the other, followed by the woman. Little Jon saw that the girl was about his own size. The boy was much larger, but he seemed no older than himself. Both wore jackets and blue jeans, like the woman.

Though the man was nearer, he moved with a slight limp, and the woman reached him first. "My goodness, honey," she said, stooping and raising him gently, "your face and hands are all scraped. Did you have a fall?"

He nodded, and the man asked, "Are you hurt badly?"

Little Jon shook his head. His eyes swung quickly from one to the other. The woman wore a green scarf around her bright hair. There were freckles across her lean cheeks, and small laughter creases at the corners of her eyes and mouth. The man had a thick

Word Bank

cowered (KOW urd) *v.*: crouched or shrank back in fear

shock of dark hair graying at the temples; his face was ruddy, but deeply lined.

The man said, "Can you tell us where you live, sonny?"

Little Jon shook his head again. There was sudden silence. The woman bit her lip, then asked quietly, "Can you understand what we are saying?"

Again he nodded, and she said, "Thomas, I believe he's had a bad shock that keeps him from speaking. I—I hate to take him to the hospital. They—they're so impersonal. I think all he needs is a hot meal and some rest."

"We're taking him home with us," the man said definitely. "If he's been lost in the mountains all day, he's had it." He jerked his head at the boy and girl. "Sally, you and Brooks ride in the back of the truck. Mary—"

"I'll carry him," she said. "He hardly weighs what Sally does."

"Mommy," said Sally, speaking for the first time. "Is—is he an Indian?"

"I doubt it, and it wouldn't make any difference if he were a horned Andalusian[6] with scales. All aboard!"

She swung Little Jon into the truck and settled him on the seat beside her. The two children scrambled into the back, and the man slid behind the wheel.

While the truck wound along the road, Little Jon sat with his hands clenched, trying to suppress the sudden tears of thankfulness that ran down his cheeks. It was so wonderful to find people who were, well, like people should be. If only he could talk to them and explain....

He tried to fit their spoken words to the thoughts he had felt in them. Their names he knew: Thomas, Mary, Sally, Brooks. His quick ears had already picked out scores of words for his eager memory to hold, but fitting them to the right thoughts would take time. He wished they would speak more to one another, but they said little during the short drive.

Even so, he was aware of questions in all of them. The man: *Odd—never saw a boy like him. Can't be from around here.* The woman: *There's something very strange about him. It isn't just his long hair. His features are so—so sensitive. And his jacket—where in the world can you find material like that?*

The truck slowed presently, and the headlights swept a small brown building with a sign that read BEAN'S ROCK SHOP, SMOKY MOUNTAIN[7] GEMS. The truck turned into a lane beside it, and climbed in second gear to a house nearly hidden by evergreens. There was a barn some distance behind the house, and Little Jon was aware of animals there, waiting. A dog barked furiously at them until he gave it an answering thought of friendliness.

They got out, and the woman carried him to the door, which the man opened with a key. Lights came on, and he was placed on a couch by a fireplace. It was a comfortable room, paneled in brown wood. He was aware of a flicker of pride in the man, who had built this home with his own hands.

The man said, "Brooks, you and Sally unload the groceries, then look after the stock."

"Aw, Dad," Brooks grumbled. "Please, can't we—"

"Do as I say, and I'll handle the milking later. There'll be plenty of time to get acquainted with him. And if your mother will whip up some supper for us, I'll build a fire and play doctor. This boy needs attention."

While the man kindled a fire, Little Jon removed his woven boots and carefully rolled

---

6. *Andalusian* (an duh LOO zhin) refers to a person from southern Spain where people's skin color is darker.
7. The *Smoky Mountains* are part of the Appalachians in North Carolina and Tennessee.

his trousers above his knees.

The man, turning, saw the bruises and whistled softly. He examined them carefully. "You sure got banged up, young fellow, but I don't believe any bones are broken. Some of the Bean family liniment[8] ought to do the trick. Good for everything from hornet stings to housemaid's knee."[9]

At that moment, as Brooks and his sister were bringing in the last of the groceries, a truck turned into the lane outside. Little Jon sat up quickly, his lips compressed. There was no mistaking the particular sound of that truck.

Brooks peered out of the window. "I think it's Mr. Gilby Pitts, Dad."

Thomas Bean frowned. "Wonder what Gilby—" He stopped, and exclaimed, "Hey, young fellow, what's come over you?"

Little Jon was on his feet, trembling, trying to limp away. It was not fear that made him tremble, but a sudden return of the morning's shock, when he had met an evil that was beyond his understanding.

Mary Bean, entering from the kitchen, put her arm around him and asked softly, "Have you had trouble with Mr. Pitts, dear?"

At his tight face and nod, she frowned at her husband. "Thomas, he's afraid of Gilby. I don't know what's happened, but I don't like—"

"Take him into our bedroom and close the door," Thomas Bean said quickly. "Knowing Gilby, I'd just as soon not—"

Save for the forgotten boots near the sofa, the room was clear when the knock sounded.

After an exchange of greetings, Gilby Pitts entered.

"You folks just git home, Tom?" he asked.

"Oh, a short while ago."

"See anything kinda unusual on the way back?"

"Saw a nice sunset. Why?"

"H'mp! I don't pay no mind to sunsets." Gilby shuffled toward the fireplace, rubbing his unshaven jaw against his high shoulder. His narrow eyes darted about the room. "There's queer things goin' on around here, Tom. I don't like it. You still got that bloodhound you raised?"

"No. Traded it to Ben Whipple over at Windy Gap for a calf. Trying to train another dog, but he's a tough one. About got me licked."

"Sure wish you had that hound. I got a mind to go over to Whipple's an' borrow him."

"What on earth for?" Thomas Bean looked at Gilby curiously.

"Might as well tell you, Tom. There's a wild boy loose in this country. Seen 'im with my own eyes. Emma can tell you. I caught the little varmint, but Emma an' me couldn't git nothin' out of him. While we were tryin' to make 'im talk, he tore loose an' took off like a streak. Never seen nothin' like it! Cleared a fence like—like—"

"A wild boy!" Thomas exclaimed. Then he asked softly, "What was he doing when you caught him, Gilby?"

"Trespassin'. An' I got signs up. I—"

"Oh, come now. No one worries about trespassing signs except in hunting season. You know that. We cross each other's land all the time. Saves miles of travel by the roads. I do it all the time when I'm out rock-hunting."

"This is a heap different. I been missing things. I—"

"Did it ever occur to you," Thomas Bean interrupted, "that this boy you're talking about could be lost, and in need of help?

---

8. A *liniment* (LIN uh mint) is a medicated semi-liquid for rubbing on the skin, to relieve soreness, inflammation, or sprain.
9. *Housemaid's knee* is a term for chronic inflammation of the kneecap caused by scrubbing floors on one's hands and knees.

Why, he could be badly hurt—"

"*He* weren't hurt! You shoulda seen 'im jump!"

"Then you must have frightened him badly. Why did you frighten him?"

"The varmint come sneakin' down to that west field o' mine with the deer. He—"

"With the *deer*!"

"That's what I said. *With the deer.* Just like he was one of 'em!"

Thomas pursed his lips, then said dryly, "You wouldn't have been taking a shot at one, would you, Gilby?"

Gilby Pitts spat angrily into the fireplace. "Fool deer been ruinin' my field. Man's got a right to scare 'em away."

"But the boy—"

"He took off, an' got tangled in the barbed-wire fence, or I'd never acaught 'im. Acted like he didn't know the barbed wire was there. But he knowed it the second time, when he busted loose. Sailed right over it like he had wings. I tell you he's wild. Wild as they come." Gilby stopped. In a lower tone he added, "An' that's not all. *He ain't natural.* I don't like *unnatural* things around. If there's more like 'im we ought to know about it."

There was a moment's silence. In the adjoining bedroom, where every word of the conversation could be heard, Mary Bean had opened the liniment bottle and was rubbing Little Jon's bruises. There was wonder in her eyes as she whispered, "Is that true about the deer? You were—friendly with them?"

He nodded, and struggled to fit new words to thoughts. But the words were too few.

"You're an odd one," she whispered. "I wish you could remember your name. Try real hard."

"J—Jon," he said. The name came unbidden[10] to his lips. There was more to it, but the rest would not come.

They fell silent, for Thomas Bean was talking.

---

10. *Unbidden* means spontaneously and not asked for.

THE FORGOTTEN DOOR / 325

"Gilby," said Thomas, "if I were you, I'd go sort of easy about this. Suppose a stray kid from over at the government camp got lost. If he fell and hurt himself, he could wander around in a daze, not even knowing who he was. If you actually found him, and scared him away instead of trying to help him, you'd be in for a lot of criticism."

"Well, mebbe…"

"What's more, this isn't hunting season, and you'd be in for more trouble if people thought you were trying to sneak some venison."[11]

"Now lissen to me, Tom—"

"I'm only telling you the truth, Gilby. Anyway, it's quite possible that some Cherokee boys from the Reservation came over this way on a hike. You know how they are in the spring."

"Aw, I dunno. Emma didn't think he was no Cherokee." Gilby shuffled around, and suddenly muttered, "I declare. Them's queer-lookin' boots yonder."

In the bedroom, Mary Bean stood up quickly, alarm in her blue eyes. She went to the door and started to slip into the hall, but at that instant Sally darted past her from the kitchen.

"Hello, Mr. Gilby," Sally chirped brightly, scooping the boots from under Gilby Pitts's nose. "My goodness, Mommy will scalp me if I don't get the mud off these." She skipped back into the kitchen, calling, "Mommy, when are we going to have supper? I'm *hungry*!"

"Coming in a minute, dear," her mother answered.

Gilby Pitts scowled, rubbed his chin on his high shoulder, and finally shambled toward the door. "Reckon I'll be goin', Tom. Let me know if you hear anything."

"Sure will. Be seeing you."

No one said a word until Gilby Pitts's truck was safely down the road. Then Thomas expelled a long breath. "Confounded old skinflint!"[12] he muttered.

"Do you think he suspected anything?" Mary said, bringing Little Jon back into the room.

"Probably not. He's just nosy. I only wish he hadn't seen the boy this morning—but maybe I've calmed him down enough so he won't do anything." He grinned suddenly at his daughter. "Thanks, Sally, for snatching the boots. That was quick thinking."

"I deserve a dime for that," Sally said pertly, holding out her hand.

"Mercenary," he growled, giving her the dime. He stooped and kissed her.

"I'm *not* mercenary," she said. "See, I can give as well as receive." She pressed the dime into Little Jon's hand. "It's yours—and—and I hope you stay with us a *long* time."

Brooks Bean, who had temporarily forgotten his chores, watched the exchange with interest. Abruptly he burst out, "Say, guy, didn't you ever see a dime before?"

"His name is Jon," said Mary Bean. "Like short for Jonathan. His name is all he can remember at the moment."

"But—but, jumping smoke," Brooks persisted, "a dime's a dime. Don't you know what money is, Jon?"

Little Jon shook his head.

"But you must know English, or you would-

---

11. The flesh of a deer or similar animal is called *venison* (VEN ih sin) when prepared for eating.
12. A *skinflint* (SKIN flint) is one who is stingy and not generous.

Word Bank   **mercenary** (MUR sih NAIR ee) *n.*: a person who acts merely for money

n't know what we're saying," Brooks went on, baffled. "So you must know about *money*!"

Mary Bean said firmly, "We've questioned him enough for one evening. After all, if you had a bump on your head as big as his, you wouldn't know which way was up. Jon's had a pretty bad day. What he needs is something to eat, and a good night's rest. Tomorrow's Sunday, and there'll be plenty of time to talk."

There was only one other surprise that evening. They had scrambled eggs for supper, along with some of Mary Bean's home-canned vegetables, generous slices of baked meat, and some fried chicken left over from the day before. Little Jon ate ravenously of everything but the meat and chicken, which he refused to touch.

He began to nod at the table, and was sound asleep before he could finish undressing for bed. He shared Brooks's bed that night and wore a pair of old pajamas, much too large for him, that Brooks had outgrown.

Chapter 3
HE LEARNS A NEW LANGUAGE

In the morning Little Jon felt nearly as well as ever. Save for the bump on his head, which was better, all his swellings had gone down during the night, and the ugly bruises had almost vanished. There was hardly a sign of the scratches that had marred[13] his hands and face. He could walk easily.

"I can't understand it," Mary Bean said at breakfast. "I *never* saw anyone heal so fast. I've heard of fast healers, but…"

"Oh, it's only our special Bean liniment," Thomas said lightly, carefully hiding his own surprise. "Jon, it's an old Indian concoction.[14] Supposed to cure everything but poverty and rabies. If it wasn't for the poverty restriction, I could sell it in the shop and make a fortune on it."

"Aw, Dad," Brooks began, but Sally said brightly, "Why don't we rub some on Jon's head? Maybe it would bring back his memory!"

Little Jon laughed. He knew she meant it, which made it all the funnier.

The others laughed with him, then looked at him curiously.

Thomas Bean said, "It's good to hear you laugh, Jon. That means your voice will be coming back soon as well as your memory. Then we can locate your folks." He paused, frowning. "What I can't understand is why there was no mention of you on the radio this morning. Ordinarily, in this mountain country, if anyone gets lost, you hear about it first thing on the local station and search parties go out. But there wasn't a word."

Mary Bean murmured, "I hope it wasn't like what happened over beyond the gap last summer."

Brooks said, "Jon, some tourists drove off the mountain, but nobody even knew about it for a week. Some hikers just happened to stumble over their car. Everybody in it was dead."

"Brooks!" his mother said despairingly. "You shouldn't—"

---

13. The scratches that *marred* (MARD) had spoiled the appearance of his face and hands.
14. A *concoction* (kun KAHK shun) is a mixture of various ingredients.

Word Bank   **ravenously** (RAV in iss lee) *adv.*: hungrily; as if starving; eagerly

THE FORGOTTEN DOOR / 327

"Aw, *he* didn't wander off from any wrecked car," Brooks told her. "I know. I asked him about it while we were getting dressed. Jon doesn't know any more about cars than he does about money."

Thomas Bean blinked. "Is that true, Jon?"

"Yes," said Little Jon, speaking his first word of English.

"He spoke!" Sally cried, delighted. "Maybe some of the liniment got on his tongue."

Neither Thomas nor Mary laughed. They glanced at each other, their eyes shadowed with questions.

Mary Bean said, "Thomas, I'm not going anywhere this morning. Why don't you take Brooks and Sally to town, and sort of nose around...."

"Um, O.K. I follow you. I'll see what I can pick up—without saying anything."

"Right. Now, Brooks," she said, "you and Sally listen to me carefully. I don't want either of you to mention a word about Jon to a soul. Understand?"

"Yes, ma'am," said Brooks. "I'm not dumb."

"But why shouldn't we mention him?" Sally asked. "I think Jon's *nice*, don't you?"

"Of course he is dear. And we want to protect him. Remember how Mr. Gilby was last night?"

"Oh, *him*!" Sally wrinkled her nose in distaste.

"So you see how it is, dear. There are too many things about Jon that people like Mr. Gilby can't understand—and they could make all kinds of, well, difficulties. Will you promise to keep Jon a secret?"

"I promise, Mommy."

"That's my girl," said Thomas, smiling at her. "Better get ready, you two. We have to get going."

> ... "you and Sally listen to me carefully. I don't want either of you to mention a word about Jon to a soul. Understand?"

When they were gone, Mary Bean went to the radio and turned it carefully to the local station. She listened to the next news report, then shook her head.

"Do you know about radios?" she asked.

Little Jon was not deceived by the casual tone of her voice. The question was important to her, for behind it were those troubling thoughts about cars and money.

"Yes," he replied. Then he remembered the politeness word, and said, "Yes, ma'am."

"Wonderful!" she exclaimed. "It's coming back. Is it hard to talk?"

"It is hard—now. But—it is coming." He liked her bright hair, and her quick blue eyes that were almost green. Sally looked much like her, but Brooks resembled his father.

"Well, we'll take it easy," she said. "Maybe I shouldn't talk to you at all for a day or two. You may have a concussion or something—I don't know too much about those things, but you've still got that bump on your head. Does it hurt this morning?"

"Only—when I—touch it. Please—talk. It—helps."

"O.K. We'll talk up a storm. I'm the biggest talker in seven counties—when I have the chance." She laughed. "Poor Thomas is too busy trying to keep the money coming in to listen to me half the time."

Word Bank   **concussion** (kun KUSH in) *n.*: an injury to the brain or spinal cord from a jarring blow

"Money?" he said. "Why?"

"There we go again! Money. You *must* know what money is! Everybody has to have it. You can't eat without it—though we manage pretty well, what with a garden and the stuff I can from it, plus chickens and a cow. They call this place a farm—but no farmer could possibly make a living from it these days, no matter how hard he worked. And we all work hard. Thomas is no farmer—but he refuses to live in cities, so he studied geology after the war, and managed to buy this place and start the Rock Shop. That's where our money comes from—mainly during the summer from tourists."

She stopped, her eyes crinkling. "Am I talking too much?"

"Oh, no! Please—please talk more."

"All right. About money. Are you absolutely certain you've never seen any before?"

"Absolutely certain."

"And the same for automobiles?"

"They are—strange to me."

"And you're getting stranger to me by the minute."

Mary Bean sat down, and he was aware of her growing bewilderment as she stared at him. His own bewilderment matched hers, but he fought it down while his mind sorted the dozens of new words he was learning. Words were used in patterns, and they had to match the patterns that thoughts came in. It was very easy—but it took time.

Suddenly she jumped up. "Jon, I'm going through the house and point out things. I want you to tell me whether they are familiar or strange. You know about radios, so you should know about TV also."

"It is like radio—but has—pictures?"

"Yes, television. We don't have a set. We've been using our extra money for books."

"Television—it seems familiar."

"Good. What about books?" She waved to the shelves of books flanking the fireplace.

"Familiar," he said instantly.

"Can you read this one?" She handed him a copy of one of Sally's books.

"No. I cannot read—this."

"That's strange. I get the feeling you're older than you look. Anyone who speaks English ought to be able to read this. Oh, dear, I didn't realize—maybe English isn't your language."

"There *is* another language I—I seem to know."

"Now we're getting somewhere!" she exclaimed happily. "If you could speak a little of it, maybe I could recognize it."

Little Jon looked out of the window, and let his mind rove over the greening valley in the distance. Suddenly he began to hum a little song about valleys. The humming changed to singing words. He wondered where he had heard it.

Mary Bean clapped her hands. "That was beautiful, Jon! Beautiful!" Her bewilderment returned. "I thought I knew something about languages—my father taught them in school. But this is a new one. How long have you known English?"

"I don't know it yet. I only began—last night."

She shook her head. "Say that again?"

"I—I am learning it from you, now," he said, and instantly wondered if he should have told her. She didn't believe him. It was strange that she couldn't understand thoughts, even strong ones—but nobody here seemed to

---

Word Bank   **geology** (jee AHL uh jee) *n.*: the study of the earth's structure and the rocks that make up its crust

be able to. Only the animals….

"Jon," she said, very patiently, "do you know the difference between truth and—and falsehood?"

"Truth? Falsehood? Truth is—is right," he managed to say. "Falsehood is—not truth. There is another word for it—but you have not spoken it yet."

"The word is 'lie,' " she said softly. "When you are not telling the truth, you are telling a falsehood—a lie."

His chin quivered a moment, then stiffened. "You think I am not telling you the truth—but —but I *must*! You are as strange to me as—as I am to you. Yesterday—in the morning—I woke up—on a mountain—far away from—from here. I hurt all over. I felt as if—as if I had fall—fallen. I did not know my name until last night, when you asked me. Everything was strange. The mountain, the trees, everything…only the deer. I—" He stopped, all at once aware of the dog he had glimpsed last night.

The dog was thirsty. It was almost a hurt to feel the dryness of its throat, the craving for water.

He told Mary Bean about the dog, but she shook her head. "Oh, I'm sure he was taken care of. Thomas wouldn't forget Rascal. Anyway, how could you possibly—"

"But he *did* forget the water. How could Rascal think a lie?"

"Jon!" There was something like fright in her eyes. "Are you trying to tell me that you can—" She shook her head, and said, "We'll go out to Rascal's pen and see—"

They had started through the doorway when they heard a car coming down the road. Instantly she drew him back inside and closed the door. They stood waiting for the car to pass. It slowed, then went on.

"The Johnsons," she said. "They would have stopped if they'd seen us. Thank goodness they didn't."

Almost in the same breath she said firmly, "Rascal will have to wait. Jon, I'm going to cut your hair, and I'm going to give you some different clothes to wear. I hope you don't mind, but I want you to look as much like other boys as possible. It's terribly important."

"I don't mind," he said, giving Rascal a quieting thought. "I'm sorry to—to make so much trouble."

"I don't mind it in the least. In fact, if I can only get used to you, I believe I'm going to enjoy this. But getting used to you…."

She got scissors and a comb, and started to cut. She found the nearly hidden clip holding his hair together at the nape of his neck.[15] "O-o-oh!" she gasped. "What workmanship! Thomas will be interested in this."

She put the clip carefully aside, and very expertly cut his hair. "I'm the family barber," she explained. "You'd be surprised what it saves. Costs a dollar-fifty in town, and nearly double that in cities. That's six dollars a month for Brooks and Thomas. Now, let's see. Clothes. Most of Brooks's old things went to the charity collection, but I saved the best for Sally to play in. They ought to fit you."

When he was finally dressed in faded jeans, a fairly good shirt, and a light zipper jacket, she surveyed him critically.

"We're short on shoes," she said, "but I think your boots will pass, if you keep your

---

15. The *nape* of the neck is the back of the neck.

Word Bank **surveyed** (sir VAYD) *v.*: inspected; examined; appraised to determine condition or size

trousers pulled over them. Next, we've got to think up a story to explain your presence here. I know—Thomas had a pal in the Marines named Jimmy O'Connor. He married a French-Moroccan girl when he was stationed in North Africa. They were both killed in the trouble there recently—so who's to know if they didn't have a son about your age? You do look, well, a bit foreign. I don't see why we couldn't call you Jon O'Connor, and say we'd sort of fallen heir[16] to you for the time being."

"But—but that would not be truth," he said, wondering.

"Oh, dear, there we go again." She sighed, and sat down, frowning. "Jon, in this day and age, with the way things are, truth—the exact truth—is often a hard thing to manage. There are times when it could cause needless trouble and suffering."

"Things must be—very wrong if—if truth can cause trouble," he replied simply.

She sighed again. "You're probably right—but that's the way the world is. Even in little things, we often tell white lies to save people's feelings."

"White lies?"

"Well, take Mrs. Johnson. She makes her own clothes, just as I do. But she's never learned to sew well, and she makes the ugliest dresses in the community. Still, I wouldn't hurt her feelings by telling her how ugly they are. I usually think of something nice to say about them."

Little Jon was puzzled. "But that's not right. How can she learn? It's wrong to make things ugly. Why, if she's wrong, should her feelings—"

"Oh Jon! I don't understand you!" She shook her head. "Listen, dear. To avoid trouble, I'm afraid you'll have to be Jimmy O'Connor's boy—until we can find out more about you. I don't dare tell the Johnsons, or the Pitts, or some other people, that—that you're a strange boy from nowhere, who has curious clothes that won't tear, and curious ideas that don't fit, who has never seen money or cars before, and who can talk to—" She stopped, and again he was aware of the flicker of fright in her mind. Quietly she said, "Let's go out and see if Rascal really is thirsty."

Rascal was a huge brown mongrel,[17] with a wide head and heavy jaws. He snarled as they approached the enclosure, and lunged to the end of his chain. The iron pan that held water was empty. Mary Bean frowned at the pan. She turned on the hose and filled it from a safe distance. Rascal quieted and drank greedily.

"How you ever knew about that pan—" she began. "Anyway, I'd better warn you about Rascal. Thomas is always picking up stray dogs and trying to train them—but this creature was a mistake. He won't let anyone but Thomas go near him. We've got to get rid of him. If he ever broke that chain…"

"He—he won't hurt you."

"I happen to know better. He's as vicious as they come, and even Thomas —No! *Don't open that gate!*"

He hardly heard her, for he had slipped quickly through the gate and all his attention was on Rascal. He held out his hands, and the big dog came over to him, uncertain, then

---

16. In this case, *fallen heir* means that the Bean family has inherited Jon from others.
17. A *mongrel* (MAHN gril) is a dog of mixed breed.

Word Bank **vicious** (VISH iss) *adj.*: savage; ferocious; very mean

whining in sudden eagerness, trembling. As he spoke silently he could feel the blackness and the lostness fade away from the brooding creature that now sprang happily upon him.

Thomas Bean, returning, glimpsed the two from the foot of the lane. He sent the truck roaring up to the house and jumped out, calling, "Hey, you crazy kid! Get out of there before—"

His voice died with recognition. Shaken, he limped over to Mary, followed by Brooks and Sally. "Didn't know him with a haircut and those clothes," he muttered. "L-rd preserve me, how did he *ever* make up to Rascal?"

"I'll try to tell you later," she whispered, "but you won't believe it. Incidentally, I've decided that he's Jimmy O'Connor's boy. We—we've got to explain him somehow."

Thomas nodded slowly. "Jimmy O'Connor is a good choice. Be hard for anyone to check up on it."

"Did you learn anything in town?"

"Not a thing. I was surprised to see Gilby and Emma there."

"They must have come to town with the Macklins—they're related, you know."

"Well, the Macklins were all there. They looked well fed on Bean hams."

"Thomas! You don't actually *know* that they stole our hams last fall."

"No, I certainly can't prove it. Anyway, I drove through town, listened around a bit, and got all the papers I could find. *Atlanta Journal*, *Asheville Times*, and a couple others. There's bound to be something in one of them about a lost boy."

"Want to make a bet on it?"

"But, Mary, he had to come from *somewhere*!"

Little Jon called from the enclosure, "Please, may—may I take Rascal out? He—he hates the chain."

"Why, say, you're getting your voice back!" Thomas exclaimed. "You're really progressing, young fellow. Er, I don't know how you made up to Rascal, but I think you'd better leave him where he is."

"He—he promises to be good."

"Oh, he *promises*, does he?" Thomas chuckled. "Well, some dogs can break promises the way people do. Maybe, tomorrow…."

Little Jon turned away to hide his disappointment. *He doesn't understand,* he silently told Rascal. *But he will. Be patient, and tomorrow we will play together.*

He heard Thomas say to Mary, "Thank heaven he's able to talk to us. Seems like a pretty bright kid, so it shouldn't be too hard to find out a few facts about him."

"Thomas," Mary whispered, "I have something to tell you about his speech. Get a double grip on yourself and come into the house."

Chapter 4
HE MAKES A DISCOVERY

The next morning, as soon as Brooks and Sally had gone to meet the school bus, Thomas Bean said, "Let's all get down to some facts and see what we can figure out."

A study of the papers had yielded not the slightest clue, and it had been decided to save all further questions until this time, when they would have the morning to themselves. Little Jon had looked forward hopefully to this moment, yet he approached it with misgivings.

Word Bank **misgivings** (mis GIV ingz) *n.*: feelings of doubt, distrust, or apprehension

His memory still told him nothing. And the Beans, much as he was beginning to love them, were still as strange to him as he was to them.

"Let's start with your clothes," said Thomas, limping over to the table on which Mary had placed them. "They should tell us a lot. Is everything here?"

"All but my boots—and my knife and belt," he said. "I'm still wearing them."

Mary Bean said, "His boots are woven of the same material as the rest of his clothes, only thicker. Even the soles."

"No leather?" said Thomas.

"Thomas," she said, "there isn't a scrap of leather in anything he owns."

"Leather" was a new word. Little Jon asked about it, and was shocked when he learned. "But how—how can you kill another creature for its skin?" he exclaimed.

"That's the way people live, young fellow," Thomas said, frowning as he wrote something on a piece of paper. "Well, that's another odd fact about you. I'm going to stop being surprised, and just jot down the facts. I learned in the Marines that if you get enough facts together, no matter how queer they may look alone, they'll always add up to something."

The pencil in Thomas Bean's hand moved swiftly as he intoned, "No leather. Doesn't believe in killing things. Will not eat meat. Seems to know how to—to communicate with animals. H'mm. Clothes, all handwoven. Material like linen…."

"It's a hundred times stronger than linen," Mary hastened to say. "The soles of his boots hardly show a sign of wear."

"Vegetable fiber," Thomas mumbled, writing. "Tougher than ramie.[18] Dove gray. Designs on hem of jacket in tan and blue. Could be Indian or Siberian—"

"But they're not," said Mary Bean, "and I don't see any sense in writing all that down when I know the answer."

"And what *is* the answer, Madame Bean?"

"I—I'm not ready to tell you," she said. "You should be seeing it for yourself. I think Jon sees it. Do you, Jon?"

He was startled by her thought. "You could be right," he told her slowly. "I almost believe you are—but I'm not sure yet. You're better able to judge. You have your memory."

"Hey, what's all this?" Thomas asked curiously.

"Skip it," Mary told him. "You're the fact finder. Have you listed his English as one of the facts?"

"I'm listing it as a language that he knows."

"That's not what I mean, Thomas."

"Oh, come on. It takes years to learn English the way he speaks it. Jon's picked it up somewhere—he'd forgotten it temporarily. That crack on the head—"

"No," said Little Jon. "Your language is new to me. I'm sure I never heard it until you spoke it. But I find it—easy."

"Oh, I don't doubt your word," said Thomas Bean, "but English just *seems* strange to you. There isn't a living soul who can pick it up in a day or two. That's absolutely impossible. The thing is, you're able to sort of know our thoughts before we speak them. That's an unusual ability—though I've heard of people who can do it. Anyway, it's an ability that's helping you to relearn English as fast as you hear it. Doesn't that sound right to you?"

Little Jon shook his head. "No, sir. I—I don't *think* in English. There's another language I—"

"We'll come to that in a minute. It's all adding up."

"What about cars and money?" Mary Bean asked quickly. "Can you add those up with

---

18. *Ramie* (RAM ee) is a tough fiber made from the stem of the *ramie* plant, a Chinese and East Indian shrub.

THE FORGOTTEN DOOR / 333

the rest of it?"

"Certainly," said Thomas. He was pacing back and forth with his awkward step, one hand rubbing his deeply lined face while he frowned at his notes. "It's beginning to make sense. Even the fact that he knows about radios, and nothing about some other things. How's this:

"Jon was raised in a foreign country, in a very remote district. He learned to speak the language of that district—probably before he learned English. Because it was a primitive sort of place, there was no money, and all trade was by barter. Naturally there'd been no cars there. But his folks had a radio so they could keep in touch with the outside world. Wouldn't be surprised if his folks were missionaries.[19] Sound right to you?"

Mary said, "Why must you be so—so reasonable, Thomas? But go ahead. Name some places like that."

"Oh, that's easy. I've been in a number of them. Parts of India, the Middle East, North Africa, and even South America. Those clothes could have been woven by Indians in the Andes."

"Nonsense," Mary said. "Those people weave only with animal fibers and cotton. The material in Jon's clothes didn't come from any of the places you mentioned."

"Well," Thomas demanded, "where *did* it come from?"

"Not from any place you know about—and while you're thinking of places, you might consider *how* he got here. That really stumps me."

"He must have flown, Mary."

"In what kind of plane, Thomas?"

"Oh, a small private one, I'd say—one that hasn't been missed yet. It *has* to be that. There's no other solution. You see, when we found him he was still wearing the clothes he must have put on when he left home. He'd hardly be wearing such odd-looking things if he had been in this country long enough to change them. I wish I'd thought of this earlier! He must have come in a plane, and it must have crashed somewhere here in the mountains. We'd better organize a search—"

Mary was shaking her head. "No, Thomas. Jon has never seen a plane in his life. He saw pictures of some in one of our magazines yesterday, and asked me what they were."

Thomas stared at her, then turned. "Is that true, Jon?"

"Yes, sir. I'm certain I've never been in a plane, Mr. Bean."

"But your memory, Jon—"

"My lost memory doesn't keep me from knowing familiar things," he said earnestly.

"H'mm. Well, what *is* familiar to you?"

"Radios are familiar, sir. Books are very familiar. Deer and—and singing birds, and birds like chickens—are all familiar. And dogs."

"Cows and horses?"

"Horses, yes. But I'm sure I never saw a creature quite like a cow before, or machines

> "Thieves? Thieves?" It was another new word with a confusing thought behind it.

---

19. *Missionaries* (MISH in AIR ees) are people sent into an area by a religious group to carry on their work.

Word Bank   **primitive** (PRIM ih tiv) *adj.*: indicating a people or society that has a simple economy and little if any technology like planes and automobiles. Of course, the *idea* of all those machines is familiar, and some of them seem familiar, like spaceships, and—"

"*Spaceships?*"

Mary Bean said, "He saw some drawings of spaceships in one of the magazines."

"But I've never been in one," Little Jon hastened to say. "It's just that I feel I've seen them. They are not strange like—like snakes and cows and—and the language you speak."

Thomas Bean sat down. He began snapping his fingers, his face blank. Speech seemed to have deserted him.

Mary laughed. "You wanted facts, Mr. Sherlock Holmes Bean. We'll toss a couple more at you. Jon, show him your knife. I'll get the clip."

The clip was gold filigree,[20] set with a blue stone. The knife, which had been entirely hidden by its woven sheath,[21] was small, with a short, thin blade that looked like gold. Its handle was of finely carved wood, with a blue stone set in the golden hilt.[21]

"Well?" said Mary, after Thomas had been examining the articles silently for several minutes. "You've been around, Mr. Bean. You're supposed to know something of gems and jewelry. Where were those things made?"

Thomas shook his head. "I've never seen such work. If these stones are real—but of course they can't be. Star sapphires like these…h'mm." He picked up a sliver of wood from the fireplace and sliced it with the knife. "Sharp as a razor! Must be a special gold alloy."[22]

Suddenly he stood up. "Let's go down to the shop. I'd like to test these stones."

As they went down the lane, Little Jon heard Rascal bark, and was aware of the eager question in it. *Soon,* he called to Rascal. *I have not forgotten.*

He watched Thomas unlock the shop door, and followed him inside. "Why do you keep the door—locked?" he asked, peering curiously and with quick interest at the rocks cramming the shelves and heaped in the corners, and at the glass case full of trays of gems.

Mary said, "Locks are to keep out thieves."

"Thieves? Thieves?" It was another new word with a confusing thought behind it.

"A thief is a person who steals," she explained. "We have a lot of valuable things here in the shop. If the windows weren't barred and the door didn't have a good lock on it, somebody would break in and take everything we own—even the safe, probably."

"B-but why—"

Thomas asked, "Don't people steal where you're from?"

"Of course not! Why, would they? It seems so stupid. They—"

"Go on!" Mary urged. "You're remembering."

"I—" He shook his head. "I almost thought of something, but it's gone. I only know that stealing is—stupid and foolish. I'm sure I've never heard of a person doing it. Why would he?"

"It's one way to make a profit—" Thomas began dryly, "if you don't mind risking jail. There are people who'll do anything for money. They'll even start a war."

"Profit? Jail? Money? War?"

"Here we go again!" said Mary. "You see, Thomas, English *is* strange to him, because it contains *ideas* that are strange."

Little Jon listened carefully, holding back his astonishment as she proceeded to

---

20. *Filigree* (FILL uh gree) is a delicate lacy work of silver, gold, or other metal.
21. A *sheath* (SHEETH) is a case or close-fitting cover for the blade of a knife; a *hilt* is its handle.
22. An *alloy* (AL loy) is a mixture of two or more metals.

explain. One subject led to another. She had finished about war, and was touching upon government and rulers and power when they were interrupted.

A man on horseback was approaching. It was the same rider who had gone by on the road Saturday evening, before the Beans appeared in their truck.

"That's Angus Macklin," said Mary. "He lives up the road beyond the Johnsons. I hope he goes on."

But Angus Macklin, seeing the door open, stopped, dismounted, and came in. He was a short, thick man with round, blinking eyes and an easy smile. Little Jon was not deceived by the smile, though he was fascinated by the repulsive[23] wad of tobacco Angus was chewing. "Howdy, folks! Howdy!" Angus said heartily. "See you're open for business. Ought to be gettin' some customers if the weather holds."

"Little early for tourists," Thomas told him. "How are things, Angus?"

"So-so. Ain't seen Tip an' Lenny around, have you?"

"Not this morning. Why aren't they in school?"

"Aw, you know kids," said Angus Macklin. "School's out tomorrow, an' it's kinda hard to make 'em go. When they heard about that wild boy, they just took off. Gilby told me about it yesterday. Soon's we got home, my kids lit out to hunt 'im. They lit out again this morning—pretended they was going fishin', but I know better. Mighty queer about that crazy wild boy. Gilby tell you how far he jumped? Near forty feet!"

"Nonsense!" Thomas said shortly. "Gilby was probably drinking. I'm sure he saw a stray Indian kid."

"Oh, I dunno," said Angus, scratching under his cap and blinking owlishly at Little Jon. "That thing he saw was plumb wild and unnatural. I've seen some queer things myself in these mountains. Lights, where there shouldn't be no lights. Heard music where there shouldn't be no music. My kids can take care of themselves, but all the same, that wild thing could be dangerous."

He paused. "Nice-lookin' boy you got here. Ain't noticed him around. He visiting you folks?"

Thomas nodded. "Jon O'Connor. Son of an old friend of mine in the Marines."

Angus smiled meaninglessly, and grunted. "Well, I'll go along. You see them fool kids o' mine, tell 'em I want 'em home."

They watched him ride away. Thomas said, a little angrily, "So, the news is out. I should have known Gilby would tell somebody like Angus. It's going to spread all over the mountains, and get wilder every time it's told."

He drew forth the knife and clip he had hidden under the workbench. As he studied them again, he began to whistle softly through his teeth.

"Out with it," said Mary. "Are the gems real?"

"They're real. I can't quite believe it. Jon, have you any idea what these things are worth?"

Little Jon looked at him intently. "They are not worth what you think they are, Mr. Bean. You're thinking they're worth more than your house, and everything in the shop—but that's all wrong. Anyway, a thing shouldn't have two values."

"*Two* values?" said Thomas, raising his eyebrows.

"Yes, sir," he said seriously. "You're judging the value of my knife by the amount of money you could sell it for. But that has nothing to do with its real value."

Thomas whistled softly. "I can't figure you

---

23. Something that is *repulsive* (ree PULSE iv) drives people away and causes a strong feeling of dislike.

out, Jon. It's a good thing we're not in business together, or we'd never make a profit."

"But—but doesn't the idea of a profit seem wrong to you?"

"I'll try to explain, Jon," Thomas said very patiently. "If Mary and I couldn't make a little profit on the things we sell, we'd soon go broke and wouldn't have enough to eat."

Little Jon looked at them helplessly. Again the dreadful feeling of lostness poured over him. He was sure of the answer now. Mary Bean had guessed it.

Suddenly he turned, peering out of the back window as he heard Rascal barking. Rascal was lost too, though in a different way, chained in a world where everything seemed wrong.

"Please," he begged, "may I take Rascal out of his pen? I promise he'll be good."

Thomas frowned, but Mary said, "Let him try it, Thomas. I'm sure he can manage Rascal."

"Um—O.K. We'll chance it this once. And here's your knife, unless you want me to keep it in the safe. You don't want to lose anything like this."

"Oh, I won't lose it, sir. I'll need it to—to—"

"Go on," Mary said quietly. "You need it to—to do what with it?"

"I don't know. Maybe it will come back if I run with Rascal. I think running will help."

As he darted out the door, Mary said, "He's upset, Thomas. I think he sees the truth. Can't you see it too? You've got facts enough—or is it that you just don't want to face the facts?"

"But, Mary, they don't make sense. I simply can't—"

"Look at him!" she gasped, staring through the rear window. "Thomas—*look!*"

In his eagerness to release Rascal, Little Jon was racing up the steep lane. Unconsciously he had made his feet light, so that his boots hardly touched the ground. Only a deer could have equaled his upward bounds.

"You win," Thomas said finally, expelling a long breath. "I don't know how he got here, and I can't understand why some things are so familiar to him—but he didn't come from this world."

"Of course not. What are we going to do?"

"H'mm. Seems like the important thing is to find out *how* he got here, if we can. I'm afraid I see trouble ahead."

Chapter 5

HE REMEMBERS SOMETHING

Sleep did not come easily that night. For a long time Little Jon lay motionless beside Brooks, thinking of the day while he listened to the sounds beyond the window—the familiar and unfamiliar sounds of a world he didn't belong in.

Somehow, by some accident, he had been lost on a planet that was not his own. It had been hard for the Beans to admit that to him, but of course there wasn't any other answer. Only, how did he get here—and why did so many of the wild creatures seem familiar?

Thomas had a theory about the wild creatures, and life on other planets. As they puzzled over it that afternoon, Thomas had said, "The latest belief among astronomers is that our Earth wasn't made by chance. There are other suns just like ours, and the same laws affect them. So there are bound to be other worlds like ours—with life developing on them in almost exactly the same way. If there are people like Jon on them, then naturally—"

"I won't dispute you," said Mary, "but that doesn't solve Jon's problem."

That was when Thomas suggested they get some help.

"Oh, good heavens, no!" she exclaimed. "How could anyone really help us? You know how people are. Don't you realize what a mess it would be if officials started buzzing around? The papers would get it, and we'd have reporters and half the world swarming all over the place. Honestly!"

"Um—guess you're right. Thank goodness someone like Angus Macklin didn't find you, Jon. It was lucky we happened on you when we did."

"No, it didn't happen that way, sir. I picked you." He explained to the Beans how he had waited for them.

"That settles it," said Thomas. "If you picked us to help you, we're sticking by you. Now, here's the crazy thing to consider: Our civilization is pretty advanced—the most advanced on Earth—yet we're just beginning space travel. We're not able to reach distant planets yet. So—how did you, whose civilization seems to be behind ours, ever reach us? You must have—"

"Thomas," Mary interrupted, "you're starting off wrong. Can't you *see* how wrong you are?"

"But, Mary, I'm judging by what I see. Jon's people haven't progressed beyond barter and the handloom. They must be tribal, for he knows nothing of money, laws, cities, and government."

"Thomas, cities come and go. Governments fall, and money becomes worthless. Is there a mill on this earth that can produce anything as wonderful as Jon's jacket?"

"Well, if we had that kind of fiber—"

"But we haven't. Can anyone on this earth learn a language as quickly as he learned ours—and read our thoughts the way he does?"

"No."

"Can anyone *move* the way he does?"

Thomas shook his head, his lips compressed.

"Thomas," she went on, "if all the people on this earth—everybody—were *absolutely* honest, would we need laws and jails—and armies and bombs and things?"

"H'mm. Guess not."

"Doesn't it seem obvious that Jon's people are actually *far* in advance of us?"

"They're certainly mighty intelligent...."

"So intelligent that they could easily have all the expensive and complicated things we have, if they wanted them. But they must not want them. They don't value them. I'm sure they've progressed way beyond them—and value other things more. Thomas, how long do you think it will take us to do away with crime and war?"

Thomas Bean shook his head. "At the rate we're going, we'll need a million years."

"Then there's our starting point. If Jon's people are a million years ahead of us, they've long known about space travel, and they've simplified it. They seem to have simplified everything else. My goodness, Thomas, they could have worked out something as simple as stepping through a door from one room to another."

"That sounds a little farfetched," said Thomas. "But maybe I'm too far behind. Does it make any sense to you, Jon?"

Something moved in his mind. "From one room to another," he repeated. "Door—door—It seems familiar—the idea, I mean."

"Think!" Mary Bean urged. "Think hard!"

It was no use. The thought, whatever it was, remained in hiding.

When Brooks and Sally came home from school, he spent the rest of the afternoon helping Brooks in the garden. Already they had begun to accept him as Jon O'Connor.

Lying awake in the night beside Brooks, he searched again for the hidden thought. It seemed important, the most important of all the hidden thoughts; but the harder he searched for it, the farther it seemed to retreat from him.

He dozed finally, and long later awoke suddenly. Rascal was barking, warning of wild creatures crossing the pasture. Deer.

Instantly, silently, he was out of bed, telling Rascal to be quiet while he drew on his clothes. In another minute he was outside, running with lightened feet to the pasture fence and bounding over it.

But the deer had been frightened by Rascal's barking. They had gone back up the forested slope, and refused to come down again.

Disappointed, Little Jon paused, and automatically glanced upward.

For the first time since his arrival he saw the wonder of the stars. Here in the open pasture, above the black bowl of the surrounding mountains, they blazed in uncounted millions. Even as he stared at them, one streaked like a flaming jewel across the sky.

A shooting star! There had been shooting stars when—when something happened. Shooting stars—and a door.

He raced back to the house, excited. It was nearly dawn, and the Beans were already stirring. As he burst into the living room he saw Thomas, still in pajamas, lighting a fire in the fireplace.

"There was a door!" he cried. "I remember that part…"

"A door?" said Thomas, as Mary hastened in from the kitchen. "What kind of door?"

"I don't know. But it seems that I was standing somewhere, looking at the stars, and I fell. And as I fell, I remembered something about a door…"

"Go on," Mary urged.

"That—that's all I can remember, as if it were part of a dream. Just stars, and thinking of a door."

"Could you have been in a ship?" asked Thomas. "You might have fallen out of one in some way."

"No—no—it wasn't like that. I suddenly fell *into* something—and when I woke up I was here on a mountain, and it was morning."

> A shooting star! There had been shooting stars when—when something happened. Shooting stars—and a door.

Thomas stood snapping his fingers, frowning. "Mary," he said finally, "it's possible you've hit on the right idea. Jon, as soon as we've finished the chores and had breakfast, we're going hunting. I want to see that spot where you found yourself."

After breakfast, Brooks and Sally went down to catch the school bus, and Thomas got out a knapsack for Mary to fill with lunch. When it was ready he thrust an odd-shaped hammer into his belt and started for the truck.

Little Jon looked curiously at the hammer. "That tool—it seems familiar. Do you—chip rocks with it?"

"It's a rock hound's[24] hammer, Jon. Thought I'd take it along and examine a few ledges while we're out. Might find a thing or two for the shop. How did you know what it's for?"

"I had the feeling I knew how to use it. Have you another I may take?"

"Why shore, podner, we'll jest go prospectin' together."[25]

Thomas found a second hammer, and they were returning to the truck when a car with a star on the side turned into the driveway. The car stopped behind them, and a lean gray-haired man got out.

At the sight of him, Little Jon was aware of sudden worry and alarm in Mary Bean, who stood watching from the steps. The man approached, studying them carefully with his hard, observant eyes. His nose was slightly hooked, and he made Little Jon think of a hawk he had seen the day before—a hawk searching for prey.

"Mr. Bean?" said the man, in a grating voice. "I'm Deputy Anderson Bush, from the sheriff's office." He opened his coat and showed a badge.

"Glad to know you, sir," Thomas said easily, extending his hand. "I've seen you around, but….This is Mrs. Bean, and my young partner here is Jon O'Connor. What can we do for you?"

"Like to ask a few routine questions, if you don't mind."

"Sure. Fire away."

Deputy Bush said, "Where were you people Saturday?"

"In town most of the day. Er, is anything wrong?"

"We'll get to that. I understand you have two children. Were they with you?"

"Yes."

"All the time?"

"Well, most of the time, except when they were in the theater. I knew where they were all the time, if that's what you want to know."

The deputy wrote something in a notebook, then looked down at Little Jon. "What about this boy?"

"He didn't arrive until Saturday evening."

"Where was he before that?"

"Traveling—on his way here."

"His parents bring him?"

"No." Thomas lowered his voice, and added, "Both Captain O'Connor and his wife were killed recently, and Jon's been pretty badly upset. Must we…."

The deputy finished writing in his notebook before he spoke. "Mr. Bean, I only want to know where the boy was all day Saturday and

---

24. A *rock hound* is an amateur collector of rocks and minerals.
25. "*Why, shore…*" "Why, sure, partner, we'll just go prospecting together." Prospecting means searching for gold, silver, and gems in samples of earth.

Word Bank **prey** (PRAY) *n.*: a creature hunted or seized for food

Sunday. That goes for your boy too. I believe Brooks is his name."

"Yes. You see, this is Jon's first trip to the mountains. Took him all day to get here. He arrived about suppertime. Sunday, he stayed home with Mrs. Bean, and I took my kids to town."

"And Sunday afternoon?"

"We were all here. No one left the place. What's this about?"

Deputy Bush made some more entries in his book. Again he glanced sharply at Little Jon. "Mr. Bean, have you heard anything about a wild boy in this part of the mountains?"

"Er—yes, I have," Thomas replied slowly. "Gilby Pitts told me about it, but I'm afraid I don't take much stock in it.[26] Do you?"

"Mr. Bean, I don't know what Mr. Pitts saw, but it seems to be very unusual. My job is to check up on it. Have you noticed any strange boy around?"

"I certainly haven't seen any boy that looks wild to me," Thomas answered, smiling. "Is he accused of any crime?"

Deputy Bush carefully closed his notebook and returned it to his coat pocket. "No one," he said, "is being accused of anything yet. Do you know the location of Dr. Holliday's summer place?"

"Of course. Dr. Holliday is an old customer of mine. Gilby Pitts takes care of the place while he's away. What about it?"

"Someone broke into it—either Saturday or Sunday. Mr. Pitts didn't learn about it until yesterday morning when he went over to finish some work he'd started last week. Some things were stolen."

"And you think a boy did it?"

"No question of it. There are foot prints and other signs. It was a boy about the size of this one, for he squeezed through a narrow window that a larger person couldn't have entered. He may have had a helper. Now, Mr. Bean, don't take any of this personally; I have to check on every boy in the area. Thank you for your help. Good day, sir."

"Good day, Mr. Bush."

Thomas stood snapping his fingers after the deputy left. "Of all the things to happen!" he burst out angrily.

"Thomas," Mary began worriedly, "do you think it likely that Anderson Bush could find out the truth about—about this wild boy thing?"

"He certainly could! He's no fool. I've never talked to him before, but I know his reputation. He's a born ferret[27] and a stickler[28] for the law—that's why he'd sure give us trouble. Bush doesn't like kids, and he never makes any exceptions. He sure had me going with those questions. If only he doesn't get too curious about Jon and start asking more…"

"There's really no reason for him to," Mary said. "It shouldn't be hard to find out who broke into the Holliday place."

"Oh, he'll find out—but that's not what worries me. It's pretty obvious who did it. Only, he doesn't know certain people like we do—he hasn't been here long enough. It'll take time to narrow things down and find out who's lying. And they'll lie. Oh, confound that fool Gilby for bringing up that tale."

"But he had to, Thomas. After all, when there's been a robbery…"

"Oh, I suppose so. Well, the thing's happened, and there's nothing we can do about it." Thomas sighed and turned back to the truck. "Let's get on with our hunting, Jon."

---

26. "*I don't take much stock in it*" is an idiom that means "I don't really believe it."
27. A *born ferret* (FER it) is a person who is naturally skilled at finding the truth. A *ferret* is a small animal used to drive out other small animals from their burrows.
28. A *stickler* (STIK ler) is someone who insists on something and won't yield.

Chapter 6

HE IS RECOGNIZED

The truck wound down toward the lower valley, and stopped briefly at the spot where Little Jon had crouched in hiding on Saturday.

"As nearly as I can guess," Thomas told him, "you must have walked ten or twelve miles through the mountains to come out here. That's all National Forest. You were heading east most of the time. Which way did you head earlier when you were following the deer to that field of Gilby's?"

"I don't know, sir. We wound around a lot. And we went over one low ridge before we got down into the valley."

"H'mm. Have you any idea how long it took you to reach the field?"

"It's hard to judge, sir. You see, I hadn't learned to count the time the way you do. And I felt so bad—it was all I could do to keep up with the doe. It may have been an hour, or even more. How far can you walk in an hour?"

Thomas chuckled. "In *this* country there's no telling. But let's say you walked a mile and a half, and mostly in an easterly direction. Gilby's place is in a pocket where the valley curves—and it isn't the same valley as this one. So what we'll do is drive past his land, and hike up the mountain to the first cove.[29] If we can't find a spot you recognize, we'll come back tomorrow and start in below Gilby's."

The truck moved on, going up and down and winding in many directions. Finally it crossed a bridge and turned into another valley. They drove past a farm, and several summer cottages that faced a noisy creek bordering the road. The next farm was nearly hidden by the dense growth of poplars[30] along the fence.

"That's Gilby's place," said Thomas, jerking his head as they went by. "Dr. Holliday's property is about a quarter of a mile farther on. We'll stop between the two."

At the first wide spot in the road, the truck was run as far over to the edge of the creek as possible, and they got out. "There's no bridge near," Thomas told him. "We'll have to wade."

"I'll jump," said Little Jon, and without thinking he made his feet light and cleared the stream in a bound. Turning, he saw the expression on Thomas Bean's face. After Thomas had splashed awkwardly over, Little Jon said apologetically, "I—I forgot. You're afraid someone might see me do that."

"I'd hate for Anderson Bush to catch you at it."

Thomas stamped water from his boots, and squinted at the forested slopes rising on three sides of them. "By the roads, we're nearly fifteen miles from home. Bet you can't tell me in what direction home is—and no fair peeking in my head for the answer!"

"I already know the answer," Little Jon told him, pointing instantly to the south. "It's a short distance over the ridge yonder. You see, I've been watching the way the roads and the valleys curve."

"I'll be jiggered![31] There's not a man in a hundred would guess that, unless he'd been raised around here. It's only two miles through a gap back of the Holliday place—if you know the trail."

"Oh!"

Thomas Bean frowned at him. "What's wor-

---

29. A *cove* (KOVE) is a recess or nook in a mountain or shoreline.
30. A *poplar* (PAHP ler) is a fast-growing tree with light wood.
31. "*I'll be jiggered*" is like saying, "Well, I'll be a fool!"

rying you, Jon?"

"I was wondering why Mr. Macklin's boys would steal—and why Mr. Macklin would let them."

"Great guns, how'd you ever get such an idea?"

"Well, you've been *thinking* they did, and Mr. Macklin *knows* they did, because yesterday when he stopped at the shop *he* was thinking about it." Little Jon paused, and looked up earnestly. "Please, Mr. Bean, you mustn't believe that I'm always looking into other people's heads. It isn't—" He groped for a word. "It isn't polite, or even right. The only reason I've been doing it is so I could learn. I *had* to do it. And sometimes you have thoughts that are so strong they—they seem to jump out at me. It goes with the way you feel. It was that way with Mr. Macklin. Yesterday he was thinking about his boys carrying things over the gap, from a house on this side. It didn't mean anything to me then, but now I understand why the thought was so strong."

"Good grief!" Thomas muttered, staring at him. He began snapping his fingers. "What a thing to know—and we can't say a word about it."

He gave a worried shake of his head, and adjusted the knapsack over his shoulder. "Let's forget about the Macklins, and see if we can find that spot we're after. It's getting more important all the time." He thrust through a tangle of laurels,[32] and began limping up a narrow ravine that opened through the trees.

Little Jon followed him easily. He could have climbed twice as fast, had Thomas been able to manage it. It was too bad, he thought, that people here couldn't make their feet light and save themselves so much trouble in getting around. It was such a simple thing. A way of thinking. But it was like so many other things that should be simple—like agreeing on something that was right, instead of trying to make it right some other way. That was why Thomas Bean limped. It had happened in a place called Korea, Brooks had said. Many men had died in Korea—and still no one agreed.

They topped the first ridge, and Thomas Bean stopped to rest. "See anything around here that looks familiar to you?"

"I don't believe I came this way," he said, studying the shadowed cove below them. "If I'd felt better Saturday, I'm sure I could have remembered everything exactly. But my head hurt, and I was so confused...."

"Don't apologize. This isn't going to be easy. I've known people to be lost for days in these mountains—and all the time they were within a half hour of a road. Let's start working east."

They followed the cove, crossed another ridge, and tramped for a winding mile or more through dense forest. By noon Little Jon had seen nothing he recognized. Finally they sat down on a mossy outcropping[33] of rock, and Thomas opened his knapsack. Little Jon had finished a sandwich and an apple when he suddenly whispered, "The doe—she's near!"

All morning he had known that many wild creatures had watched them from a distance,

---

32. A *laurel* (LAW ril) is a type of evergreen shrub.
33. An *outcropping* (OUT KRAHP ing) refers to layers of rock jutting out of the ground.

Word Bank **ravine** (ruh VEEN) *n.*: a narrow, steep-sided valley created from the erosion of running water

344 / Novella

and several times he had seen deer go bounding away. He had not tried to call them. But aware of a friend, he spoke silently, urging her to come nearer. She refused.

"What doe?" Thomas whispered. "I don't see—"

"She's way up yonder to the right—the one I followed Saturday. She knows me, but she won't come out. She's afraid of you. Mr. Pitts shot at her and hurt her—it wasn't a bad hurt because I spoiled his aim—but it makes her very afraid."

Thomas growled under his breath, "Had an idea something like that happened. I'd like to wring Gilby's neck."

"I couldn't tell you at the time—I didn't know the words. Anyway, we're getting close, Mr. Bean. The doe proves it."

"But I don't see how. These deer range for miles over the mountains."

"Yes, but she has a fawn that can't travel far, and she's still on the trail she used Saturday, only higher up. There are some—some vines she eats when she can't get anything else."

"Wild honeysuckle. Do you know the direction of Gilby's land from here?"

"Of course. It's straight over yonder," Little Jon pointed. "But we'll have to go way around, then curve to the left."

"Let's get going! I don't know how you keep these directions straight, but with a head like yours, I suppose…."

They found the doe's trail easily, and now Little Jon led the way. For Thomas Bean the next half hour was difficult. Many times Little Jon had to help him over tumbled faces of rock, slippery with green moss and running water. When they reached better ground, Thomas glanced back and grumbled, "I'm a fair mountain man in spite of my foot—but when we head for home it won't be *that* way."

"We won't have to, sir. The road's much

> "This is the place!" Little Jon cried. "I drank from the spring—see the marks of my hands?"

closer from here. We just turn left—north. Oh—I know this place! Yonder's where I first saw the doe."

He darted ahead, suddenly excited, then stopped to look slowly about him, searching.

"Was it here?" asked Thomas, limping over to him.

"It must be. It's where—no, there was a spring. I drank from it. After that I crawled…."

"There are springs all around here. You say you crawled—from where?"

"It was from a sort of dark place."

"You mean a cave?"

"It must have been. I hadn't realized till now—but there's no cave here."

"Let's try higher up," said Thomas, starting upward through a tangle of rhododendrons.[34] "There seems to be a ledge…."

There was a ledge. And there was a break in the strata,[35] marking what seemed to be a shallow cave behind the tangle. Near the mouth of it water trickled into a small pool.

"This is the place!" Little Jon cried. "I drank from the spring—see the marks of my hands? I woke up in there, where it's flat."

They crawled inside. Thomas Bean took a flashlight from his knapsack and sent the beam slowly about. The cave was much larger than it had appeared from the entrance.

"There's been a fall of rock in here recently,

---

34. A *rhododendron* (RO duh DEN drun) is a shrub or tree with clusters of showy pink, purple, or white flowers and oval leaves.
35. *Strata* (STRAT uh) are layers of rock. (The singular is *stratum*.)

Jon. Funny looking stuff. Looks igneous[36]—but only on one side."

"Igneous?"

"Volcanic. But no volcano ever melted this." He chipped experimentally with his hammer. "It's what we call metamorphic[37] granite—old, old rock that's changing. And something has seared[38] one side of it, a long time ago. I'll be jiggered!"

Thomas went farther back and straightened up. "This place is like the inside of a bottle. We've certainly found something—but don't ask me what. Think, Jon! Think about that door idea! Could this be part of it?"

"I—I don't know, sir. This place, it makes me feel sort of—tingly all over, as if something…but I can't remember."

He was aware of Thomas Bean's rising excitement as he chipped off flakes of fallen rock and examined them. Finally Thomas thrust the pieces into his knapsack, and turned the light on his pocket watch. It was later than either of them had realized.

"Pshaw!" Thomas growled. "Hate to leave—but it'll be nearly dark when we get back, and there are things to do. We'll return first thing in the morning."

They left reluctantly, their thoughts leaping as they talked of their discovery. As the shadows deepened in the forest, they fell silent and began to hurry. Little Jon led the way, following the doe's trail to the valley. At the fence he turned, skirting Gilby Pitts's land, and went through the woods to the creek.

He crossed the creek as before, though not until he had made sure that no one was around to see him.

The truck was several hundred yards around the bend ahead. They were in sight of it when Little Jon heard a car approaching. It was almost inaudible[39] above the clatter of the creek, yet his sharp ears recognized the sound.

He clutched Thomas Bean's arm in sudden uneasiness. "Mr. Bush is coming," he said. "I—I ought to hide."

"There's no reason to. He's already met you. What makes you afraid?"

"I don't know. Something…."

There was no place to hide here. The creek fell away on their left, and on their right the rocky slope rose sharply. And suddenly the car with the star on the side was swinging around a curve. It slowed as it came near them, and stopped. Gilby Pitts was sitting in the front with Anderson Bush.

"Howdy, Tom," said Gilby, his eyes sliding interestedly over Little Jon. "Heard you had a visitor. This him?"

"Yes. We've been doing a bit of rock-hunting together. How are matters up at Holliday's?"

"Been tryin' to make a list of what's been took. Some pretty valuable things. The Doctor's pet target rifle—he paid over three hundred dollars for it. Then there's some expensive fishin' rods…." Gilby Pitts rubbed his chin over his high shoulder and leaned out of the car window, squinting downward. "Them boots…."

All at once Gilby was out of the car and stooping swiftly. Little Jon knew what was coming even before Gilby's clutching hand gave his trouser leg a jerk to expose the top of the boot. And he was aware of Thomas Bean's desperate thought, *If you'll just keep quiet, Jon, and not say a word. I'll handle this.*

Thomas said, "What's come over you,

---

36. *Igneous* (IG nee iss) rocks are produced by intense heat, or are of volcanic origin.
37. *Metamorphic* (MET uh MOR fik) rock shows change as a result of natural forces, such as pressure or heat.
38. *Seared* (SEERD) means burned or scorched.
39. *Inaudible* (in AWD ih bul) means it cannot be heard.

Gilby?"

"Them's the boots I seen at your house Saturday night," Gilby Pitts said accusingly.

Thomas laughed. "What of it?"

"This kid was there all the time I was there! You never told me...."

"That we had a visitor? Why should I? Jon had had a hard day traveling, and we'd put him to bed. What's got into you, Gilby?"

"Them boots," snapped Gilby. "Ever since I seen 'em there I been wonderin' where I seen 'em before. It's come to me. That wild boy was wearin' 'em!"

Thomas laughed again, but Gilby said hoarsely, "You been hiding 'im! You cut his hair an' changed his clothes, but you ain't changed his face. I'd know that peaky face anywhere! This here's the ornery[40] little varmint that done the breakin' in and stealin'!"

"Gilby," Thomas said quietly, but with an inner fury that only Little Jon was aware of. "Take your hands off Jon—and stop accusing him before I lose my temper."

"Hold it!" ordered Anderson Bush, who had already stepped from the car and was standing, frowning, behind Gilby. "Mr. Pitts," he said in his grating[41] voice, "are you absolutely sure this is the same boy you saw the other day?"

"I got eyes!" snapped Gilby. "I'd know 'im anywhere!"

"You would be willing to swear to it?"

"On the Bible!" Gilby said emphatically.

"That's all I need to know." Anderson Bush looked hard at Little Jon, and his eyes narrowed as he turned to Thomas. "Mr. Bean, I'm afraid you haven't been honest with me. You said this boy had never been in the mountains before, and that he arrived at your place Saturday night."

"So I did."

"Why is it he was seen over here Saturday morning?"

"Pshaw!" said Thomas. "This thing's getting ridiculous. Who knows what Gilby really saw over here?"

"*I* know what I saw!" Gilby Pitts cried. "*An'—I know them boots!*"

"You see, Mr. Bean?" the deputy went on, his eyebrows raised. "I'm sure Mr. Pitts is a reliable witness. Those *are* very unusual boots the boy is wearing—and the boy himself is, well, different-looking. I'm sure I'd never forget either the boots or the boy, if I'd seen them before."

"Look here," said Thomas, his voice tighter, "this whole thing started because of a robbery that Jon couldn't possibly have had anything to do with. Are you accusing him of being a thief?"

"Mr. Bean," replied Anderson Bush, with a sort of deadly patience, "I'm only an investigating officer looking for facts. I've run into some very peculiar facts that need an explanation. We're due for another talk, Mr. Bean, so I think you'd better go home and wait for me. I'll be right over as soon as I drop off Mr. Pitts."

---

40. *Ornery* means stubborn and disagreeable.
41. A *grating* (GRAY ting) voice is one that is irritating or annoying.

Studying the Selection

First Impressions *Little Jon is troubled by behaviors and values he observes in an alien society. He, himself, is forced to change, as he realizes the necessity of concealing some of his capabilities and "gifts." What must he sacrifice to achieve a desirable end? What may he gain by doing so? Keep in mind that growth and risk often go hand in hand.*

✓ Quick Review

1. How did Little Jon come to be in his new surroundings?
2. How does the Bean family find him?
3. How do the local people react to Little Jon? How do you understand their behavior?
4. What about Little Jon's clothing and possessions attracts the interest of the other characters?

In-depth Thinking

5. Compare the reactions that Little Jon and Gilby Pitts have to animals. Which of them seems more comfortable?
6. How does Thomas Bean handle conflict? Are his wife's methods more likely to achieve positive and constructive results? Refer to the story to support your answer.
7. How would you compare the monetary worth of an article with its sentimental and personal value? Use an example from the story to illustrate the comparison.
8. How do the statements below mirror Little Jon's response to the new world?
   a. "…he couldn't quench hate with hate."
   b. "English is strange to him…it contains ideas that are strange."
   c. "Rascal was lost too, though in a different way, chained in a world where everything seemed wrong."

Drawing Conclusions

9. Little Jon encounters "human" behaviors that horrify him. List at least five. Do you think Little Jon can survive in the Beans' world? Could the Bean family make a go of it in Little Jon's world?
10. Briefly describe the physical setting of the story. Why does the locale work well? Would *The Forgotten Door* "work" in an urban (city) setting? What would need to be changed, if the events occurred in the city?

Focusing on the Novella: Characterization

Characterization is also described as **direct** and **indirect**. When the author allows the reader to observe the behavior and words of a character, the author is using **direct characterization**. However, when the reader must rely on hearsay—the words of another person in the story—for information about a character, the author is using **indirect characterization**.

With direct characterization, the reader may well assume that "seeing is believing." And since indirect characterization forces the reader to rely on a third party for "the facts," we may worry that its accuracy is open to question. But once again, we must remember that the author has invented all of this: Contrary to what we may assume, a direct characterization may involve deliberate concealment of the truth by either the character or the author; by contrast, an indirect characterization may be "right on"!

1. Select three characters from *The Forgotten Door*. Write a short sketch of each. Discuss the ways in which the author has filled in the details and made each of these characters come alive.
2. Select an additional three characters from the first part of the novella. Of the three, which are round, which flat? Support your understanding with details from the story.
3. Compare and contrast Thomas Bean and Gilby Pitts. For each man, list two important characteristics. Describe each man's goals. Has either man changed since the beginning of the story?

Creating and Writing

1. Little Jon is shocked to find himself in a world he *knows* is strange to him, in spite of his inability to recall his own life. Everything is new: the language; people's values; their relationship to animals; their reliance on money; their style of clothing. It is through what is *unfamiliar* to him in *our* world that we can draw conclusions about *his* world. What *would be* familiar to him? Two deductions that we can make are meals without meat and telepathic communication with animals by all "humans." Review the story and using this method of deduction, create a list of the features of Jon's world.
2. Write a new scene for the story either from the point of view of the Beans' dog Rascal or from the perspective of Gilby Pitts. Try to show your reader why either the dog or the human feels such savagery towards others. Try using flashbacks to move your reader towards understanding and sympathy.
3. Arrange to talk with a person who regularly provides care in a family that has a special-needs child, an elderly family member who requires frequent assistance, or a chronically ill household member that requires round-the-clock care. Talk with the caregiver about the tasks that need to be performed each day and about how one develops the physical and emotional strength to cope with such circumstances. Write up the data you have gathered and prepare an oral report. Remember to send a thank you note to your caregiver.

Blueprint for Reading

Background Bytes

The founders of the United States—those who drafted the Declaration of Independence, the Constitution, and the Bill of Rights—wanted to protect the common man from the tyranny of government. Yet modern nations enact laws to protect citizens—and to ensure their good behavior. For the benefit of "the people," modern governments also create social welfare and public safety agencies, such as police and fire departments, child welfare bureaus, food and drug administrations, and civil and criminal court systems. And so we see a tug of war between freedom and protection, between liberty and security.

Moreover, government agencies tend to move farther and farther from the common person. Increasingly, their agents and social workers are tied to written rules, rather than to the spirit of compassion that gave birth to their missions. The United States Central Intelligence Agency, for example, has repeatedly spied on private American citizens and interfered with their lives. The problem with creating a law or system to make life better is that the same law or system eventually becomes an obstacle to the humane and sensible handling of unusual human situations.

THE Forgotten Door Part II

Into *The Forgotten Door*—Part Two

Through the eyes of Little Jon, we see our own common practices, such as the payment of money for food and the killing of animals for sport. Perhaps Little Jon is capable of communicating with animals, because he knows how to listen and because he is very respectful of them. Little Jon represents the world on the other side of the door, a shadow world where innocence and gentleness are well-regarded. The villains of the piece are people who kill animals off-season, talk funny, are uneducated and thoughtless, and hate and fear what is different from them. Gilby Pitts, who really is *the pits*, is both cowardly and aggressive, perhaps too foolish to be really dangerous. But is he a symbol of modern America? There are still fine beings in this tale, even if they are few.

Focusing on the Novella: Setting

Notice Alexander Key's surprising use of setting. The world of the Beans is repeatedly seen as *less* than the magical world of Little Jon—a world we never even see. The rural countryside, which should be pleasing and beautiful, is filled with dangers. The courtroom, which might well be cold and threatening, is warmed by the protective presence of the wonderful Miss Josie, as well as the first public expression of Little Jon's power.

In the final chase scene of the story, look for details of setting and the ways in which the natural features of the region both help and hinder the protagonists. The surprise of setting echoes the betrayal of the protagonists by authorities who are supposed to help, not hurt.

Word Bank

In Chapter 8, Thomas Bean uses a variation of the idiom, *batten down the hatches.* Derived from nautical language, the words literally mean "to cover a ship's hatches with tarpaulins (to be held in place by battens)." The *hatches* are "openings in the deck of a vessel." A *tarpaulin* is a sheet of waterproofed canvas used as a protective covering. (Interestingly, *tarpaulin* has also come to mean "a sailor.") *Battens* are lengths of wood used to secure tarpaulins or to keep sails flat. What does the idiom mean figuratively? It means to prepare to meet an emergency.

aloof	evasive	recuperate
custody	materialized	reproachful

PART TWO

Chapter 7

HE IS ACCUSED

It was nearly dark when they reached the house. Little Jon glimpsed Brooks and Sally running from the barn to meet them, and he could hear Rascal whining impatiently in the enclosure, eager to see him and yet reproachful at being left alone all day. He wished suddenly that he had managed to take Rascal with them. The big dog would have loved it. Maybe, tomorrow…

"Remember," Thomas was saying, as he set the brakes and turned off the motor, "If Bush insists on asking you questions, let me think the answers before you tell him anything. He can't make us answer—only a court can do that. But I don't want him dragging us into court."

"Hi, Dad!" Brooks called. "School's out today! Yow-ee!"

"Mommy said you'd gone rock-hunting," Sally said eagerly, running ahead of Brooks. "Did you find any pretty stones?"

"A few. Where's your mother?"

"Here, Thomas," said Mary Bean, appearing from around the side of the house. "What kept you so late?"

"Trouble," Thomas said hastily. "We ran into Gilby and that deputy on the way back, and Gilby recognized Jon. Bush is on his way over to ask more questions. Keep Sally and Brooks in the kitchen. Jon, you might stay out of sight in the living room—but close enough to hear. I'll talk to Bush on the porch. Hurry—here he comes."

It was a warm evening, and the windows had been opened. Little Jon, huddled in a chair in the darkened room, heard the deputy's feet on the porch, and Thomas Bean's polite voice offering him a seat.

"Would you care for some coffee, sir?" Thomas asked. "I think Mrs. Bean has a fresh pot ready."

Word Bank   **reproachful** (re PROACH full) *adj.*: finding fault with; blaming

"No, thanks," came the deputy's grating reply. "I just want to talk to that boy. Will you get him out here, please?"

"I don't see any real reason to, Mr. Bush. I'll answer your questions."

"Mr. Bean, by your own admission, you didn't see that boy until Saturday evening. How can you tell me what he was doing the rest of the day?"

"I know where he was," Thomas said. "I know he's no thief, and I don't care to have him questioned about a matter that doesn't concern him."

"You told me his parents are dead, Mr. Bean. Are you his legal guardian?"

"I have charge of him for the time being."

"Then I gather you're *not* his legal guardian. Will you kindly tell me who is?"

Thomas stood up, and Little Jon could feel the rising anger in him.

"Mr. Bush, the only thing that concerns you is to clear up that theft. You're not going to clear it up by wasting your time here. There are other boys in this area you should be investigating."

"Mr. Bean," said Anderson Bush, in his deadly patient voice, "you're being very evasive. When people are afraid to answer questions, that means they have something to hide. What are you trying to hide, Mr. Bean?"

"I'm trying to protect an innocent boy who's had a very bad experience."

Little Jon could almost see Anderson Bush shaking his head. "You're making a mistake, Mr. Bean. I've investigated all other possible suspects, and checked them out. This boy—this Jon O'Connor—is the only one left who could have done it. He was seen, under very strange circumstances, near the Holliday place early Saturday. He's small enough to have squeezed through that window, and there are prints in the dust that could have been made by his boots."

The deputy paused, and went on slowly. "I realize how you feel, Mr. Bean. It's never pleasant to have anyone connected with you accused of a thing like this. But if it's his first offense, and all the stolen property can be recovered, we don't have to be too hard on him. If you'll just call that boy out here and let me talk to him, you'll save yourself some trouble."

"No!" Thomas said firmly. "I'll not have him questioned! He had nothing to do with this!"

Word Bank evasive (ee VAY siv) *adj.*: seeking to avoid answering directly

But Little Jon was already coming through the door. Thomas, he realized, could protect him no longer without making things worse than they were. He thrust his small hands into his pockets to hide their unsteadiness, and shook his head at Thomas Bean's silent urging to leave. How strange, he thought, looking intently at Anderson Bush, that people here would want to make life such an ugly sort of game. Somewhere, wherever he had come from, there couldn't be this ugliness, or any of these secret hates and desires that darkened everything....

"Now, Jon," Anderson Bush was saying, with a friendliness that Little Jon knew was completely false, "I'm glad you decided to come out and clear this thing up. We don't like to see young fellows like you being sent to reform school. So, if you'll tell me where you put those things you took the other day...."

"Mr. Bush," he said, "may I ask you a question, please?"

"You'd better start answering questions instead of asking them," the deputy said testily.

"I only wanted to ask you where Mr. Macklin said his boys were Sunday afternoon."

"You can't blame this on the Macklin boys. The whole family was in town all Saturday, with family the next morning, and at Blue Lake with friends all Sunday afternoon. I checked it."

Little Jon turned to Thomas. "Mr. Bean, do you remember when Mr. Macklin rode by Monday, looking for his boys? Can you tell Mr. Bush what he said?"

"Let me think," said Thomas. "H'mm. He said Tip and Lenny had skipped school and were out hunting that wild boy. Gilby Pitts had told him about it Sunday. He said—" Suddenly Thomas sat up and snapped his fingers. "I'd entirely forgotten it, but Angus said his boys were away all Sunday afternoon doing the same thing. That means Angus was lying if he said Tip and Lenny were with them at Blue Lake."

In the darkness it was hard to see the deputy's face. But his voice was cold as he spoke. "You have a very convenient memory, Mr. Bean. It proves nothing, and it doesn't explain what this boy—this Jon O'Connor as you call him—was doing when Gilby Pitts caught him Saturday. Just who *is* this boy, Mr. Bean? You've admitted you're not his guardian. Who brought him here—and why is he staying with you?"

"Blast your nosiness!" Thomas exploded. "He's the orphaned son of Captain James O'Connor of the Marines, who was killed in North Africa three months ago. The boy has lost his memory, and he was brought here by regular Marine channels because he needs a quiet place to recuperate. I happen to be O'Connor's friend, and his former commanding officer. Enough of that. The only thing that concerns you is the robbery. If you don't believe what I've told you about Macklin, you'd better go over there and have it out with him!"

"We'll all go over," Anderson Bush snapped back. "Get in the car, you two."

> He loved Thomas for trying to protect him, but the lie was a mistake.

Word Bank **recuperate** (re KOO per ayt) *v.*: recover from sickness or exhaustion; regain health or strength

It was less than a half mile up the valley. The deputy drove grimly through the night. Little Jon could feel the coiled danger in him, and he wished Thomas hadn't lost his temper and told the lie. He loved Thomas for trying to protect him, but the lie was a mistake. There were old hates in Anderson Bush, ugly things of the past that made the man the way he was now. Little Jon wished the thoughts were not there to be seen, but they leaped out as strongly as if the deputy had shouted them aloud. Anderson Bush had been in trouble in the army, and he hated all officers because of it. Later there had been trouble over a son….

The car stopped with an angry jerk before a weathered farmhouse. Anderson Bush slid out, and they followed him up to the dim porch where a hound backed away, barking. The door opened, spilling light upon them, and Angus Macklin stood there blinking. As Angus recognized the deputy, Little Jon was aware of a flicker of uneasiness in him.

"Why, it's Mr. Bush!" said Angus, smiling. "Thought you was Gilby at first."

"Are you expecting Gilby Pitts?"

"Yeah. He phoned about that wild boy, said—" Angus stopped, his eyes widening as he saw Little Jon behind Thomas. "Tom, I declare, is that really him?"

Thomas Bean ignored him. "There's Gilby coming now," he growled, as lights swung up the road. "Going to be a nice party!"

The approaching truck stopped behind the deputy's car. Gilby and Emma Pitts got out and came up on the porch. Gilby whispered hoarsely, "There's that boy!" And Emma said, "I want to see 'im—I want to see 'im in the light!"

They followed Angus into the big ugly living room where a single glaring bulb hung from the ceiling. A pinched woman, with her hands wadded nervously in her apron, stared at them from the back hall. Little Jon guessed she must be Mrs. Macklin. He was wondering about the Macklin boys when Emma Pitts suddenly grabbed his arm and jerked him under the light.

She was dressed in overalls just as he had seen her in the field that first morning. He forced himself to look steadily into her hard pebble eyes, and was surprised to see the sudden dawn of fear in them.

All at once she was backing away, exclaiming, "That's 'im! You cut his hair an' changed his clothes, Tom Bean, but you ain't hidin' what he is! He's that same wild boy, an' there's something mighty queer…"

"He ain't natural!" muttered Gilby Pitts.

"He sure ain't," said Angus Macklin, backing away. "I can see it in his face! Anything that runs with wild critters—an' jumps like 'em…"

Thomas burst out in angry disgust, "For goodness sake, Jon's not going to bite any of you—but it would serve you right if he did! Mr. Bush, I'll thank you to settle this business and take us home. We haven't had our supper yet."

"Hold your horses," Anderson Bush ordered. "Mr. Macklin, where're Tip and Lenny?"

"Round the barn somewhere," Angus replied. "They got chores."

Little Jon tugged at Thomas Bean's sleeve and whispered the thing that Angus was worried about. Thomas straighted. "Angus," he demanded, "do those chores take your boys as far over as the Johnson place?"

"How come you say that, Tom?"

"Because we just came by the Johnson place. It's not too dark to see a couple boys crossing your pasture, if you happen to be watching. Couldn't make out what they were carrying—but it's not hard to guess."

The smile had frozen on Angus Macklin's face. "You don't sound very neighborly, Tom."

"I missed too many hams last winter to be in a very neighborly mood." Thomas snapped back, finally sure of his ground. "You told Bush you'd taken Tip and Lenny to Blue Lake Sunday, but you told me they were out hunting that wild boy."

"You heard me wrong! I never said no such—"

"Pipe down!" Thomas' voice had a military ring that made Angus flinch. "I'm settling this right now! Your kids ran off Sunday and swiped that stuff from Holliday's. Lenny went through the window—he's small enough. They thought they could blame it on that so-called wild boy. But with the law buzzing around all day, you got to worrying about having stolen property on the place. So tonight you sent Tip and Lenny off to hide the things near the Johnsons'."

Thomas swung determinedly toward the door. "Come on, Bush. Get your flashlight. We don't need a search warrant for this. I'll bet those things are hidden on the edge of Johnson's woods. They won't be hard to find."

"You're taking a lot on yourself," Anderson Bush said coldly. "You'd better be sure what you're doing."

Emma Pitts cried, "If you find them things in the woods, it'll be because that wild varmint put 'em there! You've got a lot of nerve, Tom Bean, trying to blame it on Angus' boys!"

"There'll be fingerprints," Thomas reminded her, and limped outside.

Reluctantly, Anderson Bush got a flashlight from his car and they started across the pasture below the house. A mist was settling down from the ridge, making the night darker than it had been. After a hundred yards the deputy stopped.

"Mr. Bean," he grated, "I've heard enough lies for one night. It would have been impossible to have seen anyone out here when we drove by. What kind of trick are you trying to pull?"

Little Jon tugged at Thomas Bean's sleeve. "Over there," he said, pointing into the mist.

The deputy swung his light, and Thomas called, "Tip! Lenny! Come here!"

Two vague forms materialized in the beam of the light. They started to run, then halted as the deputy shouted. They came over slowly, two slender boys in soiled and patched

Word Bank materialized (muh TIR ee ul IZED) *v.*: took form or shape; appeared

jeans, with something secretive in their knobby faces that reminded Little Jon of Mrs. Macklin. Suddenly he felt sorry for Mrs. Macklin, and for Tip and Lenny.

Anderson Bush demanded, "What are you boys doing out here?"

"We got a right to be here," Tip, the taller one, said defiantly. "This here's our land."

Thomas said, "You were coming from Johnson's woods. Take us back the way you came."

"What for? We ain't been over there."

"You were seen over there. Get going!"

"You never seen us!" cried Lenny. "It musta been that wild boy."

Tip said, "We was coming back from the barn when we thought we seen something out here. Bet it was that wild boy!"

"Get going!" Thomas Bean repeated. "Take us where you hid those things."

There were loud denials. Tip cried, "How you think we gonna find something in the dark we don't know nothing about?"

They were approaching the lower fence. Poplar thickets[1] and brush loomed dimly on the other side. Anderson Bush began moving slowly along the fence, directing his light into the brush. Once Little Jon plucked silently at Thomas Bean's sleeve and pointed. Thomas nodded, and whispered, "Wait. We don't want this to look too easy."

They reached the corner near the road, and the deputy turned back. Now he crawled through the fence and very carefully began scuffling through the brush as he swung his light about. Thomas and Little Jon followed him, but Tip and Lenny stubbornly refused to leave the pasture.

The mist settled lower, and presently it became so thick that the power of the light beam was lost after a few yards.

Anderson Bush said, "It would take a hundred men to find anything out here tonight—if there's anything to find."

"Let me have the light a minute," said Thomas. "I thought I saw something gleam way over in yonder."

Thomas took the light, and guided by tugs of Little Jon's hand on his sleeve, plunged deeper into the woods.

Little Jon stopped suddenly before a clump of small cedars growing close to the ground. There was nothing to be seen until he reached in with the toe of his boot and raked out the butt of a fishing rod.

Thomas whistled softly. "They really had them hidden," he muttered. "Bush will never believe we didn't know where they were. Careful—don't touch anything with your hands."

Thomas raised his voice and called the deputy.

Little Jon watched while Anderson Bush carefully drew two fishing rods, a tackle box, and an expensive target rifle from under the cedars. The deputy remained grimly silent until he had tied the fishing rods and the tackle box together with his handkerchief, and looped the gun strap over his shoulder.

"Mr. Bean," he said at last, "you not only have a very convenient memory, but you and that boy have an exceptional ability to locate things you claim you have no knowledge of. But I'll ask you no more questions. I'll leave that to the court."

"Very well," snapped Thomas, "if that's the way you want to play it. But make sure you check all the fingerprints on those things—and in the house as well."

"You can depend on that, Mr. Bean."

---

1. A *thicket* (THIK it) is a dense growth of shrubs, bushes, or small trees.

Chapter 8

HE IS SUMMONED

Rascal was whining forlornly when they got back, begging for Little Jon to take him out. Little Jon went over and petted him, quieting him with a promise for tomorrow, then followed Thomas into the house. It had been a long and difficult day, and he knew that Thomas was badly upset by all that had happened. That was the worst of it—knowing how Thomas felt, and knowing it had all come about because the Beans were trying to help him.

Tonight, if it would have made matters any easier for the Beans, he would not have hesitated to go away. He could leave his knife in payment for Rascal, and he and the big dog could take their chances in the forest. But it was too late for that. It solved nothing, and it would only make things harder for Thomas.

Sally and Brooks were still eating when they reached the kitchen. They were bursting with questions, but Mary Bean silenced them. "You look beat," she said anxiously to Thomas. "What happened up at Macklins'?"

Thomas told her. "So," he finished wearily, "the cat's about out of the bag. Or it will be soon—if Bush has his way."

"People!" Mary blazed. "Why do they want to make so much trouble? But we'll talk about it after you eat. You two get washed. You're filthy."

They cleaned up and ate silently. Finally Little Jon said unhappily, "I'm awfully sorry about all this, Mr. Bean. I wish I could do something to—to—"

"Sorry? Why should *you* be sorry?"

"Because of the trouble I'm causing."

Thomas sat up. "If there's any apologizing to be done, *I'm* the one to do it. I apologize for the stupidity and meanness of my race. But honestly, we're not all like the ones you've met here. Actually, there are some pretty nice people in this world—only there aren't enough of them. It's the troublemaking kind that keeps all the rest of us on the jump, and makes things the way they are. Maybe nature intended it that way—to keep prodding us so we'll learn faster. I don't really know." He spread his hands. "I wish I knew what Bush is going to do."

"When he left," said Little Jon, "he was thinking about the Marines, and finding out about Captain O'Connor."

Mary Bean gasped. "Oh, no! That would tie it."

Sally, helping with the dishes, said, "Jon, how did you know what Mr. Bush was thinking?"

"I—just knew."

Sally wrinkled her nose at him. "I know how you knew." In a stage whisper, she added quietly, "*You read minds.*"

Brooks gaped at her. "You're crazy as a hoot owl!"

Mary said, "Sally!" But Sally went on quickly, "Jon can! I've known it since yesterday. It's, oh, lots of little things—like always passing me the right dish at the table before I ask for it." She made a face at Brooks. "*You* didn't know it, smartie. That proves girls are smarter than boys—except that Jon's smarter than any of us. I think it's wonderful. I wish *I* could do what he can."

"Thank goodness you can't," Brooks said with feeling. "Life wouldn't be worth living around here." He stared at Little Jon. "Sally's only kidding, isn't she?"

Thomas Bean said, "It's true, Brooks, but stow that down your hatch and keep it battened."[2] He frowned at Mary. "If Bush finds out about the O'Connors, that's all he needs

---

2. The expression "*...stow that down your hatch and keep it battened,*" means to keep that piece of information a complete secret.

to know. Fingerprints won't matter. He'll haul us into court, and we'll be forced to tell everything."

Thomas began snapping his fingers. Suddenly he lurched to his feet. "I'm going to call Miss Josie and arrange a private talk with her. She's the only really understanding person around here, and if she knows the facts ahead of time, she'll—What's the matter, Mary?"

Mary was shaking her head. "I've already tried to get her on the phone. I got so worried while you were up at Macklins' that I had to do something. Miss Josie is away tonight. Tomorrow she's got a busy morning in court, and she's flying to Washington immediately afterward. She won't be back till Monday."

Thomas sat down and began snapping his fingers again.

Little Jon asked, "Who is Miss Josie?"

"She's Mrs. Cunningham," Mary told him. "Judge Cunningham, really. But everyone calls her Miss Josie. She handles all the juvenile cases. Oh, I wish we could talk to her!"

She looked knowingly at Thomas. "Did you have any luck this morning—rock-hunting?"

"Yes. Very good luck. I'm taking Jon back first thing tomorrow. It may help his memory."

"Hey, can I go with you?" Brooks asked. "School's out, and—"

"No," Thomas said firmly. "This is too important. Jon's *got* to recover his memory. His best chance is to start over there on the mountain where he first found himself. We can't have anyone along."

"It's way past bedtime," Mary reminded them, "and it's been a day. Everybody scoot."

Little Jon awoke to a misty morning, with a threat of rain over the ridges. The rain notwithstanding, he and Thomas set out on foot at daybreak, taking the short cut through the gap that led to the other valley. This time Rascal went with them. To Thomas' amazement the big dog behaved himself, and kept quiet even when deer were sighted.

It started to pour when they reached the cave, but neither cared. There was something to be learned here if they could find it. While Thomas crawled about in the dim interior, chipping experimentally with his hammer, Little Jon sat down and tried to think.

Thomas, glancing at him once, said, "Maybe you'd better not *try* to remember. Sort of let your mind go blank. It might come to you easier."

He did as Thomas suggested. Even being here was exciting. Shadows of thoughts seemed to be crowding into the background of his mind. While he waited for them to take form, he drew out his knife and idly began to carve a twisted piece of root that lay near the cave entrance.

The thought shadows refused to take form that morning, but the piece of root did. When Thomas Bean saw it, the rain had stopped, and the root had become the striking head of a man—a man with a curious cap over his long hair, and one hand clenched under his chin as if he were lost in thought.

Little Jon was surprised that Thomas should make such a fuss over it. "But doesn't everybody do things like this?" he asked.

"Hardly. It would take a genius like Rodin[3] to produce such a head. Here, look what *I* found. It was under that fall of rock."

Thomas held out a woven cap much like the one in the carving. Little Jon put it on. It fitted him.

"The cap," said Thomas, "Proves—at least to me—that you landed here in the cave. It was probably knocked off when you fell, and covered up. It's a wonder you weren't killed.

---

3. To have created such a likeness, Little Jon would have had to be as talented as Auguste *Rodin* (aw GOOST ro DAA), the famous French sculptor.

Anyway, the cap also proves that Mary's idea of the door is correct. You see, something had to happen in here to *make* that rock fall on your cap. It isn't the kind of rock that ever splits and breaks into fragments like this—unless a force as strong as a lightning bolt hits it. Now, there's no mechanism in here, or anything that moves. That means that the door, and whatever it is that makes it work, is on the other side—I mean the distant place where your people are."

He was sure Thomas was right. He wondered, with a longing he could not express, if he had a father and mother beyond the door, and if he would ever see them again.

Thomas said, "Let's get back. I want to show Mary these things."

Mary Bean's blue-green eyes were stormy when they returned.

"It's started," she snapped, before they could show her the cap and the carving. "The phone's been ringing all day. Thomas, did you know we've been hiding a wild boy that spits fire, jumps a hundred feet, and eats live rattlesnakes? That's how the tale has grown. I'd like to choke Gilby—and stuff Anderson Bush down his throat!"

She paused for breath. "That's only the half of it. There was a reporter here about an hour ago. I told him he'd been hearing a lot of nonsense, and that we only had the young son of a friend of ours visiting us. I don't think he believed me, and I'm sure he'll be back, because he wants pictures. He had hardly left when *this* came."

Angrily she thrust out a stiff, folded paper.

"What is it?" Thomas asked.

"A summons![4] To the juvenile court. Monday morning at ten o'clock."

Thomas whistled. "Bush has found out that the O'Connors didn't have any children. He's sure worked fast! I'll bet he got on the phone first thing and called the Marine personnel office in Washington." He shook his head. "All we can do is keep Jon out of sight—and pray that his memory comes back."

"Did you make any progress today?" she asked.

"Some." Thomas opened the knapsack and took out the cap. He explained about it. "It proves you're right about the door idea—and it tells us some other things." He paused and looked around. "Where are Brooks and Sally?"

"I sent them out to pick wild strawberries, where nobody can see them. That reporter caught Sally in the yard and tried to question her."

"Well, we mustn't let Brooks, Sally, or anyone—even Miss Josie—know about the cave. If it's ever so much as mentioned, the news of it will spread and there'll be a thousand people hunting for it. It'll be torn apart and blasted and the pieces probably sold for souvenirs. But if it's never mentioned, it'll never be discovered. You can walk right by it and not know it's there. We've got to keep it that way. It's Jon's only means of getting back where he came from."

"But how—"

"How does it work? Mary, only Jon's memory can tell us that. We're just guessing, but we figure it's a sort of threshold—a place where you land when you step through from the other side. My compass goes haywire in there, so maybe the earth's magnetism has something to do with it. From the looks of it,

> We're just guessing, but we figure it's a sort of threshold—a place where you land when you step through from the other side.

---

4. A *summons* (SUM inz) is a legal notice ordering an individual to appear in a court of law.

it hasn't been used for ages."

Thomas paused, then added, "When you think about it, there's no reason why it should ever be used again—except to get Jon back."

Little Jon asked, "Why do you say that, Mr. Bean?"

"Just this: If your people are as advanced as we believe they are, what have we to offer that they'd be the least bit interested in?" Thomas laughed. "I'll bet they took one look at us, and decided we were best forgotten. They probably thought more of our wild creatures—wouldn't be surprised it they carried some young ones home with them, before we finished killing them all off."

Thomas took the carving from the knapsack. "Have a look at this, Mary. Jon made it while I was poking around."

Mary Bean studied the carving. She said nothing for a minute, but Little Jon was aware of her amazement, the quick turning of her thoughts, her sudden conviction.

"You—you think it looks like me?" he exclaimed. "That it could be my—father."

"Yes, Jon, I do. It would almost have to be. And being what he is, I'm almost sure I know what he's doing this very minute—he's moving heaven and earth to get that *door* thing repaired so he can find you."

Thomas snapped his fingers. "Of course! Jon's here by accident—and if the door were usable, he'd have been found before he left the cave. There's been no change in the place, so it means the thing hasn't been repaired yet."

Suddenly Mary asked, "Jon, can you write in your language?"

"I don't know. I haven't tried."

"Try it now. It's important. If your people came looking for you, they wouldn't know what had become of you—unless you left a message in the cave."

"But if they are like I am," he told her, "they would only have to call—and I'm sure I would hear them, even miles away. Still, if I were asleep…"

He sat down at the table with paper and pencil and tried to remember symbols that might stand for thoughts. He doodled and made marks on the paper, but they were not marks with meaning.

"I'm afraid I've forgotten how," he said.

"But you must know your language," Mary insisted. "Remember the little song you sang the other day?"

"I remember that—but I can't put it on paper. Do you suppose if I learned to write your language, that it would help bring back the other? Brooks was showing me the alphabet the other night, and I can print that already. Maybe, if you'll show me how to make words with it…."

The writing lesson was interrupted by the telephone, and later by the return of the reporter.

Little Jon hid in the front bedroom while Thomas spoke to the man. The reporter was not easily turned away this time.

"Mr. Bean," he said stubbornly, "you ought to be glad to get a little free publicity. It'll help your business. You'd be surprised at the people who'll come out to your Rock Shop to—"

"I'm quite aware of it," said Thomas, "and I don't want it. Mrs. Bean has already told you about the boy. I can't help these crazy tales that are going around, but I'd advise you to be very careful what you print."

"But at least you can let me take a picture of him, Mr. Bean. I know there's nothing in the tales, and I'd soft-pedal[5] all that. But he's news, and I could do a nice little human-interest story that would help you a lot here."

---

5. To *soft-pedal* something means to play it down and not make it obvious.

"Sorry," said Thomas, showing him the door. "No pictures, please."

"O.K. But there'll be plenty of pictures taken when Monday comes."

"What do you mean by that?"

"Mr. Bean, it's already common knowledge that the boy's a juvenile delinquency[6] case. Of course, we're not allowed to print anything like that—but the wild boy angle is something else. You can't stop news, Mr. Bean—and that boy is *news*. I'll see you Monday, Mr. Bean."

Chapter 9

HE GOES TO COURT

It was five days till Monday, and Little Jon dreaded it more each day. The phone rang almost constantly at first. Cars filled with curious people began to creep along the road. To escape prying neighbors, and the probability of more reporters, he and Thomas spent long hours at the cave.

None of this helped his memory.

When Monday finally came, Thomas and Mary took him to the courthouse in the center of town, and tried unsuccessfully to slip through the rear entrance without being noticed. A lurking photographer spotted them. Suddenly two cameras were flashing, and they were surrounded by a small crowd of ogling[7] townspeople. Thomas thrust through into the hall, where they were rescued by a policeman.

"In yonder, Mr. Bean," said the policeman, pointing to a door. "Back, everybody! You know these hearings are private."

"Hey, Mr. Bean," a man called, "can that kid really jump a hundred feet?"

The door closed behind them, shutting out the racket. Thomas, Little Jon saw, had timed their arrival carefully. The others were all present, sitting in a semicircle of newly varnished chairs facing a desk. The small room seemed overflowing with eight other people besides himself and the Beans. As he sat down on one side between Thomas and Mary, he could feel every eye upon him.

Angus Macklin and his two boys were sitting over on his left. Angus was smiling, and Tip and Lenny looked stubbornly defiant. Gilby and Emma Pitts were behind them. Anderson Bush, his hands full of papers, was talking in a low voice to a large, square-faced woman in the corner. With the woman was a long-nosed man in glasses. The man seemed aloof and officious.[8]

Little Jon glanced uneasily at the square-faced woman. She kept staring at him as if he were something unpleasant. Mary whispered, "That's Mrs. Groome. She's in charge of Welfare. The man with her is Mr. McFee, the probation officer."

The door on the other side of the desk opened, and a respectful hush fell over the room. Miss Josie entered. Miss Josie was small, gray, and precise. There was no nonsense about her, but behind her quiet, thoughtful eyes Little Jon sensed all the qualities of a friend.

As she took her seat she smiled quickly at

---

6. The term *juvenile delinquency* (JOO vuh nyl dih LINK win see) refers to antisocial or illegal behavior by children or young people (juveniles).
7. *Ogling* (OH gling) means staring at or looking at boldly or rudely.
8. To be *officious* (uh FISH iss) is to be meddling—interfering in the business of others.

Word Bank   **aloof** (uh LOOF) *adj.*: removed or indifferent

Thomas and Mary. "I've been wanting to visit the Rock Shop again, Thomas, but I haven't had time lately."

Thomas was already on his feet. "Miss Josie," he said, thrusting a folded sheet of paper across her desk, "before this thing gets any more out of hand, there are some points that I feel you—and you alone—should know about. I've jotted them down here."

"Thank you, Thomas." Miss Josie smoothed the paper out on her desk and quietly surveyed the room. "Why are you here, Gilby?"

Gilby Pitts gave a nervous twitch of his high shoulder. "Me an' Emma are witnesses, Miss Josie. I got charge of Dr. Holliday's place where all them things was stolen. An' we seen that wild boy yonder when he—"

"That's enough, Gilby!" Miss Josie's voice had the sting of a whip. "You'll not use that expression in this room. If you are called upon to say anything, you'll stick to facts, and facts only—and you'll not repeat them when you leave here."

She turned to Anderson Bush. "Mr. Bush, I've been back in town for three hours, and I've heard nothing but preposterous[9] gossip about this case. Juvenile cases of this nature are *not* for the public. When children get in trouble, they need help, not foolish gossip and publicity. Yet I find our town full of talk, and the courthouse full of curious people. It's disgraceful and disgusting."

The deputy's face had darkened, but he said smoothly, "I'm sorry, Miss Josie, but the talk had already started before I entered the case. Naturally, when someone catches a strangely dressed boy trespassing under the, er, most unusual circumstances—and then discovers that there's been a robbery…"

"Let's not waste time, Mr. Bush," she interrupted. "You were ordered to investigate a simple matter of breaking and entering, and theft—obviously committed by one or more boys. Stick to that, and tell me exactly what you learned about it."

Anderson Bush began. He told of Gilby Pitts's discovery of the forced window in the Holliday house, the small footprints inside, the missing articles and their high value. Then he related what Gilby had told him about catching a strangely dressed boy in the field. The deputy paused, and said, "Dr. Holliday's place is only three hundred yards from the spot where Mr. Pitts caught this boy Saturday morning. It was Monday morning before the theft was discovered, and naturally our suspicions centered on this strange boy. I'd like to read you a description of that boy as I got it from Mr. and Mrs. Pitts, and tell you a few facts about him I've uncovered. He—"

"That's unnecessary at the moment," Miss Josie said. "Confine yourself to the theft."

The deputy shrugged. "Yes, ma'am. As I was saying, this strange boy seemed the logical suspect. All the same, I investigated three possible suspects in Mr. Pitts's area, and checked them out. That left only the boys living in Mr. Bean's valley. Now, there's a gap behind the Holliday place, which makes it an easy hike from one valley to the other, if you happen to know the way."

"I know about the gap," said Miss Josie. "I've lived in this country sixty-four years. Proceed."

"Well, on Mr. Bean's side there's only Mr. Bean's boy—and this, er, strange boy he has with him—and the two Macklin boys up the road. I checked out the two Macklin boys. Witnesses prove they were away all Saturday and Sunday, which is the only period the theft could have happened. I also checked—"

"Pardon me," said Thomas. "You are leaving out something, Mr. Bush. I told you

---

9. *Preposterous* (pree PAHS ter iss) gossip is idle talk or rumor that is unreasonable or absurd.

Tuesday night what Mr. Macklin told Mrs. Bean and me at the shop—that his boys had been out all Sunday afternoon looking for that strange boy."

Angus burst out, "I never said no such a thing! We were at Blue Lake! We—"

"Quiet, both of you," Miss Josie ordered. "Mr. Bush, did you check a second time at Blue Lake and get the names of those witnesses?"

"I did, ma'am. Mr. Macklin and his family were visiting a Mr. and Mrs. Hinkley all Sunday afternoon. The Hinkleys swear to it."

"Mr. Bush," said Miss Josie, "did you know that Joe Hinkley and Angus Macklin were half brothers?"

Anderson Bush stiffened. "No, ma'am."

"It takes time to learn all these local relationships, and you've been here only five years. Proceed with your story."

"Well, ma'am, as I was saying, I checked out Mr. Bean's boy, Brooks. That left only Mr. Bean's visitor, this boy he calls Jon O'Connor. When I questioned him about Jon O'Connor, Mr. Bean was very evasive. He told me that Jon O'Connor was the orphaned son of Captain James O'Connor of the Marines, who was killed recently in North Africa. He said further that the Marines had brought Jon O'Connor to his house Saturday evening, and that the boy could have had nothing to do with the theft. Yet Tuesday evening Mr. Pitts saw this Jon O'Connor, and positively identified him as the strange boy he had caught in his field. Later Mrs. Pitts identified him as the same boy—the Beans had changed his clothes and cut his hair to make him look more normal—"

"But he's the same sneaky boy!" Emma Pitts exclaimed. "I'd know 'im anywhere. He ain't natural!"

"Quiet, Emma!" Miss Josie snapped. "Be careful what you say in here. Mr. Bush, this is all very interesting about Jon O'Connor, but at the moment we are concerned only with the theft. I understand that the stolen articles were recovered that very evening when you took Mr. Bean over to the Macklins'. Tell us about that."

"Yes, ma'am." The deputy pointed to a table in the corner. On it were two fishing rods, a tackle box, and a rifle.

"Those are the articles, ma'am. When we got to the Macklins', Mr. Bean insisted he'd seen the Macklin boys crossing their pasture, carrying what appeared to be the stolen things. He also insisted that Tip and Lenny were going to hide the things over in Johnson's woods, so they wouldn't be found on their own place." The deputy paused.

"Well?" said Miss Josie.

"It was a pretty dark night," said Anderson Bush. "I've got good vision, but I didn't see Tip and Lenny crossing the pasture. However, Mr. Bean insisted that we immediately search the edge of the woods. We started across the pasture, and met Tip and Lenny returning. That struck me as rather odd, and I didn't get an explanation out of them till later. Anyway, I searched the edge of the woods very carefully, and found nothing."

The deputy stopped again, and glanced at Little Jon.

"Go on," said Miss Josie. "Who found the things?"

"Mr. Bean and that boy yonder did. They found them in less than five minutes. The articles were hidden far back under a cedar clump where they couldn't have been seen even in daylight. It would have been almost impossible to find them at night unless you knew exactly where they were."

"Were there fingerprints on them, Mr. Bush?"

"Yes, ma'am. The fingerprints belonged to Tip and Lenny. When I questioned the

Macklins about it afterward, they finally said their boys had found the stolen articles during the afternoon when they were playing in the woods. They'd taken them to the barn. Mr. Macklin says when he learned about it, he made the boys return the things to the cedars, and hide them exactly as they'd found them. He says he was afraid they might be accused of the theft if they reported it."

Miss Josie asked, "Did you find any of Jon O'Connor's fingerprints on the stolen articles?"

"No, ma'am. But they could easily have been rubbed off by so much handling from other people."

"Did you find Jon O'Connor's finger prints in the Holliday house?"

"No, ma'am, I did find Tip's and Lenny's prints in there—but Mr. Pitts tells me the boys had been in the house a number of times. The doctor had them do odd jobs about the place."

"I see. Now, what have you learned about Jon O'Connor?"

Anderson Bush smiled. "There is no such person, Miss Josie. I checked with the Marines. It is true that there was a Captain O'Connor, that he was Mr. Bean's friend, and that he was killed recently. But he had no children."

"Very well," said Miss Josie. "That states things clearly. Thomas, what have you to say?"

Thomas Bean swallowed. "It's true that I lied to Mr. Bush. But I had good reasons. Miss Josie, before I try to explain, I wish you'd read those notes I gave you. They'll prepare you—"

Little Jon clutched his arm. "Please—not yet. Miss Josie," he spoke earnestly, "before you read that, will you let me say something first?"

She nodded. "Yes, Jon. We want to hear your side of it."

Little Jon took a long breath. This was not going to be easy. Because of Anderson Bush, he was forced to say and do certain things he abhorred.[10] But, if only for Thomas' sake, he had to go through with it.

"Miss Josie," he began, "Mr. Bean has been trying to protect me ever since he found me Saturday evening over a week ago. I cannot remember anything that happened before that day. I had been in some kind of accident, for I was badly bruised. And I was frightened, because I didn't know what had happened or where I was—except that I was somewhere on a strange mountain. I followed a doe and

---

10. To *abhor* (ab HOR) an action is to shrink from it with extreme hatred, loathing, or horror.

her fawn down to Mr. Pitts's field, trying to find someone to help me. Mr. Pitts tried to kill the doe, but I spoiled his aim, and—"

"That's a lie!" Gilby cried. "I never shot at no doe!"

"Gilby," Miss Josie cried icily, "hold your tongue, or it will give me great pleasure to fine you. Jon, please continue."

"Mr. Pitts caught me, but after Mrs. Pitts came, I broke away and ran. I wandered all day through the mountains until I came out on the road where Mr. Bean found me."

"Jon," said Miss Josie, "during your wanderings that day, did you find the Holliday house and enter it?"

"No, ma'am. I haven't yet seen the place. Besides, I was looking for someone to help me." Little Jon smiled. "I would hardly have expected to find any help in two fishing rods, a heavy tackle box, and a rifle. I knew nothing about such things at the time, and I couldn't have carried them if I'd wanted to. I needed a stick to walk."

He paused to plan his next move. Over in the corner he saw Mr. McFee, the long-nosed probation officer, whistle softly and shake his head. "I've heard some wild ones in my day," McFee said under his breath to Mrs. Groome, "but this kid's tale has 'em all beat."

"Mr. McFee," Miss Josie said coldly, "keep your opinions to yourself. Jon, you've just told me you knew nothing of fishing rods and rifles. For a boy of today, I find that a very strange statement."

"I'm sure you do, Miss Josie. But it's true. You see—"

"Jon," she asked suddenly, "how old are you?"

"I don't know, ma'am."

She studied him a moment, puzzled, then said, "Well, continue your story."

"That's about all, Miss Josie, except for finding the stolen things. After being taken to Mr. Macklin's house that night, I knew exactly where they were."

Miss Josie raised her eyebrows. "You did?"

"Yes, ma'am. Here is how I knew. Will you think of a number, Miss Josie? I believe it will be better if you think of a large one."

"Very well, I've thought of one. What about it?"

"The number you are thinking of is three million, seven hundred and forty thousand, nine hundred and seventy-six."

Miss Josie opened her mouth, closed it, then sat perfectly motionless while she looked at him. The room had become deathly still.

Little Jon said, "I'm not sure my pronunciation is right. I haven't known English very long, and Mrs. Bean has had so much trouble with people interrupting her lately that she hasn't had time to teach me certain things. Is the number I gave correct?"

She nodded, her lips compressed.[11]

"Do you want to try another number, Miss Josie—or something else?"

"It isn't necessary," she answered, almost in a whisper. "It's obvious, Jon, that you can read my thoughts."

"Yes, Miss Josie. It is very unpleasant to have to tell you this, but the thoughts of everyone in this room are so—so loud right now that they might just as well be shouting. So how can I help but know what the Macklins have done?"

"I don't believe it!" Anderson Bush grated. "This smooth-talking kid is full of more lies than any kid I ever—"

"Please, Mr. Bush," Little Jon said quickly, before Miss Josie could speak, "I'd rather not have to say any more. But if you won't take numbers for proof, I'll have to convince you another way. Years ago you were in the army. You were ordered to drive a truck some-

---

11. *Compressed* means pressed together.

where. On the way you had a bad accident. You—" Little Jon swallowed. "Must I tell what you did, and what happened to you afterward?"

The deputy's jaws were knotted; his face had paled. "No!" he said hoarsely. "I've heard enough." He glared at Angus Macklin. "What about it, Macklin? Have you been stringing me along all this time?"

"No—no—honest I ain't!" Angus had lost his smile. His hands were shaking. "My boys wouldn't—"

The deputy snapped. "You crazy fool, this kid really is a mind reader! Don't you realize what that means? You can't keep a secret from him. *Nobody* can!"

Emma Pitts suddenly cried, "I *told* you that kid's unnatural! Let me out of here—I don't want nothin' to do with no mind reader!" She and Gilby were on their feet, backing away. There was fear in their faces.

The room was in an uproar. From somewhere in a drawer Miss Josie produced a gavel. She pounded it vigorously on the desk.

"Sit down!" she ordered. "Quiet, all of you!"

When the room was restored to order, she said, "Angus Macklin, I've known you all my life and I happen to remember things about you I'll not mention here. Let's have the truth. Did Tip and Lenny break into the Holliday place and take those things?"

Angus swallowed and nodded. "Y-yes, ma'am."

"Where did they hide them?"

"In the barn at first. Then—then I got to worrying about it, and had 'em take the things over in the cedars."

"I see. You thought all the blame would fall on this strange boy everyone was talking about. Angus, this is a very serious matter. The value of those stolen articles is over five hundred dollars. I want you and Tip and Lenny to go home and think about how serious it is. Tomorrow I have a full day, but Wednesday I want you all back here at ten o'clock, and I'll decide what to do about you. I'm afraid Tip and Lenny are badly in need of corrective measures. You, Angus, could be prosecuted."

She turned and glanced at Mrs. Groome and Mr. McFee. "Does what I'm doing meet with your approval?"

Mr. McFee nodded; Mrs. Groome started to speak, then nodded also.

Miss Josie said, "All right, Angus. You and the boys may go. Gilby, you and Emma may go. But let me warn all of you not to say one word of what you've heard in this room this morning."

When they were gone, it was Mrs. Groome who spoke first.

"Miss Josie," she began disapprovingly, "I don't know what to make of this boy. He may be a mind reader, but I'm not at all convinced he isn't a delinquency case himself. He sounds entirely too clever to be up to any good. Furthermore, if he's really lost his memory and doesn't know where his home is, he's a Welfare case and I should be the one to handle him."

She looked coldly at Thomas. "Mr. Bean, I think you've taken a lot on yourself. Why didn't you come to me in the first place when you found this boy?"

Thomas said, "Mrs. Groome, I did what I thought was best for Jon. If Miss Josie will read what I've written for her, I'm sure she will agree with me."

Suddenly Little Jon found Miss Josie smiling at him.

He smiled back, appreciating her. "I think you'll find it easier to understand now, Miss Josie," he said.

Chapter 10

HE IS THREATENED

Miss Josie took a pair of glasses from her bag, wiped them and put them on, and unfolded the paper. It was filled with Thomas' small, neat handwriting, the facts carefully arranged as if he were making an official report. As she read, her mouth opened slightly and she bit down on her lower lip. Other than that, she gave no indication of the shock and astonishment that Little Jon knew she felt.

Thomas had listed all that the Beans knew about him—the way he had learned English, his ability to speak to animals, his strange clothing, his total ignorance of some things, and his familiarity with others. It was a long list, and Thomas had even given the value of the gems in Little Jon's knife and clip. Nothing had been omitted but the cave.

Thomas had headed the paper:

Secret—for Judge Josephine Cunningham.

At the bottom he had added:

After exhausting all possibilities, we are convinced that Jon is an accidental visitor from another planet. He is sure of this himself. A few scraps of returning memory give proof of it, and indicate how he arrived and how he may be returned. We are working on that now. Our main problem is to avoid further publicity and give him a chance to get his memory back. Our one fear is that some government agency may learn of his abilities and take him away and hold him for study. We feel this would be a tragedy. Please help us all you can.

Thomas Jamieson Bean.

Miss Josie read the paper a second time. Anderson Bush crossed and recrossed his legs, and Mr. McFee began tapping his fingers impatiently on the table beside him. Mrs. Groome seemed to be swelling momentarily. Little Jon knew she was burning with resent-

> After exhausting all possibilities, we are convinced that Jon is an accidental visitor from another planet.

ment and curiosity.

Suddenly Mrs. Groome said, "Miss Josie, if this boy—whatever his name is—is a Welfare case, I have a right to know whatever there is to know about him."

Miss Josie ignored her. Before saying anything, she carefully folded the paper and put it in her handbag with her glasses. She looked thoughtfully at Thomas, then her eyes met Little Jon's. He smiled back at her, and knew he had another conspirator[12] on his side.

"Thomas," she murmured, "it's fortunate I've known you as long as I have. You did a lot of Intelligence work[13] in the Marines, didn't you?"

"Yes, Miss Josie."

She turned to Mrs. Groome. "Jon is not a Welfare case," she said quietly.

"But—but of course he is!" Mrs. Groome protested. "He's a lost boy—he doesn't even know who he is."

"He was lost for one day," said Miss Josie.

Mrs. Groome seemed to swell even larger. "Miss Josie, I don't understand this at all. What right have the Beans to keep a boy like this—"

"Jon happens to be visiting the Beans," Miss Josie replied firmly. "That's all that is necessary for anyone to know."

"Well! This is certainly *very* strange. If the boy's parents are unknown, who gave him permission to stay at the Beans'? I think this should be looked into. I also think there

---

12. A *conspirator* (kun SPIR uh ter) works with others towards a mutual secret goal.
13. *Intelligence work* is the secret gathering of information about other people; spying.

should be a medical report on the boy. I think I have a right to insist—"

"Mrs. Groome," Miss Josie interrupted quietly, "I quite understand your feelings about the matter. But much more is known about Jon than can ever be told here. He has every right to visit the Beans for as long as they wish. It is very unfortunate that he happened to be drawn into the public eye when so much depends upon—secrecy."

Miss Josie uttered the last word as if she were touching upon high matters of state. It had an immediate effect upon her audience. Anderson Bush and Mr. McFee blinked, and Mrs. Groome was visibly deflated.[14]

"So I must insist," Miss Josie continued, "that all of you say nothing whatever about what you have learned here—not even the fact that Mr. Bean has done Intelligence work. Your silence is extremely important. There'll be questions, and you can help by making light of this—and saying it was all a mistake. And it was a mistake—a terrible one."

She stood up. "Thomas, I'll be out to see you as soon as I possibly can. Mr. Bush, please escort the Beans outside and keep those foolish people away from them."

It was over, this part of it at least, but the rest of it was just beginning. Little Jon knew that as they started for home. Miss Josie had ordered secrecy from everyone, though not for an instant had she believed no one would talk.

Money was bound to make someone talk. That thought had been in Miss Josie's mind when they left.

He said to Thomas and Mary, "I'm sorry for what happened in the courtroom. But I couldn't think of any other way to solve things."

"You had to do it," said Thomas. "There wasn't any other way."

Mary said, "You certainly gave Anderson Bush a jolt—and the rest of them too. Anyway, you prepared Miss Josie for what Thomas had written. She was able to make up her mind quickly and decide what to do. She's a remarkable woman. I wish we'd gone to her when we first found you."

"That was our mistake," Thomas mumbled. "But we had no idea something like this was going to happen. Now too many people know Jon's a mind reader."

"Oh dear," said Mary. "If the papers ever get it …."

"They'll get it. The first reporter that waves some cash under Gilby's nose will learn all about it—with trimmings. The same goes for Angus—in spite of the trouble he's in."

They turned into the driveway at last. It was good to be back, and hear Rascal barking a greeting. Little Jon got out and started happily for the enclosure, then stopped as the kitchen door flew open and Brooks and Sally raced toward them.

Something was wrong. Sally looked frightened. Brooks was angry.

"Hey, Dad! Look what somebody threw on our porch a few minutes ago!" Brooks thrust out a crumpled piece of wrapping paper. "It was folded around a stone."

After his lessons, Little Jon had no difficulty reading what was on the paper. Thomas held it for all to see. Crudely written in large letters were the words: THIS IS A WARNING. GET RID OF THAT WILD BOY AND DO IT QUICK.

He heard Mary's gasp, and was aware of Thomas' sudden fury. "Mr. Bean," he said, before Thomas could speak, "if I stay here, I might be a danger to all of you. Maybe it would be better if I went to—to that place we found. I could camp there with Rascal—"

"No!" snapped Thomas. "This is your home.

---

14. To deflate is to release air, as with a tire or balloon. When a person is *deflated* (dee FLAYT tid), their ego is depressed or reduced.

I'll be hanged if I'll let any weaselly[15] bunch of idiots drive you away from here! Brooks, did you get a look at the person who threw this?"

"No, Dad. Sally and I were in the garden when it happened. We heard Rascal bark, then the stone hit the porch. There wasn't anybody in sight. But a little later I heard a car start up somewhere down by the fork. Did you pass anybody on the road?"

"No. He must have taken the west fork when he drove away, after sneaking up here through the trees. It had to be Angus or Gilby, or a relative. There's a bunch of them, counting the Blue Lake people, and they're all related. And they're all afraid now." Suddenly Thomas laughed. "After Jon's exhibition in court this morning, they all know what he can do and they're scared to death of him."

Mary said worriedly, "I don't see anything funny in this, Thomas. Some of those people are moonshiners.[16] They could be dangerous."

"If they threaten us again, I'll have to show them that Jon and I can be more dangerous."

"Daddy," said Sally, "did Jon read minds in court this morning?"

"He sure did, honey. That's why those people are afraid."

Sally laughed. "They'd be more afraid if they knew he came from Mars or someplace, wouldn't they?"

"Sally!" Mary exclaimed. "What ever—"

Brooks said, "I told you it couldn't be Mars, Sally. There's not enough air on it. It has to be a planet like ours. Isn't that right, Jon?"

"I think so," Little Jon answered. "But since I can't remember—"

Thomas was staring hard at Brooks, and suddenly Brooks burst out, "Aw, Dad, stop trying to hide it from us! Sally and I have had plenty of time to figure it out. Why, anybody who can do all the things Jon can just couldn't be from *our* planet! He's too smart."

"O.K., son. You know the answer—but keep your hatch battened on it. Too many things are being learned about Jon already, and tomorrow the papers may be full of it. Before anything else happens, he's got to get his memory back."

Little Jon thought of the cave. He was anxious to return to it, but it was too late to start and get back before dark. He and Thomas would have to wait until morning.

Every visit had produced something, if only another carving. He had done three: the head of a man older than the first, and another of a woman who Mary Bean believed was his mother. He hoped so. She was so beautiful, and she seemed so wise. Strange how his fingers seemed to remember things that his mind couldn't. But the thought shadows were always there. Soon they would take form. He was sure of that.

Rain was slashing down in torrents the next morning. Little Jon stared out at it in dismay. Thomas said, "It ought to pass in an hour or so. We'll get ready, and leave the moment it clears a bit."

It was barely daybreak and they dawdled over breakfast. They were hardly finished when the telephone rang.

Little Jon answered it. Miss Josie was calling.

"Jon," she said, "I don't suppose any of you have seen the morning papers yet."

"No, ma'am. Mr. Bean doesn't take a daily paper."

"Well, I've just seen two, and I'll try to get more. I think we'd better have a conference. Tell Mary I'm inviting myself to lunch. It's the only time I can get away."

In spite of the rain, it was a busy morning.

---

15. A *weaselly* (WEEZ ih lee) person is a cunning, sneaky person.
16. A *moonshiner* (MOON SHY ner) is a person who distills liquor illegally.

Two cars containing out-of-town reporters and photographers came. Thomas had an unpleasant but firm session with them on the porch. They left the house, but refused to leave the area. Long-distance calls began coming over the phone. A publishing syndicate[17] wanted exclusive rights to Jon O'Connor's story. A nightclub offered a staggering amount of money for two weeks of personal appearances and mind reading. By the time Miss Josie's little car spun into the lane, Thomas was fit to be tied.

Miss Josie said, "I wish I wasn't in such a rush, but everything seems to be happening at once for all of us. Thomas, look at these."

She spread an Atlanta paper and two others on the table. On the front page of two papers were pictures snapped at the courthouse. Under them were long stories. One was headed: MIND-READING GENIUS DISCOVERED IN MOUNTAINS. Another began: WILD BOY READS MINDS, CLEARS SELF OF THEFT CHARGES. The one without pictures had a two-column box headed: WHO IS JON O'CONNOR? All the known facts had been printed. These were filled in with highly colored rumors and questions.

Mary gasped. "It's worse than I ever—"

"It's what I was afraid of," said Miss Josie. "And it's only the start." She looked at Brooks and Sally. "How much do they know?"

"Everything," said Thomas. "We didn't tell them—they guessed it."

"If they guessed," said Miss Josie, "others will too, in time. Jon, have you any idea how valuable you can be to some people?"

Little Jon was shocked by what she was thinking. "I—I didn't realize that this country has enemies. You believe they might—is 'kidnap' the word?"

"Yes. I'm just looking ahead, Jon. Nothing at all may happen, but we'll have to plan for the worst. There are some smart people in this world, and some of them are very dangerous. You said one thing in court yesterday that didn't worry me at the time, but it frightens me now. Somebody was bribed to tell it; it's in all three papers. Here it is: *'The thoughts of everyone in this room are so loud that they might just as well be shouting.'*"

"Good grief!" Thomas exclaimed. "I should have realized the danger of that myself. Why, there are agencies in our own government that, if they knew what Jon can do…"

"Exactly," said Miss Josie. "Thomas, I had a call from my brother in Washington this morning."

"The one in the War Department?"

"Yes. He had just got up; he saw a piece in his paper about Jon, and read that it had happened in my court. He was so curious he phoned me immediately. He was entirely too curious, Thomas, and he mentioned that we might have a visitor." Miss Josie paused, then asked, "Did you ever hear of a Colonel Eben Quinn?"

"H'mm. I once had to deal with a Major Eben Quinn. Tall, thin, very pale. The only thing I'll ever repeat about him is that I'm glad he's not working for our enemies."

"Well, he's a colonel now," said Miss Josie. "No one knows what department he's connected with, but he has power. Entirely too much for a colonel. Thomas, I think we'd better hide Jon. For his own safety, I think we should get him away from these mountains to someplace where he won't be recognized."

Little Jon said, "But I can't leave, Miss Josie. I *have* to stay here."

"Why, Jon?"

Thomas said, "Let me explain. Miss Josie,

---

17. A *syndicate* (SIN dih kit) is an agency that sells news articles to publications that don't have their own reporters at the scene of an event.

he doesn't dare leave here, or he'll never get back where he came from. There's a—a connection in this area, something magnetic, that forms his only means of return. He has to regain his memory here, and be close by when his people come looking for him—and from what we've learned, we're sure they will."

"Oh my, this does complicate things." She frowned and looked at Little Jon, and said almost absently, "I wish you had your memory, and that I had hours to talk to you instead of minutes. I must have read what Thomas wrote about you a hundred times last night. It gave me a glimpse of what a peaceful and wonderful place your world must be—and how strange and terrible ours must look to you. Jon, the awful part is what people here would do to you if they could. They'd use you. They'd pay no attention to the good you could give; they'd use your mind to help fight their secret battles. And no matter which side got you, nothing would be changed. It would still go on…"

Miss Josie shook her head suddenly. "I've got to think of something. Thomas, there's a legal side to this that worries me. By law, you and Mary have no real authority to keep Jon. Before some agency tries to take him away, I'd better have papers drawn up giving you temporary custody of him."

She stopped and stared out of the front window. "Oh, no! Look at those cars on the road. Silly people coming to gape. This settles it, Thomas. You'll have to have a guard here."

Brooks said, "Miss Josie, I think we need a guard. Look what someone threw on the porch yesterday." He showed her the piece of wrapping paper with the warning on it.

Her face tightened as she read it. "I don't like this, Thomas."

"What can they do?" said Thomas. "One of Gilby's bunch wrote it, I'm sure. They're just scared. Still—" Thomas paused and began snapping his fingers. "After what's in the papers, someone may try to use them. They're fools enough to let some clever person…"

"Yes," said Miss Josie. "That's exactly why they're dangerous. Thomas, I'm going to send a deputy out here this afternoon, and try to get another one for night duty. I'm not sure I can manage a night man—you know how our sheriff is: if he smelled smoke, he wouldn't believe there's fire unless it burned his nose. Anyway, I'll fix up those papers as soon as possible."

That afternoon a young deputy drove out, parked his car near the edge of the lane, and stood waving traffic on while he barred the lane to visitors. His presence, however, did not prevent a news truck from stopping under the trees at the far side of the road. Its crew set up a camera on a high platform and began taking pictures of the growing traffic and everything happening on the Bean property.

When the young deputy went off duty that evening, no one came to take his place. He had been gone hardly ten minutes when a stone crashed through one of the front windows. Wrapped around it was a piece of paper covered with another crudely lettered warning: GET RID OF THAT WILD BOY—WE MEAN BUSINESS.

"Where's this thing going to end?" Thomas muttered angrily, as he nailed a board over the broken pane.

Word Bank

custody (KUS tih dee) *n.*: the keeping, guardianship, or care of

Chapter 11

HE IS IN DANGER

The next day started badly. They had planned to leave early for the cave, but when Thomas went out to the barn at dawn he discovered that his one milk cow was missing. She had gone back into the pasture the night before; this morning the pasture was empty, and the gate to the road at the far end of it was open.

It was obvious that the cow had been stolen, and most certainly for spite. Little Jon knew that Thomas never expected to see her again. The road was jamming with cruising sightseers, and the young deputy, back on duty, was having trouble keeping a fresh batch of reporters out of the yard.

The deputy had brought Mary a paper from town. There were pictures in it showing the Bean place and the deputy standing in the lane. The story was captioned: MYSTERY BOY'S FAME SPREADS, HOUSE GUARDED. In a separate column a new question was asked: IS MIND READER FROM MARS?

Thomas glanced worriedly at the headlines, and glared at the passing cars through the unbroken window. Little Jon, watching him, was sick at heart. Who would have dreamed that his presence here would cause so much trouble? He was wondering what he could do to repay the Beans when he saw Thomas stiffen.

A long black car, driven by an army chauffeur, had turned into the lane past the protesting deputy. Two officers in uniform got out.

"That's Quinn!" Thomas exclaimed. "If he thinks he's going to see you, he's got another guess coming."

Little Jon peered uneasily at the officers from the corner of the window. Colonel Eben Quinn was the tall, pale one. The colonel paid no attention to the guard. "Official business," he snapped, without turning his head, and strode up to the house as if he owned the world.

Thomas met him on the porch.

Colonel Quinn was very pleasant at first. He shook hands with Thomas, introduced his aide, a Major Gruber, and said how delighted he was to see Captain Bean of the Marines again. It was all surface talk, Little Jon knew, for the colonel was far from pleased with the thought of having to deal with someone like Thomas.

"My department," the colonel said finally, "is much interested in Jon O'Connor. Aren't you going to invite us in to meet him?"

"No," said Thomas. "I am not."

"You are being very inhospitable, Captain Bean."

"Sorry," said Thomas. "I'll have to remain inhospitable."

"You are not acting wisely, Captain. I understand the boy has lost his memory. We have some fine doctors in Washington. We'd like to help that boy..."

Thomas' voice hardened. "Tell me another tale, Colonel. I know exactly what you want with him. You'll not have him."

Colonel Quinn suddenly chilled. "We'll see about that. Are you his guardian?"

"I am," said Thomas. It was stretching a point, for Little Jon knew Miss Josie had not yet prepared the papers.

"I doubt it," the colonel snapped. "I had a talk with Mrs. Groome before I came out. She's of the opinion that Judge Cunningham has been exceeding her authority in the case of Jon O'Connor. The whole matter is very curious, and we've been investigating it. The fact remains that nobody knows where Jon

O'Connor came from, and no one can claim him. But the government has a certain priority."[18]

The colonel paused. Little Jon was aware of Mary standing close; now he felt her hand on his shoulder, tightening. Brooks and Sally had crept nearer, and Brooks was thinking, *What right has that tall guy got to come here and try to take Jon from us?*

"Under the circumstances," said Colonel Quinn, "I think you would be wise to consider our proposal. Jon O'Connor has a rare gift we can use. In return we will give him the best of homes and care—anything he wishes, in fact. If the boy wants you and your family with him, I'm sure that can be arranged."

"No," said Thomas, turning away. "You're wasting your time. Good-by, gentlemen."

"Not so fast," Colonel Quinn said icily. "If you persist in being stubborn, we'll very quickly find legal means to take the boy off your hands."

"Try it," said Thomas. "And I'll fight you with every dollar I've got. Jon has some rights, and I intend to protect him."

"We'll see about that. In the meantime I'll warn you not to let that boy out of your sight. There are others just as interested in him as we are. You were in Intelligence—you know what they're like. If anything happens to him before we get back, we'll hold you responsible."

Colonel Quinn spun on his heel, and, followed by his aide, strode quickly out to his car.

It was a very grim Thomas Bean who reentered the room.

For long seconds no one spoke. Then Brooks, wide-eyed and half frightened, said, "Good grief, Dad, who'd have thought—I mean, what can we—"

"Yes," said Mary. "What *can* we do, Thomas? This is getting to be perfectly awful!"

"I'd better phone Miss Josie," said Thomas.

It was past noon. Thomas managed to get Miss Josie at her home. While Thomas talked, Little Jon tried to think. Everything was so unbelievably tangled on this world, with their laws and their money and their hates and their fighting for power. He could see only one solution that might help the Beans.

Thomas hung up at last. He shook his head. "Miss Josie's trying to work out something, but all this publicity—and Quinn on top of it—has stirred up a hornet's nest. Mrs. Groome is making trouble, and if the government steps in..."

"But, Thomas," Mary cried, "they just *can't* take him away."

"I'm afraid they can, Mary. If this were Jon's world, and Jon's country, it would be an entirely different matter. And if Miss Josie had more time, and could give us a chance to adopt Jon legally as our son, we'd have some rights. But there isn't time. Quinn wants Jon, and Quinn's going to get him—unless I can hide him somewhere, and fast."

"No," said Little Jon. "I've caused enough trouble, Mr. Bean, I think it would be better for everyone if I go with Colonel Quinn and do what he wants."

"Absolutely not! If Quinn gets his hands on you, you'll never see home again. We're

> "Try it," said Thomas. "And I'll fight you with every dollar I've got. Jon has some rights, and I intend to protect him."

---

18. To have *priority* (pry or ih tee) means to have the right to go before others.

going to that place we discovered. No one can find you there—and it's mighty important that you be there anyway. Mary, get us some blankets while I fill the knapsack. Jon, maybe you'd better change into your own clothes—we've nothing to compare with them for camping."

There was no changing Thomas' mind. In a very short time they were slipping out past the garden fence, carrying their equipment. Rascal trotted beside them.

They edged around the barn, skirted the pasture, and reached the road a quarter of a mile beyond the house. They crouched in the brush until no cars were in sight, then hurried across. In the woods on the other side they began angling up the slope toward the gap trail.

They were still some distance from the gap when Little Jon stopped at a warning from Rascal. "Mr. Bean," he whispered, "we're being followed."

Thomas froze. "It must be reporters," he muttered.

"No, it's Mr. Pitts and—some strangers. Men I haven't met or seen around. I—I should have known about this earlier, but there were so many people on the road…"

His mind went out, searching, and his small hands clenched as he became aware of the danger they were in—Thomas especially. They would kill Thomas to get Jon O'Connor. It shocked him to realize that men would place such terrible value on Jon O'Connor's ability.

He said quietly to Thomas, "They've been watching the house with—with field glasses, waiting till we left. They can't see us here, but they saw us cross the road. Mr. Pitts thinks we're heading for the gap."

"If we hurry," Thomas whispered, "we can lose them on the other side."

"No—they've stopped, waiting for others to come. There are four—five in all. Mr. Pitts is talking to them. He's telling them we're bound to get away, once we cross over. He's going back to get a dog—that bloodhound you once had. If the others can't catch us, they'll wait for him at the gap. He—he thinks they're some sort of government men he's helping."

Muscles knotted in Thomas' jaw. "A fool like Gilby would swallow that. They've got us checked.[19] We can't go to the cave. That bloodhound could trail us anywhere."

There was nothing to do but circle back, as quickly and as quietly as they could, and return to the house. The sun had gone down over the ridge when they finally slipped in through the kitchen door. Mary paled when Thomas told her what had happened.

"You'd better call the sheriff," she urged. "That young deputy has gone home for the night, and Jon's got to have some protection. This is an attempted kidnapping."

Thomas made several calls, all without result. The sheriff was away from town, and there were no deputies immediately available.

"If I know Quinn," muttered Thomas, "we'll soon have more protection than we want. He'll get a company of military police out here and sew us up tight."

"He was thinking of doing that when he left," Little Jon told him.

Thomas locked the doors, and began limping about the room, snapping his fingers. Once he went into the bedroom and came back with a pistol thrust in his pocket. Little Jon knew he hated weapons; Thomas had used too many in the past…

Little Jon studied the road through the windows. The twilight was deepening. A knot of coldness gathered in him as he considered

---

19. *They've got us checked* means they have got them stopped or blocked, as in a game of chess.

what might happen to the Beans. So long as he was with them, Brooks and Sally and all of them would be in danger—unless the military police came, and that probably wouldn't be till morning. Danger was out there; it wasn't close yet, but it would surely come upon them after dark. The road would be clear, and the one remaining car containing watching reporters would be gone.

Already the unknown men with Gilby had discovered that he and Thomas had not taken the gap trail. The house was in their thoughts, and they were waiting…

He wished he could understand what they were planning. But they were scattered about, and there were more men gathering. So many thoughts were confusing…

Thomas came over beside him. "Jon," he said softly, trying not to show his growing worry, "what's going on outside? Any idea?"

"I'm trying to find out."

It was hard to concentrate. Something was stirring in his mind. He tried to thrust it away, for at the moment it didn't matter. All that mattered was to draw danger away from the Beans.

As he studied the twilight again, he was aware of Rascal's uneasiness. Suddenly he knew that Gilby Pitts was somewhere over on the edge of the pasture, in the shadows. Gilby had Angus Macklin with him, and some of their friends. They were going to help the outsiders, as soon as dark came…

What was their plan?

He tried to reach Gilby's thoughts, but other thoughts kept intruding. There seemed to be a whispering in his mind.

Little Jon! Little Jon! Where are you?

All at once he gasped, and stood rigid as understanding came.

Mary, seeing him, cried, "Jon! What's wrong?"

"The Door—it must be open!" he managed to say. "My people—they are here—they are calling me…"

Chapter 12

HE ESCAPES

"Can you hear them?" Thomas exclaimed. "In your mind, I mean? They've come for you?"

"Yes—they've come through that place—it really is a sort of door…I can almost see it…it was broken on the other side, but they've got the power working, and the Door is open…it's a shimmering spot, and you step right through it as if space were nothing…"

His hands were suddenly trembling; he clenched them and closed his eyes, listening to the silent voices calling eagerly to him. He answered and told them about the Beans and what had happened. *Stay where you are,* he begged. *There is danger here. The Beans are in danger because of me. I must help them.*

He opened his eyes and looked at Thomas, and then at Mary. "They are over on the side of the mountain, waiting for me. My father is with them, and my mother…"

"Oh, Jon, I—I'm so happy for you!" Mary's chin was suddenly trembling; there were tears in her eyes.

Thomas said, in a voice that was not quite steady, "Jon, can you—is it possible—for you to make a break for it now, and reach them safely?"

Little Jon bit his lip. Alone, he could do it easily; even Rascal couldn't catch him.

"Yes," he said. "But what about you?"

"Don't worry about us," said Thomas. "We'll be all right."

"But you wouldn't—nothing here would ever be all right. If I disappeared, you couldn't explain what had happened to me. Colonel Quinn wouldn't believe you. Few people would. There'd be all kinds of trouble…"

"Confound Quinn! I'll handle him somehow."

"But what of the others?" Little Jon persisted. "The ones out there—could you make them believe it? Don't you see what would happen?"

Suddenly Thomas turned pale. "I didn't realize…"

Thomas knew now. Mary did too. Sally and Brooks would be in danger. They would surely be taken, and held to be exchanged for Jon O'Connor. Life for the Beans would never be the same. There would be questions and trouble for years. Little Jon knew they had no near relatives, no one they could turn to.

And time was getting short. It would soon be dark. They had only minutes to decide something…

He looked at them—Thomas, Mary, Brooks, and small Sally with her frightened eyes and brave chin. He loved them all, and he didn't want to leave them.

"I don't remember what it's like where I came from," he told them. "But I *know* it isn't like this. I'm sure, just from listening to what they are saying to me now, that we live in small groups, and help one another. There are not too many of us, but we have great knowledge, and we've made life so simple that we don't have laws or even leaders, for they aren't needed any more than money is needed. I think we make things—everything—with our hands, and that life is a great joy, for we have time for so much…"

They were staring at him, and Mary whispered, "Jon, what—what are you trying to tell us?"

"I—I'm trying to tell you that you'd like it there, and that I want you to come with me. I've been talking to my people, explaining what's happened to us, and telling them that I can't leave you. They—they've agreed that you must come with me."

They gasped. He read their sudden confusion. How could they drop everything?... They needed time to think, to plan...

"There's no time left," he hurried to say. "You won't need anything from here—just flashlights to see your way through the woods..."

Suddenly Sally said, "Oh, Jon, I think it would be wonderful to live in a place where all the animals were friendly, and nobody hunted them. Please, Daddy—"

"Yes," said Mary. Thomas said, "O.K., Jon. How do we manage to get away from the house?"

"After I leave, wait a few minutes," he told them. "When you hear shouts out in the pasture, get in the truck and drive as fast as you can up to the gap trail. Then climb to the gap. I'll meet you up there."

Before they could ask questions he darted to the kitchen door, unlocked it, and raced outside.

He reached the enclosure in two bounds, and released Rascal. *Stay behind me,* he ordered. *Keep quiet.*

Where was Gilby now? His flying feet took him across the garden and over the pasture fence. As he touched the pasture he heard a shrill whistle from the road, and an answering whistle ahead. It was still twilight and he had been seen already. It was better than he had hoped for.

He slowed, pretending to be undecided. In the shadows ahead he could make out Gilby and Angus and several others. He realized that their plan had been to fire the barn and draw attention from Jon O'Connor, who would be left unguarded. But Jon O'Connor was here—and he could see Angus, who carried an oil can, gaping at him in utter astonishment and disbelief, and sudden fear.

There was a quick clattering of shoes over the stones along the edge of the pasture. Other men were coming in a rush.

As he turned to dart away, a man called hoarsely, "Head the boy off! Don't let him get past! Hit him with something—but watch out for that dog!"

A hurled stone went past his head. He leaped easily beyond the frightened Angus, and saw Rascal spring growling at a second figure that tried to block his way. He listened for the sound of Thomas' truck. The way was clear, and the Beans should be leaving...

A rock grazed his shoulder, and another struck his back with such force that he stumbled and almost went sprawling. He gained his balance, but too late to avoid the next stone. There was an instant when he saw it coming, and abruptly there was the stunning impact of it across the top of his head.

Consciousness did not leave him as he fell. He heard men shouting, the pounding of approaching footsteps—and a man's sudden scream as Rascal slashed into him. The big dog was all at once a whirling, snarling fury, his charges sending men tumbling as his fangs ripped cloth and flesh.

> This was no longer Thomas Bean's world—the Beans were leaving...

Little Jon heard all this, but as his hands clutched the pasture grass it seemed for a moment that he was somewhere else—far away on a hill at home...Memory flooded over him, and he saw again the valley people on the hill, and the glittering wonder of the shooting stars they had come to watch...Then he had fallen into the hill—into the crumbling chamber with its old machine. The machine spun a force that bridged space in an instant. You stepped through the shimmering Door it made—and the threshold on the other side was somewhere else, another world.

He struggled to his knees, aware of the fury that was Rascal, of a man crawling away in pain...This wasn't home. This was the strange world, Thomas Bean's world. Only, there were too few in it like Thomas Bean, and the Door to it had long been closed...

He heard the sudden roar of Thomas' truck, and he sprang up with a glad cry. This was no longer Thomas Bean's world—the Beans were leaving...

He began to run. Behind him Rascal made one final charge, then raced to overtake him. There was pursuit, but his pursuers might have been following the wind. He and Rascal cleared the road together, and went bounding upward through the darkening woods.

He met the Beans on the trail, and led them on to where his people waited. They all carried glowing lights that made a radiance[20] in the forest. But presently, one by one, the lights vanished.

The forest grew still again, and empty save for a wandering doe and her fawn.

The Bean house stands empty. All through the mountains people whisper of it, and shake their heads. When the first investigators came, there was still food on the table, untouched. Everything the Beans owned was there, and nothing had been taken, even from the shop. Thomas Bean's truck was found up the road, abandoned. The Beans had simply vanished, empty-handed, without the least sign to indicate what had happened. And the strange boy, Jon O'Connor, had vanished with them—leaving an angry and baffled colonel who appeared the next morning, and whose men searched the mountains for days.

So the Bean place stands empty, and the pasture and the fields are overgrown. Gilby Pitts never goes by there if he can help it. Angus Macklin has moved away. Miss Josie went there only once just after the colonel left. She found three curious carvings on Thomas Bean's desk, which no one else had eyes for. She treasures them, and often wonders about them when she is alone, but she has never mentioned her thoughts to anyone.

Across a threshold, and somewhere far beyond, there is a hill where the valley people often gather when the day's work is done. From it you can watch the glittering night unfold, and see the whole magic sweep when the shooting stars begin to stream like jewels across the sky.

Even the deer come out to watch, unafraid.

---

20. They made a *radiance* (RAY dee intz) means they made a shining brightness.

Alexander Key (1904-1979) was born in La Plata, Maryland. He regarded Florida as his native state, because members of his family had been early settlers there, and spent much of his childhood on the Suwannee River. As a young person, he hoped to become a painter, and studied at the Chicago Art Institute from 1921 to 1923. At age 19, he began illustrating books; his illustrations became nationally known. His articles and short stories were popular as well.

In World War II, he served in Naval Intelligence, where he became interested in artificial intelligence and futuristic machines. Following the war, he returned to Florida, and began to write science fiction pieces, such as *Bolts—A Robot Dog*, for younger readers. His own favorite reading was science fiction. He pursued the painting of murals during the years he lived in the Carolina mountains with his wife and son. Key also wrote two adult novels. In 1965, he received the American Association of University Women Award for *The Forgotten Door*.

Studying the Selection

First Impressions

Did the Beans choose to leave their world, because they found it wanting? Or were they driven out, forced to flee down a hole to Wonderland? Would you stand up for truth and justice, if it meant leaving all that is familiar to you?

✓ Quick Review

1. What does Little Jon most value, no matter what else is going on?
2. Why is Thomas summoned to court?
3. What does Thomas Bean call the door through which Little Jon arrived?
4. What must Little Jon reveal in court to protect himself and Thomas?

In-depth Thinking

5. Why are the 'villains' so opposed to Little Jon and the Beans?
6. Why is Miss Josie willing to work outside the law to help Little Jon? How does her reaction differ from that of Mrs. Groome?
7. Anderson Bush and Miss Josie hold positions of authority. How do they differ in their approach?
8. Little Jon must work against his own values to be believed in court. How does he 'blackmail' the court into believing him?

Drawing Conclusions

9. Thomas Bean has already been to court and has not been forced to give up Little Jon. Why does Colonel Quinn of the CIA, nevertheless, threaten to use legal means to take Little Jon from Thomas Bean? Why would a federal court support the Colonel in such an undertaking? (Recall that Mrs. Groome and Mr. McFee were unable to convince Miss Josie to release the boy into their custody.)
10. What finally motivates the Bean family to go with Little Jon? Do they have any other options? Will they have any regrets when they resume their lives in Little Jon's world?

Many times Little Jon had to help him over tumbled faces of rock, slippery with green moss and running water.

Focusing on the Novella: Setting

Setting is a useful tool for an author. Which settings are described in *The Forgotten Door*? In your mind's eye, picture the Bean household, the field where Little Jon "talks" with the deer, the courtroom, and the location of the final chase. Are there other vivid descriptions of setting?

Note the elements that are important to creating a setting: (1) the time of day; (2) actual details of the environment; (3) associated passages or dialogue; and (4) the description of the characters within the scene. These four elements allow us to make a statement about another feature of setting, (5) the mood or atmosphere. Two further elements need to be considered to fully appreciate the importance of setting: (6) the deeper meaning of the scene and (7) how the scene moves the plot along.

Look at the chart below and the example we have given. Choose three examples of setting in *The Forgotten Door* and create a similar table for each one.

Location of Scene in Story	Opening scene Chapter 7
Location	The Bean home
Time of Day	Early evening
Actual Details of the Environment	Windows open; warm evening; Sally and Brooks in kitchen; John huddled in dark room
Associated Passages or Dialogue	"It was nearly dark when they reached the house." "Bush is on his way over to ask more questions."
Description of Characters in Scene	Rascal whining and impatient; Mother is concerned; Thomas is anxious
Mood/Atmosphere	Ominous
Deeper Meaning of the Scene	Trouble is brewing because Gilby Pitts has recognized Jon and Anderson Bush is on the case
How the Scene Moves the Plot Along	Turning point in the plot—first time a federal authority has come to house; Bush challenges Thomas

Creating and Writing

1. In *The Forgotten Door*, Little Jon muses, "This wasn't home. This was the strange world, Thomas Bean's world. Only, there were too few in it like Thomas Bean and the Door to it had long been closed…" How does this passage suggest the conflict of values between Little Jon's shadow world and the setting of the story?

2. Imagine that you awaken in the morning able to read minds. It dawns on you that if you reveal your telepathic ability to others, they will think of you as a freak of nature, fear being in your presence (as you will know their private thoughts), and, perhaps, try to exploit you for the scientific, military, and monetary potential of your gift. Telepathy is both a great power and a great burden. How do you resolve your dilemma?

3. Draw a picture depicting one of the following scenes:

    a. "The big dog was all at once a whirling, snarling fury, his charges sending men tumbling as fangs ripped cloth and flesh."

    b. "It's a shimmering spot, and you step right through it as if space were nothing…"

    c. "Memory flooded over him, and he saw again the valley people on the hill, and the glittering wonder of the shooting stars they had come to watch…then he had fallen into the hill…You stepped through the shimmering Door it made—and the threshold on the other side was somewhere else, another world."

    d. "He met the Beans on the trail, and led them on to where his people waited. They all carried glowing lights that made a radiance in the forest."

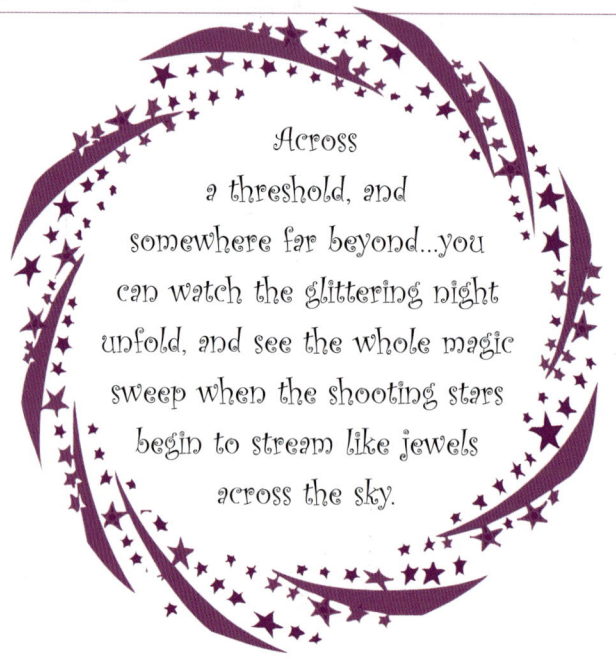

Across a threshold, and somewhere far beyond…you can watch the glittering night unfold, and see the whole magic sweep when the shooting stars begin to stream like jewels across the sky.

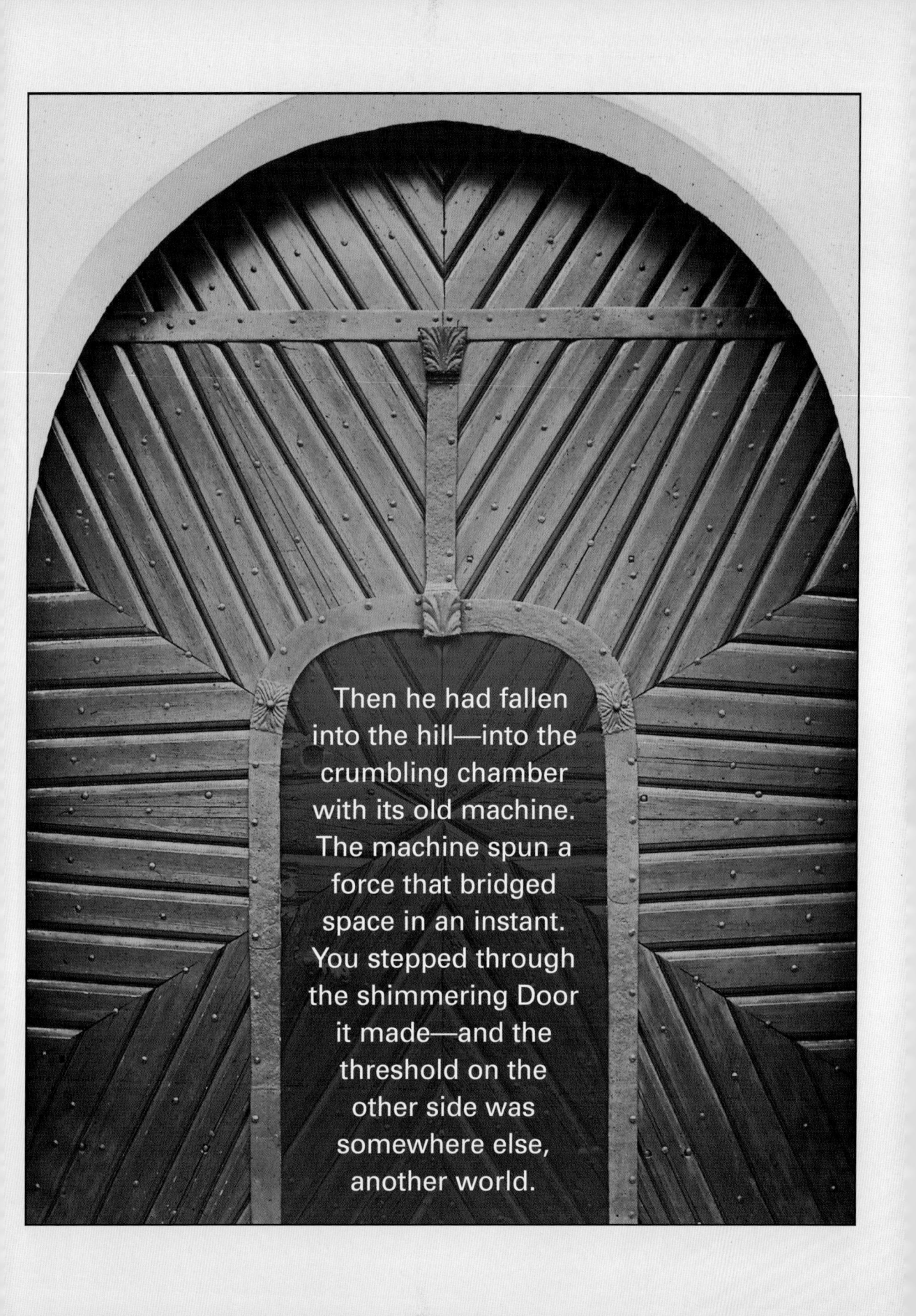

Then he had fallen into the hill—into the crumbling chamber with its old machine. The machine spun a force that bridged space in an instant. You stepped through the shimmering Door it made—and the threshold on the other side was somewhere else, another world.

The WORDS! I collected them in

poetry all shapes and sizes and hung them like bangles in My Mind.

Blueprint for Reading

Background Bytes

Try to visualize the keys on your typewriter or computer keyboard. Have you ever wondered why the letters are arranged that way? This keyboard design is called "QWERTY" and takes its name from the six letters running left to right in the second row from the top.

It is said that the QWERTY keyboard was designed to force typists to slow down, by putting important letters in hard to reach places. Actually, the letters were arranged in such a way to prevent the keys from jamming. Though electric typewriters and computers eliminated the problem of jamming keys, QWERTY overwhelmingly dominates the market, because we are so accustomed to it.

Into *takes talent*

As you read *takes talent*, think about what the theme might be. Even though the poem has a lighthearted tone, "archy" is trying to tell us something about people. What is it? Furthermore, what is he telling us takes talent?

Focusing on the Speaker of the Poem

As we can see from the signature in the last line of the poem, the **speaker** in *takes talent* is Archy. Archy was a cockroach character created in 1916 by Don Marquis, a columnist for the newspaper, the *New York Sun*. Archy writes his poems to Don Marquis by throwing himself head first at the typewriter keys. Why do you think Don Marquis would have made his 'correspondent' a cockroach? Why would a cockroach have made a newspaper columnist his 'confidante'?

Identifying the **speaker** of a poem is an important first step in reading poetry. Sometimes the speaker is **omniscient** (all-knowing), a third-person narrator, outside the events of the poem. The third-person narrator of a poem is like the third-person narrator of a short story.

As we see in *takes talent*, a poem may also be spoken using the pronoun "I." Of course this means that the poem is being told in the first person. The "I" may be the poet, or the "I" may be a character created by the poet. The character may be a person, an object, an animal, or even a cockroach named Archy!

As you read *takes talent*, consider the special perspective and skills a cockroach might possess. Is a cockroach especially qualified to offer his observations? (Have you ever heard the expression, "a fly on the wall"?) Furthermore, how does the character of cockroach-narrator contribute to the tone and mood of the poem?

takes talent

Don Marquis

there are two
kinds of human
beings in the world
so my observation
has told me
namely and to wit
as follows
firstly
those who
even though they
were to reveal
the secret of the universe
to you would fail
to impress you
with any sense
of the importance
of the news
and secondly
those who could
communicate to you
that they had
just purchased
ten cents worth
of paper napkins
and make you
thrill and vibrate
with the intelligence

archy

Studying the Selection

First Impressions *When people say, regarding a particular conversation or a particular event, that "they wish they had been a fly on the wall," they are saying that they wish they could have watched and listened in, without being observed themselves. Does Archy's size and species make him a good candidate for the proverbial fly-on-the-wall?*

✔ Quick Review

1. How has Archy determined that there are two kinds of people?
2. What does the line "namely and to wit" mean?
3. In the situation Archy imagines, what does the 'boring' person reveal?
4. What does the 'exciting' person communicate?

In-depth Thinking

5. How does Archy characterize the two types of people?
6. What *skill* is the "talent" of the title?
7. How does Don Marquis create humor throughout the poem?
8. Is there a serious message in the poem as well?

Drawing Conclusions

9. Which kind of individual do you think Archy is? Can you say why?
10. What about you?

Focusing on the Speaker of the Poem

As we have learned, Don Marquis created Archy in 1916 to voice his thoughts in Marquis's newspaper columns during the period that spanned World War I, the Roaring Twenties, and the Great Depression of the 1930s. Through Archy, a cockroach, the **speaker** of his poems, Marquis was able to offer his slant on the society of his times.

1. Instead of speaking in his own voice, Don Marquis chose to be represented by a cockroach. Using fantasy characters, especially animals, is a device of fables. Research the subject of fables. In a brief essay, explain what a fable is, and tell your reader why writers use animal actors to tell a story or express a view.
2. Look up definitions of the word *arch*. Write them down. Which definition suggests the character Archy plays? What is the etymology (the origin and development) of the word? How does the definition help us understand how Archy worked as a literary device for Don Marquis? Begin your essay with the definition and go on to describe how Archy's name suits him. Then tell your reader how he helped Marquis, in fact, put forth his *own* views?

Creating and Writing

1. Write a brief essay responding to the theme of the piece. Do you agree with Archy that there are two types of people in the world? Begin your essay by stating what it is Archy believes to be true about people. Go on to describe just what it is that takes talent. Indicate whether you agree or disagree with Archy on both his division of people and the need for talent. Support your reasoning with examples from history or from your own life. Then give a summing up or conclusion.

2. Assume the persona of Archy as fly-on-the-wall. Describe a situation you (as Archy) observed. Then tell Don Marquis what you learned from your observations.

3. Prepare a speech in which you "thrill and vibrate" your classmates about the purchase of ten cents' worth of paper napkins, or some equally 'important' subject.

Blueprint for Reading

Background Bytes

Naismithball? In December 1891, at what is now Springfield (MA) College, the chairman of the physical education department requested that James Naismith, a physical education teacher, come up with an indoor ball game to keep student athletes busy during the cold winter months.

Naismith divided his class of eighteen male students into two teams of nine players, made up thirteen rules, and started the game with a soccer ball and two half-bushel peach baskets. (The school custodian is credited with finding the peach baskets.) Points would be scored when team members dropped the soccer ball into the peach baskets. The following year, at neighboring Smith College, Senda Berenson Abbott introduced the new game to women. Almost immediately, this new sport was a hit.

Peach baskets were soon replaced by netting that hung from circular metal rims. In 1906, the net bag was cut open to allow the ball to fall through. Naismithball? No, we call it basketball!

Into *Foul Shot*

Have you ever had an experience in which skill and split-second decision-making were essential—for example while playing a game, performing a play with fellow students, or playing an instrument? As you read the poem, you will see that *Foul Shot* captures just such a moment in time; the final crucial seconds of a basketball game.

After you have read the poem through a second time, see if you can discern a theme. In a work such as this, it may be easiest to ask yourself the following questions: What is the reason for this poem? What is it that the poem expresses so wonderfully?

Foul Shot

Focusing on Diction, Connotation, Denotation

Using *Foul Shot*, we are able to discuss two literary components: **diction**, **connotation**, and **denotation**.

These literary components are important in poetry. Because poetry is so compact, the poet needs to get as much mileage as possible from every single word. (Remember, also, that creativity is intuitive. The best word is often *sensed* rather than *chosen*.)

Diction means the poet's choice of words and the way this choice expresses a particular style or mood. Examples of diction are whether the poet uses **formal** or **informal** language (for example, do you say you are "going to leave" or that you are "gonna split"?), **simple** or **complicated** language (for example, *used* or *utilized*, *pencil* or *writing implement*), or words that are **general** or **specific** (for example, *flower* or *daffodil*).

What do we mean by **connotation** and **denotation**? The **denotative** meaning of a word is its dictionary definition. The **connotative** meaning of a word includes associations with the word, not just its precise dictionary definition. For example, take the words "house" and "home." Both words may mean a physical structure where someone lives. But *house*, a more neutral word, refers to an entire building. A *home* may be a house, but it can also be an apartment in a larger building. For most of us, *home* is clearly the word with stronger emotional connotations. Not surprisingly, the word *family* is used only in the definition of *home*.

Foul Shot

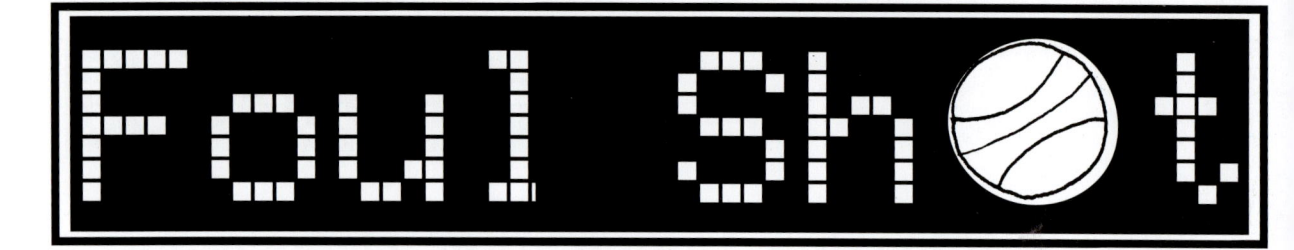

Edwin A. Hoey

With two 60's stuck on the scoreboard
And two seconds hanging on the clock,
The solemn boy in the center of eyes,
Squeezed by silence,
5   Seeks out the line with his feet,
Soothes his hands along his uniform,
Gently drums the ball against the floor,
Then measures the waiting net,
Raises the ball on his right hand,
10 Balances it with his left,
Calms it with fingertips,
Breathes,
Crouches,
Waits,
15 And then through a stretching of stillness,
Nudges it upward.

The ball
Slides up and out,
Lands,
20 Leans,
Wobbles,
Wavers,
Hesitates,
Exasperates,
25 Plays it coy
Until every face begs with unsounding screams—

And then

        And then

                And then,

30 Right before ROAR-UP,
Dives down and through.

Studying the Selection

First Impressions

Does the ball go through the basket? Did you think the ball would go through the basket?

✔ Quick Review

1. At the beginning of the poem, how much time is left in the game? What is the score?
2. What happens in lines 3-16? Lines 17-28? Lines 27-29? Lines 30 and 31? You may break the groupings down even further for your answer.
3. What adjective is used to describe the boy? What does the word mean? What does it tell us about the poet's regard for the moment? What does it tell us about the boy?
4. What does "every face" do? Look up the word *oxymoron* in your dictionary. Is this an oxymoron?

In-depth Thinking

5. How would you describe the boy in the poem? Cite words or phrases from the poem to elaborate on your answer.
6. In the first five lines, there are three suggestions of eyes. What are they?
7. How does the placement of the words on the page—as well as the line and word lengths—make the poem more effective?
8. What is ROAR-UP? Why is its placement in the next-to-last line interesting?

Drawing Conclusions

9. Why is a foul shot a good subject for a poem?

Focusing on Diction, Connotation, Denotation

1. Make a list of the very specific verbs used in *Foul Shot*. How do you think they "work" for the poem? Pay careful attention to the **connotation** of each word.
2. Write an additional two lines to the end of the poem, using **informal** language.
3. Write a factual prose account of the game, in **formal** language—as if you were writing a newscast or a newspaper article. What is lost in the prose account? Is anything gained?

Creating and Writing

1. Can you recall a time of great tension, joy, or sorrow, when you felt locked into the moment? Pick eight adjectives, eight verbs, eight nouns, and eight adverbs. Use these words to write a free verse poem that establishes the setting and conveys the feelings of that moment.
2. Write a prose narrative of the same experience.

Blueprint for Reading

Background Bytes

They were called "fire masters," "wild men," or "green men," these men who made and handled the fireworks that were essential to the celebration of military victories, state ceremonies, and royal entertainments. Running through the crowds of expectant onlookers, warning people to get back, the fire masters would set off their firecrackers to the appreciative murmurs of their enthralled audience.

Who invented fireworks? The sixth-century Chinese were responsible for the discovery of gunpowder and the invention of "war rockets." The military importance and the visual beauty of fireworks led to their rapid spread east, first to Arabia, then Mongolia, and on into Europe. Fireworks, or *pyrotechnics* (py roh TEK niks), the Greek word meaning "fire arts," have been used in the western world for more than 600 years.

Today, pyrotechnics have many uses. When we call them *flares*, they may be used as location markers by those who are lost, as illumination devices by those who need to be rescued, and as warning signals in dangerous situations. And when we call them *fireworks*, they are an indispensable part of any outdoor celebration, bringing people together with their visual beauty, with the excitement they generate, and with the special sense of shared delight.

Into *Fireworks*

As you read *Fireworks*, first appreciate its simple beauty, the ways in which the images come alive. Consider the **theme** as you read through the poem a second or third time. The keys to the theme are in the fifth and final lines. What happens ultimately to the works of humankind?

Focusing on Imagery

Poets write to help us share their perceptions—to help us see. One way to do this is through the use of **imagery**. Although we usually think of images as visual, imagery is the use of concrete details that appeal to any of the five senses: sight, sound, smell, taste, or touch. (Remember that the sense of touch embraces our physical experience of the world. For example, if the weather is very hot or very cold, or if a breeze is blowing, the heat or cold or wind that we may feel on our faces or that makes us shiver is part of the sense of touch.)

As you read *Fireworks*, look for images that appeal to the senses of sight and sound. Do any of the poet's words stimulate the sense of touch? Make a list of those images that really "touch" you.

Fireworks

Babette Deutsch

Not guns, not thunder, but a flutter of clouded drums

That announce a fiesta:[1] abruptly, fiery needles

Circumscribe[2] on the night boundless[3] chrysanthemums.

Softly, they break apart, they flake away, where

5   Darkness, on a svelte[4] hiss, swallows them.

Delicate brilliance: a bellflower[5] opens, fades,

In a sprinkle of falling stars.

Night absorbs them

With the sponge of her silence.

---

1. A *fiesta* (fee ESS tuh) is a festival or festive celebration.
2. To *circumscribe* (SIR kum SKRYB) means to encircle or limit.
3. Something that is *boundless* (BOUND liss) is infinite or unlimited.
4. *Svelte* (SVELT) means graceful and slender or smoothly agreeable and polite.
5. A *bellflower* is a plant with blue, bell-shaped flowers.

Studying the Selection

First Impressions

What was your favorite image in the poem? Is it one that surprised you?

✓ Quick Review

1. What announces the celebration? Which things do *not* announce the fiesta?
2. How many explosions of fireworks do you think there are?
3. What kind of flowers are etched on the sky? Draw a picture of one of these flowers.
4. What has "delicate brilliance"?

In-depth Thinking

5. Which characteristics of fireworks are emphasized in the poem? Which characteristics of the night?
6. What is the effect of this contrast?
7. Who is the speaker in the poem? Is there a speaker?

Drawing Conclusions

8. What is it about fireworks that makes them such a treat?

Focusing on Imagery

We defined **imagery** as the use of concrete pictures or details that appeal to the five senses. If you were trying to describe fireworks—or the experience of watching fireworks—to someone who had never seen them, what words might you use? Remember, you would need words that appeal to each of the senses affected by a fireworks display: at the very least, the senses of sight, sound, and smell. If the night were damp or sticky, your words would also need to include the sense of touch. If you drank soda pop or ate a hot dog as you watched, you would need to speak to the sense of taste. Make a list of the words and phrases you might use. You may create metaphors and similes if you wish.

Using words from your list, create a brief, free verse poem.

Creating and Writing

1. Write a brief research paper about a topic connected with the history, composition, popularity, or dangers of fireworks.
2. In *Fireworks*, Babette Deutsch draws a contrast between the sound of the fireworks and the silence of the night. Write a description of a setting that includes a contrast or comparison, such as the sun setting over the ocean or over a lake, a cat walking in the snow, the light of the street lamps at night on a wet city street. Choose images that make your reader *feel*.
3. Using any medium (pastels, water colors, crayons, pen and ink), create a fireworks display.

Blueprint for Reading

Background Bytes

When used as a verb, the word *lure* means to attract. For some people, *lure* has connotations of attracting or drawing in a deceiving way. When used as a noun, a lure is a kind of decoy, live or especially artificial bait used in fishing or trapping.

Who made the first lure? Legend has it that one day James Heddon, while waiting for some friends at Dowagiac Creek in Dowagiac, Michigan, was whittling a piece of wood, shaping it like a fish. When he cast the wood into the lake, almost immediately a bass snapped at it. Fishing lures had been invented. Some fishing lures are very beautiful— even to humans, although not to eat!—and the older fishing lures are valued by collectors.

Into *The Fish*

The Fish is quite an extraordinary poem, longer than many of the other works included in this anthology, with some very subtle **allusions**. (An **allusion** is a passing or casual reference to something, either direct or implied.) Look up the words *grunt* and *isinglass* in the dictionary, and see if you can find definitions that fit cleverly with the poem.

As you reread the poem—and it surely deserves at least three readings—see if you can begin to sense the theme. What is the poet telling us? What happens to the speaker in the poem? Think about how the speaker notices things about the fish. In the beginning of the poem, what does the speaker say about the fish that is positive? What does the speaker say about the fish that may make the fish seem distasteful or that makes you squeamish? What happens after the speaker mentally dissects the fish? By the end of the poem, what has the speaker learned? What have you, the reader learned? If you can answer these questions, it is likely that you understand the theme.

Focusing on Figurative Language and Simile

When Babette Deutsch describes fireworks as a "chrysanthemum," we are not expected to take this idea **literally**. There is, of course, no flower in the sky. We are, however, expected to take the image **figuratively**. Many of us have seen fireworks that in fact look like huge flowers.

By making such comparisons—and **figurative language** is the language of comparisons—poets help us to *see*, *hear*, *touch* (the physical experience of feeling), *smell*, and *taste*. In a figurative way, they give us eyes to see with and ears to hear with.

As you read *The Fish*, look for Bishop's use of **similes**, figurative language in which the writer makes a comparison by using the words *like* or *as*. For example, Ms. Bishop writes that the brown skin of the fish "hung in strips like ancient wallpaper." What do her similes help us see?

The FISH

Elizabeth Bishop

I caught a tremendous fish
and held him beside the boat
half out of water, with my hook
fast in a corner of his mouth.
5 He didn't fight.
He hadn't fought at all.
He hung a grunting weight,
battered and venerable[1]
and homely. Here and there
10 his brown skin hung in strips
like ancient wallpaper,
and its pattern of darker brown
was like wallpaper:
shapes like full-blown roses
15 stained and lost through age.
He was speckled with barnacles,[2]
fine rosettes[3] of lime,
and infested
with tiny white sea-lice,
20 and underneath two or three
rags of green weed hung down.
While his gills[4] were breathing in
the terrible oxygen
—the frightening gills
25 fresh and crisp with blood,
that can cut so badly—
I thought of the coarse white flesh
packed in like feathers,
the big bones and the little bones,
30 the dramatic reds and blacks
of his shiny entrails,[5]
and the pink swim-bladder
like a big peony.[6]
I looked into his eyes
35 which were far larger than mine
but shallower, and yellowed,
the irises backed and packed
with tarnished tinfoil
seen through the lenses
40 of old scratched isinglass.[7]

---

1. *Venerable* (VEN er uh bil) means worthy of respect or reverence because of old age or other admirable characteristics.
2. *Barnacles* (BAR nih kulz) are small, shelled marine creatures that attach themselves to ship bottoms and other floating objects.
3. *Rosettes* (roe ZETZ) are rose-shaped arrangements of ribbon or other material used as ornaments or badges.
4. The *gills* are the organ through which fish breathe oxygen dissolved in water.
5. The *entrails* (EN tray ilz) are the inner organs of the body, sometimes specifically the intestines.
6. A *peony* (PEE uh nee) is a plant with large, showy flowers.
7. *Isinglass* (I zin GLASS) is a thin, tough, and transparent material. The term *isinglass* also refers to a pure, translucent or transparent form of gelatin obtained from the air bladders—or swim bladders—of some fish.

They shifted a little, but not
to return my stare.
—It was more like the tipping
of an object toward the light.
45　I admired his sullen face,
the mechanism of his jaw,
and then I saw
that from his lower lip
—if you could call it a lip—
50　grim, wet, and weaponlike,
hung five old pieces of fish-line,
or four and a wire leader
with the swivel still attached,
and with all their five big hooks
55　grown firmly in his mouth.
A green line, frayed at the end
where he broke it, two
heavier lines,
and a fine black thread
still crimped from the
strain and snap
60　when it broke and he
　　　got away.
Like medals with their ribbons
frayed and wavering,
a five-haired beard of wisdom
trailing from his aching jaw,

65　I stared and stared
and victory filled up
the little rented boat,
from the pool of bilge[8]
where oil had spread raining
70　around the rusted engine
to the bailer rusted orange
and sun-cracked thwarts,[9]
the oarlocks[10] on their strings,
the gunnels[11]—until everything
75　was rainbow, rainbow, rainbow!
And I let the fish go.

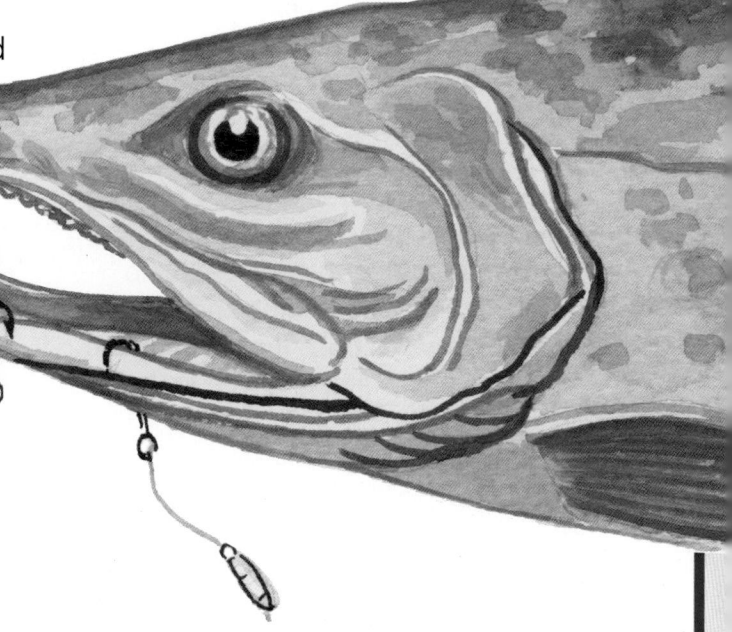

---

8. Here, *bilge* (BILJ) refers to the water, or seepage, that accumulates in the enclosed area at the bottom of a vessel.
9. The *thwarts* (THWORTS) are the seats on a boat, especially those used by the rowers.
10. The *oarlocks* (OR LOX) are U-shaped devices that provide pivots for the oars in rowing.
11. The *gunnels* (GUN ilz) refer to the gunwales or the upper edges of the side of a vessel.

Studying the Selection

First Impressions

Is *The Fish* a 'fish story'?

✓ Quick Review

1. Bishop offers a complete description of the fish. Describe its skin, its insides, its eyes, its lip.
2. Which colors does Bishop use in her description?
3. Describe the boat. Note: This boat is not a rowboat.

📄 In-depth Thinking

4. Why doesn't the fish fight back?
5. Why do you think Elizabeth Bishop gives the details of the fish's appearance in the order that she does? How does each group of details affect you?
6. The speaker's attitude towards the fish changes several times. How does the speaker feel in the beginning? In the middle of the poem? At the end? Which words or phrases does the speaker use at various points that lead you to the conclusions you have drawn?
7. What is the contrast between the fish and the boat? Why is that contrast so important?

📁 Drawing Conclusions

8. Why does the speaker throw the fish back? What is the theme of the poem?
9. Would you have thrown the fish back? Describe the thinking that would have led to your decision.
10. Do you think the speaker's experience would have a lasting effect on a person?

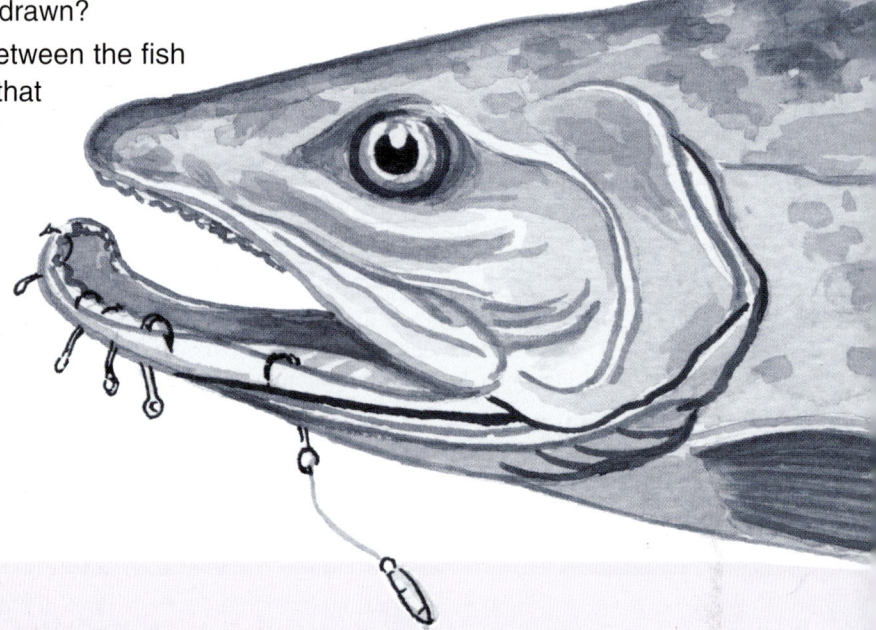

Focusing on Figurative Language and Simile

One kind of figurative language is the **simile**, a comparison between two unlike people, objects, or creatures using the words *like* or *as.* For example, if we say that a kitten's fur is as black as night, we are suggesting to the mind's eye a quality of the color of the fur. (We may also be alluding to a quality of mysteriousness!) There are many overworked or cliched similes: for example, "as warm as toast," "as stubborn as a mule," "as quiet as a mouse." When writers use similes, they try to create comparisons that offer fresh ways of seeing.

1. Find six similes in the poem. Explain the comparison in each one.
2. What other comparisons can you find in the poem that may not use the words *like* or *as*?
3. How does Bishop's use of comparisons add to our understanding of what happens to the speaker in *The Fish*?

Creating and Writing

1. Write an essay in which you discuss the "victory [that] filled up/the little rented boat."
2. Elizabeth Bishop's description of the fish is so clear that we can easily picture it. Choose an object to describe. Include two similes in your description.
3. Why would it have been a poor idea to call the poem *Victory*?
4. Design a fishing lure.

Blueprint for Reading

Background Bytes

In the poem *The Fish* by Elizabeth Bishop, we talked about fishing lures and mentioned that some people collect them. In fact, a fishing lure still in its original box may be worth as much as $2,000! Now that would surely be *alluring.*

Many other antiques and collectibles are also worth a great deal of money. Consider this: A program from the 1917 World Series is worth more than $1,800.

A first edition of the book, *The Wonderful Wizard of Oz*, is valued at $6,000.

Even a Davy Crockett lunchbox and thermos from the 1960s are worth more than $200.

Of course, many antiques and works of art are prized not just for their rarity but for their great beauty. But the value placed on so-called "collectibles" may certainly make us want to run up to our attics or down to our basements and search for treasure!

Into *Keepsakes*

What is the theme of *Keepsakes*? As you read, you may notice that the twelve-year-old girl seems concerned primarily with appearances—although consider that it may also be the case that she loves her aunt, and doesn't want to see that her aunt is getting older. To arrive at the theme, think about what the aunt is telling her niece.

Make a list of those things you consider keepsakes. If some of the items come from your early childhood, don't be embarrassed to include them. We all have treasures from an earlier time! Next to each item on your list, jot down the reason it is special to you. Save your list for the exercises that follow the poem.

Focusing on Metaphors

Another example of figurative language is the **metaphor**. Like the simile, a **metaphor** is a comparison between two unlike things. Unlike a simile, however, a metaphor does not use the words *like* or *as*. Look back at the poem *The Fish*. In *The Fish*, Elizabeth Bishop describes the barnacles as "fine rosettes of lime" and the seaweed as "rags of green weed." Those are metaphors. We are not supposed to take these descriptions literally. The barnacles are barnacles and the strips of seaweed are not rags. But these comparisons create visual images that offer fresh ways of seeing and understanding.

As you read *Keepsakes*, notice how Deloras Lane teaches us a new way of thinking about wrinkles and gray hair with the metaphors she uses.

Keepsakes
(Conversation with a twelve-year-old)
Deloras Lane

Why don't you dye your hair black
and cover the grey so
you don't look old,
my niece asked last week.
5 Oh no, I said,
those grey hairs are mistakes I made
and spun into lessons
of silver thread. Besides
I think they're rather attractive.

10 How about a little make-up
to hide those lines
around your eyes?
I like those lines, I
told her,
15 they are autographs
of smiles.

Let's go for a walk then,
she urged,
walking briskly
20 every day would help you lose
those extra pounds.
Ah those,
I answered,
are pizzas and
banana-splits
25 shared with
you—
and I savored every
one.

But let's take a walk
anyway
and see if Mr. Bennett's
roses have
30 bloomed.

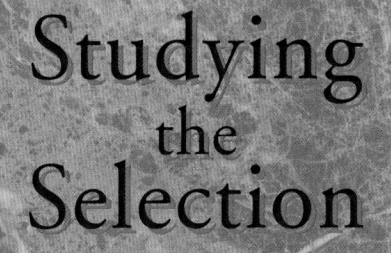

Studying the Selection

First Impressions

Would you like the woman in the poem as your aunt? Why?

✔ Quick Review

1. Which three suggestions does the niece make?
2. Does the aunt take her niece's advice?
3. What suggestion does the aunt make?

In-depth Thinking

4. To which senses does the poem appeal? Don't forget to cite those passages in your answer.
5. Why might the niece be making these suggestions? What conclusions can we draw about her character?
6. Why does the aunt suggest they go for a walk? What conclusions can we draw about her character?

Drawing Conclusions

7. What are the aunt's keepsakes? As you look at the list of keepsakes you drew up for **Into the Poem**, can you conclude that any of your keepsakes are similar to those of the aunt? Why might her "keepsakes" be different from your own?
8. In the 1960s, sociologists used the term *generation gap*, to describe the lack of communication between one generation and the other. The *generation gap* referred especially to the difficulty sociologists thought occurred in every generation: Young people and their parents had trouble understanding each other, because of differences in thinking, tastes, and behavior. Does this poem illustrate a generation gap? If so, in which ways do the aunt and the niece differ? How does the aunt bridge that gap?
9. Do you think that society discriminates against older people?

Focusing on Metaphors

Metaphors are implied comparisons, comparisons made without the words *like* or *as*. In *The Fish*, Elizabeth Bishop calls the five embedded hooks and attached lines a "five-haired beard of wisdom." This metaphor compares the hooks and lines to a beard. What makes the metaphor meaningful, however, is the addition of the word, *wisdom*. This elicits from us associations that enable us to see the fish in an entirely new light.

1. In the poem *Keepsakes*, identify the metaphors in the first stanza (lines 1-9) and the second stanza (lines 10-16).
2. Explain the ideas or associations that these metaphors stir.

Creating and Writing

1. Write an essay or story, in which you talk about aging. If you write a fictional or autobiographical piece, you need not talk directly about aging—aging may simply be at the heart of your concerns. You may take any approach.
2. Write a narrative in which you reveal a memory you wouldn't trade. Or, if you prefer, describe a keepsake you treasure, and explain why it is so important to you.
3. Why not try to bridge the *generation gap*? Visit a nursing home in your community. Perhaps you will be privileged to share someone's treasured memories.

Blueprint for Reading

Background Bytes

Unlike Hugh Lofting's Dr. Dolittle, we are not able to talk to dogs—at least not using all the subtleties of human vocabulary. We can, however, communicate with them a great deal. Dogs can understand our tone of voice and respond with overwhelming enthusiasm to affection. Some may respond to a whole range of commands. We can understand dogs, as well, if we are sensitive to what their faces, bodies, and various woofs communicate. Who doesn't know, for example, what a vigorously wagging tail means? (Of course, a vigorously "wagging" tail on a cat means quite the opposite!)

Do you know what it means when a dog's (or a cat's) small hairs stand upright? The animal is preparing for a fight, or preparing to defend itself. If you have ever walked a dog, you know from experience that all of the other dogs in the neighborhood, even those inside the houses you pass, bark blindly at the unseen, but clearly smelled, new dog. Are these barks greetings or warnings?

Into *Dog at Night*

As you read the poem, ask yourself whether *Dog at Night* has a theme. Or is Louis Untermeyer, in a gentle, comic fashion, simply describing one night—repeated over centuries, in virtually every culture—among the dogs? You may be able to draw some deeper meaning, and come up with a theme, or you may feel that this poem is just a short narrative, funny and evocative.

We could also ask, humorously, whether the poem is describing a world that has "gone to the dogs." When something has *gone to the dogs*, it has deteriorated or degenerated. This saying is one of many idioms that use dogs as a focus. A person can be described as having to *work like a dog*. Sometimes a person is *treated like a dog*. We may also warn people to *let sleeping dogs lie*—advice someone might have meant literally, if it had been said to the moon in *Dog at Night*! Find out what each of these idioms means, and write the definitions down in your notebook. Can you think of any other idioms that talk about dogs?

Focusing on Personification

Personification is a type of metaphor, and thereby involves a comparison. When we use personification, we attribute human characteristics and behaviors to non-human entities or to inanimate objects. For example, we may say that the sand creeps across the land. This is personification, because sand does not creep, people do. By using the word *creep*, we have first made a comparison with human capability, and second created an image of the gradual and encroaching movement of sand.

As you read *Dog at Night*, look for the human traits Untermeyer gives the characters in the poem.

Louis Untermeyer

Dog at Night

At first he stirs uneasily in sleep
And, since the moon does not run off, unfolds
Protesting paws. Grumbling that he must keep
Both eyes awake, he whimpers; then he scolds
5   And, rising to his feet, demands to know
The stranger's business. You who break the dark
With insolent[1] light, who are you? Where do you go?
But nothing answers his indignant[2] bark.
The moon ignores him, walking on as though
10 Dogs never were. Stiffened to fury now,
His small hairs stand upright, his howls come fast,
And terrible to hear is the bow-wow
That tears the night. Stirred by this bugle-blast,
The farmer's hound grows active; without pause
15 Summons her mastiff[3] and the cur[4] that lies
Three fields away to rally to the cause.
And the next county wakes. And miles beyond
Throats ring themselves and brassy lungs respond
With threats, entreaties,[5] bellowings and cries,
20 Chasing the white intruder down the skies.

---

1. One who is *insolent* (IN suh lint) is boldly rude or disrespectful.
2. To be *indignant* (in DIG nint) means to show righteous anger.
3. A *mastiff* (MASS tiff) is a type of large, powerful, light-colored dog with a dark muzzle.
4. Here, a *cur* (KER) refers to a dog of mixed breed.
5. Their *entreaties* (in TREET eez) are their earnest requests or petitions.

Studying the Selection

First Impressions

Initially, what is it that irritates the dog—why do his paws protest and why does he grumble? Why does he rise to his feet? At which point does he become angry? Why?

✓ Quick Review

1. How is the light of the moon described? What does the word mean?
2. What does the dog ask the intruder?
3. Which phrase tells us why the dog stiffens to a fury?
4. Who rallies to the dog's cause?

In-depth Thinking

5. To which senses does the imagery in this poem appeal? Give examples.
6. How does Louis Untermeyer show that he is familiar with a dog's body language and vocalizations?
7. Trace the dog's changing emotions in the poem. Does the moon change?
8. Does the speaker take the dog's plight seriously? How do you know?

Drawing Conclusions

9. Does the speaker in the poem appear to be a "dog person"? Are you?
10. Animals often engage in imitative behavior. In this poem, the barking of one dog leads to the barking of another. What advantages does this behavior have for a group of animals? Can you think of any disadvantages?

Focusing on Personification

When poets use **personification**, they give animals, insects, and inanimate objects the feelings, physical attributes, and behaviors we associate with people. In Elizabeth Bishop's poem *The Fish*, for example, the fish exhibits the bravery and discipline associated with a sage or war-hero. As *The Fish* magnificently demonstrates, personification deepens and broadens our thinking.

Creating and Writing

1. Write an essay in which you discuss how personification allows us to experience the dogs' reality more closely.
2. Imagine that you are either the dog or the moon and retell the story from that point of view. You may use either the first- or third-person voice.
3. Write a folktale or fable in which towns-people (or towns-animals) behave as the dogs behave in *Dog at Night*, sounding the alarm because of an imagined threat.
4. Dogs often bark at sanitation workers and the mail carrier. Their furious energy seems odd to us humans. Write a story that shows us why canines bark in these situations. If you wish, you can write a science fiction story.
5. Take a survey in your school of the number of pet owners and the kinds of pets they have. Display your results using a pie graph.

Blueprint for Reading

Background Bytes

Give me your tired, your poor,
Your huddled masses yearning to breathe free,
The wretched refuse of your teeming shore.
Send these, the homeless, tempest-tost to me,
I lift my lamp beside the golden door!

These words by Emma Lazarus are the famous last lines of her poem, *The New Colossus*, inscribed on a plaque on the Statue of Liberty.

Between 1892 and 1954, the Statue of Liberty greeted more than twelve million people emigrating to the United States. Most of those who entered the United States from the "old Empires of Europe" were processed through the nearby Ellis Island. On a single day in 1907, for example, a remarkable 11,747 people passed through the gateway of Ellis Island, which has been part of the Statue of Liberty National Monument since 1965.

More than 100 million people living in the United States today are "Americans," because of a girl or boy, woman or man, whose name was transferred from a steamship "manifest sheet" to the immigration inspector's register on Ellis Island. For many of us, our ancestors' ships docked there. Then after being examined and listed, these "huddled masses yearning to breathe free" entered the United States in search of the American dream.

Into *Ellis Island*

What is the theme of *Ellis Island*? You will find it when you contrast the first and third stanzas. As you reread the poem, are you surprised by the conflict that emerges? As you compare the message of the first thirteen lines with the message of lines 18-27, ask yourself if you have ever thought before about the conflict the poet describes. Do you know of anyone who entered the United States through Ellis Island? Where did *your* family come from? When did they come to the country where you reside? Try to gather information about your own family's genealogy that would be helpful in creating a family tree. (A **genealogy** is a record of the ancestry and descent of a person, family, or group.) Save your notes for **Creating and Writing**, activity four.

Focusing on Symbolic Language

Another form of figurative language is **symbolic language**. A **symbol** is an object, animal, or event that stands for an idea, an emotion, or even a country. A symbol has both a literal and figurative meaning. For example, the American flag is literally the flag of the United States. But its figurative or symbolic meaning may be the idea of liberty. To give you a better feel for symbols, here are more examples: George Washington, as "the father of our country"; a dove, as a symbol of peace; a $ sign as an indicator of money. By using symbolism, writers of all varieties of literature—including advertising—create another, perhaps more subtle, level of meaning.

Make a list of ten symbols you know. Share them with your classmates.

As you read *Ellis Island*, look for the symbols that give greater depth to the poem and to our lives.

Ellis Island

Joseph Bruchac

Beyond the red brick of Ellis Island
where the two Slovak[1] children
who became my grandparents
waited the long days of quarantine,[2]
5   after leaving the sickness,
the old Empires of Europe,
a Circle Line ship slips easily
on its way to the island
of the tall woman, green
10 as dreams of forests and meadows
waiting for those who'd worked
a thousand years
yet never owned their own.

Like millions of others,
15 I too come to this island,
nine decades the answerer
of dreams.

Yet only one part of my blood
    loves that memory.
Another voice speaks
20 of native lands
within this nation.
Lands invaded
when the earth became owned.
Lands of those who followed
25 the changing Moon,
knowledge of the season
in their veins.

---

1. A *Slovak* (SLO vaak) refers to a person from Slovakia. Slovakia is a republic in central Europe which was part of Czechoslovakia until 1993.
2. *Quarantine* (KWAWR in TEEN) is the strict isolation of people or animals to prevent the spread of disease.

Studying the Selection

First Impressions

Take the information in the poem and create a family tree for the speaker of the poem. Your teacher will provide a chart as a model.

✔ Quick Review

1. What is the speaker of the poem doing, and where is the speaker going, as he says these words?
2. Judging from the opening lines of the poem, what does the speaker see? What memory does it bring to mind?
3. Who is the tall woman? What does she symbolize?
4. What is the other voice that addresses the speaker? What does it say?

In-depth Thinking

5. When the speaker's grandparents arrived at Ellis Island, they were quarantined. What was the literal purpose of "the long days of quarantine"? What is the symbolic sickness?
6. Why does the speaker say "the tall woman," rather than "the Statue of Liberty"?
7. What is the dream of the speaker's immigrant grandparents? What were the repercussions of the immigrants' arrival for the Native Americans?
8. Explain the speaker's mixed feelings about the role of Ellis Island. How would you feel, if you were the speaker?

Drawing Conclusions

9. What special perspective does the speaker bring to the idea of the American dream?
10. How do you define the American dream? Consider both its more material and its less tangible (less capable of being touched, not material) meanings.

Focusing on Symbolic Language

Symbols are objects, animals, events, famous people (and so forth) that stand for or represent ideas, emotions, nations, and philosophies. Sometimes a poet uses symbols with which we are all familiar. These are universal symbols and function as a sort of shorthand, a signal, or a trigger. Symbols allow us to communicate ideas both quickly and with great subtlety. For many, Ellis Island is a symbol of a gateway to freedom. The American eagle, which is nearly extinct, makes United States citizens feel strong and proud. In *The Fish*, the long "beard" of fishing lines reminds us that the fish is old, venerable, a sage. The most obvious symbols, perhaps, are letters and words, which were long ago "invented" to represent sounds, ideas, and everyday realities. How could we do math without number symbols?

When a poet uses symbolism, the words function on two levels. On one level, there is what is literally occurring. On the second, deeper level, is the suggestion of memories stirred and the wider application of the experience.

1. When we begin reading *Ellis Island*, the symbolism of the Statue of Liberty and Ellis Island seems clear. What do they represent to the speaker's Slovakian grandparents?
2. As we continue with the poem, however, the symbolism becomes more complex. What do the Statue of Liberty and Ellis Island symbolize to the speaker's Native American grandparents?
3. What is the speaker's symbolic journey?

Creating and Writing

1. Write an essay in which you discuss how the speaker's visit to Ellis Island expresses the theme of *Ellis Island*. It may be helpful to think about how the ferry ride is a symbol of his personal journey.
2. With your classmates, brainstorm a list of questions to ask someone who emigrated to your country. Remember to be sensitive in your questions, and begin by simply talking, introducing yourself, and explaining your interest. Be sure not to treat the person like your "token immigrant." Conduct an interview with this person and write up your—and his or her—impressions.
3. Do you think that immigration is a source of strength for a nation? Remember that in the United States and Canada, except for the native peoples, we are all newcomers. We had the good fortune to come to a new country and make a fresh start. What are the dangers of the anti-immigrant sentiment that has swept the United States and much of Europe? You are a candidate for public office. Write a speech in which you talk about the history of immigration policy in your country and the importance of allowing people entry from other lands.
4. Create a family tree from your notes from **Into the Poem**.

Blueprint for Reading

Background Bytes

John Masefield was named Poet Laureate of England in 1930 by King George V. He was the sixteenth poet so honored, and was chosen over such eminent contemporaries as Rudyard Kipling and William Butler Yeats. Masefield, who became a writer only against the staunch opposition of his guardian, held the position until his death in 1967 at the age of 89.

The title "poet **laureate**" comes from the laurel tree foliage which was used to crown the victors of the Pythian games, celebrated in ancient Greece at Delphi every four years. The term laureate was also the name of a degree awarded to students for excellence in Latin grammar and poetry.

Throughout much of English history, each king and queen maintained a poet at court. The poet's task was to write poems or songs for special occasions. Of course, the poet was not awarded with laurels, but rather was maintained by the court or paid an annual fee. The first official Poet Laureate of England was John Dryden, appointed in 1668 to a lifetime term.

Into *The West Wind*

Notice the two opposite threads in *The West Wind*. This is called a **dichotomy**: a division into two parts or two opposite types of ideas. Using the first-person voice, the speaker talks of sadness, exhaustion, aging, and death in the first and second stanzas. His thoughts are countered by the voice of the west wind in the third, fourth, and fifth stanzas. The west wind beckons him with words of encouragement, awakening, blossoming, and rebirth.

So what is the theme of the poem? As you reread *The West Wind*, look for the words of the west wind. What does the west wind urge the speaker to do? Why? It is in the *why* that you will find the theme.

In your life, have you moved around or have you always lived in the same place? In your notebook, make a list of those things you miss about your former home, or if you have never moved, the things you imagine you would miss, if you were to move.

Focusing on Rhythm

When we listen to music, we often find ourselves tapping hands or feet, clapping hands, snapping fingers, or swaying to the music. What we are experiencing is the beat—or **rhythm**—of the music. (Note that rhythm is fundamental to life—think of the regularity of the beating of our hearts!)

In poetry, we define **rhythm** as the pattern of accented and unaccented syllables in each line or stanza. While the rhythm of a poem may be either regular or irregular, the beat often expresses the *meaning* or *substance* of the poem.

As you read *The West Wind*, watch for the way John Masefield uses rhythm to mimic the whooshing and blowing of wind, creating a rise and fall similar to the crest and fall of the force of the wind.

The West Wind

John Masefield

It's a warm wind, the west wind, full of birds' cries;
I never hear the west wind but tears are in my eyes.
For it comes from the west lands, the old brown hills,
And April's in the west wind, and daffodils.

5   It's a fine land, the west land, for hearts as tired as mine,
Apple orchards blossom there, and the air's like wine.
There is cool green grass there, where men may lie at rest,
And the thrushes are in song there, fluting[1] from the nest.

"Will ye not come home, brother? ye have been long away,
10 It's April, and blossom time, and white is the spray;
And bright is the sun, brother, and warm is the rain,—
Will ye not come home, brother, home to us again?

"The young corn is green, brother, where the rabbits run,
It's blue sky, and white clouds, and warm rain and sun.
15 It's song to a man's soul, brother, fire to a man's brain,
To hear the wild bees and see the merry spring again.

"Larks are singing in the west, brother, above the green wheat,
So will ye not come home, brother, and rest your tired feet?
I've a balm for bruised hearts, brother, sleep for aching eyes,"
20 Says the warm wind, the west wind, full of birds' cries.

It's the white road westwards is the road I must tread
To the green grass, the cool grass, and rest for heart and head,
To the violets and the warm hearts, and the thrushes' song,
In the fine land, the west land, the land where I belong.

---

1. Here, *fluting* (FLOOT ing) means singing in high-pitched flutelike tones.

Studying the Selection

First Impressions

What kind of music would you choose to accompany the reading of this poem? Remember that this wind is not a violent or blustering wind.

✔ Quick Review

1. What is in the west wind?
2. How does the speaker characterize the west lands, in the first two stanzas?
3. In its song, what does the west wind encourage the speaker to do? What does the wind say about the west land?
4. Which colors does the poet name? How many times does Masefield use the words *green* and *white*? What are these two colors used to describe?

In-depth Thinking

5. To which senses does the imagery in the poem appeal? What do we *feel* (as in physical sensation, for the sense of touch), *hear*, *see*, *smell*, and *taste*? Give examples from the poem of images or descriptions that speak to each of the human senses.
6. How do the words, *ye* and *brother*, affect you?
7. How would you describe the speaker's feelings? What is one of the threads that runs through the poem, as a result? What is the other thread?

Drawing Conclusions

8. It is difficult for a young person to imagine or identify with the weariness that may come with long life and wider experience. With this in mind, would the song of the west wind persuade *you* to return home? What alternatives do you imagine are available to the speaker?
9. One of the ways that John Masefield generates rhythm is through repetition. Make a list of the words and phrases that are repeated in the poem. Given the amount of detail the poet includes, you may be surprised by the extensive use of repetition. Count the number of times each repeated word is used. Write down the words and the number of repetitions.

Focusing on Rhythm

In many of the poems we have read in this unit, the poets have chosen to use irregular rhythm. In *Foul Shot*, for example, the rhythm is irregular, possibly mirroring the movement of the teasing basketball. In *Dog at Night*, on the other hand, Untermeyer uses a regular rhythm, a rhythm that moves as steadily as the moon.

The rhythms of poetry are the rhythms of life. Pleasing to the ear, basic to human physiology and the laws of mathematics, rhythm also aids memory and may add emotional intensity.

1. Read *The West Wind* aloud to yourself and to family members. Listen for the rhythm, and work at tapping it out. Is the rhythm regular or irregular? Remember that a poem can have rhythmic regularity, even if it has more than one rhythm.
2. Examine the last line of the poem. Which words are stressed? Why are these words stressed?
3. Write a brief essay of several paragraphs in which you talk about how the poet has used rhythm in the poem.

Creating and Writing

1. What is the theme of *The West Wind*? Answer this question in an essay, remembering to cite passages from the poem in presenting your reasoning.
2. Write a description of a place you remember that elicits feelings of nostalgia. This can be any place—a home where you once lived, a beach you walked on, a forest through which you hiked—any place where you felt *comfortable* and *safe*. If it is helpful, use the list of features you created for **Into the Poem**.
3. Music often reminds us of a place or a situation. Find a song that has such an association for you. In your notebook or journal, write down the words that evoke the experience. You need not write in complete sentences. Then, if you are comfortable doing so, share the song and the experience with your classmates. If you have no such memories associated with music, select another memory—it can be something you witnessed, something you heard, something you tasted, felt, or smelled—and describe your associations.

Blueprint for Reading

Background Bytes

Throughout history, human beings have been drawn to gems and precious metals and used them for crafting jewelry. Some of the best displays can be found in museums.

When your teacher reads *The Garden* aloud to you, make a list of precious and semi-precious stones mentioned in the poem. Use a dictionary and a reference text to find out more about them. A periodic table of the elements is an essential component for gathering information about gold (abbreviated *Au*), silver (*Ag*), and platinum (*Pt*). Ivory comes from the tusks of elephants, and has been so prized that elephants have been hunted nearly to extinction.

Into *The Garden*

What is the theme of *The Garden*? Are the jewels a metaphor for the actual fruits of the garden? Do they symbolize something else, equally precious? Or is Shel Silverstein writing about a "real" fantasy garden, surprising us with the final line? What does the final line suggest? Certainly it is open to more than one interpretation—and so is the theme!

Focusing on Rhyme

Rhyme is the repetition of the sounds at the ends of words. **End rhyme** occurs at the ends of lines. **Internal rhyme** occurs when words within a line rhyme.

In a poem, rhyme generally follows a pattern. This is called the **rhyme scheme**. To signify a rhyme scheme—the pattern of end rhyme—we use the letters of the alphabet, beginning with the letter *a*. For example, if a poem has rhyming couplets, so that the first two lines of a poem rhyme and the third and fourth lines of the poem rhyme (as we saw in *The West Wind*), the rhyme scheme is designated *aabb*. Sometimes poets rhyme alternating lines. Such a rhyme scheme is designated *abab*.

As you read *The Garden*, look for the rhymes that Shel Silverstein uses. When you read the poem through a second time, look to see whether his rhyming pattern is consistent or whether it is irregular. Where does he use internal rhyme?

THE GARDEN

Shel Silverstein

Ol' man Simon, planted a diamond,
Grew hisself a garden the likes of none.
Sprouts all growin', comin' up glowin',
Fruit of jewels all shinin' in the sun.
5 Colors of the rainbow,
See the sun and rain grow
Sapphires and rubies on ivory vines,
Grapes of jade, just
Ripenin' in the shade, just
10 Ready for the squeezin' into green jade wine.
Pure gold corn there,
Blowin' in the warm air,
Ol' crow nibblin' on the amnythyst[1] seeds.
In between the diamonds, ol' man Simon
15 Crawls about pullin' out platinum weeds.
Pink pearl berries,
All you can carry,
Put 'em in a bushel and
Haul 'em into town.
20 Up in the tree there's
Opal[2] nuts and gold pears—
Hurry quick, grab a stick
And shake some down.
Take a silver tater,
25 Emerald tomater,
Fresh plump coral melons
Hangin' in reach.
Ol' man Simon,
Diggin' in his diamonds,
30 Stops and rests and dreams about
One…real…peach.

---

1. *Amnythyst* (AM nih thist) is a slang word for *amethyst* (AM ih thist), a purplish-bluish gem.
2. An *opal* (O pul) is a shining, luminous, iridescent gemstone.

Studying the Selection

First Impressions

Which "fruit" from Simon's garden would you pick? Would you also prefer one real peach?

✓ Quick Review

1. According to line 2, what kind of garden did Simon grow for himself?
2. What were the colors of the fruit of jewels, as described within the first five lines?
3. What does the ol' crow nibble on? Why did the poet use amethysts for seeds?
4. What does the author suggest should be put in a bushel and hauled to town?

In-depth Thinking

5. To which senses does the poem appeal? Please give examples.
6. In line 4, when the poet writes, "Fruit of jewels all shinin' in the sun," is he using a metaphor? Explain.
7. What is the effect of using dialect like "hisself" and not pronouncing the final consonant of "old" and the final **g** in words ending **-ing**?

Drawing Conclusions

8. Did the end of the poem surprise you? Why would Simon dream of a real peach?
9. We often hear the saying, "Money doesn't grow on trees." Would there be any disadvantages if it did? Explain.

Focusing on Rhyme

People often enjoy reading poems that rhyme, perhaps especially reading them aloud. As you can see from *The Garden*, it is not rhyme alone, but **rhyme** and **rhythm** working in conjunction that makes playing with, and listening to, language so much fun. And when rhyme and rhythm work together cleverly, they aid memory and move a poem forward. As is the case in music, with the resolution of harmonies and the experience of the beat, we become good listeners because rhyme and rhythm make us anticipate the poetry to come. Often the words that rhyme are important to the ideas of the poem. Finally, rhyme, especially unusual rhymes, may delight and surprise us, and contribute to the humorous effect of a poem.

1. Chart the end rhyme of the first ten lines of *The Garden*. Is the pattern of rhyme regular or irregular?
2. Find an example of internal rhyme in the poem. Note that with **internal rhyme**, neither of the rhyming words need be the final word of the line.

Creating and Writing

1. Write an essay about the theme of the poem. Remember, the poem is open to interpretation. Just make certain that your understanding of the theme is grounded in a reasonable assessment of the poem's meaning.
2. Write a diary entry that ol' man Simon might write after a day of gardening. Add lively details to make Simon's character come to life. You may introduce thoughts—an inner conflict—that would lead us to anticipate the poem's final line.
3. Ol' man Simon is apparently good at what he does in the garden—unless it is real fruit he is trying to grow! On what practical subject do you have expertise? Give a "how to" speech on that subject to your class.
4. Choose a fruit that you love—or hate. Write a four- to eight-line poem about that fruit. Include end rhyme.

Blueprint for Reading

Background Bytes

On April 9, 1865, the Confederate General Robert E. Lee surrendered to General Ulysses S. Grant at Appomattox Court House in Virginia, ending the American Civil War. Just five days later, on April 14, 1865, John Wilkes Booth assassinated President Abraham Lincoln at Ford's Theater in Washington D.C. Devastated by Lincoln's death, which followed so closely after victory, Walt Whitman wrote the poem *O Captain! My Captain!*

Walt Whitman is considered by many to be the greatest of all American poets. *O Captain! My Captain!* was published in the New York City *Saturday Press*, and immediately met critical acclaim. Ultimately it became Whitman's most popular poem. In subsequent years, Walt Whitman was frequently asked to recite the poem during his public lectures. Today, more than a hundred thirty years later, *O Captain! My Captain!* is still widely anthologized.

Into *O Captain! My Captain!*

O Captain! My Captain! has the throbbing beat of sobbing and a beating heart. Yet the poem is also filled with the exultation of victory and the relief of finally arriving safe at home. As with the dichotomy we saw in *The West Wind*—which also speaks of coming home—the theme can be found in these double and opposite threads of heartbreak and celebration. What does the poem tell us about the death of the Commander-in-Chief? About life in general?

In *O Captain! My Captain!* Whitman compares President Lincoln to a ship's captain and the nation to a ship. As a class, brainstorm the ways these metaphors are appropriate.

Focusing on Repetition

Rhythm, we have said, is the **repetition** of stressed and unstressed syllables in a line of poetry. **Rhyme** is the **repetition** of vowel and consonant sounds at the ends of words. These are only two of the many kinds of **repetition** a poet may use. To add melody and emphasis to their poetry, poets may repeat sounds, words, phrases, or even entire lines.

    The repetition of initial word sounds is called **alliteration**.

    The repetition of vowel sounds within words is called **assonance**.

    The repetition of consonant sounds within words is called **consonance**.

As you read *O Captain! My Captain!* watch for the kinds of repetition used by Walt Whitman.

O Captain! My Captain!

Walt Whitman

O Captain! my Captain! our fearful trip is done,
The ship has weathered every rack,[1] the prize we sought is won,
The port is near, the bells I hear, the people all exulting,[2]
While follow eyes the steady keel,[3] the vessel grim and daring;
5   But O heart! heart! heart!
        O the bleeding drops of red,
            Where on the deck my Captain lies,
                Fallen cold and dead.

O Captain! my Captain! rise up and hear the bells;
10 Rise up—for you the flag is flung—for you the bugle trills,[4]
For you bouquets and ribboned wreaths—for you the shores a-crowding,
For you they call, the swaying mass, their eager faces turning;
    Here Captain! dear father!
        This arm beneath your head!
15   It is some dream that on the deck
            You've fallen cold and dead.

My Captain does not answer, his lips are pale and still,
My father does not feel my arm, he has no pulse nor will,
The ship is anchored safe and sound, its voyage closed and done,
20 From fearful trip the victor ship comes in with object won;
    Exult O shores! And ring O bells!
        But I with mournful tread[5]
            Walk the deck my Captain lies,
                Fallen cold and dead.

---

1. Here, *rack* (RAK) refers to violent strain or torment.
2. *Exulting* (eg ZULL ting) means showing lively or triumphant joy.
3. The *keel* is the central beam at the bottom of a ship's hull. It extends from stem to stern (front to back) of the ship.
4. A *trill* (TRILL) is a very rapid alternating of two musical notes.
5. A *mournful tread* is a gloomy, somber manner of walking.

Studying the Selection

First Impressions

If you hadn't known this poem was about Abraham Lincoln, would you have been able to guess? Does it add to the impact of the poem, knowing the identity of this Captain?

✓ Quick Review

1. What has happened to the ship in the poem? To the Captain?
2. What is the speaker's reaction?

In-depth Thinking

3. An **extended metaphor** is a comparison that is continued for many lines through a poem. Explain the extended metaphor in the poem. Be sure you identify the ship, the trip, the prize, the port, the captain. Has Whitman used any of the comparisons you brainstormed in **Into the Poem**?
4. What story is told in the first four lines of the first two stanzas and the third and fourth lines of the last stanza? What story is told in the last four lines of each stanza?

Drawing Conclusions

5. We often use exclamation marks when we are excited. Is that the emotion that Whitman's exclamation point conveys? Remember that we often feel and express two different feelings (or more) at the same time.
6. A dirge is a poem of mourning. An elegy is a poem of both mourning and praise for someone who has died. Which do you think is the better word to describe *O Captain! My Captain!*? Explain.
7. How might a poem like this one help a nation come to terms with a tragedy?

Focusing on Repetition

The repetition of beginning consonant sounds in words that are in close sequence is called **alliteration**. What matters is not spelling but sound. "Jolly Geoffrey" is an example of alliteration since both words begin with the "j" sound. "Good George," however, is not an example of alliteration, because the initial sounds are *not* the same (even though the initial letters *are*). Similar to other forms of repetition, alliteration adds melody to the poem, connects words, creates mood, and heightens our awareness of the playful possibilities when using language.

1. Chart the rhyme scheme of the poem. Is it regular or irregular?
2. Is the rhythm regular or irregular?
3. Which words are repeated? Phrases? Lines?
4. Find two examples of alliteration in the poem.

Creating and Writing

1. Write an essay about the theme of *O Captain! My Captain!* or, if you prefer, about the use of a dichotomy and why it may be so powerful. Remember that a **dichotomy** is a division into two different types of ideas, that are possibly contradictory, as we have seen in *The West Wind* and *O Captain! My Captain!*
2. People often respond to very sad—or very happy—events by writing poetry. Write a poem about such an event in your life. Try to include some forms of **repetition**, such as **alliteration**, **internal** or **end rhyme**, **consonance**, **assonance**, or word and line repetition.
3. What more would you like to know about President Lincoln's life and his family? The Civil War? One of Lincoln's great speeches? With your teacher and classmates, organize an Abraham Lincoln Day, during which you and the other students in your class present reports, display appropriate artwork, and dress in suitable costumes!

Blueprint for Reading

Background Bytes

Have you ever wondered where the word *dandelion* comes from? **Etymology**, the history of a word or an element of a word, is often fascinating. For example, some words are called **portmanteau** words. Portmanteau is the name of a suitcase that opens into two compartments. Thus, words created from the blending of two words are called **portmanteau** words. Examples are *smog* from *smoke* and *fog*, and *motel* from *motor* and *hotel*.

Some words are **acronyms**, which are formed from the first letter or letters of several other words. *Radar*, for example, comes from the phrase "**ra**dio **d**etecting **a**nd **r**anging." Another type of word is the **eponym**, a word that derives its name from a person or a product. For example, legend has it that John Montagu, the 18th century Earl of Sandwich, was busy one day and asked his servant to bring him some meat between two slices of bread, instead of the usual meal. The "sandwich" was born. And what of the word *dandelion*? To the French, the leaves looked like lion's teeth—in French, *dent de leon* in other words, *tooth of the lion*! (You will recognize the root word for tooth, *dent*, as appearing in *dentist*.)

Into *dandelions*

Who decides which plants are undesirable? Have you ever thought about how odd it is that we decide that some plants are simply unwelcome and must be destroyed. And then we do injury to ourselves and the environment by using dangerous herbicides and pesticides to get rid of those tiresome "weeds."

If we lived in a world with very little color, we might see that the golden dandelions are quite pretty. You will find the theme of this poem, if you think about what happens, when we decide that *we* cannot tolerate certain species of living things. Rather than appreciating them or just making room for them because they live here too, we conduct war on them—and then perceive ourselves as the victims! The poem points to the absurdity of some of our own behaviors.

This is a great poem. As you reread it, jot down your three favorite parts of the poem.

Focusing on Onomatopoeia

When poets use **onomatopoeia**, they interject words that mimic the sounds of animals, the rain, machines, liquids—various natural phenomena. In *Dog at Night*, for example, Untermeyer writes, "And terrible to hear is the *bow-wow* / That tears the night." *Bow-wow* echoes a dog's bark and gives the poem an immediacy—as if we were right there.

As you read *dandelions*, watch for Austin's delightful use of onomatopoeia. Why do the word-sounds make the poem more vivid?

dandelions

Deborah Austin

under cover of night and rain
the troops took over.
waking to total war in beleaguered[1] houses
over breakfast we faced the batteries[2]
5   marshalled[3] by wall and stone, deployed
with a master strategy no one had suspected
and now all
firing
pow
10 all day, all yesterday
and all today
the barrage[4] continued
deafening sight.
reeling now, eyes ringing from noise, from walking
15 gingerly over the mined lawns
exploded at every second
rocked back by the starshellfire
concussion[5] of gold on green
bringing battle-fatigue[6]
20 pow by lionface firefur pow by
goldburst shellshock[7] pow by

whoosh   splat   splinteryellow
    pow   by
pow   by   pow
tomorrow smoke drifts up
25 from the wrecked battalions,[8]
all the ammunition, firegold fury, gone.
smoke
drifts
thistle-blown
30 over the war-zone, only
here and there, in the shade by the
peartree
pow   in the crack by the
curbstone   pow   and back of the
35 ashcan, lonely
guerrilla[9] snipers,[10] hoarding
their fire shrewdly
never

pow

40 surrender

1. *Beleaguered* (bee LEE gerd) means surrounded or besieged by military forces.
2. *Batteries* are military units of artillery (heavy arms, such as mounted guns).
3. *Marshalled* (MAR shild) means arrayed for battle.
4. A *barrage* (buh RAZH) is a heavy barrier of artillery fire used to stop the enemy in its tracks.
5. *Concussion* (kun KUSH in) is the shock of impact from a collision or blow.
6. *Battle fatigue* is stress experienced from prolonged combat.
7. *Shellshock* is a synonym for *battle fatigue*.
8. *Battalions* are military units of ground forces.
9. *Guerilla* (guh RILL uh) warfare uses surprise raids by small, mobile groups of "irregular" soldiers operating within enemy territory.
10. A *sniper* (SNY per) is a person who shoots at others from a hidden position.

Studying the Selection

First Impressions

Who will win the war: the people or the dandelions?

✔ Quick Review

1. When did the dandelions take over?
2. What happens over breakfast?
3. How long does the barrage last?
4. Name three places new dandelions appear.

In-depth Thinking

5. Just as we have seen in *O Captain! My Captain!* this poem is an **extended metaphor**. Trace the metaphor in the poem. Be sure to identify all the words that contribute to the metaphor.
6. When you jotted down your favorite passages for **Into the Poem**, what were they? Indicate why you like these parts.
7. The imagery in the poem appeals to the senses of sight, sound, touch, and smell. Cite examples. What is unusual and interesting about the phrases, "deafening sight" and "eyes ringing from noise"?
8. Austin creates many new words in the poem. Choose two and describe why they are effective.

Drawing Conclusions

9. The poem describes the escalation of conflict between people and the dandelions. Which other conflicts exist between people and nature? To what extent are these conflicts generated by human beings? How could a new philosophical approach diminish or eradicate the conflict? What would be the global implications of such a changed attitude? You are campaigning for public office. Write a brief speech in which you try to convince your classmates to adopt a platform and a philosophy more favorable to the environment. In your speech, address each of the questions above.
10. We said that the word "dandelion" comes from the shape of the plant's leaves. After reading this poem, does the dandelion seem "lion-like" in other ways? Explain.

Focusing on Onomatopoeia

To say that bees *buzz* or crows *caw* is to use **onomatopoeia**, words that imitate sounds. When poets use onomatopoeia, they bring the poem's aural (sound) images to life. In addition, onomatopoeia adds to the melody and, consequently, to our pleasure in the poem.

1. Find three examples of onomatopoeia in *dandelions*. Which sound is each word imitating?

Creating and Writing

1. Much of our enjoyment of *dandelions* comes from the poet's fanciful use of metaphor, imagery, and sound. Write an essay in which you discuss this use of metaphor, imagery, and sound. Be sure to include specific examples in your writing.

2. Choose an object in nature that you have a strong reaction toward, perhaps a plant or an animal. Write an **acrostic poem**, a poem in which the first letter of each line, going down, spells out the name of your subject. See if you can include an onomatopoetic word. We give an example below.

   From a Young Mouse to a Little Girl
       Much as she's frightened
       I surely am smaller
       Could I learn to speak
       Eek! Would I enthrall 'er?

3. Did you know that many flowers and "weeds," including dandelions, are edible? Find a recipe that includes an unusual plant, and share it with your classmates.

Blueprint for Reading

Background Bytes

John Godfrey Saxe's *The Blind Men and the Elephant* is based on an ancient story from India. Elephants figure in many stories across cultures, and in children's stories as well. Jean de Brunhoff's elephant, Babar, fashionably dressed, accompanied by his wife Celeste, becomes king of the elephants. From Rudyard Kipling's *Elephant Child*, we learn how the elephant got its trunk. Winnie the Pooh, with his pal Piglet, digs a pit and baits it with honey, as he searches for the Heffalump in A. A. Milne's *Winnie the Pooh*. Dr. Seuss's Horton hatches an egg (an elephant bird, of course) in one story; in another, Horton hears and protects the Whos of Who-ville. Why elephants? Perhaps their impressive size, their expressive faces, their quiet dignity, and their great strength make them both moving and mysterious to us.

Into *The Blind Men and the Elephant*

In *The Blind Men and the Elephant*, each of the blind men touches a different part of the elephant. What would a person, who could not see, think an elephant looked like, if he or she were to feel only the elephant's side? What if the same person had touched only the tusk? The trunk? One of the elephant's knees or ears? The elephant's tail? In your notebook jot down your thoughts. Save your writing. These questions also bring you to the theme: What can we tell about the whole, if we know only a part of the whole?

Focusing on the Stanza

When we write a story, one of our units of organization is the **paragraph**. Each paragraph develops the idea addressed in the topic sentence (although certainly subsequent paragraphs may elaborate on the same idea). In poetry, one of the units of organization is the **stanza**. A stanza is an arrangement of lines, usually four or more, often having a fixed length, meter, or rhyme scheme, that forms a division of a poem. In poems that tell a story or describe a sequence of events, the stanzas most resemble the paragraphs of a narrative. Look back at *O Captain! My Captain!* How does each stanza work like a paragraph? When you reread *The Blind Men and the Elephant*, think about whether its stanzas work the same way.

The Blind Men & The Elephant

John Godfrey Saxe

It was six men of Indostan[1]
    To learning much inclined,
Who went to see the Elephant
    (Though all of them were blind),
5 That each by observation
    Might satisfy his mind.

The *First* approached the Elephant,
    And happening to fall
Against his broad and sturdy side,
10   At once began to bawl:
"G-d bless me! But the Elephant
    Is very like a wall!"

The *Second*, feeling of the tusk,
    Cried, "Ho! What have we here
15 So very round and smooth and sharp?
    To me 'tis mighty clear
This wonder of an Elephant
    Is very like a spear!"

The *Third* approached the animal,
20   And happening to take
The squirming trunk within his hands,
    Thus boldy up and spake:
"I see," quoth he, "the Elephant
    Is very like a snake!"

25 The *Fourth* reached out an eager hand,
    And felt about the knee.
"What most this wondrous beast is like
    Is mighty plain," quoth he;
"'Tis clear enough the Elephant
30   Is very like a tree!"

The *Fifth*, who chanced to touch the ear,
    Said: "E'en the blindest man
Can tell what this resembles most;
    Deny the fact who can,
35 This marvel of an Elephant
    Is very like a fan!"

The *Sixth* no sooner had begun
    About the beast to grope,
Than, seizing on the swinging tail
40   That fell within his scope,
"I see," quoth he, "the Elephant
    Is very like a rope!"

And so these men of Indostan
    Disputed loud and long,
45 Each in his own opinion
    Exceeding stiff and strong,
Though each was partly in the right,
    And all were in the wrong!

---

1. *Indostan* (IN doe STAN) is another spelling or pronunciation of the word *Hindustan* (HIN duh STAHN), which is a region of Northern India that includes the plain drained by the Indus, the Ganges, and the Brahmaputra Rivers. The word is also used for the entire subcontinent of India and the Republic of India.

Studying the Selection

First Impressions

Go back to the notes you made for Into the Poem. Were any of your comparisons similar to those of the blind men?

✓ Quick Review

1. Which part of the elephant did each blind man touch? What did each man, respectively, think of the elephant?
2. What does each man believe about his own opinion?

In-depth Thinking

3. What mistake do all six men make?
4. A fable is a story that teaches a lesson. What is the lesson, or theme, of this poem?

Drawing Conclusions

5. How is this poem about both literal and figurative blindness?
6. When people are so sure that they're right, how can they settle their differences?

Focusing on the Stanza

Most traditional poems are written in **stanzas**, organizing "paragraphs." Review the poems *The West Wind* and *Keepsakes*. *The West Wind* is a traditional poem, with its four-line stanzas and its consistent rhythm and rhyme. *Keepsakes*, on the other hand, has stanzas but irregular ones. Neither its rhythm nor rhyme falls into a recurring pattern. We'll take a look at this kind of poetry, free verse, in the next lesson.

1. In *The Blind Men and the Elephant*, is the rhyme scheme the same throughout the poem? How about the rhythm?
2. How are the stanzas of the poem very much like the paragraphs in a story?

Creating and Writing

1. Why would someone write a fable to share a message like this? Write an essay, short story, or poem with the same theme.
2. Have you ever been absolutely sure you were right and then learned later that you were not? Write a nonfiction narrative about such an experience—or, if you prefer, make up a story about such an experience.
3. With a group of classmates, present a dramatic reading of *The Blind Men and the Elephant*.

Blueprint for Reading

Background Bytes

In this poem by Walt Whitman, the speaker begins by saying, "When I heard the learn'd astronomer…." In 1865 when this poem was first published, *what*, in fact, would an astronomer have known? Nineteenth-century astronomers were aware that the Earth, Mercury, Venus, Mars, Saturn, Jupiter, Uranus, and Neptune orbited the Sun. This was the **heliocentric theory**. Pluto, however, would not be "discovered" until 1930.

Astronomers of that period also knew that Saturn had rings and Jupiter had moons. They used telescopes and observed comets, nebulae, and star clusters.

The men and women who studied the stars and the physics of the universe had to wait for improved technology—for example, more powerful telescopes—which would bring them greater knowledge, enhance their understanding, and create new questions.

Into *When I Heard the Learn'd Astronomer*

When you read through the poem a second time, compare or contrast the statement being made in lines 2 and 3 with the poet's words in the two closing lines. It is this contrast that will give you the theme. Remember that Walt Whitman is expressing a conflict, as he perceives it. The question he raises has long been with us and surely is important to pose. But his answer may not be *your* answer.

Do you see yourself as a scientist or an artist or something in between?
This question is founded on the notion that science and art are diametrically opposed, with the one based solely on measurement and observation, and the other the result of inspiration and intuition. Are art and science necessarily opposites? In your notebook, jot down your thoughts. Share your ideas with your classmates.

Focusing on Free Verse

Free verse is poetry that does not have a fixed line length, rhythm, or rhyme. Earlier in this unit, you read the poem *Keepsakes* by Deloras Lane. *Keepsakes* is an example of free verse written in stanzas. Although each stanza in that poem reads much like a paragraph, Lane's verse is nonetheless "free," because the number of lines in the stanzas varies, as does the length of the lines. If you refer back to *Keepsakes*, you will see, too, that the rhythm follows no set pattern and there is no end rhyme. Yet no one would argue that *Keepsakes* is not poetry. As that poem demonstrates, the traditional elements of meter and rhyme are not essential to the poetic: Instead, Ms. Lane employs vivid imagery and metaphor.

As you read *When I Heard the Learn'd Astronomer*, look for the ways Whitman makes his free verse "poetic." How does he make so powerful and persuasive a statement in only eight lines?

When I Heard the Learn'd Astronomer

Walt Whitman

When I heard the learn'd astronomer,[1]
When the proofs, the figures, were ranged in columns before me,
When I was shown the charts and diagrams, to add, divide, and measure them,
When I sitting heard the astronomer where he lectured with much applause in the lecture room,
How soon unaccountable I became tired and sick,
Till rising and gliding out I wandered off by myself,
In the mystical moist night-air, and from time to time
Looked up in perfect silence at the stars.

---

1. An *astronomer* (uh STRAHN uh mer) is a person who studies the stars and other heavenly bodies.

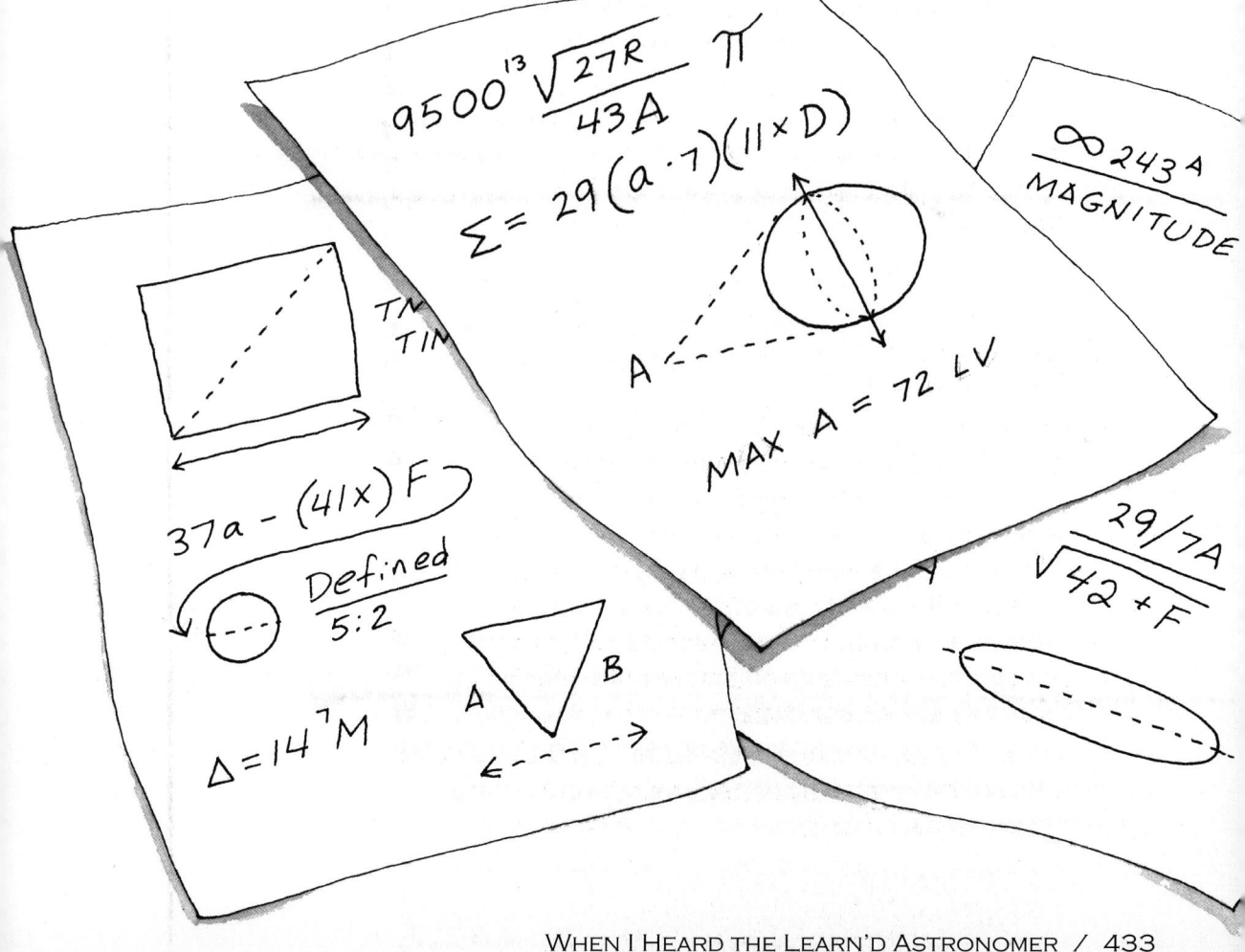

Studying the Selection

First Impressions

What do you think accounts for the speaker's unaccountable "tired and sick" feelings? Do you share his feelings? Or can you understand his feelings, but do not experience them yourself? Are his feelings a complete mystery to you?

✔ Quick Review

1. Where is the speaker in lines 1-4? In line 5? In lines 6-8?
2. What is the astronomer doing?
3. How is the astronomer being received by his audience?

In-depth Thinking

4. What makes the astronomer of the poem learned?
5. What is the contrast the poet is making in lines 1-4 and in lines 5-8?

Drawing Conclusions

6. What makes the moist night-air mystical? (Begin by looking up the definitions of *mystical* and *mystery*.)
7. How do you understand the last line of the poem? In other words, what does the speaker mean when he says that he "Looked up in perfect silence at the stars"?
8. Can a scientist also be an artist? Can a scientist be a spiritual person? How would a scientist respond to Whitman?

Focusing on Free Verse

Poets in France began using **free verse** in the second half of the 19th century. Walt Whitman found this form of poetry very appealing. He felt that language already has its own rhythms, and that his ideas would be better expressed in a less constrained form. But make no mistake: Free verse *is* poetry. Like all poetry, its form is concentrated and its language evocative.

1. Poets who write free verse often rely on repetition. How does Whitman use repetition in the first four lines? Where does he use alliteration? Beginning with line 5, are there places where the sequence of words sounds "poetic," rather than like ordinary straightforward speech? Can you think of a reason for this poetic order of words?

2. Notice that the lines gradually increase in length from line 1 to line 4. How does this changing line length serve to express the speaker's feelings in the first half of the poem?
3. The poem is all one sentence. Why would Whitman have written the poem this way?

Creating and Writing

1. Write either a free verse poem or a traditional rhyming poem that expresses the thematic conflict of *When I Heard the Learn'd Astronomer.* Include your *own* views on whether, in fact, there is a conflict between measurement and beauty, between science and fantasy.
2. Write an essay in which you compare and contrast the poetic elements of the two Walt Whitman poems, *O Captain! My Captain!* and *When I Heard the Learn'd Astronomer.* Which poem do you prefer? Is your preference related to the difference in style? Begin your work on this assignment by analyzing each poem regarding the same elements. This work will comprise the body of your essay. You will also need an introductory paragraph to tell your readers what you are going to tell them. And a concluding paragraph summing up your results and indicating your preferences.
3. Research the life and accomplishments of a famous astronomer. There are many possible subjects, one of the earliest of whom is the second-century Greek astronomer, Ptolemy. Early Islamic astronomers such as Thebit (836-901), Albategnius (858-929), Azophi (903-986), and Avicenna (981-1037) made extraordinary contributions to the field. Albiruni (973-1048) determined the Earth's circumference. Arzachel (1028-1087) invented the astrolabe, a tool that used the stars to navigate at sea. The Europeans included the sixteenth-century Nicholaus Copernicus; and the seventeenth-century Johannes Kepler, Galileo Galilei, and Vincenzo Viviani. England gave us Isaac Newton and the eighteenth-century Thomas Wright and William Herschel. Other important figures include Tycho Brahe, Edmond Halley, Edwin Hubble, and Albert Einstein. You may want to research the role of twentieth-century women astronomers, such as Wendy Freeman and Jane X. Luu. Perhaps your class can create a timeline of great astronomers with their contributions to the field.

Blueprint for Reading

Background Bytes

In 1958, at the Brussels World's Fair, a piece of music called *Poeme Electronique* was performed by four hundred loudspeakers. *Poeme Electronique* is an example of *musique concrete*, the French term for 'concrete music.' Here, the term *concrete* refers to music or sounds that are drawn from realities or actual events, rather than from *abstractions*, that is ideas or theories.

In the late 1940s, Pierre Schaeffer, a French radio broadcaster, created a piece of *musique concrete* by recording such sounds as street noises, thunderstorms, steam engines, and banging doors. He modified the taped sounds by playing them backwards, varying their speed, transforming their pitch and intensity. These sounds were then reassembled as a 'song'—a piece of *musique concrete.* This was a movement in music that paralleled a similar development in poetry. The *musique concrete* of fifty years past is the likely forerunner of today's electronic and computer-produced music.

Into *Legacy II*

Throughout history, the members of the older generation have questioned the values of the younger generation. Likewise, members of the younger generation may be mystified by the behavior of members of the older generation. But when *that* younger generation ages and takes the place of the elders who preceded them, its members easily assume the values of their predecessors. Once again the cycle repeats.

What does *Legacy II* tell us? The theme becomes clear in the last two stanzas.

What special memories do you have of an older adult, perhaps one of your grandparents, a great-aunt, or an elderly neighbor? Write down your memories and save them in your notebook.

Focusing on Concrete and Pattern Poetry

Concrete music gives musical expression new form. **Concrete poetry** does as well, but it is not as difficult for the eye as concrete music is for the ear. In concrete poetry, the poet creates visual effects, and determines the impact and the "reading" of the poem, through the spatial arrangement of words in patterns and shapes. Consider the poem, *Concrete Cat* by Dorthi Charles:

CONCRETE CAT DORTHI CHARLES

```
        A              A
       e r            e r

      eYe          eYe      stripestripestripestripe        t
   whisker       whisker       stripestripestripe        a        a i \
   whisker  m   h  whisker   stripestripestripestripes   / i / t
            o t                 stripestripestripe
            U                stripestripestripestripe

           paw paw          paw paw          ǝsnow

      dishdish                 litterbox
                               litterbox
```

Concrete Cat is certainly a lot of fun, and relies on sight, not on sound. How could you read this poem to someone? The poet who writes concrete poetry is making a visual statement that *is* the poem.

Pattern poetry is poetry in which the lines are arranged in unusual ways, in order to strengthen the emotional content of the poem. As you read *Legacy II*, note Leroy Quintana's placement of words in lines 9, 10, and 11. How does this typographic arrangement speak to the point of the poem? Lines 20, 21, and 22 provide a wonderful echo back to the midpoint of the poem.

LEGACY II

Leroy V. Quintana

Grandfather never went to school
spoke only a few words of English

a quiet man; when he talked
talked about simple things
5 planting corn or about the weather
sometimes about herding sheep as a child

One day pointed to the four directions
Taught me their names[1]
              El Norte
10 Poniente   Oriente
              El Sur

He spoke their names as if they were
one of only a handful of things
a man needed to know

15 Now I look back
only two generations removed
realize I am nothing but a poor fool
who went to college

trying to find my way back
20 to the center of the world
where Grandfather stood
that day

---

1. These are the Spanish words for the directions on a compass: the North—*El Norte* (el NOR tay); West—*Poniente* (PAHN ee YEN tay); East—*Oriente* (OR ee YEN tay); the South—*El Sur* (EL SIR).

Studying the Selection

First Impressions

If you were to place Grandfather in lines 9, 10, and 11, where would he have stood?

✓ Quick Review

1. Tell us three things the speaker mentions about Grandfather.
2. What did he teach his grandson?
3. How does the speaker characterize himself today?
4. What is the speaker still trying to do?

📑 In-depth Thinking

5. The speaker says that his Grandfather spoke as if there were only a handful of things a person needed to know. What do you think this means?
6. Why does the speaker call himself "a poor fool"?
7. What is the Grandfather's legacy?

📂 Drawing Conclusions

8. Similar to the speaker in *Ellis Island*, the speaker in *Legacy II* thinks about his heritage. Do the two speakers feel similarly? How important is the legacy of one's grandparents?
9. Do you think that the Grandfather in this poem and the aunt in *Keepsakes* are good role models? Who are your role models?

El Norte
Poniente   Oriente
El Sur

Focusing on Concrete and Pattern Poetry

Although **concrete poetry** began in the 20th century, poets have used **pattern poetry** for at least two thousand years. The major difference between the two is that pattern poetry has meaning beyond its placement of words. We can read pattern poetry aloud and still grasp its meaning. Most of *Legacy II* is a traditional poem. Lines 9 through 11, however, are comprised of a careful and well-thought-out placement of words.

1. Why has Quintana placed the four directions as he has? Where does the Grandfather go in the picture? The speaker?
2. How is the placement of the words symbolic of the speaker's sense of being lost? Of being found or of finding himself?

Creating and Writing

1. Using your notes from **Into the Poem**, write a personal narrative that goes to the heart of the theme of *Legacy II*.
2. Both *Legacy II* and *Foul Shot* are examples of pattern poetry. Write an essay in which you discuss the effect of the poet's placement of words in each poem. Conclude by expressing your own ideas about pattern poetry.
3. Try writing a concrete poem or a pattern poem. Perhaps you can use a computer, so that you can vary the fonts and sizes of your words.

Blueprint for Reading

Background Bytes

In *The Rescue*, the boy climbs a tree to rescue the family cat. Do cats, in fact, need to be rescued from trees? As you will see when you read the poem, given *this* family's obvious history of cooperation and support, this was one young man who would have never turned his back on an animal or person that appeared to be in need.

Cats are good climbers. Even those cats whose owners have had their front claws removed can ascend a tree. When they climb, cats support their weight with their strong back claws and pull themselves up with their sharper, longer front claws. Getting down from the tree, however, is not so easy. Because they cannot support their weight with their front claws, they must climb down backwards. Anyone who has befriended a cat knows that cats hate to back up or back down.

Into *The Rescue*

You will find the theme of this poem, if you look to the boy's sense of responsibility and the expression by *all of his family* of family values and unity.

Can you think of a time, when members of your family came together to help each other out—little ones and pets included? In your notebook, write down your recollection of the events.

Focusing on Narrative Poetry

The Rescue and *The Walrus and the Carpenter* (which follows the current selection) are examples of **narrative poetry**. Narrative poetry combines the characteristics of a story and a poem. Such verse has characters, who may engage in brief dialogue. Characterization is usually limited. The plot, which may include conflict and suspense, often builds to a climax. The story is generally fast-paced and, of course, is told poetically. The author uses sound effects such as rhythm, rhyme, and repetition, as well as imagery and figurative language.

As you read the next two poems, look for the combination of narrative and poetic elements.

The Rescue

Hal Summers

The boy climbed up into the tree.
The tree rocked. So did he.
He was trying to rescue a cat,
A cushion of a cat, from where it sat
5 In a high crutch of branches,[1] mewing
As though to say to him, "Nothing doing,"
Whenever he shouted, "Come on, come down."
So up he climbed, and the whole town
Lay at his feet, round him the leaves
10 Fluttered like a lady's sleeves,
And the cat sat, and the wind blew so
That he would have flown had he let go.
At last he was high enough to scoop
That fat white cushion or nincompoop
15 And tuck her under his arm and turn
    To go down—
        But oh! He began to learn
How high he was, how hard it would be.
Having come up with four limbs, to go down with three.
20 His heartbeats knocked as he tried to think:
He would put the cat in a lower chink—
She appealed to him with a cry of alarm
And put her eighteen claws in his arm.
So he stayed looking down for a minute or so,
25 To the good ground so far below.

---

1. A *crutch of branches* is an area where two branches meet and provide support.
2. Here, the term *fluorescent* (flor ESS int) means strikingly bright or glowing.

When the minute began he saw it was hard;
When it ended he couldn't move a yard.
So there he was stuck, in the failing light
And the wind rising with the coming of the night.

30   His father! He shouted for all he was worth.
     His father came nearer: "What on earth—?"
     I've got the cat up here but I'm stuck."
     "Hold on…ladder…" he heard. O luck!
     How lovely behind the branches tossing
35   The globes at the pedestrian crossing
     And the big fluorescent² lamps glowed
     Mauve-green on the main road.
     But his father didn't come back, didn't come;
     His little fingers were going numb.
40   That cat licked them as though to say,
     "Are you feeling cold? I'm O.K."
     He wanted to cry, he would count to ten first,
     But just as he was ready to burst
     A torch came and his father and mother
45   And a ladder and the dog and his younger brother.
     Up on a big branch stood his father,
     His mother came to the top of the ladder,
     His brother stood on a lower rung,
     The dog sat still and put out its tongue.
50   From one to the other the cat was handed
     And afterwards she was reprimanded.
     After that it was easy, though the wind blew:
     The parents came down, the boy came too
     From the ladder, the lower branch, and the upper,
55   And all of them went indoors to supper,
     The high branches like a white cat.
     And the tree rocked, and the moon sat
     In the high branches like a white cat.

Studying the Selection

First Impressions — At the end of this poem, the family goes indoors for supper. Form a "family" of six classmates: mother, father, sibling (brother or sister), protagonist—who may be a boy or a girl—and the family cat and dog. Act out the family's suppertime conversation and motions, with appropriate dog and cat participation.

✔ Quick Review

1. Once the boy rescues the cat, why doesn't he climb back down the tree?
2. Why does the boy almost start to cry?
3. How are the cat and boy rescued?
4. What is the last image in the poem?

In-depth Thinking

5. Why, at the beginning and at the end of the poem, does the poet repeat, "The tree rocked"? Was the boy ever in danger?
6. What is the meaning of the poem's title?

Drawing Conclusions

7. How does this poem illustrate the love of a family for each other?
8. Is this poem lighthearted or serious? Explain.

Focusing on Narrative Poetry

Dog at Night is another example of a **narrative poem**. It briefly tells the "story" of two characters in conflict. The dog wants the moon's attention and even tries speaking to it; the moon ignores the dog. As the conflict continues, the dog gets angrier and angrier until, at last, his barks summon the help of other dogs. The poem comes to a climax as all the dogs bark at the moon until they chase the intruder away. The story, of course, is told as a poem, complete with rhythm, rhyme, onomatopoeia, imagery, and figurative language.

1. In *The Rescue*, who are the characters? Is there any character development? Do the characters speak?
2. What is the plot and conflict of *The Rescue*? Is there suspense? Is there a climax?
3. Does the poem have rhythm, rhyme, or other sound effects?
4. Find two similes and two metaphors in the poem. What is personified?

Creating and Writing

1. Using your answers in the **Focus** section, write an essay explaining the elements of narrative poetry in *The Rescue*.
2. Stories, like the ones you told in **Into the Poem**, often become the stuff of family legends. Retell one of those family legends as a narrative poem.
3. Draw a 6-panel cartoon of *The Rescue*.

Blueprint for Reading

Background Bytes

Many authors have been known to write under "assumed" or invented names to conceal their identities. The terms for such created names are several: **pseudonym** (Greek for "false name"), **nom de plume** (French for "name of the pen"), and **pen name**. (However, when outlaws use an assumed name, it is referred to as an **alias** or an **a.k.a.**, which stands for "also known as"!) Writers have had various reasons for using other names. Some of the more famous authors who have done so, and who may be familiar to you, are Mark Twain, O. Henry, and Dr. Seuss. Women writers often used male pseudonyms in order to have their work reviewed and published without prejudice.

Charles Lutwidge Dodgson, who reinvented himself as Lewis Carroll, was another such author. As Charles Dodgson, he taught mathematics at Oxford University for nearly a half century. Apparently, his lectures gave no indication of his capacity for humor. To create his pseudonym, he took the Latin for his first name, *Carolus*, and the English translation of his Old German middle name, going from *Ludwig* to *Lewis*, and then he transposed them. From this comes the softer, more lyrical, Lewis Carroll. His most famous children's books? *Alice in Wonderland* and *Through the Looking Glass*.

Into *The Walrus and the Carpenter*

The Walrus and the Carpenter comes from Lewis Carroll's *Through the Looking Glass*. Alice hears the poem from the twins, Tweedledee and Tweedledum. Afterwards, she offers her opinion of the Walrus and the Carpenter. As you read the poem, determine your opinion of the two characters. Later, you can compare your opinion with Alice's.

Focusing on Narrative Poetry

Poets write **narrative** poems on all kinds of subjects. They may retell a historical event, recount the life of a famous person, or simply relate a story that the poet has invented. Narrative poems may be very serious or very silly. *The Walrus and the Carpenter* is an example of a made up story, a very humorous one. As you read the poem, look for the elements of the narrative poem as well as for the ways that Lewis Carroll creates humor.

The Walrus and the Carpenter

Lewis Carroll

The sun was shining on the sea,
    Shining with all his might:
He did his very best to make
    The billows smooth and bright—
5 And this was odd, because it was
    The middle of the night.

The moon was shining sulkily,[1]
    Because she thought the sun
Had no business to be there
10   After the day was done—
"It's very rude of him," she said,
    "To come and spoil the fun!"

The sea was as wet as wet could be,
    The sands were as dry as dry.
15 You could not see a cloud, because
    No cloud was in the sky:
No birds were flying overhead—
    There were no birds to fly.

The Walrus and the Carpenter
20   Were walking close at hand:
They wept like anything to see
    Such quantities of sand:
"If this were only cleared away,"
    They said, "it *would* be grand!"

25 "If seven maids with seven mops
    Swept it for half a year,
Do you suppose," the Walrus said,
    "That they could get it clear?"
"I doubt it," said the Carpenter,
30   And shed a bitter tear.

"O Oysters, come and walk with us!"
    The Walrus did beseech.[2]
"A pleasant talk, a pleasant walk,
    Along the briny[3] beach:
35 We cannot do with more than four,
    To give a hand to each."

The eldest Oyster winked his eye,
    But never a word he said.
The eldest Oyster winked his eye,
40   And shook his heavy head—
Meaning to say he did not choose
    To leave the oyster bed.

But four young Oysters hurried up,
    All eager for the treat:
45 Their coats were brushed, their faces washed,

Their shoes were clean and neat—
And this was odd, because, you know,
They hadn't any feet.

Four other Oysters followed them,
    And yet another four;
And thick and fast they came at last,
    And more, and more, and more—
All hopping through the frothy waves,
    And scrambling to the shore.

The Walrus and the Carpenter
    Walked on a mile or so,
And then they rested on a rock
    Conveniently low:
And all the little oysters stood
    And waited in a row.

"The time has come," the Walrus said,
    "To talk of many things:
Of shoes—and ships—and sealing-wax[4]—
    Of cabbages—and kings—
And why the sea is boiling hot—
    And whether pigs have wings."

"But wait a bit," the Oysters cried,
    "Before we have our chat;
For some of us are out of breath,
    And all of us are fat!"
"No hurry!" said the Carpenter.
    They thanked him much for that.

"A loaf of bread," the Walrus said,
    "Is what we chiefly need:
Pepper and vinegar besides
    Are very good indeed—
Now if you're ready, Oysters dear,
    We can begin to feed."

"But not on us!" the Oysters cried,
    Turning a little blue.
"After such kindness, that would be
    A dismal thing to do!"
"The night is fine," the Walrus said.
    "Do you admire the view?

"It was so kind of you to come!
    And you are very nice!"
The Carpenter said nothing but
    "Cut us another slice.
I wish you were not quite so deaf—
    I've had to ask you twice!"

"It seems a shame," the Walrus said,
    "To play them such a trick,
After we've brought them out so far,
    And make them trot so quick!"
The Carpenter said nothing but
    "The butter's spread too thick!"

"I weep for you," the Walrus said:
    "I deeply sympathize."
With sobs and tears he sorted out
    Those of the largest size,
Holding his pocket handkerchief
    Before his streaming eyes.

"O Oysters," said the Carpenter,
    "You've had a pleasant run!
Shall we be trotting home again?"
    But answer came there none—
And this was scarcely odd, because
    They'd eaten every one.

---

1. Here, *sulkily* (SUL kil lee) means moodily.
2. To *beseech* (bih SEECH) means to beg eagerly.
3. Here, *briny* (BRY nee) means salty.
4. *Sealing-wax* is a substance made from resin, that becomes soft when heated, and then hardens. It may still be used to seal letters and documents, although it was more popular in the days when there were no envelopes with glue. Often people would press their own insignia into the wax drop with a sealing ring.

Studying the Selection

First Impressions

Do you feel sorry for the oysters? Why?

✔ Quick Review

1. Sketch a picture that illustrates the first three stanzas of the poem.
2. What are the Walrus and the Carpenter discussing before they meet the oysters?
3. What invitation do the Walrus and the Carpenter make the oysters? Who accepts? How do they dress?
4. What does the Walrus want to discuss?
5. Why do the Walrus and the Carpenter need bread, pepper, and vinegar?
6. What happens to the oysters? How do the Walrus and the Carpenter react?

In-depth Thinking

7. Why does the eldest oyster wink? Does he know what is going to happen? Should he have warned the young oysters?
8. What do you think of the characters, the Walrus and the Carpenter? Compare your thoughts with Alice's in *Through the Looking Glass*.

   "I like the Walrus best," said Alice, "because you see, he was a *little* sorry for the poor oysters."

   "He ate more than the Carpenter, though," said Tweedledee. "You see, he held his handkerchief in front, so that the Carpenter couldn't count how many he took; contrariwise."

   "That was mean!" Alice said indignantly. "Then I like the Carpenter best—if he didn't eat so many as the Walrus."

   "But he ate as many as he could get," said Tweedledum.

   This was a puzzler. After a pause, Alice began, "Well! They were *both* very unpleasant characters—"

📁 Drawing Conclusions

9. Why might Hal Summers and Lewis Carroll have chosen to write *The Rescue* and *The Walrus and the Carpenter* as narrative poems instead of as short stories?
10. Are Shel Silverstein's *The Garden* and Lewis Carroll's *The Walrus and the Carpenter* too babyish for an eighth grade book? Explain.

Focusing on Narrative Poetry

Both *The Rescue* and *The Walrus and the Carpenter* are narrative poems, combining elements of stories and poetry. *The Rescue*, with its loving rescue of a boy trapped in a tree, is gently humorous. *The Walrus and the Carpenter*, Lewis Carroll's tale of the two characters and their encounter with a group of oysters, goes beyond gentle humor to laugh-out-loud silliness.

1. In *The Walrus and the Carpenter*, who are the characters? Is there any character development? Do the characters speak?
2. What is the plot and conflict of the poem? Is there suspense? Is there a climax?
3. Does the poem have rhythm, rhyme, other sound effects?
4. Find an example of personification in the poem.
5. Find examples of details, contradictions, and exaggeration that contribute to the poem's humor.

Creating and Writing

1. Which narrative poem do you prefer, *The Rescue* or *The Walrus and the Carpenter*? Write an essay in which you explain your preference.
2.
   > "The time has come," the Walrus said,
   >   "To talk of many things:
   >   Of shoes—and ships—and sealing wax—
   >   Of cabbages—and kings—
   >   And why the sea is boiling hot—
   >   And whether pigs have wings."

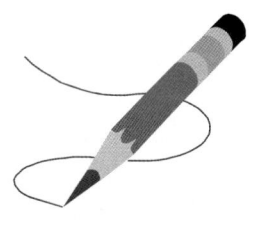

   Choose one of the topics the Walrus suggests and write a short, humorous poem on that subject.
3. Find another humorous poem you enjoy (you might choose another poem by Lewis Carroll or one by Shel Silverstein), practice reading it, then present it to your class.

Blueprint for Reading

Background Bytes

Narrative poems, such as *The Rescue* and *The Walrus and the Carpenter*, tell stories. By contrast, **lyric** poems share emotions and thoughts. However, narrative and lyric poems may *both* be examples of **lyric poetry**. Lyrical means "having the form and general effect of a song, especially one expressing the writer's feelings."

The lyre is a stringed instrument that has been in existence for several thousand years. One ancient lyre, dug up with eight others at the burial ground of Ur, is now on display at the University Museum in Philadelphia. Lyres are often associated with ancient Greece, where they symbolized wisdom and moderation. As lyres were typically made from wood or other vulnerable materials, evidence of early stringed instruments is often derived from iconographic (visual arts, visual representation) sources. For example, in Celtic society, depictions of lyres are found on early coins.

Lyres are made from a sound chamber or box—oval, round, or rectangular—usually covered with a taut, dried, animal skin (think of a banjo or a drum)—from which two arms protrude that are joined at the top by a crossbar or crosspiece. The strings, which vary in number depending on the area of origin, stretch from the crosspiece over the skin, or belly, to which they are attached by a "bridge" (think of the bridge on a violin).

The lyre was plucked with a plectrum, a small piece of metal or bone. Later, instead of plucking the lyre, musicians used a bow. A fingerboard was added, making the lyre an early relative of the violin. Singers and storytellers would play the lyre to accompany their songs and stories, which is where the word *lyric* comes from.

Into *The clouds pass* and *I Meant to Do My Work Today*

The last line of *The clouds pass* reads, "I am a rich man." Richard Garcia's words speak for the thematic experience in both *The clouds pass* and *I Meant to Do My Work Today*. What *is* the theme, or reason to be, of each of the poems that follow? Why does the speaker in *The clouds pass* close with this statement? Why does the speaker in Richard Le Gallienne's *I Meant to Do My Work Today* close by saying, "So what could I do but laugh and go?"

Focusing on Lyric Poetry

In **Background Bytes** we said that the word *lyric* comes from the word *lyre*. **Lyric poetry** is, in fact, appropriately melodic and song-like. In lyric poetry, poets share their thoughts and feelings. In *The West Wind*, for example, John Masefield shares his experience of the call of the west wind and the beauty of the west land. He does this in such a way that we *feel* and *hear* the call of the west wind. The poem is filled with vivid images and with the music of the wind—with rhythm, rhyme, and repetition. The poem is also imbued with Masefield feelings, as when he says in closing that he must return to his homeland, "the land where I belong."

As you read the next two poems, notice how these poets also share thoughts and feelings. Do you find one of the poems more lyrical, more expressive or melodic, than the other?

the clouds pass
Richard Garcia

The clouds pass in a blue sky
   Too white to be true
   Before winter sets in
   The trees are spending all their money

I lie in gold
   Above a green valley
   Gold falls on my chest
   I am a rich man.

I Meant to Do My Work Today

Richard Le Gallienne

I meant to do my work today—
    But a brown bird sang in the apple-tree,
And a butterfly flitted[1] across the field,
    And all the leaves were calling me.

5   And the wind went sighing over the land,
    Tossing the grasses to and fro,
And a rainbow held out its shining hand—
    So what could I do but laugh and go?

---
1. *Flitted* (FLIT tid) means flew swiftly or irregularly from place to place.

Studying the Selection

First Impressions

What kind of music would you choose for the singing of each of these poems?

The clouds pass

✓ Quick Review
1. In which season of the year would you place this poem?
2. List two natural phenomena that are occurring.
3. Where is the speaker? What is happening to him?
4. Where has the gold come from?

In-depth Thinking
5. To which senses does the imagery in the poem appeal? How does the imagery affect you?
6. Identify the metaphors and personification in the poem. How do these comparisons serve the theme of the poem?
7. How would you describe the speaker's mood?

Drawing Conclusions
8. Why does the speaker say, "I am a rich man"? Do you agree that the natural world makes us feel rich, or enriches our lives?
9. Richard Garcia, the author of *The clouds pass*, did not give a title to the poem. The title that is used comes from the poem's opening words. Can you think of a title that would have worked well for the poem? Why do you think the author did not name his poem?

I Meant to Do My Work Today

✓ Quick Review
1. What are five distractions the speaker encounters?
2. What choice does he make?

In-depth Thinking
3. What is the effect of the word *But* in the second line, the word *And* in lines 3, 4, 5, and 7, and the word *So* in line 8?
4. Identify the personification in the poem. What idea do these comparisons develop?
5. How would you describe the speaker's mood?

Drawing Conclusions
6. Would you have made the same decision as the speaker did in this poem? Do you think that he or she made the right choice?
7. In **Into the Poems** we suggested that the speaker in this poem, as well, would consider himself a rich man. Now that you have read the poem, do you agree? Why?

454 / POETRY

Focusing on Lyric Poetry

Narrative poetry and lyric poetry are broad categories that may overlap. In *The Rescue*, a narrative poem that tells a story, there is a lyrical description of the moon in the trees. Similarly, in *The Fish*, which primarily expresses the speaker's perceptions, feelings, and conflict about the fish, there is also a bit of a story: The speaker catches the fish, examines it, and finally throws it back into the water. (The other part of the story, of course, is the speaker's transformation from the beginning to the end of the poem.) The key to discerning the narrative and lyric components of a poem is to look at the interweaving of elements. It is this coming together that often creates memorable poems.

1. How does the speaker reveal thoughts and feelings in *The clouds pass*?
2. How does the poet make the poem "sing"?
3. Identify the speaker's thoughts and feelings in *I Meant to Do My Work Today*.
4. How does the poet make the poem "sing"?
5. Is one poem more lyrical than the other?
6. Does either poem have elements of narrative poetry?

Creating and Writing

1. Which poem do you prefer, *The clouds pass* or *I Meant to Do My Work Today*? Write an essay in which you explain your preference. If you like—or dislike—the poems equally, explain your reasons.
2. Write a personal narrative about a time you felt either literally or figuratively rich.
3. Choose a season of the year and create a collage of images you associate with that season.

Blueprint for Reading

Background Bytes

During the European Middle Ages, the armorer, who generally worked on the grounds of the feudal lord's castle, was the person who made the protective "clothing" and weaponry for the lord of the manor and his knights. In the 12th and 13th centuries, the armor of the European knights consisted of chain mail, interwoven rings of iron or steel.

In spite of the impressions most of us have from stories and from popular culture, plate armor was unknown in Western Europe during the Middle Ages. Plate armor was made of large steel or iron plates and linked by loosely closed rivets and leather, to allow freedom of movement. Plate armor had been worn by the ancient Greeks and Romans, but did not reappear in Europe until the 14th century. This was the fashion in western armor design until the 17th century. The armorer fashioned the mail to be worn underneath and fitted the plate armor individually to each knight.

Although a suit of armor could weigh more than fifty pounds, it was skillfully constructed and a properly trained individual could run, mount a horse, or lie down in the armor, which was practically indestructible. Even when dented during battle, armor could be fixed, and pounded back into shape. The armorer was a skilled and well-paid craftsman; the armorer's product was often beautiful, with designs etched into it. Some armor was covered in gold.

With the introduction of guns and gunpowder in the 1500 and 1600s, armor was increasingly outmoded: Armorers created heavier and thicker armor that would not be penetrated by bullets, but such armor interfered with the soldier's mobility. By the 1700s, plate armor was obsolete, because it was useless against improved firearms. It is interesting to consider that gunpowder, coming West as it did from China, was one of the most important elements in ending the feudal period. Castle walls, no matter how thick, could not withstand battering from cannon balls. This is an example of an invention that forced dramatic and radical social change. Can you think of any other innovations that resulted in widespread social change?

Into *Directions to the Armorer*

As you read the poem through for the first time, ask yourself what message Elder Olson is attempting to convey. We know that topically, the poem is talking about a knight or soldier, which is a strong visual and historical image for us. But Olson quickly moves to a more philosophical note—by stanza two the poem is fully devoted to the battles of the mind and soul! Our knight keeps vacillating (being indecisive, wavering in opinion) about whether he wants to fight at all and just *who* is the enemy.

Focusing on Theme

As must be clear from nearly all of the poems you have already read in this anthology, poetry, like fiction, nonfiction, and drama, has a **theme**: a statement of underlying truth, a message, a particular insight the work offers. Sometimes the theme is easy to understand—the poet lays it bare. With other works, the theme is more elusive (hard to express or define), and we have to infer its meaning. Frequently, the theme is related to the way the poem makes us *feel*. You can think of the theme as something you are more likely to *experience*, which is why it is often hard for us to describe it in thoughts and words, and why a theme is never stated.

Directions to the Armorer

Elder Olson

All right, armorer,[1]
Make me a sword—
Not too sharp,
A bit hard to draw,
5 And of cardboard, preferably.
On second thought, stick
An eraser on the handle.
Somehow I always
Clobber[2] the wrong guy.

10 Make me a shield with
Easy-to-change
Insignia.[3] I'm often
A little vague
As to which side I'm on,
15 What battle I'm in.
And listen, make it
A trifle flimsy,
Not too hard to pierce.
I'm not absolutely sure
20 I want to win.

Make the armor itself
As tough as possible,
But on a reverse
Principle: don't
25 Worry about its
Saving my hide;
Just fix it to give me
    Some sort of protection—
      Any sort of protection—
30 From a possible enemy
    Inside.

---

1. An *armorer* (AR mer er) is a person who makes and repairs armor and weapons.
2. To *clobber* (KLAH ber) is to batter severely, strike heavily, or defeat decisively.
3. *Insignia* (in SIG nee uh), here, refers to the mark, sign, or design upon the shield that identifies the division or feudal lord the knight serves.

Studying the Selection

First Impressions

What would it be like to wear armor? Which piece would be most important? Remember that armor included the cuirass (the plate armor covering the torso from neck to waist), chain mail (flexible strips of metal rings that protected the wearer from slashing strokes—although not a thrust—that ultimately was worn underneath plate armor), mail sleeves, leg harnesses, and hoods. A full suit of plate armor covered the wearer from head to toe, with holes for breathing and a small slit for the eyes in a helmet of forged metal.

✔ Quick Review

1. Which four specific instructions does the speaker give the armorer for his sword?
2. Which three specific instructions does he express for the shield?
3. Which two specific instructions for the armor?

In-depth Thinking

4. Why does the speaker want this particular sword?
5. Why does he want this particular shield?
6. Why does he want this particular armor?

Drawing Conclusions

7. Is this poem about a knight? How would you characterize this speaker?
8. Which enemies are more dangerous, the external ones or the ones within us?

Focusing on Theme

The **theme** of a poem is its underlying truth, the insight that it offers. Sometimes the theme is laid bare. For example, John Godfrey Saxe's *The Blind Men and the Elephant*, reads,

> And so these men of Indostan
>   Disputed loud and long,
> Each in his own opinion
>   Exceeding stiff and strong.
> Though each was partly in the right,
>   And all were in the wrong!

Here the theme is laid bare, although we must still sum it up: People argue the rightness of their opinions, without considering the ideas of others, even when they do not have the whole truth. In Elder Olson's *Directions to the Armorer*, the theme is fairly explicit in several lines in the final stanza.

- Find the lines that make the theme most explicit.
- Restate the theme in your own words.

Creating and Writing

1. Does the speaker in *Directions to the Armorer* give us an accurate glimpse of humankind's failings? Write an essay in which you give your opinion. Use specific examples for support.
2. In **First Impressions**, you speculated on a knight's most important piece of equipment. Finish the piece you began in response to your teacher's reading the first stanza aloud. Incorporate into your story, essay, or poem, some of these new terms. After all, what is a knight or a lady of the manor, without a *cuirass*?
3. Investigate the entertainments and food of the Middle Ages. (Chess, for example, dates back to that time period.) Did courts have court jesters at that time? Then organize with your classmates a day during the European Middle Ages—don't forget costumes!

Blueprint for Reading

Background Bytes

The Pulitzer Prizes are awarded each year to recognize outstanding achievement in American journalism, literature, drama, and music. When Joseph Pulitzer, a skillful newspaper publisher, wrote his will in 1904, he provided for prizes that would be an incentive to excellence in writing. He specified the annual award of four prizes in journalism, four in letters and drama, one for education, and four 'traveling' scholarships. In letters, awards would be made for an American play performed in New York, an American novel, a nonfiction work on some aspect of United States history, an American biography, and a work describing the historical and public service role of newspapers. But he gave the advisory board of the Pulitzer Prizes great discretionary power. In 1917, the first awards were made, and the number of awards has increased since that time to twenty-one. Their range has been broadened to include poetry (in 1922), music (1943), and photography.

At the time of the inception of the Pulitzer Prize awards, Edward J. Wheeler was president of the Poetry Society of America. He initiated a plan to bring poetry to the Pulitzers. He convinced a sympathetic patron to donate $500 for a poetry prize and turned the money over to Columbia University, where the university president announced the Pulitzer recipients each April. Wheeler did this both in 1920 and 1921. For two years in succession, then, poetry prizes were awarded. By 1922, a poetry prize came to be expected. Consequently, the Pulitzer family endowed an additional gift for poetry.

Robert Frost, author of *A Time to Talk*, won the Pulitzer Prize for Poetry in 1924, 1931, 1937, and 1940. The poem that follows shows us why.

Into *A Time to Talk*

Why is it important to respond politely to interruptions? Why do our parents raise us to have good manners, for example, to walk a guest to the door? Why say *please* and *thank you*, or answer the phone politely? How do you answer the phone?

The theme of *A Time to Talk* is closely related to the rules that regulate all of our interactions with other people. When we follow these spoken or unspoken rules, demonstrating that we have regard for others, we enhance the quality of their lives and of our own. Social and ethical rules bring a quality of graciousness into our lives.

Focusing on Theme

To understand or find the **theme** of a poem, we need to consider *what* the poet says and *how* he or she says it. First, we may look at the title. Does the title give any clues to the poem's meaning? It may, as in *Keepsakes*, and it may *not*, as in *The Fish*.

Next, we look at what the poem says. What is the relationship between the topic or subject of the poem and the events that occur? Are the behavior, words, and observations of the character(s) or the speaker what you would expect from someone doing what that person is presumably doing? Do the separate components of topic, action, words, setting, and character(s) come together in an unusual way? Are some particular aspects of the poet's observations or language very striking?

All of these considerations may provide clues that will help point the way to the meaning of the poem, to its theme. For example, in *Directions to the Armorer*, the speaker is simply not conforming to his role. In *The Fish*, the fisherwoman's thoughts are *not* what we would expect, and she does, after all, throw the fish back. The speaker in *When I Heard the Learn'd Astronomer* does *not* stay for the lecture. In fact, he is sickened, leaves the lecture hall, and goes out to look at the night sky alone. His behavior shows us the way to the point the poet is making. In *dandelions*, there is something odd about this war of weeds. Someone is taking something much too seriously and it is funny. Here, to find the theme, we really have to think about just *who* in real life is the aggressor. It is *not* the dandelions. They just grow. So what is the theme? Sometimes when we make war, it is because we feel attacked.

Sometimes, the poet gives it away in one or two or several lines, as in *Directions to the Armorer*. In *A Time to Talk*, Frost gives the reader a big clue in one of the lines. Can you find it?

A Time to Talk

Robert Frost

When a friend calls to me from the road
And slows his horse to a meaning walk,
I don't stand still and look around
On all the hills I haven't hoed,
5   And shout from where I am, "What is it?"
No, not as there is a time to talk.
I thrust my hoe in the meadow ground,
Blade-end up and five feet tall,
And plod: I go up to the stone wall
10   For a friendly visit.

Studying the Selection

First Impressions

Would you have behaved as did the speaker in this poem? Would you have stopped working?

✔ Quick Review

1. What is the speaker doing when he is interrupted?
2. What does he do with his hoe?
3. Where does he go? For what?

In-depth Thinking

4. What is a "meaning walk"?
5. What appears to be the speaker's attitude toward his work?
6. Why does the speaker make the choice he does?

Drawing Conclusions

7. Both the speaker in *A Time to Talk* and the speaker in *I Meant to Do My Work Today* are drawn away from their work. What kind of distraction does each speaker face? Which kind of distraction would you find more compelling? Why?
8. Are there ever times you would, in fact, choose to continue doing your work? Explain.

Focusing on Theme

1. Does the title, *A Time to Talk*, give any clues to the poem's theme?
2. Do you think the speaker in the poem has a conflict?
3. Describe Frost's use of simple words, alliteration, internal rhyme, and rhythm in *A Time to Talk*. Is his choice of language related to his subject or his theme? What do you think makes this poem so good?
4. What is the theme of the poem?

Creating and Writing

1. Consider these three possible titles for this poem: *Hills to Hoe*, *A Friendly Visit*, and *A Time to Talk*. Write an essay in which you discuss why the first two titles are not appropriate for the poem, and why *A Time to Talk* is just right.
2. Write a letter to your English teacher explaining why you just couldn't do your homework. You can make your reasons as ordinary (you had to babysit) or as farfetched (you were abducted by aliens) as you want. Be sure to make your reasons very specific. You may write in prose or verse.
3. Sometimes we forget to make 'a time to talk.' Why not call on an older neighbor or relative and schedule "a friendly visit"?

Blueprint for Reading

Background Bytes

Are you familiar with haiku poetry? Haiku is a form of traditional Japanese poetry, in which each poem is comprised of three lines only, which have five, seven, and five syllables respectively. With just seventeen syllables to write, some people might wonder—how difficult can it be to write a haiku? Actually, it's quite a challenge. With only seventeen syllables every word must count.

The *haijin*, the haiku poet, uses simple, direct language and concrete sensory images to describe a scene in nature. He (in Japanese society, most of the traditional poets are men) writes in the present tense, as if he is directly observing the scene. The key is catching a moment in time and place with *attention*. To do this, the haijin often starts with two seemingly unrelated images. Then the poet links the two images in a surprising or unusual way. Although the haiku may seem puzzling at first, ultimately the reader experiences the connection. The successful *haiku* produces an "Ah! I get it!" moment.

Does this haiku by the famous poet, Basho, give you a "haiku moment"?

An old quiet pond—

Frog splashes into water,

Breaking the silence

Into *Unfolding Bud*

Unfolding Bud is simple, concrete, and direct, much like a haiku. Before you read Koriyama's poem, try to write a haiku with the title of one of the poems you have read earlier in this anthology. Share your poem with your class.

Focusing on the Total Work

In the last lesson, to arrive at the theme of *A Time to Talk*, we took a look at what Robert Frost said and how he said it. Recall, even, his clever play on the word *stone wall*. But once we begin to sense a poem's theme, there is still one more step to take. What **impression** has the poem had on you? Did *A Time to Talk* make you pause and think about the value of friendship or about the simplicity of Frost's language? Did you laugh or marvel at the silly brilliance of *The Walrus and the Carpenter*? Did you find that *Dog at Night* was mysterious? Or that *The Rescue* was both lyrical and wise?

As you read and reread the next three poems—*Unfolding Bud*, *As I Grew Older*, and *Stopping by Woods on a Snowy Evening*—think about the way these poets have combined all the poetic elements we've been talking about—speaker and diction, imagery, sound, form, pattern, and theme—to create memorable works. It will be helpful to go back and review these literary components.

Unfolding Bud

Naoshi Koriyama

One is amazed
By a water-lily bud
Unfolding
With each passing day,
5   Taking on a richer color
And new dimensions.

One is not amazed,
At a first glance,
By a poem,
10 Which is as tight-closed
As a tiny bud.

Yet one is surprised
To see the poem
Gradually unfolding,
15 Revealing its rich inner self
As one reads it
Again
And over again.

Studying the Selection

First Impressions

Is Koriyama's Unfolding Bud itself an unfolding bud?

✔ Quick Review

1. In stanza one, what does the speaker find amazing?
2. What, on the other hand, in stanza two, is not amazing?
3. In stanza three, what, nonetheless, is surprising?

In-depth Thinking

4. How are an unfolding bud and a poem alike?
5. How does a poem have a "rich inner self"?
6. Which characteristics of haiku do you see in *Unfolding Bud*? When you finished reading the poem, did you experience a "haiku moment"?

Drawing Conclusions

7. Reread *Unfolding Bud*. What do you notice in the poem this time that you did not notice before?
8. To what else could you compare reading a poem?

Focusing on the Total Work

An unfolding bud is a perfect metaphor for reading poetry. As we've read poems throughout this unit, we have worked to "unfold" them, to discover their meaning. We want to be sure, however, that we put the poems back together.

As you think about *Unfolding Bud*, answer the following questions.

1. Who is the speaker of the poem? What kinds of words does the speaker use?
2. To what senses does the poem appeal? Is there figurative language?
3. Does the poet use rhythm and rhyme in the poem? Are the rhythm and rhyme regular or irregular? Is there repetition of phrases, words, or sounds? Does the poet use onomatopoeia?
4. Does the poem follow a regular pattern or is it free verse?
5. Is the poem a narrative poem? A lyric?
6. What is the theme of the poem? Now that you have "unfolded" all the elements of the poem, you are ready to put your ideas together.
7. Which of the literary components of the poem are the most important? How do they work together?

Creating and Writing

1. What is the effect of *Unfolding Bud*? Use the notes you made in **Focus** to support your opinion.
2. Another kind of Japanese poetry, the *renga*, uses a set of linked, five-line stanzas, of 5-7-5-7-7 syllables. What is interesting about a renga is that two people write it. The first person writes the first three lines of the first stanza. The second person finishes the first stanza, with the two seven-syllable lines. The second person continues and writes the first three lines of the second stanza. The first person finishes the second stanza with the two seven-syllable lines and then starts the third stanza, and so forth. A renga does not tell a story. Instead, each five-line stanza relates to the one before it, but also takes the poem off in a new direction. With a partner, try to write a three- or four-stanza renga.
3. There are many more kinds of Japanese verse. What can you find out about *waka, tanka,* and *rengay*?

Blueprint for Reading

Background Bytes

Some people complain that poetry is difficult, that it's only for scholars and for people peculiarly drawn to poetry. Robert Pinsky, the current Poet Laureate of the United States, doesn't believe that this is true—and, of course, most poets and poetry lovers would agree.

In 1997, when the Library of Congress selected him as the 39th Poet Laureate, Pinsky created the Favorite Poem Project. He wanted to make recordings of Americans reciting their favorite poems. There was a one-year open call for submissions, and during that time 18,000 people, from the ages of five to ninety-seven, from all kinds of backgrounds, education, and occupations, volunteered the poems they liked best.

The Favorite Poem Project took these thousands of letters and created several extensive collections and databases, available to the public from the Library of Congress Archive of Recorded Poetry and Literature and W.W. Norton Publishing Company. People have held "Favorite Poem Readings" across the country, from the White House, where President Clinton read *Concord Hymn* by Ralph Waldo Emerson, to the classroom. Pinsky, who has taught for more than thirty years and is a professor of English at Boston University, is proving that poetry really is for everyone.

Into *As I Grew Older* and *Stopping by Woods on a Snowy Evening*

Think about the themes of each of the poems that follow as you reread them. In Langston Hughes's *As I Grew Older*, the poet speaks to the way that the absence of light can snuff out or block the realization of a dream. What happens to him as he grows older? In *Stopping by Woods on a Snowy Evening*, is Robert Frost just describing a ride through the woods on "the darkest evening of the year," or is there greater symbolism in this poem?

Focusing on Reading Poetry

As with most poems—in fact, as with most music—*As I Grew Older* and *Stopping by Woods on a Snowy Evening* grow on the reader as we become increasingly familiar with them. Read the poems once for their general idea. Read them again. Then read each poem aloud, slowly.

Robert Pinsky has said that, "If a poem is written well, it was written with the poet's voice and *for a voice*. Reading a poem silently instead of saying a poem is like the difference between staring at sheet music and actually humming or playing the music on an instrument."

As I Grew Older

by Langston Hughes

It was a long time ago.
I have almost forgotten my dream.
But it was there then,
In front of me,
5   Bright like a sun—
My dream.

And then the wall rose,
Rose slowly,
Slowly,
10 Between me and my dream.
Rose slowly, slowly,
Dimming,
Hiding,
The light of my dream.
15 Rose until it touched the sky—
The wall.

Shadow.
I am black.

I lie down in the shadow.
20 No longer the light of my dream before me,
    Above me.
Only the thick wall.
Only the shadow.

My hands!
25 My dark hands!
Break through the wall!
Find my dream!
Help me to shatter this darkness,
To smash this night,
30 To break this shadow
Into a thousand lights of sun,
Into a thousand whirling dreams
Of sun!

Stopping by Woods on a Snowy Evening

Robert Frost

Whose woods these are I think I know.
His house is in the village, though;
He will not see me stopping here
To watch his woods fill up with snow.

5   My little horse must think it queer
To stop without a farmhouse near
Between the woods and frozen lake
The darkest evening of the year.

He gives his harness bells a shake
10   To ask if there is some mistake.
The only other sound's the sweep
Of easy wind and downy flake.

The woods are lovely, dark, and deep,
But I have promises to keep,
15   And miles to go before I sleep,
And miles to go before I sleep.

Studying the Selection

First Impressions Think about *As I Grew Older*. Would you choose colors, or the absence of colors, if you were illustrating this poem? Imagine observing the main character of *Stopping By Woods on a Snowy Evening*. Make a quick sketch of the scene in the woods.

As I Grew Older

✔ Quick Review
1. Where was the speaker's dream, and how did it appear to him, a long time ago?
2. What rose between him and his dream?
3. What rose until it touched the sky?
4. What does he say about his hands? How do you understand this?
5. What does he do to find his dream?

In-depth Thinking
6. Explain the symbolism of the wall.
7. Explain the contrast between dark and light in the poem.
8. Is the speaker black, literally or figuratively or both?

Drawing Conclusions
9. What could the speaker do to break down walls?
10. Reread the poem, varying the tone and intensity of your voice so that it is expressive of what is in the speaker's heart.

Stopping by Woods on a Snowy Evening

✔ Quick Review
1. To whom do the woods belong?
2. What is happening on that night in the woods?
3. What does the speaker imagine his horse thinks about stopping in this place?
4. Why does the speaker leave?

In-depth Thinking
5. What kind of "promises" could the speaker have to keep?
6. What is the effect of repeating "And miles to go before I sleep"?

📁 Drawing Conclusions

7. What is the mood of the poem? Is there any particular line in the poem that for you sums up the atmosphere of the poem?
8. Does this poem remind you, in any way, of *A Time to Talk*, the poem by Robert Frost that you read earlier in the anthology?
9. Would you pick either of these poems for the Favorite Poem Project? Explain your choice. If not, what poem would you pick, and why?

Focusing on Reading Poetry

The questions below are the same ones we asked regarding the poem, *Unfolding Bud*. Answer these questions for *As I Grew Older* and *Stopping by Woods on a Snowy Evening*.

1. Who is the speaker of the poem? What kinds of words does the speaker use?
2. To which senses does the poem appeal? Is there figurative language?
3. Does the poet use rhythm and rhyme in the poem? Are the rhythm and rhyme regular or irregular? Is there repetition of phrases, words, or sounds? Does the poet use onomatopoeia?
4. Does the poem follow a regular pattern or is it free verse?
5. Is the poem a narrative poem? A lyric?
6. What is the theme of the poem?
7. Now that you have unfolded all the elements of the poem, you are ready to put your ideas together. Which of the literary components of each of the poems are most important in that poem? How do they work together?

Creating and Writing

1. Write an essay in which you analyze the impact of either *As I Grew Older* or *Stopping by Woods on a Snowy Evening*.
2. Langston Hughes promises to "Find [his] dream!" Frost has "promises to keep." What kind of promises have you made? Write a poem about the promises you have made to yourself or to others.
3. With your teacher, organize a "Favorite Poem Reading" for your parents, friends, and classmates. Select a poem to memorize and recite at the reading.

the Authors

Elizabeth Bishop (1911-1979)

Elizabeth Bishop was born on February 8, 1911. Her father died while she was an infant; her mother was repeatedly hospitalized. When she was three, her maternal grandparents took her to live with them in Nova Scotia. At age six, her father's family brought her to Boston, where she grew up. She attended Vassar College, during which time she met the poet Marianne Moore. Following graduation, Bishop resided intermittently in Europe. The first of her four volumes of poetry, repeatedly rejected by publishers, was finally published in 1946. In 1951, she became ill during a trip, and the freighter on which she had traveled left her in Brazil. She lived there for the next eighteen years. In 1969 she returned to the U.S. to be Poet-in-Residence at Harvard. Bishop often spent years writing a poem. *The Fish* has received an extraordinary degree of analytical attention.

Joseph Bruchac (1942-)

Joseph Bruchac was born in Saratoga Springs, New York, where his father was a taxidermist. He studied at Cornell and Syracuse Universities, and spent three years teaching English in the West African nation of Ghana. Subsequently, Bruchac taught creative writing and African literature at Skidmore College. He considered his creative writing classes with prisoners his most important teaching experience. His Native American ancestry stimulated an interest in the literature and history of native Americans. Bruchac has spoken eloquently about the powerful experience of listening to stories: "Storytelling—sitting down and listening to someone tell a story—takes you out of time, puts you in a timeless place. And when the story's over, you kind of blink and wonder where you've been and how you got back to where you are."

Lewis Carroll (1832-1898)

Born in Cheshire, England as Charles Lutwidge Dodgson, Lewis Carroll studied at Oxford University and later became a lecturer in mathematics there. He is world-renowned for *Alice's Adventures in Wonderland* and *Through the Looking Glass,* which have entertained generations of children and adults. In addition to these timeless classics, he wrote brilliant humorous verse and enchanting prose fiction. We can only marvel at his extraordinary inventiveness. Some of the words he created entered the Oxford English Dictionary, as additions to the English language. He also wrote essays on mathematics. *The Walrus and the Carpenter* was created at Whitburn Sands, Sunderland in northern England, where a statue stands to Carroll's memory.

Babette Deutsch (1895-1982)

Babette Deutsch was born in New York City. She attended Barnard College, one of the all-female Ivy League Seven Sister Schools, which was paired at the time with the then all-male Columbia University. Following graduation, she often lectured at Columbia. She translated Russian poetry, and was also a critic. She produced an interesting variety of work, both as a poet, and as a writer of juvenile and adult fiction.

Robert Frost (1874-1963)

Robert Frost was born in San Francisco. He was eleven when his father died, and the family moved to New England. He and his wife, Elinor White, were co-valedictorians at Lawrence (MA) High School. He studied at Dartmouth College and at Harvard University, but found college curricula too confining. For ten years he wrote poetry while operating his own farm and teaching in Derry, New Hampshire. The Frosts moved to England in 1912, where his first volume of poetry was published. Three years later, they returned to the States, arriving just two days after the U.S. publication of *North of Boston*. He received the Pulitzer Prize in Poetry in 1923, 1930, 1936, and 1942. His poetry is distinguished by its "lyrics of unforgettable beauty," its dramatic conversation, its ironic commentary, and its pastoral and philosophical undertones.

Richard Le Gallienne (1866-1947)

Richard Le Gallienne, a British journalist and author, was born in Liverpool, England during the Victorian period. Le Gallienne's life spanned both World Wars. He wrote sonnets and, in the broadest sense of the word, romantic novels. For a time, he worked as a reporter in New York City. In 1927, at the age of 61, he moved to France, where he resided until his death.

Edwin A. Hoey

Edwin Hoey enjoyed a 40-year career as a writer and editor. He was strongly invested in the education of youth, and worked for many years as the managing editor of *Read*. *Read* was a magazine that functioned importantly as a literature and language arts classroom periodical.

Elder James Olson (1909-1992)

Elder Olson was born in Chicago, Illinois. He received his BA (1934), his MA (1935), and his Ph.D. (1938) from the University of Chicago, where he also taught English for many years. He moved up the ranks from Assistant Professor to Distinguished Service Professor. In fact, he was a teacher for most of his life, working as permanent or visiting professor in many universities. He received prizes and poetry awards. He lived in Albuquerque, New Mexico.

Deloras Lane

In addition to her widely published *Keepsakes*, Deloras Lane is especially appreciated for her poem, *Invisible Indian*.

Langston Hughes (1902-1967)

Langston Hughes was born in Joplin, Missouri in 1902. He was raised by his grandmother until he was twelve, when he moved to Illinois, to be with his mother. Hughes began writing poetry in high school. Following graduation, he spent a year in Mexico and a year at Columbia University. He traveled to Africa and Europe. In 1924 he moved to Harlem, and his first book of poetry, *The Weary Blues*, was published in 1926. He was strongly influenced by Paul Laurence Dunbar, Walt Whitman, and Carl Sandburg. In poignant portrayals, his work describes the experience of black Americans. His poetry is much beloved, as are his novels, short stories, and plays. Hughes's life and work were enormously important in shaping the artistic contributions of the Harlem Renaissance of the 1920s.

Don Marquis (1878-1937)

Donald Robert Perry Marquis (MAR KEE) was born in the midwestern town of Walnut, Illinois. After moving to New York, he worked as a columnist, first, for *The New York Sun*, and subsequently for *The New York Herald Tribune*. From 1913 to 1925, he honed his skills as author, humorist, and social commentator. He suffered the tragic early deaths of his wife and two children. As a satirist, he mocked social trends and fads. His popular cockroach, Archie, was inhabited by Marquis's less cynical and more endearing alter ego.

John Masefield (1878-1967)

Born in Herefordshire, England, John Masefield's childhood was filled with the emotional hardship that inspires so many to write. His mother died when he was six years old, and his father passed away soon after. He was raised by his aunt who opposed his early literary efforts. She forced him to join the merchant navy when he was only 13. On his second voyage, he deserted ship in New York. He worked there as a bartender and in a factory, and finally returned to London in 1897, determined to become a writer. In spite of his brief tenure in the merchant navy, his best-known poems are about the sea. During World War I, he worked for the Red Cross. Poet Laureate of England from 1930 until his death, he also wrote plays and novels.

Leroy V. Quintana (1944-)

Leroy Quintana was born in Albuquerque, New Mexico. From 1967 to 1969, he served in Vietnam in the Airborne Unit of the United States Army. He received his BA from the University of New Mexico in 1971 and his MA from the University of Denver in 1974. Quintana has been both a university English professor and a family counselor. Among his many literary awards is a Fellowship from the National Endowment for the Arts. Quintana's Hispanic heritage has both influenced and inspired much of his poetry.

John Godfrey Saxe (1816-1887)

Although Saxe was a minor poet who died more than a century ago, he is still widely quoted. His work was repeatedly featured in the 1916 edition of Bartlett's Quotations. Nineteenth- and early twentieth-century literary critics and historians describe the poetry of John Godfrey Saxe as characterized by humor mixed with sentiment. Saxe, himself, is referred to as a lighter lyricist, whose writing is old-fashioned and imitative. His work is clever and facile, "but does not achieve the delicate fineness" of the great writers. Nonetheless, his broadly comic verse is still very popular today. Among his other works are *Early Rising*, *Sonnet to a Clam*, and *Rhyme of the Rail*. He was also a lawyer, an editor, and a politician.

Shel Silverstein (1932-1999)

Shel Silverstein was born in Chicago, Illinois. During the Korean War, he was a cartoonist for *Stars and Stripes*, the United States Armed Forces organ, and was stationed in Japan and Korea. At the war's end, he returned to New York City, where he worked as a reporter. He was also a composer and folk singer. Silverstein wrote poetry for children that expressed sophisticated themes appropriate for adults. He illustrated his own poems with classic pen-and-ink line drawings. His work was widely loved and appreciated—some of it seemingly sheer nonsense, but much of it also exhibiting a deeply abiding cynicism and sadness. His most famous book of children's poetry is *Where the Sidewalk Ends*. He lived in Key West, Florida, as well as on a houseboat in Sausalito, California. His passing was much mourned.

Louis Untermeyer (1885-1978)

Louis Untermeyer was born in New York into a family of jewelers. He left high school when he was fifteen, and worked in the family business. At the age of 37, he left his job to write full-time. Untermeyer was known for his anthologies of modern poetry, which included a wide variety of poetic forms. He also wrote literary criticism, children's poetry and prose, and biographies. He most enjoyed poems that parodied other works; those he wrote himself were among his finest products. At the outbreak of World War II, Untermeyer joined the Office of War Information, where he met Santha Rama Rau. He was the editor of Armed Services Editions, a wartime effort that published famous works of literature for the men and women fighting overseas. Untermeyer and Robert Frost were good friends.

Walt Whitman (1819-1892)

Walt Whitman was born thirty years after George Washington was inaugurated, and was a member of the first generation of Americans in the newly-formed United States. His father, a carpenter and farmer, admired Thomas Paine. Whitman's mother was his emotional touchstone, and together they coped with a series of devastating family crises. Whitman left school at eleven; his education came from museums, circulating libraries, and public lectures. Living alone by age 14, he became a newspaper apprentice and itinerant school teacher. Early on, he opposed slavery because it threatened white laborers. However, seeing a slave auction in New Orleans radicalized his views. In the 1840s, his poetry changed from tired, sentimental rhymed stanzas to intoxicating and revolutionary free verse. Many biographers have tried to trace the source of this transformation. Whitman became America's most influential and innovative poet.

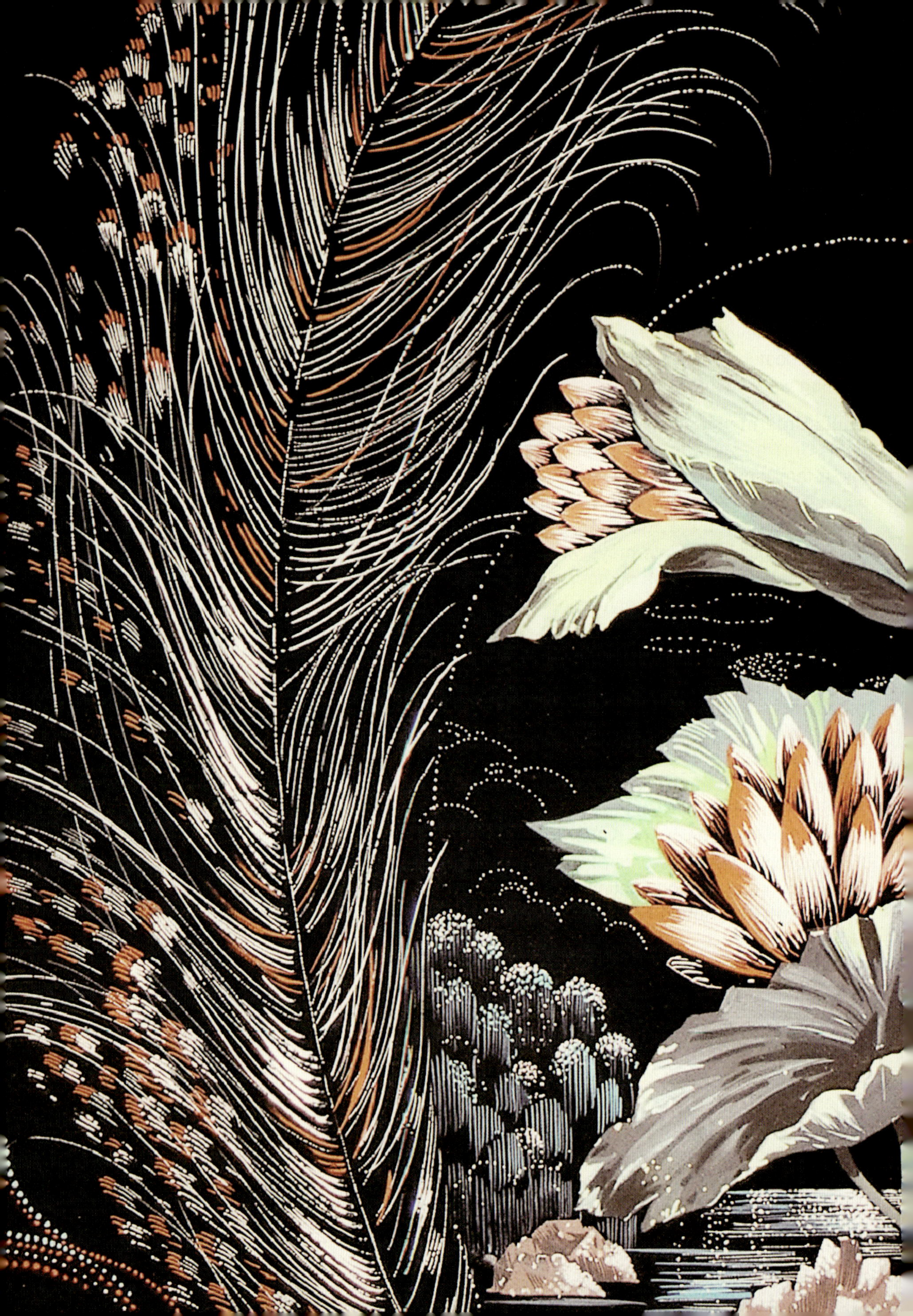

Every writer
 is a
  frustrated actor
 who recites his lines
  in the
 hidden auditorium
   of his
    skull.

DRAMA

Blueprint for Reading

Background Bytes

The time is 1940, World War II. France lies defeated, under German occupation. Life is tense and dangerous, for this is the second time this century France and Germany have fought. Their first encounter, World War I, began in 1914. After two years, Germany was winning, and France suffered heavy losses. With the entry of the United States in 1917, the tide turned against Germany. After the war, the Allies (France, Great Britain, and the United States) made the Germans pay great sums of money to the countries they had fought. Germans felt humiliated, and their determination to return Germany to its pre-war glory was a major reason for the outbreak of World War II.

During the inter-war period, France, especially Paris, became a world center for artists, writers, and musicians. Yet these creative and egalitarian people had no effect on the social structure outside the cities. In the country, hereditary landowners were considered aristocracy, the social superiors of laborers, storeowners, and farmers.

At the time of the play, the Germans have occupied northern France. Everyone must carry identity papers; those who fail to produce them on demand are arrested. Many French, including members of the upper classes, accept the Germans and even collaborate with them (assist them). Others fight, joining the Resistance, groups of loyal citizens and refugees from other countries who are determined to fight the Germans.

Into *The Pen of My Aunt*

The play opens with Madame, in her country manor house, and her only servant, Simone. (As we learn later, Madame's nephew also resides in the house.) When we are introduced to Madame and Simone, theirs is a mistress-to-maid relationship. As you read, look for dialogue and behavior that makes it clear the two women come from different social classes. Also, look for evidence that theirs is not a relationship between 'equals.' For example, Simone blurts out that strangers are coming up the avenue, while Madame lectures her on manners. What does this tell you about their individual priorities? What does this say about Madame's attitude towards Simone?

As the intruders enter, the Stranger greets Madame as 'Aunt' and asks her to identify him to the Corporal. Notice how the Stranger acts and what he says. Compare his manner with that of the Corporal. When the Stranger enters, who do you think he is? What is the Stranger's social class? His position in Occupied France? What do you suppose the author wants you to think?

"Play Within a Play"

All the elements of plot, setting, and characterization are in place:
- Madame, an upper-class woman who wants to retain her dignity and "the usages of civilization," in spite of the circumstances of war and the enemy occupation;

The Pen of My Aunt

- Simone, a 'simple' young woman, brought into Madame's home to work as a servant;
- A Stranger who says he is Madame's nephew;
- The Corporal, who represents Nazi rule.

This is the cast of the play that we are reading. But Madame, Simone, and the Stranger have also cast *themselves* in a "play within a play," which they act out among themselves in order to deceive the Corporal. Many French citizens enacted roles that were foreign and offensive to them, in order to stay alive during the terror of the Occupation.

What is meant by the term "play within a play"? In a drama, the dialogue is written down and the actors memorize their lines. For the "play within a play," the author has written the script to make it appear that Madame, Simone, and the Stranger are making up their dialogue as they go along, saying whatever comes to mind. Notice how they take cues from each other and build their story. What does this show about their attitude towards the Corporal? How does it make clear their absolute trust in each other?

Look for ways that Madame and Simone respond to the Stranger, and perhaps more interestingly, he to each of them. Notice their unspoken unity and resourcefulness: Their 'version of reality' changes whenever something new and unexpected occurs. What is your initial reaction when the Corporal returns, surprising Madame and the Stranger with his accusation against Simone? How does Madame save the situation? How important is Simone's role? How does the Stranger help to save himself?

Although from vastly different backgrounds, each of the women brings enormous courage, ingenuity, and commitment to the fight against tyranny. You will discover their strengths and see how they are used. You will see how Madame and Simone communicate with each other without actually saying what they are doing. Look for moments in the play when Madame and Simone break from their social roles and cross class lines to save the Stranger. Do Madame and Simone act independently of each other or are they working together? At which point does Madame's attitude towards Simone change?

Notice the cleverness and intensity of the angry dialogue between Simone and the Stranger. Is their meanness to each other ever 'real'? How is it a cover for the virtue that binds them? What is that virtue?

Once the "play within a play" is enacted, even the Corporal falls into its rhythm and is ensnared as one of its characters. How they keep him fooled, and the bait Madame uses to get him to unwittingly cooperate, are important elements of intrigue in *both* plays. But we realize, as the play comes to a close, that the cast has no idea how the "play within a play" really ends. At play's end consider this: *Madame and Simone get involved and risk their lives for a stranger, when they don't have to, and there is no apparent reason why they should.* Why do they do this? Is their sacrifice greater than that of the Stranger, who apparently *must* take the risk of fleeing, and whose life is already in jeopardy?

Word Bank

Occupation, Occupied, Papers, Collaborator, Credentials: Think about the terms **occupation**, **occupied**, **papers**, **collaborator**, and **credentials**. What do they normally mean? An *occupation* is a *job*, as in "What is your zebra's occupation?" *Occupied* means *busy, doing something*, as in "The children are occupied feeding the cat's food to the dog!" *Papers*? *Thin sheets for writing on*, or *newspapers*, or *scholarly essays*. One works with a *collaborator* on a literary work or a song: Rodgers and Hammerstein were famous collaborators. A person's educational and professional *credentials* are found in his or her resumé. What special definitions do these terms take on in the story?

absently	blackmail	contempt	incredulous	reflection
absurd	blunder	credentials	indignant	retards
acclimated	borne	deceitful	inexplicable	ruefully
anticipated	civilian	dryly	manhandled	speculation
assenting	combatant	fiend	miscreant	tact
barbarism	complying	hypothetical	personnel	testily
belated	consigned	implication	placidly	virtue

Focusing on Drama

The Pen of My Aunt is a classic suspense play, about World War II Resistance efforts in France. However, plays are *not* novels—in a novel, the author can take a reader inside a character's head. In a play, details of the story are communicated through speech, and we learn the characters' feelings and motivations through the words they say to and about each other.

At first, *The Pen of My Aunt* seems like a typical French comedy in which people wander through a country home, constantly misunderstanding each other. When Simone enters and Madame insists she leave and re-enter properly, we think this is going to be a comedy. But when she blurts out that German soldiers are approaching, we realize the play is set in wartime France. Notice how the tone changes at this point.

Daviot's one-act play *The Pen of My Aunt* uses plot, setting, and theme in a real world. In the country manor of an upper-class woman, we glimpse a pre-war social structure. Look for dialogue that shows this upper-class woman intent on preserving her status. Daviot paints a portrait of two women under the Occupation to show how class lines blur in the face of necessity. What shared goal brings Madame and Simone together? What might Simone feel when she rushes to help the Stranger? Does she worry about Madame's reaction? Look for dialogue that supports your opinion.

You have probably read stories that use symbols. Symbolism allows an author to use a thing or idea to express something else. Look for the important symbol in this play. How is it used, and what does it represent? Suspense is another key element in a play. How does Daviot build suspense? In most suspense stories, there is a point where the author wants us to relax, to think that all is well. When does it occur here? Once we reach it, how does Daviot restore our attention and move the plot to its conclusion?

The Pen of My Aunt

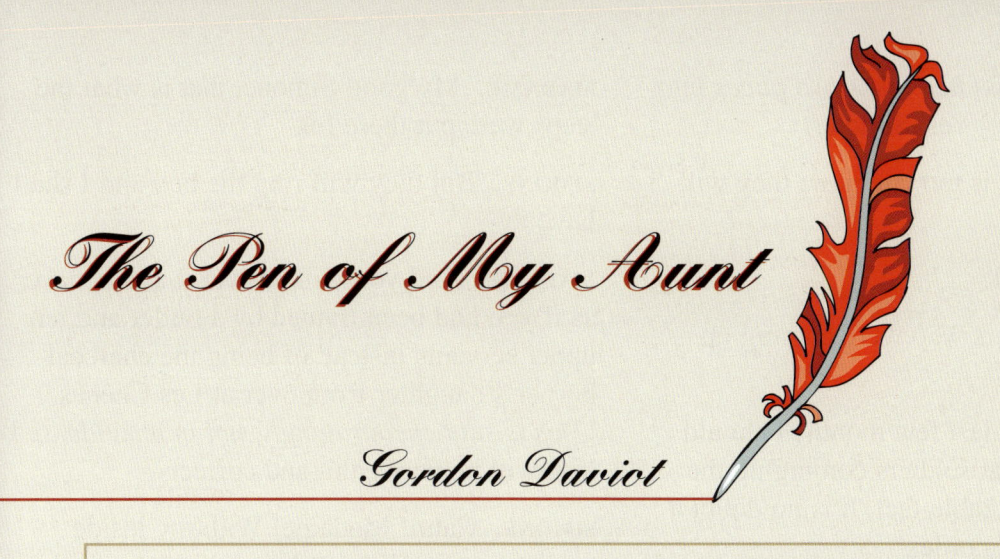

Gordon Daviot

[*The scene is a French country house during the Occupation.*[1] *The lady of the house is seated in her drawing-room.*[2]]

Characters: • Madame[3] • Simone[4] • Stranger • Corporal

SIMONE. [*Approaching*] Madame! Oh, madame! Madame, have you—

MADAME. Simone.

SIMONE. Madame, have you seen what—

MADAME. Simone!

SIMONE. But madame—

MADAME. Simone, this may be an age of barbarism, but I will have none of it inside the walls of this house.

SIMONE. But madame, there is a—there is a—

MADAME. [*Silencing her*] Simone. France may be an occupied country, a ruined nation, and a conquered race, but we will keep, if you please, the usages of civilization.[5]

SIMONE. Yes, madame.

MADAME. One thing we still possess, thank G-d, and that is good manners. The enemy never had it; and it is not something they can take from *us*.

SIMONE. No, madame.

MADAME. Go out of the room again. Open the door—

SIMONE. Oh, *madame*! I wanted to tell you—

MADAME. —Open the door, shut it behind you—quietly—take two paces into the room, and say what you came to say. [SIMONE *goes hastily out, shutting the door. She reappears,*

---

1. *The Occupation* (AHK yoo PAY shun) was the period from 1940-1944, when the Nazis "occupied"—invaded, controlled—France.
2. A *drawing-room* is a formal reception room in an apartment or house.
3. *Madame* (mah DAHM)
4. *Simone* (see MOHN)
5. *[W]e will keep the usages of civilization* means that, in spite of the Occupation, they will continue to behave in a civilized way, with good manners.

Word Bank

barbarism (BAR buh RIZ im) *n.*: a savage, primitive, uncivilized condition

shuts the door behind her, takes two paces into the room, and waits.] Yes, Simone?

SIMONE. I expect it is too late now; they will be here.

MADAME. Who will?

SIMONE. The soldiers who were coming up the avenue.

MADAME. After the last few months I should not have thought that soldiers coming up the avenue was a remarkable fact. It is no doubt a party with a billeting order.[6]

SIMONE. [*Crossing to the window*] No, madame, it is two soldiers in one of their little cars, with a civilian between them.

MADAME. Which civilian?

SIMONE. A stranger, madame.

MADAME. A stranger? Are the soldiers from the Combatant branch?

SIMONE. No, they are those beasts of Administration. Look, they have stopped. They are getting out.

MADAME. [*At the window*] Yes, it is a stranger. Do you know him, Simone?

SIMONE. I have never set eyes on him before, madame.

MADAME. You would know if he belonged to the district?

SIMONE. Oh, madame, I know everyone between here and St. Estèphe.[7]

MADAME. [*Dryly*] No doubt.

SIMONE. Oh, merciful G-d, they are coming up the steps.

MADAME. My good Simone, that is what the steps were put there for.

SIMONE. But they will ring the bell and I shall have to—

MADAME. And you will answer it and behave as if you had been trained by a butler and ten upper servants instead of being the charcoal-burner's daughter from over at Les Chênes.[8] [*This is said encouragingly, not in unkindness.*] You will be very calm and correct—

SIMONE. Calm! Madame! With my inside turning over and over like a wheel at a fair!

MADAME. A good servant does not have an inside, merely an exterior. [*Comforting*] Be assured, my child. You have your place here; that is more than those creatures on our doorstep have. Let that hearten you—

SIMONE. Madame! They are not going to ring. They are coming straight in.

MADAME. [*Bitterly*] Yes. They have forgotten long ago what bells are for.

[*Door opens*]

STRANGER. [*In a bright, confident, casual tone*] Ah, there you are, my dear aunt. I am so glad. Come in, my friend, come in. My dear aunt, this gentleman wants you to identify me.

MADAME. Identify you?

CORPORAL. We found this man wandering in the woods—

---

6. A *billeting order* directs the owner of a private home to provide lodging for military personnel.
7. *St. Estephe* (sahn ess STEFF)
8. *Les Chenes* (lay SHAYN)

Word Bank

civilian (sih VILL yen) *n.*: a person who is not on active duty with the military

combatant (kahm BAT ant) *adj.*: engaged in combat, fighting; also, ready or inclined to fight

dryly (DRY lee) *adv.*: unemotionally, indifferently, coldly

STRANGER. The corporal⁹ found it inexplicable that anyone should wander in a wood.

CORPORAL. And he had no papers¹⁰ on him—

STRANGER. And I rightly pointed out that if I carry all the papers one is supposed to these days, I am no good to G-d or man. If I put them in a hip pocket, I can't bend forward; if I put them in a front pocket, I can't bend at all.

CORPORAL. He said that he was your nephew, madame, but that did not seem to us very likely, so we brought him here.

[*There is the slightest pause; just one moment of silence.*]

MADAME. But of course this is my nephew.

CORPORAL. He is?

MADAME. Certainly.

CORPORAL. He lives here?

MADAME. [*Assenting*] My nephew lives here.

CORPORAL. So! [*Recovering*] My apologies, madame. But you will admit that appearances were against the young gentleman.

MADAME. Alas, Corporal, my nephew belongs to a generation who delight in flouting appearances.¹¹ It is what they call "expressing their personality," I understand.

CORPORAL. [*With contempt*] No doubt, madame.

MADAME. Convention is anathema¹² to them, and there is no sin like conformity. Even a collar is an offense against their liberty, and a discipline not to be borne by free necks.

CORPORAL. Ah yes, madame. A little more discipline among your nephew's generation, and we might not be occupying your country today.

STRANGER. You think it was that collar of yours that conquered my country? You flatter yourself, Corporal. The only result of wearing a collar like that is varicose veins¹³ in the head.

MADAME. [*Repressive*] Please! My dear boy. Let us not descend to personalities.¹⁴

STRANGER. The matter is not personal, my good aunt, but scientific. Wearing a collar like that retards the flow of fresh blood to the head, with the most disastrous consequences to the gray matter of the brain.¹⁵ The hypothetical gray matter. In fact, I have a theory—

CORPORAL. Monsieur,¹⁶ your theories do not interest me.

---

9. A *corporal* (KOR por uhl) is a non-commissioned officer, ranking above private, first-class.
10. *Papers* (PAY purrs) refers to documents one must carry for purposes of identification and for government or military control of individuals.
11. *Flouting* (FLOU ting) means to treat with scorn. Here, *appearances* (ap PEER enn sez) refers to outward impressions, indications, or circumstances.
12. If *convention* (kun VEN shun) is *anathema* (uh NATH uh muh) to them, this means that they hate following accepted rules and procedures.
13. *Varicose veins* (VAIR ih kose VAYNZ) are enlarged or swollen veins.
14. To *descend to personalities* is to sink to insults, disparaging, or offensive remarks.
15. The *gray matter of the brain* refers to the brain cells that make it possible for humans to reason.
16. *Monsieur* (meh SYOOHR) is French for mister or sir.

Word Bank

inexplicable (in EKS plik uh bul) *adj.*: incapable of being explained
assenting (as SENT ing) *v.*: agreeing
contempt (kun TEMPT) *n.*: scorn; disdain for anything considered base or vile
borne (BORN) *v.*: endured, tolerated
retards (ree TARDZ) *v.*: slows down, delays, hinders
hypothetical (HY poh THET ik uhl) *adj.*: assumed to exist; supposed

STRANGER. No? You do not find speculation interesting?

CORPORAL. In this world one judges by results.

STRANGER. [*After a slight pause of reflection*] I see. The collared conqueror sits in the high places, while the collarless conquered lies about in the woods. And who comes best out of that, would you say? Tell me, Corporal, as man to man, do you never have a mad, secret desire to lie unbuttoned in a wood?

CORPORAL. I have only one desire, monsieur, and that is to see your papers.

STRANGER. [*Taken off-guard and filling in time*] My papers?

MADAME. But is that necessary, Corporal? I have already told you that—

CORPORAL. I know that madame is a very good collaborator[17] and in good standing—

---

17. A *collaborator* (koh LAB oh RAYT er) is a person who works with, or assists an enemy invader of his or her country.

Word Bank speculation (SPECK yoo LAY shun) *n.*: consideration of some subject; guessing
reflection (ree FLECK shun) *n.*: careful consideration; the act of thinking; pondering

MADAME. In that case—

CORPORAL. But when we begin an affair we like to finish it. I have asked to see monsieur's papers, and the matter will not be finished until I have seen them.

MADAME. You acknowledge that I am in "good standing," Corporal?

CORPORAL. So I have heard, madame.

MADAME. Then I must consider it a discourtesy on your part to demand my nephew's credentials.

CORPORAL. It is no reflection[18] on madame. It is a matter of routine, nothing more.

STRANGER. [*Murmuring*] The great master Routine.

MADAME. To ask for his papers was routine; to insist on their production is discourtesy. I shall say so to your Commanding Officer.

CORPORAL. Very good, madame. In the meantime, I shall inspect your nephew's papers.

MADAME. And what if I—

STRANGER. [*Quietly*] You may as well give it up, my dear. You could as easily turn a steamroller. They have only one idea at a time. If the Corporal's heart is set on seeing my papers, he shall see them. [*Moving toward the door*] I left them in the pocket of my coat.

SIMONE. [*Unexpectedly, from the background*] Not in your *linen* coat?

STRANGER. [*Pausing*] Yes. Why?

SIMONE. [*With apparently growing anxiety*] Your *cream* linen coat? The one you were wearing yesterday?

STRANGER. Certainly.

SIMONE. Merciful Heaven! I sent it to the laundry!

STRANGER. To the laundry!

SIMONE. Yes, monsieur; this morning; in the basket.

STRANGER. [*In incredulous anger*] You sent my coat, *with my papers in the pocket*, to the laundry!

SIMONE. [*Defensive and combatant*] I didn't know monsieur's papers were in the pocket.

STRANGER. You didn't know! You didn't know that a packet of documents weighing half a ton were in the pocket. An identity card, a *laisser passer*,[19] a food card, a drink card, an army discharge, a permission to wear civilian clothes, a permission to go farther than ten miles to the east, a permission to go more than ten miles to the west, a permission to—

SIMONE. [*Breaking in with spirit*] How was I to know the coat was heavy! I picked it up with the rest of the bundle that was lying on the floor.

STRANGER. [*Snapping her head off*] My coat was on the back of the chair.

SIMONE. It was on the floor.

STRANGER. On the back of the chair!

SIMONE. It was on the floor with your dirty shirt and your pajamas, and a towel and what not. I put my arms round the whole thing and

---

18. *No reflection on* means no unfavorable remark was intended.
19. *Laisser passer* (less say paah SAY) is French for a "pass" that allows a person to travel freely.

Word Bank

credentials (kred EN shals) *n.*: official identification papers
incredulous (in KRED yoo less) *adj.*: disbelieving

THE PEN OF MY AUNT / 487

then—woof! into the basket with them.

STRANGER. I tell you that coat was on the back of the chair. It was quite clean and was not going to the laundry for two weeks yet—if then. I hung it there myself, and—

MADAME. My dear boy, what does it matter? The damage is done now. In any case, they will find the papers when they unpack the basket, and return them tomorrow.

STRANGER. If someone doesn't steal them. There are a lot of people who would like to lay hold of a complete set of papers, believe me.

MADAME. [*Reassuring*] Oh, no. Old Fleureau[20] is the soul of honesty. You have no need to worry about them. They will be back first thing tomorrow, you shall see; and then we shall have much pleasure in sending them to the Administration Office for the Corporal's inspection. Unless, of course, the Corporal insists on your personal appearance at the office.

CORPORAL. [*Cold and indignant*] I have seen monsieur. All that I want now is to see his papers.

STRANGER. You shall see them, Corporal, you shall see them. The whole half-ton of them. You may inspect them at your leisure. Provided, that is, that they come back from the laundry to which this idiot has consigned them.

MADAME. [*Again reassuring*] They will come back, never fear. And you must not blame Simone. She is a good child, and does her best.

SIMONE. [*With an air of belated virtue*] I am not one to pry into pockets.

MADAME. Simone, show the Corporal out, if you please.

SIMONE. [*Natural feeling overcoming her for a moment*] He knows the way out. [*Recovering*] Yes, madame.

MADAME. And Corporal, try to take your duties a little less literally in future. My countrymen appreciate the spirit rather than the letter.[21]

CORPORAL. I have my instructions, madame, and I obey them. Good day, madame. Monsieur.

[*He goes, followed by* SIMONE—*door closes. There is a moment of silence.*]

STRANGER. For a good collaborator, that was a remarkably quick adoption.

MADAME. Sit down, young man. I will give you something to drink. I expect your knees are none too well.

STRANGER. My knees, madame, are pure gelatin.[22] As for my stomach, it seems to have disappeared.

MADAME. [*Offering him the drink she has poured out*] This will recall it, I hope.

STRANGER. You are not drinking, madame?

---

20. *Fleureau* (flewr ROH)
21. *Appreciate the spirit rather than the letter* refers to the idiom "the spirit rather than the letter of the law," which means to follow the general meaning or intent of the law (its spirit) as opposed to precisely following the actual terms or wording of the law (its letter).
22. *Are pure gelatin* (JELL a tin) is similar to the idiom "legs like jello," meaning one feels weak and shaky from emotion and from a resulting sensation in the legs.

Word Bank

indignant (in DIG nant) *adj.*: feeling angry at something considered insulting or unjust
consigned (kahn SYND) *v.*: handed over; delivered to
belated (bee LAYT tid) *adj.*: coming after the customary or expected time; delayed
virtue (VURR choo) *n.*: moral excellence

MADAME. Thank you, no.

STRANGER. Not with strangers. It is certainly no time to drink with strangers. Nevertheless, I drink the health of a collaborator. [*He drinks*] Tell me, madame, what will happen tomorrow when they find that you have no nephew?

MADAME. [*Surprised*] But of course I have a nephew. I tell lies, my friend; but not *silly* lies. My charming nephew has gone to Bonneval[23] for the day. He finds country life dull.

STRANGER. Dull? This—this heaven?

MADAME. [*Dryly*] He likes to talk and here there is no audience. At Headquarters in Bonneval he finds the audience sympathetic.

STRANGER. [*Understanding the implication*] Ah.

MADAME. He believes in the Brotherhood of Man—if you can credit it.[24]

STRANGER. After the last six months?

MADAME. His mother was American, so he has half the Balkans[25] in his blood. To say nothing of Italy, Russia, and the Levant.[26]

STRANGER. [*Half-amused*] I see.

MADAME. A silly and worthless creature, but useful.

STRANGER. Useful?

MADAME. I—borrow his cloak.

STRANGER. I see.

MADAME. Tonight I shall borrow his identity papers, and tomorrow they will go to the office in St. Estèphe.

STRANGER. But—he will have to know.

MADAME. [*Placidly*] Oh, yes, he will know, of course.

STRANGER. And how will you persuade such an enthusiastic collaborator to deceive his friends?

MADAME. Oh, that is easy. He is my heir.

STRANGER. [*Amused*] Ah.

MADAME. He is, also, by the Mercy of G-d, not too unlike you, so that his photograph will not startle the Corporal too much tomorrow. Now tell me what you were doing in my wood.

STRANGER. Resting my feet—I am practically walking on my bones. And waiting for tonight.

MADAME. Where are you making for? [*As he does not answer immediately*] The coast? [*He nods*] That is four days away—five if your feet are bad.

STRANGER. I know it.

MADAME. Have you friends on the way?

STRANGER. I have friends at the coast, who will get me a boat. But no one between here and the sea.

MADAME. [*Rising*] I must consult my list of addresses. [*Pausing*] What was your service?

STRANGER. Army.

MADAME. Which Regiment?

---

23. *Bonneval* (bone ev VAHL)
24. *If you can credit it* means if you can believe it.
25. *The Balkans* (BALL kens), known as the Balkan States, refers to the countries of the Balkan Peninsula in southern Europe.
26. *The Levant* (leh VANT) consists of the lands bordering the Eastern shore of the Mediterranean Sea, known for its mixture of peoples.

Word Bank

implication (IHM plik KAY shun) *n*.: real meaning of a remark; something implied or suggested as to be naturally inferred or understood

placidly (PLASS sid lee) *adv*.: calmly, peacefully, tranquilly

STRANGER. The 79th.

MADAME. [*After the faintest pause*] And your Colonel's name?

STRANGER. Delavault was killed in the first week, and Martin[27] took over.

MADAME. [*Going to her desk*] A "good collaborator" cannot be too careful. Now I can consult my notebook. A charming color, is it not? A lovely shade of red.

STRANGER. Yes—but what has a red quill pen to do with your notebook?—Ah, you write with it of course—stupid of me.

MADAME. Certainly I write with it—but it is also my notebook—look—I only need a hairpin—and then—so—out of my quill pen comes my notebook—a tiny piece of paper—but enough for a list of names.

STRANGER. You mean that you keep that list on your desk? [*He sounds disapproving.*]

MADAME. Where did you expect me to keep it, young man? In my inside pocket? Did you ever try to get something out of your inside pocket in a hurry? What would you advise as the ideal quality in a hiding-place for a list of names?

STRANGER. That the thing should be difficult to find, of course.

MADAME. Not at all. That it should be easily destroyed in emergency. It is too big for me to swallow—I suspect they do that only in books—and we have no fires to consume it, so I had to think of some other way. I did try to memorize the list, but what I could not be sure of remembering were those that—that had to be scored off.[28] It would be fatal to send someone to an address that—that was no longer available. So I had to keep a written record.

STRANGER. And if you neither eat it nor burn it when the moment comes, how do you get rid of it?

MADAME. I could, of course, put a match to it, but scraps of freshly-burned paper on a desk take a great deal of explaining. If I ceased to be looked on with approval my usefulness would end. It is important therefore that there should be no sign of anxiety on my part: no burned paper, no excuses to leave the room, no nods and becks and winks.[29] I just sit here at my desk and go on with my letters. I tilt my nice big inkwell sideways for a moment and dip the pen into the deep ink at the side. The ink flows into the hollow of the quill, and all is blotted out. [*Consulting the list*] Let me see. It would be good if you could rest your feet

---

27. *Delavault* (dell lah VOH); *Martin* (mar TEEN)
28. Here, *scored off* means deleted or removed.
29. A *beck* is a gesture used to signal, summon, or direct someone. A *wink* is a signal conveyed by opening and closing both eyes quickly.

for a day or so.

STRANGER. [*Ruefully*] It would.

MADAME. There is a farm just beyond the Marnay crossroads on the way to St. Estèphe—

[*She pauses to consider.*]

STRANGER. St. Estèphe is the home of the single-minded corporal. I don't want to run into him again.

MADAME. No, that might be awkward; but that farm of the Cherfils[30] would be ideal. A good hiding-place, and food to spare, and fine people—

STRANGER. If your nephew is so friendly with the invader, how is it that the Corporal doesn't know him by sight?

MADAME. [*Absently*] The unit at St. Estèphe is a noncommissioned[31] one.

STRANGER. Does the Brotherhood of Man exclude sergeants, then?

MADAME. Oh, definitely. Brotherhood does not really begin under field rank, I understand.

STRANGER. But the Corporal may still meet your nephew somewhere.

MADAME. That is a risk one must take. It is not a very grave one. They change the personnel every few weeks, to prevent them becoming too acclimatized. And even if he met my nephew, he is unlikely to ask for the papers of so obviously well-to-do a citizen. If you could bear to go *back* a little—

STRANGER. Not a step! It would be like—like denying G-d. I have got so far, against all the odds, and I am not going a yard back. Not even to rest my feet!

MADAME. I understand; but it is a pity. It is a long way to the Cherfils farm—two miles east of the Marnay crossroads it is, on a little hill.

STRANGER. I'll get there; don't worry. If not tonight then tomorrow night. I am used to sleeping in the open by now.

MADAME. I wish we could have you here, but it is too dangerous. We are liable to be billeted on at any moment, without notice. However, we can give you a good meal, and a bath. We have no coal, so it will be one of those flat-tin-saucer baths. And if you want to be very kind to Simone you might have it somewhere in the kitchen regions and so save her carrying water upstairs.

STRANGER. But of course.

MADAME. Before the war I had a staff of twelve. Now I have Simone. I dust and Simone sweeps, and between us we keep the dirt at bay.[32] She has no manners but a great heart, the child.

STRANGER. The heart of a lion.

MADAME. Before I put this back you might memorize these: Forty Avenue Foch,[33] in Crest, the back entrance.

STRANGER. Forty Avenue Foch, the back

---

30. *Cherfils* (share FEE)
31. A *non-commissioned* (NAHN kuh MISH ind) officer is an enlisted person—that is, someone who has enrolled voluntarily—who can be appointed any rank between corporal and sergeant major.
32. To *keep at bay* means to keep from advancing, encroaching; to hold in check.
33. *Foch* (FOHSH)

Word Bank

ruefully (ROO fuhl lee) *adv.*: bitterly and regretfully; sorrowfully
absently (AB sent lee) *adv.*: inattentively
personnel (purr son NELL) *n.*: the people who staff an organization
acclimatized (ak KLAH mah TYZD) *v.*: accustomed to a new environment

entrance.

MADAME. You may find it difficult to get into Crest, by the way. It is a closed area. The pot boy[34] at the Red Lion in Mans.[35]

STRANGER. The pot boy.

MADAME. Denis the blacksmith at Laloupe.[36] And the next night should take you to the sea and your friends. Are they safely in your mind?

STRANGER. Forty Avenue Foch in Crest: the pot boy at the Red Lion in Mans: and Denis the blacksmith at Laloupe. And to be careful getting into Crest.

MADAME. Good. Then I can close my notebook—or roll it up, I should say—then—it fits neatly, does it not? Now let us see about some food for you. Perhaps I could find you other clothes. Are these all you—

[*The* CORPORAL*'s voice is heard mingled in fury with the still more furious tones of* SIMONE. *She is yelling:* "Nothing of the sort, I tell you, nothing of the sort," *but no words are clearly distinguishable in the angry row.*

The door is flung open, and the CORPORAL *bursts in dragging a struggling* SIMONE *by the arm.*]

SIMONE. [*Screaming with rage and terror*] Let me go, you foul fiend, you murdering foreign creature, let me go. [*She tries to kick him.*]

CORPORAL. [*At the same time*] Stop struggling, you lying deceitful little bit of no-good.

MADAME. Will someone explain this extraordinary—

CORPORAL. This creature—

MADAME. Take your hand from my servant's arm, Corporal. She is not going to run away.

CORPORAL. [*Reacting to the voice of authority and automatically complying*] Your precious servant was overheard telling the gardener that she had never set eyes on this man.

SIMONE. I did not! Why should I say anything like that?

CORPORAL. With my own ears I heard her, my own two ears. Will you kindly explain that to me if you can.

MADAME. You speak our language very well, Corporal, but perhaps you are not so quick to understand.

CORPORAL. I understand perfectly.

MADAME. What Simone was saying to the gardener was no doubt what she was announcing to all and sundry[37] at the pitch of her voice this morning.

CORPORAL. [*Unbelieving*] And what was that?

MADAME. That she *wished* she had never set eyes on my nephew.

CORPORAL. And why should she say that?

MADAME. My nephew, Corporal, has many charms, but tidiness is not one of them. As you may have deduced from the episode of the coat. He is apt to leave his room—

SIMONE. [*On her cue, in a burst of scornful rage*] Cigarette ends, pajamas, towels, bed-

---

34. A *pot boy* is a person who washes the dishes.
35. *Mans* (MAHN)
36. *Denis* (den NEE); *Laloupe* (lah LOOP)
37. *All and sundry* means everybody, collectively and individually.

Word Bank

fiend (FEEND) *n.*: a cruel or wicked person
deceitful (dee SEET fuhl) *adj.*: characterized by intentional misleading and concealment of the truth
complying (kum PLY ing) *v.*: going along with; obeying; following someone's wishes

clothes, books, papers—all over the floor like a *flood*. Every morning I tidy up, and in two hours it is as if a bomb had burst in the room.

STRANGER. [*Testily*] I told you already that I was sor—

SIMONE. [*Interrupting*] As if I had nothing else to do in this enormous house but wait on you.

STRANGER. Haven't I said that I—

SIMONE. And when I have climbed all the way up from the kitchen with your shaving water, you let it get cold; but will you shave in cold? Oh no! I have to bring up another—

STRANGER. I didn't ask you to climb the stairs, did I?

SIMONE. And do I get a word of thanks for bringing it? Do I indeed? You say; "*Must* you bring it in that hideous jug; it offends my eyes."

STRANGER. So it does offend my eyes!

MADAME. Enough, enough! We had enough of that this morning. You see, Corporal?

CORPORAL. I was so sure—

MADAME. A natural mistake, perhaps. But I think you might have used a little more common sense in the matter. [*Coldly*] And a great deal more dignity. I don't like having my servants manhandled.

CORPORAL. She refused to come.

SIMONE. Accusing me of things I never said.

MADAME. However, now that you are here again you can make yourself useful. My nephew wants to go into Crest the day after tomorrow, and that requires a special pass. Perhaps you would make one out for him.

CORPORAL. But I—

MADAME. You have a little book of permits in your pocket, haven't you?

CORPORAL. Yes. I—

MADAME. Very well. Better make it valid for two days. He is always changing his mind.

CORPORAL. But it is not for me to grant a pass.

MADAME. You sign them, don't you?

CORPORAL. Yes, but only when someone tells me to.

MADAME. Very well, if it will help you, I tell you to.

CORPORAL. I mean, permission must be granted before a pass is issued.

MADAME. And have you any doubt that a permission will be granted to my nephew?

CORPORAL. No, of course not, madame.

MADAME. Then don't be absurd, Corporal. To be absurd twice in five minutes is too often. You may use my desk—and my own special pen. Isn't it a beautiful quill, Corporal?

CORPORAL. Thank you, madame, no. *We Germans have come a long way from the geese.*[38]

MADAME. Yes?

---

38. *A long way from the geese* is a negative or disparaging reference to the source of Madame's quill pen, which is made from the feather of a large bird.

Word Bank

testily (TESS till lee) *adv.*: irritably; impatiently
manhandled (MAN hand uhld) *v.*: handled roughly
absurd (ab SURD) *adj.*: utterly, obviously senseless or illogical

CORPORAL. I prefer my fountain-pen. It is a more efficient implement. [*He writes*] For the 15th and the 16th. "Holder of identity card number"—What is the number of your identity, monsieur?

STRANGER. I have not the faintest idea.

CORPORAL. You do not know?

STRANGER. No. The only numbers I take an interest in are lottery[39] numbers.

SIMONE. I know the number of monsieur's card.

MADAME. [*Afraid that she is going to invent one*] I don't think that likely, Simone.

SIMONE. [*Aware of what is in her mistress's mind, and reassuring her*] But I really *do* know, madame. It is the year I was born, with two "ones" after it. Many a time I have seen it on the outside of the card.

CORPORAL. It is good that someone knows.

SIMONE. It is—192411.

CORPORAL. 192411. [*He fills in the dates.*]

MADAME. [*As he nears the end*] Are you going back to St. Estèphe now, Corporal?

CORPORAL. Yes, madame.

MADAME. Then perhaps you will give my nephew a lift as far as the Marnay crossroads.

CORPORAL. It is not permitted to take civilians as passengers.

STRANGER. But you took me here as a passenger.

CORPORAL. That was different.

MADAME. You mean that when you thought he was a miscreant you took him in your car, but now that you know he is my nephew you refuse?

CORPORAL. When I brought him here it was on service business.

MADAME. [*Gently reasonable*] Corporal, I think you owe me something for your general lack of tact this afternoon. Would it be too much to ask you to consider my nephew a miscreant for the next hour while you drive him as far as the Marnay crossroads?

CORPORAL. But—

MADAME. Take him to the crossroads with you and I shall agree to forget your—your lack of efficiency. I am sure you are actually a very efficient person, and likely to be a sergeant any day now. We won't let a blunder or two stand in your way.

CORPORAL. If I am caught giving a lift to a civilian, I shall *never* be a sergeant.

MADAME. [*Still gentle*] If I report on your conduct this afternoon, tomorrow you will be a private.

CORPORAL. [*After a long pause*] Is monsieur ready to come now?

STRANGER. Quite ready.

CORPORAL. You will need a coat.

MADAME. Simone, get monsieur's coat from the cupboard in the hall. And when you have seen him off, come back here.

SIMONE. Yes, madame.

---

39. A *lottery* (LOT uhr ree) is a method of raising money in which a large number of numbered tickets are sold and a drawing is held for prizes or money.

Word Bank

miscreant (MISS cree ant) *n*.: a villainous person
tact (TACT) *n*.: a keen sense of what to do or say to avoid giving offense
blunder (BLUNN dur) *n*.: a gross or careless mistake

[*Exit* SIMONE]

CORPORAL. Madame.

MADAME. Good day to you, Corporal.

[*Exit* CORPORAL]

STRANGER. Your talent for blackmail is remarkable.

MADAME. The place has a yellow barn. You had better wait somewhere till evening, when the dogs are chained up.

STRANGER. I wish I had an aunt of your caliber. All mine are authorities on crochet.[40]

MADAME. I could wish you were my nephew. Good luck, and be careful. Perhaps one day you will come back, and dine with me, and tell me the rest of the tale.

[*The sound of a running engine comes from outside.*]

STRANGER. Two years today, perhaps?

MADAME. One year today.

STRANGER. [*Softly*] Who knows? Thank you, and *au revoir*.[41] [*Turning at the door*] Being sped on my way by the enemy is a happiness I had not anticipated. I shall never be able to repay you for that. [*He goes out*] [*Off*] Ah, my coat—thank you, Simone.

[*Sound of car driving off.*]

MADAME *pours out two glasses. As she finishes*, SIMONE *comes in, shutting the door correctly behind her and taking two paces into the room.*]

SIMONE. You wanted me, madame?

MADAME. You will drink a glass of wine with me, Simone.

SIMONE. With you, madame!

MADAME. You are a good daughter of France and a good servant to me. We shall drink a toast together.

SIMONE. Yes, madame.

MADAME. [*Quietly*] To Freedom.

SIMONE. [*Repeating*] To Freedom. May I add a bit of my own, madame?

MADAME. Certainly.

SIMONE. [*With immense satisfaction*] And a very bad end to that Corporal!

---

40. *Crochet* (kro SHAY) is a kind of needlework.
41. *Au revoir* (oh rih VWAHR) is French for goodbye.

> **Word Bank**
>
> **blackmail** (BLACK mayl) *n.*: agreement or payment obtained from another person by intimidation and threats
>
> **anticipated** (an TISS sip PAYT id) *v.*: foreseen, expected

Studying the Selection

First Impressions

How do Madame and Simone act when the Stranger and the Corporal enter the house? What is our first signal that Madame is not a German collaborator? Whose point of view is used in the play?

✓ Quick Review

1. Why is Simone living in Madame's house?
2. Explain why the Corporal stopped the Stranger and brought him to Madame.
3. How do we learn the Stranger's true identity?
4. What act shows Madame's loyalties and tells us she is working for the Resistance?

In-depth Thinking

5. What does the collar symbolize in the dialogue between Madame and the Corporal?
6. What does the Stranger say about the collar? What do his words actually mean?
7. Describe the difference in attitude between the Stranger and the Corporal. If you met them, which one would you rather spend time with and why?
8. Compare Simone's submissive attitude at the beginning to her determined behavior as the story unfolds.
9. How does Madame's aid to the Stranger help the French war effort?

Drawing Conclusions

10. Why can Madame give the Stranger her nephew's papers?
11. Describe the deceptions that Madame and Simone employ to convince the Corporal that the Stranger is really Madame's nephew.
12. Why does the Corporal obey when Madame orders him to give the Stranger a pass and drive him to the Marnay Crossing?

Focusing on Drama

1. Write an essay discussing how the play weaves the idea of class structure into a tale of resistance. Back up your arguments with specific instances that illustrate Madame and Simone's desire to help the Stranger and, thereby, get the best of the Germans. Show how their action overcomes class distinction.
2. Explain the symbolism of the pen, and describe how it is used. Create a symbol that you would use in a story or play and explain how it affects the action of your story.
3. Describe how the play might end if the real nephew walked in before the Corporal and the Stranger leave.

Creating and Writing

1. Think of a situation in which you might be called on to protect someone, at the risk of your own safety. Write a brief dialogue in which you and the person you are protecting plot to outwit a third person who represents the danger. What is at stake, and how will you avoid compromising your own principles?
2. The point of view of a story controls our perception of the characters—sympathetic or unsympathetic. Writing from the Corporal's point of view, rewrite the scene in which the Corporal questions the Stranger about his papers.
3. Draw a map of the area surrounding Madame's house. Include the woods and the village, indicating German headquarters, possible Resistance strongholds and the spot where the Corporal found the stranger.

the Author   Gordon Daviot (1896-1952)

Gordon Daviot is the *nom de plume* of Elizabeth Mackintosh, better known as Josephine Tey—a second pen name associated with literate and stylish mystery novels. Bessie Mack, as she was called by her school friends, was born in Inverness, Scotland. After graduating Anstey Physical Training College, she taught at colleges in England. When her mother died in 1926, Mackintosh began to care for her invalid father and to write. Her first detective novel was published in 1929.

Mackintosh wanted to be a playwright. Her first drama, the 1932 *Richard of Bordeaux*, was a national sensation. None of her subsequent plays achieved the same success. Her mysteries are her best work; the last six were published in the final years of her life. Because Mackintosh guarded her privacy, biographers look to characterizations in her mysteries for clues.

AS IN AN EXPLOSION

I would
 erupt
  with all
the
  wonderful
   things
   I saw
    and
  understood
    in this
 world

NONFICTION

Blueprint for Reading

the Author

**Richard Lederer
(1938-)**

Richard Lederer was born in Philadelphia, Pennsylvania near the end of the Depression. His father was a textile salesman and his mother a homemaker. At age 21, he graduated from Haverford College, and in 1962 he earned a Master's Degree from Harvard.

Mr. Lederer taught English at St. Paul's School in Concord, New Hampshire, where he chaired the English Department for nearly thirty years. During his tenure at St. Paul's, he earned his Ph.D. from the University of New Hampshire. In 1989, he began writing full-time. As we see in *The Case for Short Words*, he delights in the intricacies of language. He is a fine tennis player and won the New Hampshire Doubles Championship in 1973.

Background Bytes

English has not always been spoken across six continents. Think about it! English is now the chief language of the United States, Canada, the United Kingdom, Ireland, Australia, and New Zealand—also serving as the official language of South Africa, India, and the Philippines. This is more than a tribute to the global presence of the British over the centuries; it testifies to the inherent usefulness of the English language. It has served as a national umbrella, sheltering various tongues and tribes, peoples who could not previously dream beyond a life in their village or clan. It has freed them from the tyranny of place and dialect.

Even today we have special varieties of the language—Sea English and Aviation English. Sea English uses approximately 1,500 simple English words. All navigation in international waters relies on Sea English. The alternative would be chaos. This is true, also, of air travel. All international flights use pilots who are fluent in English. Airports receiving these flights use English in their control tower transmissions. The English language provides a common denominator; a necessary element of trade and travel. It is relatively easy to learn English; simple communication is valued over verbal polish.

In the English language, nearly all basic concepts and concrete nouns (*war, Wednesday*) come from Old English, or Anglo-Saxon, as do most of the personal pronouns, auxiliary verbs, simple prepositions, conjunctions, and words for numbers.

The Case for Short Words

Into *The Case for Short Words*

The theme is hard to miss! The author urges the reader to use short words. *Why*? Answer that short question, and you have the theme. After you determine the theme, find the sentence or phrase that most strongly states the case.

Focusing on the Brief Persuasive Essay

To **persuade** is 'to convince, to advise, to induce.' Richard Lederer has used the essay form to address, as a teacher of ninth graders, a matter of concern to him. He proceeds to make his case, illustrating his point, finally, with a lean, impressive piece of student writing. Has he succeeded in persuading you?

Can *you* make a case about language use? Pick a topic to present to your classmates. Write five supporting sentences. These notes will be used for a writing exercise after you read the selection.

Word Bank

Monosyllable, Polysyllable: Most of us know what a *syllable* is, even if we cannot define the word as "an uninterrupted segment of speech." However, what are **monosyllables** and **polysyllables**? Sometimes, we can figure out the meaning of a word by dividing it into parts (here, **mono + syllable** and **poly + syllable**). If we know what *syllable* is, we can try to think of words we *do* know that use the prefixes *mono-* and *poly.* For example, do you know what a *monocle* is? Or what *monopoly* means? Both words have to do with *one*ness—the first is "an eyeglass for one eye"; the second, "sole control of a product or service." We can deduce that a **monosyllable** is "one syllable." Do you know what a *polydactyl* is? A *poloyglot*? *Polyester*? A *polydactyl* animal has many fingers or toes. A *polyglot* speaks many languages. *Polyester,* that cloth with which we are all familiar, is made up chemically of many "esters." So what is a **polysyllabic** word?

basked	eloquence	orator	prose	wrought
contemporary	hearth	plank	vigor	
descendant	monosyllable	polysyllable	vitality	

Richard Lederer

The Case for Short Words

When you speak and write, there is no law that says you have to use big words. Short words are as good as long ones, and short, old words—like *sun* and *grass* and *home*—are best of all. A lot of small words, more than you might think, can meet your needs with a strength, grace, and charm that large words do not have.

Big words can make the way dark for those who read what you write and hear what you say. Small words cast their clear light on big things—night and day, love and hate, war and peace, and life and death. Big words at times seem strange to the eye and the ear and the mind and the heart. Small words are the ones we seem to have known from the time we were born, like the hearth fire that warms the home.

Short words are bright like sparks that glow in the night, prompt like the dawn that greets the day, sharp like the blade of a knife, hot like salt tears that scald the cheek, quick like moths that flit[1] from flame to flame, and terse[2] like the dart and sting of a bee.

Here is a sound rule: Use small, old words where you can. If a long word says just what you want to say, do not fear to use it. But know that our tongue is rich in crisp, brisk, swift, short words. Make them the spine and the heart of what you speak and write. Short words are like fast friends. They will not let you down.

The title of this chapter and the four paragraphs that you have just read are wrought entirely of words of one syllable. In setting myself this task, I did not feel especially cabined, cribbed,[3] or confined. In fact, the structure helped me to focus on the power of the message I was trying to put across.

---

1. To *flit* means to fly or move swiftly.
2. Something that is *terse* is brief, concise, and forceful.
3. The words *cabined* (KAB ind) and *cribbed* (KRIBD) each indicate that someone or something is kept in an enclosure.

Word Bank

hearth (HARTH) *n.*: the floor of a fireplace, usually of stone or brick, often extending into the room

wrought (RAWT) *v.*: produced or shaped

short words are bright like sparks

One study shows that twenty words account for twenty-five percent of all spoken English words, and all twenty are monosyllabic. In order of frequency they are: *I, you, the, a, to, is, it, that, of, and, in, what, he, this, have, do, she, not, on,* and *they*. Other studies indicate that the fifty most common words in written English are each made of a single syllable.

For centuries our finest poets and orators have recognized and employed the power of small words to make a straight point between two minds. A great many of our proverbs punch home their points with pithy[4] monosyllables: "Where there's a will, there's a way," "A stitch in time saves nine," "Spare the rod and spoil the child," "A bird in the hand is worth two in the bush."

Nobody used the short word more skillfully than William Shakespeare, whose dying King Lear laments:

> And my poor fool is hang'd! No, no, no life!
>
> Why should a dog, a horse, a rat have life,
>
> And thou no breath at all?...
>
> Do you see this? Look on him, look.
>
> Look there, look there!

---

4. *Pithy* (PITH ee) means brief, forceful, and meaningful.

Word Bank

orator (OR uh tur) *n.*: a public speaker, especially one of great skill and power
monosyllabic (MAHN oh SILL LAB ik) *adj.*: consisting of one syllable

SOFT   PRAY   GLOOM   SAT   FIERCE

The Bible is a centerpiece of short words—"And G-d said, Let there be light; and there was light. And G-d saw the light, that it was good." These mighty lines live on in the twentieth century. When asked to explain his policy to Parliament,[5] Winston Churchill responded with these ringing monosyllables: "I will say: it is to wage war, by sea, land, and air, with all our might and with all the strength that G-d can give us." In his "Death of the Hired Man" Robert Frost observes that "Home is the place where, when you go there, /They have to take you in." And William H. Johnson uses ten two-letter words to explain his secret of success: "If it is to be, /It is up to me."

You don't have to be a great author, statesman, or philosopher to tap the energy and eloquence of small words. Each winter I ask my ninth graders at St. Paul's School to write a composition composed entirely of one-syllable words. My students greet my request with obligatory[6] moans and groans, but, when they return to class with their essays, most feel that, with the pressure to produce high-sounding polysyllables relieved, they have created some of their most powerful and luminous[7] prose. Here is a submission from one of my ninth graders:

For a long time we cruised by the coast and at last came to a wide bay past the curve of a hill, at the end of which lay a small town. Our long boat ride at an end, we all stretched and stood up to watch as the boat nosed its way in.

The town climbed up the hill that rose

---

5. *Parliament* (PAR lih mint) is the National Legislature of Great Britain, consisting of the House of Commons and the House of Lords.
6. Something that is *obligatory* (oh BLIG ih TOR ee) is something that is required.
7. *Luminous* (LOO mih niss) means shining or intellectually brilliant.

Word Bank

eloquence (ELL ih kwintz) *n.*: the ability to use language skillfully and powerfully
polysyllables (PAH lee SILL uh bulz) *n.*: many syllables; a polysyllabic word consists of several syllables
prose (PROZE) *n.*: the ordinary form of spoken or written language

504 / NONFICTION

small words at work

from the shore, a space in front of it left bare for the port. Each house was a clean white with sky blue or grey trim; in front of each one was a small yard, edged by a white stone wall strewn with green vines.

As the town basked in the heat of noon, not a thing stirred in the streets or by the shore. The sun beat down on the sea, the land, and the back of our necks, so that, in spite of the breeze that made the vines sway, we all wished we could hide from the glare in a cool, white house. But, as there was no one to help dock the boat, we had to stand and wait.

At last the head of the crew leaped from the side and strode to a large house on the right. He shoved the door wide, poked his head through the gloom, and roared with a fierce voice. Five or six men came out, and soon the port was loud with the clank of chains and creak of planks as the men caught ropes thrown by the crew, pulled them taut, and tied them to posts. Then they set up a rough plank so we could cross from the deck to the shore. We all made for the large house while the crew watched, glad to be rid of us.—
Celia Wren

You too can tap into the vitality and vigor of compact expression. Take a suggestion from the highway department. At the boundaries of your speech and prose place a sign that reads "Caution: Small Words at Work."

Word Bank

basked (BASKT) *v.*: lay in a pleasant warmth
plank (PLAINK) *n.*: a long, flat piece of timber; thicker than a board
vitality (vyt AL ih tee) *n.*: living force; ability to sustain or retain life; vigor and endurance
vigor (VIG er) *n.*: active strength or force; intensity; energy

Studying the Selection

First Impressions

Have you figured out the theme? Has Mr. Lederer persuaded you? Which sentence or phrase spoke to you most clearly?

✔ Quick Review

1. In regard to light, what do big words do? Small words?
2. What is not a law? But what is a sound rule?
3. The author gives a list of twenty words that presumably account for twenty-five percent of all spoken English. Make a list of the words and determine their parts of speech. Note that several act as more than one part of speech.
   - How many pronouns, that are *only* pronouns, do you find? List them.
   - How many articles?
   - How many verbs?
   - How many adverbs that are *only* adverbs?
   - How many prepositions?
   - How many conjunctions that are *only* conjunctions?
   - How many words have more than one function?

   Please list the words that belong in each category.
4. From which Shakespeare play does Lederer quote? Which Frost poem?

In-depth Thinking

5. What do you infer from the following statement: "Make them the spine and the heart of what you speak and write"?
6. Do you think "Short words are like fast friends" is an effective statement, or is Lederer overdoing matters?
7. What is the difference between a rule and a law? Before you consult the dictionary, you will want to refer to the use of the two terms in the selection.
8. Do you see any problems with the research data the author cites?

Drawing Conclusions

9. Why is the inclusion of the student composition so effective?
10. Speculate if there may be an additional reason for the author's enthusiasm for short words. Look at his comments regarding his students.

Focusing on the Brief Persuasive Essay

1. Take the five sentences you wrote before reading this selection and write a short essay, making your case. The title should read: "The Case for..."—whatever case you are making. Give several supporting arguments; try to use vivid metaphors and similes in presenting your case.
2. Go back to the limerick exercise. Using the correct form—five lines, *aabba*, and the appropriate meter—write a limerick about short words versus long.
3. Deliver a dramatic reading of the first four paragraphs of the selection. Make certain to read slowly, loudly, and to enunciate clearly. Try to use gestures to involve your audience in your presentation. You may use costumes, signs, and props if you think they are appropriate.

Creating and Writing

1. The candidates Short Words and Long Words have been running for public office. Long Words lost. Write a three-paragraph news article in which you report the five W's (**w**ho, **w**hat, **w**hen, **w**here, and **w**hy). Describe the issues, the election, the turnout at the polls. Interview both candidates and 'the people on the street.' Don't forget the headline!
2. Write a fiction piece or a travelogue using one-syllable words.

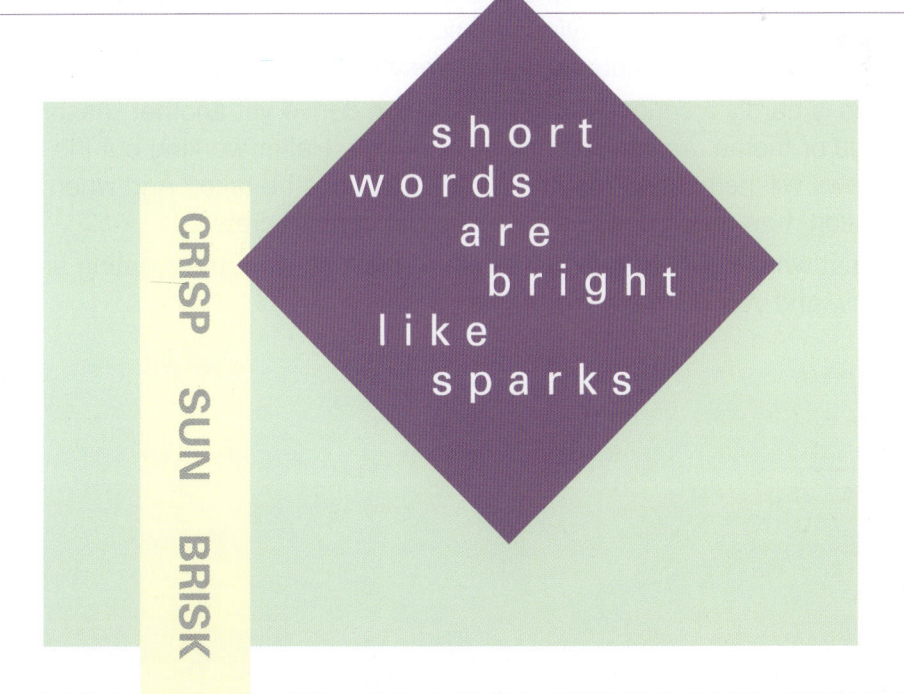

short words are bright like sparks

CRISP SUN BRISK

Blueprint for Reading

Background Bytes

Fly Away is a humorous article about a man who provides insects, and perhaps other creatures (he *does* mention "the snake room"), for use in the entertainment industry. This time, as you may guess from the title, he is asked to provide trained flies.

Do you know where flies come from? If not, this selection may be a partial answer for you. Long ago, many people believed in the theory of spontaneous generation. *Spontaneous* means 'arising from impulse,' or 'produced without external cause.' *Generation* means 'the process of coming or bringing into being.'

Spontaneous generation refers to the idea (erroneous, we now know) that living organisms—in this case, flies—grow out of non-living matter. Long ago, people saw maggots and then flies 'magically' appearing on meat. (There was no refrigeration then.) On the basis of their observations, they reasoned maggots and flies were actually *generated* by the decaying meat!

Into *Fly Away*

Sometimes, we refer to the theme of a selection as its *raison d'être* (RAY zohn DETRH), its reason to be. The most obvious reason is that the author simply wants to tell a story. In *Fly Away*, the author tells of a funny incident at work.

Now this is hardly a serious piece, but we can derive yet another reason for it to be, a message or theme. As you read, think about Mr. Helfer working out the solution. To which laws will he have to resort? What steps does he take? And when he has all the information, how much does he reveal to the camera crew?

Figure out what *Fly Away* tells us about problem solving and creating an illusion. Join the parts, and you will have the theme.

Fly Away

Focusing on Light Humor

What creates the comic effect in *Fly Away*? When we analyze humor, we should first think about the topic. Is the topic, itself, funny?

As you read, look for the lines, words, and expressions that are humorous. Write them down. What is it about these passages that catches your eye? Does everyone agree about particular lines? If not, that's fine. Humor is a personal matter.

> **Word Bank**
>
> Part of the source of humor in this piece is the relaxed tone and informal language. An example of informal language is the metaphor in, "I hoped I **hadn't bitten off more than I could chew**."
>
> As you read, you will see why the author's style can be called **informal.** The figure of speech 'bitten off more than I could chew' has a literal meaning quite different from its use in everyday conversation.
>
> The difference between the **literal and idiomatic meaning** can be shown easily. If we say someone 'bit off more than he could chew,' we mean the person 'started more than he could finish successfully.' Obviously, the literal meaning of 'stuffing more food into one's mouth than can be chewed successfully' is quite different from the ordinary use of the phrase. An unfamiliar idiom means nothing to us. Imagine what happens when translators are brought in.
>
> There are other examples of informal language in *Fly Away*. Write them down to discuss later. Are there any unfamiliar expressions that may be idioms?
>
> brood   hypnotized   skeptical   vial

Fly Away

Ralph Helfer

"I need 5,000 trained flies. Can you do it? Yes or no!" The voice at the other end of the phone was insistent.

"Well, I…"

"Of course you can't, Helfer. *Nobody* can. Look, I told the director I'd make a couple of calls. So, now I have. The answer is obviously NO!"

"I *can* do it," I said, fitting my sentence neatly in between my caller's constant jabber,[1] "but I'll need a couple of days."

The voice on the phone was silent a moment. Then: "You're kidding."

"No, really. Two days, and I'll be ready. What do they have to do?"

"There's this artificial, dead-looking 'thing' lying on the ground in the forest. The director wants thousands of flies to be crawling on it without flying away."

"Okay," I said. "Consider it done."

"No, wait. Then, he wants them *all* to fly away, on command—but not before."

"Okay, no problem," I said. "Two days."

"Wait. Did you hear what I said? They can't leave until he says okay. How are you going to keep them there, let alone have them fly away when he wants them to??"

"I'll stick each of their 20,000 legs in glue! Look, don't worry. Call me later, and I'll give you the figure. 'Bye."

Sometimes affection training was not the only answer. One could not "pet" a fly or earn its respect. I knew I would have to resort to the laws of nature for the answer to this one.

I'd had the opportunity to work with various insects in the past. But *5,000*! I hoped I hadn't bitten off more than I could chew.

I went to work, first converting an old box in which we'd been keeping crickets[2] (we raised them to feed to the tarantulas[3]). The box was about three feet high by two feet square. Patching up a few holes, I scrubbed it clean, fixed a crooked door, and set it inside the snake room.

The next day I visited a good friend of mine, Professor Jonathan Ziller, an entomologist[4] and researcher. His work area consisted of twenty to thirty lab-type cages made of fine-mesh wire. Each contained a different species of insect. Over a cup of coffee, I told him of my needs. We walked over to a cage that was being heated by a special infrared[5] lamp. Inside I could see

---

1. A person who *jabbers* (JAB burz) speaks rapidly, perhaps nonsensically.
2. A *cricket* (KRIK it) is a small, jumping insect noted for the shrill, chirping sound that it makes by rubbing its wings together.
3. A *tarantula* (tuh RAN choo luh) is a large spider with a hairy body; it has a painful bite.
4. An *entomologist* (EN tuh MAHL uh jist) studies insects.
5. An *infrared* (IN fruh RED) lamp uses the infrared spectrum to create heat.

massive swarms of maggots—fly larvae,[6] ready to be hatched into their next stage. As I stood there, the professor calculated the exact times when they would become flies. As his watch struck the "birthing" time, thousands of flies left their maggot bodies and were suddenly airborne, buzzing about the cage.

We both agreed that these flies, an unusually large type that resembled the horsefly, would be perfect. An added plus was the fact that they were all hybrid,[7] incapable of breeding. Hence, in releasing them I would not be running the risk of upsetting the natural balance of the environment.

The professor gave me a batch of fly larvae, which he'd calculated would hatch on the morning of the shoot, along with a vial of a special, harmless tranquilizer in a gas capsule. The gas would be released when the tip of the cigarette-sized plastic tube was broken. With the vial set inside the fly box, all the flies could be put to sleep within seconds. Once the gas had dissipated[8] in a matter of moments, the flies would awaken. The tranquilizer was, of course, harmless to people. A handshake later, I was off, gently carrying my brood with me.

On the morning of the shoot, all the flies hatched right on schedule. I loaded up and headed for the studio location. When I arrived, I was greeted by a crew of disbelievers with tongue-in-cheek[9] attitudes. Bets and jokes were being made in every direction, all in good-natured fun.

The director, a big, friendly sort, came over to me with a suspicious look in his eyes. "Is it true?"

"What?"

"That you can put 5,000 flies on something and they'll crawl around, but you can guarantee they won't fly right off?"

"It's true."

"Then when I tell you to let them go, they'll all fly away immediately?"

"Give or take a few."

"A few what?"

---

6. *Maggots* (MAG its) are fly larvae—the early, wingless, worm-like feeding stage in fly development.
7. Here, a *hybrid* (HY brid) refers to a species of fly that is bred from two distinct types.
8. Something that has *dissipated* (DISS ih PAY tid) has spread out and vanished.
9. The idiom *with tongue-in-cheek* means jokingly, ironically.

Word Bank

vial (VY il) *n.*: a small container, often made of glass, for holding liquids

brood (BROOD) *n.*: a number of young produced or hatched at one time

"Flies that won't fly away."

"If you pull this off, I'll double your fee," he said in disbelief.

"Ready whenever you are," I said, and headed for my fly house.

The camera was set. The "dead thing" turned out to be a special-effects monster baby that had supposedly died a while back and was now to be swarming with flies. Somebody was to walk by, and the flies would then have to fly away.

Everything was ready.

The skeptical assistant director yelled for the "fly man." One of my trainers and I carried the fly house over and set it near the camera. The loud buzzing of an enormous number of flies was obvious. Sheets of heavy paper prevented anyone from seeing into the box.

"Now, Ralph, I'll roll the camera whenever you say—okay?" asked the director.

"Sure, but everything has to be ready. I've only got 10,042 flies—just enough for two shots."

His look told me he wasn't sure whether I was putting him on or not.

"10,042—really!" he mumbled, and walked over to the camera.

With everything set, I opened the small door of the fly house. Hiding the gas capsule in the palm of my hand and reaching inside, I broke it open, closed the door, and waited for fifteen seconds. To everybody's amazement, the buzzing stopped. Next, I opened the door and scooped out three or four handfuls of flies. I shook them out as one would when counting a pound of peanuts. Putting the little sleeping flies all over the "body," I began to dramatically count the last few: "Five-thousand twenty, five-thousand twenty-one, five-thousand twenty-one...that makes it half!"

I told everyone to hold still, then I gave the flies a verbal cue: "Okay guys—Jack, Bill, Mary—come on, up and at 'em!"

Slowly the flies started to awaken, then move around. In a few moments the whole mass of them was swarming all over the "thing," but they were still too drowsy to fly, as my professor friend had told me they would be.

"Okay, roll!" yelled the director. The camera rolled on the fly swarm, and I shot a look at the crew. They appeared to be in shock. Then, having gotten enough footage, the director shouted, "Okay, Ralph, *now!*"

My great moment.

Word Bank **skeptical** (SKEP tih kul) *adj.*: doubtful

"Okay, group," I said to the flies. "Get ready: on the count of three, all of you take off."

The crew, absolutely bug-eyed[10] (forgive the pun), was hypnotized. "One," I counted. They looked from the flies to me. "Two."

"Three!" I yelled, clapping my hands and stamping my foot at the same time. Five thousand twenty-one flies flew up, up, around and around. The camera hummed, until the director, rousing himself from his amazed state, said, "Cut!"

The entire crew was silent for a moment, and then they burst into applause and delighted laughter.

"You did it, you really did it!" said the director, slapping me heartily on the back. "I'm not even going to ask you how. I don't even want to know. But if I ever need a trained *anything*, you're the man I'll call!"

Straight-faced, I said, "Well, actually, I've recently trained 432 flies to form a chorus line on my arm, and on cue they all kick a leg at the same time."

The director, poker-faced, looked straight at me. "Which one?" he asked.

"Which one what?"

"Which leg?"

"The left one, of course!"

We all broke up laughing and headed home.

---

10. To watch *bug-eyed* is to watch with eyes bulging in surprise.

Word Bank

hypnotized (HIP nuh TYZD) *v*.: transfixed; spellbound; fascinated

Studying the Selection

First Impressions

Draw a picture in which you demonstrate the literal meaning of one of the idioms you found.

✔ Quick Review

1. The author makes a joke about sticking the 20,000 legs of the 5,000 flies in glue. Since flies have six legs, what would be the actual total number of legs?
2. The author goes to visit Professor Jonathan Ziller for help with the fly project. What is Professor Ziller's field of study?
3. What kind of light bulb is used to keep the cage full of maggots at the right temperature?
4. How does Helfer put the flies to sleep briefly?

In-depth Thinking

5. When the author is originally contacted, the person calling is certain no one can fulfill the request. Why?
6. Why is it good that the flies are hybrid and cannot breed?
7. Why do the flies finally leave the monster 'body' and fly away?
8. Why does Helfer say he has recently trained a chorus line of flies to dance on his arm?

Drawing Conclusions

9. What skills are needed by someone in Ralph Helfer's profession?
10. What qualities are needed for Professor Ziller's area of research?

Focusing on Light Humor

Even when we have funny experiences, we may be unable to write humorously about them. Often the writer's style and language are what make the story funny. The following exercises will help you understand **light humor**.

1. Ask a parent or family friend to retell a true story about a funny event. Afterwards, make sure you have the facts straight. Then write up the anecdote and see if you have captured its humor. Remember to include dialogue and detailed descriptions.

2. You have copied examples of informal language from *Fly Away*. Some may be idioms. Here are some others:
   - I think he is just *getting a free ride*.
   - She is just *going along for the ride*.
   - Why does he realize that they are *taking him for a ride*?
   - I could use that one *in a pinch*.
   - The house has *changed hands* several times.
   - In the race, the two horses were *neck and neck*.
   - At the dinner, the host introduced the guests to each other in order *to break the ice*.
   - The teacher was able *to pick holes* in the student's argument.
   - Just before she performed in the school theatrical, her mother said, "*Break a leg!*"
   - After he lost the contest, he was feeling *down in the dumps*.

   List ten more idioms. Look through the dictionary to find verbs that, combined with prepositions, produce many idioms—for example, the verbs *put* (as in *put up*, *put up with*, *put away*, *put out*, and *put over*) and *beat*. Look for verbs with long entries. You may use some of the idioms above and those in *Fly Away*. Next to each idiom, write the definition and use it in a sentence.

3. Write a news article of several paragraphs reporting eyewitness reactions to the remarkable behavior of 5,000 trained flies at the filming of "Monster from the Forest Deep." Don't forget your headline, the five W's (**w**ho, **w**hat, **w**hen, **w**here, and **w**hy), and a direct quotation from someone on the set.

Creating and Writing

1. Write a description (at least five paragraphs) of how you solved a problem.
2. Describe a moment when you saw something you felt could not have been real. You can also describe someone creating such a convincing illusion you believed it for a moment. In this activity shut your eyes and remember with your 'mind's eye.' Sometimes, before falling asleep at night, it is easier to try this sort of exploration and careful recollection.
3. After doing the needed research, give an oral report to your class about fly characteristics, behavior, life cycles, or some other 'fly topic.' Draw at least one picture to go with your presentation. You need not submit a written report, but you will need notes for your presentation.

Blueprint for Reading

Background Bytes

Are you familiar with snakes? Have you actually seen one? If you have seen a snake, was it outside, in the wild, or did it star in a wildlife exhibit?

How do you feel about snakes? Do your feelings come from an *actual* encounter? If you have read Roald Dahl's *The Wish* it should be clear that the author is no fan of snakes!

In fact, if we can put aside our feelings for the moment, we might even come to appreciate the extraordinary beauty of the green mamba, with its nearly fluorescent green color. But for now, read the selection through once, just to see the events through the author's eyes. Then go back, and match it against the statements below, which come from the writings of naturalists and green mamba owners. Notice the differences!

a. The green mamba is an even-tempered snake that is not aggressive.
b. The green mamba prefers to hide from danger rather than confront it.
c. When faced with predators, green mambas will flee. Then the green mamba glides at speeds of up to seven miles per hour—twice the speed of any North American snake.
d. Green mambas often enter houses to hide in the thatched roofs.
e. The green mamba experiences the sense of smell through its tongue.
f. Although the green mamba senses vibrations through its tongue, it can also sense ground vibrations through its body.
g. The green mamba will hiss or strike when cornered or trapped. The whitish venom quickly affects the victim's nervous system.
h. The green mamba is a graceful snake and catches its prey—primarily birds and lizards—by waiting motionless for something to approach.
i. The green mamba can catch a bird in less than a second. The green mamba is different in that, after striking, it leaves its prey to die.
j. Green mambas are tree-dwellers, hiding in foliage. They favor citrus, cashew, coconut, and mango trees.
k. Although green mambas are capable of hunting on the forest floor, this is not common behavior.
l. In places with dense human populations, the green mamba becomes nocturnal (active at night).

Into *The Green Mamba*

After reading *The Green Mamba*, ask yourself if this is a story about a snake or a snake-man. Notice how the snake-man speaks to the snake. How would you describe his words and tone? Contrast the author's attitude with that of the snake-man. Who is more respectful of 'real' snakes?

The Green Mamba

Focusing on the Autobiographical Anecdote

What can we expect of an **autobiographical anecdote**? How accurate will a retelling of events be? If the reader is not relying on the author for accurate historical, scientific, or biographical details, how accurate need it be? Does it matter if bias or distortion creeps in, or if elements of drama are added? In fact, is any one of us capable of recalling events with absolute accuracy?

When we say something is exotic, we mean it is not native; it is introduced from outside or abroad. It may be foreign or strikingly unusual. We recognize immediately that this story is exotic: "Oh, those snakes! How I hated them!" (Unless we live in the tropics, most of us do not live among snakes.) Also, "Tanganyika," as a name, may be unfamiliar or foreign-sounding. The first two paragraphs are replete with details pointing to an exotic world ("replete" means "full of" or "abundantly supplied"). After your first reading of the selection, look for suggestions of a "foreign" setting in the first two paragraphs.

How does the author introduce and sustain the suspense? When you go through the selection the second time, compare the following two passages:

- "… its great size made me certain it was a creature almost as deadly as the black mamba, and for a few seconds I was so startled and dumbfounded and horrified that I froze to the spot." (This passage is from paragraph two, second sentence from the end.)

- "He was completely cool and unruffled. He didn't even raise his voice." (Here we have the final sentences of paragraph eight.)

Reread these two passages in context. Which is more frightening, generating greater suspense?

Word Bank			
abruptly	flailing	malevolent	tread
arcing	forlorn	manipulating	venom
dumbfounded	implement	millimeter	wavering

The Green Mamba

Roald Dahl

Oh, those snakes! How I hated them! They were the only fearful thing about Tanganyika,[1] and a newcomer very quickly learnt to identify most of them and to know which were deadly and which were simply poisonous. The killers, apart from the black mambas, were the green mambas, the cobras, and the tiny little puff adders that looked very much like small sticks lying motionless in the middle of a dusty path, and so easy to step on.

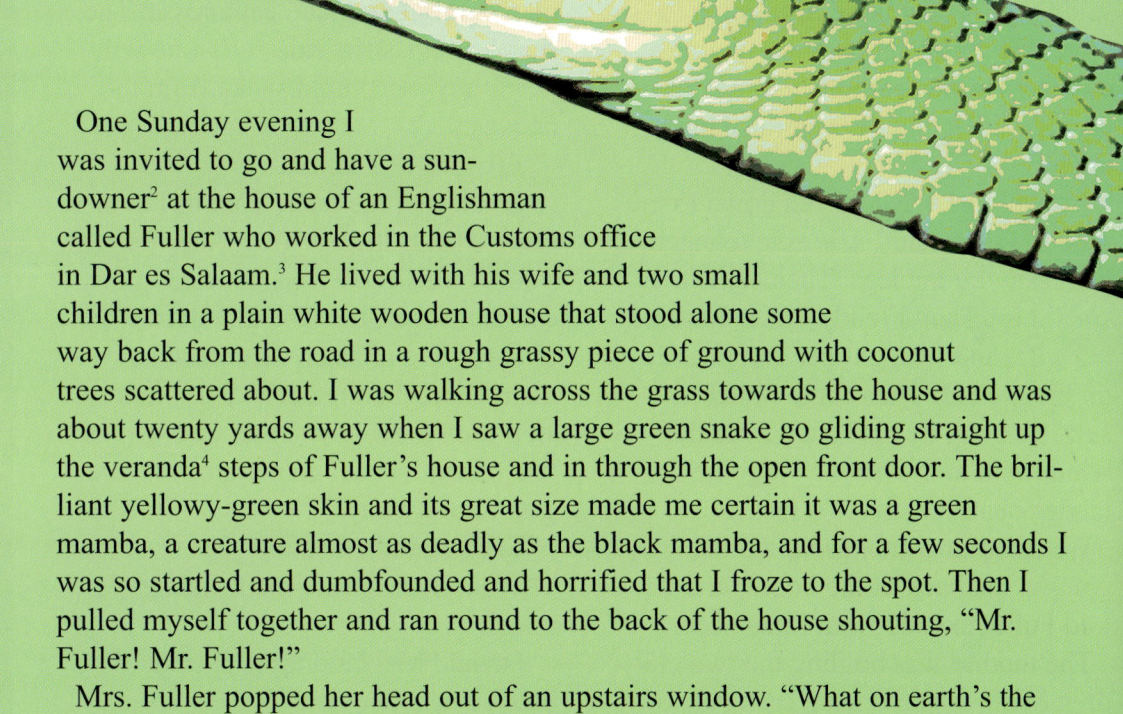

One Sunday evening I was invited to go and have a sundowner[2] at the house of an Englishman called Fuller who worked in the Customs office in Dar es Salaam.[3] He lived with his wife and two small children in a plain white wooden house that stood alone some way back from the road in a rough grassy piece of ground with coconut trees scattered about. I was walking across the grass towards the house and was about twenty yards away when I saw a large green snake go gliding straight up the veranda[4] steps of Fuller's house and in through the open front door. The brilliant yellowy-green skin and its great size made me certain it was a green mamba, a creature almost as deadly as the black mamba, and for a few seconds I was so startled and dumbfounded and horrified that I froze to the spot. Then I pulled myself together and ran round to the back of the house shouting, "Mr. Fuller! Mr. Fuller!"

Mrs. Fuller popped her head out of an upstairs window. "What on earth's the matter?" she said.

"You've got a large green mamba in your front room!" I shouted. "I saw it go up the veranda steps and right in through the door!"

---

1. *Tanganyika* (TAING un YEE kuh), now part of Tanzania, was formerly a country in East Africa.
2. A *sundowner* (SUN DOUN er) is an alcoholic drink taken after work, usually at sundown.
3. *Dar es Salaam* (DAR ESS suh LAHM) is a seaport in Tanzania, on the Indian Ocean.
4. A *veranda* (vuh RAN duh) is a partially enclosed, roofed porch; it wraps around the front and sides of a house.

Word Bank

dumbfounded (DUM FOUN did) *adj.*: astonished; amazed

"Fred!" Mrs. Fuller shouted, turning round. "Fred! Come here!"

Freddy Fuller's round red face appeared at the window beside his wife. "What's up?" he asked.

"There's a green mamba in your living room!" I shouted.

Without hesitation and without wasting time with more questions, he said to me, "Stay there. I'm going to lower the children down to you one at a time." He was completely cool and unruffled.[5] He didn't even raise his voice.

A small girl was lowered down to me by her wrists, and I was able to catch her easily by the legs. Then came a small boy. Then Freddy Fuller lowered his wife, and I caught her and put her on the ground. Then came Fuller himself. He hung by his hands from the windowsill and when he let go he landed neatly on his two feet.

We stood in a little group on the grass at the back of the house, and I told Fuller exactly what I had seen.

The mother was holding the two children by the hand, one on each side of her. They didn't seem to be particularly alarmed.

"What happens now?" I asked.

"Go down the road, all of you," Fuller said. "I'm off to fetch the snake-man." He trotted away and got into his small ancient black car and drove off. Mrs. Fuller and the two small children and I went down to the road and sat in the shade of a large mango[6] tree.

"Who is this snake-man?" I asked Mrs. Fuller.

"He is an old Englishman who has been out here for years," Mrs. Fuller said. "He actually *likes* snakes. He understands them and never kills them. He catches them and sells them to zoos and laboratories all over the world. Every native for miles around knows about him and whenever one of them sees a snake, he marks its hiding place and runs, often for great distances, to tell the snake-man. Then the snake-man comes along and captures it. The snake-man's strict rule is that he will never buy a captured snake from the natives."

"Why not?" I asked.

"To discourage them from trying to catch snakes themselves," Mrs. Fuller said. "In his early days he used to buy caught snakes, but so many natives got bitten trying to catch them, and so many died, that he decided to put a stop to it. Now any native who brings in a caught snake, no matter how rare, gets turned away."

"That's good," I said.

"What is the snake-man's name?" I asked.

"Donald Macfarlane," she said. "I believe he's Scottish."

"Is the snake in the house, Mummy?" the small girl asked.

"Yes, darling. But the snake-man is going to get it out."

"He'll bite Jack," the girl said.

"Oh!" Mrs. Fuller cried, jumping to her feet. "I forgot about Jack!" She began calling out, "Jack! Come here, Jack! Jack!…Jack!…Jack!"

The children jumped up as well, and

---

5. *Unruffled* (un RUF ild) means calm, composed, and unflustered.
6. A *mango* (MAIN go) is a large greenish-red, pear-shaped tropical fruit.

all of them started calling to the dog. But no dog came out of the open front door.

"He's bitten Jack!" the small girl cried out. "He must have bitten him!" She began to cry and so did her brother, who was a year or so younger than she was. Mrs. Fuller looked grim.

"Jack's probably hiding upstairs," she said. "You know how clever he is."

Mrs. Fuller and I seated ourselves again on the grass, but the children remained standing. In between their tears they went on calling to the dog.

"Would you like me to take you down to the Maddens' house?" their mother asked.

"No!" they cried. "No, no, no! We want Jack!"

"Here's Daddy!" Mrs. Fuller cried, pointing at the tiny black car coming up the road in a swirl of dust. I noticed a long wooden pole sticking out through one of the car windows.

The children ran to meet the car. "Jack's inside the house and he's been bitten by the snake!" they wailed. "We know he's been bitten! He doesn't come when we call him!"

Mr. Fuller and the snake-man got out of the car. The snake-man was small and very old, probably over seventy. He wore leather boots made of thick cowhide, and he had long gauntlet[7]-type gloves on his hands made of the same stuff. The gloves reached above his elbows. In his right hand he carried an extraordinary implement, an eight-foot-long wooden pole with a forked end. The two prongs of the fork were made, so it seemed, of black rubber, about an inch thick and quite flexible, and it was clear that if the fork was pressed against the ground the two prongs would bend outwards, allowing the neck of the fork to go down as close to the ground as necessary. In his left hand he carried an ordinary brown sack.

Donald Macfarlane, the snake-man, may have been old and small but he was an impressive-looking character. His eyes were pale blue, deep-set in a face round and dark and wrinkled as a walnut. Above the blue eyes, the eyebrows were thick and startlingly white, but the hair on his head was almost black. In spite of the thick leather boots, he moved like a leopard, with soft slow catlike strides, and he came straight up to me and said, "Who are you?"

"He's with the oil company," Fuller said. "He hasn't been here long."

"You want to watch?" the snake-man said to me.

"Watch?" I said, wavering. "Watch? How do you mean watch? I mean where from? Not in the house?"

"You can stand out on the veranda and look through the window," the snake-man said.

"Come on," Fuller said. "We'll both

---

7. A *gauntlet* (GAWNT lit) is a heavy glove with an extended cuff to protect the wrist and lower arm.

Word Bank

implement (IM pluh mint) *n.*: an instrument, tool, or utensil used for accomplishing work

wavering (WAY ver ing) *adj.*: feeling or showing doubt or indecision

watch."

"Now don't do anything silly," Mrs. Fuller said.

The two children stood there forlorn and miserable, with tears all over their cheeks.

The snake-man and Fuller and I walked over the grass towards the house, and as we approached the veranda steps the snake-man whispered, "Tread softly on the wooden boards or he'll pick up the vibration. Wait until I've gone in, then walk up quietly and stand by the window."

The snake-man went up the steps first and he made absolutely no sound at all with his feet. He moved soft and cat-like onto the veranda and straight through the front door, and then he quickly but very quietly closed the door behind him.

I felt better with the door closed. What I mean is I felt better for myself. I certainly didn't feel better for the snake-man. I figured he was committing suicide. I followed Fuller onto the veranda and we both crept over to the window. The window was open, but it had a fine mesh mosquito netting[8] all over it. That made me feel better still. We peered through the netting.

The living room was simple and ordinary, coconut matting[9] on the floor, a red sofa, a coffee table, and a couple of armchairs. The dog was sprawled on the matting under the coffee table, a large Airedale with curly brown and black hair. He was stone dead.

The snake-man was standing absolutely still just inside the door of the living room. The brown sack was now slung over his left shoulder, and he was grasping the long pole with both hands, holding it out in front of him, parallel to the ground. I couldn't see the snake. I didn't think the snake-

The snake-man was standing absolutely still just inside the door of the living room.

---

8. *Netting* (NET ing) is fine mesh fabric placed over windows and cribs to keep out insects.
9. *Coconut matting* (KO kuh NUT MAT ing) is a floor covering made from the branches of a coconut palm.

Word Bank

forlorn (for LORN) *adj*.: miserable; despairing

tread (TRED) *v*.: set down the foot or feet in walking; step; walk

man had seen it yet either.

A minute went by…two minutes…three…four…five. Nobody moved. There was death in that room. The air was heavy with death and the snake-man stood as motionless as a pillar of stone, with the long rod held out in front of him.

And still he waited. Another minute…and another…and another.

And now I saw the snake-man beginning to bend his knees. Very slowly he bent his knees until he was almost squatting on the floor, and from that position he tried to peer under the sofa and the armchairs.

And still it didn't look as though he was seeing anything.

Slowly he straightened his legs again, and then his head began to swivel around the room. Over to the right, in the far corner, a staircase led up to the floor above. The snake-man looked at the stairs, and I knew very well what was going through his head. Quite abruptly, he took one step forward and stopped.

Nothing happened.

A moment later I caught sight of the snake. It was lying full-length along the skirting[10] of the right-hand wall, but hidden from the snake-man's view by the back of the sofa. It lay there like a long, beautiful, deadly shaft[11] of green glass, quite motionless, perhaps asleep. It was facing away from us who were at the window, with its small triangular head resting on the matting near the foot of the stairs.

I nudged Fuller and whispered, "It's over there against the wall." I pointed and Fuller saw the snake. At once, he started waving both hands, palms outward, back and forth across the

---

10. Here, *skirting* (SKURT ing) refers to the bottom edge of a wall; wainscoting.
11. A *shaft* is a long pole forming the body of various weapons.

Word Bank **abruptly** (uh BRUPT lee) *adv.*: suddenly and unexpectedly

window, hoping to get the snake-man's attention. The snake-man didn't see him. Very softly, Fuller said, "Pssst!" and the snake-man looked up sharply. Fuller pointed. The snake-man understood and gave a nod.

Now the snake-man began working his way very, very slowly to the back wall of the room so as to get a view of the snake behind the sofa. He never walked on his toes as you or I would have done. His feet remained flat on the ground all the time. The cowhide boots were like moccasins, with neither soles nor heels. Gradually, he worked his way over to the back wall, and from there he was able to see at least the head and two or three feet of the snake itself.

But the snake also saw him. With a movement so fast it was invisible, the snake's head came up about two feet off the floor, and the front of the body arched backwards, ready to strike. Almost simultaneously, it bunched its whole body into a series of curves, ready to flash forward.

The snake-man was just a bit too far away from the snake to reach it with the end of his pole. He waited, staring at the snake, and the snake stared back at him with two small malevolent black eyes.

Then the snake-man started speaking to the snake. "Come along, my pretty," he whispered in a soft wheedling[12] voice. "There's a good boy. Nobody's going to hurt you. Nobody's going to harm you, my pretty little thing. Just lie still and relax…." He took a step forward towards the snake, holding the pole out in front of him.

What the snake did next was so fast that the whole movement couldn't have taken more than a hundredth of a second, like the flick of a camera shutter. There was a green flash as the snake darted forward at least ten feet and struck at the snake-man's leg. Nobody could have got out of the way of that one. I heard the snake's head strike against the thick cowhide boot with a sharp little *crack*, and then at once the head was back in that same deadly backward-curving position, ready to strike again.

"There's a good boy," the snake-man said softly. "There's a clever boy. There's a lovely fellow. You mustn't get excited. Keep calm and everything's going to be all right." As he was speaking, he was slowly lowering the end of the pole until the forked prongs were about twelve inches above the middle of the snake's body. "There's a lovely fellow," he whispered. "There's a good kind little chap. Keep still now, my beauty. Keep still, my pretty. Keep quite still. Daddy's not going to hurt you."

I could see a thin dark trickle of venom running down the snake-man's right boot where the snake had struck.

---

12. *Wheedling* (WHEE dling) means coaxing or persuading.

Word Bank

malevolent (muh LEV ih lint) *adj.*: wishing evil or harm to others; malicious

venom (VEN im) *n.*: the poisonous fluid that some snakes and spiders inject into or spray at their victims

The snake, head raised and arcing backwards, was as tense as a tight-wound spring and ready to strike again. "Keep still, my lovely," the snake-man whispered. "Don't move now. Keep still. No one's going to hurt you."

Then *wham*, the rubber prongs came down right across the snake's body, about midway along its length, and pinned it to the floor. All I could see was a green blur as the snake thrashed around furiously in an effort to free itself. But the snake-man kept up the pressure on the prongs and the snake was trapped.

What happens next? I wondered. There was no way he could catch hold of that madly twisting flailing length of green muscle with his hands, and even if he could have done so, the head would surely have flashed around and bitten him in the face.

Holding the very end of the eight-foot pole, the snake-man began to work his way round the room until he was at the tail end of the snake. Then, in spite of the flailing and the thrashing, he started pushing the prongs forward along the snake's body towards the head. Very very slowly he did it, pushing the rubber prongs forward over the snake's flailing body, keeping the snake pinned down all the time and pushing, pushing, pushing the long wooden rod forward millimeter by millimeter. It was a fascinating and frightening thing to watch, the little man with white eyebrows and black hair carefully manipulating his long implement and sliding the fork ever so slowly along the length of the twisting snake towards the head. The snake's body was thumping against the coconut matting with such a noise that if you had been upstairs you might have thought two big men were wrestling on the floor.

Then at last the prongs were right behind the head itself, pinning it down, and at that point the snake-man reached forward with one gloved hand and grasped the snake very firmly by the neck. He threw away the pole. He took the sack off his shoulder with his free hand. He lifted the great, still twisting length of the deadly green snake and pushed the head into the sack. Then he let go the head and bundled the rest of the creature in and closed the sack. The sack started jumping about as though there were fifty angry rats inside it, but the snake-man was now totally relaxed, and he held the sack casually in one hand as if it contained no more than a few pounds of potatoes. He stooped and picked up his pole from the floor, then he turned and looked towards the window where we were peeping in.

"Pity about the dog," he said. "You'd better get it out of the way before the children see it."

Word Bank

arcing (ARK ing) *v*.: moving in a curved line

flailing (FLAY ling) *adj*.: beating or swinging

millimeter (MILL uh MEE ter) *n*.: a unit of length equal to 1/1000 of a meter, equivalent to 0.03937 of an inch

manipulating (muh NIP yoo LAYT ing) *v*.: handling or using, especially with skill

Studying the Selection

First Impressions

How did the green mamba of the story compare with the snake described by the naturalists? Which features do they share? How are they different? How might the story differ if it were told from the viewpoint of the snake-man?

✓ Quick Review

1. What simile does Dahl use to describe the "tiny little puff adders"? Why is this a problem? What are puff adders?
2. Why does the snake-man tell Fuller and Dahl to tread softly as they walk up the veranda steps?
3. What kind of dog is Jack, and what happened to him?
4. How does the snake-man maneuver the eight-foot pole, in order to catch the green mamba?

In-depth Thinking

5. How does Roald Dahl create and sustain the suspense?
6. Why doesn't the snake-man buy captured snakes from the Africans?
7. Do you think Mrs. Fuller really believes it herself, when she tells the children that Jack is probably hiding upstairs?
8. Why does the snake-man wear thick leather boots and gauntlets?

Drawing Conclusions

9. With whom do you identify, the snake-man or Roald Dahl? Why?
10. Evaluate how the Fuller family handled the situation with the green mamba.

Focusing on the Autobiographical Anecdote

1. Reread the second paragraph of the selection. Take a personal event, one that held some element of suspense or the unknown. Write as Mr. Dahl did, using appropriate details from your own experience.

2. A writer's autobiographical perspective may be strongly biased. Why does the green mamba of the story differ from those described by naturalists and owners? Make certain you support your statements with quoted passages from the selection, the accompanying notes, or other sources, perhaps an encyclopedia. Don't forget the proper format for quotations!

3. Write an essay discussing whether *The Green Mamba* is a story about animals or man. Support your argument and conclusion with solid reasoning, citing passages from the essay. Use the correct form for any quoted passages.

Creating and Writing

1. Write a brief essay about an animal or insect you do not like. After doing your research, write a two-page paper treating your subject with respect, using your newly found facts. Include a hand-drawn illustration with your report.

2. Write the story from the snake's viewpoint. Use either the first-person voice—the pronoun "I"—or a sympathetic third-person voice—either "she" or "he."

3. Create a diorama of one of the scenes in the story. Make the figures and scenery from paper, clay, or other materials.

Blueprint for Reading

the Author

**Rita Dove
(1953-)**

Rita Dove was born in Akron, Ohio. She started writing seriously at Ohio's Miami University, where she was Presidential Scholar, National Achievement Scholar, and Phi Beta Kappa. She graduated summa cum laude and won a Fulbright. She has received honorary doctorates from the most prestigious universities. Dove is brilliant and prolific, writing poetry, plays, essays, fiction. Her awards fill two typewritten pages! She received the 1991 Pulitzer Prize for Poetry and was Poet Laureate from 1993-1995. Invited to the White House, she read a poem describing the execution of 20,000 Haitians by the dictator Trujillo. "I felt that I should show what poetry could do—that it covers many aspects of human joy and triumph and tragedy."

Background Bytes

Many of us have used clay for a school art project or in summer camp, making oddly shaped gifts—truly from our hearts and hands—for parents and friends. But why clay? When we try to shape clay, it is moist, cold, smooth, and slippery—often pleasurable to grasp and shape—a sensation missing from "dough-type" synthetics given to young children nowadays.

In many ancient cultures, clay was used to model animal figures, even before people learned how to fire pots. Early pottery provides a wonderful record of ancient life. Even today, sculptors use clay as a primary material.

In many parts of the United States, rural areas have reddish soil, evidence of red clay. Look at the crops, and you see shades of green; but look at the soil, and you see red clay. You cannot avoid it. It fills the landscape and the mind.

In this memoir, where does Ms. Dove write about clay?

Into *I Know What the Red Clay Looks Like*

The topic of this piece is Ms. Dove's becoming a writer, working at her craft. However, a memoir is more than a record; it reveals the writer's self-built world. This is Ms. Dove's creation; this she *knows*—how her writing comes to *be.* This brings us closer to the theme.

Look for the basic truths Rita Dove shares about writing and all creative art. Why does she contrast *visceral* and *cerebral* (page 533)? Where does inspiration come into play? You will know the theme, if you can state the most important point she says about the process of writing.

I Know What the Red Clay Looks Like

Focusing on the Memoir

Biography is the written record of a person's life. **Autobiography** also focuses on the individual, but it is written by that same person. A **memoir** is like an autobiography; the author is the subject. But since a memoir only deals with selected pieces of the writer's experience, the focus is on the world *outside* the author. The memoir is often short, dealing with just a *segment* of time. Ms. Dove describes universal truths (true everywhere, at all times) about creativity. These are often hard to convey and perhaps impossible to teach. The memoir, illustrating Ms. Dove's advice, is ideal for the task. This piece is well-written, and you can learn much from it. As you read, write down any sentences you particularly like. Of the ideas expressed in the piece, which is your favorite?

Word Bank

Diversity, Multiculturalism: Words may take on new connotations as our society absorbs technological innovations. (Think of the shifting meaning of the word, *compute*.) Words also vary their meanings as a result of social movements. These added meanings enable us to describe the changing attitudes that are now a part of our lives. An expanding vocabulary allows us to talk with ourselves in our own heads about the new world we see. For example, **diversity** once simply meant *variety*. Now it is often used to describe **multiculturalism**. And what is that? The concept surfaced in the early 1960s, when the results of the Civil Rights movement began to be felt and there was a lot of activism in response to the Vietnam War.

affirmation	discrete	inexhaustible	puppeteer
attributes	diversity	intimate	unified
attuned	eavesdrop	multiculturalism	validation
cello	exhilarating	precedence	yearning
compact	genre	profound	

I Know What the Red Clay Looks Like

Rita Dove

A writer is a writer all the time. I am always thinking as a writer and trying to approach the world as a writer, which means using all of my senses all of the time—being open for the breeze that comes through the window, what it smells like, and what the trees look like when the breeze touches them. It can make for a pretty scattered impression on others. But that's how a writer lives—by being deeply in the world and being attuned to it a great deal of the time, while the rest of the time is spent in the actual writing and recollection of that interaction with the world.

When I was a kid I listened to stories—the women in the kitchen, Fourth of July cookouts, folks on the porch talking—I would eavesdrop really. Listening to these stories being told and how they would affect their listeners was quite an influence on my own desire to tell stories. I also did a lot of reading. As a child, my parents really opened me and my siblings up to the glory of reading and the infinite possibilities when you open a book. It was an activity that we could do practically any time—except at the dinner table. The library was the one place we could go to without asking permission. As long as we had finished the books we had taken out from our last trip there, we could go. And we always had.

My entire childhood was imbued[1] with reading—afternoons of curling up with a book, and the pleasure of not knowing what was going to be in it until I opened it and began to read its words. The love I felt for the words on those

---
1. To be *imbued* (im BYOOD) with means to be permeated or profoundly inspired.

Word Bank

attuned (uh TOOND) *v.*: brought into harmony or agreement
eavesdrop (EEVZ DRAHP) *v.*: listen secretly to a private conversation

pages made me want to create some words of my own, and to write stories that I had not yet found.

When I began writing at maybe ten or eleven years old, it was wonderful, because I discovered that I could go wherever I wanted to go and do whatever I wanted to do. I didn't really tell anyone about it. My brother, who is a few years older than me, and I were very close as children. Every summer, we would have a newspaper, which I would usually quit about halfway through the summer to start my own newspaper. The title of my own newspaper usually made some reference to poetry. I remember one summer it was called *Poet's Delight.* Other than my brother, I really didn't show anyone what I wrote, not even my friends. It wasn't shame, it was just that writing was such an intimate act for me that it didn't really occur to me to bring it out into the world all that much.

When I got to high school, my English teacher brought a few of us to a book signing one afternoon. I hadn't shown her any of my writing either, beyond my English papers. The writer at the book signing was John Ciardi,[2] the poet and translator. I was so amazed that writers were really *people.* At that moment, I realized that this "activity" I had been doing, that I had been thinking of as somewhat of a game—some game that I would one day have to put away in order to become an adult—that this activity was really something adults did and were respected for. And it was called writing.

I did not make the conscious decision to become a writer until I was in college. It wasn't until I realized that I was rearranging my schedule to fit in creative writing courses that I thought, Well, maybe I should make a go of this, because writing had obviously become the most important thing to me. I was then able to recognize the yearning that I felt inside, the joy that I got when I wrote something I felt was halfway decent. When I was able to understand that the joy could somehow satisfy the yearning, I realized that the yearning, the joy, and the satisfaction were about wanting to write. I think I had the yearning for a long time before recognizing it; I just didn't know what

---

2. *John Ciardi* (JAHN chee AR dee) (1916-1986) wrote children's poetry. He was also an editor and translator.

Word Bank

intimate (IN tih mit) *adj.*: private; closely personal

yearning (YURN ing) *n.*: an earnest or strong desire; a longing

it was.

In my poetry, I write about what the weather is like, or what the sand feels like under a sandal—that kind of thing—and it may be drawn from an experience that I have had, or that someone I know has had. I draw from other people quite a lot, particularly family members. *Thomas and Beulah* is a good example of that because it began with a story that my grandmother told me about my grandfather. As I began to re-create the scene, the event that she told me about, imagination came in. I hadn't been there, and she hadn't been there either—only my grandfather had been there, and he had long since passed away—so by necessity I had to use my imagination. In imagining, I also put my own feelings into it—how I would have felt had I actually been there—all the while trying to slip into my grandfather's skin.

As that book of poetry grew, I went to the library and did research to find out things—like what Akron, Ohio, was like in the twenties. I also talked with my mother and drew on her memories, and then I sometimes just plain made things up. That's how I work. I did the same thing with my novel *Through the Ivory Gate*—I have played the cello, but I've never been a puppeteer—so it becomes a wonderful kind of mix, and I really don't try and sort it out that much.

I do think quite a few writers work in this same way; when we try to talk about that magical moment when the poem or the story or the scene takes off and comes alive, I know that for me it's a feeling of trying to write just to keep up with that moment. This moment is the point when all of the things I just mentioned—the memories, the imagination, the stories I've heard—all come together in such a unified piece that I don't know where the energy is coming from and all I can do is ride with it. It feels terrific. It is so exhilarating, I feel like I could write forever, that I am inexhaustible. The ideas and the words come faster than I can write them down. Although sometimes, right before that happens, there is a moment of great despair when things don't seem to be clicking; but the faith that it will come together takes me there. I learn so much in the process; it is profound discovery.

Word Bank

cello (CHELL lo) *n.*: a large, four-stringed musical instrument of the violin family
puppeteer (PUP it EAR) *n.*: a person who manipulates puppets
unified (YOO nih FYD) *adj.*: made to be a single unit; united; merged
exhilarating (ig ZILL uh RAYT ing) *adj.*: stimulating; invigorating
inexhaustible (IN ig ZAWS tih bul) *adj.*: incapable of being depleted; untiring
profound (pro FOUND) *adj.*: going beyond what is superficial or obvious; deep

There is some truth to the whole notion that something strikes the poet like a thunderbolt and she is then inspired. Inspiration is part of the writing process, and I think of it as being much more visceral[3] than cerebral.[4] I also think that there is a different kind of inspiration that comes when one is working and things begin to click together. I'll leave it up to all the scientists and psychologists to come up with the right terminology for it, but I do think that I try to engage all of my senses when I write. Absolutely and completely. I try to get *in* it. And then I need to find a word that will best describe being in it, which is very cerebral. The mind, the soul, the heart, and the heartbeat try to get into sync,[5] and when they do, it is very difficult to say which takes precedence, in fact I don't think any one thing does.

When the writing doesn't gel[6] together, I just keep working. For example, since I am both a poet and a fiction writer, let me try to explain the differences I feel between these two genres. With poetry, very often there are the days and hours of a lot of frustration when things are not coming together. When things finally do click, I find the moments of connection are usually much more brilliant and unequivocal.[7] With prose, I find that the periods when things are not clicking are not quite as depressing because there is so much to do in prose besides working on those connections. I guess you could call it housekeeping—tidying up ragged paragraphs, creating an atmosphere, checking dialogue—so that I can keep active in the work and not despair that it won't come together. Maybe it is because I consider myself more of a poet than a fiction writer, but I also find the moments that come together in prose are not as epiphanal[8] as those in poetry. So it's a trade-off. I prefer the higher highs and the deeper depths in poetry.

---

3. *Visceral* (VISS er il) means "of the intestines"—from instinct, not intellect.
4. *Cerebral* (SIR ee bril) means of the brain—the intellect.
5. When the mind, the soul, and the heart are in *sync* (SINK), they are all working together.
6. To *gel* (JELL) means to have all the parts come together in a solid form.
7. *Unequivocal* (UN ee KWIV uh kul) means having only one possible interpretation.
8. An *epiphanal* (ih PIF ih nil) moment is one in which a sudden intuitive understanding of the essential meaning of something bursts upon the person.

Word Bank

precedence (PRESS ih dintz) *n*.: the right to be placed before others; priority in order, rank, or importance

genre (ZHAHN ruh) *n*.: a class or category of artistic endeavor having a particular form, content, or technique

For me, there is simply a deep and basic pleasure in seeing words come alive. The simpler the word, the better. Because words are amazingly compact; they carry so much power in such a small package. I think the simpler the word, the more power it contains, because our first words were very simple, one-syllable words. If I can find a way to bring back all the power of the word *bread*, not Wonder bread, but *bread*—the stuff that gives us life—if I can restore the freshness and magic to that word in a prose passage or in a poem, then I've got it all. What an incredible power—I smell it, I feel it, I am alive. I run through all the different attributes of a word when I am trying to find the right one. A word not only has a meaning—it also has a sound, a feeling in the mouth, a texture, a history. Very often, if a word has the right meaning, but not the sense, the deeper sense I need, I try to think of words that rhyme, or I look up its etymology.[9] Writing for me means that intense pleasure of dealing with language, working with the language like a potter works with clay. I think most writers have an almost shameless love of language, of words and the way they work.

When we are children, we love to play with language; we like feeling sounds in our mouth. Then as we start to grow up, what begins to happen is that the pleasure of mouthing words has to be compromised because words are also used for daily interactions. Using charcoal or paint to create art is an activity that can be kept discrete. But the use of words can't be. We have to use them to talk and to communicate. Many people forget the pleasure of words for the purpose of expediency[10]—they have to get on with their lives. I also think that this is why a lot of poets and writers are not great conversationalists. We are not the kind of people who sit around at the party spouting off witty and glib repartee.[11] And a lot of that has to do with this intense love of words. To constantly make the switch between honoring every word and using them just to get on with things is very difficult. It's almost schizophrenia.[12]

---

9. The *etymology* (ET ih MAHL ih jee) of a word is its origin and history.
10. *Expediency* (ik SPEE dee in see) is a regard for what is advantageous rather than for what is right.
11. *Glib repartee* (GLIB) (REP ar TAY) is conversation filled with superficial, easy, witty replies.

Word Bank

compact (kum PAKT) *adj.*: closely packed; solid; concise
attribute (AT trib YOOT) *n.*: a quality or characteristic of a person, thing, or group
discrete (diss KREET) *adj.*: separate; distinct

I've recently been named poet laureate[13] of the nation, and I am still trying to decide what that title means. It is a kind of public or outward affirmation, not so much that I'm a good writer, but that the writing reaches an audience. And that is gratifying. Unless you do a lot of public readings, every time you sit down to write or finish a piece, there is that fear of being misunderstood. You say to yourself: What I'm writing is *really* crazy; no one is going to relate to this. So to have this sort of official recognition not only as a poet and writer, but also as someone who can stand forward and be a channel[14] for literature in this country, is marvelous.

It doesn't really matter to me what kind of validation the title may give me as a poet—I don't really worry about that kind of stuff. Every time I sit down to write, it's a new ball game. The poem, or the story, or the scene, that I'm working on has its own problems, and there is always the fear that the poem or passage will not work or mean anything to anyone else. The intensity of this sort of hand-to-hand combat never goes away.

It is very exciting to think that the country thinks enough about literature to appoint a younger poet laureate, which may encourage the idea of writing in children and engage our youth by saying in effect: See? This can be done. That the country chose to honor a black woman is also tremendously exciting. On the one hand, it declares that there is value and richness in diversity. But it also shows that multiculturalism and diversity do not mean being separate. My ultimate desire is to be considered as part of the human family—to be recognized and respected as a black woman, but not to have that fact make any earth-shaking difference. It is significant that I am a black woman, but it is not the end-all-be-all in terms of being poet laureate.

---

12. *Schizophrenia* (SKITZ oh FREN ee uh) is a severe mental disorder, associated with brain abnormalities, disorganized speech and behavior, and delusions and hallucinations.
13. In the United States, a *Poet Laureate* (PO it LAW ree eht) is the national poet. The position is official recognition of the poet's achievements.
14. A *channel* (CHAN nil) is a route through which something passes, or a course into which something may be directed.

Word Bank

affirmation (AF fur MAY shun) *n.*: the assertion that something exists or is true
validation (VAL ih DAY shun) *n.*: confirmation; approval
diversity (dy VURS ih tee) *n.*: being of various kinds or forms; variety
multiculturalism (MULL ty KULL chur uh liz im) *n.*: the existence, recognition, or preservation of different cultures within a unified society

Studying the Selection

First Impressions *Which were your favorite sentences in the selection? Your favorite ideas? We are looking for your visceral (or gut) reaction. There is no right answer, but it is important to try to state the reasons for your choices.*

✔ Quick Review

1. When is a writer a writer?
2. For writers, when is the magical moment?
3. Is *inspiration* visceral or cerebral? Use the selection and the dictionary to make your choice.
4. According to Ms. Dove, why is it exciting that the country would appoint a *younger* poet laureate?

In-depth Thinking

5. What does the author mean by the glory of reading?
6. What does she mean by stories that she had not yet found?
7. Compare and contrast the concepts, *visceral* and *cerebral*. Please include the definition of each of the words in your discussion.
8. What do you think the author means when she writes of her ultimate desire "to be considered part of the human family"?

Drawing Conclusions

9. What might the author mean when she says the moment when things start to come together is *unequivocal* and *epiphanal*? Consult the dictionary for definitions.
10. What does the comparison with a potter suggest?

Focusing on the Memoir

1. Write a brief memoir, describing yourself somewhat, but focusing mostly on your perception or experience of your small world and those living there. Write the memoir in the first-person, using either present or past tense. Remember—your focus is outward. Even though the perceptions are your own, it is the memoirist's world that is the focus. Write so the reader sees you reflected in your choice of powerful but soft images.

2. Write a memoir, but use the imagined voice of anything that cannot speak: an infant, an animal, a tree, a piece of furniture. You want to show us—or give us a feel for—some important part of this world. Use the pronoun "I." Try both present and past tense, to see which works best for you.

3. Pair off with a classmate. Select two paragraphs you particularly like from *I Know What the Red Clay Looks Like*. Read the paragraphs aloud to each other several times. Discuss what the two paragraphs tell us about the world of writing. Present your conclusions to the class by first reading aloud the paragraphs slowly and clearly. Now give your classmates some added insight or understanding of each of the paragraphs.

Creating and Writing

1. Write a short essay about the process of creativity being both visceral and cerebral. Ms. Dove makes it clear that writing is not simply a matter of making an outline and proceeding. If you wish, you may include an experience of your own as a starting point, or you may use Ms. Dove's examples of the meshing of heart and mind.

2. Choose ten to twenty words or phrases from the selection. Write each word or phrase on a separate piece of paper. Arrange the pieces of paper to make a skeleton of a 'poem' about writing. Then add your own words to flesh out these 'bones.'

3. You might want to make a collage to go with your poem.

Blueprint for Reading

the Author

**Bruce Brooks
(1950-)**

Brooks was born in Washington, D.C. He attended the University of North Carolina at Chapel Hill, receiving his B.A. in 1972. Later, he received his M.F.A. from the University of Iowa in 1982. Besides writing, he worked as a letterpress printer, a newspaper and magazine reporter, and a teacher. He has received many awards for his children's and young adult literature. He also writes nonfiction, novels, and stories. His interests include music, nature, sports, and reading. In an interview with *Authors & Artists for Young Adults* he said, "We are capable as readers of a wild and intricate world of thought and response and feeling—things going on in different layers at the same time. I hope to write books that involve all those layers of the thinking and feeling in my reader."

Background Bytes

Do you know anything about wasps? The female paper wasp described in *Animal Craftsmen* builds her nest from a paper-like material, made by chewing wood into a paste.

Each nest holds about 100 cells for larvae (or babies). The female provides a store of food in each cell. The larvae eat insects caught by the female parent, so wasps are an important natural form of insect control.

Into *Animal Craftsmen*

Nonfiction pieces do not always have an underlying theme. Instead, there may be a main point, or several main points. At times, therefore, the main point and the topic closely overlap. As you read *Animal Craftsmen*, think about *why* the author is telling us this remembrance. What point (or points) is he making?

Notice that the *why* of this piece changes two-thirds of the way through the selection. Look first for a sentence where the *attitude* of the speaker changes. In the next paragraph, both the tone and focus of the discussion change. When this occurs, the point of the essay, the theme, changes. *Animal Craftsmen* has a primary theme or story to tell in its first section—the author explains his discovery and his childhood fascination. In the second section, there are more themes, or main points. The author reflects on his childhood discovery and the fascination he still feels as an adult.

Where does the first section end and the second section begin? What do you find most interesting about each section?

ANIMAL CRAFTSMEN

Focusing on the Childhood Memoir

Think back on yourself at age five. Would your parents have permitted you to go off on your own, as the author did? At that age would you have climbed to the top of an icy ladder?

When we think about *how* stories come into being, especially nonfiction stories, we might view both the story and author differently. The act of writing is both interesting and instructive. When we recollect, how much do we remember on our own? How much of our memory comes from family stories about earlier events? Perhaps our recollection is a joining of *both*—a **composite memory**. We remember an experience, *and* we remember what others said about it. But where does one end and the other begin? Where in Bruce Brooks's recollection might you wonder if this is an *actual* memory or a *learned* memory?

The author might not have intended to separate his essay into two parts, but it happened. Can you still describe the entire piece as a childhood memoir?

Word Bank

Sphere: When you see a word, such as **sphere**, in which the letters **ph** have the sound of the letter **f**, you know that the word comes to us from Greek, not Latin. In Greek, the **f** sound—or rather, the **ph** sound—is represented by the letter **phi** (FEE). Some examples of English words that use **ph** for the **f** sound are *phonograph, telephone, physician, photograph,* and *elephant.* Can you think of any others?

adhesiveness	empathy	intricately	uncanny
agility	fungus	migrant	vault
architecture	genetic	rung	vigil
attributing	improvise	sphere	wary
cell	ingenious	subtle	
dismantling	instinct	taut	

ANIMAL CRAFTSMEN

One evening when I was about five, I climbed up a ladder on the outside of a rickety[1] old tobacco barn at sunset. The barn was part of a small farm near the home of a country relative my mother and I visited periodically; though we did not really know the farm's family, I was allowed to roam, poke around, and conduct sudden studies of anything small and harmless. On this evening, as on most of my jaunts,[2] I was not looking for anything; I was simply climbing with an open mind. But as I balanced on the next-to-the-top rung and inhaled the spicy stink of the tobacco drying inside, I *did* find something under the eaves[3]—something very strange.

It appeared to be a kind of gray paper sphere, suspended from the dark planks by a thin stalk, like an apple made of ashes hanging on its stem. I studied it closely in the clear light. I saw that the bottom was a little ragged, and open. I could not tell if it had been torn, or if it had been made that way on purpose—for it was clear to me, as I studied it, that this thing had been *made*. This was no fruit or fungus. Its shape, rough but trim; its intricately colored surface with subtle swirls of gray and tan; and most of all the uncanny adhesiveness with which the perfectly tapered stem stuck against the rotten old pine boards—all of these features gave evidence of some intentional design. The troubling thing was figuring out who had designed it, and why.

I assumed the designer was a human being: someone from the farm, someone wise and skilled in a craft that had so far escaped my curiosity. Even when I saw wasps entering and leaving the thing (during a vigil I kept every evening for two weeks), it did not occur to me that the wasps might have fashioned it for themselves. I assumed it was a man-made "wasp house" placed there expressly for the purpose of attracting a family of wasps, much as the "martin hotel," a giant birdhouse on a

---

1. A *rickety* (RIK ih tee) barn is one that is likely to fall and collapse and is in a state of disrepair.
2. A *jaunt* (JAWNT) is a short, pleasurable trip.
3. The *eaves* (EEVZ) are the overhanging, lower edges of a roof.

Word Bank

rung (RUNG) *n*.: one of the crosspieces forming the steps of a ladder

sphere (SFEAR) *n*.: any round, globular body

fungus (FUN guss) *n*.: a plant—such as mold, mildew, and mushrooms—that lacks chlorophyll and reproduces by spores

intricately (IN trih kit lee) *adv*.: in a way that is full of elaborate detail

subtle (SUT il) *adj*.: fine, or delicate

uncanny (un KAN nee) *adj*.: seeming to be supernatural or unexplainable; extraordinary

adhesiveness (ad HEE siv niss) *n*.: the tendency to adhere; stickiness

vigil (VIJ il) *n*.: a period of watchful attention

BRUCE BROOKS

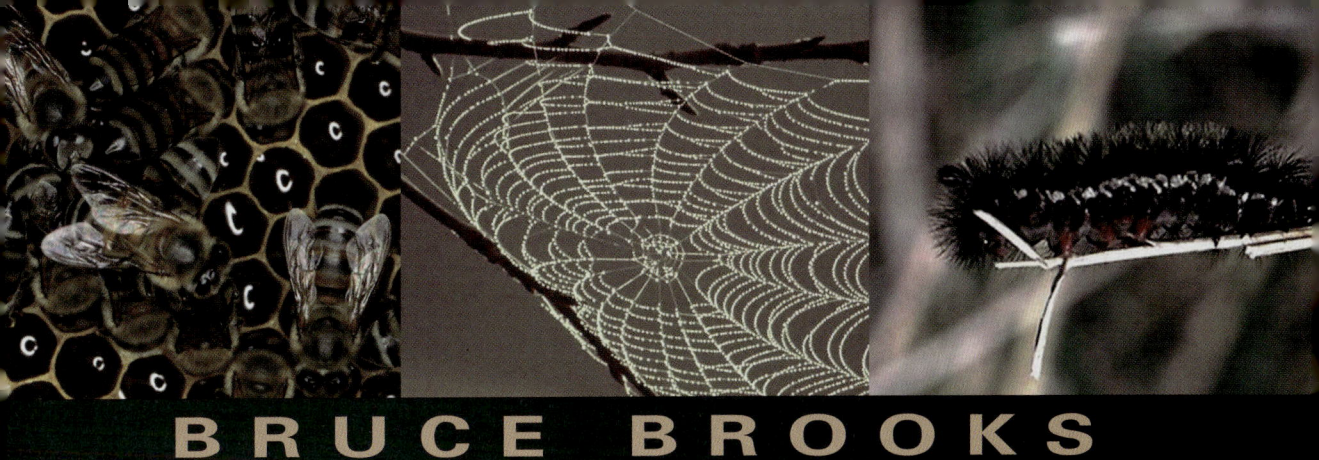

pole near the farmhouse, was maintained to shelter migrant purple martins who returned every spring. I didn't ask myself why anyone would want to give wasps a bivouac;[4] it seemed no more odd than attracting birds.

As I grew less wary of the wasps (and they grew less wary of me), and as my confidence on the ladder improved, I moved to the upper rung and peered through the sphere's bottom. I could see that the paper swirled in layers around some secret center the wasps inhabited, and I marveled at the delicate hands of the craftsmen who had devised such tiny apertures[5] for their protection.

I left the area in the late summer, and in my imagination I took the strange structure with me. I envisioned unwrapping it, and in the middle finding—what? A tiny room full of bits of wool for sleeping, and countless manufactured pellets[6] of scientifically determined wasp food? A glowing blue jewel that drew the wasps at twilight, and gave them a cool infusion[7] of energy as they clung to it overnight? My most definite idea was that the wasps lived in a small block of fine cedar the craftsman had drilled full of holes, into which they slipped snugly, rather like the bunks aboard submarines in World War II movies.

As it turned out, I got the chance to discover that my idea of the cedar block had not been wrong by much. We visited our relative again in the winter. We arrived at night, but first thing in the morning I made straight for the farm and its barn. The shadows under the eaves were too dense to let me spot the sphere from far off. I stepped on the bottom rung of the ladder—slick with frost—and climbed carefully up. My hands and feet kept slipping, so my eyes stayed on the rung ahead, and it was not until I was secure at the top that I could look up. The sphere was gone.

I was crushed. That object had fascinated me like nothing I had come across in my life; I had even grown to love wasps because of it. I sagged on the ladder and watched my breath eddy[8] around the blank eaves. I'm afraid I pitied myself more than the apparently homeless wasps.

But then something snapped me out of my sense of loss: I recalled that I had watched the farmer taking in the purple martin hotel every November, after the birds left. From its spruce[9]

---

4. A *bivouac* (BIV WAK) is a military camp with tents. In this context, it means a temporary home.
5. An *aperture* (AP er cher) is an opening, a hole or gap.
6. A *pellet* (PELL it) is a small, rounded piece, as of food.
7. An *infusion* (in FYOO zhun) of energy is the introduction of energy by permeating or instilling.
8. *Eddy* (ED dee) means whirl in spirals.
9. Here, *spruce* (SPROOS) means neat or trim.

Word Bank

migrant (MY grint) *adj*.: moving from one climate or region to another, as done by certain birds, animals, and fishes

wary (WAIR ee) *adj*.: watchful; on guard against danger

appearance when he brought it out in March, it was clear he had cleaned it and repainted it and kept it out of the weather. Of course he would do the same thing for *this* house, which was even more fragile. I had never mentioned the wasp dwelling to anyone, but now I decided I would go to the farm, introduce myself, and inquire about it. Perhaps I would even be permitted to handle it, or, best of all, learn how to make one myself.

I scrambled down the ladder, leaping from the third rung and landing in the frosty salad of tobacco leaves and windswept grass that collected at the foot of the barn wall. I looked down and saw that my left boot had, by no more than an inch, just missed crushing the very thing I was rushing off to seek. There, lying dry and separate on the leaves, was the wasp house.

I looked up. Yes, I was standing directly beneath the spot where the sphere had hung—it was a straight fall. I picked up the wasp house, gave it a shake to see if any insects were inside, and, discovering none, took it home.

My awe of the craftsman grew as I unwrapped the layers of the nest. Such beautiful paper! It was much tougher than any I had encountered, and it held a curve (something my experimental paper airplanes never did), but it was very light, too. The secret at the center of the swirl turned out to be a neatly made fan of tiny cells, all of the same size and shape, reminding me of the heart of a sunflower that had lost its seeds to birds. The fan hung from the sphere's ceiling by a stem the thickness of a pencil lead.

The rest of the story is a little embarrassing. More impressed than ever, I decided to pay homage[10] to the creator of this habitable[11] sculpture. I went boldly to the farmhouse. The farmer's wife answered my knock. I showed her the nest and asked to speak with the person in the house who had made it. She blinked and frowned. I had to repeat my question twice before she understood what I believed my mission to be; then, with a gentle laugh, she dispelled[12] my illusion about an ingenious old papersmith fond of wasps. The nest, she explained, had been made entirely by the insects themselves, and wasn't that amazing?

Well, of course it was. It still is. I needn't have been so embarrassed—the structures that animals build, and the sense of design they display, *should* always astound us. On my way home from the farmhouse, in my own defense I kept thinking, "But I couldn't build anything like this! Nobody could!"

The most natural thing in the world for us to do, when we are confronted with a piece of animal architecture, is to figure out if we could possibly make it or live in it. Who hasn't peered into the dark end of a mysterious hole in the woods and thought, "It must be pretty weird to live in there!" or looked up at a hawk's nest atop a huge sycamore and shuddered at the thought of waking up every morning with nothing but a few twigs preventing a hundred-foot fall. How, we wonder, do these twigs stay together, and withstand the wind so high?

It is a human tendency always to regard animals first in terms of ourselves. Seeing the defensive courage of a mother bear whose cubs are threatened, or the cooperative determination of a string of ants dismantling a stray

---

10. To pay *homage* (AHM ij) means to show respect for another.
11. A *habitable* (HAB ih tih bul) sculpture is a sculpture that is fit to be lived in.
12. *Dispelled* (diss PELD) means disbursed, caused to vanish.

Word Bank
cell (SELL) *n.*: a small compartment forming part of a whole
ingenious (in JEEN yiss) *adj.*: cleverly inventive; resourceful
architecture (AR kih TEK cher) *n.*: the action, process, or design of building; construction
dismantling (diss MANT ling) *v.*: taking apart

chunk of cake, we naturally use our own behavior as reference for our empathy. We put ourselves in the same situation and express the animal's action in feelings—and words—that apply to the way people do things.

Sometimes this is useful. But sometimes it is misleading. Attributing human-like intentions to an animal can keep us from looking at the *animal's* sense of itself in its surroundings—its immediate and future needs, its physical and mental capabilities, its genetic instincts. Most animals, for example, use their five senses in ways that human beings cannot possibly understand or express. How can a forty-two-year-old nearsighted biologist have any real idea what a two-week-old barn owl sees in the dark? How can a sixteen-year-old who lives in the Arizona desert identify with the muscular jumps improvised by a waterfall-leaping salmon in Alaska? There's nothing wrong with trying to empathize with an animal, but we shouldn't forget that ultimately animals live *animal* lives.

Animal structures let us have it both ways—we can be struck with a strange wonder, and we can empathize right away, too. Seeing a vast spiderweb, taut and glistening between two bushes, it's easy to think, "I have no idea how that is done; the engineering is awesome." But it is just as easy to imagine climbing across the bright strands, springing from one to the next as if the web were a new Epcot attraction, the Invisible Flying Flexible Space Orb. That a clear artifact of an animal's wits and agility stands right there in front of us—that we can touch it, look at it from different angles, sometimes take it home—inspires our imagination as only a strange reality can. We needn't move into a molehill to experience a life of darkness and digging; our creative wonder takes us down there in a second, without even getting our hands dirty.

But what if we discover some of the mechanics of how the web is made? Once we see how the spider works (or the hummingbird, or the bee), is the engineering no longer awesome? This would be too bad: we don't want to lose our sense of wonder just because we gain understanding.

And we certainly do *not* lose it. In fact, seeing how an animal makes its nest or egg case or food storage vaults has the effect of increasing our amazement. The builder's energy, concentration, and athletic adroitness[13] are qualities we can readily admire and envy. Even more startling is the recognition that the animal is working from a precise design in its head, a design that is exactly replicated[14] time after time. This knowledge of architecture—knowing where to build, what materials to use, how to put them together—remains one of the most intriguing mysteries of animal behavior. And the more *we* develop that same knowledge, the more we appreciate the instincts and intelligence of the animals.

---

13. The builder's *adroitness* (uh DROYT niss) refers to his clever skill.
14. *Replicated* (REP lih KAY tid) means copied or duplicated.

Word Bank

empathy (EM puh thee) *n.*: intellectual or emotional identification with another
attributing (uh TRIB yoot ing) *v.*: considering as a quality or characteristic of the person, thing, or group
genetic (juh NET ik) *adj.*: passed biologically from one generation to the next; of the genes
instinct (IN stinkt) *n.*: an inborn pattern of activity, or tendency to action, common to species; intuitive sense
improvised (IM pruh VYZD) *v.*: performed without preparation
taut (TAWT) *adj.*: tightly drawn; tense; not slack
agility (uh JILL ih tee) *n.*: quickness; coordination
vault (VAWLT) *n.*: a room or compartment used for storage

Studying the Selection

First Impressions

Were you able to find the transition paragraph where tone and focus change? Which of the two sections of Animal Craftsmen do you prefer? Do you think the two sections fit together?

✓ Quick Review

1. Who owned the farm where five-year-old Bruce found the "paper sphere"?
2. In the second paragraph, what simile does the author use to describe the wasp's nest?
3. As a child, when the author went home at the end of the summer, what did he do in his imagination? What did he find?
4. What thought snapped the author out of his sense of loss, when he saw that the nest was no longer hanging from the eaves?

In-depth Thinking

5. Describing his childhood self, the author says he "had even grown to love wasps because of it." What made him grow to love wasps? Why do you think he felt this way?
6. Find the paragraph beginning with the sentence, "The rest of the story is a little embarrassing." Do you think the sentence provides a smooth transition from the previous paragraphs? Or does the change in tone break the magical spell of the story?
7. The author makes several assumptions about people in the last seven paragraphs. What are these assumptions? Do you agree with him?
8. Why might people lose their sense of wonder as they gain understanding? Aside from insect architecture, is this a valid concern when regarding other marvels and mysteries?

Drawing Conclusions

9. Think about the author of *The Green Mamba*. How do you think Dahl might have reacted, as a five-year-old or as an adult, to finding a wasp nest?
10. Examine the first sentence of paragraph twelve. Do you think the author is embarrassed *now* as he recalls his childhood misunderstanding regarding the source of the nest? Support your answer with information from the selection.

Focusing on the Childhood Memoir

1. Write your own childhood memoir. Think of a fascinating discovery you made as a child. Write two paragraphs explaining your discovery and how you felt at the time. Then, change your viewpoint and write a closing paragraph explaining how you feel about your childhood discovery now.

2. Find an interesting or humorous photo of yourself as a child. Using that photo as your starting point, write about what happened before, during, and after the picture was taken. Make sure to include the actual photo in your story.

3. Write the first three paragraphs of a childhood memoir from the viewpoint of a wasp. The wasp sees the boy in *Animal Craftsmen* return repeatedly to the nest and watch in fascination. How might the wasp tell the story?

Creating and Writing

1. Prepare a one-page report about some aspect of wasp society, behavior, or physiology. Create at least one illustration to include in your report.

2. Develop a wasp alphabet. This means you need a symbol for each letter in the alphabet. (Remember that you don't want your symbols to look too much alike.) For example, let us say you designed the following alphabet:

    a = ♋   b = ♌   c = ⌘   d = ❖

    and so forth. (*Waspese* does not have capital letters!) Now, you are a wasp living in the nest. In *Waspese* write a brief letter to the young boy in the story. Make certain you include the *Waspese* equivalents of the English alphabet, so your teacher can read your letter!

3. Complete one of the following activities:
    a. With a group of your fellow students, create a newspaper or magazine. Write articles about amazing animal (or insect) architecture. Be sure to give your publication a clever title and include pictures or photos of amazing animal craftsmanship.
    b. Team up with one or more students to research the communal lives of social wasps. Present the play, *A Day in the Life of an Extended Wasp Family*. Use appropriate costumes and props.
    c. Phyllo dough is laid in 'papery' layers to make Near Eastern and Turkish recipes. Since the sheets are like the papery layers of the wasp nest, the assignment is to make baklava, a Near Eastern dessert, for your family or classmates. You may work in teams of two. Phyllo dough is available in the freezer section of the supermarket. Confer with your parents before you begin. Your teacher will distribute a good recipe for baklava.

Blueprint for Reading

the Author

James Herriot (1916–1995)

Herriot was born in England as James Alfred Wight. He was the son of a musician and a professional singer. He became a veterinary surgeon at the early age of 24, but he also loved to write. He choose the pen name James Herriot because the British government didn't allow veterinarians to advertise, and the pen name allowed him to write about his experiences as a veterinarian. He wrote his first book at age 50, thinking it would be his only one. Combining his love for animals and his love of writing, however, he wrote many novels. He is probably best known for his All Creatures Great and Small series that he began in 1972. These were novels about the love of animals and their place in the world. Many of his writings were for a young adult audience.

Background Bytes

The history (or etymology) of a word or word part can be both interesting and useful. If you recognize word roots, you can increase your vocabulary and figure out the meaning of unfamiliar words. *The Recital* is a humorous memoir.

How did the word 'humor' come into the English language?

Linguists—people who study the formation of language—believe the word entered English in the 14th century from the French *humeur.* The word had come to France from the Latin *humere,* 'to be moist.'

How is being 'moist' related to something being amusing?

The shifts in meaning reflect changing use over time.

Today 'humor' can mean a bodily fluid, such as blood or lymph. In medieval times, this was the chief meaning of the word. Science held there were four 'Humors' or fluids interacting within the body, determining the person's health and temperament. The belief that bodily humors or fluids were responsible for one's personality or disposition led to other definitions of 'humor.' For example, when we say 'she is in no *humor* to listen,' we are talking about 'a temporary state of mind.' And just as the neutral word 'temperament' became 'temperamental,' meaning 'excitable, erratic, or moody,' the expression 'out of humor' came to mean 'out of sorts' or 'irritable and depressed.'

'Humorous,' which originally meant 'of the four bodily humors,' came to mean being absurd, laughable, or inappropriate—someone a little off-balance from an excess of one humor. Our modern-day definition of 'humor,' as 'the ability to express or appreciate the laughable or absurd,' also includes that which is comical or amusing.

THE RECITAL

Into *The Recital*

Although *The Recital* is neither heavy nor serious, it has a serious theme, as well as an important secondary message or subtheme. From the initial listening exercise, we have seen how people in Darrowby are 'different' from each other. The primary theme, however, suggests just the opposite, and it is one reason why the piece is so funny. What might the theme be? What does this story tell us about people?

The secondary message can be found in Jimmy's experience and conduct at the keyboard. What happens to him? How does he respond on each occasion?

Focusing on Humor

The Recital is a funny piece of writing. Why? What makes it so? Read the piece through just to enjoy it. Then read it again, noting where you laughed. Why did you laugh?

Humor is a stimulus causing spontaneous laughter: an involuntary motor reflex, created by the contraction of 15 facial muscles, just like the automatic upward kick when we are hit below the knee with that little silver hammer. And yet, the laughter reflex puzzles scientists.

Philosophers have long talked about the nature of comedy. Aristotle (Greece, 384-322 B.C.E.), a pupil of Plato and the teacher of Alexander the Great, thought laughter was related to ugliness, a matter of 'putting other people in their place'; Descartes (France, 1596-1650) felt laughter was an expression of joy mixed with surprise or hatred or both; Thomas Hobbes (England, 1588-1679) called it a rejoicing in our superiority over others.

We are taught not to laugh at the less fortunate. But the negative, aggressive element in humor is subtle and unconscious—we don't really think about it. Surely, a part of the humor in *The Recital* lies in our relief at not being in that situation. In fact, if you take the events seriously, these parents, and some children, are suffering. Their extreme reactions—and the hyperbole (exaggeration) used by James Herriot—make us laugh with them or at them.

Often, our feelings of tense expectation overwhelm us, and we laugh, perhaps nervously. When Jeff Ward's face looks 'hideously mottled' as his daughter Margaret plays the wrong notes repeatedly, we do not expect her to get it right and move on effortlessly. If we laugh, it is a nervous laugh.

Also, look for linked events or words that are not normally placed together. For example, look at the sentence "My son, Jimmy…had been practicing without much enthusiasm for the big day." When we see 'without much enthusiasm,' we don't expect 'the big day' to follow. These two phrases express contrary feelings about the same event. The clash is humorous.

> **Word Bank**
>
> **Ghastly, Martyrdom; Convulsively, Flailing, Shuddering:** In this funny story, the author uses words *hyperbolically* (hy pur BOLL ick uhl lee), or with great exaggeration. This is partly what makes us laugh out loud as we read. For example, **ghastly** means "dreadful, horrible, frightful; resembling a ghost." **Martyrdom** means "extreme suffering, torment." (A **martyr** is one who suffers torment or death for refusing to renounce her or his beliefs.) These are words the author uses to describe his experience attending his son's piano recital! What other words of extremity does he include? **Convulsively, flailing**, and **shuddering**. Find their meanings in the Word Banks and think about whether you would expect to find them in a comedy.

abdomen	erupted	impassively	rapturously
atmosphere	eternity	indulgent	shuddering
audible	finale	lingering	succession
blotchy	flourish	martyrdom	tempo
commenced	ghastly	notable	vibrant
convulsively	hovered	palpable	virtuosity
crucial	immobility	perceptibly	wayward

The Recital

James Herriot

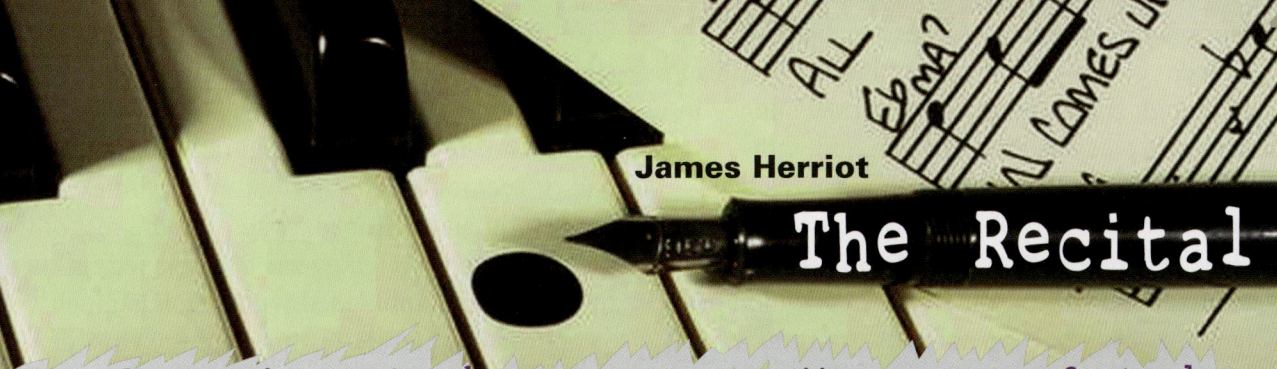

Mr. Garrett's words about parents needing nerves of steel have come back to me many times over the years. One notable occasion was the annual recital given by Miss Livingstone's piano class.

Miss Livingstone was a soft-voiced, charming lady in her fifties who started many of the local children in piano lessons, and once a year she held a concert for her pupils to show their paces. They ranged from six-year-olds to teenagers, and the room was packed with their proud parents. My son, Jimmy, was nine at the time and had been practicing without much enthusiasm for the big day.

Everybody knows everybody else in a small town like Darrowby, and as the place filled up and the chairs scraped into position, there was much nodding and smiling as people recognized each other. I found myself on an outside chair of the center aisle, with my wife, Helen, on my right. Just across from me was Jeff Ward, who tends old Willie Richardson's cows, sitting very upright, hands on knees.

He was dressed in his Sunday best, and the dark serge[1] was stretched tightly across his muscular frame. His red, strong-boned face shone with intensive scrubbing, and his normally wayward thatch[2] of hair was plastered down with brilliantine.[3]

"Hello, Jeff," I said. "One of your youngsters performing today?"

He turned and grinned. "Now, then, Mr. Herriot. Aye, it's our Margaret. She's been comin' on right well at t'piano, and I just hope she does herself justice this afternoon."

"Of course she will, Jeff. Miss Livingstone is an excellent teacher. She'll do fine."

He nodded and turned to the front as the concert commenced. The first few performers who mounted the platform were very small boys in shorts and socks or tiny girls in frilly dresses, and their feet dangled far above the pedals as they sat at the keyboard.

Miss Livingstone hovered nearby to prompt them, but their little mistakes were greeted with indulgent smiles from the assembly, and the conclusion of each piece was greeted with thunderous applause.

I noticed, however, that as the children grew bigger and the pieces became more difficult, a certain tension began to build up in the hall. The errors weren't so funny now, and when little

---

1. *Serge* (SURJ) is a smoothly-finished fabric used for suits.
2. A *thatch* (THATCH) of hair is thick hair resembling thatch on a roof.
3. *Brilliantine* (BRILL yen TEEN) is a greasy substance used to make the hair stiff and shiny.

Word Bank

notable (NO tuh bul) *adj.*: worthy of notice; remarkable; outstanding
wayward (WAY werd) *adj.*: disregarding or rejecting what is considered right or proper
commenced (kuh MENST) *v.*: began; started
hovered (HUV erd) *v.*: waited near at hand; lingered; hung over
indulgent (in DULL jint) *adj.*: showing kindly tolerance; permissive

Jenny Newcombe, the fruiterer's daughter, halted a couple of times, then bowed her head as though she were about to cry, the silence in the room was absolute and charged with anxiety. I could feel it myself. My nails were digging into my palms and my teeth were tightly clenched. When Jenny successfully restarted and I relaxed with all the others, the realization burst upon me that we were not just a roomful of parents watching our children perform; we were a band of brothers and sisters, suffering together.

When little Margaret Ward climbed the few steps to the platform, her father stiffened perceptibly in his seat. From the corner of my eyes I could see Jeff's big, work-roughened fingers clutching tightly at his knees.

Margaret went on very nicely till she came to a rather complicated chord that jarred on the company with harsh dissonance.[4] She knew she had got the notes wrong and tried again…and again…and again, each time jerking her head with the effort.

"No, C and E, dear," murmured Miss Livingstone, and Margaret crashed her fingers down once more, violently and wrongly.

"Good heavens, she's not going to make it," I breathed to myself, aware suddenly that my pulse was racing and that every muscle in my body was rigid.

I glanced round at Jeff. It was impossible for anybody with his complexion to turn pale, but his face had assumed a hideously mottled[5] appearance and his legs were twitching convulsively. He seemed to sense that my gaze was on him, because he turned tortured eyes towards me and gave me the ghastly semblance[6] of a smile. Just beyond him, his wife was leaning forward. Her mouth hung slightly open and her lips trembled.

As Margaret fought for the right notes, a total silence and immobility settled on the packed hall. It seemed an eternity before the little girl got it right and galloped away over the rest of the piece, and though everybody relaxed in their seats and applauded with relief as much as approval, I had the feeling that the episode had taken its toll on all of us.

I certainly didn't feel so good and watched in a half-trance as a succession of children went up and did their thing without incident. Then it was Jimmy's turn.

There was no doubt that most of the performers and parents were suffering from nerves, but this couldn't be applied to my son. He almost whistled as he trotted up the steps, and there was a hint of swagger in his walk up to the piano. This, he clearly thought, was going to be a dawdle.[7]

In marked contrast, I went into a sort of rigor[8] as soon as he appeared. My palms broke out in an instant sweat, and I found I was breathing only with difficulty. I told myself that this was utterly ridiculous, but it was no good. It was how I felt.

Jimmy's piece was called "The Miller's Dance," a title burned on my brain till the day I

---

4. *Dissonance* (DISS uh nintz) means inharmonious sounds.
5. *Mottled* (MAHT ild) means spotted or blotched.
6. A *semblance* (SEM blintz) of a smile is a hint of a smile.
7. *A dawdle* (a DAW dil) is an informal British expression for "something easy to do."
8. *Rigor* (RIG er) is a sudden coldness or stiffening.

Word Bank

perceptibly (pur SEP tib lee) *adv.*: recognizably; discernibly; in a way that could be perceived

convulsively (kun VULSS iv lee) *adv.*: with violent, involuntary muscular contractions

ghastly (GAST lee) *adj.*: haggard and pale; ghostlike in appearance

immobility (IM mo BILL ih tee) *n.*: the state of being incapable of movement or motion; motionless

eternity (ee TUR nih tee) *n.*: a seemingly endless period of time

succession (suk SESH in) *n.*: a number of persons or things following one another in order

die. It was a rollicking[9] little melody which, of course, I knew down to the last semi-quaver,[10] and Jimmy started off in great style, throwing his hands about and tossing his head like a concert pianist in full flow.

Around the middle of "The Miller's Dance," there is a pause in the quick tempo where the music goes from a brisk *ta-rum-tum-tiddle-iddle-om-pom-pom* to a lingering *taa-rum, taa-rum*, before starting off again at top speed. It was a clever little ploy[11] of the composer and gave a touch of variety to the whole thing.

Jimmy dashed up to this point with flailing arms till he slowed down at the familiar *taa-rum, taa-rum, taa-rum*. I waited for him to take off again, but nothing happened. He stopped and looked down fixedly[12] at the keys for a few seconds, then he played the slow bit again and halted once more.

My heart gave a great thud. Come on, lad, you know the next part—I've heard you play it a hundred times. My voiceless plea was born of desperation, but Jimmy didn't seem troubled at all. He looked down with mild puzzlement and rubbed his chin a few times.

Miss Livingstone's gentle voice came over the quivering silence. "Perhaps you'd better start at the beginning again, Jimmy."

"Okay." My son's tone was perky as he plunged confidently into the melody again, and I closed my eyes as he approached the fateful bars. *Ta-rum-tum-tiddle-iddle-om-pom-pom, taa-rum, taa-rum, taa-rum*—then nothing. This time he pursed his lips, put his hands on his knees and bent closely over the keyboard as though the strips of ivory were trying to hide something from him. He showed no sign of panic, only a faint curiosity.

In the almost palpable hush of that room, I was sure that the hammering of my heart must be audible. I could sense Helen's leg trembling. I knew we couldn't take much more of this.

Miss Livingstone's voice was soft as a zephyr,[13] or I think I would have screamed. "Jimmy, dear, shall we try it once more from the beginning?"

"Yes, yes, right." Away he went again like a hurricane, all fire and fury. It was unbelievable that there could ever be a flaw in such virtuosity.

The whole room was in agony. By now the other parents had come to know "The Miller's Dance" almost as well as I did, and we waited together for the dread passage. Jimmy came up to it at breakneck speed. *Ta-rum-tum-tiddle-iddle-om-pom-pom*, then *taa-rum, taa-rum, taa-rum*...and silence.

Helen's knees were definitely knocking now, and I stole an anxious glance at her face. She was pale, but she didn't look ready to faint just yet.

As Jimmy sat motionless except for a thoughtful drumming of his fingers against the woodwork of the piano, I felt I was going to choke. I glared around me desperately, and I saw that Jeff Ward, across the aisle, was in a

---

9. A *rollicking* (RAHL ik ing) tune is a playful, lively tune.
10. A *semi-quaver* (SEM ee KWAY ver) is a sixteenth note.
11. A *ploy* (PLOY) is simply a trick, a strategy.
12. To look *fixedly* (FIX id lee) means to look steadily or stare.
13. A *zephyr* (ZEFF er) is a gentle, mild breeze.

Word Bank

tempo (TEM po) *n.*: the rate of speed of a musical passage or work
lingering (LIN ger ing) *adj.*: remaining or staying in a place longer than usual or expected
palpable (PAL puh bul) *adj.*: capable of being touched or felt; tangible
audible (AW dih bul) *adj.*: capable of being heard; loud enough to be heard
virtuosity (VUR choo AH sit ee) *n.*: excellence and brilliance in musical technique or execution

bad way. His face had gone all blotchy again, his jaw muscles stood out in taut ridges and a light sheen[14] of perspiration covered his forehead.

Something had to break soon, and once more it was Miss Livingstone's voice that cut into the terrible atmosphere.

"All right, Jimmy, dear," she said. "Never mind. Perhaps you'd better go and sit down now."

My son rose from the stool and marched across the platform. He descended the steps and rejoined his fellow pupils in the first few rows.

I slumped back in my seat. Ah, well, that was it. The final indignity. The poor little lad had blown it. And though he didn't seem troubled, I was sure he must feel a sense of shame at being unable to get through his piece.

A wave of misery enveloped me, and though many of the other parents turned and directed sickly smiles of sympathy and friendship at Helen and me, it didn't help. I hardly heard the rest of the concert, which was a pity because as the bigger boys and girls began to perform, the musical standard rose to remarkable heights. It was a truly splendid show—by everybody but poor old Jimmy, the only one who hadn't managed to finish.

At the end, Miss Livingstone came to the front of the platform. "Well, thank you, ladies and gentlemen, for the kind reception you have given my pupils. I do hope you have enjoyed it as much as we have."

There was more clapping, and as the chairs started to push back, I rose to my feet, feeling slightly sick.

"Shall we go then, Helen?" I said, and my wife nodded back at me, her face a doleful[15] mask.

But Miss Livingstone wasn't finished yet. "Just one thing more, ladies and gentlemen." She raised a hand. "There is a young man here who, I know, can do much better. I wouldn't be happy going home now without giving him another opportunity. Jimmy." She beckoned toward the second row. "Jimmy, I wonder…I wonder if you would like to have one more try."

As Helen and I exchanged horrified glances, there was an immediate response from the front. Our son's voice rang out, chirpy and confident. "Aye, aye, I'll have a go!"

I couldn't believe it. The martyrdom was surely not about to start all over again. But it was true. Everybody was sitting down, and a small, familiar figure was mounting the steps and striding to the piano.

From a great distance I heard Miss Livingstone again. "Jimmy will play 'The Miller's Dance.'" She didn't have to tell us—we all knew.

As though in the middle of a bad dream, I resumed my seat. A few seconds earlier, I had been conscious only of a great weariness, but now I was gripped by a fiercer tension than I had known all afternoon. As Jimmy poised his hands over the keys, a vibrant sense of strain lapped around the silent room.

The little lad started off as he always did, as though he hadn't a care in the world, and I began a series of long, shuddering breaths designed to carry me past the moment that was fast approaching. Because I knew he would stop again. And I knew just as surely that when he did, I would topple senseless to the floor.

---

14. A *sheen* (SHEEN) of perspiration is seen when light reflects on the sweat.
15. *Doleful* (DOLE full) means sorrowful or mournful.

Word Bank

blotchy (BLAH chee) *adj.*: covered with spots
atmosphere (AT muh SFEER) *n.*: a surrounding or pervading mood, environment, or influence
martyrdom (MAR tur dum) *n.*: extreme suffering or torment for a cause
vibrant (VY brint) *adj.*: pulsating with vigor and energy
shuddering (SHUD der ing) *adj.*: convulsive trembling, as from horror or cold

I didn't dare look round at anybody. In fact, when he reached the crucial bars I closed my eyes tightly. But I could still hear the music—so very clearly. *Ta-rum-tum-tiddle-iddle-om-pom-pom, taa-rum, taa-rum, taa-rum*...There was a pause of unbearable length, then, *tiddle-iddle-om-pom, tiddle-iddle-om-pom,* Jimmy was blissfully on his way again.

He raced through the second half of the piece, but I kept my eyes closed as the relief flooded through me. I opened them only when he came to the finale, which I knew so well. Jimmy was making a real meal of it, head down, fingers thumping, and at the last crashing chord, he held up one hand in a flourish a foot above the keyboard before letting it fall by his side in the true manner of the concert pianist.

I doubt if the hall has ever heard a noise like the great cheer which followed. The place erupted in a storm of clapping and shouting, and Jimmy was not the man to ignore such an accolade.[16] All the other children had walked impassively from the stage at the end of their efforts, but not so my son.

To my astonishment, he strode from the stool to the front of the platform, placed one arm across his abdomen and the other behind his back, extended one foot and bowed to one side of the audience with the grace of an eighteenth-century courtier. He then reversed arms and pushed out the other foot before repeating his bow to the other side of the hall.

The cheering changed to a great roar of laughter which continued as he descended the steps, smiling demurely.[17] Everybody was still giggling as we made our way out. In the doorway we bumped into Miss Mullion, who ran the little school our son attended. She was dabbing her eyes.

"Oh, dear," she said breathlessly. "You can always depend on Jimmy to provide the light relief."

I drove back home very slowly. I was still in a weak condition, and I felt it dangerous to exceed twenty-five miles an hour. The color had returned to Helen's face, but there were lines of exhaustion round her mouth and eyes as she stared ahead through the windshield.

Jimmy, in the back, was lying full-length along the seat, kicking his legs in the air and whistling some of the tunes that had been played that afternoon.

"Mum! Dad!" he exclaimed in the staccato[18] manner so typical of him. "I like music."

I glanced at him in the driving mirror. "That's good, son, that's good. So do we."

Suddenly he rolled off the back seat and thrust his head between us. "Do you know why I like music so much?"

I shook my head.

"Because it's"—he groped rapturously for the phrase—"because it's so soothing."

---

16. An *accolade* (AK uh LAYD) is an award, honor, or expression of praise.
17. Someone who speaks *demurely* (dih MYOOR lee) speaks with shyness.
18. *Staccato* (stuh KAH toe) notes are shortened and detached.

Word Bank

crucial (KROO shil) *adj.*: of vital or critical importance

finale (fuh NAL ee) *n.*: the last piece, division, or movement of a concert, opera, or composition

flourish (FLUR ish) *n.*: a showy or dramatic gesture or display

erupted (ee RUPT id) *v.*: burst forth with

impassively (im PASS iv lee) *adv.*: without feeling or emotion

abdomen (AB duh min) *n.*: the lower part of the body, containing the digestive organs and intestines

rapturously (RAP chur iss lee) *adv.*: ecstatically

Studying the Selection

First Impressions

Share the passages you found funny with your classmates. Do they agree with your assessment of the humor at each point?

✔ Quick Review

1. Give the names of the following: (a) the author; (b) the author's wife; (c) their son; (d) Margaret's father; (e) the piano teacher; (f) the fruiterer's daughter; (g) the musical composition Jimmy plays; and (h) the administrator of Jimmy's school.
2. Miss Livingstone is characterized in at least four passages in the narrative. How is she described?
3. How many times altogether does Jimmy start the piece? How many times does he complete it?
4. How is Jimmy described in the following situations: (a) when he is playing the piano successfully; (b) when he halts in the middle of the piece; (c) when he is asked to come back on stage and try once more; (d) when he is being applauded at the end?
5. In contrast, how does the author describe his own feelings when Jimmy is on stage? Give ten examples, quoting short phrases from the selection.

In-depth Thinking

6. Why are the parents of the young performers so emotional about their children's performance?
7. What is the theme or message of the story? Write a short paragraph several sentences long. Remember, if you can support your understanding with examples from the piece, you can make a persuasive case—even if your viewpoint differs from that of your classmates.

Drawing Conclusions

8. The author describes Jeff precisely. Describe the author as Jeff might see him. For guidance, review the details the author uses to describe Jeff. Be creative if facts are absent. For example, do we know how the author is dressed?
9. Have you ever given a performance? You may include any activity carried out before others. (a) Describe how your experience was similar to some aspect of *The Recital*. (b) Describe how it was different. (c) Using *The Recital* as a model, write ten phrases, using original adjectives, to show how you were affected by the occasion.

Focusing on Humor

The following three exercises focus on the literary component, **humor**.

1. Compile a list of five jokes, choose one, and write a brief analysis of why it is funny. Arrange with your teacher to perform your joke before your classmates.
2. With your teacher's or your parents' guidance, select a short, humorous piece of writing to present to your class. This may be an essay, a poem, or a short story. Prepare for your presentation by privately reading or reciting the piece aloud many times. Afterwards, write a brief statement telling how the performance felt to you. Perform with costume if possible!
3. Types of humor also include cartoons, caricatures, limericks, 'nonsense' rhymes, plays on words, tongue-twisters, jokes, and so forth. Choose one type of humor; on a piece of cardboard, state the type of humor, giving the definition and an example. Be creative and artistic!

Creating and Writing

1. Can you think of a situation where people from different groups engage in a shared activity? Why might they avoid bringing outside attitudes to the new situation? Write an essay about your observations.
2. Write a 'fictional' piece with the theme of an awkward encounter between two people. Your 'actors' could be from different places, or they might be of different ages or interests.
3. Choose one of the following:
   - With your parents' approval, attend a music recital with family or friends. Review the performance for your class.
   - Draw a map of the United Kingdom and locate Thirsk, the real-life Darrowby. Try to describe the lives of the people as you imagine them.

Blueprint for Reading

the Author

James (Grover) Thurber (1894-1961)

Thurber was born in Columbus, Ohio. As a staff member for *The New Yorker* magazine from 1927-1933, Thurber wrote short stories and drew humorous cartoons. He became popularly known for his witty humor and cartoon drawings, known as one of America's great humorists. He also wrote many children's books. He lost sight in his left eye as a child, and later lost all of his sight in his mid-forties. This didn't stop him from writing, however, as he still wrote and contributed to *The New Yorker* magazine until his death.

Background Bytes

This selection contains many factual and fascinating details of Columbus, Ohio as it existed nearly a century ago.

Factual information can make us want to know *more.* For example, the reader of *The Day the Dam Broke* might wish Thurber had included a map. But you, the reader, from the details of the city areas described, should be able to draw such a rough sketch. Where would you find the details for such a map? There are clues.

The author mentions a movie theater, "motor lorries," "an electric," and cars that had to be cranked. It is March 12, 1913. When were motion pictures and automobiles invented? When could an ordinary family afford a car? Does anyone make a phone call? When were telephones used widely? We are told of a visitor in an airplane, "looking down on the straggling, agitated masses." Did passenger airplanes exist in 1913? Were there *any* airplanes? Or is this the author's point of view, twenty years later? When Thurber says businessmen were "computing," does he mean they were using computers?

We are looking at an earlier version of a modern city, but the people might seem a bit strange to us, more than a bit backward. Surely they could have behaved in a more sensible manner. They have motor vehicles—why can't they use them to escape more quickly? The year is 1913, why can't anyone use the telephone to check facts? Surely a soldier wouldn't behave like a civilian and panic also. Or is it just possible that modern gadgets aren't enough to bring about 'modern' behavior?

Into *The Day the Dam Broke*

This is a 'tongue-in-cheek' story; that is, it is told as an extended gentle joke. The author begins by claiming he "would gladly forget" what he and his family endured during the 1913 flood in Ohio. Does he mean it, or is he joking? Could he have written the story, if he had forgotten what they endured?

The Day the Dam Broke

Keep in mind the *why* of this story. Where does Thurber go thematically, as he recalls these events? Read the story for fun—because it should be fun—and then reflect on the qualities shown by the people in the story. What generalization could you make about 'human nature' as you look at their behavior? *That* is the theme of *The Day the Dam Broke*.

Focusing on the Humorous Historical Recollection

This reminiscence is ironic, a bit of a joke. By **irony**, we mean the words convey a meaning opposite to their **literal** or strict meaning. For example, the story is called, *The Day the Dam Broke*. Yet the first paragraph tells us the dam did *not* break. In the story we see people fleeing for their lives, believing the dam has broken. Would it be funny if it were to happen to us? Probably not! If elderly people and children were trying to escape, with everyone abandoning houses, pets, and possessions to an onrushing flood, that would be frightening. How is the story told to make it *funny*, not *upsetting*?

Finally, the story is **history**. We have a record—an eyewitness account—of people, places, and events. Sometimes we look at our own efforts and ask why our story is flat. Thurber's writing is full and rich. Read the story and make a list of details that bring these people to life. Then make a list of the statements that could help you create a map of the city.

> ### Word Bank
> **Phenomena:** One of the vocabulary words is *phenomenon*, meaning "a fact, occurrence, or circumstance that is observed or can be observed." Note that **phenomenOn** is the singular form of the word. **Phenomena** is the plural.
>
> | | | | |
> |---|---|---|---|
> | authentication | dispelled | intercepted | phenomenon |
> | brandishing | engulf | militiamen | refuge |
> | calamity | exhorted | misconception | staid |
> | coherent | frothing | oblivion | thoroughfare |
> | demoralized | grotesque | perilous | |

James Thurber
The Day the Dam Broke

My memories of what my family and I went through during the 1913 flood in Ohio I would gladly forget. And yet neither the hardships we endured nor the turmoil and confusion we experienced can alter my feeling toward my native state and city. I am having a fine time now and wish Columbus were here, but if anyone ever wished a city ill it was during that frightful and perilous afternoon in 1913 when the dam broke or, to be more exact, when everybody in town *thought* that the dam broke. We were both ennobled[1] and demoralized by the experience. Grandfather especially rose to magnificent heights which can never lose their splendor for me, even though his reactions to the flood were based upon a profound misconception; namely, that Nathan Bedford Forest's cavalry[2] was the menace we were called upon to face. The only possible means of escape for us was to flee the house, a step which grandfather sternly forbade, brandishing his old army saber[3] in his hand. "Let 'em come!" he roared.

Meanwhile hundreds of people were streaming by our house in wild panic, screaming "Go east! Go east!" Grandfather had to be restrained for his own safety. Grandfather promptly fainted. Impeded as we were by the inert[4] form of the old gentleman—he was taller than six feet and weighed almost a hundred and seventy pounds—we were passed, in the first half-mile, by practically everybody else in the city. Had grandfather not come to, at the corner of Parsons Avenue and Town Street, we would unquestionably have been overtaken and engulfed by the roaring waters—that is, if there had *been* any roaring waters.

Later, when the panic had died down and people had gone rather sheepishly[5] back to their homes and their offices, minimizing the distances they had run and offering various reasons for running, city engineers pointed out that even if the dam had broken, the water level would not have risen more than two additional inches in the West Side. The West Side was, at the time of the dam scare, under thirty feet of water—as, indeed, were all Ohio river towns during the great spring floods of forty years ago. The East Side (where we lived and where all the running occurred) had never been in any danger at all. Only a rise of some ninety-five feet could have caused the flood waters to flow over High Street—the thoroughfare that divided the east side of town from the west—and engulf the East Side.

The fact that we were all as safe as kittens

---

1. To be *ennobled* (en NOBE ild) is to be made noble, dignified, or exalted.
2. *Nathan Bedford Forest's cavalry* was a group of mounted Confederate soldiers led by Nathan B. Forest (1821-1877), a Confederate general.
3. A *saber* (SAY ber) is a slightly curved sword with a single sharp edge. It was widely used during the Civil War.
4. *Inert* means not moving.
5. *Sheepishly* (SHEEP ish lee) means with embarrassment or bashfully.

Word Bank

perilous (PER ih liss) *adj.*: involving grave risk; dangerous
demoralized (dee MOR uh LYZD) *adj.*: thrown into confusion; deprived of spirit and courage
misconception (MISS kun SEP shun) *n.*: an incorrect interpretation or misunderstanding
brandishing (BRAN dish ing) *v.*: shaking or waving (a fist or sword, for instance) in a threatening manner
thoroughfare (THUR oh FAIR) *n.*: a major road or highway
engulf (en GULF) *v.*: swallow up; envelop or overwhelm completely

under a stove did not, however, assuage[6] in the least the fine despair and the grotesque desperation which seized upon the residents of the East Side when the cry spread like a grass fire that the dam had given way. Some of the most dignified, staid, cynical, and clear-thinking men in town abandoned their wives, stenographers, homes, and offices and ran east. There are few alarms in the world more terrifying than "The dam has broken!" There are few persons capable of stopping to reason when that clarion[7] cry strikes upon their ears, even persons who live in towns no nearer than five hundred miles to a dam.

The Columbus, Ohio, broken-dam rumor began, as I recall it, about noon of March 12, 1913. High Street, the main canyon of trade, was loud with the placid hum of business and the buzzing of placid businessmen arguing, computing, wheedling, offering, refusing, compromising. Darius Conningway, one of the foremost corporation lawyers in the Middle West, was telling the Public Utilities Commission in the language of Julius Caesar that they might as well try to move the Northern Star as to move him. Other men were making their little boasts and their little gestures. Suddenly somebody began to run. It may be that he had simply remembered, all of a moment, an engagement to meet his wife, for which he was now frightfully late. Whatever it was, he ran east on Broad Street (probably toward the Maramor Restaurant, a favorite place for a man to meet his wife).

Somebody else began to run, perhaps a newsboy in high spirits. Another man, a portly[8] gentleman of affairs, broke into a trot. Within ten minutes, everybody on High Street, from the Union Depot to the Courthouse was running. A loud mumble gradually crystallized[9] into the dread word "dam."

"The dam has broke!" The fear was put into words by a little old lady in an electric,[10] or by a traffic cop, or by a small boy; nobody knows who, nor does it now really matter. Two thousand people were abruptly in full flight. "Go east!" was the cry that arose—east away from the river, east to safety. "Go east! Go east! Go east!"

Black streams of people flowed eastward down all the streets leading in that direction; these streams, whose headwaters were in the dry-goods stores, office buildings, harness shops, movie theaters, were fed by trickles of housewives, children, cripples, servants, dogs, and cats, slipping out of the houses past which the main streams flowed, shouting and screaming. People ran out leaving fires burning and food cooking and doors wide open. I remember, however, that my mother turned out all the fires and that she took with her a dozen eggs and two loaves of bread. It was her plan to make Memorial Hall, just two blocks away, and take refuge somewhere in the top of it, in one of the dusty rooms where war veterans met and where old battle flags and stage scenery were stored. But the seething throngs, shouting "Go east!" drew her along and the rest of us with her.

When grandfather regained full consciousness, at Parsons Avenue, he turned upon the retreating mob and exhorted the men to form ranks and hold off the rebel dogs, but at length he, too, got the idea that the dam had broken and, roaring "Go east!" in his powerful voice, he caught up in his one arm a small child and in the other a slight, clerkish man of perhaps forty-two, and we slowly began to gain on those ahead of us.

---

6. To *assuage* (uh SWAYJ) means to soothe or calm.
7. A *clarion* (KLAIR ee un) cry is a cry that is clear and shrill.
8. One who is *portly* (PORT lee) is rather heavy or fat.
9. To *crystallize* (KRISS tuh LYZ) is to assume definite and concrete form.
10. An *electric* was a battery-powered car.

Word Bank

grotesque (GRO tesk) *adj.*: fantastically ugly or absurd; bizarre
staid (STAYD) *adj.*: serious or dignified in character
refuge (REF yooj) *n.*: shelter or protection from danger or trouble
exhorted (eg ZORT id) *v.*: gave urgent advice, recommendations, or warnings

A scattering of firemen, policemen, and army officers in dress uniforms—there had been a review at Fort Hayes, in the northern part of town—added color to the surging billows[11] of people. "Go east!" cried a little child in a piping voice, as she ran past a porch on which drowsed[12] a lieutenant-colonel of infantry. Used to quick decisions, trained to immediate obedience, the officer bounded off the porch and, running at full tilt,[13] soon passed the child, bawling "Go east!" The two of them emptied rapidly the houses of the little street they were on.

"What is it? What is it?" demanded a fat, waddling man who intercepted the colonel. The officer dropped behind and asked the little child what it was. "The dam has broke!" gasped the girl. "The dam has broke!" roared the colonel.

"Go east! Go east! Go east!" He was soon leading, with the exhausted child in his arms, a fleeing company of three hundred persons who had gathered around him from living rooms, shops, garages, back yards, and basements.

Nobody has ever been able to compute with any exactness how many people took part in the great rout[14] of 1913, for the panic, which extended from the Winslow Bottling Works in the South End to Clintonville, six miles north, ended as abruptly as it began and the bobtail and ragtag and velvet-gowned groups of refugees melted away and slunk home, leaving the streets peaceful and deserted. The shouting, weeping, tangled evacuation of the city lasted not more than two hours in all. Some few people got as far east as Reynoldsburg, twelve miles away; fifty or more reached the Country Club, eight miles away; most of the others gave up, exhausted, or climbed trees in Franklin Park, four miles out. Order was restored and fear dispelled finally by means of militiamen riding about in motor lorries[15] bawling through megaphones: "The dam has *not* broken!" At first this tended only to add to the confusion and increase the panic, for many stampeders thought the soldiers were bellowing "The dam has *now* broken!" thus setting an official seal of authentication on the calamity.

All the time, the sun shone quietly and there was nowhere any sign of oncoming waters. A visitor in an airplane, looking down on the straggling, agitated masses of people below, would have been hard put to it to divine[16] a reason for the phenomenon. It must have inspired, in such an observer, a peculiar kind of terror, like the sight of the *Marie Celeste*,[17] abandoned at sea, its galley fires peacefully burning, its tranquil decks bright in the sunlight.

An aunt of mine, Aunt Edith Taylor, was in a movie theater on High Street when, over and above the sound of the piano in the pit[18] (a W. S. Hart[19]

---

11. Here, *billows* (BILL ohz) refer to the surging masses.
12. As he *drowsed* (DROUZD) means as he lay half-asleep.
13. The idiom *at full tilt* means at maximum speed; with great energy.
14. A *rout* (ROWT) is a tumultuous and disorderly crowd of people.
15. *Lorries* (LOR eez) is a British word for trucks.
16. To *divine* (dih VYN) means to discover.
17. The *Marie Celeste* (muh REE suh LEST) was a ship that vanished in the Atlantic while traveling from New York to Italy. It was later found abandoned with its entire crew missing.
18. In the era of silent movies, there was a *piano in the pit*, an area beneath the movie screen. During the movie, a pianist played suitable music to the action.
19. *W. S. Hart* (1872-1946) was a popular actor in early Western silent movies.

Word Bank

intercepted (IN ter SEP tid) *v.*: halted someone or something on its way from one place to another

dispelled (dih SPELD) *v.*: caused to disburse, vanish

militiamen (muh LISH uh MEN) *n.*: a group of citizens enrolled for military service, called out periodically for drill, but serving full-time only in emergencies

authentication (aw THEN tih KAY shun) *n.*: validation as genuine

calamity (kuh LAM ih tee) *n.*: a great misfortune or disaster; a catastrophe

phenomenon (fih NAHM uh NAHN) *n.*: something that is remarkable or extraordinary; a fact, occurrence, or circumstance observed or observable

picture was being shown), there rose the steadily increasing tromp of running feet. Persistent shouts rose above the tromping. An elderly man, sitting near my aunt, mumbled something, got out of his seat, and went up the aisle at a dogtrot. This started everybody. In an instant the audience was jamming the aisles. "Fire!" shouted a woman who always expected to be burned up in a theater; but now the shouts outside were louder and coherent.

"The dam has broke!" cried somebody. "Go east!" screamed a small woman in front of my aunt. And east they went, pushing and shoving and clawing, knocking women and children down, emerging finally into the street, torn and sprawling.

Inside the theater, Bill Hart was calmly calling some desperado's[20] bluff and the brave girl at the piano played "Row! Row! Row!" loudly and then "In My Heaven."

Outside, men were streaming across the statehouse yard, others were climbing trees, a woman managed to get up onto the "These Are My Jewels" statue, whose bronze figures of Sherman, Stanton, Grant, and Sheridan[21] watched with cold unconcern the going-to-pieces of the capital city.

"I ran south to State Street, east on State to Third, south on Third to Town, and out east on Town," my Aunt Edith has written me. "A tall spare woman with grim eyes and a determined chin ran past me down the middle of the street. I was still uncertain as to what was the matter, in spite of all the shouting. I drew alongside the woman with some effort, for although she was in her late fifties, she had a beautiful easy running form and seemed to be in excellent condition. 'What is it?' I puffed. She gave me a quick glance, and then looked ahead again, stepping up her pace a trifle. 'Don't ask me, ask G-d!' she said.

"When I reached Grant Avenue, I was so spent that Dr. H. R. Mallory—you remember Dr. Mallory, the man with the white beard who looks like Robert Browning?—well, Dr. Mallory, whom I had drawn away from at the corner of Fifth and Town, passed me. 'It's got us!' he shouted, and I felt sure that whatever it was *did* have us, for you know what conviction Dr. Mallory's statements always carried. I didn't know at the time what he meant, but I found out later.

"There was a boy behind him on roller skates, and Dr. Mallory mistook the swishing of the skates for the sound of rushing water. He eventually reached the Columbus School for Girls, at the corner of Parsons Avenue and Town Street, where he collapsed, expecting the cold frothing waters of the Scioto to sweep him into oblivion. The boy on the skates swirled past him, and Dr. Mallory realized for the first time what he had been running from. Looking back up the street, he could see no signs of water, but nevertheless, after resting a few minutes, he jogged on east again. He caught up with me at Ohio Avenue, where we rested together. I should say that seven hundred people passed us.

"A funny thing was that all of them were on foot. Nobody seemed to have had the courage to stop and start his car; but as I remember it, all cars had to be cranked in those days, which is probably the reason."

The next day, the city went about its business as if nothing had happened, but there was no joking. It was two years or more before you dared treat the breaking of the dam lightly. And even now, many years after, there are a few persons, like Dr. Mallory, who will shut up like a clam if you mention the Afternoon of the Great Run.

---

20. In the early days of the American West, a *desperado* (DESS puh RAH doh) was a bold, reckless criminal or outlaw.
21. *Sherman*, *Grant*, and *Sheridan* were all famous Union generals during the Civil War; *Stanton* was Secretary of War during the Civil War.

Word Bank

coherent (ko HEAR int) *adj.*: logically connected; consistent
frothing (FRAWTH ing) *adj.*: bubbling; foaming
oblivion (uh BLIV ee un) *n.*: the state of being completely forgotten; the state of forgetting completely or of being completely unaware

Studying the Selection

First Impressions

Which brief passage does most to bring the story to life for you? Which part do you find most amusing?

✔ Quick Review

1. What was Grandfather's profound misconception?
2. What does the author mean, when he says that he and his family were *impeded* by Grandfather's *inert* form?
3. How much of a rise in the water level would have caused the waters to flow over High Street?
4. What was the name of the river that "imperiled" them?

🗏 In-depth Thinking

5. Compare and contrast James Thurber's recollection in *The Day the Dam Broke* with that of Bruce Brooks in *Animal Craftsmen*. Are there any similarities? What are some of the differences?
6. Would *The Afternoon of the Great Run* have been a good name for this piece? Would it have been better than *The Day the Dam Broke*?
7. In *The Recital*, James Herriot uses exaggeration as a way of creating absurdity. Find ten instances where James Thurber's language overstates or understates events and behavior and makes them even funnier.
8. What can we tell about Civil War attitudes in Columbus, Ohio? Which passages in the selection give us the needed information?

📁 Drawing Conclusions

9. How effective is the first paragraph of the selection? Does it draw you in? Is it difficult to understand? Is it too long or too short, or just right in length? Give a detailed answer, with quotations from the paragraph to support your opinions.
10. Rewrite the first paragraph, telling of that day, as if the dam actually *did* break.

Focusing on the Humorous Historical Recollection

1. Use your list of streets, directions, sections of town, and landmarks to create a map. Think about the order of the streets running north to south. You won't need to draw a detailed, careful map. It can be more of a cartoon, but it should include stores, movie theater, houses, and other landmarks. Use your list of clues from the story, but use your imagination and your artistic sense as well.

2. How might James Thurber have gathered information for this story, if he felt his own memories were insufficient? Pretend you are James Thurber and want to write this story. Make a list of the needed resources—including your own memories. Create a schedule over an imagined two-week period, indicating *when* and *where* you will do your research and *whom* you will interview. In your 'James Thurber' diary, make at least eight entries. Describe your imagined experience at the library or at City Hall, examining town records and old newspapers, talking with family, searching for old friends, and recollecting your own experiences.

3. Pick a person from *The Day the Dam Broke* and write a recollection of the event from that person's point of view. Write in the first-person, using "I." You may use either the present tense (as if it were happening at the time of the writing and the person were speaking) or the past tense.

Creating and Writing

1. Write an essay about a theme in this piece. Your essay might describe how "the best of us behave foolishly at times," or respond to the idea that "the influence of the mob is very powerful." If you can make a case for a different theme, you may use that as the focus of your essay. You may argue for or against a theme.

2. Write a dialogue in which Tommy from *The Recital*, eight-year-old Bruce Brooks from *Animal Craftsmen*, and young James Thurber swap stories about playing piano, finding wasp nests, and fleeing the cold, frothy waters of the Scioto.

3. Choose one of the following activities:
   - Make a large-scale map of Columbus, Ohio in 1913. Present it to your classmates, explaining how you used the clues in the story to construct it.
   - Draw a picture of a scene in *The Day the Dam Broke*.
   - Give a dramatic reading of one of the funnier passages in the selection.

Blueprint for Reading

the Author

Santha Rama Rau (1923-2009)

Rau was born in Madras, India. She attended Wellesley College in the United States, and graduated with honors in 1944. She became an instructor at Sarah Lawrence College and a freelance writer. She has written many travel books. She lived in New York, New York and died in 2009.

Background Bytes

What do you know about India, or about *Bharatavarsha*, as its people refer to it in the Hindi language? India is located in South Asia and is the second most populous country in the world, with more than one-sixth of the globe's total population.

India is a subcontinent, separated from the rest of Asia to the north by the Himalayan mountain range. During its history, India endured partial "conquests" by Arab, Turkish, and Persian invaders. But when the British navy achieved supremacy during the 19th century, India fell completely to the British.

By 1858 the British ruled the country, with Queen Victoria also proclaimed Empress of India. British culture was entirely different from that of India. But India was a rich center of trade, and that mattered most to the British. The British made contributions to Indian society, but they transformed the Indian economy and Indian industry to suit the needs of the British Empire, using the wealth of India to benefit England. Even upper-class, wealthy Indians were treated as second-class citizens in their own country. Eventually Indian political movements gave way to more active struggles, with no success and little change.

Then, Mohandas Gandhi led a national nonviolent protest movement during the 1920s and 1930s. Various boycotts began. Indians were to give up British titles or honors. They were to stop wearing British clothes. They were to stop paying taxes. During these years, thousands of Indians were imprisoned. Although many Indians served with the Allies during World War II, India, as a country, refused to join the war effort. They did not want to be associated with the British. It took until 1947 for India to finally achieve independence.

By Any Other Name

Into *By Any Other Name*

Read the story completely. Then read it again. As you read it the second time, try to understand why it is important to read a story such as this. Moreover, ask yourself why Santha Rama Rau wanted to write it. You are looking for the theme.

What happens when children cannot wear traditional clothes, eat familiar food, or think of their actions as normal? What happens if someone is ridiculed for personal habits, language, and beliefs? What happens when one's natural behavior becomes a source of humiliation? Consider these questions as you think about the theme.

As you read, copy phrases that contrast British and Indian culture. Keep a list, as well, of vocabulary words that appear to come from Indian or Anglo-Indian culture.

Focusing on the Childhood Memoir

By Any Other Name is a beautifully written memoir about the author's childhood world. The piece is vivid in its exotic details, and touches us with its subtle description of how British culture in India reached into the private lives of two sisters.

The **childhood memoir**, written by this upper-class observer, gives the reader a sharp portrait of social inequality. The clear and simple writing is filled with a child's wonder, and the ending is so satisfying that we can only love this tale.

As you read, note those passages appealing to the senses of sight, sound, and touch. Remember, the sense of touch includes the physical experiences of heat and cold.

Word Bank

Incomprehensible, Insular, Intensity, Intimidated: The vocabulary words for this story include four that begin with the prefix *in-*: **incomprehensible**, **insular**, **intensity**, and **intimidated**. What does the prefix *in-* tell us, anyway? When something is *comprehensible*, we can understand it. When it is **incomprehensible**, it cannot be understood. Clearly, sometimes *in-* is like the English word *not*. But this is not always the case. **Insular** comes from *solus*, "alone." In Latin, *insula* means "an island"—a piece of land by itself, separated. Here *in-* means "of, on, by." The Latin *tendere, tensus* means "to stretch, to stretch toward" (English *tension*) and "to lean towards" (*attend* and *tendency*). The Latin word *intendere* meant "to stretch into" and came to mean "eager." Here *in-* has the effect of **intensifying** the root word. The word *timid* means "fearful." The *in-* of **intimidated** means "to be in a state of" or, for **intimidate**, "to put in a state of."

baffled	peevishness	provincial	sprinted
incomprehensible	precarious	sedately	tepid
insular	procession	semidarkness	valid
intensity			

Santha Rama Rau[1]

By Any Other Name

At the Anglo-Indian day school[2] in Zorinabad[3] to which my sister and I were sent when she was eight and I was five and a half, they changed our names. On the first day of school, a hot, windless morning of a north Indian September, we stood in the headmistress's study and she said, "Now you're the *new* girls. What are your names?"

My sister answered for us. "I am Premila, and she"—nodding in my direction—"is Santha."

The headmistress had been in India, I suppose, fifteen years or so, but she still smiled her helpless inability to cope with Indian names. Her rimless half-glasses glittered, and the precarious bun on the top of her head trembled as she shook her head. "Oh, my dears, those are much too hard for me. Suppose we give you pretty English names. Wouldn't that be more jolly? Let's see, now—Pamela for you, I think." She shrugged in a baffled way at my sister. "That's as close as I can get. And for *you*," she said to me, "how about Cynthia? Isn't that nice?"

My sister was always less easily intimidated[4] than I was, and while she kept a stubborn silence, I said, "Thank you," in a very tiny voice.

We had been sent to that school because my father, among his responsibilities as an officer of the civil service, had a tour of duty to perform in the villages around that steamy little provincial town, where he had his headquarters at that time. He used to make his shorter inspection tours on horseback, and a week

---

1. *Santha Rama Rau* (SAHN thuh RAHM uh ROW)
2. The *Anglo-Indian day school* was a non-boarding school in India with British administrators.
3. *Zorinabad* (zor IN uh BAHD) is a village in northern India.
4. *Intimidated* means easily threatened by the actions of others.

Word Bank

precarious (pree KARE ee iss) *adj.*: uncertain; dangerously insecure or unsteady
baffled (BAF ild) *adj.*: confused, bewildered, or perplexed
provincial (pruh VIN shil) *adj.*: not city-like; unsophisticated

before, in the stale heat of a typically post-monsoon[5] day, we had waved goodbye to him and a little procession—an assistant, a secretary, two bearers,[6] and the man to look after the bedding rolls and luggage. They rode away through our large garden, still bright green from the rains, and we turned back into the twilight of the house and the sound of fans whispering in every room.

Up to then, my mother had refused to send Premila to school in the British-run establishments of that time, because, she used to say, "you can bury a dog's tail for seven years and it still comes out curly, and you can take a Britisher away from his home for a lifetime and he still remains insular." The examinations and degrees from entirely Indian schools were not, in those days, considered valid. In my case, the question had never come up, and probably never would have come up if Mother's extraordinary good health had not broken down. For the first time in my life, she was not able to continue the lessons she had been giving us every morning. So our Hindi[7] books were put away and we were sent to the Anglo-Indian school.

That first day at school is still, when I think of it, a remarkable one. At that age, if one's name is changed, one develops a curious form of dual personality. I remember having a certain detached and disbelieving concern in the actions of "Cynthia," but certainly no responsibility. Accordingly, I followed the thin, erect back of the headmistress down the veranda to my classroom feeling, at most, a passing interest in what was going to happen to me in this strange, new atmosphere of school.

The building was Indian in design, with wide verandas opening onto a central courtyard, but Indian verandas are usually whitewashed, with stone floors. These, in the tradition of British schools, were painted dark brown and had matting on the floors. It gave a feeling of extra intensity to the heat.

I suppose there were about a dozen Indian children in the school—which contained perhaps forty children in all—and four of them were in my class. They were all sitting at the back of the room, and I went to join them. I sat next to a small, solemn girl who didn't smile at me. She had long, glossy-black braids and wore a cotton dress, but she still kept on her Indian jewelry—a gold chain around her neck, thin gold bracelets, and tiny ruby studs in her ears. Like most Indian children, she had a rim of black kohl[8] around her eyes. The cotton dress should have looked strange, but all I could think of was that I should ask my mother if I couldn't wear a dress to school, too, instead of my Indian clothes.

I can't remember too much about the proceedings in class that day, except for the beginning. The teacher pointed to me

---

5. *Post-monsoon* (POST mahn SOON) refers to a dry period following the monsoon season of winds and heavy rains.
6. *Bearers* (BAIR erz) carry heavy loads of materials and supplies.
7. *Hindi* (HIN dee) is the official language of India.
8. *Kohl* (KOLE) is a dark powder used as eye makeup in the Middle East and India.

Word Bank

procession (pro SESH in) *n.*: a line or body of people or vehicles moving in a formal, orderly way

insular (IN suh ler) *adj.*: narrow-minded

valid (VAL id) *adj.*: legally sound, effective, or binding

intensity (in TEN sih tee) *n.*: great force, strength, or energy

and asked me to stand up. "Now, dear, tell the class your name."

I said nothing.

"Come along," she said, frowning slightly. "What's your name, dear?"

"I don't know," I said, finally.

The English children in the front of the class—there were about eight or ten of them—giggled and twisted around in their chairs to look at me. I sat down quickly and opened my eyes very wide, hoping in that way to dry them off. The little girl with the braids put out her hand and very lightly touched my arm. She still didn't smile.

Most of that morning I was rather bored. I looked briefly at the children's drawings pinned to the wall, and then concentrated on a lizard clinging to the ledge of the high, barred window behind the teacher's head. Occasionally it would shoot out its long yellow tongue for a fly, and then it would rest, with its eyes closed and its belly palpitating, as though it were swallowing several times quickly. The lessons were mostly concerned with reading and writing and simple numbers—things that my mother had already taught me—and I paid very little attention. The teacher wrote on the easel blackboard words like "bat" and "cat," which seemed babyish to me; only "apple" was new and incomprehensible.

When it was time for the lunch recess, I followed the girl with braids out onto the veranda. There the children from the other classes were assembled. I saw Premila at once and ran over to her, as she had charge of our lunchbox. The children were all opening packages and sitting down to eat sandwiches. Premila and I were the only ones who had Indian food—thin wheat chapatties,[9] some vegetable curry,[10] and a bottle of buttermilk. Premila thrust half of it into my hand and whispered fiercely that I should go and sit with my class, because that was what the others seemed to be doing.

The enormous black eyes of the little Indian girl from my class looked at my food longingly, so I offered her some. But she only shook her head and plowed her way solemnly through her sandwiches.

I was very sleepy after lunch, because at home we always took a siesta.[11] It was usually a pleasant time of day, with the bedroom darkened against the harsh afternoon sun, the drifting off into sleep with the sound of Mother's voice reading a story in one's mind, and, finally, the shrill, fussy voice of the ayah[12] waking one for tea.

At school, we rested for a short time on low, folding cots on the veranda, and then we were expected to play games. During the hot part of the afternoon we played indoors, and after the shadows had begun to lengthen and the slight breeze of the evening had come up we moved outside to the wide courtyard.

I had never really grasped the system of competitive games. At home, whenever

---

9. *Chapatties* (chah PAT eez) are thin griddlecakes of unleavened bread used in Northern India.
10. *Vegetable curry* (VEJ tuh bul KUR ee) is a pungent dish of vegetables cooked in a sauce with curry powder.
11. A *siesta* (see ESS tuh) is a midday or afternoon rest or nap.
12. In India, an *ayah* (AH yuh) is a native maid or nanny.

Word Bank **incomprehensible** (IN kahm pree HEN sih bul) *adj.*: impossible to understand

we played tag or guessing games, I was always allowed to "win"—
"because," Mother used to tell Premila, "she is the youngest, and we have
to allow for that." I had often heard her say it, and it seemed quite reasonable to me, but the result was that I had no clear idea of what "winning" meant.

When we played twos-and-threes[13] that afternoon at school, in accordance with my training, I let one of the small English boys catch me, but was naturally rather puzzled when the other children did not return the courtesy. I ran about for what seemed like hours without ever catching anyone, until it was time for school to close. Much later I learned that my attitude was called "not being a good sport," and I stopped allowing myself to be caught, but it was not for years that I really learned the spirit of the thing.

When I saw our car come up to the school gate, I broke away from my classmates and rushed toward it yelling, "Ayah! Ayah!" It seemed like an eternity since I had seen her that morning—a wizened,[14] affectionate figure in her white cotton sari,[15] giving me dozens of urgent and useless instructions on how to be a good girl at school. Premila followed more sedately, and she told me on the way home never to do that again in front of the other children.

When we got home we went straight to Mother's high, white room to have tea with her, and I immediately climbed onto the bed and bounced gently up and down on the springs. Mother asked how we had liked our first day in school. I was so pleased to be home and to have left that peculiar Cynthia behind that I had nothing whatever to say about school, except to ask what "apple" meant. But Premila told Mother about the classes, and added that in her class they had weekly tests to see if they had learned their lessons well.

I asked, "What's a test?"

Premila said, "You're too small to have them. You won't have them in your class for donkey's years." She had learned the expression that day and was using it for the first time. We all laughed enormously at her wit. She also told Mother, in an aside, that we should take sandwiches to school the next day. Not, she said, that *she* minded. But they would be simpler for me to handle.

That whole lovely evening I didn't think about school at all. I sprinted

---

13. *Twos-and-threes* is a game similar to tag.
14. A *wizened* (WIZ ind) person has withered, shriveled features and skin.
15. A *sari* (SAR ee) is a garment worn chiefly by Indian women. It consists of a long cloth wrapped around the body with one end draped over one shoulder or over the head.

Word Bank

sedately (sih DAYT lee) *adv.*: calmly, quietly, or in a composed manner

sprinted (SPRIN tid) *v.*: raced or moved at full speed for a short distance

barefoot across the lawns with my favorite playmate, the cook's son, to the stream at the end of the garden. We quarreled in our usual way, waded in the tepid water under the lime trees, and waited for the night to bring out the smell of the jasmine.[16] I listened with fascination to his scary stories, until I was too frightened to cross the garden alone in the semidarkness. The ayah found me, shouted at the cook's son, scolded me, hurried me in to supper—it was an entirely usual, wonderful evening.

It was a week later, the day of Premila's first test, that our lives changed rather abruptly. I was sitting at the back of my class, in my usual inattentive way, only half listening to the teacher. I had started a rather guarded friendship with the girl with the braids, whose name turned out to be Nalini[17] (Nancy in school). The three other Indian children were already fast friends. Even at that age it was apparent to all of us that friendship with the English or Anglo-Indian children was out of the question. Occasionally, during the class, my new friend and I would draw pictures and show them to each other secretly.

The door opened sharply and Premila marched in. At first, the teacher smiled at her in a kindly and encouraging way and said, "Now, you're little Cynthia's sister?"

Premila didn't even look at her. She stood with her feet planted firmly apart and her shoulders rigid, and addressed herself directly to me. "Get up," she said. "We're going home."

I didn't know what had happened, but I was aware that it was a crisis of some sort. I rose obediently and started to walk toward my sister.

"Bring your pencils and your notebook," she said.

I went back for them, and together we left the room. The teacher started to say something just as Premila closed the door, but we didn't wait to hear what it was.

In complete silence we left the school grounds and started to walk home. Then I asked Premila what the matter was. All she would say was "We're going home for good."

It was a very tiring walk for a child of five and a half, and I dragged along behind Premila with my pencils growing sticky in my hand. I can still remember looking at the dusty hedges, and the

---

16. *Jasmine* (JAZZ min) is a fragrant, flowering shrub of the olive family.
17. *Nalini* (nuh LEEN ee)

Word Bank

tepid (TEP id) *adj.*: moderately warm; lukewarm
semidarkness (SEM ee DARK niss) *n.*: partial darkness

tangles of thorns in the ditches by the side of the road, smelling the faint fragrance from the eucalyptus[18] trees and wondering whether we would ever reach home. Occasionally a horse-drawn tonga[19] passed us, and the women, in their pink or green silks, stared at Premila and me trudging along on the side of the road. A few coolies[20] and a line of women carrying baskets of vegetables on their heads smiled at us. But it was nearing the hottest time of day, and the road was almost deserted. I walked more and more slowly, and shouted to Premila, from time to time, "Wait for me!" with increasing peevishness. She spoke to me only once, and that was to tell me to carry my notebook on my head, because of the sun.

When we got to our house the ayah was just taking a tray of lunch into Mother's room. She immediately started a long, worried questioning about what are you children doing back here at this hour of the day.

Mother looked very startled and very concerned, and asked Premila what had happened.

Premila said, "We had our test today, and she made me and the other Indians sit at the back of the room, with a desk between each one."

Mother said, "Why was that, darling?"

"She said it was because Indians cheat," Premila added. "So I don't think we should go back to that school."

Mother looked very distant, and was silent a long time. At last she said, "Of course not, darling." She sounded displeased.

We all shared the curry she was having for lunch, and afterward I was sent off to the beautifully familiar bedroom for my siesta. I could hear Mother and Premila talking through the open door.

Mother said, "Do you suppose she understood all that?"

Premila said, "I shouldn't think so. She's a baby."

Mother said, "Well, I hope it won't bother her."

Of course, they were both wrong. I understood it perfectly, and I remember it all very clearly. But I put it happily away, because it had all happened to a girl called Cynthia, and I never was really particularly interested in her.

---

18. *Eucalyptus* (YOO kuh LIP tiss) is a tree of the myrtle family with sweet-smelling evergreen leaves.
19. A *tonga* (TAHN guh) is a two-wheeled, horse-drawn vehicle.
20. *Coolies* (KOO leez) are workers hired at low wages for unskilled work.

Word Bank

peevishness (PEEV ish niss) *n*.: fretfulness; irritability

Studying the Selection

First Impressions

As you read, which were the three strongest phrases, sentences, or passages that appealed to the sense of sight, sound, or touch?

✔ Quick Review

1. What was the headmistress's "helpless inability"?
2. Why had the sisters been sent to the school in Zorinabad, despite their mother's opposition to English-run schools?
3. What did Santha do during a lovely evening?
4. What event brought about the sisters' leaving school?

In-depth Thinking

5. Why do you think examinations and degrees from all-Indian schools were not considered valid in those days?
6. Is the author correct in thinking that a change of name—as hers was changed—at the age of five and a half, encourages a curious form of dual personality? Support your argument with material from the selection.
7. Compare and contrast Indian and British educational practices as they are described in the selection.
8. Why do you think Santha wanted to ask her mother if she could wear a cotton dress to school?

Drawing Conclusions

9. How would you behave towards new neighbors, if the young girls in the family wore gold bracelets, saris, and applied kohl around their eyes? Would you be prepared to welcome them?
10. Why do you think Premila, who had so willingly conformed to the school's expectations, walked out in the end?

Focusing on the Childhood Memoir

1. Explore the etymology of five 'foreign' words used in the selection. Give your list to your teacher—with their definitions, history, and any related English words.
2. With your teacher's help, find some writings by civil rights leaders. Explore how they were influenced by Mohandas Gandhi's stand on nonviolent non-cooperation. On index cards, make notes for an oral report to your class. Submit the cards to your teacher, making sure all quotations use the proper citation form.
3. Imagine you are Premila. In the first-person voice, describe what happened to you at the school in Zorinabad.

Creating and Writing

1. Write an essay on Premila's nonviolent, non-cooperative reaction to the school's classroom practices. Relate her response to the teachings of Mohandas Ghandi.
2. You are the school headmistress. Write a letter to the mother of Premila and Santha, 'explaining' school policies.
3. Draw a map of India, indicating mountain ranges, rivers, and major cities. If possible, outline the various states.

Blueprint for Reading

Background Bytes

The Encyclopedia Britannica considers drought the "most serious physical hazard to agriculture in nearly every part of the world." Do you know the cause of drought or how it affects your weekly grocery bill? In fact, in many regions, drought control literally means giving life to millions of people and animals.

Drought is an insufficiency or lack of rain over a long time—a condition resulting in water shortages, crop damage, and loss of soil moisture. Without enough rain, or if too much plant moisture is lost into the air (a process called transpiration), a complex imbalance results that is often difficult or impossible to reverse.

Into *Drouth*

In Ben Logan's essay, the topic (a severe drought and its effects) is somewhat more separated from the theme than has been the case elsewhere. As you read, ask yourself, "What lesson does the selection teach?" Sometimes it is hard to find the theme. Here, you ask, "What have the characters learned?" That is the theme.

Photographs
by Dorothea Lange
from Library of Congress

Drouth

Focusing on the Reminiscence

As in *Animal Craftsmen* and *The Day the Dam Broke*, *Drouth* is a piece of nonfiction, an **autobiographical episode**. The author tells of a childhood experience, an encounter with nature. Unlike *The Day the Dam Broke*, however, this piece is absolutely serious, and takes place over a period of time. Unlike the wasp nest that captures one boy's attention in *Animal Craftsmen*, the lack of rain in *Drouth* concerns everyone in the family—and everyone in the region, for that matter.

The writing style is well suited to the **reminiscence**; much of it is poetic, even as the reality is painful. The rhythm of the writing is slow-paced, well-suited for looking back—especially to a hot, dry time. Look for passages or phrases that are especially powerful or vibrant, full of imagery and feeling. As you read the selection a second time, make a list of the words, phrases, or sentences that particularly impress you.

Word Bank

Wither: The word, **wither**, is related to the English word *weather*, and comes to us through Northern Europe. Wither has a fascinating array of "relatives" in many other languages. In Old Slavic, *vedro* meant "good weather" and *vetrô*, "the state of the air." In Lithuanian, *vÂtra* means "bad weather, especially a storm." So how do we get **wither**, which means "shrivel, fade, decay" from *weather*? We look to old, middle, and modern German: *gewitere* meant "bad weather." *Gewitter* is "a thunderstorm." The word, *verwittern*, is the key. It means "to be weatherworn, hence to deteriorate, decay."

caravan	drouth	pungent	whittled
contour	geologist	stunted	withered
cultivating			

Ben Logan

DROUTH

There was a gentleness in most summers, the land staying green and moist even in the boiling sun of August. The summer the drouth was at its peak was different. That summer had violence in it. The thirsty land dried, cracked open as though to better receive the rain—and the rain didn't come. The stunted corn curled up its leaves, trying to save moisture. The oats, which needed cool weather when the grains were forming, cooked in the hot dry sun, producing grains light as chaff.[1] The alfalfa[2] was short-stemmed and had the pale green look of cured[3] hay even before it was mowed.

Down in the valleys the creeks ran warm and sluggish, half clogged with moss and slime. The leaves on the elm trees in our yard rattled like the dried oak leaves of fall and began to turn yellow by the middle of July. By then the pastures were brown as old straw, the cattle thin, ribs showing halfway across a forty-acre field, and we could milk any two of them into one twelve-quart pail.

As the land dried out the days grew hotter. The sun came up a violent red through the dust and smoke, heat pulling at the moisture in us before we had finished the morning milking. For the first time anyone could remember, there was no morning fog filling the big valley that led down to the Kickapoo.

The bawling[4] of cattle woke us at night. Any other summer it would have meant a cow had been left in the

---

1. The *chaff* (CHAF), part of the husk, covers the grain until it is removed during threshing.
2. *Alfalfa* is a grass-like crop used for animal feed. Normally it can be mowed several times during the growing season.
3. Freshly cut hay is usually dark green. It must be dried, or *cured* (KYURD), before it can be fed to livestock.
4. The cattle were *bawling*, loudly complaining.

Word Bank

drouth (DROWTH) *n.*: also spelled *drought*; a period of dry weather, especially one that is harmful to crops

stunted (STUN tid) *adj.*: stopped, slowed down, or hindered in growth or development

barnyard by accident when the others were put out to night pasture. This summer it meant they wanted to get back into the barnyard for water.

"Even the grass doesn't have any moisture in it," Father said.

The drouth was not ours alone. Day after day the northwest wind carried the soil of the Great Plains to us in a never-ending cloud of yellow-brown. The fine dust that rode the wind was everywhere. It gritted between our teeth when we ate. Freshly washed clothes turned brown on the clothesline. I could draw faces on the dark wood of a tabletop that had been wiped clean an hour before.

Newspapers carried pictures of houses half-covered with dust, roads being cleared of dust drifts with snowplows, and caravans of farmers leaving the land, possessions piled high in old pickup trucks. There was talk that half the soil of the Great Plains was going to end up east of the Mississippi.

The endless summer went on. Father suffered with the suffering land. Each morning his eyes swept the horizon, looking for some sign that rain might come. He walked out into the fields, feeling the wilted plants, poking at the concrete hardness of the dry soil. He would come back to the house, face drawn, shaking his head. "If there was just something a man could do. I don't know anything to do but wait for it to rain."

Lyle tried to cheer Father up. "You always said it would be nice to have one of those rich Iowa farms. Few more weeks of this dust and you'll have one, delivered right to you."

The old men at the filling station, who whittled and argued their days away, compared the summer to the ancient-sounding past. Any time we stopped there they were at it. "Figure it's the worst one we ever had," old Charlie said. "Lot worse than back in ninety-five. I tell you, there's never been a summer like this one before."

He said it with great authority, and no one argued. I had never seen that happen before.

Men reacted to the drouth in different ways. Some gave up and moved away. Some prayed to G-d for help. Some went through the days condemning the weatherman, the Republicans, and whoever invented farming in the first place.

Some, like Lyle, kept trying to make jokes. "Joking about it is a lot better than shooting yourself," he said.

A neighbor offered Lyle a chew of tobacco one day.

"Nope," Lyle said. "Had to give it up."

"How come?"

"Too dry. Last time I tried some, I chewed all day. It was seven o'clock that night before I worked up enough juice to spit. Going to try it again some day if it ever rains."

Word Bank

caravans (KARE uh VANZ) *n*.: groups of travelers journeying together for safety through hostile territory

whittled (WIT ild) *v*.: carved, trimmed, and shaped (a piece of wood) by cutting off bits with a knife

It didn't rain.

The grasshoppers came in a horde, as though they were blown in from the West with the dust. There was a story about them, too, passed on by one of the men at the filling station.

"I heard a fellow over by Mount Zion was out cultivating corn. He noticed the grasshoppers was pretty thick but didn't pay them no mind. Finally he got thirsty. He was in a field close to the house so he left the horses there and started to go get some water. It was when he was climbing over the fence he noticed them grasshoppers had gone through all the grass along the fence row and was starting on the fence posts."

"Wood fence posts or steel fence posts?" someone interrupted.

"Fellow didn't say.

Anyway, he went on to the house and got his drink of water. When he got back to the field, the cultivator and team of horses was gone. He figured they'd run away until he saw what the grasshoppers was doing. You know they'd ate up the horses and cultivator and was pitching horseshoes to see who got him."

As the summer went on, a new and pungent blue joined with the brown of the dust. Forest fires were raging out of control in the pine woods to the north.

Along the ridge wells began drying up. Neighbors came in wagons and pickup trucks to fill ten-gallon milk cans or sometimes drove a whole herd of cattle to water at our stock tank. Father kept checking the flow from our pump, but it held out, the windmill going steadily.

Storms rolled up the northwest. We watched them coming, hopeful even when they looked violent and

Word Bank

cultivating (KULL tih VAYT ing) *v.*: preparing and working on land, in order to raise crops

pungent (PUN jint) *adj.*: sharply affecting the organs of taste or smell; biting; acrid

dangerous. White windclouds boiled ahead of black clouds, the day going so dark the nighthawks came out and filled the sky with their whirling and diving. But the storm had a way of going around us or just seeming to dissolve into the dry air. Or they came on, driving us to cover, and turned out to be nothing but a giant wind.

Someone said, "The wind's doing its best to bring us rain. It's like there just ain't any rain out there to bring."

We put up forty-eight loads of hay that summer. No one could remember a year when we had put up less than a hundred. One field of oats was so light we cut it for hay and made a stack behind the barn. That night one of the rainless windstorms came. Lightning struck the hay poles and set the stack on fire. The flickering glow coming through the window woke Father. We rushed out, but all we saved were the hay poles and rope.

Father reported the loss to the fire-insurance company and a check came in the mail. He opened the letter at the dinner table, looked at it, and started shaking his head.

"They didn't pay very much?" Laurance asked.

"They paid too much. They must think that was good hay—like alfalfa."

And in that violent summer, when the crops were a failure, the cows drying up, money short, and it seemed it might never rain again, Father sent the check back to the insurance company and said he'd take half that much.

Mother suffered through that summer, worrying about Father, worrying about her garden and about a fall and winter coming with a family to keep fed. Her garden withered, only the brave-colored zinnias[5] seeming to flourish in the drouth. Birds were scarce. "Gone on farther north maybe," she said, "to where it's cooler." And having said that, she began to worry about the birds getting caught in the forest fires.

Looking ahead to a lean harvest, we canned all the summer apples we could, even searching in the old orchards of deserted farms. Lee and I picked more than a hundred quarts of blackberries, still a decent crop, deep in the shaded woods along the moist ditches. When the ears of the field corn were in the milk stage, we picked bushels of them and cut off the kernels for canning.

"Good idea," Lyle said. "We won't be able to put it in the corncrib[6] anyway."

"What are you talking about?"

---

5. *Zinnias* (ZINN yuhs) are flowers with bright colors.
6. A *corn-crib* (KORN KRIB) is a roofed storage bin. Its widely separated slats allow the corn to dry.

Word Bank

withered (WITH erd) *v.*: shriveled; faded; dried out

Father asked.

Lyle had on his deadpan[7] look. "Why the ears are so small they're just going to come rolling out through the slats in the crib fast as we can shovel them in."

Father didn't even smile.

Rain finally came in the fall, breaking the drouth, and the land began to heal itself. But the costs of drouth were not yet paid. Ditches appeared where none had ever been as the rain pounded at soil that was cracked and protected only by the stunted plants and close-cropped grass. Hundreds of oak trees stood bare of leaves the following spring. Some of the wells and springs that had dried up never had water again.

We didn't farm quite the same after that summer. The reaction of the land to the drouth told us we had made mistakes, had taken the harvest too much for granted, and left the land too little safety margin to allow for the dry years.

We learned to cultivate corn just deep enough to cut off the weeds, leaving the moisture protected instead of rolling it up to dry out in the sun.

Most important of all, we began laying out fields in long narrow strips, planted alternately in oats, hay, and corn so that a plowed field and a cultivated crop never laid open a wide piece of hillside to the rain. When water had a free run across a big cornfield, it picked up enough speed to carry the soil with it. In the new strip-cropping,[8] water was slowed by running into the hay or oats before it could pick up the soil.

Laurance came home from high school with word that strip-cropping had been used more than fifty years before by farmers from Switzerland who lived in Mormon Coulee, near La Crosse, sixty miles to the north.

At first we laid out our strips in straight lines, but the hillsides were not straight. Later, we ran them along the contours of the hills and our fields began to look like pictures in my geography book of mountainside terraces in China.

From the drying up of the wells we learned that the need to protect the land was not just local. A state geologist explained what he thought had happened. Much of the well water in southwestern Wisconsin came from a layer of limestone buried three hundred feet or more below the surface of the ridges. That layer of limestone slanted upward, to the north, so that a hundred miles away, in north central Wisconsin, the limestone lay at the surface. There, it picked up water. That water seeped slowly southward through the limestone to our wells,

---

7. A man with a *deadpan* expression does not facially reveal that he is joking.
8. The farmers placed different *crops* side-by-side, in narrow *strips*, so water would be absorbed by the soil.

Word Bank **contour** (KAHN toor) *n.*: the outline of a figure or body; the line that defines a shape or object

taking perhaps seventy-five years to make the trip. And about seventy-five years before, the geologist pointed out, men had drained the surface water from the north central Wisconsin marshes to make more farmland.

The story of the seventy-five-year-old well water and the draining of the marshes made a deep impression on Father. "There's just too much we don't know," he said. "How could somebody way up there know he was draining away our water supply? For that matter, what are we doing right here that's changing things someplace else? We know what cutting off the timber has done—making floods in the valleys."

"I guess we can't be expected to know everything in advance," Mother said gently.

"That's right. But we can go slow when we start changing things. We can admit that we're playing around with something that's a lot bigger than we are."

I suddenly remembered old Charlie Harding, teetered[9] back in his chair at the filling station, fussing about the timber being cut out of the Mississippi bottoms. "I don't know just what it's all about," he said. "Might even be a good idea. But it's another thing being changed that ain't ever going to be changed back again."

An age of innocence had ended. Father had thought of man in general as being an enemy of the land. The summer of the drouth made him examine everything we were doing to see in what ways we, personally, were enemies of the land.

---

9. He balanced himself, swaying, as he *teetered* (TEET erd) back and forth in his chair.

Word Bank

geologist (jee AHL uh jist) *n.*: one who studies the physical history of the land and the rocks of which it's composed

Studying the Selection

First Impressions

Which words, phrases, and sentences in Drouth are especially strong, beautiful, or revealing?

✔ Quick Review

1. In the summer of the drought, what does "the thirsty land" do? How does the author describe the corn, the oats, the alfalfa, and the leaves on the elm trees?
2. What happens that no one can remember happening before?
3. Ordinarily, why do cattle cry at night? Why do they cry at night during the drought?
4. As the summer goes on, "a new and pungent blue join[s] the brown of the dust." What does the pungent blue indicate?

In-depth Thinking

5. Does the family live within the "borders" of the Great Plains? Cite passages from the selection to support your reasoning.
6. What does Lyle mean when he jokes with Father that one of those rich Iowa farms will soon be delivered to him?
7. The author writes that "birds were scarce." What does Mrs. Logan surmise (guess) has happened to the birds?
8. In contrast to earlier farming practices, what does the Logan family change after the summer drought? What do they realize as the wells begin to dry up?

Drawing Conclusions

9. Why does Father return the insurance check? Is his decision a surprise to you?
10. In many states the drought lasted longer than it did in Wisconsin. Was it logical for farmers in those states to remain on their farms? Why do you think they stayed?

Focusing on the Reminiscence

1. The following quote is from a farmer during those times: "I felt I was becoming a slave to the land. But I held on to the thought that this land had to be stopped from blowing. Often I was so full of dust that I drove blind, unable to see even the radiator cap on my tractor or hear the roar of the engines." Why do people record their difficult experiences in journals and diaries? Write a short essay in which you discuss the why of journals and diaries. Or you can write about another reminiscence you have read.

2. The federal government began various relief programs during the 1930s. Use reference resources to identify them. Write a brief paper about one of these programs. In your paper, discuss what might have happened if aid were not available.

3. Arrange to visit a home for the aged. Interview someone who has lived through the Depression, the drought of the 1930s, or a similar difficult time. Make a list of questions beforehand. A good researcher will befriend the person before asking questions. Prepare for at least one follow-up session after you digest the answers to your questions. Then write a first-person account of that person's experience. (Don't be afraid to say "I.") Make certain you give your subject a copy to critique. Try to maintain this new friendship with monthly visits.

Creating and Writing

1. Obviously, we can't predict the results of seemingly harmless actions. Write about a personal experience, in which you learned that lesson.

2. Select one or two of the passages that are particularly meaningful for you. Try to imagine yourself in that time and place, actually witnessing the event. In the first-person voice, present tense, write a letter to one of your classmates describing your observations and feelings. That classmate will read your letter aloud to the class.

3. Dorothea Lange and Ben Shahn worked as photographers for the U.S. Farm Security Administration during the 1930s. Dorothea Lange's photographs appear in this section. Write to the proper government agencies for copies of their photographic work. Using the photographs, along with material you cut from newspapers or magazines supplied by your teacher, create a collage that speaks to the spirit of those times.

Literature is the art of writing

literature is the art

Novel

something that will be read twice

of writing something that will be read twice

Blueprint for Reading

the Author

**Jack Bennett
(1934-)**

Jack Bennett could well serve as our imagined ideal Australian—that is, he arrived from somewhere else. Born in colonial South Africa, he worked and traveled throughout Africa and the Far East. Starting as an artist, he held various non-technical jobs before settling in as a journalist. Bennett worked for various newspapers before trying his hand at fiction. His experiences in Hong Kong provided background for his novels, especially *The Voyage of the Lucky Dragon*, with its tale of temporary refugee camps and hint of forced repatriation.

Background Bytes

War hasn't occurred on American soil since the Civil War of the 1860s. Vietnam, on the other hand, has known war for most of the 20th century. The longest war—between North and South, although longer than America's Civil War—lasted over twenty years.

Vietnam is in Southeast Asia. To the north lies southern China. To the west are Laos and Cambodia. South and east, the South China Sea forms the border of Vietnam. This is a country rich in rivers and harbors, ideal for rice farmers and fishing. Unfortunately for Vietnam, its potential wealth creates envy, and it has not known peace for much of its history. *The Voyage of the Lucky Dragon* is set at the end of the Second Indochina War, otherwise known as the Vietnam War.

The First Indochina War involved the French, the original colonial power. After World War II, they tried to regain their prewar possession, but were forced to withdraw after 1954. The North became home to the victorious Communists. They continued their fight against the democratic South. America became part of the Vietnam conflict, fighting with the South from 1965–1973. In 1975 the war was over. American aid stopped and the North invaded Saigon, signaling the defeat of South Vietnam. Peace and unification, however, meant danger for citizens in the South who had identified with the Americans and democracy. They feared execution or separation from their families—deportation to "New Economic Zones" and re-education camps. These government programs were meant to break their attachment to particular areas and to promote communist doctrines. Many people fled—some on American airplanes—others by boat, often forced to bribe corrupt officials, hoping for asylum in neighboring and Western countries.

Into *The Voyage of the Lucky Dragon*—Part One

The family in *The Voyage of the Lucky Dragon* is filled with fear when North Vietnam defeats the South and unifies the country. Having fought for the *wrong* side, they fear revenge by the new government. Events at school prove their fears are well-grounded, for the government sees them as hostile to communist ideals.

THE VOYAGE OF THE LUCKY DRAGON

The father, Phan Thi Chi, hopes for a better life in the village where his father lives and owns a fishing boat. He plans to move his family there without government knowledge. Given the uncertainty, family support is all that matters. After years of war and hardship, the extended Thi Chi family wants only to stay together. Their relationships are intricately woven into a tight fabric. When one member despairs, another triumphs, never letting their hopes be dashed entirely.

Focusing on Setting

In the first section of this novel, setting is crucial. Intrigue, suspense, and danger are appropriate to a war-ravaged country. There have, however, been many wars, many refugees. Why, then, did Bennett choose to set his story in Vietnam? As recent history, the Vietnam War still affects us, giving the setting greater weight. Also, authors choose to write from strength. Jack Bennett is Australian, and his country welcomed many Vietnamese boat people. Likely, Bennett wanted to tell the story of his country's newest immigrants.

Many of Bennett's readers live in Western countries and haven't known war or been exposed to Southeast Asia or its people. Bennett must establish a sense of place early on. In his opening chapters, background material on the conflict helps readers understand North and South Vietnam, the two halves of an artificially divided nation. Individual family members show us the personal side of war. Events—after 'peace'—become real, as the family meets the new government in action. This material brings Vietnam, a foreign place, alive for Western readers.

Word Bank

Paranoia and **parapet** are two of the many words that begin with *para-*. In *paranoia*, which comes from Greek, *para* is a preposition meaning "at one side of, beside." Similar words are *paragraph*, *paralyze*, and *parallel*. *Paranoia* comes from *para-* + *nous*, "mind," and literally means "out of one's mind." In *parapet*, *para-* comes from a Latin verb meaning "(to guard) against." *Parapet's* two roots, "against" + *petto* "the chest," don't explain its current meaning. Similar words are *parasol*, "to guard against the sun," and *parachute*, "to guard against a fall."

accord	entranced	intricate	repatriate	threshold
animated	exploited	jetty	scapegoats	tirade
contempt	flaccid	lurched	scathingly	torrent
conviction	grimaced	naively	shards	triumphal
decadent	harangue	ominous	sinister	upheavals
deteriorating	indispensable	paranoia	steadfastly	
dismantled	inscrutable	parapet	sullen	

The Crossroads of Southeast Asia

The Voyage of the Lucky Dragon

Jack Bennett

❀ Part One

Foreword

In the latter half of the 1970s a great many Vietnamese[1] made a terrible discovery: they could no longer live in the country of their birth.

So they left. Illegally, risking arrest and execution. They left everything except the clothes they stood up in. In large boats, small boats, stolen boats and hired boats they put to sea by the hundred, the thousand, the tens of thousands and the hundreds of thousands.

They died in the same numbers. Their bones lie like dead coral in the Gulf of Thailand, the South China Sea, the western Pacific, the Indian Ocean, the Timor Sea, the Arafura Sea. They were robbed, murdered, drowned, starved, ignored.

This is the story of one boat, the aging fishing boat Lucky Dragon, and the family she carried out of Vietnam.

Lucky Dragon's people—like all the other Vietnamese who fled—wanted one simple thing:
    A home.

御 Chapter 1

Home.

Home was a small flat[2] over a general dealer's shop in Bach Dang[3] in the Gia Dinh[4] suburb of Ho Chi Minh City.[5] Before the liberation, before the French and then the Americans had left, it was called Saigon.[6]

There always seemed to be a war. Before Quan[7] was born the French were the enemy. His mother, whose name was Xuyen,[8] sometimes told exciting stories about carrying messages for the Viet Minh,[9] the Vietnamese nationalists who were fighting the French. Xuyen was only twelve, the age of her daughter, Ly,[10] when she used to slip through the French lines with information for the Viet Minh.

---

1. *Vietnamese* (vee ET nuh MEEZ)
2. A *flat* is a residential apartment that runs from the front to the back of a building.
3. *Bach Dang* (BAHK DAWNG) is a section or part of Gia Dinh.
4. *Gia Dinh* (GEE DIN) is a suburb on the outskirts of Ho Chi Minh City.
5. *Ho Chi Minh* (HO CHEE MIN) *City*
6. *Saigon* (sy GAHN), the former name of Ho Chi Minh City, was the capital of South Vietnam from 1954 to 1976.
7. *Quan* (KWAN) is a Vietnamese name for a man.
8. *Xuyen* (NOO YEN) is a Vietnamese name for a woman.
9. The *Viet Minh* (VEE et MIN) were a Vietnamese group that fought against French rule.
10. *Ly* (LY) is a Vietnamese name for a female.

Xuyen's stories angered Uncle Tan (who wasn't really an uncle, but a cousin, several times removed). He had lost his right leg fighting the Viet Cong at Hue[11] in 1968.

"Perhaps it would have been better for all of us if we'd let the French stay," he would snarl and then, picking up his crutch, swing himself awkwardly out of the shop.

Then that war ended and most of the French left and for a while it seemed that everything was going to be fine. But it wasn't, of course. Nothing stayed fine in Vietnam for long. After the French had left, the country was split in two along the seventeenth parallel of latitude[12] and the people were promised—by statesmen meeting in Geneva[13]—that in two years elections would be held which would reunite the whole country. But the elections were never held, and the war began again. But this time the Vietnamese were fighting one another: the people in the south, or most of them, were fighting the Viet Minh, most of whom were northerners, and who had been renamed (by the government in Saigon) the Viet Cong, which means Vietnamese communists.[14]

So once again the streets of Saigon were full of soldiers—foreign soldiers, too; Americans and Koreans and Australians and New Zealanders and Thais as well as Vietnamese.

Quan's earliest impression of the war was one of noise. All day long and well into the night, trucks full of soldiers, or piled high with boxes of ammunition, rumbled past his parents' shop. Sometimes tanks passed with a horrible clanking, leaving scars on the street.

Then there were the planes. Gia Dinh was about ten kilometers from Than Son Nhut[15] Airport, and, for part of that war, Than Son Nhut was the busiest airport in the world. The sky was always full of planes. The sound of them never went away; it was like a great wave, or a waterfall, a torrent of noise made up of separate sounds: the clatter of helicopters, roar of jets, whine of turbo-props.[16] Quan and his friends made a game of spotting them, the way children in other countries made a game of spotting things like migratory birds or locomotives.

By the time he was ten, war planes were a part of his landscape. Children in parts of the world where there was no war had swallows and crows and pigeons in their skies: Quan and his friends had Phantoms and Intruders and C-130's and Galaxy Starlifters and Skyhawks and Skyraiders and whole flocks of helicopters, from the little single-rotor ones which fired rockets from racks on their landing skids[17] to the big twin-rotored troop-carrying Chinooks and the terrifying gunships. One night Quan stood on the roof of their flat above the shop and watched a gunship firing on Viet Cong across the Saigon River. The gunship's massed battery of mini-guns made a terrible sound: a long unending tearing scream, and the red tracers, so many of them

---

11. The *Viet Cong* (vee ET KAHNG) were a Communist-led guerilla force in the Vietnam War. *Hue* (HWAY) is a seaport.
12. *Seventeenth parallel...* is the seventeenth of the imaginary lines drawn east to west on the globe to mark the latitude.
13. *Geneva* is a major Swiss city, often the site of international peace talks.
14. *Communists* support a political system in which all property is owned by the government, to create a social system presumably with no poverty and no social classes.
15. *Than Son Nhut* (THAN SUN NOOT)
16. *Turbo-props* were WWII planes with turbo-propeller engines.
17. *Landing skids* are a helicopter's landing gear.

Word Bank

torrent (TOR int) *n.*: a rushing or abundant stream flowing with great rapidity and violence

that they formed one solid shaft of light, licked the ground like a breath of flame. Quan knew that night that he had seen a real dragon, and that the ones in the storybooks would never frighten him any more, even in his dreams.

And all the time, behind the truck noise and plane noise, there was the gunfire. The gunfire had been there for so long that Quan hardly noticed it. It was not very close, just a constant low grumbling all around the city, as, night and day, big field-pieces fired on real or imagined Viet Cong trails. H and I fire, it was called: Harassment and Interdiction[18] fire.

For many nights of the war Saigon never had a natural night, a night of real darkness. The sun set as usual, of course—even the war couldn't stop that—but as the twilight faded small aircraft would take off from Than Son Nhut and drop big magnesium parachute flares[19] over the city: they bloomed like horrid white flowers and floated slowly down beneath nylon parachutes. People looked like corpses in their ghastly light. Sometimes there were twenty in the sky at once. They were supposed to prevent the Viet Cong from sneaking into Saigon under cover of darkness, by destroying the darkness. In the morning the parachutes hung flaccid from the palm trees.

A soldier told Quan that the flares cost ninety American dollars each, and Quan and his friends wondered how the Viet Cong thought they could ever defeat a country that had so much money to waste.

His father went away to the war. So did the fathers and elder brothers of most of his friends. The only men left were old or crippled. Even the teenagers went to the war in the end. Quan and Ly helped their mother in the shop: old Ah Soong, the Chinese amah,[20] left her private kingdom in the flat above and came down to help in the shop. It seemed as though their whole world had suddenly dwindled to the shop, which was really a tiny slit in the high walls of Bach Dang, with a sad stock of cheap threads, needles, buttons, plastic toys and poor clothes from Taiwan.[21] But as the war came closer the family clung to it.

As they grew older Quan and Ly thought more and more about Ah Soong. The old Chinese lady had been part of their lives for as long as they could remember: she had been nursemaid, teacher, cook, housemaid, a stern quiet figure who was always there; quick to scold, when they had done something wrong; slow to praise, because her standards were so high that they seldom did anything she deemed worthy of her praise. But Ah Soong's praise, when it came, was worth waiting for: to see that ivory-colored old face, as immobile as a carved mask, suddenly melt with approval and affection, was a delight which never palled.

> His father went away to the war. So did the fathers and elder brothers of most of his friends. The only men left were old or crippled. Even the teenagers went to the war in the end.

---

18. *Harassment and Interdiction* fire is the steady use of ground fire to repeatedly disturb (harass) and hinder (interdict) enemy troops.
19. *Magnesium flares* burn with a dazzling light. They were attached to *parachutes* that fell slowly into the city.
20. *Amah* is an Asian word for female servant.
21. *Taiwan* (ty WAN) is an island, the seat of the Republic of China since 1949.

Word Bank

flaccid (FLAS sid) *adj.*: soft and limp; not firm; flabby; lacking force

But of course Ah Soong was always a foreigner to them. She was not Vietnamese, after all: she was a Hoa,[22] as Chinese living outside China were called in Vietnam. One day Ah Soong would go back to the China she had left fifty years before. If not alive, then dead, with her bones in a burial urn. Ah Soong, like many Chinese living in foreign countries, cherished a dream of being buried in China.

She even managed to save a few dong[23] from the tiny wage of a few piastres[24] a month she earned, and put them in a savings account at the Hong Kong and Shanghai Banking Company's branch in Chuong Duong Street. Quan and Ly had seen her savings account book, so they knew this was true.

At this time Ah Soong was in her late sixties. She had worked hard all her life and like most Cantonese was lithe and strong although small. She had come from China when she was a girl of fifteen to marry a distant cousin: the young man had died of cholera before the wedding could take place. The marriage had been arranged years before, when Ah Soong and her bridegroom-to-be were babies; she had never met him before coming to Vietnam, and felt nothing but a formal grief when he died. Many other people had died of cholera that year and his death was but one drop in a bucket of water. But the cholera had killed many other young men among the Hoa, and Ah Soong realized that her chances of finding another husband, either in Vietnam or China, were few.

But she did not want to return to China. To have come home, penniless and husbandless, to live out her life as a pitied, dependent old maid among her family would have meant great loss of face. Nor did she want to fill the same position among her dead husband-to-be's family, although they would, of course, have taken her in.

But, although the young woman who was to become Ah Soong the amah had no other friends or relatives among the Hoa, she had people she knew among the half-Hoa: Quan Thi Chi's grandfather's wife had been a Hoa, a Wong from Quandong Province (or Kwantung, as it was known in those days) in South China, and the Wongs had intricate ties of family and obligation with the people Ah Soong had left behind to marry in a strange land.

So she had picked up her cheap, dented cardboard suitcase and traveled, by bus, train, and riverboat, across the width of southeast Vietnam, from Qui Nhon to Saigon. Quan Thi Chi's grandfather's wife had taken her in, being well aware of the Chinese obligations of family, and there she had stayed, through several

---

22. *Hoa* is Vietnamese for Chinese expatriate.
23. The *dong* is Vietnamese currency.
24. *Piastres* (pee AST erz) are a former French monetary unit.

Word Bank   **intricate** (IN trih kit) *adj.*: having many interrelated parts or facets; entangled or involved; complex

wars, floods, famines, pestilences,[25] revolutions, depressions, and family upheavals. Whatever happened, Ah Soong, like a stout headland on a wave-battered coast, remained, in the quiet eye of many a storm.

She nursed generations of children: Quan Thi Chi's father, Phan,[26] was the youngest of eleven. Some had died of cholera.[27] Diptheria had killed another, and an unknown fever had killed two. It was a time in which many children died. Then wave after wave of wars and turmoil had scattered the rest of the family so that by 1970 only Phan, a much older brother, and their father, now an old man of eighty, were left. The old man had wearied of the city, become sickened by the changes in it, and had given the shop to his youngest son; the rest of his money—small enough crop to harvest after a lifetime's work—he had taken south to Rach Gia[28] with the older son, and there they had bought a boat, named Lucky Dragon, and become fishermen.

The old man hoped to find in the sea a peace that had evaded him on the land. Of course he was too old to help actively with the handling of the boat; but his son employed some lively young men from Rach Gia, which is southwest of Saigon, on the Gulf of Siam, and they got on well enough. The Lucky Dragon streamed big nets from long booms swung out amidships[29] on either side, and they netted prawns in season and with lines and nets caught shark and other fish which the old man recognized from seeing in the markets and called by the names his Chinese wife had taught him: the *hung-mei-tsee yue*, the red-tailed mackerel scad, which has protective scales like plate armor where its tail joins the body to prevent bigger fish taking it from behind; the big gold and silver surface-swimming *wong-cheung*; the brilliantly colored coral cod, the *pak-mei-paan*, the *naam-dim-paan* and the red and black-spotted *cheung-may-paan*. The old man was proud of knowing the names of the fish and would rattle them off as they were brought aboard while he sat in the bows and mended the nets or kept the boat's books (because he was determined to run the Lucky Dragon like a business). But the young men from Rach Gia called the fish by their Vietnamese names, which was natural enough, and laughed at the old man behind his back, which in the East is not natural. But then they were of a generation which had never known any of the old ways: only war and disturbances.

Then the war came close to Rach Gia, to the many wide and tangled channels of the mighty Mekong[30] River delta, which was west of Rach Gia. The army took the young hired men, and they were never seen again. Then the older son was taken: he was shot by the Viet Cong while on a river patrol with the Americans. So the old man lived alone on his boat, tied to a slowly collapsing jetty at Rach Gia, and wrote to his youngest son, Phan, in Saigon:

"When the war is over, Phan, I think you should sell the shop and come and work on the boat. It will be better down here for you and your family than the city."

---

25. *Pestilences* (PES til lintz iz) refer to a series of deadly epidemic diseases.
26. *Phan* (FAHN) is a Vietnamese man's name.
27. *Cholera* (KAHL er uh) is a severe, contagious infection of the small intestine, causing profuse diarrhea and dehydration, transmitted via contaminated drinking water.
28. *Rach Gia* (RAHK GEE) is a village on the Gulf of Siam.
29. *Amidships* means located in the middle part of the ship.
30. *Mekong* (MAY kawng)

Word Bank

upheavals (up HEE vilz) *n.*: strong or violent changes

jetty (JET ee) *n.*: a pier or structure of stones or piles projecting into a body of water to protect a harbor from the water current

Then the old man sat on his boat and lived very simply on rice and vegetables and sometimes fish, which he caught with a handline from the boat, and waited for the war to end.

CHAPTER 2

The war ended at last. One day the city was full of foreign soldiers; the next it was not. The planes flew in and out of Than Son Nhut day and night, leaving full of Americans and their Vietnamese friends, and coming back empty for more.

And then it was over. People who had the yellow and red flag of South Vietnam in their homes or shops hastily destroyed or hid them and displayed instead the red and blue banner of the Viet Cong.

The city was full of confusion. The Viet Cong and the North Vietnamese Army were only a day's march away, and the peasants hurrying to get out of the way of the final battle between them and the Army of the Republic of South Vietnam spilled down the roads from the north and east into Saigon.

Aunt Binh[31] was with them: she arrived at the shop one day hot and tired and upset with nothing but the cheap dress she was wearing. Her husband had been killed fighting for the south near Da Nang. He had been killed by mortar fragments,[32] only a few blocks from his home. Then the Americans and the southern soldiers had pushed the Viet Cong out of the village. Unfortunately they had destroyed the village at the same time. Aunt Binh's house had been hit by a friendly plane's bomb: Aunt Binh had been knocked unconscious by the blast, that was all, but her only child, a daughter of nine, had been killed instantly.

Aunt Binh, when they let her out of the hospital the next day, never went back to the wreck of her house. She just walked out of the hospital and joined the thousands of people fleeing south. Sometimes she rode on a crowded bus, or got a lift in a truck. Mostly she walked. She lived on a handful of rice a day and slept beside the road. When she arrived at her younger sister's house in Bach Dang, something had happened to her mind. For days she just sat staring down the street and crying without making a sound; just letting the tears run down her thin face.

After a while she got better. She washed and mended her dress and began to help around the house and in the shop. Sometimes, listening to the news or watching politicians talk on television, she would laugh in a way that sent shivers down Quan's spine.

And then it really was all over. The old government fled with the Americans; or most of the big shots, the "fat cats," did. When the northern army marched into the city, Phan Thi Chi and his whole family—Ah Soong, Uncle Tan and Aunt Binh—went in to Tu Do Street to watch the triumphal parade.

"It might be wise," said Quan's father nervously. So they all went and stood in a forest of red and blue flags on the crowded pavement and cheered.

"Perhaps it won't be so bad after all," said Quan's mother afterwards, as they walked slowly home. "They say they won't punish anyone for working with the old government, or with the Americans."

---

31. *Binh* (BIN)
32. *Mortar fragments* are pieces of shells thrown from a mortar cannon. Mortar cannons are short in proportion to their barrel and eject shells at a high angle.

Word Bank   **triumphal** (try UM fil) *adj.*: highly successful or victorious; celebrating a triumph

Uncle Tan grunted and dug his crutch viciously into the pavement, his face twisted with weariness. Aunt Binh laughed shortly, and Quan's father looked worried. He had looked worried for a long time.

On the way home they stopped and had rice and vegetables at a food stall. All the small tables were full of people talking and laughing. But among the animated faces were many with the same shadow that Quan saw in the faces of his parents.

Lying in bed that night Quan felt uneasy. He couldn't sleep. There was something different about the city. He got up and pulled on a pair of shorts. Quietly he opened his door. The house and the shop below were dark and silent. He walked softly up the short, narrow hall, his bare feet silent on the boards. He jumped when a voice in the darkness just below his left ear whispered: "Quan? Is that you?"

"Of course it is," he hissed back crossly. "Who did you think it was?"

Ly giggled in the dark.

"I'm sorry if I gave you a fright. But I couldn't sleep."

"Nor can I. I'm going up to the roof for some fresh air."

"I'll come with you."

"All right. But be quiet."

He felt Ly's small hand slip into his.

"All right. You go first."

Quietly, so as not to wake the sleeping house, they groped their way up the stairs in the dark. Quan fumbled with the bolt of the roof door and then the small door swung open and they stepped on to the tiny flat roof where Ah Soong hung the family wash on long bamboo poles. The roof was still warm with the heat of the day. Hand in hand Quan and Ly leaned over the low parapet and looked at the long silent sweep of Bach Dang, deserted and bleak in the cold blue light of the few mercury vapor street lamps that still worked. The sandbagged gun emplacement[33] on the roof of the house opposite, which for as long as Quan could remember had housed a big belt-fed American M50 machine gun and its crew, was dark and silent. The gun was gone.

Then he realized what was different about the city. The night was not dark: there were bright stars and a half moon was riding behind some wisps of cloud; but there were no parachute flares shedding their ghastly light. And there were no planes in the sky, and no noise of planes. Over to the east, Than Son Nhut was dark and silent.

He realized for the first time what nights were like in the city before the war.

They stood there a long time, until the dew began to fall.

In the morning it was strange not to see the dirty white flare parachutes hanging from the trees.

---

33. A *sandbagged gun emplacement* is a makeshift stand for weapons. The sandbags protect against incoming fire.

Word Bank

animated (AN ih MAYT id) *adj.*: full of life, action, or spirit; lively

parapet (PAIR uh PET) *n.*: a low, protective wall or barrier at the edge of a roof or balcony; a wall or elevation in a fortification

Studying the Selection

✓ Quick Review

1. What is the Thi Chi family business?
2. What is Ah Soong's role in the family?
3. Who shot magnesium parachute flares over the city and why?
4. Why can't Quan and Ly sleep after the northern army marched into the city?

In-depth Thinking

5. Dragons are common to stories around the world. Why won't Quan ever be frightened by storybook dragons after seeing helicopter gunships firing?
6. Ah Soong, Uncle Tan, and Aunt Binh come to live with Quan's family and are taken in. What does this teach about Vietnamese tradition?
7. What might cause Aunt Binh to laugh in such a way that it "sent shivers down Quan's spine," when she watches the news or politicians on TV?
8. Although people from other lands differ from us, similarities do exist. What about Quan's life seems foreign? What similarities have you seen so far?

Drawing Conclusions

9. The Lucky Dragon is used as the name of the grandfather's boat. Chinese tradition, which greatly influenced the Vietnamese, sees the dragon as a good luck symbol. What clues suggest the "Lucky Dragon" will live up to its name?
10. We're told that when the family stops for lunch after the parades "…among the animated faces" in the café were "many with the same shadow that Quan saw in the faces of his parents." What accounts for the shadow?

CHAPTER 3

For a few weeks things did not change much in Bach Dang, Gia Dinh. The sandbagged gun-pit on the house across the road was dismantled. Tanks and guns the Americans had left behind were displayed at street corners.

There was not much to sell, but Phan Thi Chi kept his shop open and made a few piastres a day. Ah Soong went out earlier than usual to buy food for the household and came back late, obviously tired, and complaining about the cost of rice and fish. But then Ah Soong had always complained about the cost of food.

Quan and Ly went to school as usual. Some of their old teachers, who had left during the war, returned. Others did not, and somehow the children knew that it would not be wise to inquire after them. They had some new teachers, too: hard-faced young men and women from the north, who made no attempt to hide their contempt for the southerners.

Saigon was named Ho Chi Minh City, after Ho Chi Minh (which means He Who Enlightens), the Vietnamese leader who had led both the south and the north against the French, and then the north against the south and the Americans and their allies.

"Now they will be satisfied," said Quan's mother.

Aunt Binh laughed.

Uncle Tan shouldered his crutch, hobbled to the door and spat into the street.

"It's only the beginning," he said. "You wait and see."

The next day it was announced on the radio that neighborhood "re-education committees" were to be formed, and the day after that one of the hard-faced young men from the north came down the street. He stopped at every house and told the families there that they would have to attend a meeting once a week.

Two days later Ly came home from school in tears. One of the teachers from the north had made her stand in front of the class while he explained that she was the daughter of a capitalist.[34] Poor Ly hadn't the least idea what a capitalist was. Most of the teacher's tirade went right over her head; but she knew deep shame and humiliation. Afterwards, her classmates were afraid to talk to her. She ran all the way home, weeping.

"Are you a capitalist, father?" she asked, while her mother tried to soothe her.

Her father looked around the tiny shop from which he had scratched a bare living for years. He looked at the bare shelves with their pathetic displays of cheap goods. He sat down at the kitchen table as though suddenly weak.

"Yes, Ly," he said. "I suppose I am."

His daughter looked at him in horror. It was as though he had admitted being a murderer or a robber. The teacher's harangue, the bitter venom of it, had made a cruel impression on her.

In the sudden silence Aunt Binh cackled shrilly.

"It's starting," said Uncle Tan, rapping the floor angrily with his crutch. "It's starting."

"Nonsense," said Quan's father, angrily. "I've done nothing wrong. I run a small shop. I have nobody working for me. I've exploited nobody."

"You'll see," said Uncle Tan grimly. "You'll

---

34. Here, *capitalist* is a negative label for any merchant.

Word Bank

dismantled (diss MAN tild) *v.*: taken apart
tirade (TY rayd) *n.*: a prolonged, bitter, negative outburst
harangue (huh RANG) *n.*: a scolding or a verbal attack
exploited (ex PLOY tid) *v.*: taken advantage of or used selfishly for one's own benefit

see. And don't forget—we're not even pure Vietnamese. We're half-Hoa, our family. They want scapegoats, you know. They want someone to blame for the country's misfortunes, and we'll do."

"Nonsense," said Phan Thi Chi again, but without much conviction.

Aunt Binh laughed again.

"I wish I had died at Da Nang," she said. "With my husband and my child."

"That is wicked talk," said Quan's mother, who was a religious woman, even though she had helped defeat the French, who had introduced her religion to Vietnam. It was a silent family that ate its simple evening meal that night. Phan Thi Chi picked at his rice, deep in thought. He knew that Tan was right: this was just the beginning. He had listened to all the market and food stall talk. People were being publicly criticized by the young men—cadres,[35] they were called—from the north, and shouted down when they tried to defend themselves. It seemed that these days almost everything that Phan Thi Chi and people like him regarded as normal, worthwhile activities, were "anti-social" or "capitalist" or "reactionary."[36]

There were more sinister rumors, too: of people, whole families at a time, being sent out of the city to "New Economic Zones" in the mountains or jungles, where they were forced to hack[37] farms and rice paddies from the virgin bush for a handful of rice a day, people who had never done any manual work in their lives.

But in the depths of his despair Phan Thi Chi had one straw to grasp at: his father's boat. Later that night he got the old man's letter out of the drawer where he kept his best shirt and, smoothing out the crumpled paper, read the shaky script again. Yes, he would sell the shop and go and help his father work the Lucky Dragon. And if he couldn't sell the shop, or if the cadres wouldn't let him, he would give away what stock he couldn't carry to Rach Gia. Things were sure to be different in a little fishing village like Rach Gia. His family would be able to live quietly there and fish for a living. Let the cadres and the politicians have Ho Chi Minh City.

He folded the letter and put it carefully away. For the first time in months he felt quite lighthearted.

I'll tell the family tomorrow, he thought as he fell asleep. Quan will like working on a boat. But I must think of some way to continue his and Ly's education. They must take all their school books with them. The schools in Rach Gia may not be as good as those in Ho Chi Minh City.

He fell asleep and dreamed he and Quan were hauling in a net bulging with shining silver fish.

記 CHAPTER 4

But Phan Thi Chi didn't tell his family anything the next day. Because the next day turned out to be Quan's day of humiliation.

Of course, being a boy, and a tough one,

---

35. Here, *cadres* (KAHD reez) means a unit of communist soldiers used to train and harass South Vietnamese.
36. *Anti-social* and *reactionary* are negative political labels for people who wanted to keep their small businesses and not be told what to do by the government.
37. To *hack* is to clear by cutting away vines, trees, or other growth. Here, it means to create farms from untouched wilderness.

Word Bank

scapegoats (SKAYP GOATS) *n.*: persons or groups used as a focus for blame, accused of the mistakes or crimes of others

conviction (kun VIK shun) *n.*: a fixed or firm belief; the state of being convinced

sinister (SIN is ter) *adj.*: wicked, evil, or dishonest

although misleadingly quiet, he didn't, as his sister had, come home in tears.

He came home rigid with rage instead. Oh, the tears were there, of course, behind the frozen mask of his face, but Quan believed he would have died rather than let them run.

He refused to say anything until after the evening meal. Then he told them, his face still frozen in a rictus of anger and mortification,[38] how the northern teacher—who only two weeks ago had replaced the old, kindly, easy-going Tiet Quoc Lien[39]—had called five of the older boys in the class out and made them line up in front of the blackboard—"like thieves," spat Quan, angry as a wet cat.

There was Quan, son of a "capitalist" small shop-owner. Then there was his friend Duong Van Minh, who was also half-Hoa (his mother was Chinese), whose father was an artist in the new Ministry of Culture and who, Quan thought, would have been safe as—as gold; then there was Le Van Dung; well, one would have known he would be picked on—his father, who was now dead or in America, nobody seemed to know—had worked in the United States Air Force PX at Than Son Nhut for many years. But it seemed unfair that Van should be punished for something his father had done, whatever it was.

Also chosen were Huyn Ngoc Ba,[40] whose father had five other children besides and had lost an arm fighting near the Y bridge in Ho Chi Minh City (or Saigon as it then was) in the Tet Offensive in 1968.[41] Ngoc's father had made the mistake of fighting for the wrong side, and now his son was paying for it; as was the fifth boy in the shameful parade, Sik-nin Chau, who had made the mistake of being born to parents of pure Chinese stock, which was not wise at a time when the government had decided that the Hoa were, if not actually traitors, a potentially hostile community. After all, didn't most of them live among their own people, marry their own people? And didn't most of them still regard China as home? And—most annoying of all—weren't they good businessmen who made money?

The family listened in stunned horror. Ly wept anew at the revived memory of her own mortification. Aunt Binh rocked in silent grief and refused to talk to anyone for the rest of the evening.

"I'm not going back to school," wailed Ly. "I can't. I can't! Quan, you won't go back, will you? It's too bad!"

Quan looked at his father.

"Must I, father?"

Phan Thi Chi nodded his head slowly. "Yes. I'm afraid you must. For two reasons, Quan. One is that education is so valuable that you can't just throw it away. Perhaps, later, when this madness has blown over, we can find you another school. The second reason is that if you didn't go back to school, you'd draw even more attention to yourself. They might even send you to a—a…" he hesitated, groping for words.

Quan grimaced. "A re-education camp. Yes, I've heard of them. Or to pull weeds in one of the New Economic Zones."

"So you must go back to school," said his

---

38. *Rictus* (RIK tuss) is a gaping grin. *Mortification* (MOR tih fih KAY shun) is anger and humiliation.
39. *Tiet Quoc Lien* (TYET KWOKE LEEN)
40. *Huyan Ngoc Ba* (HWAN NOKE BAH)
41. *The Tet Offensive of 1968* was a major North Vietnamese assault against the South and the American military that occurred during the Tet Festival.

Word Bank **grimaced** (grih MIST) *v.*: made an ugly or contorted facial expression indicating disapproval or pain

mother. "And Ly, so must you."

"But I can't," wailed Ly, weeping afresh.

"It might not be for long," said their father. "There's something—something else I'm thinking of. But you must go back to school and above all don't show any resentment. Do you understand?"

"Yes," said Quan. "I understand. Ly, stop crying. When I'm an engineer we'll all move to—to America, or France." He paused, and looked at his father. "But what's this 'something else,' father? Are we going to go away?"

A sudden look of fear swept over Phan Thi Chi's face and he quickly laid his hand over the boy's mouth. He glanced at the window opening on to the sweltering night.

"Quan, don't say things like that! If we even talked about going away they'd watch us like hawks! They never let anyone do what they want, go where they want! If we said we wanted to go south, they'd send us north! I've heard that, listening around the shops!"

His wife asked, quietly: "Who are *they*?"

Her husband shrugged. "I'm not sure. The government, of course, but more than the government. It comes right down to street level. The Bureau of Public Security. The neighborhood committees. The cadres. They are everywhere. There's a cadre in every public office. At the railway station, the bus depot, everywhere. They watch everyone."

"Then we'd better make sure that we don't give them any more cause to watch us," said his wife sensibly, and Phan Thi Chi glanced at her approvingly. "Quan and Ly, go to bed now. And let's have no more silly talk about going away. What about our shop? And your grandpa down in Rach Gia? Eh?"

Reluctantly, the children went to bed. In the corner Aunt Binh covered her face with her hands and wept silently. The widow seemed to be deteriorating more each day. She spent her waking hours in a sort of daze. The simplest household tasks became too much for her, much to the exasperation of Ah Soong, whose own reaction to the tension and anxiety in the household and the city was to work harder. As Aunt Binh faded, Ah Soong bloomed. She was up first and to bed last, washing, ironing, mending, cooking, shopping in the fruit, fish and vegetable markets—and still managing to come home with tasty bargains while other housewives were wailing about the impossibility of getting anything.

> The ex-soldier had plenty of news for his old friend, all of it bad. Yes, people were being sent to the New Economic Zones. Families were being split up, the children sent north, the parents south, or the other way around.

"You come to the markets with me," she had suggested to Aunt Binh one day. "It will do you good. Get out of the house. Meet people."

"I can't," whined Aunt Binh. "I can't face people." And then—they were washing up at the time, squatting beside the cold tap in the tiny backyard—she dropped a pretty blue and white rice bowl on the wet cement slab beneath the tap. The bowl burst like a little bomb, and Aunt Binh collapsed into tears. "I can't do anything," she cried, retreating into the house. "I'm a useless woman. I might as well be dead."

Ah Soong shrugged philosophically and picked up the shards of rice bowl. She finished the washing up alone. Aunt Binh never offered to help again, nor did she ever go to the markets, which didn't really bother Ah Soong,

---

Word Bank

deteriorating (dee TEER ee uh RAYT ing) *v.*: worsening; being worn away; disintegrating

shards (SHAHRDZ) *n.*: fragments, broken pieces

who privately regarded her as a silly woman and had only made the suggestion out of politeness. Besides, Ah Soong went to the markets to gossip as much as to shop, and there was no doubt that Aunt Binh would have got in the way. Ah Soong was a very tough old lady.

旺 CHAPTER 5

Uncle Tan was not present when Quan told his family about his painful day at school. Early that afternoon Tan had shouldered his crutch and heaved himself halfway across the city to visit a friend—also a crippled ex-soldier—who now ran a cooked food stall. The ex-soldier had plenty of news for his old friend, all of it bad. Yes, people were being sent to the New Economic Zones. Families were being split up, the children sent north, the parents south, or the other way around. Yes, the authorities seemed to take a cruel delight in forcing city people to do backbreaking labor in the country. Yes, it was the same all over Vietnam.

"The north is getting its own back," said Uncle Tan's friend grimly, jerking the stump of his left arm—lost at the battle of Long Tan—for emphasis.

"Hanoi has sent many young cadres down here to shake us up. They say, the leaders in Hanoi say, that we in the south have become soft and decadent from living under the old government and under the Americans. Well, they may be right. I can't say I like the way some of our young people became so westernized. Juke-boxes and Coca-Cola! And that terrible music! But the—"

"I know," said Uncle Tan. "The new way doesn't seem to be much better."

Uncle Tan had a few small beers with his friend, using up his last few dong, and then had to hobble all the way home across crowded, noisy central Ho Chi Minh City. He got home very late, tired and irritable. His crutch had blistered his armpit and his stump was aching.

He flung himself down on a chair and rested his arms on the table. Silently Ah Soong put a bowl of rice and vegetables before him. He ate listlessly. Phan Thi Chi and his wife watched him without speaking. Their faces gave them away.

Uncle Tan stopped eating. He looked at them. He pushed his unfinished meal away and stood up, balancing on one leg while he groped for his crutch.

"Oh G-d," he said. "Bad news. More bad news. It's in your faces! You might as well take an advertisement in the newspaper! Well, I don't want to hear it, do you see? I don't want to hear it! Tell me tomorrow. All day I've heard nothing good! I'm going to sleep!"

He stumped angrily away. His passage could be heard all over the small house. Thump thump thump, went his crutch, stabbing at the floor.

In the silence left by his departure Quan's mother said softly: "What is this something else you're thinking of?"

Phan Thi Chi told her of his father's boat. She sat thinking for a while.

"Would they let us go?"

"We won't ask them. We'll just go. Once we have jobs on the boat at Rach Gia, I don't think they'll find us. The country is still in a mess, you know. We'll just go quietly, one or two at a time. Quan and Ly can go down together by bus. If anyone asks they can say

---

Word Bank

decadent (DEK uh dint) *adj.*: characterized by moral decay

they're going to spend the weekend with their grandpa. There's nothing wrong in that, surely?"

"I don't know, these days. So many things seem wrong to them."

Phan Thi Chi sighed. "Yes. But I think we'll get away with it. Then Aunt Binh can go with Tan. G-d knows she couldn't go alone. And then you and I will go separately, last—"

"I don't want to go without you!"

"You must. It would arouse suspicion if we went together. And one of us must catch a bus from Cholon or some other part of the city, not from here. We must take only what we can get into small suitcases, that's all. We'll have to leave almost everything in the shop."

"There's not much to leave, anyway."

"No. That's true."

"What about Ah Soong?"

"Ah Soong will have to go back to China. She still has people there and I heard today that the government is making plans to repatriate the Hoa to China."

"Ah Soong won't go. She won't leave us," said his wife decidedly.

"We can't take an old woman to work on a fishing boat! And you know how small my father's house is!"

"She won't go. I can tell you that."

"Well, we'll see. I'll find out more about the government plan to send people like her home."

"She won't go, I tell you. It would break her heart, too."

"I know. Don't you think I've thought about it? I've known Ah Soong for more than thirty years! She's part of the family. But she's almost seventy! Can you ask an old woman to travel hundreds of kilometers by bus through a country in a mess like this one is, and then work on a boat? Of course not! And if she didn't work on the boat she'd have to clean fish or something! There's a fishing commune at Rach Gia, you know, she wouldn't be allowed to do nothing! No, it's better if she goes home. China is a safer place than Vietnam just now."

His wife shook her head.

"You're wasting your breath talking. She won't go."

"We'll see about that," he said with a conviction he did not feel.

中 CHAPTER 6

Phan Thi Chi did not tell the rest of his family about the plan the next day, or the day after that. He was by nature a cautious man, and wars and the aftermath of wars had intensified that caution almost to the point of paranoia. Not that he was not still determined to go. He knew there was no place for him or his family in Ho Chi Minh City any more; he believed their only hope for a peaceful happy future lay in some small village such as Rach Gia where they would be left alone as long as they did no harm to the new regime. And, naively, he believed that things would be different in a small village. Country people would always be the same, he told himself. It was harder to plant new ideas in the country. The peasants would listen politely to the northerners, to the political commissars,[42] and when the strangers had gone back to the cities the peasants would live the lives they had always led. After all, they had done it for centuries—under Thai

---

42. *Political commissars* were communist officials who tried to persuade the peasants to communist practices.

Word Bank

repatriate (ree PAY tree AYT) *v.*: send back (a refuge, prisoner of war) to his or her country
paranoia (PAIR uh NOY uh) *n.*: baseless or excessive distrust of others
naively (ny EEV lee) *adv.*: in an unsophisticated, simplistic way; in an innocent and overly trusting way

invaders, Chinese invaders, French colonialists, under the old emperors, under the Japanese, and under the Diem and Thieu regimes[43] when the French left. Why should things be different now?

So he made his quiet plans, checked bus schedules to the south, worked out with his wife who would go with whom, and what they would take from the shop. He wrote his father a very careful letter and mailed it from the central post office.

"Tomorrow," he told his wife after he had posted the letter to his father, "we'll tell the family."

"What about Ah Soong?" asked his wife.

"I've explained about Ah Soong," he said irritably because he was tired and hot and worried. "There is a plan by the government to send the Hoa back to China. She'll have to go, that's all."

"She won't," said his wife. "I know that old lady. She thinks we can't do anything without her."

"Nobody's indispensable," said Phan Thi Chi; but in his heart he was worried. He had lived with Ah Soong for many years and regarded her as one of the family. But his heart sank at the prospect of getting his own family unseen, unmolested and unquestioned through a disturbed and suspicious country; to add an old woman to his responsibilities would, he thought, be asking too much.

The next few days were busy ones for Phan Thi Chi and his wife. Like Ah Soong, they each had a small savings account, and there was always some cash in the shop's old till—not much, it is true—but in those days even a few piastres was something. Now they set about turning this small store of money into something that they could take with them, for they were afraid that if they left Ho Chi Minh City and tried to use their savings accounts they would be tracked through the banks. They wanted something they could conceal easily, and something more reliable than paper money, which could be devalued at the government's whim, something of universal value. They chose what Asian people have always chosen in times of crisis: gold. Slowly, bit by bit, dealing with widely separated goldsmiths, they turned their scanty store of piastres and dong—and a few illegal American dollars—into thin strips of gold. Each strip weighed a tael,[44] thirty Western grams. By the time they had finished, they had ten tael. Phan Thi Chi had five and his wife had five, clipped into little booklets, like stamps.

With this, and a few piastres left for bus fares and food on the way to Rach Gia, Phan Thi Chi felt he could move his family in with his father without straining the old man's slender resources.

"Why, we can have the Lucky Dragon painted," he said to his wife. "And perhaps even get something done about that terrible old engine. Why, when I was on the Lucky Dragon it coughed and choked and smoked and stopped every five minutes."

"You worry about the boat once we're safely at Rach Gia," said his wife. "And you haven't said anything to Ah Soong yet."

---

43. A *regime* (ray ZHEEM) is the period in which a system of rule is in power. *Diem* (1901-1963) was brutal and corrupt. *Thieu* (1923-2001) was the dictatorial south Vietnamese president, 1967-1975.
44. A *tael* (TAY il) weighs a little more than an ounce, which equals 28.5 grams.

Word Bank

indispensable (IN diss PEN sih bul) *adj.*: absolutely necessary or essential

"I will, woman," he said irritably. "I will. I will tomorrow."

"Hmmm," said his wife, and went out to help Ah Soong prepare supper. Phan Thi Chi frowned. Then he got up and climbed the stairs to the flat roof. He stood there a while, looking at the rooftops of Ho Chi Minh City. It was purple dusk and the street lights were coming on. Below him Bach Dang was quiet with only a few people on the pavements outside their houses and shops, though from the next block came the roar and shriek of traffic. Almost every vehicle in Ho Chi Minh City seemed to have a two-stroke engine and a defective silencer.

He stood there in the warm evening and thought of Rach Gia and the Lucky Dragon. He had not seen the old boat for years. Not since the war against the north started. But he remembered having fun aboard it many years ago. And he remembered how quiet and peaceful Rach Gia was, with its several quiet fingers of water slipping into the Gulf of Siam. He had thought Rach Gia a boring old village then and had resented every day spent away from Saigon. Now times had changed and so had he: peace and quiet seemed very precious.

CHAPTER 7

There was no letter from Phan Thi Chi's father the next day. But that evening, while the whole family was having supper around the big table in the back room, a young man came into the shop. He rapped rudely on the counter and Ly ran out to serve him.

She came back in a few seconds, her face pale. "Father," she said. "Please come. There's a—a young man to see you. He's strange—" Phan Thi Chi and his wife got up hastily, their food unfinished. Ah Soong, Uncle Tan and Quan and Ly exchanged uneasy glances. Then, with one accord, they crowded into the narrow, short passage between the back room and the shop.

The strange young man was quietly dressed in a white short-sleeved shirt, black trousers and black shoes. He was about twenty-two or twenty-three; no older. His young face held authority and, as he glanced around the little shop, a cold contempt. He put back in his pocket a card he had just showed Phan Thi Chi and glanced at the expectant faces crowding the passage.

"Family?" he asked.

"Yes," said Phan Thi Chi. After all, he thought, defensively, Ah Soong is family.

The young man unfolded a sheet of typewritten paper.

"You are Phan Thi Chi, shopkeeper, of thirteen Bach Dang, Gia Dinh?"

"Yes."

"You have heard of the government decree of March twenty-third?"

"It is only March twenty-four today and I have heard no news all day."

Word Bank

accord (uh KORD) *n.*: agreement; harmony

contempt (kun TEMPT) *n.*: disdain or scorn for anything considered vile or worthless

"From March twenty-three—that is yesterday—all trading and business operations by bourgeois elements[45] of the population are abolished. Do you know what that means?"

"Yes," said Phan Thi Chi quietly. "It means you take my shop away from me."

"That is right. This shop is now owned by the state. You will remain in control of it until the state sends a manager to take over."

"How do I and my family live?"

There was suddenly a deadly hush in the room: it was as though everyone had stopped breathing. Out in the street a dog barked suddenly. It seemed very loud. The young man read from his piece of paper:

"Phan Thi Chi will be sent to a re-education camp in Ho Chi Minh City. After showing progress, he will be sent to a New Economic Zone in An Gian Province—"

"I know nothing about farming," said Phan Thi Chi.

The young man shrugged. "You'll learn. It will be part of your re-education."

"And my family?"

"Your wife will go to a re-education center at Long Thanh. Your children will be sent to a New Economic Zone at Le Minh Xuan."

"Will we be allowed to visit each other? To write?"

The young man shrugged again.

"I don't know. That depends on the authorities, I suppose."

Phan Thi Chi felt himself growing angry despite the cold fear that gripped him.

"What about the rest of my family?" He pointed to Ah Soong, her face inscrutable, to Aunt Binh and Uncle Tan. Uncle Tan balanced on his crutch, his eyes on the young man.

The young man consulted his paper again.

"I have no instructions about these people," he said. He looked at Uncle Tan.

"Where did you lose your leg?"

"It's buried at Hue."

"With a lot of Americans and traitors," said the young man.

Uncle Tan just stared at him. The young man folded his paper and put it in his pocket.

"Well, I have no instructions about you, one-leg. Nor about these two ladies—" he nodded at Ah Soong and Aunt Binh.

"No doubt you will hear from the authorities soon enough." He turned to the ashen-faced Phan Thi Chi. "You may operate your shop until the state official arrives. That may take a few days or a week. You must not sell any goods which have been declared subject to state control—"

"How do I know what they are?"

"You must find out. Don't ask me how. But you must find out. Go to the Public Security Bureau. It is a serious offense to trade in state-controlled goods, you know."

And then he was gone, leaving a shocked silence which Phan Thi Chi was the first to break.

"Shut the door," he said to his wife. "Quan, shut the back door. Lock it. Then all come upstairs, to the roof. Nobody can hear us there."

When they were all on the roof, dodging Ah Soong's washing, he told them of his plan to escape to Rach Gia, and start a new life on his old father's boat. When he had finished talking, he watched their faces anxiously.

Quan was the first to speak. To his father's relief, he was delighted. Quan was a strange boy sometimes, with his own ideas.

---

45. *Bourgeois* (BOOR zhwah) elements is a negative label for middle-class merchants.

Word Bank

inscrutable (in SKROOT uh bul) *adj.*: mysterious, unfathomable; incapable of being investigated, analyzed

"When do we go?" was all he said. "I'd love to be a fisherman—"

"You mustn't forget your schoolwork," said his mother. "There'll be a school at Rach Gia, you know—"

"Not like the one here, I hope," said Ly, wrinkling her nose.

"Things will be different in Rach Gia," their father promised them. "It's a little village. People are different down there."

"If I like working on the boat, I might become a marine engineer," said Quan. "Eh, mother? I could see the world!"

"I don't like the sea," said Aunt Binh mournfully. "I went out on a junk[46] at Da Nang. I got sick. And boat people aren't like us. But don't worry about me, please. I know I have to do as I'm told."

"No you don't," said Phan Thi Chi rather cruelly. "You can always go to one of their New Economic Zones, and learn to be a rice-farmer."

Aunt Binh turned her heard away, sniffling quietly, and Phan Thi Chi felt guilty.

"Well, if that is decided then, I'd better go and get some food ready for the trip," said Ah Soong, as though Phan Thi Chi had announced that a bus was waiting below to whisk them to Rach Gia on the instant.

Phan Thi Chi cleared his throat nervously and his wife glanced at him with a sly smile.

"Ah, well," said Phan Thi Chi, and the old woman looked at him sharply.

"We—ah, I, had thought, Ah Soong, that, ah, you—well, it could be a rough life down at Rach Gia and ah, well, we don't know what sort of house we will find, you know, and so—"

"And so you thought I'd go back to China! At my age! After nearly half a century in Vietnam! What nonsense!"

"Now just listen, Ah Soong," said Phan Thi Chi nervously, rolling a desperate eye at his wife, who was gazing steadfastly over the rooftops as though entranced by some sight in the general direction of the National Assembly Building.

"Besides," said Ah Soong, "besides the fact that I haven't written to my family in China for years, have you forgotten who runs the country now? When I left it was the Kuomintang, and now it is the communists. Well, I didn't like the Kuomintang when I was a girl in China, and I don't like what I've seen of the Vietnamese communists. Why should the Chinese communists be different? Or better? No, I'm coming with you. I have some money of my own. Besides—" and the old woman drew herself up and glanced scathingly at the rest of the family, "you couldn't get on without me! Now I have things to do." And she shuffled off downstairs, leaving Phan Thi Chi embarrassed behind a flapping wet sheet.

"I told you," said Ly's mother after a short silence.

"Are you coming, Uncle Tan?" asked Quan.

Uncle Tan twirled his crutch.

"I saw a movie about a one-legged pirate once," he said with a grin. "And he had only one eye, too. Yes. I'm coming."

So it was decided.

There was no letter from Phan Thi Chi's father the next day. But the state official didn't come to take charge of the shop, either.

---

46. A *junk* is a ship used primarily in Chinese waters, that has square sails, a high stern, and a flat bottom.

Word Bank

steadfastly (STED FAST lee) *adv.*: fixedly; with firm purpose
entranced (en TRANST) *v.*: filled with delight or wonder
scathingly (SKAYTH ing lee) *adv.*: with bitter severity

Chapter 8

Three days since the cadre's ominous visit and still no letter from Rach Gia. The time had come to go, letter or not. Any day now they would get their orders to leave.

Phan Thi Chi looked at the calendar in his shop. The cadre had called on Monday; today was Thursday. They would go on Saturday: many people would be traveling over the weekend; they would be able to disperse and lose themselves in the crowded buses.

Phan Thi Chi tried not to worry about the lack of a letter from his father. Perhaps the old man was ill. Perhaps he had written and the letter was lost in the mail—that often happened. He had heard many people complaining about the postal service. The country was in a disturbed state still and the mail service had suffered. Other fears swirled thickly in his troubled mind but he pushed them aside.

That night, after closing the shop, he helped his wife and children choose the few personal things they would be able to take with them: some clothes, Quan's and Ly's school books, some old photographs of weddings and holidays, his wife's old Bible, a prize she had won at school. Very little else. It did not seem much after half a lifetime. But it was much more, Phan Thi Chi knew, than many other people had. And they had the gold! Ten taels! Gold was, that day, two hundred American dollars an ounce. After all, he consoled himself, that's a lot of money. We can start a new life with that amount of money. If they let you keep it, whispered a small doubting voice in his head.

He slept badly that night, pursued by disturbing dreams about his father's letter. In the next room, his son Quan dreamed of steering the Lucky Dragon out on to a wide blue sparkling sea. The Lucky Dragon, in Quan's dream, looked rather like a huge ChrisCraft cruiser he had seen, years ago, in an American magazine he'd found on a bus: it was about thirty meters long, gleaming with chrome and brass, had a high flying bridge and its big twin diesels grumbled like chained tigers beneath his feet. When he awoke it was still dark and a wet wind was blowing from the river and the nightsoil collector's truck was rattling down the street.

Ly slept without dreaming, or at least without dreaming dreams she could remember.

Ah Soong sat up late mending clothes.

Aunt Binh lay awake in the dark for a long time and went back to Da Nang in her mind.

Uncle Tan folded his two spare shirts, washed and ironed that day by Ah Soong, his spare pair of trousers and his one good shoe into a neat bundle which he wrapped in newspaper and tied with string. He stumped backwards and forwards across the kitchen, where he slept on a thin mattress, and tried to imagine using his crutch on the rolling deck of a fishing boat. I'm going to do a lot of falling, he thought, smiling wryly. Perhaps I'll get a peg-leg. Any good carpenter could make me one. If Grandpa Phan Thi Chi has any tools in his boat I'll make one myself.

Then he slept and dreamed he was back in the field hospital at Hue. It was crowded and noisy and thick with terrible smells and sounds and they were cutting away his uniform to do something to his leg—something horrible! Horrible! He struggled but he seemed to be weighted with lead in every limb: he couldn't move and when he turned his head he could see a perfect forest of arms and legs in the corner. He woke groaning and

---

Word Bank

ominous (AHM in us) *adj.*: foreshadowing evil or harm; threatening

sweating and lay there panting in the dark.

Quan's mother dreamed she was back at school.

Friday was wet and windy: the palm fronds slapped one another and shook water on to the passers-by. The gutters ran full and dirty in Bach Dang. Few people came to the shop. In the afternoon there was thunder and jagged lightning over towards the west. The thunder rolled away under the clouds, sullen as distant artillery. Or like B52's dropping their tons of bombs in the Iron Triangle from nine thousand meters during the war. The Viet Cong had called the B52 attacks Rolling Thunder. The bombs had set up ground shock waves which made glasses ring on tabletops in Saigon, fifty kilometers away. But they hadn't won the war.

That afternoon Phan Thi Chi and Quan put on their yellow plastic raincoats and walked to the district post office in the warm rain.

There was a letter from Rach Gia. Trembling, Phan Thi Chi put it in his shirt pocket, away from the wet, and he and Quan hurried home, almost running.

"Don't bring those wet things into the shop," said Quan's mother when they got back. Then she saw her husband's face: "It's come? It's come."

"Yes. Quickly. Come upstairs. Quan, stay in the shop."

Still in his dripping yellow raincoat, Phan Thi Chi took the stairs two at a time. His wife followed more slowly, laughing and protesting.

"Slower, slower! It won't run away!"

Upstairs, safely out of sight of anyone in the street, Phan Thi Chi took the rain-spotted letter from his pocket and tore it open. He ran his eyes swiftly across the half-dozen lines in his father's spidery handwriting and grunted as though he had been suddenly, savagely hurt.

"Oh G-d," he said. "Oh G-d!" He sat on the bed, his face hidden in his hands, rocking to and fro.

His wife, smiling a moment before, shrieked in terror.

"What is it? What is it? Oh, please tell me—the letter—the letter! Let me see."

She took the letter from his clenched fingers and read it. And read it again. Then she let it drop and sat down beside her husband.

"All our plans," his wife said, weeping too, "All that! For nothing! Nothing!"

Ly, just back from school, heard her mother crying and ran into the room. She stopped on the threshold, shocked. Her mother pointed at the letter, lying crumpled on the floor, with a trembling finger. Ly picked it up, flattened out the paper, and read the few lines it contained: "My dear son, they have taken my boat for the commune. They say I will get a share of the fish they catch with her but so far I have had only a few pieces of fish. The boat is not the Lucky Dragon any more. It is VN 507. Remember that if you ever come looking for it. I am not feeling well and am in the commune hospital."

Phan Thi Chi sobbed quite openly in the suddenly silent room. Ly turned and fled, still clutching the letter.

Ah Soong had prepared a grand dinner for that night. It was going to be a celebration—to mark the end of an old life and the start of a new. She had spent hours in the markets, walking several kilometers with her plastic string bag, a remarkable bag which seemed to have no limits to its expansion.

Word Bank

sullen (SULL in) *adj.*: gloomy or dismal; moody

threshold (THRESH hold) *n.*: the entrance to a house or building; the sill of a doorway

There was *pho*, of course, the delicate beef soup which Vietnamese love and without which no meal is considered complete; and that was just the beginning. There was a light crab omelette. There was a chicken which had obviously had a hard life but which Ah Soong had transformed into *Ga xao bun tau*—one of Quan's favorite dishes, chicken with papery, almost transparent noodles. There was a fish dish, too, and mountains of rice, and *nuoc cham*, the pungent sauce made from fish juices, garlic and chiles. And there was the salad traditionally eaten with the *pho*—bean sprouts, fat white onions, firm tomatoes. There were bottles of beer for the men and pale clear tea for the women. And some violently orange soft drinks sweating in a plastic bucket of ice.

Oh yes, Ah Soong had excelled herself. It was a pity that no one—not even Quan or Ly—had any appetite.

They picked at the good food. Only Ah Soong ate with gusto.

"No sense wasting it," said the old lady. "We might not get another good meal for a long time."

Quan toyed with some crab.

Phan Thi Chi sat staring at his plate. He took his father's letter out and read it again, for the tenth time, trying desperately to change its meaning. But it stayed horribly clear. The boat was gone, gone forever. And their hopes with it.

Quan's mother said, hesitantly: "Perhaps they took his boat because he was too old to use it. Perhaps he couldn't handle the crew. Young men—after all, he's almost eighty—"

Phan Thi Chi snorted. "He's as tough as a bamboo. You know that."

"I haven't seen him for years," replied his wife.

"That's true," said Phan Thi Chi sadly. "Nor have I."

"Is it a good boat?" asked Quan.

"Of course," said his father automatically. "Of course. A very good boat."

To tell the truth, Phan Thi Chi had only the vaguest idea of what the Lucky Dragon looked like; he had only been on it once, on a hurried visit to Rach Gia in 1971, almost eight years ago. Phan Thi Chi was a city man, not much interested in boats or the sea, and besides, there was a war on at the time and he had other things on his mind.

So now he grunted and snapped irritably: "Of course, yes, a very good boat."

But Quan, who loved boats, wanted to know everything about the Lucky Dragon. How long was it? What was its beam? How big an engine did it have? Did it have sails? Was it built like a Chinese junk? When his persistent questioning in the face of his father's obvious ignorance became embarrassing, his mother intervened.

"Maybe," she said, putting her hand lightly on her husband's arm, "maybe, if we went down there and said we would help your father run the boat—"

Phan Thi Chi laughed bitterly. "Maybe they'd give it to us? Do you think they would? Nonsense!"

Uncle Tan nodded his head. "You're right. What the communes take, they keep. You've lost your boat, I'm afraid."

Ah Soong cleared her throat. There was a strange glint in the old lady's eye: for a fleeting moment, as Phan Thi Chi looked at her, it was as though half a century had sloughed away, and he was looking at the face of a naughty teenager. Then Ah Soong's full, curved lids came down, hooding the bright eyes, and she was once more an old, work-hardened

> She took the letter from his clenched fingers and read it. And read it again. Then she let it drop and sat down beside her husband. "All our plans," his wife said, weeping too, "All that! For nothing! Nothing!"

THE VOYAGE OF THE LUCKY DRAGON / 609

Chinese woman. She pushed back her chair and started collecting the used dishes.

"We could go and take the boat," she said as she noisily clattered the dishes into the washing up basin.

There was a stunned silence. Quan was the first to recover.

"We could, father," he said. "We could! We could go and—and take it, when no one was looking—it wouldn't be stealing! Grandfather would have given it to you, wouldn't he?"

"Don't talk nonsense," said his father angrily. "You don't know what you're talking about." He glared at Ah Soong. "Old woman, it's better you went to China than talk such nonsense!"

Ah Soong, her back to them, splashed and clashed the dishes.

"It is nonsense," said Phan Thi Chi defensively, looking around the table. "Nonsense! We would all be shot! Or sent to labor camps!"

"You are already booked for a labor camp," said Ah Soong, without turning around. "A New Economic Zone will be the same thing for us. We are all dead already."

Uncle Tan laughed. It was the first time anyone had laughed for a long time. He opened the beer and passed the bottle to Phan Thi Chi. Little peaks of foam formed at the necks of the brown bottles.

"The old lady's right," said Uncle Tan. "She's right! Let's go and take the boat—and go—go anywhere—"

"To Malaysia!" said Quan excitedly, while his father glanced swiftly from his son to the crippled soldier as though not believing his ears.

"A toast!" said Uncle Tan. "A toast—to the—to the—what's the boat's name?"

"Lucky Dragon," said Quan.

"Right then," said Uncle Tan. He lurched on to his remaining leg, clutching the table for support with one hand, and raised his foaming beer bottle high in the other.

"A toast—to the voyage of the Lucky Dragon!"

"*Yum sing!*" echoed Ah Soong from the washing up dish, her ivory face crinkled into the biggest, most delighted smile Quan had ever seen on that dignified visage.[47] "*Yum sing,*" she cried—the traditional Chinese toast, meaning "bottoms up—drink up!"

Slowly, unbelievingly, his eyes darting from Ah Soong to Uncle Tan to his son and back again to all three, Phan Thi Chi raised his bottle and drank. Ly poured her mother a glass of orange soft drink and they clinked plastic glasses in imitation of the men. Aunt Binh sniffed and sipped her tea.

Then, as though a heavy cloud which had hung over the house all day had been dispersed by a fresh wind, they were suddenly laughing and chattering and calling for fresh plates and eating Ah Soong's good food until they could eat no more.

Only Phan Thi Chi and Aunt Binh sat silent. Aunt Binh sat silent because that was her way. She liked to hug her injuries to herself without interruption. Phan Thi Chi was trying to remember the only occasion he had been to sea on the Lucky Dragon. He *must* have learned something about handling a boat that day! But his mind remained blank. (For a good reason, too: he had learned nothing because he had done nothing. He had dozed in

---

47. *Visage* (VIZ ij) means the face—the shape, features, and expression. A dignified visage has gravity and formality.

Word Bank **lurched** (LERCHT) *v.*: rolled or pitched suddenly; swayed abruptly; staggered

the sun and wished the day was over while his father and the young men from Rach Gia had raised and lowered the anchor, rigged and baited the lines, caught the fish, run the engine, and made fast to the jetty at the end of the day. Phan Thi Chi had come ashore smelling of fish, nursing a slight headache, and very glad to get the night bus back to Saigon.)

Phan Thi Chi felt something close to panic. He had looked forward to working the Lucky Dragon with his father: in fact, he had planned that his father, Tan, and Quan (when he was not at school) could handle the boat, while he did the bookwork—sold the catch or negotiated with the commune, whatever was required these days. He had never seen himself as a working seaman. Least of all as captain of a boat bound—on the open sea, and quite illegally—for Malaysia.

But he was caught on the helter-skelter of the rest of the family's enthusiasm, and was carried away with it. That, and the realization that it was Lucky Dragon or forced labor in a New Economic Zone. Of the two unknown terrors, a sea passage in the stolen Lucky Dragon seemed the less menacing.

Finishing his beer, Phan Thi Chi sighed and realized that he would soon have to tell his son two things: that he knew nothing about handling boats.

Or how to get to Malaysia.

Studying the Selection

First Impressions

This is the story of a unit. Who then, if anyone, stands out as a family leader and why? If one person is not in charge, what enables the family to function so well? How has the war affected their individuality?

✓ Quick Review

1. Why does Ly return from school in tears and Quan close to tears a day later?
2. How does his wife react when Phan Thi Chi suggests Ah Soong should go to China instead of heading to Rach Gia with the family?
3. What information does the young visitor to the store present to Phan Thi Chi that increases the pressure to escape to Rach Gia?
4. After waiting to hear from his father, Phan Thi Chi becomes upset when he finally does receive a letter. What does his father tell him that is so upsetting?

🗐 In-depth Thinking

5. What angers Quan most when his teacher ridiculed him and four other classmates in front of the class?
6. Phan Thi Chi writes his father a "very careful letter." What might that mean, and why does he write in such a way?
7. The young man adds that Uncle Tan's leg is buried at Hue with "a lot of Americans and traitors." What does Uncle Tan's reaction—"just star[ing] at him"—tell us about Uncle Tan?
8. What is ironic about Ah Soong coming up with a solution to the problem of the Lucky Dragon being owned by the government?

📂 Drawing Conclusions

9. One boy in Quan's school, Sik-nin Chau, "made the mistake of being born to parents of pure Chinese stock, which was not wise at a time when the government had decided that the Hoa were, if not actually traitors, a potentially hostile community … And—most annoying of all—weren't they good businessmen who made money?" Discrimination—for reasons of nationality, religion, or race—has occurred throughout history. In a few sentences, describe another instance you are aware of.
10. Think about those things you value in your daily life. Now try to imagine your feelings if everything you "regarded as normal, worthwhile activities" were seen as 'anti-social' or 'reactionary'? Write your response.

Focusing on Setting

1. Imagine your family is sponsoring an exchange student from Thailand, a democratic country near Vietnam. The student has studied English but has never visited America. You are close in age and are looking forward to helping the student adjust. Write a letter describing your community and home. Include any suggestions you might have for the student.

2. Think of a past vacation. Describe your feelings—awe of the beauty, fear of great heights, or perhaps exhilaration at the crashing waves. Write a short vignette, to evoke similar feelings in the reader. Include details that allow the reader to see, feel, hear, taste, and touch the place. Share your effort with the class.

3. Ask your teacher to recommend a story or novel with a wartime setting. Go beyond reporting—write five diary entries in a character's voice. The entries should give a sense of place, time, and situation.

Creating and Writing

1. In Chapter 8, Bennett spends several paragraphs describing what each person in the family dreamt or did the night Phan Thi Chi helps them choose items to take on their journey. Reread this section. Write what is revealed about each character through their actions and dreams. What do you learn about their personalities and feelings? Explain your conclusions.

2. Imagine you will be leaving your home for a new, unfamiliar place. Your destination and future are both uncertain. In a letter, describe your fears, expectations, and feelings about this situation.

3. Investigate some aspect of Vietnam's rich history. Areas of interest might be: Chinese influence on the country; Vietnamese or tribal cultures; landscape and the economy; independence before the French conquest or Vietnam under the French; America's role in the Vietnam War; differences between the North and South. Present your findings to the class using a poster or collage.

Blueprint for Reading

Background Bytes

In Vietnam, water is life. The country depends on two major rivers—the Red River in the north and the Mekong in the south. As the Mekong drops to the South China Sea, it splits into nine main branches and is renamed the Mekong Delta, or Cuu Long, the Nine Dragons.

These wetlands are perfect for rice, a major source of food and income. Along the coast, fishing thrives, but it is a hard way to earn a living. After the war, the waterways were even more vital as families fled the country. Despite the dangers, they sailed their rickety boats into an uncertain future.

Into *The Voyage of the Lucky Dragon*—Part Two

As the story of the Thi Chi family unfolds, dreams become reality, often as nightmares. Phan Thi Chi, as father and head of his household, must make many difficult decisions. Affected by the war, his fears hamper his ability to act. Then grief over his father brings him close to despair.

The will to leave, avoiding the fate decreed by the Communists, is provided by Quan. As in *Accounts Settled*, a son takes over when a father can't go on. In Part Two, Quan begins to assert himself. So begins Quan's coming of age. During the rest of the novel, try to chart Quan's progress from child to man. Note those instances where you see particular growth or bravery.

The whole family is courageous, as they work out their dream of escape. As guards aim guns at the dock, the family must leave undetected. At any moment they can be seen, arrested, or killed. The impetuous Quan, known to act without thinking, is fearful, amazed at what they are trying to do. Admiration for his father grows, as he sees how difficult it is for this cautious man to launch his scheme. Mark Twain, the American author, had it right: "Courage is resistance to fear, mastery of fear—not absence of fear." Have you ever resisted fear and gone on? What did you accomplish because of your courage?

THE VOYAGE OF THE LUCKY DRAGON

Focusing on Point of View

Jack Bennett makes effective use of **point of view**. It is obvious that the novel uses a third-person omniscient (*all-knowing*) narrator. Yet, most often, the perspective is limited to only one character, as we see events mainly through the eyes of this character, learning this person's thoughts and feelings.

The author deliberately shifts the point of view to give us new insights. In one chapter Quan's perspective lets us see him forced to grow up—in another we use Phan's eyes and sense his fear. Later the narrator is truly omniscient, revealing thoughts, feelings, and actions of more than one character. For example, Chapter 1 gives us Quan's perspective, as we're told, "Quan's earliest impression of the war was one of noise." Later, in Chapter 3, a section is firmly anchored in Phan Thi Chi's perspective. After he comes to a decision about his family, we're told that, "For the first time in months he felt quite lighthearted."

Bennett deals with Xuyen in an interesting manner. She is rarely named, usually referred to as Phan's wife, or the mother of Quan and Ly. Examine the novel, and see how these references relate to point of view.

Point of view is particularly related to the 'coming of age' theme. As the story continues, and Quan grows into the role of family leader, his perspective is used more and more. At first this is a family's story, then Phan's. Now Quan's eyes become our way of viewing the family's experiences.

In Part Two you will encounter many unfamiliar boating and seafaring terms. Please see the glossary on the next page for a quick reference.

Word Bank

In French, some consonants, such as **z**, **t**, and **s**, are not pronounced when they are the final letter of a word. The Word Banks of *The Voyage of the Lucky Dragon* define **rendezvous** and **ricochet**. Clearly these two words are French: *Ricochet* is pronounced RIHK oh shay with no final t sound; the word itself is of uncertain etymology. *Rendezvous*, pronounced RAHN day VOO, comes from the French *rendez* (give, present, render) and *vous* (yourselves): Give yourselves up! Present yourselves! (Notice the relationship to the English *surrender*.)

acuteness	effrontery	inquisitive	magnitude	rendezvous
agonizingly	exasperation	intricate	maliciously	shrapnel
apparition	garish	irrevocably	mortally	skepticism
canted	imperturbably	lamented	prostrate	strident
capacious	incongruous	lenient	rakish	tendril
covertly	ingenuously	lout	refuse	

Blueprint for Reading

Boating Glossary

Abaft	Toward or at the stern.
Aft	The area that is near or toward the back (stern) of a ship.
Bilge	The lowest point of a ship's inner hull.
Bollard	A post on a wharf around which to fasten mooring lines.
Bow	The front of a ship.
Coaming	A raised frame around a hatchway to keep out water.
Deck	A platform stretching across and along a boat, serving as a floor.
Eddies	Currents of water circling against the main current.
Fairlead	A block or ring that serves to guide a line on board a boat.
Fulcrum	The support, or point, about which a lever turns.
Gunwale	The upper edge of a ship's side.
Hold	The space inside the ship's bottom, used to store cargo and food.
Hull	The outer shell of a ship.
Jetty	A barrier sunk in the water to affect the current or protect a harbor.
Junk	A Chinese boat with bamboo-ribbed sails.
Keel	The main rib running the length of the hull's bottom, its backbone.
List	To lean to one side.
Mast	A long pole rising from the keel or deck of a ship to carry the sails.
Mooring	A place where a boat can be tied up.
Piles	Long, slender columns supporting a pier.
Port	The left side of a ship, also an order to turn to the left.
Raked	Slanted or sloped.
Rudder	A large piece of timber or metal hinged to a post fitted to a ship at the back. The rudder is moved side to side to change direction.
Starboard	The right side of a ship, also an order to turn to the right.
Stern	The rear of a ship.
Wake	The track left in the water by a ship.

MAST

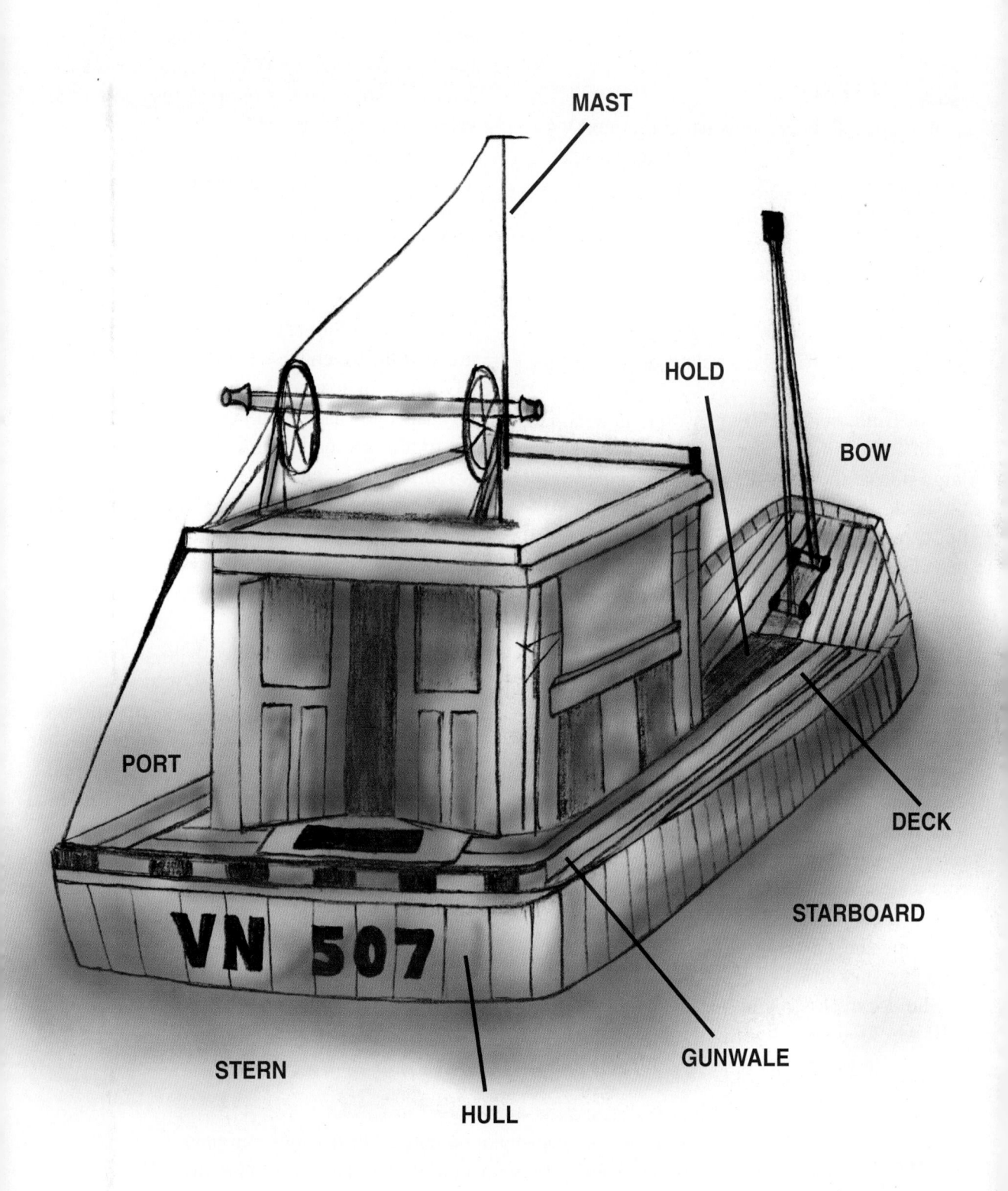

HOLD

BOW

PORT

DECK

STARBOARD

STERN

GUNWALE

VN 507

HULL

PART TWO

CHAPTER 9

They opened the shop as usual the next morning. Not to do so would have aroused suspicion.

The family started slipping away at ten o'clock. Ah Soong went first, clutching the inevitable shopping bags. Today they were full instead of empty, but that would not cause remark. Asian women, young and old, are always visiting friends or relatives with gifts of food.

Aunt Binh, her worldly possessions wrapped in old copies of the *Saigon Post* (there was a large pile of the now-defunct[1] newspaper in the back of the shop) and carried in a cheap but capacious black plastic carry-all, went next. She left with the air of a martyr going to the stake to meet Ah Soong at a bus station near Cholon.

"She had better come with me," said Ah Soong. "Or she will get lost. Besides, I understand her nonsense."

As no one else understood Aunt Binh's nonsense, and everyone was certainly too preoccupied to try to understand it now, Aunt Binh was consigned to the old lady with sighs of relief. Quan's mother was worried, though. She watched Aunt Binh disappear into the morning crowds and sighed.

"I hope she's all right. She can't do much for herself, you know."

"She doesn't try," said her husband.

"If Ah Soong said she'll take her to Rach Gia, she'll get to Rach Gia," said Uncle Tan. "I wish everything else was that certain."

Quan and Uncle Tan left at noon. Uncle Tan had made himself a bag with a shoulder strap, but he still had only one free hand, and Quan had to carry most of Tan's luggage as well as his own. They made slow progress down the crowded pavements, made slower by the fact that everyone Tan knew in Ho Chi Minh City seemed to be out on the street—and with nothing to do but talk—that hot afternoon.

They had almost cleared Gia Dinh, and Quan was congratulating himself on not running into any of his schoolmates, when a loud voice behind him said: "Hullo, Quan—where are you off to, eh?"

Quan spun around, his heart racing. A big boy, his eyes narrowed maliciously although his mouth grinned, was standing behind him, leaning on a bicycle.

He saw Uncle Tan's stained and scratched suitcase, the broken locks reinforced with string, and raised his eyebrows.

"Going on holiday, Quan? Or—running away, eh?" He laughed.

Quan had always vaguely disliked Nguyen Hung.[2] He was a lout, a bully. And it was rumored in the school that he was an informer for the new northern teachers. Nguyen's father held a small local government job, and in his spare time had an ill-defined job with the local sub-branch of the party. No one, certainly not Quan, knew what this party job was, but that didn't matter. The fact of it alone made him—and his son—people to be placated, if not feared.

---

1. *Now-defunct* (dee FUNKT) means no longer in effect or use.
2. *Nguyen Hung* (NYEN HAWNG)

Word Bank

capacious (kuh PAY shus) *adj.*: capable of holding a lot; spacious or roomy
maliciously (muh LISH iss lee) *adv.*: with a desire to inflict harm; spitefully
lout *n.*: a clumsy, boorish person

Quan forced himself to be calm. Today he was prepared to be friendly even to a slug like Nguyen. Out of the corner of his eye he could see Uncle Tan talking animatedly to yet another of his friends. Not for the first time that day Quan thought with exasperation, my G-d, does he know everyone in Ho Chi Minh City? He made himself smile.

"Hullo, Nguyen," he said, trying to sound friendly, pleasantly surprised. He was surprised, all right, but not pleasantly.

Nguyen was waiting for his answer, his head cocked a little on one side, his smile knowing. And suddenly he thanked G-d he was with Uncle Tan. He jerked his finger over his shoulder in the direction of the garrulous ex-soldier.

"Him," he said. "He's been sent to one of the—the NEZs. I'm helping him take his stuff to his assembly point. Down in Tu Do Street."

Nguyen's suspicious eyes flicked towards Uncle Tan, who had finished his farewells (Quan hoped he had been discreet) and was bobbing through the crowd towards them like a buoy bucking a strong tide.

"Huh," said Nguyen, losing interest. "What's he going to do in an NEZ, eh? Punch holes with his tin leg for the rice planters?" He shrugged and turned away. "Good luck. You'll need it. See you at school."

He mounted his bicycle and rode off, leaving Quan trembling with relief.

"Who was that?" asked Uncle Tan, sweat streaming from his face. "Phew! Well, let's go."

"Just a—a friend," said Quan. "From school."

"A friend, eh?" said Uncle Tan, looking at him shrewdly. "I hope so."

"So do I," said Quan. "We'd better keep moving or we'll miss the bus to My Tho."[3]

"And that's only the first stop!" lamented Uncle Tan. "My Tho, then another hundred uncomfortable kilometers to Can Tho and then—"

"I know," said Quan. "But you've missed out Vinh Long. That's another hundred kilometers. Then one more hundred from Can Tho to Rach Gia."

Uncle Tan sighed. "That's about, ah, five or six hundred clicks in all," he said.

"What?"

"Clicks. The soldiers—well, the American soldiers, anyway—used to call kilometers clicks. 'They's a buncha gooks ten clicks uppa road,' they used to say," said Uncle Tan, in a fair imitation of an east coast American accent. "That meant there were some Viet Cong ten kilometers up the road," he explained kindly.

"Thank you," said Quan dryly. They walked on in silence for a few minutes. Well, not exactly silence. Uncle Tan traveled in a little wake of sound: a regular thump as the rubber-shod tip of his crutch hit the pavement, followed by a dry shirr as he swung his body on it, followed by the slap-slop of his single sandal. Thump. Shirr. Slap. Thump. Shirr. Slap. It was exhausting work in a temperature of thirty degrees Celsius and humidity of almost ninety per cent. Uncle Tan's face glowed and the sweat ran from him in a steady stream: it ran down his leg and his single foot left a wet print in the dust. Uncle Tan was not a big man—few Vietnamese are—but he was as tough as new bamboo: what the war had left of his body was lean and sinewy, and he had a mind to match. He had left all he had ever had

---

3. *My Tho* (MY TOE)

Word Bank

exasperation (ig ZAS puh RAY shun) *n.*: extreme annoyance or irritation

lamented (luh MEN tid) *v.*: mourned deeply and vocally

and loved in his bloody shambles around Hue, including his leg, but he never gave way to despair or self-pity, and he never asked, as he had heard many others do, "Why me?" because, as he ingenuously explained to Quan's father one night, "If I ask 'Why me?' I must also ask 'Why not me?' and I'll go around in circles. I'm not the first soldier to lose his leg. I won't be the last. Not by a long way."

So now he tramped on uncomplaining beside the silent Quan, glancing anxiously at the boy now and again.

The unexpected meeting with Nguyen had upset Quan. Had he followed them? They weren't in the same class, but the whole school knew which students had been publicly criticized by the cadres for having bourgeois or reactionary parents.[4] Perhaps Nguyen was even now telling his father—who would scurry to the Public Security Bureau. No, Quan reassured himself. He stole a glance at Uncle Tan's cheap Japanese watch. Three-twenty. His father and mother would still be in the shop. As far as anyone dropping in was concerned, it was business as usual. Phan Thi Chi and his wife were going to keep the shop open all day and slip away with Ly after dark. Then they would head southwest by bus and train and rendezvous with the rest of the family near the Rach Gia post office—the only place they could think of on the spur of the moment—at noon on Monday. But say Nguyen tells his father he saw me and Uncle Tan, and his father tells the Public Security Bureau, and the PSB comes to the shop? Well, mother and father will be there. And they'll tell them—with a horrible sinking sensation Quan realized that the family had failed to prepare mutually-corroborating stories.[5] Although he was sweating almost as much as Uncle Tan he actually shivered. What an incredible oversight! My poor father, he thought. He's really not cut out for this sort of thing. Well, it's no good worrying about it. Just keep moving.

But he did worry about it, for hours. And when he had got them two seats and hauled Uncle Tan aboard the eight o'clock bus for My Tho—and seen that wiry old soldier fall instantly into the deep sleep of exhaustion—Nguyen's knowing face floated before him in the hot and dusty gloom as the old, grossly over-loaded bus rumbled through the night. He slept very little. Uncle Tan got his full hundred clicks' worth.

CHAPTER 10

Phan Thi Chi put up the shutters for the last time at seven o'clock that Saturday evening. He and his wife and daughter ate some cold rice and had a glass of tea and then they picked up their bags and went quietly out of

---

4. *Bourgeois* (BOOR zhwah) *or reactionary parents* refer to parents who were members of the middle class and owned small family businesses.
5. *Mutually-corroborating stories* confirm each other.

Word Bank

ingenuously (in JEEN yus lee) *adv.*: naively; artlessly; without restraint, openly

rendezvous (RAHN day VOO) *v.*: meet at an agreed-upon time and place

the back door, leaving the kitchen light burning so that inquisitive passers-by—and there were many these days—would think that the family was in the kitchen as usual. Then, by dark back lanes, foul with the day's refuse, and by ill-lit side streets, they gradually worked their way further and further away from thirteen Bach Dang, Gia Dinh, their home for so many years. They were too terrified to grieve.

In the empty shop the big cockroaches came out cautiously at first, twitching their antennae nervously, expecting a trap: then they got bolder and soon their scurryings made a soft whispering through the whole shop and up into the empty rooms above: a sound of dead leaves blowing.

After a while a rat came out, too, a big fat brown fellow who climbed on to the table and saw the remains of the family's last meal: he ate the rice very delicately, watching the busy cockroaches with eyes bright as sapphire chips.

So they all came to Rach Gia: by train, bus, riverboat, ferry and pedicab.[6] Ah Soong would have used a rickshaw,[7] if she had needed to, and had that shameful vehicle still been available. But the big old Japanese buses got her and Aunt Binh to Rach Gia early on Monday morning; in time for them to wash their faces and brush their hair—so stiff with red dust that each woman seemed to be wearing an ungainly helmet. Ah Soong was an old woman; she had spent the previous twenty-four hours in circumstances of extreme discomfort—South Vietnamese buses are old, worn, badly sprung. Ah Soong had stood for more than two hundred kilometers so that Aunt Binh could squeeze herself into the only few centimeters of seat available, and on Sunday morning, in the gray, gritty confines, rank with the stink of raw sewage, of a bus station north of My Tho, Ah Soong found some boiling water. With it she made several cups of tea for herself and the prostrate Aunt Binh, heated some rice and washed both their faces. Then she straightened her black amah's skirt (dreadfully creased overnight) and sponged some stains from her blouse; and when the bus began the next bouncing stage of its journey southwest, well, Ah Soong looked as fresh, capable, and tough as ever. Only someone who knew her very well (and they had all died a long while ago, of old age, poverty, war and disease) would have noticed that there were just a few more lines around those fine eyes, that the face was a little more strained. But who notices things like that in the faces of servants, anyway? Servants are like mothers: Ah Soong had never been a mother, but she had always been a servant. But, like a mother, she had always been taken for granted. Ah Soong would always be there.

And, this steamy Monday in Rach Gia, Ah Soong was still there. She was there in the dusty square near the post office when Phan Thi Chi arrived, hot and weary, with his daughter and wife; she was there when Uncle Tan, still joking despite the exhaustion which showed on his face and the agony which turned his stump to flame, arrived with Quan.

Gradually the family drifted to tea tables and

---

6. A *pedicab* (PED ee KAB) is a three-wheeled public vehicle operated by pedals. It typically has a hooded cab mounted behind the driver and holds two passengers.
7. A *rickshaw* (RIK shah) is a small, two-wheeled passenger vehicle pulled by one person. It was widely used in China and Japan.

Word Bank

inquisitive (in KWIZ ih tiv) *adj.*: curious; eager for knowledge; unduly curious; prying
refuse (REF yooz) *n.*: rubbish; trash; garbage; something that is discarded as useless
prostrate (PRAHS trayt) *adj.*: physically weak or exhausted; lying flat, at full length, face down on the ground; utterly dejected

food stalls under the trees. They found three tables away from the street and slowly, when they saw that no one was paying any attention to them, ordered tea and rice and fish and had a cheap and simple meal. They talked, keeping their voices low. But to the stall-holders they were just a group of stained and obviously tired travelers. The stall-holders had their own private worries, no doubt, so they paid little attention to the family as it refueled itself and gathered collective courage for the next move. A move which would put them, all of them, finally and irrevocably outside the law.

Quan told Ly of his chance meeting with Nguyen Hung, whispering so as not to alarm his parents. Ly, who knew Nguyen Hung, was as alarmed as Quan.

"He'll tell," she said with nervous conviction. "Oh, he'll tell. He'll tell the teacher, or a cadre, or his father."

"He's not in my class, and he's not in yours," said Quan, trying to be optimistic. "Perhaps he won't notice we're not at school."

"Of course he will," said Ly. "Everyone will! Ever since we were criticized everyone always notices us!"

"What are you children whispering about?" asked Phan Thi Chi irritably.

"I'm just telling Ly about something funny that happened on the bus on the way here," said Quan hastily. A white lie, he thought. But the truth would terrify him.

Uncle Tan looked at him sharply. "Something funny?" he said dryly. "I wish I'd seen it. I could have done with a laugh." He fell silent again, nursing his stump. Not for the first time since leaving the US military hospital at Hue, he wondered if they had got all the shrapnel out. Sometimes he could *feel* something in there....

"You were asleep," said Quan.

A short while after that, the family split up again to find plain lodgings for the night. There were several small private guesthouses operating in Rach Gia. It was a field of activity the government had not yet entered. Cheap rooms were found and then Phan Thi Chi set out to see what he could find out about his father.

Quan sat glumly under an aging mango tree[8] with Ly and in mutual gloom they worried about Nguyen Hung.

They were not to know it ever, of course, but Nguyen's very malice had saved them. Quan and Ly, two of the many marked children in the school, had been missed at nine o'clock that morning, when it was obvious that they were not coming to school. The alarm had been given by ten by the senior political cadre attached to the school, who knew what was in store for Phan Thi Chi's family that week. And meanwhile the state-appointed manager had arrived at the shop to find it empty and cockroach-haunted and apparently in the charge of a big brown rat. So by noon, after the various officials had exchanged views, the fat was in the fire and the alarm was out. Now the local branch of the Public Security Bureau knew of Phan Thi Chi's old father in Rach Gia —there was little the PSB didn't know about most of the families in its precinct—and would quickly have put two and two together; and the product of that sum would have been a quick phone call to Rach Gia and the arrest and imprisonment (pending return to Ho Chi Minh City) of Phan Thi Chi, his wife, Quan,

---

8. A *mango tree* produces tropical fruit, that is pear-shaped and greenish-red, and has a sweet, pulpy interior.

Word Bank

irrevocably (ih REV ih kuh blee) *adv.*: unalterably; in a manner that could not be undone

shrapnel (SHRAP nil) *n.*: fragments scattered by a bursting artillery shell, mine, or bomb

Ly, Aunt Binh, Ah Soong and Uncle Tan.

But before the PSB had time to consult its files on Phan Thi Chi's out-of-town connections, an excited teacher arrived at the PSB office with a self-important Nguyen Hung, who was babbling a tale about seeing Quan and his crippled Uncle Tan in suspicious circumstances on Saturday. Nguyen had also seen Uncle Tan talking to a one-armed man at a tea stall near Tu Do Street. He was sure he would recognize the man if he saw him again.

So Nguyen and the teacher and a northern political cadre and three PSB men got into an old Renault and drove across the city to where Nguyen had seen Quan and Uncle Tan on Saturday: it was near a bicycle shop (now state-owned) which Nguyen knew, so he had no difficulty in finding the place again. And then he found the strip of pavement on which he had startled Quan, and there, sure enough, were the tea stalls; and at one of them was the one-armed man he had seen, over Quan's shoulder, talking to Uncle Tan.

"Stop the car," Nguyen shouted, and they all got out.

The one-armed man (who had lost his arm in the same battle as that in which Uncle Tan had lost his leg) watched them coming through the crowd: the panting schoolboy, the glacial political cadre,[9] the grim-faced men from the PSB. He whistled softly under his breath. Phew. He knew it was Tan they were after. Tan had not said anything, but he had seen the boy waiting in the background and sensed that something was up. Well! And now they were after Tan. Wait. Tan had said something. About having a few days down in—in—ah! Rach Gia. A little fishing village away to the southwest. Yes. The one-armed man smiled inwardly.

"That's him," said Nguyen shrilly. "That's him!" pointing rudely at the one-armed man, who sipped his tea imperturbably. Then the men from the PSB took over. Had he seen the man known as Uncle Tan, a one-legged ex-soldier? Yes, he had. Had chatted to him on Saturday. Was there anything suspicious about him? The one-armed man thought deeply. No. Yes. Wait a minute! Of course. There was a young fellow hanging around, keeping in the background, carrying Tan's luggage. Now why, he asked himself, would Tan have so much luggage if he were just going away for the weekend? Eh? It's not as though a one-legged man would need a lot of luggage, would he? Only one shoe, for example. Well, had the man Tan said where he was going for the weekend? Where? Yes, where? Oh. Ah, yes. The one-armed man thought rapidly. Yes. He remembered now. Tan said he and the boy were going to Da Nang. The PSB was astounded. Da Nang? For the weekend?

The one-armed man shrugged. That was what Tan had said. Perhaps he had heard wrong. His hearing wasn't any too good, you know. The war.…The PSB held a whispered consultation. The one-armed man, suddenly developing a remarkable acuteness of hearing, heard the words "Hong Kong" and "Manila" and grinned inwardly. Then the PSB and the cadre and the self-important schoolboy rushed away, the PSB to set telephone and telex wires[10] to Da Nang buzzing with orders to find and arrest a man and a boy believed to be heading for Da Nang to stow away aboard a ship bound for Hong Kong or Manila.

---

9. The *glacial political cadre* means that the cadre is cold and aloof.
10. *Telex wires* are similar to telegrams, but they are used by subscribers, and not the general public.

Word Bank

imperturbably (IM per TERB uh blee) *adv.*: calmly; without agitation

acuteness (uh KYOOT niss) *n.*: sensitivity even to slight details or impressions

The one-armed man had another cup of tea and smiled quite openly. He had always liked Tan. He pictured the PSB launching a wild goose chase in Da Nang and his smile grew broader.

Da Nang is not only three times as far from Ho Chi Minh City as Rach Gia. It is also in the opposite direction.

中 CHAPTER 11

Phan Thi Chi staggered back into the brilliant sunshine of the post office square like a drunken man. His face was ashen and he was trying to choke back violent sobs.

Quan and Ly ran to him and helped him to a seat, shielding him from the inquisitive eyes of passers-by. Phan Thi Chi hid his face in his hands for a while, trying to compose himself. At last he lifted his head and looked wildly at his son and daughter.

"Dead," he said. "Dead! My father's dead!"

They sat in stunned silence on the bench. After a while Phan Thi Chi spoke, bitterly.

"Heart, they said at the commune. His heart killed him. Yes, I'm sure it was his heart. They broke it!" He wept silently again, more in rage, frustration and pure fear than in true sorrow. Then he wiped his face and stood up.

"Well, then. There's nothing for it. We must give ourselves up to the authorities. Perhaps they'll be lenient."

Quan put his arm around his father's shoulders.

"Did they say—where he was—buried?"

Phan Thi Chi nodded. "Of course. Here—" he unfolded a grimy piece of paper he had been clutching. "Here. They wrote down where to find it."

"I'll get mother," said Ly, and sped away.

The old man's grave was a low mound of red earth marked with a stick bearing a crudely painted number. It lay among dozens of equally anonymous graves on the edge of town. Already the jungle from which the cemetery had been hacked was returning. Within a few years the graves would be swallowed up.

Quan's mother placed a few frangipani[11] flowers—already wilting in the blistering heat—on the grave and read a few verses from her prayer book. There was nothing more they could do, or had the heart to do.

Walking back in the late afternoon to their guesthouses, they passed the fishing jetties. The boats were returning, followed by the fast brown brahimy kites[12] which are to be found, peace or war, around any Vietnamese fishing village. The birds rode the air currents in the boats' wakes, diving for scraps of fish as the day's catch was cleaned.

Phan Thi Chi averted his eyes as he passed the boats. It was too painful to see them, to realize that all his hopes were dashed, and that he and his family now faced nothing but separation and forced labor on raw farms in a strange part of the country.

But Quan plucked at his arm.

"Father—the boat. The Lucky Dragon must be down there! Let's go and look at her—please. Perhaps—"

---

11. *Frangipani* (FRAN juh PAN ee) *flowers* are from a tropical tree and used to make perfume.
12. *Brahimy* (BRAH him mee) *kites* are hawk-like birds that fly above fishing areas. They signal the arrival of the fishermen at the end of the day.

Word Bank   **lenient** (LEE nee int) *adj.*: agreeably tolerant; not strict or severe; indulgent

His father shook him off, angrily.

"Are you mad? What can we do? What do we know about boats?"

His son stared at him, open-mouthed.

"But—but I thought you could handle a boat! You said—"

His father's voice was strident, almost breaking with shame and guilt and grief.

"Yes! I've been out on the boat! As a passenger! I couldn't sail across a pond, let alone to Malaysia!"

Quan backed away, horrified.

"At least let's look at the boat," he said quietly. "We've come so fa—"

"No!" shouted Phan Thi Chi. His face was glistening with sweat and he seemed on the verge of screaming, of running away shrieking up the street. His family looked at him, terrified by the change the past few days had wrought.

Uncle Tan saved the situation. He stopped swinging himself along on his crutch and mopped his streaming face. "Phew! Let me get my breath. Look," he said reasonably to Phan Thi Chi, "look, tell you what. Just let's have a look at the boat, eh? Do no harm. We'll come down later when the fishermen have gone and just have a look at her. After all, as Quan says, we've come all this way."

Phan Thi Chi, calmer and a little ashamed of his outburst, shrugged.

"All right. If you want to. Don't blame me if you get into trouble, that's all." Then he turned and walked stiffly away up the road, as though they had mortally offended him.

"Thanks, Uncle Tan," said Quan.

"He's right, you know," said Uncle Tan. "We're finished."

"Not yet," said Quan. "Not yet."

Standing on the almost deserted main jetty with Uncle Tan an hour later Quan saw the Lucky Dragon—now VN 507—for the first time.

He almost wept. He was not sure what he had expected. He had hoped—although he knew it was not likely—that the Lucky Dragon would be sleek, trim, glowing with brass and glass. At least *something* like the boats he had seen in old American magazines. Or, if that was too tall an order, something like a Chinese junk, with a high stern, raked mast,[13] solid, seaworthy lines. The Lucky Dragon could never, he had convinced himself, be anything like the chunky, graceless cargo boats he had seen chugging up and down the Saigon River.

But she was, and uglier: twenty meters long, with a stern which seemed to run forwards a long way before entering the water; a clumsy rudder which seemed to be made of a chunk of rusty steel; high flared bows which met at a heavy, rusted roller fairlead.[14] The whole boat seemed to be made of huge, rough-hewn balks[15] of timber, silvery with age and salt and sun. Not a speck of varnish or brass anywhere. Such rigging as Quan could see was of ordinary steel, red with rust. The bridge, set aft behind the gaping shallow holes of the four fishholds, was a poor mockery of the rakish affair Quan had imagined. The windows were of ordinary cheap house glass; set in ordinary window frames with chipped putty, and behind them loomed—not the brass-bound varnished wooden wheel of Quan's dreams—but a

---

13. A *raked mast* is one that is tilted back rather than perpendicular to the deck.
14. A *roller fairlead* is a pulley mechanism that prevents the rope from wearing out from friction.
15. *Rough-hewn balks* are roughly carved, heavy pieces of wood.

Word Bank

rakish (RAY kish) *adj.*: jaunty; dashing; stylish
strident (STRY dint) *adj.*: harsh in sound; grating
mortally (MOR tuh lee) *adv.*: severely; grievously; fatally

cheap, skeletal circle of steel. An attempt had been made, long ago, to brighten the wheelhouse by painting the wooden panels below the windows in gay colors: now the garish blue and yellow and red paint wept in big flakes on to the dirty deck, and the wheelhouse had the sad and tawdry[16] look of an abandoned circus caravan. And this shabby seagoing disappointment was crowned, so to speak, by a tottering galvanized iron smokestack, all dented and stained, which left the deck through a crude hole just abaft[17] the shameful wheelhouse and poked two meters into the sky, secured by several rusted metal stays.

Lucky Dragon seemed aware of her deficiencies. She was the outermost boat in a string of five secured to each other by ropes and plank ladders, and she leaned tiredly against her neighbor, creaking slightly as she moved on the water. So she leaks as well, thought Quan bitterly, noting the list.[18]

Uncle Tan, sensing the boy's disappointment, stayed silent. But the silence stretched on and on, with Quan gazing at the boat as though in a trance, until at last Uncle Tan, sitting on a bollard,[19] stirred him up with his crutch.

"We'd better go," he said. "See, the sentry's come on." He nodded towards the seaward end of the quay, where a young man armed with an old American M-1 rifle was sitting in a small shelter.

"It's all we have," said Quan, as though talking to himself.

"And it's not enough," said Uncle Tan, shouldering his crutch.

"It's all we have," repeated Quan. He pointed down through the sun-warped boards of the jetty to the water swirling around the piles.[20]

"See that? Tide's still coming in. And there's no moon. I noticed last night. We must take her tonight, Uncle Tan, before they start looking for us."

Uncle Tan stopped walking and grinned wryly.

"Quan," he said. "Look—" he nodded towards the man at the end of the jetty again. "There's him. And look over there—across the river. I only noticed it a few minutes ago. See—just above that moored boat. A machine gun post."

"I see it," said Quan, after a discreet glance. He walked up the jetty deep in thought. When they had passed the guard, he suddenly said to Uncle Tan:

"Could you start her engine?"

Uncle Tan, who rather prided himself on his mechanical knowledge—he had been a truck driver before being drafted into the army—bridled.[21] "Of course. Any engine can be started if it's not broken, you know."

"Say it needs an ignition key, and the key isn't there?"

"Then you jump the ignition switch with a piece of wire," said Uncle Tan. "Easy. How do you think car thieves work?"

"So you could do it on Lucky Dragon if you had to?"

"Of course. But—Quan, my boy, forget it. Your father's right. We're finished. Have you seen the size of that boat?"

"Yes."

---

16. *Tawdry* (TAW dree) is showy and cheap.
17. *Abaft* (uh BAFT) means behind.
18. Here, *list* (LIST) means leaning to one side.
19. A *bollard* (BAH lerd) is a thick, low post mounted on a wharf to hold mooring lines of vessels.
20. The *piles* (PY ilz) are cylindrical pieces of wood hammered into the soil near the edge of the water to support the pier.
21. *Bridled* (BRY dild) means draw up the head and draw in the chin, in disdain or resentment.

Word Bank

garish (GAIR ish) *adj.*: crudely or tastelessly colorful or showy

"Besides, Quan, even if we sneak aboard Lucky Dragon—and how do we get past that man on the gate, eh?—what will happen as soon as I start the engine? Bang, bang, bang—that's what happens. From the jetty guard and that machine gun across the river."

"We won't start the engine, Uncle Tan," said Quan. "Not until we're well down the river."

"I don't get it," said Uncle Tan.

"The tide," said Quan. "The tide! It's a spring tide and still rising! When it begins to fall, it will run out fast. We cut Lucky Dragon loose and let the tide take her out. With no noise, in the dark. They won't see us or hear us."

"The jetty guard—"

"We go under him. Get on to the beach and swing ourselves along under the jetty, along the piles!"

It seemed to Uncle Tan that there was something Quan had forgotten, but by then they had arrived at the food stall at which they had all arranged to meet for the evening meal, so he shrugged and sat down in the chair Ly pulled out for him.

Phan Thi Chi had chosen a table well back from the street; or rather two tables pulled together, under some sheltering seacoast mallow trees in yellow bloom. Quan's calm suggestion that they cut out Lucky Dragon and face the unknown terrors of the sea in her horrified him. At first he would not listen. Then he rebuked Quan for his effrontery, reminding him who was father and who son.

At last his wife said quietly: "Let us just listen to Quan's plan, dear. We have nothing to lose."

"I think so," said Ah Soong, nodding. "Let's listen, Phan Thi Chi."

"You mad old woman," said the tormented Phan Thi Chi. "I should have sent you to China."

"Plenty of time for that," said the old lady philosophically.

"Whatever happens we will all die," said Aunt Binh drearily. "I'm just sorry to be such a nuisance to you all."

Ly felt very much like shaking her.

"The boy's quite mad," said Uncle Tan. "But listen to him."

So, speaking softly while they ate their rice, Quan told them his plan: two of the men should get aboard Lucky Dragon late that night, as the tide started to fall, by crawling from piling to piling under the jetty. Once aboard Lucky Dragon, they would cut her free and let the falling tide take her seawards. Quan had noticed that, about a kilometer below the village, a sand spit jutted into the river. The rest of the family could wait there. The boat would be allowed to run aground so that they would not have to get out of their depths to wade out and climb aboard. This would have to be done quickly, or Lucky Dragon would be stranded by the falling tide. Once everyone was aboard, the tide would be allowed to take them again, carrying them down to the sea….

"And anyway," said Quan, "once we're clear of Rach Gia, Uncle Tan can start the engine."

"What about the jetty guard and the machine gun across the river?" asked Ly.

"There's no moon," explained Quan. "It's very dark. And we'll make no noise. Just cut the ropes and let the river take us."

"If it's so dark, how will you see where you're going? You might run into the bank," said Ly.

"We'll be able to see the bank by the stars," said Quan. "I think."

Word Bank

effrontery (ee FRUN ter ee) *n.*: shameless or impudent boldness

"I hope you're right," said Ly, with a sister's skepticism.

"Well, father?" asked Quan.

Phan Thi Chi sighed. He seemed to have aged years in a few days. "Yes. It could work. But if we get the boat away, and out of the river, and into the sea, and if a gunboat doesn't catch us—well, how do we get to Malaysia? Can you navigate? Of course not! We will drift around until we starve to death!"

"No, we won't," said his son. "I looked at a map at school. Malaysia is due west of Rach Gia. We just follow the setting sun and we must hit Malaysia."

"When?" said Phan Thi Chi, refusing to be cheered. "When, that's the point."

"In four or five days, father," said Quan. "Or, to be even safer, we can head northwest—that is, to the right of the setting sun, and go up into the Gulf of Siam. That way we must hit land. We have to, because there's no seaway out of the Gulf."

"There's pirates in the Gulf," said Aunt Binh. "My late husband told me about them." She settled herself down lower in her chair, shrugging her travel-stained clothes around her rather like a depressed crow ruffling its feathers on a wet day. "But don't listen to me. I won't be a nuisance for much longer. I feel it, you know."

"Please, woman," said Uncle Tan testily. He broke off and looked at his watch. "Was that tide full when you looked at it, Quan?"

"Almost. I noticed the marks of the last tide on the jetty."

"Then if we're going, we had better go soon," said Uncle Tan. "I think they will be looking for us here tomorrow or the next day at the latest." He paused. "And who is going to swing under the jetty like a monkey with you to cut the boat free, eh?"

Quan looked at him, surprised. "Why, you of course, Uncle Tan. I thought—" And then he stopped, embarrassed.

Uncle Tan laughed. "Sorry, Quan. I couldn't do it. I'd fall into the water and wake the guard."

"I'll come with you, Quan," said Phan Thi Chi quietly.

They were about to leave when Ah Soong asked innocently: "And have you a sharp knife?"

Quan and his father exchanged glances. They had forgotten all about a knife.

Ah Soong clicked her tongue.

"I thought so. Well, I'll have to lend you my best kitchen knife. Mind you don't lose it, now. And be careful. It's very sharp."

She handed Quan the knife, wrapped for safety in several layers of cloth, and disappeared into the dark where the rest of the family waited.

The memory of that nightmare climb under the jetty stayed with Quan for a long time. It was pitch dark except for infrequent pale strips of starlight which fell through gaps in the planking. The tide turned before they were halfway along the jetty's hundred-meter length, and began to fall with startling rapidity, exposing as it did dripping piles covered with razor-edged small oysters and slimy weed.

The receding water sucked and gurgled around their feet and there were strange scurryings and ploppings as unknown sea creatures made off into the deeper darkness at their approach. Quan suddenly remembered all he had ever read about sea snakes and giant octopi and squid and fierce eels.

Word Bank   **skepticism** (SKEP tih siz im) *n.*: doubt or disbelief

All his sea-going dreams died then, in that dripping dark beneath the jetty. With painful clarity he saw himself for what he was: not a dashing hero in some novel or movie, but a frightened schoolboy in a most dangerous position. He had a sudden urge, agonizing in its intensity, to call the whole thing off. To cancel out the past two days. To wake up in his room above the little shop at thirteen Bach Dang. To get dressed and have his breakfast and walk quietly to school with his sister. He gritted his teeth and swung himself on to the next diagonal pile brace. He was bleeding from dozens of tiny cuts by now. There seemed to be sharp-edged shells everywhere he put a hand or foot. His sweat got in the cuts and they stung viciously. He wondered what his father was thinking. Quan was no philosopher but he knew that his father was more frightened than he was: and that, Quan knew, made him a very brave man. There in the damp dark beneath the jetty, scrabbling from pile to pile crab-like, Quan felt more admiration and affection for his father than he ever had before in his whole life.

Suddenly, heaving himself across a stretch of water gleaming like black ice below him, Quan slipped on some weed: he kept his hold on a crossbeam with his hands, but his feet slid out from under him and his lower body hit the water with a violent smash, sending the water—thick with phosphorescence[22]—exploding in a silver shower.

They froze, flattening themselves against the sodden timber. After what seemed an age, in a silence broken only by the soft slap of water around the piles and the cry of some night bird on the river, measured footsteps thumped down the jetty above them. A flashlight's pale beam flickered through the slits in the planks above them and cast a yellow circle on the rushing black water.

The footsteps advanced until the guard stood right overhead: looking up, terrified, they could see him as a foreshortened shadow blocking out the pale strips of sky.

The guard cleared his throat noisily, spat lustily into the water, and walked slowly back the way he had come.

They let out their pent-up breath in long sighs. But they waited for almost twenty minutes before moving again. Phan Thi Chi shivered as he thought of the man sitting there in the dark with his rifle cocked and ready, just waiting for them to give themselves away. He had a lively imagination and his flesh crept as he thought of a .30 bullet punching its way through his soft body.

After a while his heart stopped pounding and he patted Quan on the shoulder. Quan's eyes caught the starlight and gleamed briefly in the darkness. Phan Thi Chi leaned closer and hissed: "The tide!" and Quan nodded. It was running out fast.

They started their slow painful progress again. Then something occurred to Quan, a thought so incongruous that he almost laughed aloud. There was no music! No music at all! In all the movies he had ever seen, greet deeds of daring were always accompanied by music. Why, you could sit blindfolded in most movies and know what was happening just by listening to the music. So this is the difference between real life and the movies, he mused,

---

22. *Phosphorescence* (FAHS fuh RESS intz) here refers to ocean life that emits luminous radiation at night.

Word Bank   **incongruous** (in KAHN groo iss) *adj.*: out of place; inappropriate; not fitting

sucking a splinter of shell from his thumb. No music. Just fear and discomfort and pain. And at this moment more fear than anything. Once again the magnitude of what they were doing struck him and his heart sank.

Then he gritted his teeth and swung himself on to the next pile.

There was a four-meter rise and fall during spring tides at Rach Gia. By the time they got to the end of the jetty, the water level had dropped a meter, and the moored boats with it. The deck of the inshore boat, which had been slightly above jetty level when Quan and Uncle Tan had inspected the Lucky Dragon several hours earlier, was now almost a meter below it, so Quan and his father could slither aboard unnoticed by the sentry, who would otherwise surely have seen them silhouetted against the stars, even on such a dark night, or against the few scattered lights of houses on the opposite shore.

They crawled across the intervening boats on their stomachs, like snakes, inhaling at close range mixed smells of fish and oil and paint and damp rope and wet nylon nets and cockroaches and bilge water and unwashed bucket toilets.

Then they were aboard Lucky Dragon. She was lying with her bows upstream. The river caressed her forefoot with urgent ripples, trying to swing her seawards.

"Cut her loose," whispered Phan Thi Chi. "I'll take the wheel." Which was fine seamanlike sentiment for someone who didn't know port from starboard.

Quan looked at the rushing water, saw it straining the bows, trying to swing Lucky Dragon away from the wharf. Yes, he thought, I must cut the bowline first, let the tide swing her, and then get aft and cut the stern line. That way the tide will swing her across the river and turn her so that we don't run down headfirst, or bows first, he corrected himself, trying to think like a seaman.

Ah Soong's best knife winked at him in the starlight when he unwrapped it. The thin blade, honed to razor sharpness, slid through the taut five-centimeter manila hawser[23] like the proverbial knife through butter. Lucky Dragon instantly swung away from the jetty, pushed by the fast-falling tide. Quan scrabbled frantically aft as Lucky Dragon's stern, pivoting on the fulcrum[24] of her stern rope, drove hard against the jetty with a muted wooden groan.

Ah Soong's knife flashed again: one strand of the thick hawser held, stretched, and parted, and Lucky Dragon swung, free, across the river. Starlight twinkled on the widening gap of dark water between them and the jetty.

Quan wrapped Ah Soong's knife carefully and put it inside his shirt. Then he crawled back along the deck and hauled himself into the wheelhouse where his father was standing at the big metal wheel. Phan Thi Chi angled Lucky Dragon across the tide so that, as far as he could judge, they were in the middle of the stream, being pushed at about three knots by the falling tide.

In mutual, terrified silence father and son watched the jetty and the lights of Rach Gia drop behind. They scanned the darker far bank anxiously, watching for the first signs of alarm at the invisible machine gun post, the first

---

23. A *hawser* (HAW zer) is a heavy rope used for mooring or towing.
24. The *fulcrum* (FULL krim) is the support on which the rope, acting as a lever, turns the boat.

Word Bank

magnitude (MAG nih TOOD) *n.*: great size; extent; or dimensions

flickers of fire as the big gun caught them against the glow of the village.

Agonizingly slowly, they crept away, the only sound the chuckle of water at the bows. Then they rounded a slight bend, shutting out the lights of Rach Gia, and the sand-spit was a few hundred meters ahead, a pale tongue against the darker river. At the tip of the tongue were several dark blobs crouched like drying cormorants.[25]

Phan Thi Chi, terrified of running hard aground on an ebbing tide, cut it very fine. So fine that Quan thought they would miss the spit altogether. Lucky Dragon, moving faster now, slid past the outer edge of the tongue of sand. There were muffled squeaks from someone on the shore—Ly, Quan guessed. Then Phan Thi Chi put the helm over and Lucky Dragon swung sharply to port. There was a long soughing[26] rumble as the bilge keels[27] ran on to the sand, and then the boat was stopped, heeled slightly, broadside to the stream but partly protected by the sand-spit from the tide which would have quickly sucked it away.

"Quickly—quickly," hissed Quan. He had found a heavy rope on the afterdeck. He slung it now towards the dark shapes splashing through the shallows. It fell rattling and splashing and someone grabbed it—Uncle Tan; the starlight winked briefly on his metal crutch.

Quan realized instantly that they had overlooked something: Lucky Dragon, riding high with her fishholds empty, had almost two meters of freeboard, increased now by the heel caused as she rested on her starboard bilge keel.

And they had no ladder! Quan cursed himself for his forgetfulness.

Phan Thi Chi came padding down the deck.

"What's the matter?" he hissed. "Get them aboard! Get them aboard! We'll be stuck here!"

"They can't get on!" said Quan, feeling panic rising in him. "It's too high!"

His father groaned.

"I'll get over and heave them up," said Quan. "They can use my shoulders. You heave them aboard. Here." He gave his father the rope and leaped lightly over the side, landing with a small splash in the warm water.

The family was petrified with fear, milling around in the water like frightened cattle. Aunt Binh was moaning softly and clutching Ah Soong.

"You first, Ly," said Quan authoritatively. "You can help father pull us aboard."

"No, I'll stay and help—" began Ly, but he slapped the wet rope into her hands.

"Do as I say—now!"

And Ly, after one glance at his taut face in the starlight, went up the rope like a monkey.

"Good girl," he said. The rope splashed back to him.

"Aunt Binh." Ignoring her moaning protests he got the rope around her middle, forced her to hold it, and hissed "Pull!"

He got behind and pushed, his feet sinking into the soft sand, and Aunt Binh went aboard, sagging like a bundle of badly packed washing.

Ah Soong. Then his mother. Working frantically, all the while feeling the tide dropping

---

25. *Cormorants* (KOR mor intz) are dark-colored seabirds.
26. A *soughing* (SUF ing) rumble is a rushing, rustling sound.
27. *Bilge keels* (BILJ KEELZ) are projections at the point where the bottom and sides of a vessel meet. The keels prevent the boat from rolling.

Word Bank   **agonizingly** (AG uh nyz ing lee) *adv.*: very distressingly; extremely painfully

about his legs, seeing Lucky Dragon heel more sharply.

He put his shoulder against the hull and heaved.

"Uncle Tan! Help me push—get her off a bit before she sticks."

They heaved, sweating. Lucky Dragon, pushed also by the river, slid into deeper water and rolled back on to an even keel.

Over the gunwale[28] his father and Ly watched, their faces white blobs against the sky.

"Now, Uncle Tan." Quan gave him the rope.

"I can't," panted Uncle Tan, breath coming in harsh gasps. "Bloody crutch—stuck in the sand—and my leg!"

Quan felt like laughing. It was just too much. After all that, to be caught because Uncle Tan's crutch was stuck in the mud!

He felt the strain on the rope as Lucky Dragon moved on the tide.

"Father," he whispered.

"Yes?"

"Tie your end of the rope. There's a bollard behind you. Tie it, and leave us—"

"Leave you? Don't talk—"

"No. Listen. Leave us and get back to the wheel. Let the tide pull us off. I'll hang on to Uncle Tan."

"Are you sure?"

"Yes. Yes, be quick." The pull on the rope was hard, urgent. Quan looped it about both of them. What knot? Oh yes, he remembered. He had been interested in knots once, when he had gone through a brief phase of wanting to be a seaman when he grew up. He had got a book out of the library and spent hours over its step-by-step instructions on how to tie the most intricate bends and hitches imaginable. Now, standing up to his waist in the rushing dark river, it all came back to him, and he encircled them with a creditable bowline on the bight,[29] a hitch which makes a loop which will not turn into a dangerous slipknot.

He had barely finished it when Lucky Dragon, swinging clear of the lee of the sand-spit and taking the full force of the tide along her beam, snapped the rope drum-taut and popped them out of the clinging sand like corks out of a bottle. Uncle Tan's crutch and all.

They twirled helplessly as Lucky Dragon swung away downstream, bumping against the fishing boat's rough sides, coughing and spluttering.

Ly's pale face appeared over the gunwale above them.

"Are you all right, Quan?"

"Yes," he panted. "Fine. I'm coming up. Uncle Tan, you hang on—"

"Take my crutch," spluttered Tan. He had it hooked awkwardly under one arm.

Quan slid it out from Uncle Tan's armpit and, holding it by the tip, passed it to Ly, who managed to grab it.

---

28. The *gunwale* (GUN il) is the upper edge or side of a vessel.
29. The *bight* (BYT) is the middle or slack part of an extended rope. A bowline is a knot that creates a nonslipping loop at the end of a rope.

Word Bank

intricate (IN trih kit) *adj.*: hard to understand, work, or make; complex; involved

"Don't fall in," hissed Quan.

Ly giggled. "I won't. Ah Soong's got one foot and Aunt Binh's got the other!"

Quan was next. Bracing his feet against the hull, he hauled himself aboard in three long pulls. Then he and Ly and the other women leaned on the rope and Uncle Tan was soon floundering on the deck, panting and blowing, close to exhaustion.

But he was the first to speak. He propped himself against the gunwale and laughed softly. It was a strange sound.

"Well," he said. "We really have done it!"

Lucky Dragon moved slowly and silently down the dark river. "Where's my knife?" asked Ah Soong.

旺 CHAPTER 12

The tide was almost on the turn, and the river ran gently into the sea. The two bodies of water melted together with quiet swirls and bubblings. Flat and pearl gray with scarcely a swell, barely a ripple. The east was pink and lemon behind them, the land still shadowed in the valleys.

Lucky Dragon ran slowly out of the river and swung in the eddies of river and sea. It was very quiet. Seabirds called over the water as they went to their feeding grounds.

The horizon stretched flat as a knife blade ahead of them. There was not another boat in sight.

Quan stretched, his limbs aching. He had spent the night, what was left of it, on the wet deck beside Uncle Tan. The rest of the family had huddled in the wheelhouse, too frightened to look for more comfortable resting places.

Quan looked at Lucky Dragon in the growing light. She was ugly, no doubt about that.

Ugly and uncared for. He noticed that since they had inspected her covertly at the jetty the previous afternoon, the hatches had been secured on three of the four fishholds. The lid of the fourth was leaning against its coaming.[30] He shrugged; so someone was careless.

Uncle Tan sighed, grunted, and woke. He caressed his stump, kneading it.

"Unnhh," he said. "Ooh. What a night." He found his crutch and levered himself upright, swinging away across the deck. He returned seconds later, carrying a plastic bucket with a length of rope tied to its handle.

"Spotted this yesterday," he said. He slung it over the side, and hauled it aboard full of water. Then he washed his face with great splutterings and splashings.

"Ah," he said. "That's better. Now to look at the engine."

"There's a hatch behind the wheelhouse," said Quan, preparing to scoop up some water for himself.

"I saw it," said Uncle Tan. He swung aft, pausing only to rattle his knuckles on the salt-caked wheelhouse windows. The family awoke, reluctantly. Phan Thi Chi came out, yawning and stretching, his face changing as he looked out at the sea and remembered where they were.

Quan drew him a bucket of water and Phan Thi Chi washed himself.

Quan threw the bucket overboard again, jerking the rope to sink it.

"Uncle Tan?" asked his father.

"Starting the engine."

"I hope he can," he said grimly.

Even as he spoke a series of long mechanical

---

30. A *coaming* (KOME een) is a raised border around an opening in a deck, that is designed to keep water out.

Word Bank   **covertly** (KUV ert lee) *adv.*: in a secret or concealed manner

grunts came from behind and below, then—ufufufuf-boom-boom-uff.

Then silence.

Ufufuuffauffauffa.

Silence.

A thick tendril of blue smoke leaked from the rusty smokestack.

Ufufufufufboomboomboomboom.

The steady, hearty thump of a big diesel. Uncle Tan appeared, his face and hands oil-streaked. He grinned.

"Left the key in the ignition! Can you imagine!"

"No trouble starting her?" asked Phan Thi Chi.

"None! Lovely big new Yanmar. Japanese. The old man must have sunk all his money in it."

"Well, that's good news. The old one was falling apart. I wish he'd told me—I've been worrying about that old engine ever since we left home."

It was now full light. The sun was just behind the hills: a glowing orange nimbus.[31]

Quan carried buckets of water to the family, now sitting on the forward deck on the hatches of the fishholds. Ah Soong was unpacking her capacious black bag. She produced a huge vacuum flask decorated with pink peach blossoms and a nest of plastic glasses. The tea—pale amber, milkless and sugarless in the Chinese fashion—was still hot. There was enough for half a glass each. Quan wondered what else Ah Soong had in her bag.

The sun was now above the hills and Phan Thi Chi was nervous. He scanned the horizon anxiously. The diesel burbled[32] to itself.

"We'd better not hang around here," said Uncle Tan.

"I was wondering—" began Phan Thi Chi, "which—"

"Keep the sun behind us," said Quan. "That's all we have to do. Run due west."

The two men and the boy went into the wheelhouse. The engine controls were simplicity itself. A throttle—a metal rod with a moulded black plastic handle. A brass lever set on a quadrant marked ahead and astern. And that was all. No gauges. No revolution counter. Nothing. No radio.

"Simple, eh?" grinned Uncle Tan. "Shall we go?"

Phan Thi Chi, at the wheel, nodded. He seemed overwhelmed by it all.

Uncle Tan pushed the throttle lever forwards. The diesel's burbling changed note. Beneath their feet they could feel the big single screw bite into the water. Lucky Dragon stopped twisting aimlessly on the slack water and moved ahead. The lopping of the water about her forefoot changed to a steady chatter.

Phan Thi Chi glanced over his shoulder to line up the sun and turned Lucky Dragon slightly to head due west. They moved swiftly over the calm water, lifting ever so gently to a long and very low ground swell. The sun came up and burned off the sea mists and the water sparkled.

"Malaysia, here we come!" said Quan.

Uncle Tan slapped him on the shoulder.

"We've done it, boy, done it! Two, three days, and we're there!"

They stood there, side by side, watching the waves slip past them, letting the sun warm them, watching some terns[33] diving on a school of small surface-swimming fish.

---

31. Here, the term *nimbus* (NIM biss) means halo or aura.
32. *Burbled* (BUR bld) means simply bubbled or gurgled.
33. *Terns* (TURNZ) are web-footed aquatic birds resembling seagulls, although typically smaller and slimmer.

Word Bank tendril (TEN drill) *n.*: a threadlike, spiraling shape

Lucky Dragon, although Quan didn't know it, was in fact a very good boat. Not pretty, certainly, but she was designed as a work boat, not a yacht. Her high flared bows and strange stern—which seemed to curl back on itself and run unnecessarily far forwards again—were designed to give her what seamen call a "good entry." In other words, they allowed her engine to push her along with the least possible resistance. Now, with the big Yanmar diesel thumping away and imparting maximum revolutions to the large brass screw, Lucky Dragon lifted her skirts, so to speak: her bows came up, her funny stern dropped, and she fairly planed across the placid early morning sea.

Even Phan Thi Chi smiled.

And then Aunt Binh shrieked.

A monstrous figure was rising from the forward fishhold: a round, olive-green, metallic head, tilted blindly towards them. Then they saw the muscular arms hauling the rest of a man's powerful body out of the hold. A thick leg followed next, then the metal head canted back to reveal a wide, high-cheekboned, rather coarse face.

The figure completed the laborious process of hauling itself from the fishhold and sat puffing on the coaming, eyeing the terrified women uncomprehendingly.

The figure—that of a man in his mid-forties, powerfully built, but with a thick band of fat around his middle—removed the old army helmet which had given him such a bizarre appearance when he first emerged from the hold, and revealed a round, bullet head, on which the thick black hair had been cropped to a stiff metallic fuzz. Still regarding the women with a puzzled expression, he took a dirty piece of rag from the crumpled, ragged shorts he wore and mopped his face.

"Phew. Oh. Ah." He winced as the sunlight shattered on the sea and hastily replaced his helmet, tilting it over his eyes.

"Phew," he said, "Well—" and then he saw Phan Thi Chi, Uncle Tan and Quan, who had hastily abandoned the bridge at the sight of the apparition on the foredeck. Lucky Dragon, throttle wide and wheel unmanned, began drawing a large, lazy circle over the Gulf of Siam.

The stranger half rose, then sat down again, hastily. He wore nothing besides the shorts, and his big chest and shoulder muscles twitched nervously, the way a horse does when a fly lands on it.

Quan spoke first. He got between his mother and the stranger.

"Who are you?" It was all he could think of.

The stranger grinned. Despite his appearance, it was rather a pleasant grin. His teeth winked gold in the sunlight.

"No," he said. "Who are you? When I went to sleep last night—all right, I was drunk, that's why I slept in the fishhold, couldn't get ashore—this was my boat, at least the boat I work on. And when I wake up there are strangers aboard and we're—" he looked around, wincing, at the sea and the distant land—no longer receding, because Lucky Dragon was now looping back towards it, crossing her own wake with a bit of bumping and rolling—and finished "—we're at sea, and going around in circles!"

Phan Thi Chi stepped forward.

"It's my boat! My father's, anyway."

The stranger considered this for a few minutes. Then he shook his head.

"No. The old man died. The boat belongs to

Word Bank

canted (KANT tid) *v.*: tilted; inclined

apparition (AP uh RISH in) *n.*: a ghostly appearance of a person or thing

the commune now."

Phan Thi Chi was silent.

"And where," asked the stranger, "are you taking it?" He was fully awake now and confident in his strength.

"To Malaysia," said Quan boldly.

"We are," said Uncle Tan, hobbling to stand beside him, clutching a rusty shifting spanner he had found in the cubbyhole which passed for Lucky Dragon's engine room.

The stranger shook his head and winced again.

"You?" he asked incredulously. "You—?" He ran his eyes over them, grinning again. He was silent for a few seconds. He noticed the bucket and rope.

"Get me some water," he said to Quan. "Please."

Quan got him a slopping bucketful and the stranger took off his helmet and poured it over himself. Then he shook himself like a dog and put on the helmet again. There was a sinister triangular rent[34] in the metal on one side.

"All right," he said. "Why?"

They told him, all speaking at once, about the threat of the NEZs, the shop, the school, the cadres, Uncle Tan's leg, Aunt Binh's husband. Everything. The stranger listened silently.

When they had finished he said quietly to Phan Thi Chi: "You'd better stop us going around in circles and head that way." He pointed. "West."

They gaped at him.

"Go, man," he said to Phan Thi Chi. He leaned against the gunwale and waited while Lucky Dragon was put on course again. Then he spat over the side before speaking.

"Name's Cu." He took off the steel helmet and touched three faded white vertical bars painted on its front. "This was an American infantry captain's helmet. Killed at Da Lat. I knew him. Kept his helmet. So they call me Captain Cu now. Okay?" He smiled and stuck a finger through the ugly wound in the metal.

"AK-47 bullet. Not straight on. A ricochet. All twisted out of shape when it hit him."

He put the helmet back on.

"So you're going to Malaysia. In a big boat like this. Phew! Two women—" He looked at the trembling Aunt Binh. "Tell her not to be frightened. I won't eat her! An old lady! And a girl. And a city boy and his father and a cripple! Phew!"

He mopped his face again.

"All right. I'll come with you. You'll never get there—anywhere—without me. Out there—" he gestured ahead of them, at the wide empty sea, pale under the low sun, "pirates. All sorts of bad people."

"Why?" asked Quan.

Captain Cu lifted his huge shoulders and laughed briefly.

"Why not? There's nothing to keep me back there. No family. I don't hate the communists. Oh, I fought them, and sooner or later they'd discover what I did in the war, and do something to me. But I'd be safe at Rach Gia for a while. But they bore me, you know that? You know why you got away with this boat, this

---

34. There was a *sinister triangular rent*—a threatening, evil-looking triangular tear in the metal helmet.

Word Bank ricochet (RIK uh SHAY) *n.*: the rebound or skip of an object after it hits a striking blow against a surface

VN 507—?"

"She's not VN 507," said Quan, startled by his own boldness. "She's PK 507, and anyway her name's Lucky Dragon, not a number!"

Captain Cu chuckled and winced, holding his head.

"You wouldn't have a beer, would you? No? Listen, boy, PK means private registration. And private registration doesn't exist any more. She's the VN 507 now. A government boat. Lucky Dragon? Never heard of it! Anyway, you know why you got this far? Because the communists are boring, that's why!"

"I don't understand," said Quan. Ly was squatting beside him, watching Captain Cu with terrified fascination, and Quan gave her a comforting hug.

Captain Cu snorted. He swept his arm around, taking in the empty sea from horizon to horizon.

"Know why this is empty? I'll tell you. Because all the boats are tied up at Rach Gia while the crews attend a political lecture! That's why! Lecture, lecture. Talk, talk, talk. It bores me to sleep. But you have to go, or you get into trouble. People call you counter-revolutionary. You've got to be careful of being called that. So you go and get bored." He shrugged again. "So we go to Malaysia. You ever been there?"

"No," said Quan.

"Nor me. But so what. It'll be new. And not boring, I hope." He stopped, looking incredulously at Quan, then up at his father, whose pale anxious face could be seen through the wheelhouse window.

"And you're going just by steering west? No navigation? No charts?"

"Haven't got any," said Quan briefly.

Captain Cu removed his helmet and scratched his stubble. "You're right, of course. Keep going west and you must hit Malaysia. But where? North? South? You might be pushed north by a current and hit Thai territory—and they might send you back." He replaced the helmet. "I've got a better way. Put you right ashore in the Malaysian state of Trengganu. No trouble."

"What do we do?" asked Quan.

Captain Cu stretched himself on the deck, sliding his helmeted head into the small patch of shade provided by the forward fishhatch's canted cover.

"Wait until dark," said Captain Cu. "Wait until dark." He folded his arms across his wide chest. Quan turned to go. "One moment," said Captain Cu, closing his eyes. "Get my bed out of the hatch and spread it on the deck—"

"Your bed?"

"Net," said Captain Cu. "I slept on the net. Get it out. Spread it on the deck. If you see any boat, *any* boat, no matter how far away, you wake me, quick. Okay? Now let me sleep."

Quan, Ly, and Phan Thi Chi dragged the heavy nylon net with its marker buoys and floats from the fishhold while Uncle Tan manned the wheel. They untangled the green net, laying it in long folds forward to aft.

Lucky Dragon motored on undisturbed, laying a ruler-straight wake which quickly disappeared across the calm pale green sea.

Captain Cu slumbered on, snoring heartily, his helmet tilted over his nose.

Ah Soong continued unpacking her amazing bag and produced a small charcoal stove. The Yanmar rumbled happily.

Studying the Selection

First Impressions — *Now that you have read Chapters 9–12, consider the options open to this family. Even the way to Rach Gia was dangerous. Did they have real choices? That is, could they have chosen freely among available alternatives? Would you have tried their scheme? What would you have done?*

✓ Quick Review

1. Why was Quan's encounter with Nguyen Hung so disturbing?
2. How did Uncle Tan's friend help the family?
3. What is Phan Thi Chi's reaction to Quan's suggestion that they "cut out Lucky Dragon and face the unknown terrors of the sea"?
4. Why does Captain Cu decide to go with the family to Malaysia?

In-depth Thinking

5. How did the description of the cockroaches and rat in the shop affect you? Why might Bennett have chosen to include these details?
6. Why is it ironic that "Nguyen's very malice had saved them" from being caught by the PSB?
7. Phan Thi Chi's "shame and guilt and grief" are extreme, as Quan says, " 'But—but I thought you could handle a boat!' " Why should this be so?
8. Describe some scenarios the family might have imagined as Captain Cu emerged from the fishhold. What might they have feared?

Drawing Conclusions

9. Explain what Uncle Tan means in Chapter 9 when he says, "If I ask 'Why me?' I must also ask 'Why not me?' " How is his logic helpful?
10. What is your impression of Quan at this point? How has it changed or been reinforced since the beginning of the novel? Include details from the text.

Focusing on Point of View

1. In the story we mainly use the viewpoints of Quan and Phan Thi Chi. The women's feelings are less apparent. Thinking about what's happened so far in the story, write an article from the perspective of any of the female characters. You could be that character herself, therefore writing in first-person, or a reporter interviewing the character after she has settled in Australia. Recount the family's struggle to Chapter 12 from the woman's point of view. What would be her main concerns and fears? Describe her thoughts and feelings surrounding the events.

2. Authors often choose a narrator or particular point of view with an audience in mind. Skim this novel up to Chapter 12, other stories in this book, or one of your favorite stories or novels. Who is the intended audience? How do you know? Did the point of view or type of narration chosen help you determine the intended audience? In an essay, discuss your answers to these questions.

3. Share with the class a true story, one told in family gatherings. Often these stories are filled with drama, but they are usually told from one point of view. Think about facts that bother you, or details another perspective might add. Now talk to someone familiar with the event. Prepare questions to assure a thoughtful response. As a follow-up activity, tell the story to the class again, adding the new elements. Ask the class how this story differs from the first version. What have you learned from this activity?

Creating and Writing

1. Consider the personality of Xuyen. We rarely learn about her except through the observations of others. Why might Bennett describe Xuyen this way? Discuss your thoughts in a short essay.

2. Although most of us haven't lived through the dangers the Thi Chi family encountered, we have all found inner reserves that enabled us to overcome fears. Are you aware of someone close to you who showed courage? Tell this incident in a short story or essay, using your best narrative voice. Consider your audience. What details should they have if they are to understand the situation? Give the reasons for the fear, to illuminate the bravery involved.

3. America is a land of immigrants. Look for these people in the community. Interview someone who has come to the United States. Discuss the details of their departure. Why did they choose to come here? What did they leave behind? What dangers did they encounter? Present this person's story to your classmates in a creative and unique way. Perhaps you might videotape or record the interview; perhaps the person would be willing to visit your class; perhaps you could write and perform a skit with friends to tell this person's story. Share your ideas with your teacher before deciding on your presentation.

Blueprint for Reading

Background Bytes

Where would 500,000 refugees find new homes? The Vietnamese sought asylum in Southeast Asia—Thailand, Hong Kong, the Philippines, and Malaysia. They had limited space and few resources. Although refugee camps were set up, the host countries wouldn't give permanent status to the refugees. These 'first asylum' countries sheltered the refugees only until they could find homes in other, more prosperous, countries.

The mass flight from Vietnam went on so long that first-asylum countries eventually turned hostile. Refugees waited months (or years) for second-asylum visas. Some refugees had to moor (anchor) offshore, as the neighboring Southeast Asian countries would not let them land. Sometimes they were given rations of fuel and food and sent out to sea again. Others, after questioning about their reasons for leaving Vietnam, were repatriated—from *patria,* father—returned to their *father*land. Fights were common, as the refugees tried to avoid this fate.

Leaving Vietnam was just the beginning of their hardships. As one twelve-year-old boy told John Isaac, the United Nations' official photographer, "If you're a Vietnamese refugee, there are two happy days in your life. The first is when you leave Vietnam… The second is when you get out of this camp—and go to another country, where you can finally live in peace."

Into *The Voyage of the Lucky Dragon*—Part Three

By Part Three the family seems to be moving toward a better future. Lucky Dragon has evaded the government net. True to the promise of its name, it has a capable fisherman aboard, helping the family on their journey. They even have enough food and fuel to reach Malaysia, a couple days' sail away. Yet Phan Thi Chi's gloomy mood alerts the family and the reader to possible problems ahead.

The family is refused entry to Malaysia, and their hopes are dashed. Their options seem to be a return to Vietnam or a stay in the refugee camp on Bidong Island for months or even years. At this point, "…something snapped in Quan." The family *does* have another choice; they won't give up their hard-won freedom.

In this section, we watch the characters reacting differently in difficult situations. We'll examine their personalities closely. Notice how each person is affected by adversity. Before you start, try to predict how each character will respond to the coming turmoil. As you read, are you surprised by their actions? What might lie ahead as they put out to sea again?

The Voyage of the Lucky Dragon

Focusing on Characterization

Unlike the writer of short stories, a novelist can introduce many characters. Short stories typically center on just one or two fully developed characters. The good author adheres to the unwritten rule of literature: bring the character to life—make the character **dynamic**. Dynamic characters change and grow as they face challenges. If short story writers include too many characters, the possibility of fully developing any one is lessened.

Although novels also have one or two *main* characters, minor characters can be introduced and developed sufficiently to interact with the main characters, to reveal more about them. Relationships are established, and these often drive the plot. *The Voyage of the Lucky Dragon* is filled with interesting and intertwined characters, all working together. Of course, the main character is Quan, yet we know quite a bit about Phan Thi Chi, Ah Soong, Aunt Binh, and Uncle Tan. While not much is learned of Captain Cu's past, he is a strong presence in the second half of the novel, as he develops a relationship with Quan and the family. Xuyen and Ly are less developed, yet their presence enriches the story.

Jack Bennett's plot is a complicated one, based on real experiences of the boat people. It is a good stage for the dynamic characters to play out their drama. They experience so many trials, disappointments, and victories that they can't avoid being affected. Each character is distinct, however, and developed enough so that we can believe the motivation behind the action. We know that the family is motivated to leave Vietnam out of fear of the communists and a desire for freedom. Yet, each character reacts differently to the decision to leave.

Previously, you charted Quan's progress from child to adult. Now note in your journal any new character changes you observe. How do the changes affect your enjoyment? Would you be as interested if the characters remained **static**? Why or why not?

Word Bank

Lurid is an example of words with meanings that have shifted over time. When this happens, often the **connotative** meaning replaces the **denotative** meaning. In other words, the real meaning of the word, the dictionary definition (**denotative** meaning), is replaced by associations people have with the word (**connotative** meaning). In the Victorian period (1850 to 1900), *lurid* meant *a red fiery glow*. We see this use in the Sherlock Holmes' books. *Lurid* went from *a fiery light* to *shocking* to its current popular meanings, *gruesome* and *horrible*.

ancillary	flotsam	khaki	mirthlessly	sluicing
consternation	guttering	legacy	myriad	vulnerable
	hovels	lurid	precariously	wallowing
epaulette	impassive	miasma	prudently	

Part Three

Chapter 13

Ly saw it first: the long low shape of a patrol boat sliding out of the mid-morning glare. A black angular craft with the sun behind it.

Quan woke Captain Cu. He leaned on the line-scored gunwale, squinting into the sun.

"Not from Rach Gia," he said. "She's coming up from the south." He thought for a minute, watching the strange boat. "A gunboat, for sure. And Vietnamese, not Thai, coming from that direction. She's about six kilometers away. We've got time. But we've got to move. Fast."

Under Captain Cu's guidance Quan, Ly, and Phan Thi Chi—barking their shins,[1] knocking their knuckles and stubbing their toes—swung clear the outrigger booms and rigged the big net. In twenty minutes Lucky Dragon, considerably slowed by the drag of the net, was wallowing through the gentle swell like any Asian trawler going about her lawful business.

The gunboat altered course to cross their bows. Captain Cu watched it with narrowed eyes.

"Just inquisitive," he said. Sunlight winked from glass on the gunboat's bridge.

"They've got the glasses on us," said Captain Cu. They watched the boat in silence. The booms creaked and swayed. The gunboat was parallel to them now, about a kilometer away. They could see the gun on its foredeck. Once again light twinkled on field glasses. Then abruptly the boat's silhouette changed, shortened, as it turned away. Captain Cu let out his breath in a big whoosh.

"The nets fooled them," he said. He looked at the gunboat's disappearing stern. White foam boiled around the gray hull as the boat increased speed.

Half an hour later, with the gunboat a black dot on the horizon, they took the nets in and Lucky Dragon turned due west again with the old Yanmar thumping at full revolutions.

Captain Cu took over the wheel from Phan Thi Chi, and Quan and his father sat on the stern watching Vietnam, the only home they had ever known, disappear over the eastern horizon. No longer could they see the shore and trees and lumpy hills; the land had become a flat green line. And then it was gone, and there was nothing but sea on every side: a quiet, flat, shimmering sea, pearl-gray now in the noon haze.

"Look," shouted Ly, pointing. "Look!"

Small shimmering fish darted in a shower from the bow wave, flashed in the light, and dropped back into the water.

"Flying fish," said Captain Cu. "You'll see plenty more of them."

They did, too, as the afternoon wore on: dozens of them, fluttering like locusts. Once one of them came skittering aboard, shedding bright scales on the deck, and came to rest, gasping, against the wheelhouse.

"Poor thing," said Ly, and threw it back only seconds before Ah Soong could seize it.

The old lady was briefly angry.

"You never throw food away," she said.

"But we'll be in Malaysia in—in a day or two, won't we?" asked Quan's mother, nervously.

Captain Cu shrugged. "Tomorrow night,

---

1. The idiom *barking their shins* means scraping their legs.

Word Bank   **wallowing** (WAHL oh ing) *v.*: rolling about or lying in water, mud, or dust

maybe. But the old lady's right. Food is food."

"It was so beautiful," said Ly.

"Take the wheel," said Captain Cu to Quan. The fat man clambered down into the engine compartment behind the wheelhouse and inspected the fuel tank. He swung himself back on deck a few minutes later, frowning and moving his lips in some calculation. He leaned past Quan on the wheel and closed the throttle so that the Yanmar was barely turning over. The way fell off and Lucky Dragon settled deeper by the stern.

"Using too much fuel," said Captain Cu briefly. "There's just about enough to get us to Trengganu if we take it easy and don't burn it like a speedboat."

He took off his helmet and scratched his head, sweeping the horizon with his eyes.

"What are you looking for?" asked Quan.

"Land," said Captain Cu. "Islands." He frowned, thinking hard. "I'm trying to see it in my mind. Yes. First there's the Damas, then, further south, Hon Chuoi. I think we'll see Damas only. Then we turn almost south—"

"South—not west?" asked Quan.

"We keep going west, we run across the widest part of the gulf. We might use all our fuel and just drift around until we starve to death. Or get killed by pirates—pirates! Every fisherman on the gulf seems to be a pirate these days. Every Thai fisherman, anyway. But in any case, we don't want to go to Thailand. The Thais are sick of people like us. They've got too many. Up north, they've got camps full of refugees. Thousands. Starving to death. No food. No work. No doctors. Nothing! We've got a better chance in Malaysia! Maybe even Singapore." He broke off, pointing forward with a thick finger.

"What's that woman doing?"

Aunt Binh, changed into black trousers rolled up to the knees, was hauling water aboard with the rope and bucket and sluicing down the deck. Even though Lucky Dragon was moving slowly, making about five knots, the sudden drag of the bucket as it filled was almost enough to pull the frail widow overboard. Quan and Ly ran forward to help her. She was sweating, her hair hanging around her face. But for the first time in years she was animated. She paused, balancing the bucket on the gunwale, and said indignantly:

"This is a dirty boat! If we're going to spend days in it, it's got to be cleaned! Look at it—fish scales everywhere. Oil! All sorts of filth!" She threw the bucket overboard again and the stringy muscles on her thin arms strained. Quan pulled the full bucket aboard for her and dodged as she splashed the deck. She was right, of course: Lucky Dragon was very dirty. And the fishholds stank terribly. The sun seemed to be sucking the stench out of them.

Quan and Ly helped Aunt Binh clean most of the fish refuse off the decks. Ly found an old, balding broom in the wheelhouse and after two hours' non-stop hot work the deck was reasonably clean.

And then Ly made another discovery. There was no lavatory. Nothing. Not even a primitive bucket. On the extreme stern, high above the water, was an open lattice-work platform with a wooden cleat to hang on by; that was all. The lattice was stained and foul. Quan drew several more buckets of water and scrubbed the offensive woodwork with the broom. When he had finished he threw the broom overboard.

Captain Cu watched him in amazement.

"That was a good broom," he said mildly.

"Not any more. Captain Cu, can Ly take the

Word Bank

sluicing (SLOOS ing) *v.*: flushing or cleansing with a rush of water

wheel for a while? I want you to help me."

"With what?"

"I want to carry the hatchcovers[2] to the stern and build a shelter—a wall. For the lavatory."

"But it doesn't need one!" protested Captain Cu. "Oh, all right. Forgot you were city people. Too rough for you, eh? Want a flush toilet? Well, if it gets rough, you'll get a flush! Waves come right up through the slats at you!" He laughed uproariously.

But he helped Quan and Phan Thi Chi rig the shelter, while Ly steered Lucky Dragon. They hauled one of the heavy wooden hold covers aft and braced it with lengths of netboom.

Then they sat, sweating, and laughed at Ly's steering. Under Ly's inexpert hands Lucky Dragon was weaving across the sea like a drunken man.

"You'll have us back in Rach Gia soon!" called Captain Cu, and Ly blushed.

"Perhaps that wouldn't be such a bad idea," said Phan Thi Chi bitterly. They looked at him in amazement. He glared at Quan and Captain Cu.

"Yes, I mean it. Madness! This is madness! Where are we going? Sailing to nowhere! No food! It'd be better if we turned back now, before it's too late—" His voice broke and he turned his face away, staring out over the sea. "We must have been mad."

"Too late to turn back now," said Captain Cu. "And besides, there's not enough fuel—"

Quan sat down beside his father. He felt quite helpless.

"We'll be all right, father," he said. "Look, we'll be in Malaysia tomorrow. Next day at the latest, Captain Cu says—"

"And if the Malaysians let us land, what do we do then, eh? How do we live?"

"I can work. Ly can work. You can start another shop."

"We're all dead," said his father dully. "All dead." He got up and walked forward and sat alone on the bow fairlead, shoulders hunched in misery.

Captain Cu slapped Quan on the back.

"Come on, boy, let's go 'n show your sister how to steer, eh?"

Despondently, Quan followed him into the wheelhouse where Ly, brows furrowed and lips pursed in concentration, was trying to keep Lucky Dragon on a straight course. She was not doing very well. Although the sea was calm, a long low swell had developed from the southeast which gave Lucky Dragon a gentle nudge now and again.

Captain Cu looked at their wake, twisting like a silver worm behind them, and grinned. Then he showed Ly a few tricks of the helmsman's trade:

"Don't use too much wheel. Don't panic when the bows swing off—don't over-correct. See—little, little wheel movements. Okay?"

Eventually, Ly got it right, to her delight. Then Uncle Tan was given a lesson.

They had a small meal towards the middle of the afternoon: cold rice and fish. Ah Soong boiled some of the boat's water—kept in two rusty, dented twenty-liter jerry cans in the wheelhouse—and made tea. Phan Thi Chi, still gloomy, ate very little. He snapped at his wife when she tried to cheer him up by talking of the new future they were sailing to.

"There's no future for us," he said. "None." The meal was finished in silence. Phan Thi Chi's gloom was infectious.

Late that afternoon Ly spotted a low island several kilometers off the port beam. Captain Cu squinted at it, cupping his hands around his eyes against the glare.

"Damas," he said. "I think. I hope—anyway, we must change course now. South and a bit of east."

He put the wheel over and Lucky Dragon

---

2. The *hatchcovers* (HACH KUV erz) are the covers of openings in the decks of the vessel.

swung on to the new course. The island slid behind, into the sea, and there was nothing ahead of them except the long steady swell, golden in the late sunlight.

As darkness fell it grew colder and they all huddled in the wheelhouse for warmth.

Captain Cu gave Quan the wheel and curled, like a large golden dog, at the boy's feet.

"Wake me if you see anything," he said. "Anything, you hear?"

And then he was asleep, snuffling and twitching, his head pillowed on the dented helmet.

Lucky Dragon slid across the dark sea, her wake a pale phosphorescent glow. Captain Cu snored loudly.

中 CHAPTER 14

Uncle Tan, on the wheel, dug the tip of his crutch into Quan's ribs. Quan woke with a start. For a moment he did not know where he was and looked wildly about, quite disorientated.

"Shsss!" said Uncle Tan. "Get up."

Quan got up, his knees cracking as he straightened his legs for the first time in hours.

"What's that?" asked Uncle Tan, pointing through the forward windscreen, which Aunt Binh had cleaned of its film of salt.

Far ahead of them something glowed in the sky, a lurid pulsing glare. Quan watched it in silence for several seconds.

"There's another one," said Uncle Tan. "See? Over to the left."

Quan bent down and shook Captain Cu awake. He grunted and sat up, fumbling for his helmet. Then the rest of the sleepers woke, and the tiny wheelhouse was suddenly full of pale anxious faces, all watching the eerie lights on the horizon. But Captain Cu eyed the lights with satisfaction, nodding to himself.

"Good," he said. "On the button, as the Americans say."

"What is it? Those lights—what are they?" asked Phan Thi Chi.

Captain Cu chuckled.

"Malaysia, my friend. Malaysia! Well, not actually Malaysia, but almost. Those lights are waste gas being burned on the deep-sea oilfields off Trengganu. About a hundred and ninety or two hundred kilometers offshore. We'll be in Malaysia tomorrow, if our fuel lasts!"

Then he went back to sleep. But the family was too excited to sleep. Leaving Uncle Tan on the wheel, they clustered on the foredeck, shivering in the cool morning air, and watched the lights grow bigger and brighter as Lucky Dragon thumped across the black sea towards them.

When the east paled from black to indigo and then pale lemon and pink they slipped between the two lights, which they could now see were huge metal drilling platforms, twenty meters high, each topped by an orange torch of blazing gas ten meters tall, guttering and flaring, trailing black smoke which coiled like dark serpents across the water. Each tower was also illuminated by powerful spotlights, bright even in the growing dawn.

They gaped in silent wonder, awed, as Lucky Dragon passed the nearest of these monsters. A tiny figure appeared on an upper platform and waved, and they waved back, nervously.

They drew seawater and washed themselves and Phan Thi Chi, in better spirits than he had been for days, insisted on taking the wheel. Ah Soong found them some cold rice and they ate it while the drilling platforms were left behind.

Word Bank

lurid (LUR id) *adj.*: shining with an unnatural, fiery glow; garishly red; wildly dramatic or sensational

guttering (GUT er eeng) *adj.*: burning low or being blown so as to be nearly extinguished

"A few hours now," said Captain Cu, "and we'll see Malaysia—" He suddenly dived into the engine compartment and emerged smiling and oil-streaked a few minutes later. "We'll just make it!" He leaned across Phan Thi Chi and nudged the throttle with the heel of his hand. "Let's speed it up a bit!"

The sun exploded out of the sea and sucked up the mist and they warmed themselves, chattering like children, making a million plans.

As the green coast of Malaysia heaved itself above the horizon, Quan's mother unpacked her small suitcase and hung up her clothes to get the creases out. Ah Soong disappeared behind the wheelhouse and reappeared in clean black trousers, a new white blouse and a jade-green quilted jacket. Aunt Binh and Ly combed each other's hair. The men stood on the lavatory grating and poured buckets of seawater over each other. Uncle Tan, teetering precariously on one foot, almost fell overboard when Lucky Dragon lurched suddenly on the back swell from the shore, but Captain Cu clamped on to him with a vice-like hand. Lucky Dragon rang with shouts and laughter.

They turned southeast a few kilometers offshore and ran slowly down the coast. The jungle, dark green, reared up behind the empty white sand beaches. There were a few small fishing boats offshore. People waved to them and they waved back.

Phan Thi Chi leaned on the gunwale with his wife and let out a long breath of relief. It seemed to him that he had been holding his breath for days. Weeks, even. Ever since that day the cadre called…and now it was almost over. Well, the worst part of it. For the first time in weeks he felt hopeful, even cheerful.

He smiled at his wife.

"I didn't think it would be so easy," he said.

"Not so easy."

"There's a big boat," said his wife, pointing. A large official-looking boat was bustling around a low headland a kilometer ahead, and heading straight for them.

"It's the welcome party," shouted Captain Cu. He closed the throttle and disengaged the screw and Lucky Dragon drifted idly on the swell, the Yanmar burbling softly into the warm clear water.

The big boat came nearer: the Malaysian flag snapped at its masthead. Uniformed figures eyed the Lucky Dragon curiously as the boat made a wide circle around the sun and sea-stained fishing boat.

A voice crackled at them in a strange language through a loudspeaker. The Malaysian boat came abeam of them and water boiled white around its stern as its engines went astern. It lay there, a few meters off, its big diesels growling powerfully, and the tinny voice blared at them again.

Phan Thi Chi cupped his hands around his mouth and shouted, first in Vietnamese, then in Cantonese, "We are Vietnamese! We want to come ashore!"

The loudspeaker crackled again.

Captain Cu balanced precariously on the gunwale, clinging to the stowed net boom, and bellowed in his American-accented English: "Vietnamese! Vietnamese refugees! We want to live in Malaysia!"

Silence for a few seconds. Then a new voice blared at them from the loudspeaker, in odd, nasal English:

"You are in Malaysian waters. You cannot stay here. Proceed to sea at once, please. I repeat: you are in Malaysian territorial waters. You must leave at once."

The family stared at one another in absolute

Word Bank   **precariously** (pree KAIR ee iss lee) *adv.*: dangerously; unsteadily or insecurely

consternation. To be turned away! They were prepared for all sorts of disasters, but not this! To be refused entry!

Phan Thi Chi, standing next to his wife, Xuyen, gaped at the Malaysian boat, his mouth open, as though physically stunned.

"Captain Cu," whispered Quan. "What are we going to do? We can't go back—"

"We can't go anywhere," said Captain Cu. "We've got no fuel left."

"Or food," said Uncle Tan quietly.

The loudspeaker directed another tinny blast at them: "I repeat: you must leave Malaysian territorial waters immediately."

Captain Cu turned back to the Malaysian boat.

"We have no fuel," he roared. "None! We can't go anywhere."

The officers on the bridge of the patrol boat went into a huddle.

"We're coming alongside," said the loudspeaker. Water bubbled around the Malaysian boat's stern as it was skillfully maneuvered alongside Lucky Dragon. Ropes pattered down on to the deck forward and aft and were secured by brisk, uniformed sailors.

Two officers, young men in neat uniforms, came aboard.

"I am very sorry," said the senior one (Quan judged him to be the senior man because he had two gold braid rings on the epaulettes of his khaki uniform shirt), "I'm sorry, but no refugees are being allowed ashore in Malaysia. It is illegal to try to land."

"We have no fuel," said Captain Cu.

"Show me your tank," said the officer. Captain Cu shrugged. "Sure." He took them into Lucky Dragon's tiny engine compartment. The officers looked at the gauge and tapped the tank.

"Another tank anywhere?" asked the junior man.

"No," said Captain Cu. "You can look."

The junior officer shouted an order and the two seamen who had secured the lines holding Lucky Dragon to the patrol boat swiftly checked the fishing boat from stem to stern. It didn't take long.

"I'll give you two drums," said the senior officer. "And then you must go."

He was a decent-looking man and it was obvious that he felt sorry for them. He snapped an order and the seamen on the patrol boat began rigging canhooks and a sling for getting the fuel across.

It was all done very efficiently and within twenty minutes the drums were aboard and lashed down. The junior officer went back aboard the patrol boat and the senior man prepared to follow him. The seamen prepared to slip the bow and stern lines.

"You're free to go," said the senior man.

"And starve," said Uncle Tan quietly.

The Malaysian looked startled.

"Have you food?" he asked.

"None at all," said Uncle Tan.

The officer looked at them, his face worried. He shouted something to his second in command in Malaysian and the man disappeared below with two seamen. Minutes later they reappeared, hauling a large sack of rice. They tumbled it over the gunwale into Lucky Dragon.

"It's all we have," said the Malaysian. "I'm sorry. Now you must go. Please."

He jumped lightly back aboard his own boat, the seamen cast off, and the patrol boat's big diesels churned the water to foam. Soon there

---

Word Bank

consternation (KAHN stir NAY shun) *n.*: a sudden, alarming amazement that results in utter confusion; dismay

epaulette (EP uh LET) *n.*: a decorative shoulder piece found chiefly on the uniforms of military officers

khaki *n.*: a heavy beige or tan fabric, used especially in making uniforms and trousers

was a widening gap of oil-slicked sea between the two boats. Someone waved from the Malaysian boat's bridge and the family waved back. Then Captain Cu ordered Uncle Tan to the wheel while he set about refilling the main fuel tank with Phan Thi Chi and Quan.

When they had finished, the patrol boat was a black chip on the horizon.

Captain Cu watched it disappear as Lucky Dragon motored due east at half-speed.

"They'll keep us in sight until dark," he said, "to make sure we leave Malaysian waters."

"It was good of them to give us the fuel and rice," said Ly.

Captain Cu spat over the side. "They're used to it," he said. "I spoke to the officer while we were getting the fuel aboard. They do it all the time. Their orders are: give them fuel and food, and get rid of them. Don't let them ashore. Malaysia has too many refugees and won't take any more. So the government's getting tough." He laughed mirthlessly. "I wish I'd known before I got on this boat."

"You didn't get on," pointed out Quan. "You were on."

"Yes," said Captain Cu, thoughtfully, "I was." He grinned suddenly. "I should have arrested you all and turned the boat around."

"But you didn't," said Ly. "So what do we do now?" Captain Cu frowned in the sun. He watched Ah Soong, helped by Aunt Binh, slitting open the bag of rice and scooping out several handfuls of the browny-white grain. He looked up at the sky. There were no clouds and the sun was almost directly overhead. Their shadows were shapeless black blobs on the deck.

"North or south?" asked Uncle Tan. "We can't go east, and if we go north we'll run out of sea finally and hit Thailand."

"And the Thais don't want us either. We know that. And up north in the Gulf, up near the Isthmus of Kra, well, it's full of those pirates who call themselves fishermen," said Captain Cu.

"So?" asked Quan.

Captain Cu swept his right arm across a big arc of ocean and sky.

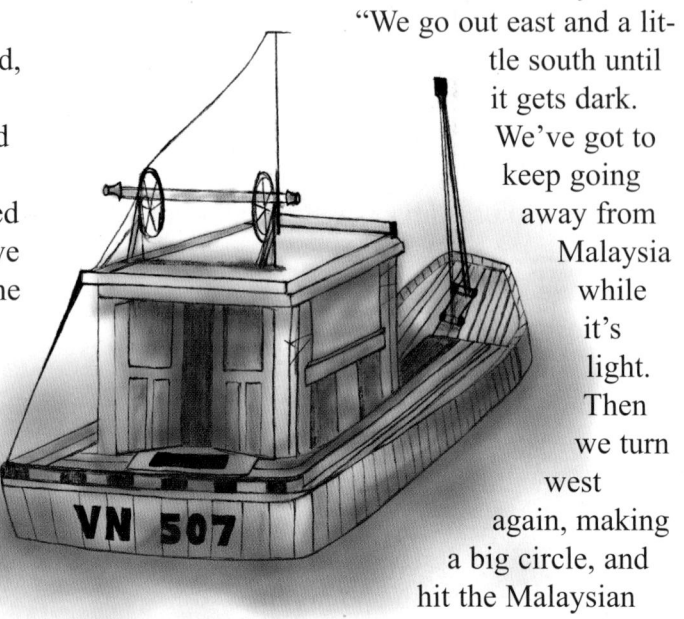

"We go out east and a little south until it gets dark. We've got to keep going away from Malaysia while it's light. Then we turn west again, making a big circle, and hit the Malaysian coast a hundred or so kilometers further south."

"They'll just chase us off again," said Quan.

"I've heard of an island down there—" Captain Cu gestured vaguely—"Bidong. It's a Malaysian island but the United Nations has something to do with it, I've heard. The Malaysians allow refugees to land at Bidong, and the United Nations people find countries that will let them in. So I've heard."

"I hope you've heard right," said Uncle Tan.

"It's just what I've heard," said Captain Cu. "It may not be true."

"If it's not true," said Phan Thi Chi, his eyes still on the distant patrol boat, "then we're all

---

Word Bank   **mirthlessly** (MERTH liss lee) *adv.*: joylessly; unhappily

dead." He spoke flatly, without emotion.

At sunset—a beautiful, flaming red and gold and purple sunset—they ate a meal of plain rice cooked by Ah Soong.

Then Captain Cu put the wheel over and Lucky Dragon turned south and then southwest across the darkening sea. When it grew truly dark Quan switched on Lucky Dragon's red and green port and starboard navigation lights, but Captain Cu switched them off again.

"We're running dark," he said. "These are dangerous waters."

So they slipped southwest through the night, a dark shape lost on the darker sea, their passage marked only by the glowing white wake. The Yanmar thumped steadily away. The stars came out and wheeled above them and Quan, who knew something about astronomy, pointed out Venus and the dull red eye that was Mars to Ly and Captain Cu while the others slept.

At midnight a big cruise line passed them, a towering brilliantly lit mountain of steel and glass. It passed less than two hundred meters from them; they could hear very loud music and see figures on the lighted decks. Then it was gone, leaving Lucky Dragon rolling heavily in its wash, taking its sound and light with it. Quan watched the liner's lights disappear and heard the last scraps of music fade on the night breeze and shivered. He felt very alone. He wished he and Ly, all of them, were safely aboard a big liner.

When he awoke it was sunrise and Uncle Tan was on the wheel. The sea was flat and the last stars were fading.

Uncle Tan pointed through the wheelhouse screen. Green hills, still dark in the early light. Malaysia again.

Captain Cu woke up and took the wheel and Lucky Dragon changed course again to run south along the coast.

They breakfasted on cold rice and weak tea. It was a silent, depressing meal. When they had finished eating, Ah Soong and Aunt Binh washed the dishes in seawater. Phan Thi Chi and his wife sat silently, apart, watching the sea slip past them.

The second patrol boat found them at noon. It came storming up from the southwest, an officious, chunky craft with the Malaysian flag at its masthead. A breeze had risen with the sun and a small chop[3] was laid over the long swell from the southeast. The patrol boat dug its bows in and sent the spray flying in glittering showers.

Captain Cu cut the engine. It died away with a few reluctant grunts and Lucky Dragon wallowed in the swell.

The family watched the patrol boat dully. They had no more illusions. The wind turned Lucky Dragon across the swell and spray pattered aboard. A few gray-backed gulls soared about the boat, idly, hopefully, and then sheered away. A few meters inshore of them, seven or eight black and white terns were fishing, dropping like small bombs with little explosions of spray on to a surface-swimming shoal of fish. And beyond them lay Malaysia, green as Vietnam.

The Malaysian patrol boat slowed, sinking deeper into the water as its way fell off. It made one wide circle around Lucky Dragon. Then it edged closer, so that the two hulls, on opposite rolls, almost touched. The loudspeaker crackled, the words whipped away by the wind. "You are in Malaysian territorial waters. You must leave instantly."

"Ignore them," said Captain Cu. "See what they do."

They did not have long to wait. The loudspeaker barked once more. Then the patrol boat ran smartly alongside Lucky Dragon, fenders made of motorcar tires were hastily rigged, lines snaked aboard forward and aft followed by lithe young seamen, and within a

---

3. A *chop* is a short, brief irregular motion of the waves.

few minutes the two boats were lashed together, creaking and groaning and grinding as they rolled in the beam swell.

Ah Soong hastily hid her rice.

Two officers came aboard. They were friendly and polite but quite insistent: Lucky Dragon was to leave Malaysian waters immediately. They were sorry. That was the law.

"We have no fuel," said Captain Cu.

"Or food," said Phan Thi Chi. "Do you want us to die at sea?"

The officers were plainly embarrassed. No decent man would happily condemn an innocent family to death by thirst and starvation aboard a helpless, drifting fishing boat. The Malaysians, whose faces held the blank, frozen look of men forced to do distasteful things, held a whispered conference. Quan held his breath. What if they searched the boat and found that Captain Cu had lied about the fuel? Then they certainly *would* be ordered to sea again, and with an escort, probably.

He held his breath. Ly, standing close beside him, squeezed his arm as the two Malaysians ran their eyes over the boat. To his relief he saw that the spare two hundred-liter drum of fuel, which had been lashed to the front of the wheelhouse, was hidden under a pile of net. He glanced down at Ly and she winked. "Aunt Binh and I pulled the net over it while they were tying up alongside," she whispered. Quan gave her hand a grateful squeeze.

The Malaysians made up their minds quickly. Lucky Dragon would be towed to Bidong Island. It was about forty kilometers south. There were Malaysian and United Nations people there who would decide what to do. Phan Thi Chi asked nervously how long they would be allowed to stay on Bidong. The officers shrugged in unison. Six months. A year. Two years. Some people had been there for three years. Until a country could be found to take them. But they would not be allowed to stay in Malaysia. That was certain. The family listened in stunned silence. Quan's mother wept silently. Ah Soong pulled her quilted jade-green jacket about her and sat, stolid, impassive as an ivory carving, on the coaming of the second fishhold while the lithe young seaman took a heavy towing hawser from the patrol boat, ran it over Lucky Dragon's bow fairlead, and turned it up around the midships bollard.

Then the Malaysians returned to their own boat, the towing cable was paid out so that there was a hundred meters between the boats. Then the patrol boat picked up speed and the hawser snapped taut, spraying sea water in a shower of sparkling drops which made, briefly, a lovely, miniature rainbow: and then they were heading south again, engine silent, wallowing and yawing astern of the Malaysian boat.

Captain Cu, on the wheel, grunted in satisfaction.

"Sooner have them use their fuel than ours."

"But this Bidong—" Quan began.

Captain Cu pursed his lips. "We don't have much choice," he said quietly.

"Three years some people have been there," Phan Thi Chi murmured.

Quan swallowed. "We have the boat," he protested, "And some fuel. We can fish. We can feed ourselves and sell fish and make money. It maybe won't be so bad."

Being towed is always an uncomfortable proceeding. The breeze became a young wind and the swell increased. Lucky Dragon developed a horrible motion, half pitch, half roll, and soon Aunt Binh was being noisily seasick.

Word Bank

impassive (im PASS iv) *adj.*: showing or feeling no emotion; unmoved

Studying the Selection

✓ Quick Review

1. The family encounters four boats on their way to Malaysia. Describe each boat's purpose and the family's encounter with it.
2. We're told Aunt Binh is "animated" in this chapter. What actions show her renewed energy?
3. What does each family member do as Malaysia appears on the horizon?
4. After the patrol boat tells them they must leave Malaysian waters, why does the family sail away and then return?

📑 In-depth Thinking

5. What might Quan and Phan Thi Chi have thought, as they watched Vietnam "become a flat green line" in the distance and then disappear, leaving them surrounded only by water?
6. What might account for Aunt Binh's sudden transformation?
7. What might the family be feeling as Malaysia "heaved itself over the horizon"? How do their actions support your response?
8. What is dangerous about Captain Cu's suggestion that the family return to Malaysia? What might happen if they did not do so?

📁 Drawing Conclusions

9. While everyone else is excited about the prospect of a new home in Malaysia, Phan Thi Chi continues to worry. What accounts for his outlook?
10. How would you describe the relationship between Captain Cu and Quan? What need, if any, does Captain Cu fill?

中 Chapter 15

"There it is," said Captain Cu. "Bidong."

Clustered in the wheelhouse, the family watched the island grow out of the sea ahead of them.

At first it was a dark speck on the glittering sea. Then it changed shape, grew, developed hills and palm trees. And houses. Hundreds of houses. Except they weren't houses when one got closer. They were shacks. Shacks of all shapes and sizes. Plastered against the hillside like flotsam after a flood. Hovels made of packing cases and cardboard and flattened tins and drums.

About a kilometer offshore the Malaysian patrol boat cast off the towline and turned away seawards. Captain Cu started the Yanmar and slowly, reluctantly, Lucky Dragon slipped through the sea, calm now in the late afternoon, towards Bidong's solitary wharf.

Quan watched with mounting horror as the island unfolded before them. A tapestry of misery and despair. Narrow muddy tracks between rows of crazy hovels. And the smell! It reached out and lapped around Lucky Dragon as though it were the tentacles of some foul monster. A raw ripe miasma of human excrement, dirty clothes, rotting fruit, decaying household refuse: a truly foul cocktail of evil smells. And despair, resignation, stagnation. Dull faces, blank stoic masks of surrender and defeat, stared idly, unwonderingly, at Lucky Dragon as she neared the wharf.

"Take the line ashore, Quan," said Captain Cu, deflated by the sights and smells of Bidong even before he landed.

Listlessly Quan picked up and coiled the bowline. He looked at the ghastly place they had come to. A seething garbage dump of unwanted people. Three years! Maybe forever! Perhaps no country would ever take them!

Lucky Dragon was fifty meters from the wharf when something snapped in Quan. He threw down the bowline and hurled himself into the wheelhouse. He grabbed the wheel from the startled Captain Cu and put it hard over. Lucky Dragon heeled sharply, turning away from the wharf and its small crowd of ragged, beaten-looking spectators.

"What the——" said Captain Cu. "What *are* you doing?"

"We're not going to that dreadful place," said Quan, his jaw set. "Look at it! You heard what that patrol boat man said—we could stay there for years! We'll rot there!"

He put the wheel amidships, holding Lucky Dragon on a course to take her away from Bidong.

Captain Cu took off his helmet and scratched his dark stubble.

"That's fine," he said. "But where *are* we going?"

"Yes," said Ly. "Where, Quan?"

Quan hesitated. He realized that he had not the slightest idea of where he was going. He just knew that it would never be Bidong. Suddenly a thought struck him and he laughed aloud.

"Australia!" he shouted. "Yes, that's where we'll go. Australia!"

Captain Cu grinned and slapped him on the back. "You're right," he said. "Australia! They take anyone! I met plenty Australians in the war! Diggers, they call them. Bloody dinkum, mate,"[4] he said. "Fair bloody go!"

---

4. The expression *bloody dinkum, mate* is a somewhat offensive Australian way to express surprise.

Word Bank

flotsam (FLAHT sum) *n.*: refuse or wreckage of ships floating on the water

hovels (HUV ilz) *n.*: small, humble dwellings; dirty disorganized dwellings

miasma (my AZ muh) *n.*: vapors harmful to health from rotting organic matter; poisonous vapors

THE VOYAGE OF THE LUCKY DRAGON / 653

"What's a fair go?" asked Ly.

"Don't know," said Captain Cu, "but the Australian soldiers I met said everyone got a fair go—"

"Perhaps it's something the government gives people," said Ly. "Like a pension."

"I don't know," said Captain Cu. "But we'll find out! We're going to Australia!" He put his head out of the wheelhouse, grinning at the rest of the family, who were clustered at the starboard rail, watching, with complete bewilderment, Bidong rapidly retreating into the late afternoon haze. "Hey, we're going to Australia! Yes, to Australia."

"We'd better eat," said Ah Soong, and set up her charcoal stove.

"They have kangaroos in Australia," said Aunt Binh authoritatively as she helped Ah Soong. "I've seen them in the movies. Funny things." She shook her head. "It's a long way away."

It was a very worried Phan Thi Chi who voiced the doubt lurking in Quan's mind.

"How do we find Australia?" he asked, very quietly and reasonably. "How, Quan?"

There was silence. A long silence. Behind them the coast of Malaysia had shrunk to a thin wrinkled line on the horizon; Bidong Island was a dot on the sea. Ahead lay the South China Sea, ruffled by the wind, empty as far as the eye could see. Lucky Dragon creaked as she lifted to the long low swells.

"Your father is right," said Quan's mother. "How will we get to Australia?"

Quan looked at Captain Cu. The fat man took off his helmet and scratched his head.

"Don't look at me. I can steer, I can work the nets. But I can't navigate. Never had to learn, on these fishing boats. Out for a day, back at night, always near land. Why should I learn about the stars and such things?"

"We haven't any navigational equipment, anyway," pointed out Uncle Tan. "No compass. No charts even. Nothing."

"Charts!" shouted Quan. "Yes, we have!" He darted to the forward fishhold, clambered in, and returned with his battered school suitcase. He opened it and produced a dog-eared school atlas, plastic ruler and a ballpoint pen.

"Here," he said excitedly, folding the atlas. "Here! Here's Vietnam, and Malaysia, and the Gulf of Siam, and Singapore—"

Phan Thi Chi glanced at the map. "Where's Australia?" he asked.

"Well, it's not on this page," conceded his son. "But, see, here, this page ends just south of Singapore—and just shows the top of Borneo. Now—" he ruffled the pages hastily. "See! Here—this map shows more of Borneo, and most of Indonesia and look—there, where my finger is—that little piece of land and that city, Darwin—that's the top of Australia!"

"And without a compass how do we know which way to go?" asked Uncle Tan.

"I know," said Ly. "I learned in geography. If you want to go south, the sun in the morning must be on your left."

"That's right," said Quan. "I learned that too. Keep the sun on your left in the mornings and on your right in the afternoon and you can't go wrong."

"G-d help us," said his father. "Truly, G-d help us."

Captain Cu looked at the atlas and shook his head. "It's going to be a long trip. I'll see how much water we have. And whether someone's left a fishing line aboard. I don't think it's much use working the nets out here. Water's too deep."

"It's deep enough to drown in," said Phan Thi Chi somberly. "Quite deep enough."

"We won't drown," said his wife. "We've got Captain Cu and Quan and Uncle Tan to drive the boat. And Ly knows how to keep us going in the right direction. And I and Ah Soong and Aunt Binh can—we can cook—"

"Cook what?" said Phan Thi Chi bitterly. "That rice won't last long."

"Then you must catch fish," said his wife, briskly, determined to look on the bright side of things. "Captain Cu will find a fishing line."

Poor woman. She sensed that her husband was close to panic, the panic of utter despair. In the past few months he had lost everything: his shop, modest though it was, and with it his livelihood; his father, his country. And now, uprooted, stateless, rejected by the country he had confidently believed would take him in and give him the chance of a new life, he believed he had lost his future as well. Xuyen could see him clinging desperately to the last few rags of his self-respect.

Phan Thi Chi was a simple man who had earned a modest income in a community in which he and his family were known and respected. Even through the war certain standards, certain traditions, had remained intact: and he had believed that they always would. Then had come peace and the new ideas, and his world had collapsed about his ears.

Now here he was, a man in his mid-forties, a city man, sailing across terrifying unknown seas to a strange unknown country. And how did they know Australia would take them in? Australia was a land of Europeans, not Asians. And would this old boat get them there? Every creak and groan as Lucky Dragon breasted a swell sent shivers of fear through Phan Thi Chi. And he hated looking at the sea: he hated the huge watery desert which swept with a soft menacing sighing from horizon to horizon. He shuddered at the vastness, the emptiness of it. He had come from a crowded street in a crowded suburb in a crowded city. And now there was nothing, nobody, within—his mind reeled—thousands of kilometers.

He hunched himself up into a ball beside his wife, hugging himself to himself, and tried to shut out the sea and the pale sky.

Up forward, Quan and Ly were trying to remember everything they had learned about Australia. It was not much. "It's big," said Ly vaguely.

They had both learned English at school, and now they began practicing it on one another. Most urban Vietnamese spoke some English, anyway; a legacy of the war years, when hundreds of thousands of Vietnamese had worked with Americans and Australians and Thais and Filipinos and New Zealanders and Koreans in the armed forces, where English was the *lingua franca*, as it was in the myriad bars, American PXs, hotels, rest and recreation resorts and restaurants which had sprung up swift as mushrooms after rain in Saigon (as it then was), Da Nang, Da Lat, Cam Ranh Bay and dozens of other places. The bars and other ancillary services provided for the well-paid soldiery were all gone now, of course; but their language remained.

So Quan and Ly practiced their English and tried to recall facts about Australia.

Ah Soong and Aunt Binh separated the gift rice into meal-sized packets—made from old newspapers found in the fishholds—and stowed them in different parts of the wheelhouse; that way, there was not one single vulnerable central store of rice to be rained on,

> He hunched himself up into a ball beside his wife, hugging himself to himself, and tried to shut out the sea and the pale sky.
> Up forward, Quan and Ly were trying to remember everything they had learned about Australia.

Word Bank

legacy (LEG uh see) *n.*: anything handed down from the past; bequest
myriad (MEER ee id) *adj.*: of an indefinitely great number; innumerable
ancillary (AN sih LAIR ee) *adj.*: secondary; supplemental; subordinate
vulnerable (VUL ner uh bul) *adj.*: open to being hurt physically or emotionally

swept overboard, or turned into a salty, sodden mass by a stray wave.

Captain Cu tuned the Yanmar to its leanest rate of fuel consumption, reducing Lucky Dragon's speed to about five knots—as accurately as he could estimate by watching the passing sea—and then took over the wheel from Uncle Tan.

Uncle Tan sat on the forward fishhold cover with an incredibly tangled old nylon fishing line Captain Cu had found, a cat's cradle of fouled monofilament loops and knots[5] and rusty hooks, and patiently set about untangling it: a task that was to take hours.

Several times that afternoon flying fish had pattered into the sea across Lucky Dragon's bows; but none landed on board. The sea still breathed with a slow, heavy sigh and the sky turned a strange murky gray. The wind fell away completely and the long swells shone like oil as they slid by.

The Yanmar thumped away industriously with a slow, regular bombombombom and the occasional bubbling gulp as a steeper swell lifted the water intake ports clear of the water.

A thousand kilometers east of Lucky Dragon, in the southern waters of the South China Sea, powerful, invisible forces were stirring: air, heated by the sun and the blood-warm sea, began to rise. As it rose, atmospheric pressure dropped. The air outside the affected area, sucked in to fill the vacuum left by the rising air and the low pressure zone it created, began to move, slowly but steadily, in a spiraling, clockwise motion. As yet the movement was slow: but it had begun. Unimaginable forces had been awakened. Enormous powers stirred in the upper air and on the surface of the sea. Far-ranging seabirds sensed it and winged landward. Porpoises, sensitive to the slightest change in the ocean's mood, stopped feeding and playing and joined the whales, who had already prudently started moving south, away from the disturbance which was as yet only a murmur in the skies.

Aboard Lucky Dragon, Captain Cu was on the wheel. The family slept. Captain Cu did not have the inbuilt weather gauge of a porpoise, seabird, or whale. But he felt uneasy as he ran south-southeast throughout the night. The big swells, shining in the three-quarter moon, rushed to meet him, lifted Lucky Dragon, and passed sighing beneath. Captain Cu wished they had a compass. And charts. And a radio. There were so many things he wished they had.

Once he got a fright: something huge, black and shining surfaced with an explosive gasp beside Lucky Dragon. Captain Cu saw puffs of spray burst above the long shape as it arched its back and disappeared; he saw a stubby fin against the moon as Lucky Dragon dropped into a trough. Then another sigh and whistling gasp and strange whiff of some animal smell and he saw two whales falling astern, driving hard across the swells, swimming strongly and decisively towards some unknown destination. During the night he heard them blowing again and again as they passed him in the darkness. He envied the whales. This was their world. They knew where they were going. He wished he did.

---

5. *Monofilament* (MAHN oh FILL uh mint) *loops and knots* refers to a large synthetic fishing line knotted in a series of loops and knots.

Word Bank

prudently (PROO dint lee) *adv.*: wisely; cautiously; carefully with an eye towards the future

Studying the Selection

First Impressions — *At the end of this section Quan makes his decision. Do you sympathize with him? Has he put his family in greater danger, or has he made the best choice? How do the other characters react to his choice? What motivates them to act in such a way? Are you surprised by their actions? Why are you surprised?*

✓ Quick Review

1. Describe what the family sees and smells as they draw near Bidong Island.
2. Where does Quan decide the family will go instead of staying on the island?
3. What question does Phan Thi Chi ask Quan about this decision?
4. How does Xuyen reassure Phan Thi Chi about his fear they will all drown?

In-depth Thinking

5. Why is Quan so determined to avoid Bidong Island? Is his response in character? Why or why not?
6. Earlier in the novel, we saw that Phan valued education highly. His children must go to school, no matter how frightening it becomes. How is their education helping the family?
7. We're told Phan Thi Chi's "world had collapsed about his ears." We know that the same is true for other family members. Why is his situation worse?
8. As Phan Thi Chi "hunched himself up into a ball beside his wife," others busied themselves in various ways. How do their actions reflect their personalities?

Drawing Conclusions

9. In Chapter 13 a flying fish landed on Lucky Dragon, to be thrown back by Ly. Ah Soong scolds her for throwing away food. In Chapter 15, flying fish abound, but never reach the deck. What might this detail foreshadow?
10. Until the final paragraphs of Chapter 15, Captain Cu has been a reassuring presence, confident in his abilities, flexible enough to change. Do you think he'll tell the family of new concerns? Do his concerns affect your interest?

Focusing on Characterization

Complete the following activities:

1. Individually, or in two or three person teams, outline the personality of each character in *The Voyage of the Lucky Dragon.* What role does each person play in the family? How have the characters changed so far? Are any characters unchanging, not dynamic? If so, what might account for the lack of change? Is it due to author intent or personality? (Is there a difference?) Share your responses, to see if others view the characters differently.

2. Consider the stories you have read in this textbook. Choose one that features dynamic main characters, a story that emphasizes growth and change. In a short essay write about a character, answering the following questions: What was this character like at the beginning of the story? What events caused growth in the character? What motivates the actions? Were the changes positive or negative? What lessons can be learned from this story?

3. Use your local phonebook to find a name for a character in a short story you will be writing. Some names are quite common, while others stand out as unusual. Choose a name that sparks your imagination. Using that name, bring your character to life. How does this person look? What is the person's family history? Assign a social status and an appropriate job. What events have shaped this person? Is this person motivated by fear, anger, optimism, or curiosity? Once you flesh out your character, share your ideas with another classmate who has also created a character. Together, write a story using the two characters. Think how each character will act or react in the jointly created situation. Share the story with the class.

Creating and Writing

1. To help you better understand the developing personalities of the characters in the story, answer the following questions.
   a. Who seems most positively affected by the turn of events? Why and how?
   b. Who seems most negatively affected? Why and how?
   c. Which *type* of person does each character resemble; for example, are any of the characters impetuous—that is, do they act without sufficient thought?
   d. Are any particularly pessimistic, or do any always look on the bright side?
   e. Are their reactions appropriate for their personality type?
   f. Do their actions seem realistic? Why or why not?

Creating and Writing *cont.*

2. Can you generalize about people's reactions when they are placed in an extreme situation? Who is most likely to thrive, who to withdraw? Explain.

3. One chapter of the family's life has ended, and another begins as they sail toward Australia. How do you imagine the family will fare on this next part of their journey? What do you think they might encounter along the way? Write your own version of the next chapter of their lives. Share your ideas with the class. As you continue to read the novel, it will be fun to compare your versions with what actually happens.

4. In many parts of the world, especially in the 20th century, refugees have lived in camps while awaiting return to their own country or transfer to a new home. With help from your teacher or librarian, find information on a refugee situation in a location that interests you. Consider these questions.

   a. Why did so many people flee the country?
   b. How did the first asylum country acquire its role as a stopover?
   c. What were conditions like in the refugee camps?
   d. How were the refugees treated?
   e. How long did they stay in the camps?
   f. Where did most of them hope to go?
   g. Did many reach their goal?

   In an oral report, present your findings to the class. To help your audience appreciate the situation you are describing, use visual aids such as creative posters, photographs, drawings, or objects that might symbolize the situation.

Blueprint for Reading

Background Bytes

Typhoons, pirates, starvation! The words evoke images of action on the high seas, of excitement and heroism. Yet these facts of the refugee experience brought an eventual end to the refugee exodus. There was terrible excitement in the refugee experience, but no glory—rather fear, pain, and death.

Of approximately 500,000 boat people who left Vietnam, some 75,000 died. Rough waters often swamped the overcrowded, rickety boats, drowning thousands. Thai pirates saw helpless prey in the Vietnamese boat people. Most boats were attacked at least four times. One boat survived twenty-three attacks!

Starvation, perhaps the cruelest blow, took thousands. Anxious to leave, families often didn't take enough food. Others were unready for a long journey, not anticipating being sent back to sea. Small children and the elderly suffered most from lack of food and fresh water, as destinations became unreachable.

Heroes were made on these journeys. Survivors forged new lives. Yet many paid the final price for freedom—a privilege we, all too often, take for granted.

Into *The Voyage of the Lucky Dragon*—Part Four

The trip has been challenging enough so far, but nothing can match the Thi Chi family's experiences in Part Four. Life and death struggles almost overwhelm them. How will they survive? As before, the family rises to the occasion. Now, more than ever, they must work as a team or perish. Characters draw on their inner resources. For some, the challenges are too much—there is nothing left.

By the middle of Chapter 19, we are awed by their resilience. What else can happen to this family? Would *we* have been able to endure as they did? What keeps them going? Are there any characters you are particularly concerned about? Why? The answers to these questions will cast light on the theme of this fourth section, holding tightly to one's dreams.

Focusing on Plot

Our earlier examinations of plot—the story line—focused on tension and suspense. Without these elements, stories drag, and the reader's attention wanders. So the author is continually challenged to supply tension and suspense. One way is to have the characters undergo increasingly difficult situations, each more difficult than the last. Think about *The Voyage of the Lucky Dragon*. These characters overcame *many* difficulties, but now they are about to go through their most trying time. With its raging waters and dangerous pirates, Part Four may feel like the climax, but the story is not over.

The Voyage of the Lucky Dragon

In his book, *What's Your Story?*, Marion Dane Bauer speaks of the role of tension in plot. The plot must center on something the main character wants. This goal is the reason a character acts, and—to keep readers interested—the goal should be difficult to achieve. The character must struggle. Bauer speaks of the "magic of three." In a short story, he suggests, characters should make three attempts to achieve the goal, or endure three trials before reaching the goal. The goal can be internal, such as desiring a better relationship with someone, or it can be external, such as climbing a mountain. Each obstacle should require more of the character, each obstacle being more difficult to scale.

The number three works well, he says, because two hurdles would seem like no struggle at all. Readers would feel cheated out of a full encounter with the characters. More than three can become tiresome in a short story format.

In the novel, however, the author can include many plot complications and introduce subplots as well, those smaller stories that occur within the larger context. Bennett's characters are good examples of Bauer's advice, for they are pursuing a definite goal. In just Part Four alone, the novel's characters face three grave challenges. Each is more life-threatening than the last, heightening tension for the reader. We read to find out what will happen next, and this is true throughout the novel, not just in Part Four. The entire focus of the plot is on the Thi Chi family as they face obstacles in their flight toward freedom.

Plot without good characters, however, also falls flat. Without rounded characters, the reader would not be as interested in these people. We root for them, as they struggle to survive. The combination, then, of well-developed, sympathetic characters and a suspenseful plot provides a worthwhile mix in *The Voyage of the Lucky Dragon*.

Word Bank

Linguists use the word **cognate** for words, roots, or letters "related to each other" or "having the same parentage." English *cold*, German *kalt*, and Russian *cholod* are cognates. *W* and *gu* are cognate letters, as in the obviously related, *guarantee* and *warranty*. But sometimes a word relationship is a surprise, since the cognates have opposite meanings. *To garnish* is "to provide or supply with something ornamental." Its cognate *warn* means "to give notice of impending danger." What is the connection? In Old German and Old Northern French, *warn* came to mean "to provide for, to provision"—the rest is history!

bulbous	flayed	inexorably	rogue	tumultuous	yawning
counterpoint	garnished	parlance	succumbed	unobtrusively	
crouched	impotently	reverently	tracery	vitals	

Part Four

Chapter 16

Dawn broke fiery red and black, the sea still a meadow of long low swells, but with an undercurrent of different movement, as though some unseen force was tugging at the water.

Captain Cu slept curled up dog-like, his ugly head resting on the olive-green helmet with its sinister scar.

Phan Thi Chi was on the wheel. Inexperienced as he was, he could feel that the sea was—well, different. He smiled at the sight of Uncle Tan stumping about the foredeck like some rough seafaring character out of a movie, looking at the waves and sky, sniffing the wind.

Ah Soong was crouched over her charcoal stove, cooking breakfast. Her incredible bag had yielded—from some deep, secret recess—enough dried fish to make a meal.

"And then," she had said, "you must catch some."

So Uncle Tan had streamed his untangled fishing line astern, the hook garnished with a strip of cloth teased into a tempting lure by Captain Cu, and every ten minutes hauled it in to see if any passing fish had succumbed. So far, none had.

Ly saw the strange boat first, which annoyed Quan, who was beginning to rather fancy himself as a seaman.

"Where? Where?" he shouted in exasperation, as his sister, balancing precariously on the wheelhouse roof—at the very great risk of being pitched off into the sea—waved and pointed.

Then Lucky Dragon breasted a low swell, and he saw it. About four or five kilometers away, a jagged black shape against the low sun, running steadily on a course which, Quan realized, would cross their own in a few minutes.

Reluctantly, because he knew the former fisherman had been on the wheel for most of the night, he woke Captain Cu. Then, apologetically, seeing the puzzlement and secret hurt in his father's eyes, he said: "There's a boat—there—" and he pointed to the strange vessel, now much closer.

Captain Cu got up, groaning. He had been dreaming: vague dreams which had left him strangely unhappy—strangely, because he couldn't remember them. But then he mused, as he put on his helmet, how many happy dreams were there? Most dreams left one feeling uncomfortable. Well, most of his did.

Then he saw the strange boat. His eyes narrowed as he squinted into the flare of the rising sun.

"A fishing boat," said Captain Cu. "Thai, I think."

"A proper fishing boat?" asked Phan Thi Chi nervously, glancing apprehensively at the strange vessel. They could see the shapes of men now, lining the forward rail.

Captain Cu shrugged.

"I hope so."

"Quan," said Captain Cu urgently, "get on the roof of the wheelhouse. Quick. See if you can see anything on that boat's deck, under the nets—"

"Anything?"

"Men—men hiding. Quickly."

Word Bank

garnished (GAR nisht) *adj.*: adorned; provided or supplied with something ornamental; decorated

succumbed (suh KUMD) *v.*: gave or given way to a superior force; yielded

662 / Novel

The Thai boat was abeam[1] of them now, matching Lucky Dragon's speed and course exactly: voices barked across the water in broken Vietnamese.

"They want to sell us water, fuel, and fish," said Captain Cu. "They know we're on the run."

"How?" asked Quan.

"What else would a Vietnamese boat be doing so far south? Don't worry, they know who we are."

"Can we trust them?" asked Phan Thi Chi.

"Looks like we'll have to," said Captain Cu. "Look, they're edging closer so that if we don't slow down we'll ram them." He sighed. "Well, perhaps they're just fishermen. We need food, anyway. We'll have to pay in that gold you've got hidden. Just don't let them see how much you've got."

Phan Thi Chi looked startled. "Gold? How do you know we've got any gold?"

Captain Cu laughed shortly. "All people who run from Vietnam have gold. What good would Vietnamese paper money be outside Vietnam? Toilet paper!"

Captain Cu closed the throttle and the steady thump of the Yanmar died away to a slow pulsing. Lucky Dragon slowed. Half a dozen men appeared on the foredeck of the Thai boat, busy with old rubber tire fenders and ropes.

The Thai boat was slightly bigger than Lucky Dragon, and newer. And, judging by the boil of white water around its stern, it had a large and powerful engine. So we can't run, thought Captain Cu, watching the men with the lines and fenders. Nobody on the stern. So he's going to get a bowline aboard us and then pull his stern in with his engine. An awkward way of doing things. But why is he concentrating all his men up forward? To distract our attention from something in the stern? He looked across at the boat, piled with nets and booms and floats, but could not see anything suspicious. And yet alarm bells were clamoring in his brain.

The Thai seamen were shouting and waving, calling for someone to go forward and take their line.

"Quan," said Captain Cu urgently, "get on the roof of the wheelhouse. Quick. See if you can see anything on that boat's deck, under the nets—"

"Anything?"

"Men—men hiding. Quickly. Uncle Tan, come up to the bows with me. Quan, if you see anything, shout. Shout loud."

Captain Cu, followed by Uncle Tan, left the wheelhouse and went forward, stopping briefly by Ah Soong to ask for the old woman's sharp knife, the one that had cut Lucky Dragon loose at the jetty in Rach Gia. Ah Soong gave it to him without a word: just a brief raising of her thin eyebrows.

The Thai boat's line rattled aboard Lucky Dragon. Captain Cu seized it and prepared to run it through the big fairlead and turn it up around the midships bollard. The Thai fishermen prepared to scramble aboard Lucky Dragon. The two boats were bow-to-bow now, held apart by the creaking, squealing fenders, lying almost at right angles to one another. The water boiled around the Thai boat's stern as the engine was put astern and the big screw began pulling the boats together as it thrust water against the hard-over rudder.

Quan scrambled on to the wheelhouse roof. Spread-eagled, he hooked toes and fingers around the shallow cleats on either side of the roof. From the wheelhouse he could look down, as Lucky Dragon rolled, into the Thai boat's amidships section, hidden from view at deck level by the high gunwale. He could see the piled nets and floats and booms. And he could see, crouched up against the gunwale so

---

1. *Abeam* means at right angles to.

they could not be seen from Lucky Dragon's deck, eight men armed with stout wooden clubs and knives—eight men waiting for their boat to be swung, beam to beam, with Lucky Dragon so they could swarm aboard.

The first Thai seaman was already swinging his leg on to Lucky Dragon's forecastle, and Uncle Tan was reaching out a hand to heave him aboard, when Quan shrieked his warning:

"Pirates! Captain Cu, pirates! Stop!"

Uncle Tan acted with incredible speed. The pirate got one leg aboard, and then the other: and then Uncle Tan, whipping his aluminum crutch out from his armpit, stabbing with it like a rapier,[2] caught the man in the midriff, doubling him up and sending him crashing into the sea between the boats. The next man shouted something and leaped the narrow gap between the bows, a knife flashing in his right hand. Uncle Tan was caught off balance, and would probably have died then, but Captain Cu, covering the space between them with two long strides and swinging a heavy spanner from Lucky Dragon's engine compartment, shattered the man's wrist as the knife snaked towards Uncle Tan. And then there were three more men, shouting and swinging clubs and knives, and Uncle Tan and Captain Cu were hard-pressed on the narrow forecastle to keep them off. Only the fact that the two boats had swung on the sea and were now only joined bow-to-bow—leaving space for only one man at a time to tread—saved them. Uncle Tan's crutch flashed, Captain Cu's spanner flickered in and out with deadly effect: but the result was a foregone conclusion. Two men, one a cripple, cannot hold off more than a dozen tough and determined thugs for long.

And now the Thai boat's big motor was roaring, relentlessly pulling the stern closer to Lucky Dragon. Once both boats were locked together, the pirates would swarm aboard from both ends. And Captain Cu and Uncle Tan would be dead very quickly.

Phan Thi Chi stood at the wheel, frozen with fear and indecision, his eyes blank. Quan, swinging down from the wheelhouse roof, saw that his father was in a state of shock.

Quan watched the rapidly narrowing gap of water between the two boats. The Thai boat's big screw was dragging them inexorably together. The pirates who had been hidden behind the gunwale revealed themselves now, strong dark men eager for plunder: they ranged the rail, shouting and laughing, as the gap between the boats narrowed. What easy pickings!

Ly, shaking and terrified, joined Quan outside the wheelhouse.

"What can we do?" she asked, her voice trembling. "What can we do?"

Quan's eyes took in two things at once: two separate things that clicked together in his mind like magnets: the Thai boat's threshing screw, winching them together; and the untidy pile of nets aboard Lucky Dragon.

He grabbed Ly's hand, hauling her with him as he ran for the nets. She staggered after him, her eyes wide with horror.

Quan stopped at the nets.

---

2. A *rapier* (RAY pyur) is a small, narrow 18th-century sword, or a long, heavy, double-edged 17th-century blade.

Word Bank

inexorably (in EX or ih blee) *adv.*: unyieldingly; unalterably; immovably; mercilessly

"Get them over," he shouted. "Over—into the screws!"

Panting, sobbing, they hauled and tugged at the heavy nets: Aunt Binh and Ah Soong, without knowing what they were doing, ran to help them. So did Quan's mother.

The nets splashed into the rapidly narrowing strip of sea between the boats. The Thai boat's churning screw sucked hungrily at the nets, drew them in, wrapped them around itself and the whirling propeller shaft, and knitted them into a huge writhing triple-knotted web of monofilament and floats. Gears whined and the engine's smooth rumble changed to a labored groan as the shaft whipped and shuddered. Hastily the engineer disengaged the clutch. The Thai boat stopped its slow edging toward the Lucky Dragon.

Quickly Quan and Ly tumbled the rest of the nets overboard.

Fighting for his life against three men at once, Captain Cu at first didn't realize what Quan had done. He saw, out of the corner of his eye, the nets splash overboard, but didn't realize the significance of it until he heard the note of the pirate boat's engine change, and saw several men leaning over the stern, shouting and pointing.

Captain Cu gave a roar of exultation. With one long sweep of Ah Soong's knife he drew a bloody furrow across the chest of his nearest opponent: the man fell back with a shriek, his blood brilliant in the sunlight.

Uncle Tan, hopping on one leg, now using his crutch like a sword, now like a club, sent another man reeling with a smash to the head: then Captain Cu bent down and cut the line holding Lucky Dragon to the Thai boat.

Slowly, agonizingly slowly, the boats drifted apart: not fast enough. The pirates were running forward with new lines. The gap between Lucky Dragon was still narrow enough for an agile man to leap. Captain Cu was panting, his chest heaving. Uncle Tan was exhausted, drained by the effort of supporting himself on one leg and fighting at the same time. If two or three men jumped aboard at once, there was no way they could be stopped.

Quan raced to the wheelhouse. Phan Thi Chi still stood behind the wheel, gazing in horror at the scene on the foredeck.

Unceremoniously, Quan shouted at his father: "In gear! Put her in gear!"

Uncomprehending, Phan Thi Chi gaped at him. Impatiently, Quan pushed him aside. He slammed the still-idling Yanmar into astern and pushed the throttle wide open.

The screw bit into the water and hauled Lucky Dragon astern as three pirates, ropes trailing from their waists, leaped for the Vietnamese boat.

Too late! Captain Cu roared with laughter as the three, arms and legs flailing, fell into the sea with great splashes.

Quan took Lucky Dragon astern for a hundred meters. Then he put the engine ahead and put the boat back on course, making a wide detour around the Thai boat, which now had half a dozen men in the water around its stern, hacking at the crippling net. Captain Cu helped Uncle Tan up.

"How are you?" he asked.

Uncle Tan grimaced. "I'm all right. But look at my crutch! That last man I hit must have had a hard head."

The strong aluminum tubing had a great U-shaped dent in it. Captain Cu took it, straightened it as best he could, and handed it back to its owner.

"You can get a new one in Australia," he said.

Uncle Tan looked at him. Slowly he grinned and nodded.

"You know," he said, "I think I will."

Pushed by the thudding Yanmar, Lucky Dragon rapidly left the disabled pirate boat

THE VOYAGE OF THE LUCKY DRAGON / 665

astern. The family watched it dwindle to a dot on the horizon, too dazed by their good fortune to be exultant. But Captain Cu shook hands with Quan and awkwardly patted Ly on the shoulder and told Phan Thi Chi and Xuyen that they had a pair of brave and clever children there and it was times like this that made him wish he was not just an old bachelor. Aunt Binh shed a tear or two and Ah Soong hugged Ly, and Uncle Tan shook hands with Captain Cu and Quan several times and showed everyone his dented crutch.

Only Phan Thi Chi remained frozen, his face quite frightening in its mask-like rigidity. He gripped the wheel so hard that his knuckles stood out white on his slim golden-brown hands.

"They'll come back," he said. "They'll come back." His wife tried to comfort him, but he rebuffed her almost rudely. "I tell you, woman, they'll come back. Or other boats like them will come. Tonight, tomorrow."

"They'll come again. And again. We'll never see Australia. Never. We'll all die on this sea. We should have stayed at home."

Quan looked at him, open-mouthed with dismay. His father caught his glance and laughed, a short, bitter bark.

"We don't even know where Australia is—look! That's our navigation equipment—that!" He pointed at the school atlas map which Captain Cu had nailed to the bulkhead beside the wheel, and on which, in consultation with Captain Cu, Quan had drawn a line representing the Lucky Dragon's course (or what he guessed was Lucky Dragon's course) in blue ballpoint pen.

"But it's all we have, father," said Ly gently.

"Yes," said her father savagely. "That's what I mean! That's all we have."

In tears, Ly slipped quietly from the wheelhouse, followed unobtrusively by Aunt Binh.

"I'll make some tea," said Ah Soong. "And we still have some rice. One of you men must catch a fish."

"My line!" said Uncle Tan. "I'd forgotten about it."

He stumped aft, followed by Quan. Eagerly the line was hauled in. But the hook was bare, the cloth lure faded by the sea.

"I'll make another lure," said Uncle Tan. "Perhaps if I had some red cloth—ah yes, I have a red shirt in my bag—"

Quan left Uncle Tan busily twisting a strip of cloth from his favorite red shirt into a lure which, he boasted, would lure the cleverest fish from the deep when he had finished it. In only a few days Uncle Tan had turned into quite a seaman.

Quan found Ly sitting in the lee of the wheelhouse, her back against the warped, sea-stained planks. Aunt Binh was with her: she had her thin arm about Ly's shoulders, and he could see that his sister had been crying.

Quan sat down beside his sister, feeling quite helpless.

He look at Aunt Binh inquiringly.

"She'll be all right," said the elder woman. "It's just fright. Those men…" Her dark eyes flashed fiercely. "Why, if they'd got aboard I'd have—I'd—I'd have knifed them myself! I'd have—" and here Aunt Binh said something very crude indeed, something Quan had never heard her say before. He looked startled, and Aunt Binh had the grace to look embarrassed.

"Don't tell your father I said that," she said hastily, "—or your mother."

"I won't," said Quan. He wondered what Ly was thinking. "I didn't know you knew talk

Word Bank unobtrusively (UN ub TROO siv lee) *adv.*: in a manner that does not intrude or interrupt

like that, Aunt Binh."

"Mmm," said Aunt Binh. She pursed her lips primly. "Don't you worry about what I know or don't know, young man," she said, giving him a hard glance. Quan looked at her in amazement: this—this determined woman was the same Aunt Binh who used to mope and weep around the house in Bach Dang and drive his mother and Ah Soong to distraction!

Captain Cu came up from behind Quan and lowered his wide bottom onto the fender Quan was sharing with Ly.

"I must help Ah Soong," said Aunt Binh, and scurried away.

"She's changed," he said.

"More than you know," said Quan.

"Do you think we've lost the pirates for good?" asked Ly anxiously.

"We haven't lost them at all," said Captain Cu. He took off his helmet and scratched his head. "Not at all. That clever trick with the nets delayed them for a few hours, that's all. They've already cut them loose and they're after us again."

Quan gazed at him in disbelieving horror. "But—but how do you know?"

"I climbed on the roof of the wheelhouse an hour ago. From up there I could see a boat behind us. What other boat could it be?"

"I don't believe it," said Quan.

Captain Cu shrugged.

"Look for yourself."

"I will!" Quan flung away and hauled himself on to the swaying roof of the wheelhouse, clinging to the funnel stay for support.

He was back beside Captain Cu and Ly two minutes later, his face ashen.

"It's there! You can see it! Straight astern of us!"

Ly, her voice trembling, asked: "How long will it take them to catch us?"

"They're faster than us," said Captain Cu. He squinted at the sun, hidden behind scudding[3] thin gray cloud. "It'll be dark in about three hours. They'll be within a few kilometers of us by then. They'll keep us in sight through the night and board us in the morning."

"You can see it from here now," said Ly flatly. She had stood up and was staring into the wake. "Yes—there!"

A black speck bobbed briefly on the heaving horizon, sank, and reappeared.

"He's moving," said Captain Cu. "Must have a real big engine." He watched the small speck that was the pirate boat with professional interest. "Yes, be up with us around sunset."

"You don't seem very worried," said Quan. A horrible thought struck him. "You're not going—going to leave us, are you? Join them, the pirates?"

Captain Cu laughed. "No way. I'm not worried about them because we'll have other things to worry about pretty soon."

Quan and Ly gaped at him, puzzled.

"Out there—" Captain Cu waved towards the southeast, "—out there, my children, something is being born right now."

"What?" asked Ly, gazing anxiously at the rushing sea as though expecting some fearsome, nightmarish monster to suddenly rend the waves.

"A typhoon," said Captain Cu.

命 CHAPTER 17

Typhoon! The supreme wind, the Chinese *tai-fung*, a monstrous rotating wall of gale and rain, terror of sailors in Far Eastern seas since man first ventured on the waters.

The typhoon now being spawned[4] was a long way from Lucky Dragon: far out in the South China Sea, it had now ceased being a formless swirl of air and moisture and had been entered

---

3. *Scudding* (SKUD ing) clouds are clouds driven by the wind.
4. *Spawned* means produced or born.

on the charts in meteorological stations in Hong Kong, Manila, Singapore and Guam as a tropical depression. Slowly, as it gained shape and size, it began to move. It moved northeast, towards Hong Kong, and away from Lucky Dragon. As it moved, it was constantly photographed by United States weather planes and by orbiting weather satellites.

As the tropical depression grew and solidified, it was upgraded in the weathermen's parlance to a tropical storm, and telexes began chattering warnings to shipping and aircraft in the entire western Pacific. Soon it became a severe tropical storm, and then a full-fledged typhoon: and it was named, by the weathermen in Guam, Typhoon Caroline.

If Caroline had moved southwest instead of northeast, the voyage of the Lucky Dragon would have come to an abrupt end. Shallow-draft Vietnamese fishing boats are not built to stand two hundred kilometer-an-hour winds and huge seas which seem to come from every direction at once, roaring like berserk green mountains of water.

But even though she was moving away, Caroline left a massive meteorological disturbance in her wake. The southwest monsoon, which normally blows across the Gulf of Thailand between Malaysia and Vietnam between June and September, was sucked into Caroline's wake, and began, late that afternoon, to lash the shallow sea with unusual fury.

By sunset the wind had increased to almost gale force: the foam from the breaking tops of the racing waves was blown flat on the water, streaking the backs of the swells as they passed Lucky Dragon.

Captain Cu was on the wheel: hours before, he had made sure that everything loose aboard the boat was lashed down, the spare fuel drum held as tightly as he could rope it to the gunwale. There was nothing else they could do. Lucky Dragon would just have to fight it out.

Now in the late afternoon, with the last sunlight an angry red through the torn cloud, Captain Cu braced his feet and prepared for a long night. He had long ago stopped looking astern: he was not worried about the Thai pirate boat any more. Lucky Dragon was about to meet a far tougher foe.

The Yanmar was throttled back to quarter speed: just enough to keep Lucky Dragon moving into the waves and wind. Captain Cu was saving fuel for a long fight. Ahead of him the flaring bows soared skyward as Lucky Dragon rode a big swell: torn white water gushed through the bow fairleads. Spray rattled against the windscreen like heavy rain, and within minutes there was rain, too, thick tropical rain, raindrops thick as pencils, blotting out the sea, sky, even the foredeck in a driving, solid curtain which roared on the deck and wheelhouse and churned the wild sea to foam. The rain thundered on the foredeck and the scuppers[5] could not handle it: it lay fifteen centimeters deep on the deck and Captain Cu felt Lucky Dragon stagger beneath the weight of water. It gushed over the side in huge white and green gouts.[6] The rain burst in white explosions on the fishhold covers, and Captain Cu thanked G-d that he had replaced them in time. Otherwise....

Then the sun was gone. In the last few minutes of light, Captain Cu glanced at the family

---

5. *Scuppers* (SKUP erz) are the openings at the edge of the ship's deck that allow accumulated water to drain into the sea.
6. *Gouts* (GOWTS) are splashes or spurts of liquid.

Word Bank   **parlance** (PAR lintz) *n.*: way or manner of speaking; jargon; vernacular

huddled around him in the creaking wheelhouse: Ah Soong was crouched in a corner, clutching her bag and stove: beside her was Aunt Binh, rigid with terror. Uncle Tan, bracing himself against the door frame with his single leg, was trying to shelter Phan Thi Chi and Xuyen from wind-driven rain squirting through a crack in the wheelhouse's thin planking. Quan had his arms around Ly and was shouting what sounded like encouragement above the howl of the gale.

Then it was dark. Captain Cu steered by feel, by the pressure of wave and wind on hull and rudder. Sometimes, through a rent in the cloud, starlight would glitter briefly and coldly on the rearing waves marching endlessly to the horizon. Lucky Dragon rose and fell heavily, smashing through the swells instead of riding them as she got heavier with the great weight of water she was taking, through her deck planks and through the old, creaking, ill-seasoned planking of her hull.

Captain Cu could feel the whole boat shaking beneath him. As she rolled, the moving mass of water in her fishholds slammed from side to side, tons of it, putting unbearable strains on timbers already subjected to unendurable pressures.

Captain Cu nudged Quan with his foot. The boy looked at him, his eyes wide with terror.

"The wheel," said Captain Cu. "Take the wheel. I'm going on the pump."

Outside, even on the afterdeck, which was partially protected by the wheelhouse, it was a dark and howling wilderness of noise and sea. The gale wrenched at the engine hatch cover when Cu unlatched it, almost tearing it from his hands. He slid over the coaming and pulled the cover close after him, bolting it from the inside.

It was dark as a coal sack inside the engine compartment. The Yanmar roared in the dark, a wild mechanical wail that put Cu's teeth on edge and pounded his eardrums. The deck planking wept water which spattered, hissed and turned into steam on the Yanmar's hot engine block. Outside the sea roared past within a few centimeters of him: the gale howled, and Lucky Dragon seemed to be shaking herself to death.

Desperately, fighting panic, Captain Cu forced himself to remember the layout of the tiny engine compartment. For a frightening moment he could not work out which way he was facing—forward or aft. He took a tighter hold on himself and worked it out. Yes. If that was forward, the pump was on the starboard side—groping for the pump handle, he touched one of the Yanmar's battery leads. The violent, high-voltage shock snapped him backwards, smashing his head hard against a heavy bulkhead. But for his helmet, he would have been knocked out. As it was, he felt sick and dizzy and had to stand quietly in the dark for several minutes, getting his breath and his courage back.

Then it began again, this dreadful groping in the dangerous, tumultuous dark, cringing at the thought of another shock. He felt something cold lick his feet. Water! Water over the floorboards in the engine compartment! The cold invisible tide ebbed as Lucky Dragon pitched and rolled, and then came back higher

> The rain thundered on the foredeck and the scuppers could not handle it: it lay fifteen centimeters deep on the deck and Captain Cu felt Lucky Dragon stagger beneath the weight of water. It gushed over the side in huge white and green gouts.

Word Bank

tumultuous (tuh MUL choo iss) *adj.*: full of violence and noise; uproarious; turbulent

than before. It was around his ankles now. A few more centimeters and it would lap the hot engine block itself: and then either the sharp differences in temperatures inside and outside the block would crack the metal, or the Yanmar's electrical system would short circuit in a shower of sparks.

Whatever way it happened, the result would be the same: Lucky Dragon would die. Without an engine she would roll helpless as a log before the waves. With no forward speed, her rudder would be unable to hold her head into wind and sea. She would swing beam on, presenting her broad, high sides to the gale and the swells. Her tired, battered planking would open and she would sink like a stone, dragged down by the weight of the dead Yanmar. Or she would wallow for a while before turning turtle.[7]

Panting, sobbing with fear and frustration, fighting growing claustrophobia, Captain Cu groped desperately for the pump handle. He received one more savage electric sting from the Yanmar—and then he found the pump handle!

Almost weeping with relief, he began pumping. The first few strokes rasped dryly and then he felt the beautiful pressure of water in the cylinder and the hearty slurp and thrust of a good pump drawing well. He spread-eagled[8] himself against unseen timber in the dark and settled down to a long driving rhythm.

Invisible in the dark, torn by the wind and waves, a steady, life-saving jet of water gushed from Lucky Dragon's side.

Sweating in the dark, his arm a throbbing piston which hardly seemed to belong to him, Captain Cu could not see the results of his efforts. But his feet were no longer licked by oily water when Lucky Dragon rolled and he knew that he had at least saved the Yanmar. And that was something. He kept pumping.

He kept pumping for hours. At least he thought it was hours. It could have been days. In that pitch-black hole, battling to stay on his feet as Lucky Dragon staggered from wave to wave, he had no way of telling time. He tried counting pump strokes, promising himself a rest after a hundred; then he gave up. His mind wandered. He thought of sleep. He longed for sleep. He would give anything to lie down and sleep. Once, towards dawn although he did not know it, he stopped pumping. He leaned against the bulkhead and closed his eyes. It was delicious. He didn't even have to lie down. He could sleep right there, standing. Just a little sleep. Just a little, little sleep. It wouldn't matter if he had just a very small sleep.

Then something cold touched his ankle in the dark. The water was rising again. He seized the pump handle again. He was too tired to stand and his right arm was a lump of burning flesh. So he knelt beside the pump in the dark and pumped with his left hand. After a while it grew lighter in the engine compartment. Looking up, Captain Cu saw pale streaks of light through the working deck planks. Dawn.

He stopped pumping and hauled himself aloft, lurching on to the deck like a drunken man. The family stared at him as though they had seen a ghost.

He staggered into the wheelhouse and pushed Quan from the wheel.

"Go below," he gasped. "And pump! Pump! Pump!" He leaned against the wheel, closing his eyes. Spray rattled on the glass. He stirred himself when someone shook him gently by the shoulder. It was Phan Thi Chi.

"Sleep," he said. "I'll take the wheel. Quan and Uncle Tan will pump. They've had some rest. You've had none."

---

7. The idiom *turning turtle* means capsizing or overturning.
8. He lay *spread-eagled*, with his arms and legs outstretched.

Lucky Dragon rolled, and Captain Cu rolled with it: as though in slow motion, he fell into a corner. His helmet came off and clanged on the deck. Aunt Binh picked it up and Captain Cu put it back on, mumbling. Then his head fell back and his eyes closed.

For the next four hours, while Lucky Dragon heaved and rolled and groaned and pitched, Captain Cu slept. Sometimes he rolled with the boat, unresponding as a corpse. Once an especially fierce roll almost pitched him out through the wheelhouse door and over the side; but Aunt Binh and Ah Soong and Xuyen grabbed his legs.

And Lucky Dragon fought for her life.

Studying the Selection

✓ Quick Review

1. Why was Quan annoyed when Ly spotted a strange boat?
2. What did the Thai fishermen say they wanted from the family?
3. What finally stopped the pirate attack?
4. What was Captain Cu looking for in the dark engine room?

In-depth Thinking

5. What keeps Phan Thi Chi from helping, as Quan and the other men hold the pirates at bay? How might he feel as his son pushes him aside?
6. We're told the Thai pirates were "strong dark men eager for plunder," that they considered the Thi Chi family "easy pickings." What do you think most surprised them about their encounter with the family?
7. What might be the significance of Uncle Tan's getting a new crutch when they reach Australia?
8. Why was it dangerous for Captain Cu to enter the engine room during the storm? What might have happened had he not found the pump?

Drawing Conclusions

9. How would the family have fared without Captain Cu in these two chapters? Why? How did his presence assure their survival?
10. How has the Lucky Dragon lived up to its name in Chapters 16 and 17?

Chapter 18

Captain Cu woke with a grunt of pain and discomfort. His arms ached. He was a mass of bruises. The engine compartment bristled with knobs, levers, sharp corners, brackets, projections of every sort, and he had been hurled repeatedly against them by Lucky Dragon's violent movement.

He sat up, wincing, while Ah Soong, Aunt Binh and Xuyen watched him with a concern which for the moment almost—but not quite—made them forget their own terror.

Phan Thi Chi was on the wheel. Captain Cu forced himself to stand up. He hauled himself out on deck and the wind and flying water tore at him as he looked over the starboard side. He smiled with his dry, salt-caked lips.

A steady jet of water, thick as his arm, pulsed steadily from Lucky Dragon's side. The pump was still working.

The waters of the southern gulf of Thailand, the southern South China Sea and the Java Sea, the region Lucky Dragon was then in, are not deep. But the tidal influences of the Indian and Pacific Oceans overlap in this area, and set up strange whirls of current and countercurrent. The shallow water, when whipped as well by the monsoon or the edge of a typhoon, becomes a nightmare of short, steep, confused waves.

So Lucky Dragon lurched south-southeast, making increasingly heavy weather of the shorter, steeper seas, constantly yawing and falling off into troughs when hit by one of the many rogue cross-waves. The boat's timbers groaned, a long never-ending moan which made Quan shudder.

But at noon they were still afloat. Ly and her mother were on the pump; Uncle Tan was asleep, exhausted. Aunt Binh was helping Ah Soong ladle out a handful of cold rice—a fire was out of the question—for each person.

Captain Cu was on the wheel again, and Phan Thi Chi was sleeping beside Uncle Tan. Everyone was wet, cold and terrified. But everyone was still alive. Which, thought Quan as he ate his cold rice, was—well, almost a miracle. He looked at the map pinned to the wheelhouse bulkhead. It was torn by the wind and stained by spray and rain now, and some of the colors had run. But it was there, and the little bit of Australia it showed was still there. Quan noticed that some time during the morning, someone—it had to be Captain Cu—had extended the wavy ballpoint pen line to indicate the distance they had traveled during the night. It was a wavering line, to be sure, but it brought Lucky Dragon appreciably closer to Australia.

It had stopped raining. The squalls were moving away west. And, unbelievably, there were patches of blue sky. But the seas were still steep and confused and broken along their tops by the wind. Yet the wind speed had dropped, too: the spray was flying now, not being driven flat on to the backs of the swells. From the wheelhouse one looked on to a dreary waste of gray-green water and flying spray. The departing rain squalls hid the horizon behind gray curtains of water.

Somehow they got through the day. The Yanmar kept thudding away. Captain Cu reduced speed even more. The fuel supply was dangerously low. During the morning he and Quan and Phan Thi Chi had manhandled the spare drum to the engine room hatch and managed to fill the main tank without spilling too much: it was a horrible, exhausting operation. The sea had almost wrenched the heavy drum

Word Bank

yawing (YAW ing) *v*.: straying temporarily from a straight course

rogue (ROAG) *adj*.: destructive, not conforming to a desired standard; vicious

from them as they slipped and staggered in the gale on the heaving deck. Once, indeed, the drum had got away from them and smashed against the wheelhouse with a terrifying splintering of timber. But they had got it under control again and coupled it to the short rubber hose Uncle Tan had thrust up from the main tank through the hatch. When it was all over and the spare drum and what remained of its contents was again safely lashed, they had sprawled gasping on the deck, hardly noticing the seas surging over them as Lucky Dragon rolled. It had taken two hours. And for the rest of the day the spilled fuel flashed green and pink and gold on the wet planks, and trickled overboard to lay a long oil trail astern.

At sunset that day they ate more cold rice and washed it down with cold tea. The rain returned with the night and the wind rose again, shrieking around the wheelhouse.

Once, about midnight, or so he supposed, Quan saw a star, a brief wink of light. Then it was gone. But just that brief glimpse made him feel somehow happier. It was as though it were a sign, a reassurance that there was another world: a world of sun and moon and stars and houses and trees and warmth and hot food and drink and dry clothes and beds, not just a world of dark and cold and violent movement and wind and slashing rain and noise.

Then the wind shattered two panes of the wheelhouse windscreen: they burst with a high sharp tinkle. The wind blew the shards inwards and in the dark Quan felt the sting of the sharp glass and then the trickle of warm blood down his face. He stood there at the wheel in the dark and felt his blood running down his face and his arms too and fought down rising panic. Bleeding in the dark when you can't see the wounds is unnerving. But the wind and rain and spray howled through the broken windows and soon Quan couldn't tell which was blood and which was rain or salt spray; the blood tasted like spray and the spray tasted like blood. The wind and rain in the wheelhouse woke the rest of the family—Captain Cu was alone below on the pump—and they muttered and groaned with wet and fear and hunger and misery in the dark. Then the remaining two windows blew in, shattering with explosive tinklings, and everyone was cut a little. Sharp slivers of glass stuck like thorns and could not be found in the dark.

Someone began to cry: horrible gasping sobs that made Quan's flesh creep. He couldn't see who it was. The sobbing went on and on. And he could smell blood and rain and sea and oil and despair and fear. There was nothing he could do about any of these things so he gritted his teeth and tried to hold Lucky Dragon into the wind. The wind, salty and wet, blew hard through the broken windows. It seemed to slap his face with spiteful hands. His eyes stung with salt. But still he could just see the phosphorescent loom of the breaking wave tops and kept the boat lumbering in to them. And he tried not to hear the sobbing.

The night ended at last: it became pale green and sickly and trickled through the shattered windows into the wheelhouse. Captain Cu had been relieved on the pump by Uncle Tan: he slept heavily, snoring. Phan Thi Chi lay with his eyes open, staring at something beyond the windows. For a moment Quan thought he was dead: then he saw his chest heaving. The family lay like bundles of dirty washing, filthy, streaked and spotted with blood. Glass crackled beneath their bodies as the boat rolled and pitched. The broken glass spilled out on to the streaming decks and sparkled like ice before being swept away.

Then the sun was up, a pale yellow ghost behind scudding cloud. The wind had dropped, fallen away to a light breeze. The sea still heaved huge and gray about them, waves rushing from every quarter: but they were not breaking any more.

Reluctantly, moving like an old, old man, Phan Thi Chi relieved his son on the wheel. The women slept on, clutching each other in their sleep. Quan swung himself out of the wheelhouse, stretching his aching arms and legs. He saw for the first time that Lucky Dragon had lost her smokestack some time during the night: the funnel's stays had snapped and the whole ungainly affair of badly-jointed galvanized iron had snapped off at deck level. The Yanmar's exhaust now spewed out at deck level, coiling across the afterdeck and spilling off astern before the wind tore it into dirty shreds.

We made it, thought Quan. Two nights. And we made it through that storm. He looked around the horizon. Nothing. No ship. No land. But we made it! The sun came through a rent in the clouds and was warm on his face. He yawned and the dried blood from his cuts cracked and fell in a little shower of black flakes.

He was washing his face, trying to get the blood and salt off, using the sea which swirled and rushed up through the scuppers with every heavy roll, when Ly came out of the wheelhouse. Her eyes were hooded with fatigue and she had a tracery of small glass cuts on one cheek.

"You were crying this morning," said Quan gently. She shook her head.

"Not me." She scooped water and dabbed at her face. He looked at her.

"Who, then? Mother?" She shook her head, looking away from him, over the wild heaving sea.

"Father."

By noon the wind had gone completely. The sea was down, too, reduced to a heavy, oily ground swell. The clouds thinned and in the early afternoon the sun burst through. The deck steamed.

Ah Soong spread the last of her charcoal out to dry. The old woman had aged terribly in two days: her eyes glittered in her sunken face. Even though the sun was out she still wore her best jade-green quilted jacket. She seemed to move with difficulty, as though under a great weight. Ah Soong looked very ill.

Late in the afternoon, while Quan was on the pump, the stout Yanmar began to run rough. The engine block was so hot that it made the small engine compartment almost unbearable.

Quan called out, and Captain Cu swung himself through the hatch.

He listened to the uneven grumblings of the engine and swore. Then he cut the ignition.

"Overheated," he said. "It's been running nonstop for days. Have to give it a rest."

The block clicked and groaned as the tortured metal cooled. With no way on, Lucky Dragon swung her beam on to the swell and began a sickening rolling which soon had Aunt Binh retching again.

"What do we do now?" asked Quan.

Captain Cu shrugged. "Let it cool. And hope we can start it again tomorrow."

"Has it done this before?"

"No. But then it's never worked so hard

Word Bank

tracery (TRAY sir ee) *n.*: a delicate, interlacing work of lines or threads

before. I'd better check the oil." He withdrew the dipstick, wiped it on a piece of waste, replaced it and withdrew it again.

"Hmmm. Lower than it should be."

"Will it get us to Australia?"

"G-d knows, Quan. I don't."

By the last light Quan, using Captain Cu's estimate of their course and speed, worked out their position and extended the ballpoint line on the chart. It put the boat about two hundred kilometers east of Singapore. And a long way from Australia.

They ate their supper—a cupful of cold rice each—as the sun went down in a glorious blaze of red and purple. In the sudden dark the big swells rushed at them, big as mountains against the stars. Lucky Dragon rolled and complained, her timbers, strained by the storm, creaking and shrieking. The boat was still making water and there had to be someone on the pump all the time, but at least there was no longer rain or spray coming through the deck, and the pump seemed to be handling the leak. But it was numbing, exhausting work.

Throughout the night the steady clank and suck of the pump provided a counterpoint to the myriad other noises—splash of sea, fast rush of passing swell, groan of working bulkheads.

At first light Captain Cu went below to restart the Yanmar. On deck, the family held their breaths as the starter motor groaned—urururururrrr—reluctantly. Then the engine coughed, faltered, and settled down to its familiar, comforting ufufufufboomboom. With Quan on the wheel, Lucky Dragon swung back on course.

Captain Cu, dripping sweat, heaved himself out of the engine hatch. He sat on the coaming for a while, getting his breath back and idly looking at the sea. Below him, Aunt Binh's wiry figure labored at the pump.

Suddenly Captain Cu leaped to his feet. He dashed to the stern like a man berserk, seized Uncle Tan's fishing line and began to haul it in, hand over hand, panting with effort. Fifty meters astern a long thin fish broke the surface, flashing silver-green in the sun. It dived, and the line ran out through Captain Cu's fingers, burning them, cutting painful grooves in the sea-softened flesh. The line hissed through the water, leaving a thin line of foam. Then the angle changed and it rose as the fish broke surface again, flashing in a writhing leap. Then Captain Cu hauled it alongside, and swung it aboard with a triumphant shout: more than a meter of long thin body, ending in a long thin spike: it looked like a miniature marlin, but was in fact a needlefish, the biggest Captain Cu had ever seen. Its beak snapped angrily and its wide crescent tail slapped the deck.

"Hey, that was my fishing line!" Uncle Tan protested, laughing with pride and excitement. "My line!"

"Sorry I couldn't wait for you," said Captain Cu. "I was frightened it would get away. You can have the next one."

Leaving Uncle Tan to fashion another lure—the needlefish's sharp teeth had shredded the original one—Captain Cu dispatched the fish with a sharp blow on the head from the engine room monkey wrench, and presented the long fish to Ah Soong.

"There you are, old lady," he said, grinning. "Let's see what you can do with that."

Clutching the fish as though afraid it would come to life again and leap overboard, Ah Soong shuffled forward. Carefully the old

---

Word Bank   **counterpoint** *n.*: any element contrasted or juxtaposed with another

woman and Xuyen loaded the small earthenware stove with the dried charcoal. It took a lot of puffing and blowing, but eventually the fire was lit.

Twenty minutes later they were eating their first real meal for days: boiled fish and rice—and warm, too! Then Ah Soong still moving strangely heavily, made some weak tea. Oh, it was a feast. Quan sat and sucked the fish bones until there was not a shred of flesh left on them.

That night they ate the last of the rice. And Uncle Tan's new lure fluttered untouched astern.

Chapter 19

The next day was so bright that it hurt. The sky was a burnished blue bowl, the sun a harsh flare which flayed the skin and, shattering on the sea into a million dancing points of light, pricked the eyes until they ached. And the Yanmar was ailing. There was a thready mechanical whine underlying the cheery boomboomboom now, a thin wail of pain, of aching metal. Captain Cu kept popping down the hatch, listening, checking the oil level—which was dropping every day—muttering encouragement to the Yanmar as though it were a horse or water buffalo.

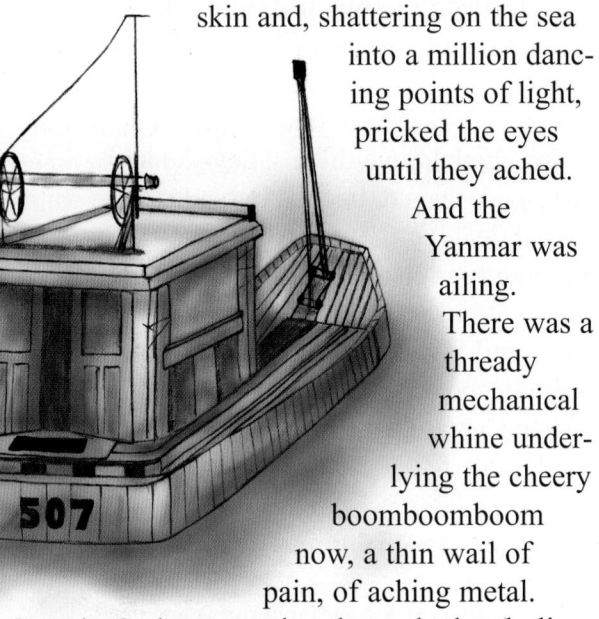

And Aunt Binh, her gaunt frame gaunter, seemed to be always on the pump. Her eyes glowed in her strained face as she worked. They seemed to shine in the hot gloom of the engine hatch.

Captain Cu regarded her with wonder.

"I thought at first she was a dreadful woman," he confided to Quan once. "Always moaning! And lazy. But I was wrong."

"She's changed," said Quan. "She's changed wonderfully. She's a different woman."

"She's a good woman," said Captain Cu. He looked at Quan with sudden sympathy. "Other people have changed too," he said. "It's not their fault. This boat—the storm—"

"My father," said Quan. "Yes. We're very worried about him. He won't talk. Just does his turn on the wheel or pump and sits and thinks. He blames himself for everything."

"That's rubbish," said Captain Cu. "You couldn't have stayed in Ho Chi Minh City. You told me that yourself. You'd all be separated now. In work camps. On farms."

"I know," said Quan. "He's forgotten that, I think. He just knows that we've lost our shop and are hungry and in danger. And he says it's his fault. My mother can't make him stop blaming himself."

Captain Cu shook his head sadly and left to relieve Uncle Tan on the wheel. Phan Thi Chi was sitting against the side of the wheelhouse, his face lined and old in the hard white sunlight, his eyes staring across the sea without seeing. His wife sat beside him.

Hunger came slowly at first, and they kept it at bay with frequent glasses of very weak tea. Then the tea was gone, too. Ah Soong's wonderful bag was empty at last: and the hunger

---

Word Bank **flayed** (FLAYD) *v.*: stripped off the skin or outer covering, as by whipping

came back fiercer than ever, a constant dull ache in their bellies.

Ah Soong, that tough old lady, began to fade before their eyes: her eyes retreated into dark pools of shadow, her cheeks became sunken. She moved slowly, dragging herself across the deck. But she never uttered one word of complaint. She sat in what shade she could find, silent as a statue for hour after hour. In the blazing sun her prized jade-green jacket, now sadly salt-stained, faded to a pale lime. The old lady refused to remove her jacket, clutching it to her with a fierce possessiveness which made Quan fear that her mind was going. But he was always reassured by her eyes, which were as sharp and knowing as ever.

"I am dying of uselessness," she said to Quan one day. "All my life I have worked. Now there is no work. No cooking, nothing. I can do nothing for the family. I am a useless old woman, and will die soon, killed by the uselessness."

And the hunger grew, and grew, until it crouched in all of them like a ravening[9] monster, clawing at their vitals. They could not sleep. They dreamed of food: Quan had tantalizing dreams of huge white mounds of rice, of chicken, fish, sliced beef, piles of fruits. He would wake with the taste of food in his mouth: and there would be nothing but the wide empty sea, the aching blue sky, the uncaring sun, the groaning of timber and the Yanmar's nagging metallic complaint.

On the fourth day after the storm they saw a ship. It came fast from the east, a big Japanese container ship heading for the Straits of Malacca.

Captain Cu hastily dived into the engine compartment and emerged with a can of black sump oil and a stiff, paint-clogged brush. While the family watched, he printed on the side of the wheelhouse, in thirty centimeter-high letters:

HELP! VIETNAMESE REFUGEES
NO FOOD PLEASE HELP

Then he took the wheel from Ly and altered course so that Lucky Dragon's track intersected that of the approaching ship.

"They must see us," Captain Cu muttered. "They must! We must have shown on their radar."

The container ship came nearer and nearer. It was enormous: it towered above them, a huge slab of steel. It passed so close that they could hear the whisper and rush of the sea cleaved by its bulbous Mitsubishi bow, and hear the deep rumble of its engines. They read the name on the stern as it passed: Hokkaido Maru.

A small figure appeared on the wing of the bridge, high above them. They shouted, screamed, waved, begged, whistled. The ship passed, leaving the Lucky Dragon tossing impotently in its wake.

They stood watching it, willing it to stop, to turn, until it slid over the western horizon. Nobody spoke.

Then Captain Cu went wild: he screamed, waving his fist at the empty sea. "Devils! You Devils!"

---

9. A *ravening* (RAY vin ing) monster is one that is starving, prowling for food.

Word Bank

crouched (KROUCHT) *v.*: stooped with knees bent as if ready to pounce
vitals (VY tilz) *n.*: the bodily organs essential to life, such as the brain, heart, liver, lungs, and stomach
bulbous (BUL biss) *adj.*: bulb-shaped
impotently (IM puh tint lee) *adv.*: powerlessly

"Perhaps they didn't see us," said Quan quietly.

Captain Cu turned on him angrily. "You believe that? You really believe that?"

"It's better than believing the other thing," said Quan. "Isn't it?"

"What's that?" asked Captain Cu, puzzled.

Quan glanced at his father, still gazing after the vanished container ship. Quan hesitated, and Phan Thi Chi turned away from the empty horizon, his face twitching. "Say it," he said. "Yes, say it. Say that nobody wants us! Nobody will help us! We'll be left to starve!"

Quan could only stare at his father, helplessly. After a while Phan Thi Chi grew calmer: his wife took his arm, whispering to him, and they went and sat in the lee of the wheelhouse.

"Perhaps he's right," said Captain Cu thoughtfully. "But it sure won't help us to believe so. Now—" he slapped his forehead. "That woman—she's still on the pump!"

Quan watched as Captain Cu bustled down the hatch. He heard Aunt Binh's voice raised in protest, and then saw the widow being ordered from the engine room compartment by Captain Cu's booming voice. And he thought how strange it was that the dreary woman who had spent her whole day back at thirteen Bach Dang in reciting an endless litany of complaints had never mouthed one word of regret or disappointment since leaving Rach Gia. He shook his head at the wonder of it and went aft to inspect Uncle Tan's line. The lure was untouched, the rusting hook empty. Sighing, he streamed it again.

The next day, four big flying fish came aboard. They took off, a small fluttering shower of frightened fish, from a big swell on Lucky Dragon's port beam. Several flashed right over Lucky Dragon as she rolled; several more thumped against the hull: but four landed, skittering and flapping, on the deck, and Quan and Captain Cu leaped upon them with cries of joy. One slipped out of Quan's grasp and was flapping over the side when Uncle Tan lashed out with his crutch and scooped it back aboard.

They laid the four fish on the deck and gazed at them reverently. Bigness is relative: a big flying fish is only twenty centimeters long. But the family gazed at these fish as though they were made of the rarest jade.

"And now," said Captain Cu jubilantly, "it's up to you, old lady!"

"I'll light the stove," said Quan's mother, and hurried away. Slowly, Ah Soong cleaned the fish: that is to say, she scaled them. The scales were small and came off easily in little showers. The intestines were too precious to throw away: Ah Soong squeezed the contents from them, washed them in sea water collected by Aunt Binh, and replaced them in the tiny belly cavities.

Then, miraculously, she made a creditable fish stew over the last of the charcoal: she turned her bag inside out and recovered long-lost rice from the seams; she coaxed a few drops of soy sauce out of an empty bottle; she found a dried stalk and withered leaf of cabbage—pale souvenirs of a long-ago shopping trip in easier times.

And, miracle of miracles, Ah Soong recovered enough spilled tea to make a weak—very weak—glassful for each of them.

And they ate! How they ate! Nothing was wasted, nothing. Eyes, gills, fins, stomach—all was eaten, turned over and over in the mouth, swallowed reluctantly. The delicate bones

---

Word Bank **reverently** (REV er int lee) *adv.*: with deep respect

were sucked until they gleamed, and then cracked for their thin salty marrow.

That night, after he had finished his spell on the wheel, Quan slept properly for the first time in days. He woke just before dawn. Ly was already on deck, walking around as though looking for something.

He padded silently across the planking and she started when he touched her shoulder.

"What are you looking for?"

"More flying fish," she said. "I hoped some might have come in the night."

Together they scoured the deck, but there were no more fish. Then the sun reared above the wrinkled dark line of sea: a deep red ball at first. Then it seemed to shoot into the sky, turned a blinding white. And the decks smoked as the dew turned to steam and the mist was sucked from the whispering calm ocean.

Ah Soong sat in the cool shadow of the wheelhouse and talked to Quan and Ly. She was in a strange mood: detached, her gaze a long way away, looking, it seemed to Quan, past him and his sister, past the boat, past the sea—to where? China? Her youth, so long ago? Her life at thirteen Bach Dang?

Ah Soong was talking about Australia. He was surprised that the old woman knew anything about Australia; but then he realized that although he had known her all his life he knew very little about Ah Soong: he had never really spoken to her. And he didn't know much about Aunt Binh either; or Uncle Tan; or his father. It seemed that he knew his mother best of all: she had always been there, the way she was there now; except that she was no longer comforting and protecting and reassuring a child who had stubbed his toe, or who was frightened of his first day at school: she was doing all these things for her husband.

"When I was young, in China," said Ah Soong, "many young Chinese wanted to go to Australia. In the last century many did go, you know. In the eighteen sixties. They called Australia the Golden Mountain—"

"Why?" asked Ly.

"Because they thought there was a lot of gold there," said the old woman. "Oh, there were good stories in Canton and all over Kwangtung Province and Swatow, which is the city all the clothworkers and lacemakers come from. Stories that you could just put your spade in the ground and dig up gold!"

"And were they true?" asked Quan.

"Of course not! Are these silly stories ever true?"

"But the Chinese stayed in Australia?" said Ly.

"Probably because they couldn't afford to come back," said Ah Soong. "Fools! Still, some of them must have made money. I know they were treated very badly by the Australians at first—now, that would be in my great-great-grandfather's time—but things have got better, I believe." She paused, musing. "You know, I have never met an Australian! Still, I suppose they are like all *gwai-lo*."

"Well, you will soon meet your first Australian 'foreign devil,' Ah Soong." said Quan. The old woman shrugged.

"We shall see."

So they slipped south-southeast, past the Tambelan Islands, past Bangka and Belitung, past the high mass of Borneo, hidden by cloud and distance, past Sumatra, through the Straits of Karimata at night, and into the Java Sea,

> Quan traced it all on his school atlas chart and watched the slowly lengthening ballpoint pen line with wonder. "We're going to make it," he told Ly. "We're going to make it!"

flat and clean and brilliant blue as a peacock's feather.

Uncle Tan's tattered lure caught them another fish—a plump bonito. They had no more charcoal so they made a fire of splinters torn from the deck and wheelhouse timber.

North of the Indonesian city of Surabaja they were stopped by an Indonesian gunboat. The Indonesians were polite and sympathetic but firm: no Vietnamese refugees were wanted in Indonesia.

The Indonesian captain was a young and kindly man. He gave them a bag of rice and filled their fuel and water tanks, and then pointed the Lucky Dragon towards the Lombok Straits.

Quan traced it all on his school atlas chart and watched the slowly lengthening ballpoint pen line with wonder.

"We're going to make it," he told Ly. "We're going to make it!"

Studying the Selection

First Impressions — Who might be seen as the greatest hero or heroes in Part Four? Why? Was there any place where you felt the family might not endure? Where did this occur? Are you concerned about the survival of a particular character? Who and why? How has the family managed to survive their challenges?

✓ Quick Review

1. Why does the glimpse of a star through the clouds make Quan feel happier?
2. What caused everyone to bleed during the second night of the storm?
3. What happened to the engine?
4. What is "the other thing" that Quan can't get himself to say when the Japanese boat passes by without helping them?

In-depth Thinking

5. Look at the passage in Chapter 18, where Quan—cut and bleeding—is at the wheel during the storm. Bennett provides much description before he says someone began to cry. How many of the senses does his description involve? Why might he go into such detail here? How does this affect you?
6. Who seems to have been affected most by the storm? Give evidence from the text to support your response.
7. Why would the Japanese container ship pass by the damaged Lucky Dragon?
8. Many times Ah Soong's ability to make a meal from almost nothing has been described as miraculous. How does this description affect your image of Ah Soong? What makes the meals in Chapter 19 particularly miraculous?

Drawing Conclusions

9. Why does Ly look away from Quan when she tells him who was crying in the night? How might the children regard their father at this time?
10. Captain Cu calls Phan Thi Chi's fears of endangering the family "rubbish." Why? Why might this response be helpful after all they have endured?

Focusing on Plot

Complete the following activities for greater understanding of plot.

1. Review Parts 1–4. List the obstacles the Thi Chi family had to overcome in their attempt to find a home away from Vietnam. Which section had the most obstacles? Which of them was the most dangerous? Explain. Next, think about the characters in the story. Do any of the characters have personal goals or desires? How might

this journey affect those goals? Do they encounter any obstacles? Compare your answers to those of a classmate. Are they similar?

2. Use the character you created in **Focusing on Characterization** from Part Three, and write a short vignette. Think about the character's drives, and build a simple plot around a goal. The character's struggle to reach the goal needn't be dangerous. It could be as simple as befriending a neighbor. To create a bit of tension and suspense, include three obstacles your character must overcome before reaching the goal. Share your story with the class.

3. Recall a favorite or familiar story. Determine what the main character in this story wants. What is the goal? What problems must be overcome to reach the goal? Now, change the goal and build a new plot. For example, in the tale of Little Red Riding Hood, the main character wants nothing more than to deliver goodies to her grandmother. Try placing her in a large city. What difficulties would she encounter? This might lead her on a journey through various neighborhoods. Have fun, and share your story with the class.

Creating and Writing

1. Answer the following questions in a short essay. What do most family members want? Which are most determined to pursue this dream? How does their attitude affect their efforts to continue despite the hardships? Why are some characters more determined than others? Do any characters have goals that undermine the others? Are these differences crucial? Should the family have the same goal? Explain your answer in terms of the theme of Part Four.

2. Using the "I" voice of a character, write what might be said to another character. Express these thoughts in a letter or speech. Which character might have thoughts that are difficult to express? What words might they struggle for, as they try to express their thoughts? Remember, family members may find it difficult to express gratitude, disappointment, fear, love, or other emotions. Share your work with your class.

3. The Thi Chi family sought help during times of need. Sometimes they were given fuel, food, or other aid—such as Captain Cu provided. Other times they were scorned. Often our neighbors around the world, or in our own country, find themselves in need as a result of fires, floods, earthquakes, or similar disasters. Many organizations help with relief efforts in these stricken areas. With your teacher's help, contact one of these organizations to ask where they are currently sending aid. Find out what the victims need most. Often they need supplies of clothing or canned goods. As a class, decide which group or cause you would most like to help. Then organize a school-wide drive for supplies needed by that relief effort.

Blueprint for Reading

Background Bytes

As the refugees neared their destinations—ending weeks, months, or years of waiting and hardship—many had mixed emotions. Excitement often blended with apprehension. What surprises awaited them in these strange lands? Could they adjust to their new home? What would become of those left behind?

In Australia, as in America, kind volunteers tried to help Vietnamese immigrants adjust to new surroundings. Often, however, the cultural differences were so great that the helpers could not even imagine which questions had to be answered. Many refugees were unfamiliar with items we take for granted, ending up confused on first encounter. Many had never seen can openers, toothpaste, or refrigerators; doorknobs were new to some immigrants.

The need for bravery—although a different kind—followed the Vietnamese boat people even after they had finally found freedom.

Into *The Voyage of the Lucky Dragon*—Part Five

Believe it or not, the Thi Chi family has yet to encounter their most difficult challenges. Not everyone faces the challenges successfully, however, and a new question emerges: Why do some succumb to hardship, while others endure? We might also ask, when is hardship too much? At what point will each of us break? Although similar questions were asked earlier, they should again be asked about the events in Part Five.

We might also ask about the Lucky Dragon itself as the family nears Australia. How meaningful is the name of this boat? How often does good fortune play a part in survival? Some might call it luck; others say luck favors those who are prepared. Regardless, how often might this family have perished, given a slight change of fortune? What if the storm had lasted another day? What if Quan hadn't used the nets during the pirate attack? What if the guard's flashlight had located Phan Thi Chi and Quan back in Rach Gia? How many times had the family barely survived a seemingly hopeless situation? Despite all the hardships, in what ways are they truly fortunate?

The Voyage of the Lucky Dragon

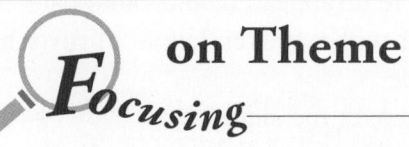

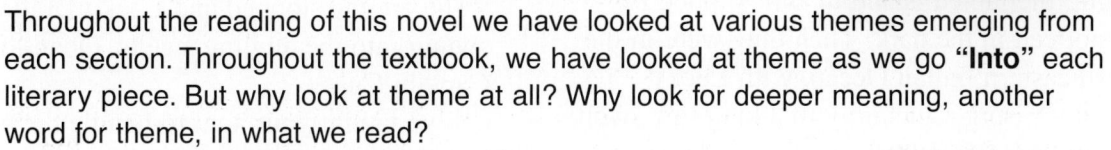

Focusing on Theme

Throughout the reading of this novel we have looked at various themes emerging from each section. Throughout the textbook, we have looked at theme as we go **"Into"** each literary piece. But why look at theme at all? Why look for deeper meaning, another word for theme, in what we read?

As human beings, we want our activities to enrich our lives in some way. Playing games, we look for fun as well as exercise. While shopping, we look for more than price; we want the item to be pleasing to the eye as well. Reading literature is no different. We gain much from reading fiction—enjoyment being a main component—but also knowledge and insight. We read hoping for more than information. We want the time spent to be meaningful.

By definition writers express ideas—they set their readers to thinking. At times they just have a great story to tell or a strong sentiment to express in poetry. This is called the writer's purpose, but embedded in a piece of writing lies some additional worth, some meaning that we refer to as theme. Because fiction and poetry are expressions of our shared human experience, we—the readers—naturally focus on these deeper truths.

We have gained much from the truths embedded in *The Voyage of the Lucky Dragon*. We have learned about the power of hope, the value of family, and the need to work together to accomplish goals. We have experienced a boy's coming of age and seen ordinary people accomplish extraordinary deeds by overcoming their fears. We've learned how individuals handle situations differently, and how some are more likely to succeed than others. And we have seen and will see how each individual has a different breaking point. We will also see how a positive outlook can hold off the seemingly inevitable breakdown.

Jack Bennett gives us more than the story of a desperate family. He teaches us about ourselves, about our world. That, ultimately, is the function of theme.

Word Bank

The word *feint* means "a movement made in order to deceive (an adversary); an assumed appearance." The verb *feint* is "to make a false show of, simulate, pretend." The root appears in *counterfeit*, *feign*, *figment*, *fiction*, and *effigy*. Do you know what these other words mean? They all came from the Latin *fingere*, meaning "to model in clay" hence "to fashion in any plastic material," then "to fashion or form," and finally, "to invent, imagine," even "to pretend."

congeal	feint	morbid	revulsion

Part Five

Chapter 20

They came through the Lombok Straits at night; the fabled island of Bali slipped by unnoticed in the dark. Then they were in the northeastern Indian Ocean, with Lucky Dragon rising reluctantly to a long low swell from the southwest.

Quan was still half asleep when he heard the thudding: a harsh violent hammering against the hull. He rushed on deck: it was early morning. Lucky Dragon was breasting an awkward, broken ground swell. And something was banging her timbers with a bone-jarring thump as she took every wave.

Quan leaned over the side. Captain Cu, hastily waking Uncle Tan and putting him on the wheel, joined him.

"Nightmares," he said quietly. "Bloody nightmares!" Lucky Dragon was a round-bilged boat, designed to be run ashore and careened—that is, left high and dry by the falling tide—when her bottom needed scraping. To prevent her rolling over when high and dry, and to give her something to settle on evenly, she was fitted with bilge keels—long, thick slabs of wood bolted to her hull at the outermost edge of its curve.

Lucky Dragon's bilge keels were five meters long, thirty centimeters wide, and ten centimeters thick. They were admirable pieces of timber. But the boat builder had bolted them to Lucky Dragon's hull with three long bolts of mild steel, instead of using brass or copper, or a saltwater-resistant alloy. And now the two forward retaining bolts, rusted away, had sheared; and the long and heavy bilge keel, held only by the after bolt, was moving up and down with a scissor-like action in the heavy swell, and slamming hard against Lucky Dragon's already strained timbers.

"That's going to knock a hole in us pretty soon," said Captain Cu. "We'll have to cut it loose." He disappeared, and came back minutes later with a broken length of rusty hacksaw blade.

"I'll go over the side."

The engine stopped and Lucky Dragon swung into the angling swells. Quan looked at Captain Cu.

"I've taught your aunt to handle the controls," said Captain Cu. "She's a very clever woman. Hardworking too."

"Yes," said Quan, dryly. "Very."

Captain Cu had uncoiled the long mooring rope from the forward bollard. Now he secured one end around his waist and gave the other end to Quan.

"You see any sharks," he said, "you shout bloody loud and haul me back up bloody quick. No, on second thought, you haul first and then shout."

"Sharks?" said Quan.

"Plenty of sharks down here," said Captain Cu, poised on the gunwale with the hacksaw blade between his teeth.

"Big ones, too. Tigers." He jumped.

It was not easy work. Lucky Dragon was rolling and pitching. The junction of thick rusty bolt and heavy timber bilge keel was a murderous combination of moving wood and steel. Captain Cu, clinging to the moving bilge keel with one hand, sawing with the other, was flung violently up and down as Lucky Dragon rolled broadside to the swell. One second he was high out of the water, slammed against the side: the next he was choking a meter

> His mother saw the shark first, and screamed, a shocking sound in the bright morning. It was a big tiger shark, almost four meters long, and it was hungry and excited.

below the surface. And the work was agonizingly slow. Finally, exhausted, ripped and torn by the barnacles on the lower hull, Captain Cu was hauled back on board with the bolt only half severed.

He lay panting and blowing on the deck in a spreading pool of pink-tinged sea water.

"A few minutes' rest and I'll try again," he said, wincing at the sting of his cuts.

"No," said Quan. "I'll go." He tied the rope around his waist and leaped overboard before Captain Cu could protest.

The water was warm, salty, and very clear: when he opened his eyes he could see the weeds and barnacles on Lucky Dragon's hull. A shoal of small silver fish were feeding along the main keel. Then the boat rolled heavily and Quan, hanging on to the bilge keel, was lifted clear of the water and banged against the hull: he felt the wasp-sting as the razor-sharp barnacles slashed his legs. Looking down through the clear water he saw delicate pink tendrils of blood.

He filled his lungs with air, ducked his head into the water again, and began sawing the bolt. He could see the bright silver line of Captain Cu's cutting and he slid the hacksaw blade into it.

It was awkward, exhausting and dangerous work. The blade kept jerking from the bolt as Lucky Dragon rolled and pitched. The heavy bilge keel whipped up and down, churning the water to foam—foam which turned pale pink as Quan leaked blood from a hundred tiny barnacle cuts.

As Quan grew tired, the water, which had been so warm, seemed to turn colder: soon he was shivering uncontrollably as he sawed at the bolt. Every time an exceptionally violent roll hurled him clear of the sea, he caught a wild inverted glimpse of the family's anxious faces lining the gunwale: they reminded him of so many dolls on a shelf.

And then his efforts began to tell: the thick mild steel bolt bent, worked the other way, bent again, displaying more bright unrusted steel—and snapped. The bilge keel, with Quan clinging to it, panting, floated clear.

His mother saw the shark first, and screamed, a shocking sound in the bright morning.

It was a big tiger shark, almost four meters long, and it was hungry and excited. It had been hunting turtles on a steep reef-edge a few hundred meters away when it picked up the vibrations caused by Captain Cu and Quan kicking and thrashing about as they worked on the bilge keel. To a shark, vibrations in the water mean something in trouble.

Now it came up in a long shallow run, swinging its great chisel-shaped head from side to side, all its sensor alarms ringing. Its distinctive tiger stripes shimmered light and dark as the food message sent pulses of excitement through its body.

It broke water about five meters from Quan, tearing the water with its wide shining back, made a small broadside feint as it tried to unscramble the confused vibrations which had attracted it, and then came straight in, hard and fast as a bull charging. The lower jaw dropped, the upper jaw raised, and the whole fearsome armory slid forward, a lethal cone of razor-sharp teeth.

Xuyen screamed again, and so did Aunt Binh and Ly. Captain Cu hurled himself away from the rail so violently that he knocked Uncle Tan sprawling.

The shark lifted itself high out of the water as it hit the bilge keel. The powerful jaws

---

Word Bank

feint (FAYNT) *n.*: a movement made in order to distract an opponent; an attack aimed at one place or point to distract from the real target

which could slice through a green turtle's tough upper and lower shells closed on the timber centimeters from Quan's arm. Then the shark violently jerked the front half of its body sideways, its high tail lashing the water. This is the way the tiger usually feeds: its terrible teeth are designed for a shearing cut. On the first bite the victim—turtle, man, or dolphin—is seized: two or three violent shakes, and the prey is usually cut completely in half.

For Quan it was a moment out of stark nightmare: the shark's terrifying teeth were centimeters from his arm. Its cold flat eyes, utterly expressionless, were level with his own as he cowered behind the keel. The pupils were black holes rimmed by a narrow golden iris. Looking into them, Quan felt hypnotized: he couldn't move. He couldn't even move his arm to get it away from the big sideways-raked teeth.

Then the shark jerked its head sideways in the second phase of the eating ritual, and the teeth embedded in the bilge keel snapped off with high sharp crackings. Messages flowed back to the tiny brain hidden in the great grisly head: this is not flesh. This is not food. But the sensors kept pouring in other data: yes, there is food here. We can feel it. We can smell it.

The great jaws opened and the tiger slid back into the water. It made an excited half-circle, its stripes changing color as a dim anger grew. Then it got a clear food image from its sensors. Quan's legs, which he had drawn up against his body in terror, swung below the confusing image of the bilge keel.

In its excitement and blind hunger, the tiger reared half out of the water as its big tail fin drove it towards Quan. The big wide head swung sideways in readiness for the first fatal shearing bite: the shark was aroused, and there was going to be no grab and hold, no ritual.

Then something flashed briefly in the sun. There was a strange wet thud, and the shark veered away in mid-run, trailing a strange dark cloud as it passed below Quan's legs.

Lucky Dragon's heavy monkey wrench, hurled with all the strength of Captain Cu's powerful arm, had struck the tiger hard in the gills. Sharks don't have hard protective gill covers like other fish. A shark's gills are guarded by nothing but thin slits in the skin. The heavy spanner, moving fast, tore two gill slits and lacerated the delicate oxygen-gathering organ inside.

It was not a fatal wound, but the sudden shock was enough to distract the tiger from its attack. It passed below Quan in a long shallow dive, trailing ropes of blood from its damaged gill.

Seconds later Quan was lying sobbing on the deck, with his mother's arms around him. Xuyen was sobbing, too, and so was Ly, from shock and relief.

"Sorry I knocked you down," said Captain Cu to Uncle Tan. "But I was in a hurry."

"Don't mention it," said Uncle Tan. "But give me time to get my crutch out of the way next time, will you? It's bent again."

Phan Thi Chi couldn't speak. He took Captain Cu's hand and held it while the tears squeezed slowly from his closed eyes.

Captain Cu was embarrassed. He stood there for a few minutes squinting with embarrassment, scratching his head beneath the helmet with his free hand.

Quan got up. He was still trembling but calm.

"Thank you," he said.

"That's all right," said Captain Cu. "It's a good thing I didn't miss him."

That just did not bear talking about, even thinking about. Uncle Tan got a sudden clear vision of what might have been and closed his eyes, feeling sick.

"I wonder where he is now?" said Quan. "That shark. Oh, he was big."

"He'll probably be back," said Captain Cu.

"He wasn't hurt too badly, I think. They're tough. He'll—hey, hey—there he is!"

The tiger surfaced in a swirl of foam about ten meters away, on the other side of the boat. He swam side on to Lucky Dragon, his tail and dorsal fins out of the water. Through the clear water they could see that he was still leaking blood from the damaged gill.

"That tough old tiger," muttered Captain Cu. "That tough old war-fish. I wish I had a gun."

Suddenly the big fish jerked out of the water as though an explosive charge had been set off beneath him. The whole long striped body jerked clear of the water and fell back, thrashing; then it was in two pieces, and they glimpsed a huge head, a meter wide, shaking the way a dog does when it worries something it has caught: and the sea exploded into white foam and blood as other, smaller sharks homed in on the blood and vibrations released by the giant tiger when it attacked its injured younger brother.

The big tiger dived, then reappeared, with two meters of torn shark trailing from its jaws. It rolled, its body, wide as a two-hundred-liter oil drum, flashing in the sun. The big dorsal fin was like a small sail. Then it was gone, and the smaller sharks moved in and the sea boiled white and red.

For a long while after the sharks had gone Quan leaned on the gunwale, staring at the sea. Ly touched him gently on the shoulder, and he started.

"What are you thinking about?" asked his sister.

"Just wondering," said Quan. "Just wondering."

"Wondering what?"

"Just wondering where I'd be now if that big shark had arrived first."

Ly put her fingers on his lips, her eyes wide with horror.

"Don't even think about that," she whispered. "No, don't even think about it."

Then all morbid thoughts were swept away in a flurry of activity. The pump had been unmanned for twenty minutes. Aunt Binh had scrambled on deck from the engine compartment at Xuyen's first scream. Now the water was well up over the floorboards again, and rising.

The steady, measured pumping routine Captain Cu had drilled into them could not stem the flow: Lucky Dragon's aging, strained planks were letting in the sea all along her length. Now each person had to pump with all his or her strength: hard and fast, long full strokes, sweating and bumping shins and elbows in the hot engine compartment. They pumped and pumped for hours. To Ly it seemed as though she had never done anything else. They each had half an hour at a time. Half an hour of violent, frenzied activity in the stifling gloom. Their empty stomachs cramped and the smell of hot oil and bilge water made them retch. Once Aunt Binh fainted and hit her head on the Yanmar engine block as she fell. Ah Soong tore up her second-best blouse and bandaged the ugly cut; and Aunt Binh went back on the pump. By late afternoon the water was below the floorboards in the engine compartment, and Captain Cu deemed it safe

---

Word Bank

morbid (MOR bid) *adj.*: unwholesomely gloomy; gruesome

to start the Yanmar.

The engine was hard to start. Finally, though, it grumbled into life. Captain Cu and Quan held a long consultation over the school atlas chart, now very torn and stained and faded, by wind, sun, and salt water.

By the day's last light Quan drew in Lucky Dragon's estimated track. At the end of the day's run—it had been a very short one, thanks to the shark and the time lost pumping—he put a small cross and wrote the time and the date. The cross showed Lucky Dragon as being about two hundred kilometers west of the Indonesian island of Sumba.

They changed course slightly, heading almost due south, or in the direction they thought south must be.

"There are a lot of small islands around here," said Captain Cu. "Look at the map. There must be many very small ones they don't even show on this map. We don't want to hit them—or Sumba, even, if we're closer than we think—in the dark. So we go south until tomorrow, then turn east." He tapped the map. "We must hit Darwin. Well, we must hit the Australian coast near Darwin."

"And if we miss?" asked Quan.

"Well, we'll hit Cape York—see, it sticks up further north than Darwin."

"And it's also about a thousand kilometers east," pointed out Quan. "I think we should run south until tomorrow afternoon at least, then turn east. That way, we must hit Australia. Somewhere."

"Unless we miss it completely and go right on to the South Pole," said Captain Cu. He shrugged. "All right. We'll turn east at sunset tomorrow. That should take us well south of Cape York. If the engine doesn't die before then."

"Do you think it will?"

"It's pretty sick. And getting very hot. Something's going to go soon. I don't want to stop it again. I'll never get it started."

The sun went down in reds and golds which turned to green and then indigo and the stars came out quite suddenly, as though switched on.

Rolling in the low swell from the west, Lucky Dragon thumped south across the Timor Sea at five knots.

Quan slept briefly, lying on the warm deck planking. He dreamed the great shark had returned and was swimming below the boat, staring at him through the planking with its great dark eyes. He woke cold with terror. Then the dream faded and the dull hunger pain in his stomach returned. He could not go back to sleep so he lay looking at the stars and thinking about food. He wondered what sort of food they would have in Australia. Well, it didn't matter. Food was food. But he wondered what the Australians ate? They must eat like everyone else. Perhaps they ate those strange animals whose pictures he had seen. Kangaroos and wombats and koala bears. Well, whatever they ate would be welcome.

中 CHAPTER 21

Phan Thi Chi was using the primitive lavatory when the sharks returned. The sea was flat and oily and the first sunlight had just lapped Lucky Dragon in an orange glow when the two slender shapes, blacker than the dark water, slid out of the gloom astern of the boat. Phan Thi Chi saw them through the toilet lattice and his blood seemed to congeal: he

---

Word Bank   congeal (kun JEEL) *v.*: solidify or thicken by cooling; curdle

couldn't move, couldn't call out. His hand froze to the cleat he was clutching. He would have been a comic figure, locked there on the stern, except for the stark terror on his face. His mouth worked, but no words came out, only a strange gibbering.

They were not the same sharks, of course; they had not returned, as Phan Thi Chi imagined they had, to follow Lucky Dragon like remorseless sea demons through the night. They were two big blues who had merely crossed the boat's wake, picked up some interesting smells and vibrations, and changed course to investigate. It is quite probable that they could not even see the terrified man squatting on the lattice two meters above them.

Captain Cu looked straight into Phan Thi Chi's wide and terrified eyes. He leaped to his feet: "What's wrong with the old man? Quan!"

Together they raced to the stern. Phan Thi Chi could not talk: his lower jaw had sagged, and was now locked open. Strange gurglings came from his throat. Then they saw the sharks. They had dropped slightly astern. The nearest one was about three meters long. The other one was slightly bigger, about four meters long, and more heavily built. They swam with their straight high dorsal fins out of the water and sometimes the tip of their big tails broke the surface with a soft rippling.

Captain Cu and Quan had to prise[1] Phan Thi Chi's fingers from the cleat one by one. Then they carried him, his muscles still locking him into a rigid half-crouch. Gently they laid him on the deck and spoke to him. He took no notice. Xuyen cradled his gaping head and sobbed. Gradually the mouth closed, the limbs unlocked. Then came another change, almost as horrible. Phan Thi Chi seemed to melt against the deck, as though trying to force himself into the wood, to squeeze himself away from the light. They sat around him in an agony of helplessness. After a while Phan Thi Chi got on to his hands and knees. Still making strange sounds deep in his throat, he crawled forward, past the wheelhouse. They watched in cold horror as he crawled into one of the fishholds and scuttled, like a great crab, into a corner. They watched as, with thin trembling hands, he pulled the few fragments of nets which remained over him. When he was completely hidden, they turned away, unable to look into each other's faces.

Late that afternoon Xuyen came to her son as he relaxed in the last sun after his stint on the pump. Quan stopped massaging his aching right arm and looked at her.

"He—?"

"Is sleeping," said Xuyen. Her face was swollen with tears. She clasped and unclasped her hands nervously. At last, as the light died, she spoke:

"Your father is—is ill. His mind—it's broken—" She broke off, crying softly.

Quan put his arms around her.

"Mother, it will be all right," he said. "When this is over—when we get to Australia—"

She pushed him away, but gently.

"Quan, Quan, that's nonsense, you know, we'll never get to Australia. You know that. We were mad. All of us. It's too far. Too, too far. Now—"

"We will get there," said Quan. "Look how far we've come! Do you think that everything has been for nothing? Of course not."

"We should have stayed under the communists," said his mother.

"Who says so? Ah Soong? Aunt Binh? Uncle Tan? Ly? Me? Or you, mother?"

She shook her head.

"Your father. And I think he's right."

"Father is sick. He doesn't know what he's saying. And anyway, it's too late now. We

---

1. To *prise* (PRYZ) means to pry up.

couldn't go back. We couldn't find our way back, for a start!" As though suddenly remembering something, Quan left his mother hastily and darted into the wheelhouse. Over startled protests from Captain Cu, he ripped the school atlas chart from the bulkhead.

His mother was standing where he had left her, passive, quiet, watching the fading red glow in the west. Quan waved the chart before her. He stabbed it with his finger.

"See! That's Rach Gia and—" another stab— "that's where we are. At least, that's where Captain Cu and I think we are. And—" another jab—"that's Australia! We're almost there."

Then he tore the chart across and across and threw the pieces over the stern. They fluttered and twirled in the breeze like dying leaves.

"Now we can't go back," said Quan. "We really couldn't find our way."

"Then you must take us to Australia," said his mother with sudden firmness. She put her thin hand on his shoulder.

"You see, Quan, you are head of the family now. Your father is too sick. It is all up to you. Everything."

Quan hesitated.

"I will do my best. Until father is better."

His mother shook her head.

"No. Even if he gets better, he will never be the same. No, Quan, you are head of the family now."

She turned and went forward, leaving him alone on the dark stern. He was still sitting thinking in the dark when he felt Lucky Dragon turn. Looking up, he saw that Captain Cu had swung the boat so that the last faint glow in the west was dead astern. Lucky Dragon was lined up on her final easterly run in to Australia.

They each had a glass of warm water for supper. Uncle Tan hauled in his line a dozen times during the night. The hook seemed to mock him with its emptiness.

Their hunger refused to let them sleep. They sat and talked, remembering the old times, trying to reassure each other that the coming new times would be better. They created huge banquets, trying to outdo each other in sheer extravagance. And then it got too painful to even talk about food.

Phan Thi Chi lay beneath the dirty nets in the filthy fishhold and refused to speak.

In the first pale light of dawn Quan, waking from a shallow doze troubled by vague, uneasy dreams, was startled to see Aunt Binh in her torn black skirt, faded to a grubby gray by sea water and sun, crawling up and down the decks, scrabbling with her fingers in the seams, probing the cracks where the wheelhouse planking met the deck.

He thought of his father in the fishhold and shuddered. Not Aunt Binh too! And who next? Would they all go mad? Would a boatful of insane people drift ashore in Australia?

He was lying just in front of the wheelhouse, and Aunt Binh, lifting her head, saw that he was awake. She smiled and waddled towards him on her knees, her hands cupped together in front of her. He eyed her apprehensively. Her eyes were shining wildly. Well, she's only a poor thin woman, he reassured himself as she approached. I can hold her down and call Captain Cu if she gets violent.

Aunt Binh shoved her cupped hands out to him.

"Look!"

Sticking to her dirty palms were about five dozen equally dirty grains of rice.

"I knew we must have spilled some," she said happily. "No matter how careful you are, you always spill rice!"

"Aunt Binh," said Quan feelingly, "you are wonderful!"

Ah Soong cooked the grubby rice with all the care which, in other days, she would have bestowed on the very best chicken or fish Gia Dinh market could have provided. It swelled in the cooking, as rice does, so that there was enough for one small teaspoonful each, washed down with the water in which it had been boiled. They drank the dusty-tasting, gritty rice-water for two reasons: because some of the rice goodness would be in it, and because Ah Soong, drawing the water for the meal, had made an alarming discovery: there were only about five liters of fresh water left.

CHAPTER 22

When Quan was not steering or pumping he watched the sharks. There was nothing else to do. Sometimes he would pull in Uncle Tan's line and make a new cloth lure for the rusty hook. But mostly he just watched the sharks.

He hated and feared them but he had to admit they were beautiful. Their backs were a deep, deep blue and their bellies were a brilliant white which flashed silvery through the pale green water. Each shark had a passenger: a sixty-centimeter-long pilot fish stuck to its head. Sometimes the pilot fish detached themselves and swam on their own. But most of the time they sat tight and let the sharks do the swimming, which they did very easily with lazy movements of their big tails. Quan had read somewhere that the pilot fish got their name because they were supposed to lead sharks to food. As far as he could see, this pair did not do much leading. They gave the impression of just having come along for the ride.

"A pretty nice life you have, don't you?" he asked them bitterly one hot afternoon. "A pretty nice life."

That was the afternoon they drank the last of the fresh water. The sky was a pale blue, like denim which has been washed and beaten and washed and dried in the sun so that there is only a shadow of color left. The sea was flat and sighing with a long low swell from the west and quite empty from horizon to horizon.

That was also the afternoon the Yanmar died. It died quite suddenly: one moment it was thudding away, and then it stopped. Just like that. Lucky Dragon's deep metallic heartbeat had stopped. They sat silent, appalled. A thin oily tendril of smoke coiled out of the broken smokestack and trickled across the sea. Hot oil hissed and bubbled as it ebbed from the Yanmar's veins and arteries. There was the slow ticking of hot metal cooling.

Uncle Tan, who was on the pump, put his face over the engine hatch coaming and said, quite unnecessarily, "Engine's stopped."

Lucky Dragon slowed and stopped. The sharks were puzzled. They swam right up under the stern. The pilot fish detached themselves and swam about agitatedly. Then the pilot fish reattached themselves and the sharks left, swimming strongly southeast as though they had just remembered an important engagement.

Without the Yanmar it was very quiet: the rasp and splash of the pump seemed a gross intrusion on the huge silence of the sea.

The moon was nearly full. It laid a golden track across the water. Several times they thought they saw boats moving in the moon track. They shouted and whistled and made a fire. They exhausted themselves trying to attract the attention of wave tops and moon shadows.

Just before dawn a small breeze came from the northwest. It was a warm, soft wind, barely stirring the sea. Captain Cu felt it on his face and prayed for it to blow Lucky Dragon to Australia. But it died as the sun rose.

The day was calm and very hot. Lucky Dragon ached in the sun. Her boards cracked

> Several times they thought they saw boats moving in the moon track. They shouted and whistled and made a fire. They exhausted themselves trying to attract the attention of wave tops and moon shadows.

and bent. Her fishholds stank.

The family sat in the shade of the wheelhouse, moving as the sun moved, or as Lucky Dragon turned on the swell, following the wheelhouse shadow on the burning decks. At noon there was hardly any shadow at all.

Quan wished he had not thrown the chart away. He tried to remember it in his mind, to extend the ballpoint track to where they would be now.

"We can't be far from Australia," he said to Uncle Tan one broiling afternoon, two days after the last of the water. Uncle Tan shrugged. His face had grown so thin that his cheekbones jutted like shelves over the lower half of his face.

"It doesn't matter," he croaked. "We're not going to make it, anyway. Look at that." He stuck out his stump. "The sharks won't get much off that, will they?"

The flesh had shrunk so that Quan could see the shape of the thighbone. Quan shuddered.

That afternoon Quan's father came out of the fishhold and tried to jump into the sea, screaming. Although he had never been a particularly strong man, and had not eaten for days, it took Quan and Captain Cu all their strength to hold him. He screamed all the while, his eyes staring at something beyond them. Then, quite suddenly, he stopped struggling.

They helped him into the shadow of the wheelhouse and he sat down.

"It's all right," he said calmly. "It's all right now." He sat there for the rest of the day, smiling. As the sun set he stirred briefly, looking around at the boat and the family with the surprised air of someone who has been awakened from a deep sleep.

"It's all right," he said. "It's really quite all right."

He died quietly some time during the night. When they found him the next morning he was leaning against the stern gunwale. His eyes were open and he seemed to be smiling slightly. He was facing north.

"He was looking at Vietnam," said Ah Soong softly. It was the first time she had spoken for days. Gently the old lady closed the staring eyes and Quan and Captain Cu laid Phan Thi Chi on the deck.

That evening a rain squall came out of the east. It was a small line squall cutting a narrow path across the moonlit sea and it took them by surprise. The rain made a sharp hissing noise as it cut the flat warm water. It passed Lucky Dragon in a few minutes and they had no time to catch more than a cupful each. Captain Cu raged. "That's what you get for being stupid," he said, angrily. "Ignorant! I heard it long before it got here. I should have known what it was. But I haven't been at sea long enough."

"But we got some," said Ly. "I got a whole glassful."

"Make it last," growled Captain Cu. "Make it last."

The rain slicked Phan Thi Chi's hair down and plastered his clothes to him so that he looked like a boy asleep in the moonlight. Xuyen crouched beside him and wept. Quan cried, too, but he went up to the bows and cried alone. And wished that you could weep tears enough to drink.

And after the weeping was over, there was still the matter of Phan Thi Chi's body.

It was Uncle Tan who broached the idea. He did it hesitantly, aware of the revulsion it

---

Word Bank **revulsion** (ree VUL shin) *n.*: a strong feeling of disgust, distaste, or dislike; loathing

would arouse.

The family listened with mounting horror. Xuyen fled, weeping, to the bows. Ly followed her, and put her arms around her mother's heaving shoulders. Quan, sick with disgust, forced himself to listen to Uncle Tan's idea.

When Uncle Tan had finished, Quan looked around in anguish.

"What shall I do?" he asked, his cheeks wet with tears. "It's horrible—horrible! I must ask my mother—my sister—"

Captain Cu said, brutally: "No. It is your father. You are head of the family. You decide."

Quan stood up. He looked at the thin bodies of the family, the tired faces. From below came the hoarse rasping of the pump. That will go soon, he thought: and then we will fill and sink. Perhaps this terrible thing Uncle Tan suggests will give us a chance. He nodded.

"All right. Captain Cu?"

"I'll do it," said Captain Cu. "And Tan will help me."

Quan turned his eyes away while Captain Cu and Uncle Tan manhandled a fishhold cover aft and lashed his father's wasted body to it. Quan could not watch while they tied a flat board to the dead man's chest and wrote on it in sump oil: PLEASE! WE ARE VIET RUFUGEES ADRIFT WEST OF DARWIN! NO FOOD OR WATER! PLEASE HELP US!

There was a scrape as the hold cover was dragged over the gunwale; a splash. And Phan Thi Chi drifted away on his last journey. Quan stifled a sob. All the rest of the day he never looked back, and the next day there was no sign of his father.

But when his mother looked at him there was sheer horror in her eyes.

Quan started from an uneasy sleep with the knowledge that something was wrong. Some sound—he sat up abruptly. No—no sound.

Silence except for the soft slapping of the sea. Then he realized what was missing. The pump's metallic rattle and cough. He got up, his head spinning with the effort.

Captain Cu was sitting on the engine hatch coaming. His face was pale in the moonlight: a sickly, deathlike pallor.

"Yes," he said, before Quan could speak. "Pump's gone. Piston worn to nothing. What could you expect? Days and days and days of pumping. And now...." His voice died away.

"We can't be far from Australia now," said Quan.

"Far enough," said Captain Cu. "I've measured the leak. We'll stay afloat about thirty-six hours. No more. Then—" He snapped his fingers. "Pouff! All for nothing."

Quan tried to picture Lucky Dragon sinking: the slow dying. The water first around their ankles, then around their necks. Then floating free, with nothing beneath their feet. Like a man being hanged. He wondered how far down the bottom of the sea was. He closed his eyes and saw Lucky Dragon sinking slowly, turning over and over; and them following, feet kicking in the black sea. Through shoals of fish, floating weed, turtles, sharks, cleaving a sparkling darkness to the final mud. He shivered. Then realized that Captain Cu was shaking him.

"Yes," he said, dreamily, because he was very tired. "Yes?"

"I said thirty-six hours," said Captain Cu. "That may be long enough! Look—! West, there where the stars stop!"

Where the stars stop. For a moment Quan thought Captain Cu had lost his mind. Then he saw what the fisherman meant. The myriad stars bent over them in a brilliant bow against the black vault of the sky—and suddenly stopped, a long way above the horizon. It was as though someone had ruled a line across the sky.

"Clouds," said Captain Cu. "Clouds coming

from the west. Rain, Quan! And wind, maybe—enough wind to push us ashore in Australia before we sink!"

When the rain and wind arrived it was startlingly cold: they sheltered behind the wheelhouse, but as Lucky Dragon kept turning in the wind and choppy sea, no position was in the lee of the weather for long.

So they huddled together like terrified sheep in the corner of a slaughter pen, listening to the wind and sea in the dark. It seemed as though the sun would never rise again. They were so weak and so tired that they did not think of catching any of the cold rain. They just let it run into their mouths.

During the cold gray hour before dawn Quan heard another sound between the rush of wind and the hissing rain: the long heavy swash of water in Lucky Dragon's holds. He almost cried with relief when the sun rose, pale yellow at first, then quickly a golden flare as it burned away the cloud and mist. It would be hateful to drown at any time, but somehow to go down in the dark seemed specially horrible. It made his skin crawl.

The wind died with the sun and the sea was flat with a long low swell which scarcely lifted Lucky Dragon as it passed. Now that the pump was finished Lucky Dragon was making water fast: she had developed a noticeable list to port during the night so that it was rather comfortable to lean against the sloping starboard side of the wheelhouse in the early sun. So easy to go to sleep, too. A long, long sleep....Quan forced himself to get up. He shook the dozing Captain Cu.

"Wake up! Wake up!" He looked at the bedraggled, sleeping family and felt terror rising in his throat.

"Wake up! Wake up!" he screamed again, his voice cracking. He knelt beside his sister and seized her shoulders. He shook her roughly.

"Ly! Wake up. You must wake up!"

Exhausted eyes, glazed with hunger, stared at him resentfully. "Just a little longer, Quan," mumbled Ly. "Just a few minutes." He dragged her to her feet. She spat at him resentfully, tried weakly to pull away.

The others watched them dully.

"You must get up," he said. "Don't you see? If we just lie here, we'll sleep until we die! We must start getting the water out of the boat! We must be near Australia now—we must watch for ships!" He stopped, panting. His head spun.

Captain Cu got up, swaying a little, and helped Uncle Tan to his single foot.

"You're right, Quan. To have come so far—"

Gradually, muttering protests, herded by Captain Cu and Quan, the family awoke.

Xuyen leaned on the gunwale, staring at the sea. "No Australia," she said flatly. "It was all a dream. All a dream."

The tears ran unchecked down her face. Quan put his arms around her and his mother seemed to crumble away in his embrace. She seemed suddenly as small and vulnerable as a child. He stood there, helpless.

Then Uncle Tan shouted. And shouted again. He pointed with his dented crutch.

And Captain Cu bellowed with delight.

Across three-quarters of the eastern horizon a thin, wavery line had appeared, looking like a line drawn in charcoal pencil on a watercolor seascape. It lifted, sank, appeared and disappeared from view as Lucky Dragon moved on the sea. But always it came back.

Land.

Land!

They gaped at it, open-mouthed. Then they laughed and cried at the same time. They lined the gunwale and stared at it as though frightened it would go away.

"How far do you think it is?" Quan asked Captain Cu.

Captain Cu took off his helmet and scratched his head. He squinted into the sun.

"Oh, about thirty, forty kilometers. Not

more."

"If only we had the engine still."

"Or sails. Or oars."

"Well, we don't have anything," said Aunt Binh. "Except water in the holds. So stop wishing and start working, eh? Come on, come on."

She shooed Captain Cu and Quan aft to get buckets and empty cans from the engine compartment to use as bailers.

Keeping Lucky Dragon afloat was murderous work for starving, exhausted people. After a few hours it seemed to Quan that he was no longer in his body, but outside it, looking on while a strange glassy-eyed puppet with his face made futile scoops at the rising tide of oily water in the holds.

They realized soon enough that the sea was winning. It crept up inexorably, mocking their efforts. Lucky Dragon settled deeper in the water and her list to port increased two or three degrees an hour. Simple arithmetic told Quan that they had another day at most before the tired boat turned turtle.

And so they dashed at the water all day, lifting their eyes now and then to assure themselves that the land was still there.

It had shape and form now: a low shore, rising into ragged brown hills. And a huge blue sky rearing behind it, a sky which seemed to pulsate with a strange light. A sky which seemed to shimmer above limitless space.

It was like nothing they had ever seen before.

Ah Soong did not move all day. The old woman lay in the angle of the wheelhouse wall and deck, an angle turned into a comfortable couch by Lucky Dragon's list, and gazed at the sea.

Quan knelt beside her in the blazing afternoon and asked her if she wanted to get into the shadows. Ah Soong shook her head. She seemed to have shrunk inwards upon herself, like a doll from which the stuffing has leaked. In the hot sunlight she drew her stained, faded, once-best jade-green jacket about her as though cold, clutching it jealously to her with papery hands.

They stopped bailing at sunset. The land was still there, a little closer, and a tide or current was pushing the listing Lucky Dragon slowly towards it. And they were simply too exhausted to do anything more.

A feathery touch on his shoulder wakened Quan. He sat up, startled. The moon had just risen, full and orange, riding on the sea's rim.

Ah Soong stood before him in the bright moonlight. She put a finger to her lips and motioned him to follow her. Surprised, he stood up. The family slept like the dead around him. Ah Soong walked slowly forward and sat down with a sigh in the bows. The big rising moon was behind her: her skin seemed to glow. The old lady turned and looked at the moon. Quan sat beside her, waiting. He was very tired.

"I am not going to the Golden Mountain," said Ah Soong after a while. She paused. "I am going to my ancestors," she said. She sighed. "I always wanted to go home to China. Even when I was dead. To be buried there. Every Chinese wants to go back to China. Some day. But now—" She sighed again, a thin whisper of sound. Quan was silent. What could he say?

Then, briskly, she rose. She took off her once-best

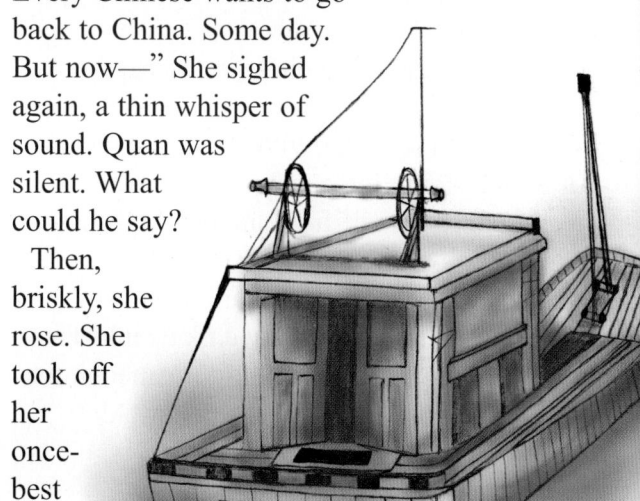

jade-green jacket and handed it to Quan.

He protested: "Ah Soong, I don't—" Then he stopped. The jacket was heavy. It dragged his arm down.

"Put it on," said Ah Soong. The jacket had always been big for her, and it fitted Quan's slim frame, although a bit tight under the armpits.

"Feel the hems," whispered Ah Soong, hunching her thin old shoulders against the cool evening breeze.

He felt the gold sewn there, thin strips in a sausage of cloth sewn along the hem of the jacket.

"Fifteen taels," sighed Ah Soong. "All my savings. All my life. There."

Quan opened his mouth in protest, but Ah Soong raised her hands.

"No. You are the head of the family now. You will need it in Australia."

"I'll keep it for you, Ah Soong, and you can put it in a bank in Australia," said Quan.

The old woman smiled.

"You just keep it," she said. She shivered slightly.

"You're cold," said Quan. "Here—take your jacket back—"

"No. There's another one—in my bag."

"I'll get it," said Quan.

When Quan returned with her jacket, he saw Ah Soong stumbling against the gunwale. Too weak to keep herself from falling, Ah Soong tumbled into the sea.

She had gone over the moonless side of the boat, where the shadows lay dark as ink. They called her name and wept and screamed at the sea and the night, but they never saw Ah Soong again.

CHAPTER 23

Lucky Dragon was dying. They could feel it as the first pale light came across the sea. During the night the water in the holds had deepened and the list had increased so that the port gunwale almost touched the sea.

There was a small sea running, breaking on the muddy, mangrove shore which lay now only a few hundred meters to the east. Behind the mangroves a long beach, empty in the dawn, stretched for kilometers.

Now the small waves rushing towards the beach began breaking against Lucky Dragon. The boat groaned and rolled, dipping her port gunwale, staggering under each blow. Spray, warm and salty, soaked the family.

Then, with an impact that set her quivering from bow to stern, Lucky Dragon struck something—a rock, a reef, Quan did not know. They clung to the wheelhouse in terror as waves broke white against the hull and ominous crackings and grindings came from beneath their feet. The first line of mud and mangroves was only a hundred meters away now, but a rising spring tide was driving the low surf, and the surging white-streaked water looked frightening. Besides, none of them were good swimmers.

During the night, Quan had improvised a sort of communal life-belt—there were no individual ones aboard the boat—from the empty water container and three other smaller plastic bottles he had found in the fishholds. Now he pushed the unwieldy contraption over the high starboard gunwale, hanging on to it by a length of thick line from the remains of the fish nets.

Grimly, the family clung to the starboard gunwale as Lucky Dragon fought her last fight with the sea. A wave larger than the rest wrenched her suddenly free from the obstruction. Lucky Dragon surged forward sluggishly. The next wave swung her stern over: the tons and tons of water in the fishholds, still traveling in the original direction, surged to port. The sudden changing of her center of balance was more than Lucky Dragon could stand. The port gunwale dipped, another wave burst against the starboard gunwale, the sea poured in over the submerged port gunwale, and Lucky Dragon died. The family struggled over the starboard hull and keel as she rolled, with huge whooshes of escaping air, and clung, panting with fatigue and fright, to the upturned, barnacle-covered bottom.

Quan was the last to leave. He stood up, the raft line still about his wrist, and prayed briefly that Ah Soong's heavy jacket wouldn't drag him to the bottom. Then he remembered something. He bent, briefly, and touched Lucky Dragon's scarred, stained planking.

"Thank you," he said. "Goodbye." Then he jumped, as Lucky Dragon started her final voyage.

For a few horrifying moments he thought Ah Soong's gold would drown him. Then his head broke water and he was clinging to one of the raft's plastic bottles. A gleaming oil slick, some fishnet floats and few pieces of timber marked Lucky Dragon's grave.

"Swim," shouted Captain Cu at him, "swim!"

Kicking, thrashing with their free arms, they inched towards the beach. Sometimes the undertow pulled them back: sometimes the waves pushed them shorewards. Soon they were shivering with cold and exhaustion. The salt water stung their eyes.

Then Quan felt mud beneath his feet: sticky mud, gritty with broken shells. A wave lifted him and his feet trod water. Then the mud was back. He felt the shells slice his water-softened feet but he scrabbled desperately for a foothold. Then they were all standing, still clutching the remains of the raft. Swaying like drunken people they staggered ashore, clinging to the slimy mangroves for support.

They collapsed on the dry sand beyond the mangroves. Nobody said anything. There did not seem to be much to say. They slept for a while, right there on the sand in their wet clothes. When they awoke the sun was high in a cloudless blue sky. Quan thought it the bluest sky he had ever seen.

"Listen," said Uncle Tan, holding up his hand. Two hundred meters to the east the beach rose to a low ridge which hid the coastline beyond. From behind the ridge came a muted roaring.

"A car—a truck—" said Captain Cu. They were all standing now, their hearts pounding.

Something shot over the ridge in a spray of wet sand, bouncing and swerving.

"Jeep," said Captain Cu.

Apprehensively they watched the vehicle approach, weaving as the driver picked the hardest spots on the wet sand.

Quan looked at Captain Cu questioningly, but the former fisherman shook his head firmly.

"No. Australia was your idea. And you speak good English. And—" he grinned despite his tiredness, "besides, you're head of the family now."

The Land-Rover—Captain Cu was wrong—stopped in a flurry of wet sand. A large man in white shirt and shorts got out and looked at the little group of Vietnamese doubtfully.

Quan, followed by Ly and Captain Cu, walked across the sand to the stranger.

"Please," he said, pronouncing as carefully as he could the speech he had rehearsed over two thousand kilometers of tropic sea, "please, we are Vietnamese refugees. We want to stay in Australia."

The man gaped at them.

Ly stepped forward and stood beside Quan.

"And we want," she said slowly and clearly, as though reciting a lesson, "we want a fair go."

Then she fainted.

"Bloody dinkum," said the big man. "Bloody dinkum." He turned to the Land-Rover, from which two more big men were already scrambling.

"Ray. Norm. Give us a hand here. Bloody dinkum!"

國 EPILOGUE

A big orange and black grouper lives in Lucky Dragon's wheelhouse now: he spends most of his time floating half in and half out of the doorway, watching with his great goggle eyes the little bright reef fish flash and sparkle among the young coral growing on the tilted foredeck. The forward fishhold is occupied by a thick, quick tempered purple-gray moray eel with fierce eyes and teeth like a ripsaw.

On stormy days, when the short steep swells run in from the Timor Sea, Lucky Dragon stirs slightly. Faint tremors run through her timbers, and the old boat sighs and groans as though sailing again. But every day the industrious coral polyps[2] add more tiny cells to their crystalline castle, and soon Lucky Dragon will be hidden forever.

Quan is in his last year at school. He has done well, and won a scholarship to university. He still wants to be an engineer.

Ly has also done well at school.

She is also very popular. She is good at tennis and swimming, and represents her school in both sports. She wants to be a nurse when she leaves school.

After a hard first year in Australia, Xuyen has adapted to her new life. She works in an import-export company during the day, and at night attends English classes. These days her English is almost as good as her children's.

Captain Cu married Aunt Binh. He still says she is the most remarkable woman he has ever known. He still has his old helmet with its ragged hole, but never wears it. Captain Cu works very hard in a car factory. He saves most of his money for the restaurant he and his wife hope to open soon. Sometimes, it is true, he stops off to visit with friends after work, but Aunt Binh never nags him. After all, she says, if a man who works hard can't have some fun, what is the point of working? Today's Aunt Binh, in fact, is so unlike the Aunt Binh of the old days that Quan often finds himself staring at her as though she were a stranger. He agrees with Captain Cu that she is a remarkable woman. She has a job in a knitwear shop and is well-liked by everyone.

Uncle Tan works as a mechanic in a car-repair shop and has a new leg, a proper, shaped, knee and ankle-jointed leg which, he says, is almost as good as the one he left at Hue. He lives with Xuyen and Quan and Ly.

Quan added Ah Soong's gold to Phan Thi Chi's gold and it made a good little pile. Then he divided it equally between them all. He did it so tactfully that nobody protested too much.

Xuyen used her share to put a deposit on a small semi-detached house. Uncle Tan helps with the mortgage repayments, which are not too large.

The only souvenir of the old days in Ho Chi Minh City is a five-year-old photograph of the family. It was taken by a neighbor. The cheap print is turning yellow now, and the image was never too sharp. But it shows Phan Thi Chi, Xuyen, and Quan and Ly, outside thirteen Bach Dang. And behind them, smiling, stands Ah Soong.

---

2. The *coral polyps* are the little cylindrical-shaped animals that make up the coral reef.

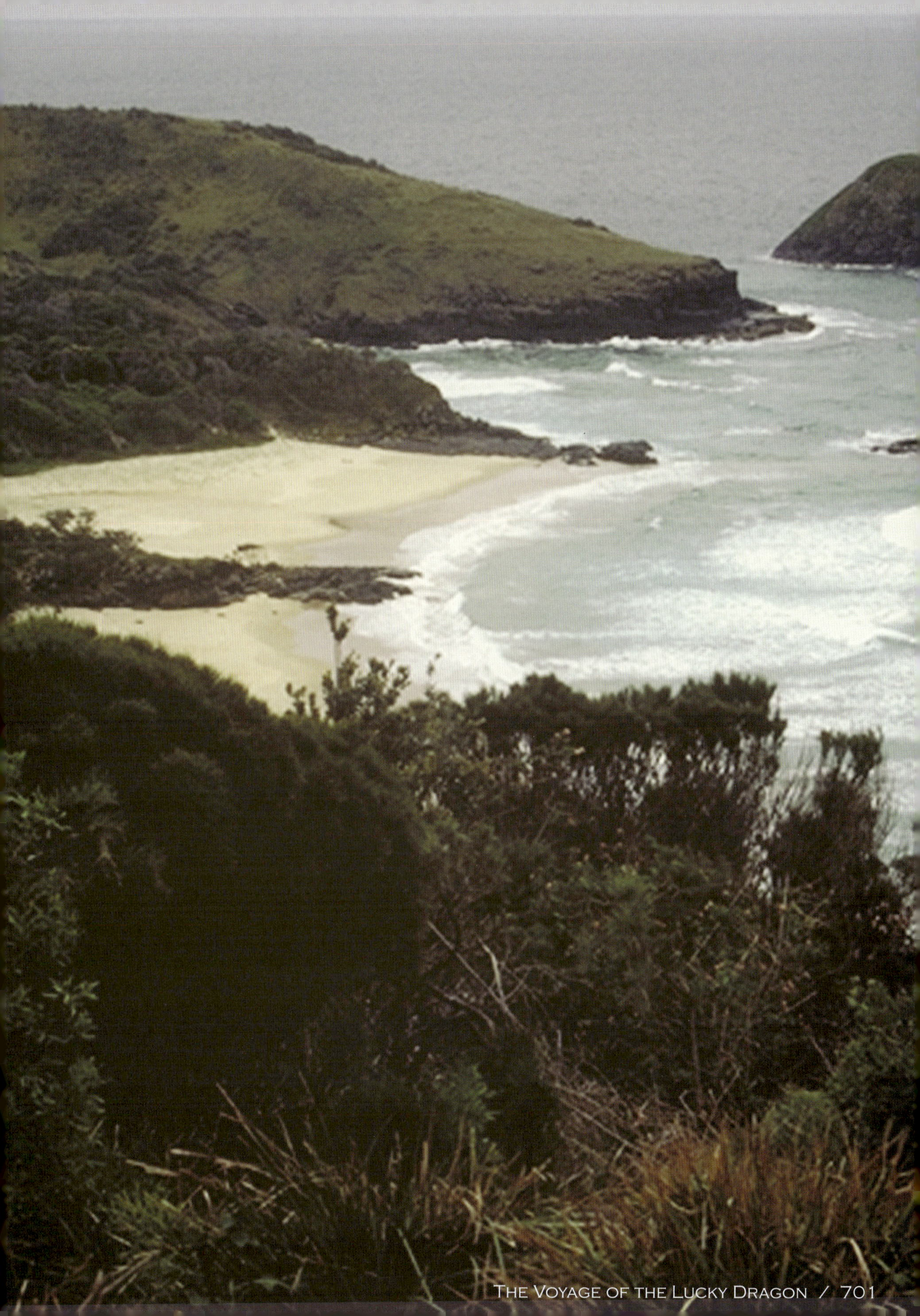

Studying the Selection

First Impressions *What might the family have felt, as they came ashore? What might they have thought? How did you feel on finishing the novel? How did the epilogue add to your experience? Would the story have been as satisfying without it?*

✓ Quick Review

1. How did Quan avoid being injured by the tiger shark?
2. Why does Xuyen tell Quan he is now the head of the family and must take the family to Australia?
3. Chapter 22 is filled with loss. Name at least four losses.
4. What did Quan build that helped the family reach shore safely?

In-depth Thinking

5. Why might the author have included the scene where a larger shark attacks the one Quan encountered?
6. What might have caused Quan to tear up the map he relies on so completely?
7. Of all the family losses experienced in Part Five, which are the greatest and why?
8. In what way is the story's end similar to the family's discovery of Captain Cu aboard the Lucky Dragon?

Drawing Conclusions

9. Of the many characters in *The Voyage of the Lucky Dragon*, why is it significant that Phan Thi Chi is the one who is defeated by the voyage?
10. How do Phan Thi Chi and Ah Soong continue to live within the family?

Focusing on Theme

Complete the following activities for greater understanding of theme.

1. Which theme do you feel is strongest in *The Voyage of the Lucky Dragon*? This could be a theme already discussed, or one you've just uncovered. Write an essay showing why this theme is so important to the novel. Include supporting passages from the novel.

2. Write a brief essay explaining the purpose of theme in literature, drawing on information from the text and other literature you've read this year. How has theme enriched your reading?

3. Try this: Think of a truth or theme of great importance to you. Make an outline for a story built around that truth and share it with a classmate. Then, think of a recent event that should be more widely known. This could be something that happened to you or an acquaintance. Discuss the event with others and see what themes emerge. Why is this event important to relate? Now, which method is most effective in getting across meaning? The story written around the theme, or the story that had to be told? Why?

Creating and Writing

1. In Part Five of the novel we see a character breaking under stress. In our 'real' world, many people have similar problems. Although research has helped us understand the causes of mental illness, people are often unwilling to recognize these ailments as real. Many are still frightened by people with these problems and find it difficult to reach out to them. As a way to deepen your own understanding, research some area of a mental disorder or a related problem. Ask your teacher to help you find suitable material. What are the causes? Are treatments available today? What had been the treatment and understanding of the disorder in the past? What progress has been made in recent years? Write an essay about the subject, and share it with the class.

2. Imagine a year has passed since the Lucky Dragon sank and the family landed in Australia. Use the voice of one of the characters in writing a letter to someone back in Vietnam. Describe the challenges of the past year. What was most difficult about your adjustment? What were the highlights? What were your feelings during this first year? What hopes do you have for the person back home? What questions do you have about your homeland? For this activity, you may need your teacher's help in finding information on the experience of Vietnamese immigrants in America or Australia.

3. In some form, other than an essay, recreate your favorite scene from *The Voyage of the Lucky Dragon.* You might create a diorama, drawing, poster, or collage. You might join a group to act out the scene. One student might serve as the character/subject of a group interview and answer interesting questions about that particular scene. Your recreation of the scene should bring out the excitement, tragedy, or joy of that event. In closing, tell your audience why this scene is the most memorable for you.

Mosdos Press Literature

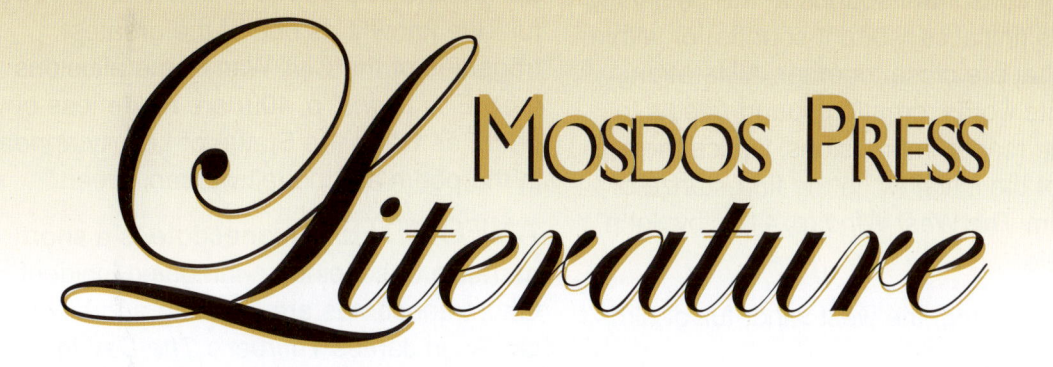

- Glossary of Literary Terms
- Glossary
- Index of Authors and Titles

Glossary of Literary Terms

ALLITERATION: **Alliteration** is the repetition of consonant sounds at the beginning of words (initial consonant sounds) or within words that are close together. Alliteration highlights words, creating sound effects to reinforce reader impressions. Notice the repetition of the initial "w" in the first stanza of the poem *The West Wind* (p. 413), by John Masefield:

It's a warm wind, the west wind, full of birds' cries;
I never hear the west wind but tears are in my eyes.
For it comes from the west lands, the old brown hills,
And April's in the west wind, and daffodils.

This repetition builds a musical foundation, unifying the ideas presented in the stanza. The reader can almost hear the west wind as an accompaniment to the poem.

ALLUSION: **Allusion** is the use of references to famous persons, places, events, objects, literature, and art in fiction, poetry, and nonfiction. Allusions are important social, cultural, and historical symbols, used by authors as cues for the reader and in order to bring a story to life. Often, we have only a superficial familiarity with an allusion—we may have never read Shakespeare or Homer, listened to Bach or Beethoven, or seen the Taj Mahal—but these allusions *still* create images and associations. In *In the Middle of a Pitch* (p. 108), the wooden fences of the ball field advertise CHEER, BRYL CREEM, and COLGATE WITH GARDOL—details that make the scene *real*, because *we know these words*. In Ray Bradbury's *The Drummer Boy of Shiloh*, the general (p. 148) considers a phrase "fitting for Mr. Longfellow"—Henry Wadsworth Longfellow. The use of *Shiloh* itself is powerful—we know it as one of the greatest tragedies of the Civil War. Some allusions (see *Ellis Island*, p. 409) are made less obviously, as when the Statue of Liberty appears in the poem as "the tall woman, green."

ANECDOTE: An **anecdote** is a short narrative describing an intriguing incident. Often, anecdotes are amusing and biographical. As in James Thurber's *The Day the Dam Broke* (p. 558), which is a comical nonfiction piece, an anecdote may be the basis for an essay or short story. Since all of the events of the story issue from a single episode—here a mock catastrophe—anecdotes do not have complicated plots. *Dandelions* (p. 425), the poem by Deborah Austin, is also anecdotal in its marvelous description of dandelion guerrilla warfare. Anecdotes may also be described as having an off-the-cuff, unstudied quality; such accounts generally describe events of a less-than-serious nature.

ANTAGONIST: An **antagonist** works against (opposes) the hero of the story or poem. The antagonist may be a person, a force of nature, a ruler, a segment of society, or the conscience working within the hero's mind. In the one-act drama *The Pen of My Aunt* (p. 483) by Gordon Daviot, the intruding Nazi Corporal is the antagonist. He has invaded Madame's home and seems intent on taking the stranger into custody. Thus the antagonists here are the Corporal, the entire German Army, and World War II, which is the backdrop of the story. See *Conflict* and *Protagonist*.

AUTOBIOGRAPHY: **Autobiography** is a category of nonfiction in which the author tells of his or her life. The excerpt from *I Know What the Red Clay Looks Like* (p. 530) by Rita Dove, tells the reader how Ms. Dove was influenced to become a professional writer by family events during her childhood. For example, in the following lines we see clearly why Ms. Dove chose her life's work: "Listening to these stories being told and how they would affect their listeners was quite an influence on my own desire to tell stories. I also did a lot of reading." Notice she writes her story in the first-person, using the pronouns "I" and "my."

BALLAD: A **ballad** is a poem with a story line, often treating adventure, romance, or universal ideas. Most ballads are written in four or six-line stanzas with regular rhyme and rhythm. Many ballads contain a refrain, a repeated stanza. Ballads were originally unwritten and sung by balladeers, to spread news or tell important stories. Thus, they were passed along orally, and only later written down; some have survived for thousands of years. Of course, many ballads are more recent. *The Walrus and the Carpenter* (p. 446) by Lewis Carroll, is a ballad from Carroll's famous satirical novel, *Alice in Wonderland.* In this ballad, the reader learns of a walrus and a carpenter who go for a walk on a beach. They persuade some unsuspecting oysters to join them. Finally, after the oysters are tired and hungry, the walrus and the carpenter eat the oysters for dinner. Each stanza is six lines long, there is no refrain, and the rhyme scheme is A-B-C-B-D-B. The number of syllables in each line of each stanza is 8, 6, 8, 6, 8, 6, with the accent on every second syllable. This gives this ballad a singsong quality. For instance:

Four other Oysters followed them,
And yet another four;
And thick and fast they came at last,
And more, and more, and more—
All hopping through the frothy waves,
And scrambling to the shore.

CHARACTER: A **character** is a person (or animal) taking part in the action of a literary work. A **main**, or major, character is the most important character in the story, novel, poem, or play. This character is often referred to as *the hero*, *the heroine*, or *the protagonist.* For instance, Patsy Barnes is the main character of the story *The Finish of Patsy Barnes* (p. 225), by Paul Laurence Dunbar. A **minor** character plays a smaller role in the development of a literary work; nonetheless, this character is needed to build the plot and theme of the work. For example, in the one-act play *The Pen of My Aunt* (p. 483) by Gordon Daviot, the maidservant Simone has a small but important role. She is vital to The Stranger's escape from the Nazis. A **flat** character is one-sided or a stereotype, not well-developed. The Grandfather in James Thurber's *The Day the Dam Broke* (p. 558) is a flat character. We see him as a befuddled old man overreacting to a perceived dangerous situation. He faints and must be carried around by his family until he regains consciousness. Thurber never tells the reader any more about this old man, so he is seen as somewhat incompetent. On the other hand, a **round** character is well-developed and exhibits varied traits and characteristics throughout the literary work. The character of Walter Plummer, the untalented clarinetist in *The No-Talent Kid* (p. 78) by Kurt Vonnegut, is written as a determined, never-say-die character who lacks musical talent but has no lack of creativity when it comes to getting what he wants. A **dynamic** character is one who changes and matures during the course of the work. In the story *Accounts Settled* (p. 30) by Paul Annixter, the main character, Gordon Bent, is a young, frightened sixteen-year-old boy with too much responsibility. By the end of the story, he has matured into a self-confident young man, proud of all he has done. On the other hand, a **static** character is one who does not change. In the poem *The Walrus and the Carpenter* (p. 446) by Lewis Carroll, the Walrus never changes; he remains the trickster who, through wordplay and guile, charms the unsuspecting Oysters into joining him and the Carpenter for dinner—only the Oysters are the dinner.

CHARACTERIZATION: Authors use **characterization** to create and develop believable literary characters. Basically, there are two methods of characterization—direct and indirect. When using direct characterization, the author directly tells the reader what a character is like in appearance and in personality. An example of **direct characterization** occurs at the beginning of *The Finish of Patsy Barnes* (p. 225) by Paul Laurence Dunbar, as Dunbar introduces the title character to the reader: "His name was Patsy Barnes, and he was a denizen of Little Africa. In fact, he lived on Douglass Street….He was black, and very much so….Patsy was incorrigible. Even into the confines of Little Africa had penetrated the truant officer and the terrible penalty of the compulsory education law." The reader learns many things about Patsy in the first sentences because the author has revealed so much. But with **indirect characterization**, the author reveals the character's personality through appearance, words, and actions. Sometimes the reader is told what other characters in the work say or think about this person, and this allows the reader to judge the character. In Jack London's *To Build a Fire* (p. 118), the reader is not given a lot of direct description of the man who is the main character. However, the reader sees this man make serious mistakes that eventually cost him his life. He hadn't listened to the more experienced men and had ignored their advice about extreme temperatures. "It certainly was cold, was his thought. That man from Sulphur Creek had spoken the truth when telling how cold it sometimes got in the country. And he had laughed at him at the time! That showed one must not be too sure of things. There was no mistake about it, it was cold." Thus, the reader realizes that this man is stubborn and overly self-confident. Instead of heeding good advice and staying alive, he ignored the advice and died. Just through the man's actions and reactions to others, including his dog, the reader can draw conclusions about this man's character.

CLIMAX: **Climax** is either the turning point in a story or the point of greatest intensity, drama, interest, or suspense. In James Herriot's *The Recital* (p. 549), the climax occurs as Herriot's son Jimmy, in his second attempt, makes it through "The Miller's Dance" at a piano recital, winning the approval of the audience. Herriot, telling the story in the first-person, conveys his own anxiety and feelings when he writes: "He raced through the second half of the piece, but I kept my eyes closed as the relief flooded through me. I opened them only when he came to the finale, which I knew so well….I doubt if the hall has ever heard a noise like the great cheer which followed. The place erupted in a storm of clapping and shouting…"

CONCRETE POEM: A **concrete poem** contains lines whose shape represents, or makes visible, the subject of the poem. In the poem *Concrete Cat* (p. 437) by Dorthi Charles, the words of the poem form the shape of a cat (dead mouse under its tail, litter-box nearby) sitting over its food dish. The poem is part art and part language, revealing itself in an amusing and interesting manner.

CONFLICT: The opposition of two forces results in **conflict**, and this usually sets off the action in most literary works. There are two types of conflict: **external** and **internal**. In the category of external conflict we have: man vs. man, man vs. society, and man vs. nature. An **internal conflict** is called man vs. himself; it takes place within the mind of a character. Many works of literature contain more than one conflict. In the story *The Countess and the Impossible* (p. 60) by Richard Y. Thurman, we have a **man vs. man** conflict. The first-person narrator recounts his encounter at age 13 with an elderly neighbor, known only as "The Countess" for her regal bearing. She intimidates and frightens everyone. This conflict sets the plot in motion. **Man vs. society** is seen in the nonfiction work *By Any Other Name* (p. 566), by Santha Rama Rau, at the end of the memoir. Santha's sister tells their mother why they left school early and will not return. "Mother looked very startled and very concerned, and asked Premila what had happened. Premila said, 'We had our test today, and she made me and the other Indians sit at the back of the room with a desk between each one.'" On hearing this, the mother asks why this happened, and Premila responds, "'She said it was because Indians cheat...so I don't think we should go back to that school.'" Here the reader sees how unjustly the British treated Indians. The British are distrustful of the Indian people, whose land they have taken over and now rule. One of the best examples of **man vs. nature** can be found in Jack London's *To Build a Fire* (p. 118). In this famous short story, the main character tries to survive the icy Yukon cold by outwitting nature. However, in the end, the man is no match for temperatures that fall to 70 degrees below zero; thus, he freezes to death, and the cruel environment wins out. The conflict in *The Drummer Boy of Shiloh* (p. 148) by Ray Bradbury is internal. The story is set during the American Civil War with Joby, the main character trying to get some sleep before the Battle of Shiloh. He is a frightened and homesick drummer boy, and he doesn't think he is up to leading the troops into battle. As Joby lies crying, the third-person narrator reveals Joby's thoughts: "If he stayed very still, when the dawn came up and the soldiers put on their bravery with their caps, perhaps they might go away, the war with them, and not notice him living small here, no more than a toy himself." Joby's conflict lies within. He wants to be brave and strong like the others, but he is a scared young boy, filled with self-doubt.

DIALECT: **Dialect** is an offshoot of a standard language. A dialect is a variety of speech used by members of a particular class, trade, profession, race, or religion. It is used by writers to make their characters more believable. When immigrants use the language of their new country imperfectly, it can also be considered dialect. In the story, *The First Day* (p. 176) by George and Helen

Papashvily, the Russian immigrant (who is also the narrator and also the main character) speaks English with Russian overtones. When he tries to find out the correct time, he asks, " 'What watch?' " Later on, he asks, " 'How man clock?' " Yet the first-person narrator tells us, "A wonderful place. Rapidly, if one applies oneself, one speaks the English." This "broken" English is a realistic representation of immigrant speech until the new language becomes second nature.

DIALOGUE: Conversation between characters in a literary work is **dialogue**. In poetry, novels, short stories, and nonfiction, dialogue is usually set off by quotation marks. When the speaker changes, there is usually a new paragraph. In drama, however, the dialogue follows the names of the characters, usually shown in bold type, but with no quotation marks. Here is an example of dialogue from *The Pen of My Aunt* (p. 483), a one-act play by Gordon Daviot:

SIMONE. (*Approaching*) Madame! Oh, madame! Madame, have you—
MADAME. Simone.
SIMONE. Madame, have you seen what—
MADAME. Simone!
SIMONE. But madame—
MADAME. Simone, this may be an age of barbarism, but I will have none of it inside the walls of this house.

DRAMA: A **drama** is a story written for the stage and can be fiction or nonfiction. A drama implies a 'watched' performance, but we also have a written version (or script) and we can imagine the characters, setting, and action. A script has both dialogue and stage directions. Stage directions are usually written in *italics*. They describe how the characters in the play should look, speak, and move. They also describe the play's setting, sound effects, and lighting. A drama may or may not be divided into segments called acts. Often, each act is divided into even smaller parts called scenes. However, some plays are short and only contain one act and one scene, or setting. *The Pen of My Aunt* (p. 483) by Gordon Daviot is a one-act play with only one scene.

DYNAMIC CHARACTER: See *Character.*

ESSAY: An **essay** is a short nonfiction work on a single subject. Most essays have an introduction to present the subject and its background. The main part of the essay is the body, which contains details, examples, illustrations, and explanations. It is the longest part of the essay, and must support the writer's view for the essay to succeed. The conclusion pulls together all parts of the introduction and the body, highlighting the main ideas and then either drawing a conclusion or asking the reader to form an opinion. There are different types of essays. A **narrative essay**, like *By Any Other Name* (p. 566) by Santha Rama Rau, tells a story about real people and real events. *Animal Craftsmen* (p. 538), by Bruce Brooks, is a fine example of a **descriptive essay**, presenting its subject in detail through imagery and figurative language. It is also a good example of a reflective essay because it communicates the author's thoughts and feelings about his subject.

EXPOSITION: **Exposition** is the part of a literary work devoted to giving information and background on characters and their situation. It can also tell us about the setting of the piece. The author usually provides this exposition at the beginning of a work or when a new character is introduced. For instance, in the first two paragraphs of *Accounts Settled* (p. 30) by Paul Annixter, the reader is told the main character, Gordon Bent, a young boy of 16, has to tend to a trap line alone after his father had come down with flu-pneumonia. The reader also learns there is something sinister and frightening about the area. "This spruce valley was a dark, forbidding place even in summer; now the winter silence under the blue-black trees was more than silence—it was like a spell.... Gordon Bent was sixteen...already six feet tall and scantling thin....Timber-bred, he knew the woods and creatures as well as his father...But something about this valley had filled him with dread from the first." Thus, in the first two paragraphs of this story, the reader learns a great deal about the main character, his situation, and the setting of the story.

EXTENDED METAPHOR: An **extended metaphor** is a comparison between two things that does not use the words *like* or *as*; it is then developed (extended) at length. Shel Silverstein's poem *The Garden* (p. 417) is an excellent example of an extended metaphor. Throughout the poem, Silverstein compares Ol' man Simon's garden to a diamond, and each type of fruit represents jewelry: "Take a silver tater,/ Emerald tomater,/ Fresh plump coral melons/ Hangin' in reach,/ Ol'man Simon,/ Diggin' in his diamonds...."

FANTASY: Fantasy is highly imaginative literature containing elements not found in real life. The novella *The Forgotten Door* (p. 316), by Alexander Key, deals with a young boy who accidentally falls through a 'door' in his utopian world, landing in a world similar to our own. He has to fend off dangerous people and animals in this new world, until he is able to return to his family. Falling from one world into another is obviously impossible, but the author's seemingly 'authentic' invented details carry the reader along with him.

FICTION: Fiction refers to any work of imaginative literature in which the characters and events are invented by the writer. Short stories, novels, plays, novellas, and even some dramatic poetry can be fictional as long as they contain at least some imaginary events and characters. Fiction is often based on real events and people; but, if the author adds invented characters, dialogue, settings, and action, the work is still considered fiction. This is called **fact-based fiction** or **fiction based on fact**. Nevertheless, most works of fiction depend on the author's imagination and not on real events or people. The writers of this type of imaginative literature must create everything that goes into the work—characters, setting, action, and dialogue.

FIGURATIVE LANGUAGE:
Figurative language is meant to be understood imaginatively rather than literally. It conveys a figure or a likeness, provides images without filters, and suggests comparisons. Figurative language often uses *symbols.* The varieties of figurative language are called **figures of speech** and include *metaphor, simile, personification, onomatopoeia,* and *hyperbole* (exaggeration). Certainly figurative language is a component of prose writing, but it is perhaps most obvious in poetry. *Fireworks* (p. 395) by Babette Deutsch derives wonderful visual images from its *metaphors.* Walt Whitman's *O Captain! My Captain* (p. 421) is an *extended metaphor* for the assassination of Abraham Lincoln. Elizabeth Bishop's *The Fish* (p. 398) has *simile* ("his skin hung in strips like ancient wallpaper") and closes with superb *hyperbole* ("until everything was rainbow, rainbow, rainbow!"). In Louis Untermeyer's *Dog at Night* (p. 406), both dog and the moon (with its insolent light) are *personified.* Both *Dog at Night* and Austin's *Dandelions* (p. 425) have wonderful examples of *onomatopoeia*—sounds. Figurative language gives us eyes to see with and ears to hear with.

FIGURE OF SPEECH: See *Figurative Language.*

FLASHBACK: A **flashback** is a break in the chronology of a story, showing an episode or scene occurring earlier. The episode or scene itself is also referred to as a flashback. In Patrick McCallum's story *The Song Caruso Sang* (p. 256), the narrator employs the use of flashback to tell about his father: "Before he came to America, Papa played the violin-cello in the string quartet at the Ristorante Ricco, one of the best places to eat in Naples, in case you ever go there." Although this information interrupts the sequence of the story, it provides the reader with valuable information about Papa's character, as well as the rest of the family.

FLAT CHARACTER: See *Character.*

FORESHADOWING: Foreshadowing in a story gives the reader hints, indications, or suggestions about later events. Writers use foreshadowing to create reader expectations and build suspense. In Jack London's *To Build a Fire* (p. 118), the dog gives the reader clues about the danger of the extreme cold the man and dog are facing: "The dog did not know anything about thermometers. Possibly in its brain there was no sharp consciousness of a condition of very cold such as was in the man's brain. But the brute had its instinct. It experienced a vague but menacing apprehension that subdued it and made it slink along at the man's heels, and that made it question eagerly every unwonted movement of the man as if expecting him to go into camp or to seek shelter somewhere and build a fire." Thus, the reader is prepared for the later danger the man faces.

FREE VERSE: Free verse is poetry without rhyme or meter; but free verse poems still use rhythm, figurative language, and other poetic techniques. Walt Whitman, a poet known for his use of free verse, wrote the poem *When I Heard the Learn'd Astronomer* (p. 433). Notice how the lines of this poem vary in length and stress, while still showing other poetic features.

How soon unaccountable I became tired and sick,
Till rising and gliding out I wandered off by myself,
In the mystical moist night-air, and from time to time
Looked up in perfect silence at the stars.

Whitman uses alliteration, rhythm, and figurative language in this example of free verse.

GENRE (ZHAN ruh)**:** A **genre** is an artistic or literary division or type. In literature, fiction, nonfiction, poetry, and drama are the main genres. **Fiction** and **nonfiction** are usually written in prose, our everyday form of written language—without rhyme or meter. **Poetry** makes use of rhyme, meter, and other poetic techniques. **Drama** uses dialogue, with stage directions showing actors where to move and how to speak their lines, and to show the designer how the set should look.

HAIKU: Haiku is an ancient Japanese verse form written in three lines of five, seven, and five syllables respectively. These poems usually describe natural phenomena in an extremely tight form, employing many of the poetic techniques discussed on these pages, including imagery, personification, figurative language, etc.

HERO/HEROINE: The **hero** (male main character) or the **heroine** (female main character) is also known as the **protagonist** in a work of fiction. Every work of fiction in this anthology has a hero or a heroine. In the story *Accounts Settled* (p. 30) by Paul Annixter, the hero, or protagonist, is sixteen-year-old Gordon Bent. In *Mr. Brownlee's*

Roses (p. 164) by Elsie Singmaster, the heroine, or protagonist is the young Swedish girl, Jennie Swenson. We identify with the heroes and heroines of stories and are often motivated to continue reading, to see what will happen to them.

IMAGE:
An **image** (French for *picture*) is a word or phrase that appeals to one or more of the five senses, making the poem or literary work more vivid and real. Images capture how people or things appear, taste, smell, feel, or sound. A successful image gives the reader a powerful sense of the person or object being described, thus enriching the work. The poem *Fireworks* (p. 395), by Babette Deutsch, makes use of vivid images as the poet describes the sights and sounds of fireworks. The reader can almost feel present, watching and listening as the fireworks explode in the night air.

Not guns, not thunder, but a flutter of clouded drums
That announce a fiesta: abruptly, fiery needles
Circumscribe on the night boundless chrysanthemums.
Softly, they break apart, they flake away, where
Darkness, on a svelte hiss, swallows them.

These words enliven the poem and make it seem more vivid for the reader.

IRONY:
Irony involves surprising, interesting, or amusing contradictions. In verbal irony, words suggest the opposite of their usual meaning. For example, "It rained all day. What a great picnic we had!" In dramatic irony, there is a difference between the character's thoughts and what the readers know to be true. For instance, in Jack London's *To Build a Fire* (p. 118) the audience knows the man is doomed in the frozen Yukon, but the man believes he can beat nature and survive. In irony of situation, an event occurs in direct opposition to the expectations of the characters and audience. At the end of the story *A Man Who Had No Eyes* (p. 52) by MacKinlay Kantor, the readers and the blind beggar are both shocked to discover that Mr. Parsons, the hero of the story, is also blind. Since the author had not dropped any hints or clues about this situation, no one, including the other character, expects it.

LYRIC POEM:
A **lyric poem** expresses the poet's personal emotions or sentiments rather than just telling of external events. Sonnets, elegies, odes, and hymns are all lyric poems. An excellent example of a lyric poem is Richard Garcia's *The Clouds Pass* (p. 452), as the speaker describes the end of summer and the beginning of fall. In the last line of Stanza One, he says, "The trees are spending all their money." In the second stanza, the speaker says he lies in gold (the fallen leaves) and proclaims his wealth. The reader is able to see the author's comparison of falling leaves to gold, and the reader can appreciate the author's feelings about lying in a pile of fallen leaves on a crisp, clear autumn day. He is rich! The poet's feelings

about the change of season are evident and can be easily appreciated by the reader.

MAIN CHARACTER: See *Character* or *Hero/Heroine*

MEMOIR (MEM wahr)**:** A memoir is a type of **autobiographical** writing. It usually focuses on one incident, event, or influential person in the writer's earlier life, and it is extremely personal in nature. Santha Rama Rau's piece *By Any Other Name* (p. 566) is an example of a well-written memoir. In this work, Rau recalls an incident involving a change of names and its effect on her personality and behavior. When Santha and her sister Premila were sent to an Anglo-Indian school for the first time in their lives, the headmistress immediately gave each of them English names, explaining that their Indian names were much too difficult for her to remember. Later, Santha recalls in this memoir, "That first day at school is still, when I think of it, a remarkable one. At that age, if one's name is changed, one develops a curious form of dual personality. I remember having a certain detached and disbelieving concern in the actions of 'Cynthia,' but certainly no responsibility." Thus, the reader is able to enter Santha's mind and feel the effect of this event at such a young age.

METAPHOR: A **metaphor** is a figure of speech in which one thing is likened to something else and treated accordingly. An example of this type of metaphor is Shakespeare's famous line, "All the world's a stage." A metaphor may also be an implied comparison in which a word or phrase ordinarily used in one area is applied to another. Examples are: "a storm of protest" or "screaming headlines." The poem *Keepsakes* (p. 403) by Deloras Lane, is filled with metaphors. The poem is supposed to be a conversation between a twelve-year-old girl and her elderly aunt. When the girl asks her aunt to dye her grey hair black, the aunt responds, "those grey hairs are mistakes I made/ and spun into lessons/ of silver thread." When the girl suggests her aunt put on make-up to hide the lines around her eyes, the aunt says the lines "...are autographs/ of smiles." Later the young girl suggests they go for a walk, so her aunt could lose some weight. The aunt responds that her extra pounds "are pizzas and bananasplits/ shared with you—/ and I savored every one." The aunt is able to compare all her physical shortcomings with the strength, knowledge, and good times she treasures in her journey through life. The reader (and, hopefully the young girl) can easily realize how the process of aging can be positive and joyous.

METER: **Meter** is the regular pattern of stressed syllables that give a line of poetry a predictable rhythm. For example, there is a strong beat in Walt Whitman's poem *O Captain! My Captain!* (p. 421). Beginning with the second syllable, every other syllable is stressed. Thus, in each line (except for the refrains between stanzas) the second, fourth, sixth, eighth, and tenth syllables are stressed, while the other syllables are unstressed. The second and third lines of the first stanza give us an example of the steady meter Whitman uses throughout: "The ship has weathered every rack, the prize we sought is won,/ The port is near, the bells I hear, the people all exulting." The poet uses iambic pentameter; the stress is on the second syllable of each poetic foot (making it *iambic*), and there are five (*penta-*) feet to each line. This produces a serious, slow rhythm, one that mirrors regular speech.

MINOR CHARACTER: See *Character*.

MOOD: **Mood**, or atmosphere, is the feeling a work of literature creates in the reader. The mood of a literary work can be set by dialogue, setting, action, or the author's choice of words. Sometimes the mood is sustained throughout the entire piece, and sometimes the mood changes according to circumstances. In *The Finish of Patsy Barnes* (p. 225) by Paul Laurence Dunbar, the mood at the beginning of the story is one of tension and sadness. By the end, the mood is one of triumph and hope. At the beginning, Dunbar writes of Patsy's reaction to his father's untimely death: "The little fellow had shed no tears when he looked at his father's bleeding body, bruised and broken….Patsy did not sob or whimper, though his heart ached, for over all the feeling of his grief…." At the end of the story, Patsy wins a major horse race and is able to pay for a doctor and medicine to save his mother's life. "Then the band thundered, and Patsy was off his horse, very warm and very happy, following his mount to the stable….An hour later he walked into his mother's room with a very big doctor, the greatest the druggist could direct him to. The doctor left his medicines and his orders, but when Patsy told his story, it was Eliza's pride that started her on the road to recovery." One can see the sharp, dramatic contrast between the mood at the beginning of the story and the mood at the end.

MOTIVATION:
Motivation is the reason for a character's thoughts, feelings, actions, and speech. The motives of the characters, especially the main characters, must be clear to the reader, or the characters will not be believable. Characters (since they *are* people) are motivated by their feelings or emotions—fear, love, or competitiveness—or by their physical needs, such as food, shelter, and safety. In the story *You Need to Go Upstairs* (p. 186), by Rumer Godden, the main character, a young blind girl named Ally, is motivated to leave the safety of the yard of her house (and her mother's company) by her physical need to use the bathroom upstairs, inside her house. However, Ally is also motivated by pride, to go by herself without asking for help, even though the yard, the house, and its stairs present many challenges and a certain degree of danger. She feels the need to prove to her mother's guest and to herself that she can accomplish this task on her own, and she does.

NARRATION/NARRATOR:
Narration is the act of telling a story, and a narrator is the one who tells the story. There are different kinds of narrators. One type is a **first-person limited narrator**. This occurs when a character tells the story from a single point of view. A first-person narrator may also be involved in the action and thus, not always objective. If the first-person narrator is not objective, we have an unreliable narrator; the reader gets only the information this narrator knows and/or wants to give the reader. The story *The First Day* (p. 176), by George and Helen Papashvily, is an example of first-person limited narration. The narrator recounts, from his own viewpoint, the events that occurred during his first day in America. The reader has no idea what the other characters think or how they view the main character who is telling the story. In first-person narration, the narrator refers to him or herself as "I" or "me." Another type of narration is called **third-person omniscient narration**. Usually the omniscient (*all-knowing*) narrator is not a character in the story. Rather the narrator knows everything about the story being told, including the characters and their thoughts. An example of third-person omniscient narration occurs in Jack London's *To Build a Fire* (p. 118). In this story, the narrator is not a character, but he knows everything about the main character, his motives, his dog, the weather, and the eventual outcome of the action. The reader even knows what the man is thinking: "The man held

steadily on. He was not much given to thinking, and just then, particularly, he had nothing to think about save that he would eat lunch at the forks and that at six o'clock he would be in camp with the boys." The narrator knows everything and is anxious to share this knowledge with the reader. Another type of narrator is **third-person limited narrator**. A third-person limited narrator is usually a minor character who relates the events from a single point of view. This type of narration is similar to first-person limited narration because the action, character's personalities, and the outcome are told only through the point of view of this one character. Thus, the reader might be missing out on some important information, and the narrator may not be totally reliable. The story *Charles* (p. 70), by Shirley Jackson, is a good example of a story told by a third-person limited narrator. The story is told from the viewpoint of the mother of the main character (Laurie), and the audience knows only what she knows about the events in her son's kindergarten class. The narrator is a minor figure in the story, and the audience learns only what the mother knows. We are not getting an objective account, but rather an account colored by the narrator's feelings and knowledge of these events.

NARRATIVE POEM:

A **narrative poem** tells a story in verse. Narrative poetry has all the elements of fiction, including characters, conflict, setting, and plot. An example of a narrative poem is *The Rescue* (p. 442) by Hal Summers. This poem tells of a young boy who climbs high in a tree to rescue a cat that is stuck there. When the boy realizes how high he is and how windy it is, he calls for the help of his parents, his brother, and his dog. They take turns helping the boy bring the cat down to the ground, and then they all go inside the warm house and eat supper. "Up on a big branch stood his father,/ His mother came to the top of the ladder,/ His brother stood on a lower rung,/ The dog sat still and put out its tongue./ From one to the other the cat was handed/ And afterwards she was reprimanded./ After that it was easy, though the wind blew;/ The parents came down, the boy came too…" The poem reads like a story with action, conflict, characters, and a conclusion. The only difference is that it is told in verse with rhyme, rhythm, and meter.

NONFICTION:

Nonfiction uses prose to explain ideas or tell about real people and their lives. Nonfiction also deals with real places, objects, or events. There are many types of nonfiction: essays, reports, letters, biographies, autobiographies, newspaper articles, and other factual items. Most nonfiction is objective, presenting only the facts about the subject of the piece. However, some nonfiction, particularly essays and letters, can be slanted to reflect the writer's point of view. The reader should look for bias when reading any work of nonfiction. For instance, the memoir *By Any Other Name* (p. 566), by Santa Rama Rau, is an autobiographical work that is not totally objective. The author tells the reader of a painful experience from her childhood, and the reader only learns what Rau wants to remember.

NOVEL:

A **novel** is a long work of prose fiction. Novels contain all the elements of fiction—characters, plot, setting, and theme. The novelist develops these elements more fully and extensively in a novel than in a short story because there are fewer limitations than there are in a short story or other genre. A novel may contain more than one theme, and it may have more than one plot. These extra plots, which are minor compared to the main plot, are called subplots. *The Voyage of the Lucky Dragon* (p. 590) by Jack Bennett is an example of a novel. *The Forgotten Door* (p. 516), by Alexander Key, is an example of a short novel, sometimes called a novella.

ONOMATOPOEIA (AHN uh MAHT uh PEE uh):
Onomatopoeia refers to the formation of a word by imitating the natural sound associated with the object or action involved (e.g. tinkle, buzz, chickadee, hiss). The poem *Dandelions* (p. 425), by Deborah Austin, contains many good examples of onomatopoeia. The poet compares the growth of dandelions in a yard to enemy soldiers taking over a battlefield. The poem is filled with the sounds of battle and the images of yellow dandelions creeping up all over:

exploded at every second
rocked back by the starshellfire
concussion of gold on green
bringing battle-fatigue
pow by lionface firefur pow by
goldburst shellshock pow by
whoosh   splat   splinteryellow   pow by
pow   by   pow

The reader/listener can almost hear the sounds of the fierce battle taking place as the dandelions attack the lawn and win.

PERSONIFICATION:
Personification occurs when an author endows inanimate objects or abstract qualities with human characteristics. In *Dog at Night* (p. 406) by Louis Untermeyer, the poet compares the moon, which keeps the dogs awake at night, to a living being with human qualities. First, the moon is compared to a stranger who breaks "the dark with insolent light." Instead of answering the dog, "The moon ignores it, walking on as though/ Dogs never were…" At the end of the poem, all the dogs are howling at the moon and "Chasing the white intruder down the skies." The moon has become a human stranger, an intruder, who wakes the dogs with its "insolent" light and adds insult by ignoring them.

PERSUASION (pur SWAY zhun):
Persuasion is the term used when the author's aim—serious or less so—is to bring the reader over to his or her position on an issue, change the reader's mind, or encourage the reader to perform an action. Richard Lederer's essay, *The Case for Short Words* (p. 502), is surely written to guide good writing, as much as to make the author's preferences known. Rita Dove's biographical piece, *I Know What the Red Clay Looks Like* (p. 530), entices the beginning writer with its shimmering language. The example Dove sets, with her anecdotes and with the writing itself, is persuasion in its finest form: inspiration. Works, such as Santha Rama Rau's biographical *By Any Other Name* (p. 566) and Langston Hughes's poem *As I Grew Older* (p. 470), can surely be said to be persuasive, as they show the reader how the other guy feels.

PLOT:
The **plot** of a work of fiction is the working out of events occurring throughout the piece. Usually, one event leads to the next, and so on, until the **conflict** of the story is resolved. The characters involved act out the central conflict. The plot begins with **exposition**, or background information, which introduces the characters, the setting, and the situation. After the exposition, there is the **rising action**, which introduces the central conflict and develops it. The conflict then heightens until it reaches the point of greatest suspense and interest, the **climax**. After the climax, the **falling action**, or end of the central conflict, takes place. Any events occurring after the falling action are referred to as the **resolution** of the plot. Not every work of fiction contains all of these elements; for example, some stories do not begin with an exposition, and some do not end with a resolution. An example of a fiction work containing all these elements is the novel *The Voyage of the Lucky Dragon* (p. 590).

POETRY: A **poem** is a composition, usually in verse, and characterized by rhythm, or meter, and the use of heightened, precise language. No word is wasted as the poet observes the subject. Poetry often examines some aspect of life, nature, or history through the eyes of the poet. Poets usually make use of figurative language and imagery with metaphors, similes, personification, and symbolism. The rhythm, the rhyme, the use of stanzas, the compactness of language, the engagement of the reader's senses, and the use of imagery are all used in poetry, but not every poem contains all of these elements. Major types of poetry include *lyric poetry, narrative poetry, and concrete poetry*. In *dramatic poetry*, characters speak in their own voices. In *epic poetry*, the poet tells a long, involved story about battles and heroes or heroines. *The clouds pass* (p. 452) and *I Meant to Do My Work Today* (p. 453) are both examples of lyric poetry. Narrative poetry is represented in this text by *The Rescue* (p. 442) and by *The Walrus and the Carpenter* (p. 446), which is also a good example of dramatic poetry. Concrete poetry is found in the delightful poem, *Concrete Cat* (p. 437).

POINT OF VIEW: See *Narration/Narrator*.

PROSE: The ordinary form of written language is **prose**. It usually consists of sentences and paragraphs, and is used in both fiction and nonfiction. Prose is generally not used in poetry, drama, or song.

PROTAGONIST: The **protagonist** is the main character in a work of literature. If the protagonist is a male, he is the hero of the story; if the protagonist is female, she is the heroine of the story. The protagonist is involved in some sort of conflict with the *antagonist*, or opposing force. The reader usually identifies with the protagonist and is interested in the protagonist's triumph over the antagonist. In Jack London's famous short story *To Build a Fire* (p. 118), the protagonist is the man at risk in the bitter cold of the Yukon. The antagonist is the weather and the other harmful elements of nature affecting the man and his dog.

REPETITION: **Repetition** is a literary device (used for emphasis and effect) featuring a recurring sound, word, or phrase. The device is used in the poem *O Captain! My Captain!* (p. 421) by Walt Whitman. In the first line of the first stanza, the audience reads, "O Captain! my captain! our fearful trip is done." The first line of the second stanza reads, "O Captain! my Captain! rise up and hear the bells." The emphasis is placed on calling the Captain, asking him to acknowledge the finality of the situation. The last two lines of each stanza are repetitious, stressing the fact that the Captain lies cold and dead on the ship's deck. In stanza one, the lines are, "Where on the deck my Captain lies,/ Fallen cold and dead." In stanza two, the final lines are, "It is some dream that on the deck/ You've fallen cold and dead." In the third and final stanza, the final two lines are, "Walk the deck my Captain lies,/ Fallen cold and dead." Again, the stress is on the fact that the Captain lies cold and dead on the deck. The reader is never allowed to forget this.

RHYME: **Rhyme** is the exact repetition of sounds in the final accented syllables of two or more words. In John Masefield's poem *The West Wind* (p. 413), each stanza has four lines. The final accented syllables and/or words of the first and second lines rhyme, and the final accented syllables and/or words of the third and fourth lines rhyme. For example, the final word of line one, stanza one is "cries." The final word of line two, stanza one is "eyes." These two words rhyme. Then in line three, stanza one, the final word is "hills," while the final word in line four, stanza one is "daffodils." Again, the final word of line three, "hills," rhymes with the final accented syllable of line four, "dils," the final syllable of "daffodils." The rhyme is pleasant to the ear, an aid to memory, and helps emphasize the meaning and mood of the poem. Rhyme also gives a songlike quality to the verse.

RHYME SCHEME: A **rhyme scheme** is the regular pattern of rhyming words in a poem. The rhyme scheme of the poem is indicated by lower case letters that follow each line. Each rhyme is assigned a different letter. The following lines are a stanza from Lewis Carroll's *The Walrus and the Carpenter* (p. 446):

The Walrus and the Carpenter	a
Were walking close at hand:	b
They wept like anything to see	c
Such quantities of sand:	b
"If this were only cleared away,"	d
They said, "it would be grand!"	b

Therefore, the rhyme scheme of this stanza is *abcbdb*.

SCIENCE FICTION: Science fiction stories and novels tell of events involving science and/or technology and are often set in the future. Sometimes they deal with aliens visiting our planet. The setting can be Earth, space, another planet, or even another solar system. The novella, *The Forgotten Door* (p. 316) is a good example of science fiction. The main character comes from another world—possibly a different solar system. He is trying to return to his own world with the assistance of his adoptive earthling family.

SETTING: Setting is the time and place of a work's action. However, historical time and geographical place are not the only components of setting. Setting may also include the social, economic, and cultural environment of a work. In some works, setting is not important and serves only as background. In other works, setting takes on the importance of a character and is crucial to the development of the plot. Setting plays a major role in Ray Bradbury's *The Drummer Boy of Shiloh* (p. 148). The Civil War setting creates a mood of nervous expectation, as the story takes place just before a major Civil War battle. The two characters speak to each other and confess their fears and longings in this atmosphere. Jack London's *To Build a Fire* (p. 118) also has a setting that plays a major role in the story's development. The hostile and barren setting causes the protagonist to feel afraid and alone. The reader can identify with these feelings, in part because of the mood created by this setting.

SHORT STORY: A **short story** is a brief fictional work with a plot, characters, conflict, and setting. The central idea is the story's theme. A short story is concise, usually creating a single effect for the reader. Thus, it is not as complex in plot, characters, theme, or conflict as a novel or a novella. A short story should be read in one sitting, so the effect can be better absorbed by the reader.

SIMILE (SIM ih lee)**:** A **simile** is a figure of speech making a direct comparison, using "like" or "as," between two items that are usually not related. Hal Summers' narrative poem *The Rescue* (p. 442) uses a vivid simile in the following lines:

So up he climbed, and the whole town
Lay at his feet, round him the leaves
Fluttered like a lady's sleeves,
And the cat sat, and the wind blew so
That he would have flown had he let go.

Summers describes the attempted rescue of a cat stuck high in a tree. The boy making the rescue is surrounded by leaves that "fluttered like a lady's sleeves." This simile is a powerful comparison, showing how the leaves fluttered during the rescue attempt. It adds color and life to the poem, providing more meaning for the reader.

SPEAKER: The **speaker** is the imaginary voice assumed by the poet. In other words, the speaker is a character speaking out to the audience. This character, or voice, is often not identified by name, but the speaker's attitude toward the subject may communicate a tone or attitude to the reader. For example, in the poem *Ellis Island* (p. 409) by Joseph Bruchac, the speaker of the poem, not Joseph Bruchac, tells of his grandparents' quarantine on Ellis Island and of his own trip to this island to relive their experience. The speaker's attitude is contemplative and serious, as he questions the immigrants' invasion of this land that once belonged to the Indians. This tone reaches beyond the poem, to create an introspective mood in the reader.

STANZA: A **stanza** is a group of lines in a poem that are meant to be understood as a unit. Stanzas are usually separated by spaces. A stanza of poetry can often be compared to a paragraph of prose. Stanzas are labeled according to the number of lines they contained:

Couplet: two-line stanza
Tercet: three-line stanza
Quatrain: four-line stanza
Cinquain: five-line stanza
Sestet: six-line stanza
Heptastich: seven-line stanza
Octave: eight-line stanza

Most traditional poetry is divided into stanzas that use rhymes. For instance, *The West Wind* (p. 413), by John Masefield, has stanzas that are quatrains. In each stanza the first and second lines rhyme, as do the third and fourth lines, giving the poem an *aabb* rhyme scheme. Yet a poem can have stanzas but no rhyme at all. So, in the poem *The clouds pass*, by Richard Garcia (p. 452), each stanza is a quatrain, but there are no rhymes.

SURPRISE ENDING: A **surprise ending** occurs when the reader assumes the conflict has been resolved, but a plot twist changes the outcome. A surprise ending has elements of **irony**. It is an unexpected outcome, given the information supplied up to that point. For instance, in O. Henry's story *The Last Leaf* (p. 42), the conclusion surprises the reader. In the short story *A Man Who Had No Eyes* (p. 52) by MacKinlay Kantor, the reader discovers at the end that the blind beggar isn't the only blind man in the story. A surprise ending makes for satisfying reading, especially if the reader can guess the ending beforehand.

SUSPENSE: **Suspense** is the feeling authors evoke in their readers about the outcome of a literary work. An author creates suspense through setting, mood, tone, plot turns, and other literary devices, raising questions in the reader's mind. In *The Voyage of the Lucky Dragon* (p. 590), suspense is created as the reader worries about the family's safety. Suspense is heightened by each turn of events. Will the family reach a safe haven or will pirates, hunger, or other hardships overtake them? The play *The Pen of My Aunt* (p. 483) by Gordon Daviot is another example of a suspenseful literary work. The audience wants to know if the Stranger will succeed (with the help of Madame and Simone) in getting away from the Nazi Corporal who has come to take him along as a prisoner. Thus, suspense often sustains and heightens interest in a literary work as we wait to see how things will turn out.

SYMBOL: A **symbol** is anything that stands for something else. A flag can symbolize a country or patriotism. Dark clouds can symbolize danger. A dove with an olive branch in its beak is a symbol of peace. In his poem *The Garden* (p. 417), Shel Silverstein uses precious gems to symbolize the fruits and vegetables a farmer grows in his garden. In the poem *The Blind Men and the Elephant* (p. 429) by John Godfrey Saxe, the six blind men of Indostan symbolize the ignorance of people who only see things in part and not in full. Thus, symbolism is a literary technique that authors use to emphasize a point and make it more obvious to the reader.

THEME: A **theme** is the central message or insight of a literary work. It can be **directly stated** by a character in a story or by the speaker in a poem. However, the theme is usually **implied**—hinted at or suggested by the content of the literary work. In the story *The Man Without a Country* (p. 235), by Edward Everett Hale, the theme is stated directly by the main character, Philip Nolan. The theme is one of patriotism, and the reader sees it in Nolan's final words: "Bury me in the sea; it has been my home, and I love it. But will not someone set up a stone for my memory, that my disgrace may not be more than I ought to bear? Say on it: In Memory of PHILIP NOLAN, Lieutenant in the Army of the United States 'He loved his country as no other man has loved her; but no man deserved less at her hands.' " On the other hand, there is a strong implied theme (not directly stated) in the short story *The Song Caruso Sang* (p. 256) by Patrick McCallum. The implied theme of this story is that a strong sense of family will help its members become strong, exercising sound judgment about important matters. The theme includes the idea that family rituals and values are more important than money. By the end of the story, the narrator, a family member, declares, "We're a family again and still have the record. Maybe someday we'll save enough money to move to that farm in Jersey. Right now it's just something nice to dream about."

TONE: **Tone** is the author's attitude toward the audience and subject. The tone of a literary work can be formal or casual, serious or humorous, bitter or sympathetic, happy or sad, straightforward or ironic. In the poem *Foul Shot* (p. 392) by Edwin A. Hoey, the author's tone is one of urgency and suspense—the same way a spectator feels during an important play in an athletic event. His tone is also casual because he is writing about a basketball game where most people behave casually and not formally. However, even though Hoey is casual, he is still serious about his subject matter because most sports fans are serious about their favorite sports and teams. Thus, the subject matter and the reader's relation to it have a great deal to do with the tone adopted by any author.

Glossary

A

abdomen (AB duh min) *n.*: the lower part of the body, containing the digestive organs and intestines

abruptly (uh BRUPT lee) *adv.*: suddenly and unexpectedly

absently (AB sent lee) *adv.*: inattentively

absurd (ab SURD) *adj.*: utterly, obviously senseless or illogical

access (AK sess) *n.*: ability or right to enter or use

acclimatized (ak KLAH mah TYZD) *v.*: accustomed to a new environment

accord (uh KORD) *n.*: agreement; harmony

acute (uh KYOOT) *adj.*: sharp or severe in effect; intense

acuteness (uh KYOOT niss) *n.*: sensitivity even to slight details or impressions

adept (uh DEPT) *adj.*: very skilled; proficient; expert

adequately (AD ih kwit lee) *adv.*: sufficiently

adhesiveness (ad HEE siv niss) *n.*: the tendency to adhere; stickiness

affirmation (AF fur MAY shun) *n.*: the assertion that something exists or is true

affronted (uh FRUNT id) *adj.*: offended by an open display of disrespect; insulted

agility (uh JILL ih tee) *n.*: quickness; coordination

agonizingly (AG uh nyz ing lee) *adv.*: very distressingly; extremely painfully

allusion (uh LOO zhin) *n.*: a passing or casual reference to something, either directly or implied

aloof (uh LOOF) *adj.*: removed or indifferent

ancillary (AN sih LAIR ee) *adj.*: secondary; supplemental; subordinate

anguish (AYN gwish) *n.*: acute suffering or pain

animated (AN ih MAYT id) *adj.*: full of life, action, or spirit; lively

annals (AN ilz) *n.*: historical records; chronicles

anticipated (an TISS sip PAYT id) *v.*: foreseen, expected

apathetically (AP uh THET ik lee) *adv.*: having or showing little or no emotion

apparition (AP uh RISH in) *n.*: a ghostly appearance of a person or thing

appeasingly (uh PEEZ ing lee) *adv.*: in a pacifying way; in such a way as to please

appraisingly (uh PRAY zing lee) *adv.*: with an eye towards estimating the nature, quality, or importance of

apprehension (AP ree HEN shun) *n.*: suspicion or fear of future trouble

arbitrarily (AR bih TRAIR ih lee) *adv.*: unreasonably; done according to one individual's will; on a whim

architecture (AR kih TEK cher) *n.*: the action, process, or design of a building; construction

arcing (ARK ing) *adj.*: moving in a curved line

aristocracy (AIR iss TAHK rih see) *n.*: a class of persons holding high rank and privileges, especially the nobility

aromatic (OW ROW MAT ik) *adj.*: having a pleasant smell; fragrant or sweet-scented

artifacts (AR tih FAKTZ) *n.*: handmade objects, or their remains from an earlier time, found at an archaeological excavation

askew (uh SKYOO) *adj.*: to one side; crooked

assenting (as SENT ing) *v.*: agreeing

assurance (uh SHUR intz) *n.*: a positive declaration intended to give confidence; freedom from doubt; self-confidence

atmosphere (AT muh SFEER) *n.*: a surrounding or pervading mood, environment, or influence

attribute (AT trib YOOT) *n.*: a quality or characteristic of a person, thing, or group

attributing (uh TRIB yoot ing) *n.*: considering as a quality or characteristic

attuned (uh TOOND) *v.*: brought into harmony or agreement

audible (AW dih bul) *adj.*: capable of being heard; loud enough to be heard

augmented (awg MEN tid) *v.*: enlarged in size, number, strength or extent; increased

authentication (aw THEN tih KAY shun) *n.*: validation as genuine

availed (uh VAY ild) *v.*: used to his advantage, made use of

B

baffled (BAF ild) *adj.*: confused, bewildered, or perplexed

banister (BAN iss tur) *n.*: a handrail and its supporting posts, especially on a staircase

barbarism (BAR buh RIZ im) *n.*: a savage, primitive, uncivilized condition

barnacle (BAR nih kul) *n.*: a sea-dwelling, hard-shelled creature that often attaches itself to ship bottoms and timber

basked (BASKT) *v.*: lay in a pleasant warmth

belated (bee LAYT tid) *adj.*: coming after the customary or expected time; delayed

bereaved (bih REEVD) *adj.*: greatly saddened by the loss of a loved one

blackmail (BLACK mayl) *n.*: a payment extorted by intimidation and threats

blight (BLYT) *n.*: a disease in plants that causes them to stop growing and wither

blotchy (BLAH chee) *adj.*: covered with spots

blunder (BLUNN dur) *n.*: a gross or careless mistake

borne (BORN) *v.*: endured, tolerated

brandishing (BRAN dish ing) *v.*: shaking, or waving (a fist or sword, for instance) in a threatening manner

brood (BROOD) *n.*: a number of young produced or hatched at one time

bulbous (BUL biss) *adj.*: bulb-shaped

burgh (BERG) *n.*: a town; an incorporated town

C

cajoling (kuh JOE ling) *adj.*: persuading by flattery or promises; wheedling; coaxing

calamity (kuh LAM ih tee) *n.*: a great misfortune or disaster; a catastrophe

callous (KAL iss) *adj.*: insensitive; indifferent; unsympathetic

cane (KANE) *n.*: sugarcane

canted (KANT tid) *v.*: tilted; inclined

capacious (kuh PAY shus) *adj.*: capable of holding a lot; spacious or roomy

capsized (KAP syzd) *v.*: turned bottom up; overturned

caravans (KARE uh VANZ) *n.*: groups of travelers journeying together for safety through hostile territory

cell (SELL) *n.*: a small compartment forming part of a whole

cello (CHELL lo) *n.*: a large, four-stringed musical instrument of the violin family

channel (CHAN il) *n.*: a navigable route between two bodies of water; a waterway; a route along which anything passes

charade (shuh RAYD) *n.*: an obvious fake or deception; a mockery

chastise (chass TYZ) *v.*: discipline, especially using physical punishment; criticize severely

chivalric (shiv AL rik) *adj.*: considerate and courteous; knightly in behavior

chivalry (SHIV il ree) *n.*: a combination of qualities that include courage, generosity, and courtesy

circumvent (SIR kum VENT) *v.*: go around or bypass

citations (sy TAY shunz) *n.*: awards for outstanding achievement

civilian (sih VILL yen) *n.*: a person who is not on active duty with the military

clamor (KLAM er) *n.*: a loud uproar, as from a crowd of people

clod (CLAHD) *n.*: a lump or mass of earth or clay

coherent (ko HEAR int) *adj.*: logically connected; consistent

combatant (kahm BAT ant) *adj.*: engaged in combat, fighting; also, ready or inclined to fight

commenced (kuh MENST) *v.*: began; started

compact (kum PAKT) *adj.*: closely packed; solid; concise

compelled (kom PELD) *v.*: forced or driven to a course of action

complying (kum PLY ing) *v.*: going along with; obeying; following someone's wishes

concussion (kun KUSH in) *n.*: an injury to the brain or spinal cord from a jarring blow

congeal (kun JEEL) *v.*: solidify or thicken by cooling; curdle

congenial (kun JEEN yil) *adj.*: suited in tastes, temperament; compatible

consigned (kahn SYND) *v.*: handed over; delivered to

consternation (KAHN stir NAY shun) *n.*: a sudden, alarming amazement that results in utter confusion; dismay

contempt (kun TEMPT) *n.*: disdain or scorn for anything considered vile or worthless

contour (KAHN toor) *n.*: the outline of a figure or body; the line that defines a shape or object

converge (kun VURJ) *v.*: move toward one point; come together by gradual approach

conviction (kun VIK shun) *n.*: a fixed or firm belief; the state of being convinced

convulsively (kun VULSS iv lee) *adv.*: with violent, involuntary muscular contractions

corroded (kuh RODE id) *adj.*: rusted; eaten or worn away gradually

counterpoint (KON ter POYNT) *n.*: any element contrasted or juxtaposed with another

covertly (KUV ert lee) *adv.*: in a secret or concealed manner

cowardice (COW er diss) *n.*: lack of courage; lack of mental and emotional strength

cowered (KOW urd) *v.*: crouched or shrank back in fear

credence (KREED intz) *n.*: belief in the truth of something

credentials (kred EN shals) *n.*: official identification papers

crimson (KRIM zen) *n.*: deep purplish red

crouched (KROUCHT) *v.*: stooped with knees bent as if ready to pounce

crucial (KROO shil) *adj.*: of vital or critical importance

culminating (KUL min ate ing) *v.*: arriving at a final or climactic stage

cultivating (KULL tih VAYT ing) *v.*: preparing and working on land, in order to raise crops

curt (KERT) *adj.*: rudely brief; abrupt in manner

custody (KUS tih dee) *n.*: the keeping, guardianship, or care of

D

decadent (DEK uh dint) *adj.*: characterized by moral decay

deceitful (dee SEET fuhl) *adj.*: characterized by intentional misleading and concealment of the truth

deed (DEED) *n.*: a document executed under seal and delivered to finalize an acquisition, especially of real estate

deluged (DEL yoojd) *v.*: covered with liquid; flooded

delusion (dih LOO zhin) *n.*: a type of mental turmoil; a false belief

demoralized (dee MOR uh LYZD) *adj.*: thrown into disorder or confusion; deprived of spirit and courage

deteriorating (dee TEER ee uh RAYT ing) *v.*: worsening; being worn away; disintegrating

disconcerting (DISS kun SURT ing) *adj.*: disturbing; unsettling; throw into confusion

discrete (diss KREET) *adj.*: separate; distinct

dismantled (diss MAN tild) *v.*: taken apart

dismantling (diss MANT ling) *v.*: taking apart

dispatches (diss PATCH iz) *n.*: messages or official communications sent with speed

dispelled (dih SPELD) *v.*: caused to disperse, vanish

dissociate (dih SO see ate) *v.*: draw apart from; disconnect; separate

dissolution (DISS uh LOO shun) *n.*: separation into parts or elements; disintegration

diversity (dy VURS ih tee) *n.*: being of various kinds or forms; variety

droning (DRONE ing) *adj.*: continuous, low, monotonous

drouth (DROWTH) *n.*: also spelled *drought*; a period of dry weather, especially one that is harmful to crops

drove (DROVE) *n.*: a number of oxen, sheep or swine driven in a group; herd; flock

dryly (DRY lee) *adv.*: unemotionally, indifferently, coldly

dubious (DOO bee iss) *adj.*: marked by doubt; questionable; inclined to doubt

dumbfounded (DUM FOUN did) *adj.*: astonished; amazed

E

eaves (EEVZ) *n.*: the overhanging lower edge of a roof

eavesdrop (EEVZ DRAHP) *v.*: listen secretly to a private conversation

edible (ED ih bul) *adj.*: fit to be eaten as food; eatable

effrontery (ee FRUN ter ee) *n.*: shameless or impudent boldness

elaborate (ee LAB rit) *adj.*: worked out in great detail; painstaking

elicited (ee LISS ih tid) *v.*: drew out or brought forth

elongation (EE long GAY shun) *n.*: a lengthening or extending

eloquence (ELL ih kwintz) *n.*: the ability to use language skillfully and powerfully

ember (EM ber) *n.*: a small burning piece of coal or wood, as in a dying fire

empathy (EM puh thee) *n.*: intellectual or emotional identification with another

engulf (en GULF) *v.*: swallow up; envelop or overwhelm completely

enigmatic (EN ig MAT ik) *adj.*: mysterious; perplexing

enigmatically (EN ig MAT ih klee) *adv.*: perplexingly; mysteriously

enthralled (en THRAHLD) *adj.*: captivated or charmed; spellbound

entice (en TYC) *v.*: lead on by exciting hope or desire; tempt

entranced (en TRANST) *v.*: filled with delight or wonder

epaulette (EP uh LET) *n.*: a decorative shoulder piece found chiefly on the uniforms of military officers

equilibrium (E kwill LIB ree um) *n.*: a state of rest or balance

erupted (ee RUPT id) *v.*: burst forth with

eternity (ee TUR nih tee) *n.*: a seemingly endless period of time

etiquette (ET ih kit) *n.*: formally approved requirements for proper behavior in a given situation

evasive (ee VAY siv) *adj.*: seeking to avoid answering directly

exasperation (ig ZAS puh RAY shun) *n.*: extreme annoyance or irritation

exhilarating (ig ZILL uh RAYT ing) *adj.*: stimulating; invigorating

exhorted (eg ZORT id) *v.*: gave urgent advice, recommendations, or warnings

expedient (eks PEED ee int) *n.*: a handy means to an end

expedition (EK spuh DISH un) *n.*: a journey or voyage made for a specific purpose

expiring (ek SPY ir ing) *v.*: breathing the last breath; dying

exploited (eks PLOY tid) *v.*: taken advantage of; used or abused

extricated (EX trih kayt id) *v.*: freed or released from entanglement; disengaged

F

façade (fuh SAHD) *n.*: the front of a building, especially an imposing or decorative one

feint (FAYNT) *n.*: a movement made in order to distract an opponent; an attack aimed at one place or point to distract from the real target

ferocity (fuh RAHS ih tee) *n.*: fierceness; wildness

fervent (FUR vint) *adj.*: very warm or intense

fiend (FEEND) *n.*: a cruel or wicked person

fiendishly (FEEN dish lee) *adv.*: in an outrageously cruel way; wickedly

finale (fuh NAL ee) *n.*: the last piece, division, or movement of a concert, opera, or composition

flaccid (FLAS sid) *adj.*: soft and limp; not firm; flabby; lacking force

flailing (FLAY ling) *adj.*: beating or swinging

flayed (FLAYD) *v.*: stripped off the skin or outer covering, as by whipping

flotsam (FLAHT sum) *n.*: refuse or wreckage of ships found floating on the water

flourish (FLUR ish) *n.*: a showy or dramatic gesture or display

forlorn (for LORN) *adj.*: miserable; despairing

frigate (FRIG it) *n.*: a fast naval vessel of the late 18th and early 19th centuries

frothing (FRAWTH ing) *adj.*: bubbling; foaming

fungus (FUN guss) *n.*: a plant—such as mold, mildew, and mushrooms—that lacks chlorophyll and reproduces by spores

furrow (FUR oh) *n.*: a narrow groove-like or trench-like depression in any surface

futile (FYOO till) *adj.*: incapable of producing any result; useless; not successful

G

gait (GAYT) *n.*: the manner of walking, stepping, or running

galoshes (guh LAHSH iz) *n.*: waterproof boots or overshoes, usually high ones

garish (GAIR ish) *adj.*: crudely or tastelessly colorful or showy

garnished (GAR nisht) *adj.*: adorned; provided or supplied with something ornamental; decorated

garrison (GAIR ih sun) *n.*: a body of troops stationed in a fortified place

gaudily (GAW dil lee) *adv.*: showily and tastelessly; flashily

gaudy (GAW dee) *adj.*: showy in a tasteless way; flashy

genetic (juh NET ik) *adj.*: passed biologically from one generation to the next; of the genes

genre (ZHAHN ruh) *n.*: a class or category of artistic endeavor having a particular form, content, or technique

geologist (jee AHL uh jist) *n.*: one who studies the physical history of the earth and the rocks of which it's composed

geology (jee AHL uh jee) *n.*: the study of the earth's structure and the rocks that make up its crust

ghastly (GAST lee) *adj.*: haggard and pale; ghostlike in appearance

gingerly (JINJ er lee) *adv.*: with great care or caution; warily

gnarled (NAR ild) *adj.*: full of or covered with knot-like shapes; bent; twisted

gnawing (NAW ing) *n.*: biting on or chewing on persistently; troubling or tormenting by constant annoyance

grandeur (GRAN jer) *n.*: impressiveness, importance, distinction

gravely (GRAYV lee) *adv.*: seriously or solemnly

grimaced (grih MIST) *v.*: made an ugly or contorted facial expression indicating disapproval or pain

grotesque (GRO tesk) *adj.*: fantastically ugly or absurd; bizarre

grotesquely (gro TESK lee) *adv.*: in an odd or unnatural way

guttering (GUT er eeng) *adj.*: burning low or being blown so as to be nearly extinguished

H

habitation (HAB ih TAY shun) *n.*: a place of residence; dwelling; community

harangue (huh RANG) *n.*: a scolding or a verbal attack

haunches (HAWN chez) *n.*: the hips or fleshy part of the body about the hips; the hindquarters of an animal

havoc (HAV ik) *n.*: great destruction or devastation

hearth (HARTH) *n.*: the floor of a fireplace, usually of stone or brick, often extending into the room

hefts (HEFTS) *v.*: lifts; heaves

hogshead (HAWGZ HED) *n.*: a large wooden barrel

hold (HOLD) *n.*: the cargo space in the hull of a vessel, especially between the lowermost deck and the bottom

hovels (HUV ilz) *n.*: small, humble dwellings; dirty; disorganized dwellings

hovered (HUV erd) *v.*: waited near at hand; lingered; hung over

hulls (HULZ) *n.*: outer coverings of seeds, fruits, or other objects

hypnotized (HIP nuh TYZD) *v.*: transfixed; spellbound; fascinated

hypothetical (HY poh THET ik uhl) *adj.*: assumed to exist; supposed

I

imminent (IM ih nint) *adj.*: likely to occur at any moment

immobility (IM mo BILL ih tee) *n.*: the state of being incapable of movement or motion; motionless

impassive (ihm PASS iv) *adj.*: showing or feeling no emotion; unmoved

impassively (im PASS iv lee) *adv.*: without feeling or emotion

impeding (im PEED ing) *v.*: causing delay, interruption, or difficulty

impenetrable (im PEN ih truh bul) *adj.*: incapable of being penetrated, pierced, or entered

imperative (im PAIR ih tiv) *adj.*: absolutely necessary or required

imperceptible (IM pur SEPT ih bul) *adj.*: very slight, gradual, or subtle

imperturbably (IM per TERB uh blee) *adv.*: calmly; without agitation

implement (IM pluh mint) *n.*: an instrument, tool, or utensil used for accomplishing work

implication (IHM plik KAY shun) *n.*: real meaning of a remark; something implied or suggested as to be naturally inferred or understood

impotently (IM puh tint lee) *adv.*: powerlessly

improvised (IM pruh VYZD) *v.*: performed without preparation

inaccessible (IN ak SESS uh bul) *adj.*: impossible to approach; unreachable

inaudible (in AW dih bul) *adj.*: too low or distant to be heard

incompetence (in KAHM pih tintz) *n.*: lack of ability or fitness; mental deficiency

incomprehensible (IN kahm pree HEN sih bul) *adj.*: impossible to understand

incongruous (in KAHN groo iss) *adj.*: out of place; inappropriate; not fitting

incorrigible (in KOR ih juh bul) *adj.*: unruly; uncontrollable; bad beyond reform

incredulous (in KRED yoo less) *adj.*: disbelieving

indignant (in DIG nant) *adj.*: feeling angry at something considered insulting or unjust

indignation (IN dig NAY shun) *n.*: strong displeasure at something considered unjust or insulting, righteous anger

indispensable (IN diss PEN sih bul) *adj.*: absolutely necessary or essential

indulgent (in DULL jint) *adj.*: showing kindly tolerance; permissive

inestimable (in ESS tih muh bul) *adj.*: too precious to be estimated or appreciated; invaluable

inexhaustible (IN ig ZAWS tih bul) *adj.*: incapable of being depleted; untiring

inexorably (in EX or ih blee) *adv.*: unyieldingly; unalterably; immovably; mercilessly

inexplicable (in EKS plik uh bul) *adj.*: incapable of being explained

infernal (in FUR nil) *adj.*: extremely troublesome, annoying; outrageous

ingenious (in JEEN yiss) *adj.*: cleverly inventive; resourceful

ingenuously (in JEEN yus lee) *adv.*: naively; artlessly; without restraint; openly

inimical (in IM ih kul) *adj.*: unfriendly; hostile

inordinately (in OR dihn it lee) *adv.*: excessively; unrestrainedly

inquisitive (in KWIZ ih tiv) *adj.*: curious; eager for knowledge; unduly curious; prying

inscrutable (in SKROOT uh bul) *adj.*: mysterious, unfathomable; incapable of being investigated or analyzed

insignia (inn SIG nih yuh) *n.*: a badge or distinguishing mark of office or honor

insinuated (in SIN yoo ate id) *v.*: suggested or hinted; placed (herself) into a position between

insolent (IN suh lint) *adj.*: haughtily contemptuous, extremely disrespectful

insolently (IN suh lint lee) *adv.*: in a boldly rude way

insoluble (in SAHL yuh bul) *adj.*: incapable of being solved

instinct (IN stinkt) *n.*: an inborn pattern of activity, or tendency to action, common to a species; intuitive sense

instinctively (in STINKT iv lee) *adv.*: arising from a natural or inborn impulse, inclination, or tendency

insular (IN suh ler) *adj.*: narrow-minded

intangible (in TAN juh bul) *adj.*: not definite or clear to the mind; vague; elusive

integral (in TUH gril) *adj.*: essential to the whole; necessary to completeness

intensity (in TEN sih tee) *n.*: great force, strength, or energy

intent (in TENT) *adj.*: firmly or steadfastly fixed or directed; having the attention sharply focused on something

intercepted (IN ter SEPT id) *v.*: secretly listened to or recorded; took, seized, or halted

interminable (in TUR min uh bul) *adj.*: having no apparent limit or end

intimate (IN tih mit) *adj.*: private; closely personal

intricate (IN trih kit) *adj.*: having many interrelated parts or facets; entangled or involved; complex

intricately (IN trih kit lee) *adv.*: in a way that is full of elaborate detail

irate (i RATE) *adj.*: angry; enraged

irrevocably (ih REV ih kuh blee) *adv.*: unalterably; in a manner that could not be undone

J

jeers (JEERZ) *n.*: rude and mocking shouts or taunts

jetty (JET ee) *n.*: a pier or structure of stones or piles projecting into a body of water to protect a harbor from the water current

judiciously (joo DISH iss lee) *adv.*: having or characterized by good judgment

K

khaki (KACK ee) *n.*: a heavy beige or tan fabric, used especially in making uniforms and trousers

L

lagoon (luh GOON) *n.*: an area of shallow water open to the sea but separated from the ocean by low sandy dunes

lamented (luh MEN tid) *v.*: mourned deeply and vocally

ledgers (LEJ urz) *n.*: account books for keeping records

legacy (LEG uh see) *n.*: anything handed down from the past; bequest

lenient (LEE nee int) *adj.*: agreeably tolerant; not strict or severe; indulgent

liberality (LIB er AL ih tee) *n.*: generosity and open-mindedness

lingering (LIN ger ing) *adj.*: remaining or staying in a place longer than usual or expected

lithe (LYTH) *adj.*: flexible; bending readily; pliant

lout (LOUT) *n.*: a clumsy, boorish person

ludicrously (LOO dih kris lee) *adv.*: ridiculously

lunar (LOON er) *adj.*: resembling the moon; round or crescent-shaped

lurched (LERCHT) *v.*: rolled or pitched suddenly; swayed abruptly; staggered

lurid (LUR id) *adj.*: shining with an unnatural, fiery glow; garishly red; wildly dramatic or sensational

lynx (LINX) *n.*: a fierce wildcat with short tail and tufted ears

M

magnitude (MAG nih TOOD) *n.*: great size; extent, or dimensions

malevolent (muh LEV ih lint) *adj.*: wishing evil or harm to others; malicious

maliciously (muh LISH iss lee) *adv.*: with a desire to inflict harm; spitefully

maneuvered (muh NOO verd) *v.*: moved skillfully to avoid obstacles

manhandled (MAN hand uhld) *v.*: handled roughly

manipulating (muh NIP yoo LAYT ing) *v.*: handling or using, especially with skill

martyrdom (MAR tur dum) *n.*: extreme suffering or torment for a cause

materialized (muh TIR ee ul IZED) *v.*: took form or shape; appeared

mercenary (MUR sih NAIR ee) *n.*: a person who acts merely for money

mesmerized (MEZ mer ized) *adj.*: hypnotized; spellbound; fascinated

miasma (my AZ muh) *n.*: vapors harmful to health from rotting organic matter; poisonous vapors

migrant (MY grint) *adj.*: moving from one climate or region to another, as done by certain birds, animals, and fish

militiamen (muh LISH uh MEN) *n.*: a group of citizens enrolled for military service, called out periodically for drill, but serving full-time only in emergencies

millimeter (MILL uh MEE ter) *n.*: a unit of length equal to 1/1000 of a meter, equivalent to 0.03937 of an inch

minute (my NOOT) *adj.*: extremely small, as in size, amount, extent, or degree

mirage (mih RAHZH) *n.*: something illusory; an optical effect created by the reflection of light over hot sand or pavement

mirthlessly (MERTH liss lee) *adv.*: joylessly; unhappily

misconception (MISS kun SEP shun) *n.*: an incorrect interpretation or misunderstanding

miscreant (MISS cree ant) *n.*: a villainous person

misgivings (mis GIV ingz) *n.*: feelings of doubt, distrust, or apprehension

mite (MYT) *n.*: a very small creature, person, or thing

monosyllabic (MAHN oh SILL LAB IK) *adj.*: consisting of one syllable

morbid (MOR bid) *adj.*: suggesting an unhealthy mental attitude; unwholesomely gloomy

mortally (MOR tuh lee) *adv.*: severely; grievously; fatally

mottled (MAHT ild) *adj.*: marked with spots or blotches of different colors or shades

multiculturalism (MULL ty KULL chur uh liz im) *n.*: the existence, recognition, or preservation of different cultures within a unified society

mutton (MUTT un) *n.*: the flesh of a mature sheep, used as food

myriad (MEER ee id) *adj.*: of an indefinitely great number; innumerable

N

nag (NAG) *n.*: an old horse

naively (ny EEV lee) *adv.*: in an unsophisticated, simplistic way; in an innocent and overly trusting way

notable (NO tuh bul) *adj.*: worthy of notice; remarkable; outstanding

novel (NAHV il) *adj.*: of a new kind; different from anything seen or known before

O

objective (ub JEK tiv) *adj.*: not influenced by personal feelings or prejudice; unbiased

oblivion (uh BLIV ee un) *n.*: the state of being completely forgotten; the state of forgetting completely or of being completely unaware

oblivious (uh BLIV ee us) *adj.*: unmindful or unaware

obscure (ub SKYOOR) *adj.*: not readily seen, heard, noticed, or understood

ominous (AHM in us) *adj.*: foreshadowing evil or harm; threatening

onslaught (AHN SLAWT) *n.*: an onset or assault, especially a vigorous one

orator (OR uh tur) *n.*: a public speaker, especially one of great skill and power

ovation (oh VAY shun) *n.*: an enthusiastic, public show of approval, marked especially by loud, prolonged applause

overhauled (O ver HAWLD) *v.*: gained upon, caught up with; overtook

P

palled (PAWLD) *v.*: had a wearying or tiresome effect; made dull; became distasteful

palpable (PAL puh bul) *adj.*: capable of being touched or felt; tangible

palpitated (PAL pih tayt id) *v.*: quivered; trembled; pulsated

paranoia (PAIR uh NOY uh) *n.*: baseless or excessive distrust of others

parapet (PAIR uh PET) *n.*: a low, protective wall or barrier at the edge of a roof or balcony; a wall or elevation in a fortification

pardoned (PAHR dund) *v.*: forgave, especially an offender

parlance (PAR lintz) *n.*: way or manner of speaking; jargon; vernacular

peevishness (PEEV ish niss) *n.*: fretfulness; irritability

pensively (PEN siv lee) *adv.*: in a dreamily or wistfully thoughtful way

perceived (per SEEVD) *v.*: became aware of, identified by means of the senses; recognized

perceptibly (pur SEP tib lee) *adv.*: recognizably; discernibly; in a way that could be perceived

perilous (PER ih liss) *adj.*: involving grave risk; dangerous

perimeter (puh RIM ih ter) **cord** *n.*: a rope marking the boundary or outer limits of an area or object

persevered (PUR suh VEERD) *v.*: persisted in pursuing a goal in spite of obstacles or opposition

persimmon (per SIM in) *n.*: a large orange fruit that is edible and sweet when very ripe and soft

personnel (purr son NELL) *n.*: the people who staff an organization

petulance (PECH oo lintz) *n.*: sudden irritation

phenomena (feh NAHM ih nuh) *n.*: facts, occurrences, or circumstances that are observable; things that are remarkable or extraordinary

phenomenon (fih NAHM uh NAHN) *n.*: something that is remarkable or extraordinary; a fact, occurrence, or circumstance observed or observable

placid (PLASS id) *adj.*: pleasantly calm or peaceful

placidly (PLASS sid lee) *adv.*: calmly, peacefully, tranquilly

plaintively (PLAIN tiv lee) *adv.*: sadly; with sorrow or melancholy; mournfully

plank (PLAINK) *n.*: a long, flat piece of timber, thicker than a board

polysyllables (PAH lee SILL uh bulz) *n.*: many syllables; a polysyllabic word consists of several syllables

potential (po TEN shill) *n.*: possibility; latent ability that may not be developed

precarious (pree KARE ee iss) *adj.*: uncertain; dangerously insecure or unsteady

precariously (pree KAIR ee iss lee) *adv.*: dangerously; unsteadily or insecurely

precedence (PRESS ih dintz) *n.*: the right to be placed before others; priority in order, rank, or importance

preeminence (pree EM ih nintz) *n.*: superiority to all others

prestige (press TEEZH) *n.*: reputation or influence arising from "success"

prey (PRAY) *n.*: a creature hunted or seized for food

primitive (PRIM ih tiv) *adj.*: indicating a people or society that has a simple economy and little, if any, technology

primly (PRIM lee) *adv.*: properly; in a formally precise way

procession (pro SESH in) *n.*: a line or body of people or vehicles moving in a formal, orderly way

profound (pro FOUND) *adj.*: going beyond what is superficial or obvious; deep

prose (PROZE) *n.*: the ordinary form of spoken or written language

prostrate (PRAHS trayt) *adj.*: physically weak or exhausted; lying flat, at full length, face down on the ground; utterly dejected

protruded (pro TROOD id) *v.*: projected; jutted out

provincial (pruh VIN shil) *adj.*: not city-like; unsophisticated

prudently (PROO dint lee) *adv.*: wisely; cautiously; carefully with an eye towards the future

pungent (PUN jint) *adj.*: sharply affecting the organs of taste or smell; biting; acrid

puppeteer (PUP it EAR) *n.*: a person who manipulates puppets

Q

quarry (KWOR ee) *n.*: an excavation or pit from which building stone and slate are obtained by cutting or blasting

quench (KWENCH) *v.*: satisfy; extinguish

R

rakish (RAY kish) *adj.*: jaunty; dashing; stylish

rapturously (RAP chur iss lee) *adv.*: ecstatically

ravager (RAV ij er) *n.*: someone or something that damages or destroys

ravenously (RAV in iss lee) *adv.*: hungrily; as if starving; eagerly

ravine (ruh VEEN) *n.*: a narrow, steep-sided valley created from the erosion of running water

rebuked (ree BYOOKT) *v.*: sternly disapproved of; reprimanded

recuperate (re KOO per ayt) *v.*: recover from sickness or exhaustion; regain health or strength

reflection (ree FLECK shun) *n.*: careful consideration; the act of thinking; pondering

refuge (REF yooj) *n.*: shelter or protection from danger or trouble

refuse (REF yooz) *n.*: rubbish; trash; garbage; that is discarded as useless

reminiscence (REM ih NISS intz) *n.*: a recalling of the past; a personal remembrance from the past

rend (REND) *v.*: separate into parts with force or violence; tear apart

rendezvous (RAHN day VOO) *v.*: meet at an agreed-upon time and place

repatriate (ree PAY tree AYT) *v.*: send back (a refugee, prisoner of war) to his or her country

reproachful (re PROACH full) *adj.*: finding fault with; blaming

resolute (REZ uh loot) *adj.*: firmly set in purpose or opinion; determined

respite (RESS pit) *n.*: a delay or stopping for a time, especially of anything distressing or difficult; an interval of relief

retards (ree TARDZ) *v.*: slows down, delays, hinders

reverently (REV er int lee) *adv.*: with deep respect

revulsion (ree VUL shin) *n.*: a strong feeling of disgust, distaste, or dislike; loathing

ricochet (RIK uh SHAY) *n.*: the rebound or skip of an object after it hits a striking blow against a surface

robust (roh BUST) *adj.*: strong, healthy, hearty

rogue (ROAG) *adj.*: destructive, not conforming to a desired standard; vicious

routine (roo TEEN) *n.*: a rehearsed act, performance, or part of a performance

ruefully (ROO fuhl lee) *adv.*: bitterly and regretfully; sorrowfully

rung (RUNG) *n.*: one of the crosspieces forming the steps of a ladder

S

scanty (SKAN tee) *adj.*: insufficient; very brief

scapegoats (SKAYP GOATS) *n.*: persons or groups used as a focus for blame, accused of the mistakes or crimes of others

scathingly (SKAYTH ing lee) *adv.*: with bitter severity

schooner (SKOON er) *n.*: any sailing vessel with both a foremast and a mainmast

scoured (SKOW erd) *v.*: removed by hard rubbing

sedately (sih DAYT lee) *adv.*: calmly, quietly, or in a composed manner; undisturbed

semblance (SEM blintz) *n.*: an appearance or outward aspect; slightest appearance or trace

semidarkness (SEM ee DARK niss) *n.*: partial darkness

serrated (SIR ayt id) *adj.*: notched on the edge like a saw

shaft (SHAFT) *n.*: a long pole or handle serving to balance a weapon or tool

shards (SHAHRDZ) *n.*: fragments

shrapnel (SHRAP nil) *n.*: fragments scattered by a bursting artillery shell, mine, or bomb

shuddering (SHUD der ing) *adj.*: convulsive trembling, as from horror or cold

simultaneously (SY mul TAY nee iss lee) *adv.*: concurrently; occurring at the same time

sinister (SIN iss ter) *adj.*: threatening or hinting at evil, harm, or trouble

skeptical (SKEP tih kul) *adj.*: doubtful

skepticism (SKEP tih siz im) *n.*: doubt or disbelief

sluicing (SLOOS ing) *v.*: flushing or cleansing with a rush of water

smiting (SMYT ing) *v.*: afflicting or attacking with deadly or disastrous effect

solemnly (SAHL em lee) *adv.*: seriously; earnestly

solicitously (suh LISS ih tuss lee) *adv.*: anxiously or concernedly; in a kindly way

solitude (SAHL ih tude) *n.*: the state of being or living alone

sorghum (SORE gum) *n.*: a sweet syrup made from the sorgo plant

sovereignty (SAHV rin tee) *n.*: supreme and independent power or authority

spare (SPAIR) *adj.*: lean or thin

speculation (SPECK yoo LAY shun) *n.*: consideration of some subject; guessing

sphere (SFEAR) *n.*: any round globular body

spits *n.*: pointed rods for skewering and holding meat over a fire for cooking

spontaneous (spahn TAY nee iss) *adj.*: coming from a natural feeling without effort; unplanned

sprinted (SPRIN tid) *v.*: raced or moved at full speed for a short distance

staid (STAYD) *adj.*: serious or dignified in character

stance (STANTZ) *n.*: position or posture of the body while standing

steadfastly (STED FAST lee) *adv.*: fixedly; with firm purpose

steerage (STEER ij) *n.*: the cheapest accommodations for travelers, usually providing minimal comfort and convenience

strident (STRY dint) *adj.*: harsh in sound; grating

stripling (STRIP ling) *n.*: a youth

stunted (STUN tid) *adj.*: stopped, slowed down or hindered in growth or development

subtle (SUT il) *adj.*: so slight as to be difficult to detect; not obvious

subtler (SUT ler) *adj.*: finer or more delicate in meaning or intent; more difficult to perceive or understand

succession (suk SESH in) *n.*: a number of persons or things following one another in order

succumbed (suh KUMD) *v.*: gave or given way to a superior force; yielded; died

sullen (SULL in) *adj.*: gloomy or dismal; moody

sullenly (SUL in lee) *adv.*: gloomily and irritably

surveyed (SIR vaid) *v.*: inspected; examined; appraised to determine condition or size

symmetrical (sih MET rih kul) *adj.*: well-balanced; having harmonious proportions in shape, size; having corresponding parts, so that the right and left sides are mirror images

T

tact (TACT) *n.*: a keen sense of what to do or say to avoid giving offense

tapestry (TAP iss tree) *n.*: a woven, ornamental fabric

taut (TAWT) *adj.*: tightly drawn; tense; not slack

teeming (TEEM ing) *adj.*: occurring or existing in great quantities or numbers; swarming

tempo (TEM po) *n.*: the rate of speed of a musical passage or work

tenaciously (tih NAY shiss lee) *adv.*: holding fast; characterized by keeping a firm hold

tendril (TEN dril) *n.*: a threadlike, spiraling shape

tepid (TEP id) *adj.*: moderately warm; lukewarm

testily (TESS till lee) *adv.*: irritably; impatiently

thoroughfare (THUR oh FAIR) *n.*: a major road or highway

threshold (THRESH hold) *n.*: the entrance to a house or building; the sill of a doorway

tirade (TY rayd) *n.*: a prolonged, bitter, negative outburst

tithe (TYTH) *n.*: a tenth part or small part of something

torrent (TOR int) *n.*: a rushing or abundant stream flowing with great rapidity and violence

tracery (TRAY sir ee) *n.*: a delicate, interlacing work of lines or threads

traipsing (TRAYP sing) *v.*: walking or going aimlessly or idly, without finding or reaching a goal

transient (TRAN shint) *adj.*: not lasting or enduring; temporary

traversing (truh VERS ing) *v.*: passing or moving over, along, or through; crossing

tread (TRED) *v.*: set down the foot or feet in walking; step; walk

treason (TREE zohn) *n.*: violation of allegiance to one's state; the betrayal of a trust or confidence; treachery

triumphal (try UM fil) *adj.*: highly successful or victorious; celebrating a triumph

triumphantly (try UMF ant lee) *adv.*: successfully; victoriously

tumultuous (tuh MUL choo iss) *adj.*: full of violence and noise; uproarious; turbulent

U

unamiably (un A mee uh blee) *adv.*: unpleasantly; in an unfriendly way

uncanny (un KAN nee) *adj.*: seeming to be supernatural or unexplainable; extraordinary

uncoiling (un KOY ling) *v.*: unwinding from a spiral

undermining (UN der MYN ing) *adj.*: impairing, weakening, or destroying (health, morale, etc.) in barely noticeable stages

unified (YOO nih FYD) *adj.*: made to be a single unit; united; merged

unobtrusively (UN ub TROO siv lee) *adv.*: in a manner that does not intrude or interrupt

upheavals (up HEE vilz) *n.*: strong or violent changes

V

valid (VAL id) *adj.*: legally sound, effective, or binding

validation (VAL ih DAY shun) *n.*: confirmation; approval

vault (VAWLT) *n.*: a room or compartment used for storage

vender (VEN dur) *n.*: (also spelled vendor) a seller

venom (VEN im) *n.*: the poisonous fluid that some snakes and spiders inject into or spray at their victims

vial (VY il) *n.*: a small container, often made of glass, for holding liquids

vibrant (VY brint) *adj.*: pulsating with vigor and energy

vicious (VISH iss) *adj.*: savage; ferocious; very mean

vigil (VIJ il) *n.*: a period of watchful attention

vigilance (VIJ uh lintz) *n.*: the state or quality of being on guard; watchfulness; alertness

vigor (VIG er) *n.*: active strength or force; intensity; energy

virtue (VURR choo) *n.*: moral excellence

virtuosity (VUR choo AH sit ee) *n.*: excellence and brilliance in musical technique or execution

visor (VY zer) *n.*: the projecting front brim of a cap

vitality (vyt AL ih tee) *n.*: living force; ability to sustain or retain life; vigor and endurance

vitals (VY tilz) *n.*: the bodily organs essential to life, such as the brain, heart, liver, lungs, and stomach

vulnerable (VUL ner uh bul) *adj.*: open to being hurt physically or emotionally

W

wallowing (WAHL oh ing) *v.*: rolling about or lying in water, mud, or dust

waning (WAY ning) *adj.*: gradually decreasing in strength, intensity, or size

warily (WEAR ih lee) *adv.*: watchfully; watching against danger

warped (WORPT) *adj.*: bent or twisted, especially from a straight or flat shape

wary (WAIR ee) *adj.*: watchful; on guard against danger

wavering (WAY ver ing) *adj.*: feeling or showing doubt or indecision

wayward (WAY werd) *adj.*: disregarding or rejecting what is considered right or proper

wheedled (WEED ihld) *v.*: tried to influence by using flattering words or acts

whittled (WIT ild) *v.*: carved, trimmed, and shaped (a piece of wood) by cutting off bits with a knife

widish (WYD ish) *adj.*: rather wide; tending to be wide

withered (WITH erd) *v.*: shriveled; faded; dried out

wolverine (WOOL ver EEN) *n.*: a carnivore of the weasel family, native to Canada and the northern United States

wraith (RAITH) *n.*: a vision or apparition

wretched (RECH id) *adj.*: characterized by misery and sorrow; miserable

writhing (RYTH ing) *adj.*: twisting about, as in pain or effort

wrought (RAWT) *v.*: produced or shaped

Y

yawing (YAW ing) *v.*: deviating temporarily from a straight course

yearning (YURN ing) *n.*: an earnest or strong desire; a longing

Index of Authors and Titles

Accounts Settled, 30
Adolf, 270
Animal Craftsmen, 538
Annixter, Paul, 30, *28*
As I Grew Older, 470
Bennett, Jack, 589, *586*
Bishop, Elizabeth, 398, *474*
Blind Men and the Elephant, The, 429
Bradbury, Ray, 148, *146*
Brooks, Bruce, 538, *536*
Bruchac, Joseph, 409, *474*
By Any Other Name, 566
Carousso, Georges, 92
Carroll, Lewis, 446, *474*
Case for Short Words, The, 502
Charles, 70
Children of the Harvest, 204
Clouds Pass, The, 452
Concrete Cat, 437
Countess and the Impossible, 60
Dahl, Roald, 216, 518, *214*
Dandelions, 425
Daviot, Gordon, 483, *497*
Day the Children Vanished, The, 292
Day the Dam Broke, The, 558
de Maupassant, Guy, 194, *192*
Deutsch, Babette, 395, *474*
Directions to the Armorer, 458
Dog at Night, 406
Dove, Rita, 530, *528*
Drouth, 576
Drummer Boy of Shiloh, The, 148
Dunbar, Paul Laurence, 225
Ellis Island, 409
Fetch, 285
Finish of Patsy Barnes, The, 225
Fire!, 156
Fireworks, 395
First Day, The, 176
Fish, The, 398

Fly Away, 510
Forgotten Door, The, 316
Foul Shot, 392
Frost, Robert, 463, *475*
Garcia, Richard, 452
Garden, The, 417
Godden, Rumer, 186, *184*
Godfrey Saxe, John, 429, *476*
Gordon, Arthur, 16, *14*
Green Mamba, The, 518
Hale, Edward Everett, 235, *232*
Helfer, Ralph, 510
Hemingway, Ernest, 280, *278*
Herriot, James, 549, *546*
Hoey, Edwin A., 392, *475*
Hudson, Lois Phillips, 204, *202*
Hughes, Langston, 470, *475*
I Know What the Red Clay Looks Like, 530
I Meant To Do My Work Today, 453
In the Middle of a Pitch, 108
Jackson, Shirley, 70, *68*
Kantor, MacKinlay, 52, *50*
Keepsakes, 403
Key, Alexander, 316, *379*
Lane, Deloras, 403, *475*
Last Leaf, The, 42
Lawrence, D. H., 270, *268*
Lederer, Richard, 502, *500*
Legacy II, 438
Le Gallienne, Richard, 453, *475*
Logan, Ben, 576
London, Jack, 118, *116*
MacDonald, John D., 156, *154*
Man Who Had No Eyes, A, 52
Man Without a Country, The, 235
Marquis, Don, 387, *476*
Masefield, John, 413, *476*
McCallum, Patrick, 256
Meissner, Bill, 108, *106*
Mr. Brownlee's Roses, 164
No-Talent Kid, The, 78

O Captain! My Captain!, 421
O. Henry, 42, *40*
Old Man at the Bridge, 280
Olson, Elder, 458, *475*
Papashvily, George & Helen, 176, *174*
Pen of My Aunt, The, 483
Pentecost, Hugh, 292, *290*
Piece of String, The, 194
Quintana, Leroy V., 438, *476*
Rau, Santha Rama, 566, *564*
Recital, The, 549
Rescue, The, 442
Sea Devil, The, 16
Silverstein, Shel, 417, *476*
Singmaster, Elsie, 164, *162*
Song Caruso Sang, The, 256
Stopping By Woods on a Snowy Evening, 471
Stuart, Jesse, 136, *134*
Summers, Hal, 442
Takes Talent, 387
This Farm for Sale, 136
Thurber, James, 558, *556*
Thurman, Richard Y., 60
Time to Talk, A, 463
To Build a Fire, 118
Unfolding Bud, 466
Untermeyer, Louis, 406, *477*
Vonnegut, Kurt, 78, *76*
Voyage of the Lucky Dragon, The, 589
Walrus and the Carpenter, The, 446
Warden, The, 92
West Wind, The, 413
When I Heard the Learn'd Astronomer, 433
White, Robb, 285, *284*
Whitman, Walt, 421, *477*
Wish, The, 216
You Need to Go Upstairs, 186

Acknowledgments

Accounts Settled: "Accounts Settled" by Paul Annixter. Copyright © 1966 by Scholastic Magazines, Inc. Reprinted by permission.

Adolf: "Adolf," copyright 1936 by Frieda Lawrence. Copyright renewed © 1964 by The Estate of the late Frieda Lawrence Ravagli; from PHOENIX 1: THE POSTHUMOUS PAPERS OF D. H. LAWRENCE by D. H. Lawrence, edited by Edward McDonald. Used by permission of Viking Books, an imprint of Penguin Publishing Group, a division of Penguin Random House LLC. All rights reserved.

Animal Craftsmen: From *NATURE BY DESIGN* © 1991 by Bruce Brooks. Reprinted by permission of Farrar, Straus, Giroux Books for Young Readers. All Rights Reserved.

As I Grew Older: "As I Grew Older" from THE COLLECTED POEMS OF LANGSTON HUGHES by Langston Hughes, edited by Arnold Rampersad with David Roessel, Associate Editor, copyright © 1994 by the Estate of Langston Hughes. Used by permission of Alfred A. Knopf, an imprint of the Knopf Doubleday Publishing Group, a division of Penguin Random House LLC. All rights reserved.

By Any Other Name: "By Any Other Name" from *Gifts of Passage* © 1951 by Santha Rama Rau. Copyright renewed 1971 by Santha Rama Rau. Reprinted by permission of William Morris Endeavor Entertainment.

The Case for Short Words: From THE MIRACLE OF LANGUAGE by Richard Lederer. Copyright © 1991 by Richard Lederer. Reprinted with the permission of Atria Books, a division of Simon & Schuster, Inc. All rights reserved.

Charles: "Charles" from THE LOTTERY by Shirley Jackson. Copyright © 1948, 1949 by Shirley Jackson. Copyright renewed 1976, 1977 by Laurence Hyman, Barry Hyman, Mrs. Sarah Webster and Mrs. Joanne Schnurer. Reprinted by permission of Farrar, Straus and Giroux.

Children of the Harvest: "Children of the Harvest" from *Reapers of the Dust* by Lois Phillips Hudson, reprinted by permission of Minnesota Historical Society Press.

The Clouds Pass: Copyright Richard Garcia. Used by permission of the author.

Concrete Cat: "Concrete Cat" by Dorthi Charles, from *Literature: Eleventh Edition* (Pearson Publishing, copyright © 2010 by X. J. Kennedy and Dana Gioia). Reprinted by permission.

The Countess and the Impossible: "The Countess and the Impossible" by Richard Y. Thurman, originally published in Reader's Digest. Copyright © 1958 by Trusted Media Brands, Inc. Used by permission. All rights reserved.

Dandelions: Deborah Austin, "Dandelions", from the Paradise of the World, 1964. Copyright © 1964 by The Pennsylvania State University Press. Reprinted by permission of The Pennsylvania State University Press.

The Day the Children Vanished: "The Day the Children Vanished"; copyright © 1958, 1986 by Hugh Pentecost. Originally appeared in This Week Magazine. Reprinted by permission of Brandt & Hochman Literary Agents, Inc.

The Day the Dam Broke: "The Day the Dam Broke" by James Thurber from *My Life and Hard Times*. Copyright ©1933 by Rosemary A. Thurber. Reprinted by arrangement with Rosemary Thurber and The Barbara Hogenson Agency.

Dog at Night: "Dog at Night" from STARS TO STEER BY by Louis Untermeyer. Copyright © 1941 by Houghton Mifflin Harcourt Publishing Company, renewed 1969 by Louis Untermeyer. Reprinted by permission of Houghton Mifflin Harcourt Publishing Company. All rights reserved.

Drouth: From The Land Remembers by Ben Logan. Reprinted by permission of the University of Wisconsin Press. © 2017 by the Board of Regents of the University of Wisconsin System. All rights reserved.

The Drummer Boy of Shiloh: Reprinted by permission of Don Congdon Associates, Inc. Copyright (c) 1960 by the Curtis Publishing Co., renewed 1988 by Ray Bradbury

Ellis Island: "Ellis Island" by Joseph Bruchac from THE REMEMBERED EARTH, edited by Geary Hobson. University of New Mexico Press 1981.

The Finish of Patsy Barnes: "The Finish of Patsy Barnes" from THE STRENGTH OF GIDEON AND OTHER STORIES. With permission granted from Ayer Company Publishers. 1899.

Fireworks: "Fireworks" from *Babette Deutsch Collected Poems: 1919-1962*, Indiana University Press, 1963, reprinted by permission of Michael Yarmolinsky for the Estate of Babette Deutsch.

The Fish: "The Fish" from POEMS by Elizabeth Bishop. Copyright © 2011 by The Alice H. Methfessel Trust.

Publisher's Note and compilation copyright © 2011 by Farrar, Straus and Giroux. Reprinted by permission of Farrar, Straus and Giroux.

Fly Away: "Fly Away" from *The Beauty of the Beasts: Tales of Hollywood's Wild Animal Stars* by Ralph Helfer, reprinted by permission of Richard Curtis Associates, Inc.

The Forgotten Door: Selection from *The Forgotten Door* by Alexander Key is reprinted with permission of Westminster John Knox Press. All rights reserved.

Foul Shot: From Read Magazine, January 2004. Copyright © 2004 by the Weekly Reader Corporation. Reprinted by permission of Scholastic Inc.

The Garden: COPYRIGHT (C) 1974, renewed 2002 EVIL EYE MUSIC, LLC. Reprinted with permission from the Estate of Shel Silverstein and HarperCollins Children's Books.

I Know What the Red Clay Looks Like: "Rita Dove" first appeared in *I Know What the Red Clay Looks Like: The Voice and Vision of Black Women Writers*, Edited by Rebecca Caroll, New York: Crown Trade Paperbacks, 1994. © 1994 by Rita Dove. Reprinted by permission of the author.

In the Middle of a Pitch: "In the Middle of a Pitch" by Bill Meissner, as seen in HITTING INTO THE WIND by Bill Meissner.

Keepsakes: "Keepsakes" by Deloras Lane, used by permission of the author.

Legacy II: "Legacy II" by Leroy V. Quintana, reprinted by permission of the author.

The No-Talent Kid: © Kurt Vonnegut LLC. Used by permission.

Old Man at the Bridge: From THE SHORT STORIES OF ERNEST HEMINGWAY by Ernest Hemingway. Copyright © 1938 by Ernest Hemingway. Copyright renewed 1966 by Mary Hemingway. Reprinted with the permission of Scribner, a division of Simon & Schuster, Inc. All rights reserved.

The Pen of My Aunt: "The Pen of My Aunt" by Gordon Daviot (Josephine Tey), published by Samuel French Ltd, reprinted by permission of David Higham Associates.

The Recital: From THE LORD GOD MADE US ALL © 1981 by James Herriot. Reprinted by permission of St. Martin's Griffin, an imprint of St. Martin's Press. All Rights Reserved. Reprinted by permission of Harold Ober Associates Incorporated. Copyright © 1981 by James Herriot.

The Rescue: Reprinted by permission of the author.

The Sea Devil: Reprinted with permission from the Estate of Pamela and Arthur Gordon.

Stopping By Woods on a Snowy Evening: "Stopping by Woods on a Snowy Evening" by Robert Frost from the book THE POETRY OF ROBERT FROST edited by Edward Connery Lathem. Copyright © 1923, 1969 by Henry Holt and Company. Copyright © 1951 by Robert Frost. Reprinted by permission of Henry Holt and Company. All rights reserved.

Takes Talent: "Takes Talent," copyright © 1926 by P.F. Collier & Son, Company; from THE LIVES AND TIMES OF ARCHY AND MEHITABEL by Don Marquis. Used by permission of Doubleday, an imprint of the Knopf Doubleday Publishing Group, a division of Penguin Random House LLC. All rights reserved.

This Farm for Sale: Appeared in "Progressive Farmer", 1954, "Scholastic" and "Junior Scholastic" 1955, 1958. Copyright Jesse Stuart and the Jesse Stuart Foundation. Used by permission of Marian Reiner on behalf of the Foundation.

A Time to Talk: "A Time to Talk" by Robert Frost from the book THE POETRY OF ROBERT FROST edited by Edward Connery Lathem. Copyright © 1916, 1969 by Henry Holt and Company. Copyright © 1944 by Robert Frost. Reprinted by permission of Henry Holt and Company. All rights reserved.

Unfolding Bud: From Christian Science Monitor, July 3, 1957 © 1957 Christian Science Monitor. All rights reserved. Used by permission and protected by the Copyright Laws of the United States. The printing, copying, redistribution, or retransmission of this Content without express written permission is prohibited.

The West Wind: The Society of Authors as the Literary Representative of the Estate of John Masefield.

The Wish: "The Wish" from SOMEONE LIKE YOU by Roald Dahl, published by Michael Joseph, reprinted by permission of David Higham Associates.

You Need to Go Upstairs: Copyright © 1944, 1968 by Rumer Godden. Copyright renewed 1971, 1966 by Rumer Godden. First appeared in *Harper's Magazine*. Reprinted by permission of Curtis Brown, Ltd.

Note: We have expended much effort to contact all copyright holders to receive permission to reprint their works. We will correct any omissions brought to our attention in future editions.